IT Essentials v8
Companion Guide

Cisco Press

IT Essentials v8 Companion Guide

Published by:
Cisco Press

7 2024

Library of Congress Control Number: 2023938352

ISBN-13: 978-0-13-816610-6
ISBN-10: 0-13-816610-2

Editor-in-Chief
Mark Taub

Alliances Manager, Cisco Press
Arezou Gol

Director, ITP Product Management
Brett Bartow

Executive Editor
James Manly

Managing Editor
Sandra Schroeder

Development Editor
Roopali Satija

Production Editor
Mary Roth

Copy Editor
Kitty Wilson

Editorial Assistant
Cindy Teeters

Cover Designer
Chuti Prasertsith

Composition
codeMantra

Indexer
Timothy Wright

Proofreader
Barbara Mack

Warning and Disclaimer

This book is designed to provide information about the Cisco Networking Academy IT Essentials course. Every effort has been made to make this book as complete and as accurate as possible, but no warranty or fitness is implied.

The information is provided on an "as is" basis. The authors, Cisco Press, and Cisco Systems, Inc. shall have neither liability nor responsibility to any person or entity with respect to any loss or damages arising from the information contained in this book or from the use of the discs or programs that may accompany it.

The opinions expressed in this book belong to the author and are not necessarily those of Cisco Systems, Inc.

Trademark Acknowledgments

All terms mentioned in this book that are known to be trademarks or service marks have been appropriately capitalized. Cisco Press or Cisco Systems, Inc., cannot attest to the accuracy of this information. Use of a term in this book should not be regarded as affecting the validity of any trademark or service mark.

Microsoft and/or its respective suppliers make no representations about the suitability of the information contained in the documents and related graphics published as part of the services for any purpose. All such documents and related graphics are provided "as is"

Special Sales

For information about buying this title in bulk quantities, or for special sales opportunities (which may include electronic versions; custom cover designs; and content particular to your business, training goals, marketing focus, or branding interests), please contact our corporate sales department at corpsales@pearsoned.com or (800) 382-3419.

For government sales inquiries, please contact governmentsales@pearsoned.com.

For questions about sales outside the U.S., please contact intlcs@pearson.com.

Feedback Information

At Cisco Press, our goal is to create in-depth technical books of the highest quality and value. Each book is crafted with care and precision, undergoing rigorous development that involves the unique expertise of members from the professional technical community.

Readers' feedback is a natural continuation of this process. If you have any comments regarding how we could improve the quality of this book, or otherwise alter it to better suit your needs, you can contact us through email at feedback@ciscopress.com.

Please make sure to include the book title and ISBN in your message.

We greatly appreciate your assistance.

CISCO

Americas Headquarters
Cisco Systems, Inc.
San Jose, CA

Asia Pacific Headquarters
Cisco Systems (USA) Pte. Ltd.
Singapore

Europe Headquarters
Cisco Systems International BV Amsterdam,
The Netherlands

Cisco has more than 200 offices worldwide. Addresses, phone numbers, and fax numbers are listed on the Cisco Website at www.cisco.com/go/offices.

Cisco and the Cisco logo are trademarks or registered trademarks of Cisco and/or its affiliates in the U.S. and other countries. To view a list of Cisco trademarks, go to this URL: www.cisco.com/go/trademarks. Third party trademarks mentioned are the property of their respective owners. The use of the word partner does not imply a partnership relationship between Cisco and any other company. (1110R)

About the Contributing Authors

Allan Johnson entered the academic world in 1999, after 10 years as a business owner/operator, to dedicate his efforts to his passion for teaching. He holds both an MBA and an MEd in training and development. He taught CCNA courses at the high school level for 7 years and has taught both CCNA and CCNP courses at Del Mar College in Corpus Christi, Texas. In 2003, Allan began to commit much of his time and energy to the CCNA Instructional Support Team, providing services to Networking Academy instructors worldwide and creating training materials. He now works full time for Cisco Networking Academy as curriculum lead.

Dave Holzinger has been a curriculum developer, project manager, author, and technical editor for the Cisco Networking Academy program in Phoenix, Arizona, since 2001. Dave has helped develop many online courses, including IT Essentials, CCNA, and CCNP. He has been working with computer hardware and software since 1981. Dave has certifications from Cisco, BICSI, and CompTIA, including the A+.

Contents at a Glance

Contents

Command Syntax Conventions

The conventions used to present command syntax in this book are the same conventions used in the IOS Command Reference. The Command Reference describes these conventions as follows:

- **Boldface** indicates commands and keywords that are entered literally as shown. In actual configuration examples and output (not general command syntax), boldface indicates commands that are manually input by the user (such as a **show** command).

- *Italic* indicates arguments for which you supply actual values.

- Vertical bars (|) separate alternative, mutually exclusive elements.

- Square brackets ([ ]) indicate an optional element.

- Braces ({ }) indicate a required choice.

- Braces within brackets ([{ }]) indicate a required choice within an optional element.

Introduction

IT Essentials v8 Companion Guide is a supplemental book to the Cisco Networking Academy IT Essentials: Version 8 course. The course includes information to allow you to develop working knowledge of how computers and mobile devices operate. It covers information security topics and provides practice experience in computer procedures, networking, and troubleshooting.

Cisco Networking Academy is a comprehensive program that delivers information technology skills to students around the world. *IT Essentials v8 Companion Guide* provides you with the foundational knowledge to be successful in employment in many areas of IT. You will learn techniques to successfully problem-solve and troubleshoot IT functions, understand virtualization technologies, recognize security threats, use mitigation methods and tools, identify and install infrastructure and system components, and enhance your customer service skills.

This book provides a ready reference that explains the same concepts, technologies, protocols, and tools as the online curriculum. You can use the online curriculum as directed by your instructor and then use this *Companion Guide*'s study tools to help solidify your understanding of all the topics.

The course is designed to prepare you to take and pass the CompTIA A+ 1000 series exams. By reading and completing this book, you have the opportunity to review all key concepts that the CompTIA A+ exams cover. If you use this book along with its study tools, you can reinforce those concepts with hands-on exercises and test that knowledge with review questions and exercises.

The IT Essentials: PC Hardware and Software course aligns with the CompTIA A+ (220-1001) exam and CompTIA A+ (220-1002) exam. You must pass both exams to earn the CompTIA A+ certification.

Who Should Read This Book

This book is intended for students in the Cisco Networking Academy IT Essentials: Version 8 course. Such students are usually pursuing careers in information technology (IT) or want to understand how a computer works, how to assemble a computer, and how to troubleshoot hardware and software issues.

Book Features

The educational features of this book focus on supporting topic coverage, readability, and practice of the course material to facilitate your full understanding of the course material.

Topic Coverage

The following features give you a thorough overview of the topics covered in each chapter so that you can make constructive use of your study time:

- **Objectives:** Listed at the beginning of each chapter, the objectives reference the core concepts covered in the chapter. The objectives match the objectives stated in the corresponding chapters of the online curriculum; however, the question format in the *Companion Guide* encourages you to think about finding the answers as you read the chapter.

- **Notes:** These are short sidebars that point out interesting facts, timesaving methods, and important safety issues.

- **Chapter summaries:** At the end of each chapter is a summary of the chapter's key concepts. It provides a synopsis of the chapter and serves as a study aid.

- **Practice:** At the end of each chapter is a full list of all the labs, class activities, and Packet Tracer activities to refer to at study time.

Readability

The following features assist your understanding of the networking vocabulary:

- **Key terms:** Each chapter begins with a list of key terms, along with a page-number reference from inside the chapter. The terms are listed in the order in which they are explained in the chapter. This handy reference allows you to find a term, flip to the page where the term appears, and see the term used in context. The Glossary defines all the key terms.

- **Glossary:** This book contains an all-new Glossary with more than 1000 terms.

Practice

Practice makes perfect. This *Companion Guide* offers you ample opportunities to put what you learn into practice. You will find the following features valuable and effective in reinforcing the instruction that you receive:

- **Check Your Understanding questions and answer key:** Review questions are presented at the end of each chapter as a self-assessment tool. These questions

Packet Tracer
☐ Activity

Video

Interactive
Graphic

match the style of questions that you see in the online course. Appendix A, "Answers to 'Check Your Understanding' Questions," provides an answer key to all the questions and includes an explanation of each answer.

- **Labs and activities:** Throughout each chapter, you are directed to the online course to take advantage of the activities created to reinforce concepts. In addition, at the end of each chapter is a Practice section that lists all the labs and Packet Tracer activities to provide practice with the topics introduced in this chapter.

- **Page references to online course:** After headings, you will see, for example, (1.1.2.3). This number refers to the page number in the online course so that you can easily jump to that spot online to view a video, practice an activity, perform a lab, or review a topic.

About Packet Tracer Software and Activities

Packet Tracer
☐ Activity

Interspersed throughout the chapters you'll find a few Cisco Packet Tracer activities. Packet Tracer allows you to create networks, visualize how packets flow in the network, and use basic testing tools to determine whether the network would work. When you see this icon, you can use Packet Tracer with the listed file to perform a task suggested in this book. The activity files are available in the course. Packet Tracer software is available only through the Cisco Networking Academy website. Ask your instructor for access to Packet Tracer.

How This Book Is Organized

This book corresponds closely to the Cisco Networking Academy CCNA IT Essential v8 course and is divided into 14 chapters, an appendix, and a glossary of key terms:

- **Chapter 1, "Introduction to Personal Computer Hardware":** This chapter introduces you to all the components that go inside a computer case. A computer system consists of hardware and software components. This chapter discusses hardware components in a computer system as well as safety guidelines you should follow to prevent electrical fires, injuries, and fatalities while working inside a computer. You will also learn about electrostatic discharge (ESD) and how it can damage computer equipment if it is not discharged properly.

- **Chapter 2, "PC Assembly":** In this chapter, you will learn about PC power supplies and the voltages they provide to other computer components. You will learn about the components that are installed on the motherboard, including the CPU, RAM, and various adapter cards. You will learn about different CPU architectures and how to select RAM that is compatible with the motherboard and the chipset. You will also learn about various types of storage drives and the factors to consider when selecting the appropriate drive.

■ **Chapter 3, "Advanced Computer Hardware":** This chapter covers the computer boot process, protecting a computer from power fluctuations, multicore processors, redundancy through multiple storage drives, and protecting the environment from hazardous materials present in computer components.

■ **Chapter 4, "Preventive Maintenance and Troubleshooting":** In this chapter, you will learn general guidelines for creating preventive maintenance programs and troubleshooting procedures. Troubleshooting is a systematic process used to locate the cause of a fault in a computer system and to correct the relevant hardware and software issues. In this chapter, you learn general guidelines for creating preventive maintenance programs and troubleshooting procedures. These guidelines are a starting point to help you develop your preventive maintenance and troubleshooting skills.

■ **Chapter 5, "Networking Concepts":** This chapter provides an overview of network principles, standards, and purposes. IT professionals must be familiar with networking concepts to meet the expectations and needs of customers and network users.

■ **Chapter 6, "Applied Networking":** Virtually all computers and mobile devices today are connected to some type of network and to the Internet. This means that configuring and troubleshooting computer networks is now a critical skill for IT professionals. This chapter focuses on applied networking, with a discussion on the format and architecture of Media Access Control (MAC) addresses and Internet Protocol (IP) addresses, both IPv4 and IPv6, that are used to connect computers to a network. Technicians must be able to set up, configure, and troubleshoot networks. This chapter also teaches you how to troubleshoot problems when networks and Internet connections fail.

■ **Chapter 7, "Laptops and Other Mobile Devices":** This chapter focuses on the many features of mobile devices and their capabilities, including configuration, synchronization, and data backup. With the increase in demand for mobility, the popularity of mobile devices will continue to grow. During the course of your career, you will be expected to know how to configure, repair, and maintain these devices.

■ **Chapter 8, "Printers":** This chapter provides essential information about printers. You learn how printers operate, what to consider when purchasing a printer, and how to connect printers to an individual computer or to a network.

■ **Chapter 9, "Virtualization and Cloud Computing":** Organizations both large and small are investing heavily in virtualization and cloud computing. It is therefore important for IT technicians and professionals to understand these two technologies. While the two technologies do overlap, they are, in fact, two different technologies. Virtualization software allows one physical server to run several individual computing environments. Cloud computing is a term used to describe the availability of shared computing resources (software or data) as a service and on demand over the Internet. In this chapter, you will learn about both virtualization and cloud computing.

- **Chapter 10, "Windows Installation":** As a technician, you will be required to install operating systems of many types, using a variety of methods. This chapter focuses on the Windows 10, Windows 8.x, and Windows 7 operating systems. The components, functions, system requirements, and terminology related to each operating system are explored. The chapter also details the steps to install a Windows operating system and the Windows boot sequence.

- **Chapter 11, "Windows Configuration":** In this chapter, you learn about support and maintenance of the Windows operating system after it has been installed. You learn how to use tools that optimize and maintain the operating system. You also learn methods for organizing and managing Windows computers on a network, the domain, and the workgroup, and how to share local computer resources, such as files, folders, and printers, on the network. This chapter also explores the CLI and PowerShell command line utility.

- **Chapter 12, "Mobile, Linux, and macOS Operating Systems":** In this chapter, you learn about operating systems such as iOS, Android, macOS, and Ubuntu Linux and their characteristics. The portable nature of mobile devices puts them at risk for theft and loss, so this chapter discusses mobile security features.

- **Chapter 13, "Security":** Technicians need to understand computer and network security. Failure to implement proper security procedures can have impacts on users, computers, and the general public. This chapter covers why security is important, security threats, security procedures, how to troubleshoot security issues, and how you can work with customers to ensure that the best possible protection is in place.

- **Chapter 14, "The IT Professional":** As a computer technician, you not only fix computers but also interact with people. In fact, troubleshooting is as much about communicating with customers as it is about knowing how to fix computers. In this chapter, you learn to use good communication skills as confidently as you use a screwdriver. You also learn about scripting to automate processes and tasks on various operating systems.

- **Appendix A, "Answers to 'Check Your Understanding' Questions":** This appendix lists the answers to the "Check Your Understanding" review questions that are included at the end of each chapter.

- **Glossary:** The Glossary provides definitions for all the key terms identified in each chapter.

Figure and Text Credits

Figure 3-1, Figure 3-4, Figure 13-16: American Megatrends, Inc

Figure 5-17, Figure 5-26, Figure 6-16, Figure 6-41A, Figure 7-17A, Figure 7-41, Figure 7-44, Figure 7-51 through Figure 7-53, Figure 8-50, Figure 12-3, Figure 12-6, Figure 12-12 through Figure 12-16, Figure 12-19, Figure 12-22, Figure 12-25, Figure 12-28, Figure 12-32, Figure 12-33, Figure 12-36, Figure 12-38 through Figure 12-44, Figure 12-47, Figure 12-51, Figure 12-57 through Figure 12-63, Figure 12-68, Figure 12-73, Figure 12-75: Apple, Inc

Figure 6-41B, Figure 7-49, Figure 7-50, Figure 12-2, Figure 12-7, Figure 12-9 through Figure 12-11, Figure 12-18, Figure 12-21, Figure 12-24, Figure 12-27, Figure 12-30, Figure 12-31, Figure 12-35: Google, Inc

Figure 12-49, Figure 12-76: Ken Thompson

Figure 12-50, Figure 12-65 through Figure 12-67, Figure 12-70 through Figure 12-72, Figure 12-77 through Figure 12-89: The Linux Foundation

Figure 12-52 through Figure 12-56, Figure 12-74: Canonical Ltd

Figure 6-8: Wireshark Foundation

Figure 6-42: Sony

Objectives

Upon completion of this chapter, you will be able to answer the following questions:

- What are the components in a computer?
- What electrical and ESD safety procedures should you follow when working on a computer?
- What are computer cases and power supplies?
- What are motherboards?
- What are CPUs?
- What are the types of memory?
- What are adapter cards and expansion slots?

- What are hard disk drives and SSDs?
- What are optical storage devices?
- What are ports, cables, and adapters?
- What are input devices?
- What are output devices?
- What are the features and functions of each component in the technician's toolkit?
- How do you disassemble a computer?

Key Terms

This chapter uses the following key terms. You can find the definitions in the glossary at the end of the book.

Accelerated Graphics Port (AGP) page 30

adapter page 45

adapter card page 28

Advanced Technology (AT) page 11

alternating current (AC) page 10

AT Extended (ATX) page 11

ATX12V page 11

audio port page 42

augmented reality (AR) page 56

barcode scanner page 50

basic input/output system (BIOS) chip page 14

cache memory page 27

capture card page 28

central processing unit (CPU) page 18

chipset page 14

converter page 45

digital camera page 50

Introduction to Personal Computers (1.0)

People prepare for work in the information technology fields by earning certifications, seeking formal education, and gaining experience through internships and jobs. In this chapter, you will learn about all the components that make up a PC, including the case, which houses all the internal components. Computers, computer components, and computer peripherals all contain hazards that can cause severe injury. Therefore, this chapter begins with safety guidelines you should follow to prevent electrical fires, injuries, and fatalities while working inside a computer. You will also learn about electrostatic discharge (ESD) and how it can damage computer equipment if it is not discharged properly.

This chapter will introduce you to all the components inside a computer case, starting with the motherboard. You will learn about all the internal components connected to the motherboard, such as the power supply, the central processing unit (CPU), random access memory (RAM), expansion cards, and storage drives. You will also learn about the connectors, ports, and cables that physically connect devices to the motherboard.

It is important for a technician to learn about computer components and also build hands-on skills. This chapter includes a lab in which you will disassemble a computer so you can become more familiar with all the components and how they are connected.

Personal Computer Safety (1.1)

What Is in a Computer? (1.1.1)

A computer is an electronic machine that performs calculations based on a set of instructions. The first computers were huge, room-sized machines that took teams of people to build, manage, and maintain. The computer systems of today are both exponentially faster and only a fraction of the size of those original computers.

A computer system consists of hardware and software components. *Hardware* is the physical equipment. It includes the case, keyboard, monitor, cables, storage drives, speakers, and printers. *Software* includes the operating system and programs. The operating system manages computer operations such as identifying, accessing, and processing information. Programs or applications perform different functions. Programs vary widely, depending on the type of information that is accessed or generated. For example, instructions for balancing a personal budget are different from instructions for simulating a virtual reality world on the Internet.

Video Explanation 1.1.1.1: What's in a Computer?

Electrical and ESD Safety (1.1.2)

Safety is an important topic and practice in the workplace. Safety guidelines help protect individuals from accidents and injury. They also help protect equipment from damage.

Electrical Safety (1.1.2.1)

Follow electrical safety guidelines to prevent electrical fires, injuries, and fatalities.

Some printer parts, such as power supplies, contain high voltage. Check the printer manual for the location of high-voltage components. Some components retain a high voltage even after the printer is turned off.

Electrical devices have certain power requirements. For example, AC adapters are manufactured for specific laptops. Exchanging AC adapters with a different type of laptop or device may cause damage to both the AC adapter and the laptop.

Electric equipment must be grounded. If a fault causes metal parts of the equipment to become live with electrical current, the ground will provide a path of least resistance for the current to flow harmlessly away. Typically, computer products connect to ground via the power plug. Large equipment such as server racks house network devices that must also be grounded.

ESD (1.1.2.2)

Electrostatic discharge (ESD) can occur when there is a buildup of an electric charge (static electricity) on a surface that comes into contact with another, differently charged surface. ESD can cause damage to computer equipment if not discharged properly. Follow proper handling guidelines, be aware of environmental issues, and use equipment that stabilizes power to prevent equipment damage and data loss.

At least 3000 volts (V) of static electricity must build up before a person can feel ESD. For example, static electricity can build up on you as you walk across a carpeted floor. When you touch another person, you both receive a shock. If the discharge causes pain or makes a noise, the charge was probably above 10,000V. By comparison, less than 30V of static electricity can damage a computer component. Static buildup can be discharged by touching a grounded object prior to touching any electronic equipment. This is known as self-grounding.

ESD can cause permanent damage to electrical components. Follow these recommendations to help prevent ESD damage:

- Keep all components in antistatic bags until you are ready to install them.
- Use grounded mats on workbenches.
- Use grounded floor mats in work areas.
- Use antistatic wrist straps when working inside computers.

Interactive Graphic

Check Your Understanding 1.1.2.3: ESD Characteristics

Refer to the online course to complete this activity.

PC Components (1.2)

Personal computers (PCs) are made up of hardware and software components that must be chosen with specific features in mind. All the components must be compatible to work as a system. PCs are built based on how a user works and what needs to be accomplished. They may need to be upgraded when work needs are not being met.

Case and Power Supplies (1.2.1)

Computer cases are the enclosures that house the internal computer components. They come in different sizes, also known as form factors. The case you choose influences what motherboards you can use and what computer components you can install. Case, motherboard, and *power supply* form factors must be compatible. The power supply is a critical component and is used to convert the current provided from an AC outlet into DC current that is usable by many parts inside the computer case.

Cases (1.2.1.1)

The case of a desktop computer houses the internal components, such as the power supply, motherboard, central processing unit (CPU), memory, disk drives, and assorted adapter cards.

Cases are typically made of plastic, steel, or aluminum and provide the framework to support, protect, and cool the internal components.

A device *form factor* refers to its physical design and look. Desktop computers are available in a variety of form factors, including:

- Horizontal case

- Full-size tower

- Compact tower

- All-in-one

This list is not exhaustive, and many case manufacturers have their own naming conventions (for example, super tower, full tower, mid tower, mini tower, cube case, and more).

Computer components tend to generate a lot of heat; therefore, a computer case contains a fan that moves air through the case. As the air flows past warm components, it absorbs heat and then exits the case. This process keeps the computer components from overheating. Cases are also designed to protect against static electricity damage. A computer's internal components are grounded via attachment to the case.

Note

A computer case is also referred to as a computer chassis, cabinet, tower, housing, or simply box.

Horizontal Case

A horizontal case, as shown in Figure 1-1, is horizontally oriented on the user's desk, often with the monitor positioned on top. This type of case was popular in early computer systems. This form factor is often used for home theater PCs (HTPCs).

Figure 1-1   Horizontal Case

Full-Size Tower

A full-size tower, as shown in Figure 1-2, is a vertically oriented case typically located under or beside a desk or table. It provides room for expansion to accommodate additional components, such as disk drives, adapter cards, and more.

Figure 1-2   Full-Size Tower

Compact Tower

Figure 1-3 shows a compact tower, which is a smaller version of a full-size tower. It is a common form factor in the corporate environment. It might also be called a mini-tower or small form factor (SFF) model. It can be located on the user's desk or on the floor. It provides limited room for expansion.

Figure 1-3   Compact Tower

All-in-One

In an all-in-one computer, as shown in Figure 1-4, all of the computer system components are integrated into the display. An all-in-one typically includes touchscreen input and a built-in microphone and speakers. Depending on the model, all-in-one computers offer little to no expansion capabilities. The power supply is often external to the computer.

Figure 1-4   All-in-One

Power Supplies (1.2.1.2)

Electricity from wall outlets is provided in *alternating current (AC)*; however, all components inside a computer require direct current (DC) power. To obtain DC power, computers use a power supply, as shown in Figure 1-5, to convert AC power into lower-voltage DC power.

Figure 1-5   Power Supply

The list that follows describes the various computer desktop power supply form factors that have evolved over time:

- *Advanced Technology (AT)*: This was the original power supply form factor for legacy computer systems and is now considered obsolete.

- *AT Extended (ATX)*: This updated version of AT is also considered obsolete.

- *ATX12V*: This is the most common power supply on the market today. It includes a second motherboard connector to provide dedicated power to the CPU. There are several versions of ATX12V available.

- *EPS12V*: This was originally designed for network servers but is now commonly used in high-end desktop models.

Connectors (1.2.1.3)

A power supply includes several different connectors, as shown in Table 1-1. These connectors are used to power various internal components, such as the motherboard and disk drives. The connectors are "keyed," which means they are designed to be inserted in only one orientation.

Table 1-1   Connectors

Type	Example Image	Description
A 20-pin or 24-pin slotted connector		<ul><li>Connects to the motherboard</li><li>The 24-pin connector has two rows of 12 pins each</li><li>The 20-pin connector has two rows of 10 pins each</li></ul>
SATA keyed connector		<ul><li>Connects disk drives</li><li>Connector is wider and thinner than a Molex connector</li></ul>

Type	Example Image	Description
Molex keyed connector		■ Connects hard drives, optical drives, or other devices
Berg keyed connector		■ Connects to a legacy floppy drive ■ Smaller than a Molex connector
4-pin to 8-pin auxiliary power connector		■ Connector has two rows of two to four pins and supplies power to different areas of the motherboard ■ The auxiliary power connector is the same shape as the main power connector but smaller
6/8-pin PCIe power		■ Connector has two rows of three to four pins and supplies power to internal components

Power Supply Voltage (1.2.1.4)

The different connectors provide different voltages. The most common voltages supplied are 3.3V, 5V, and 12V. The 3.3V and 5V supplies are typically used by digital circuits, and 12V supplies are used to run motors in disk drives and fans.

Power supplies can also be *single rail*, *dual rail*, or *multi rail*. A *rail* is the printed circuit board (PCB) inside the power supply to which the external cables are connected. A single rail has all the connectors connected to the same PCB. Dual rail splits the total amperage among four circuits; this can allow for safer operation because you're not forcing loads of power through a single rail. A multi rail has separate PCBs for each connector.

A computer can tolerate slight fluctuations in power, but a significant deviation can cause the power supply to fail.

Interactive Graphic

Check Your Understanding 1.2.1.5: Cases and Power Supplies

Refer to the online course to complete this activity.

Motherboards (1.2.2)

A motherboard is one of the most crucial parts of a computer system because it houses key computer components. There are a variety of motherboard types, with different form factors. They are constructed to operate with specific types of memory (RAM) and processors, so all these components must be compatible.

Motherboards (1.2.2.1)

The *motherboard*, also known as the *system board* or the *main board*, is the backbone of the computer. A motherboard is a *printed circuit board (PCB)* that contains buses, or electrical pathways, which interconnect electronic components. These components may be soldered directly to the motherboard or added using sockets, expansion slots, and ports.

Motherboard Components (1.2.2.2)

A motherboard has some connections where computer components can be added, as shown in Figure 1-6 and described in the list that follows:

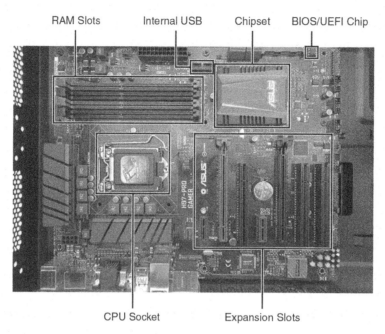

Figure 1-6 Motherboard Connections

- **Central processing unit (CPU):** This is considered the brain of the computer.

- **Random access memory (RAM):** This is a location that temporarily stores data and applications.

- **Expansion slots:** These provide locations to connect additional components.

- *Chipset*: This consists of the integrated circuits on the motherboard that control how system hardware interacts with the CPU and motherboard. It also establishes how much memory can be added to a motherboard and the type of connectors on the motherboard.

- *Basic input/output system (BIOS) chip* and *Unified Extensible Firmware Interface (UEFI) chip*: BIOS is used to help boot the computer and manage the flow of data between the hard drive, the video card, the keyboard, the mouse, and other components. Recently, the BIOS has been enhanced by UEFI. UEFI specifies a different software interface for boot and runtime services but still relies on the traditional BIOS for system configuration, power-on self-test (POST), and setup.

The Serial Advanced Technology Attachment (SATA), shown in Figure 1-7, is a disk drive interface used for connecting optical drives, hard drives, and solid-state drives to the motherboard. SATA supports hot swapping, which is the ability to replace devices without powering off the computer.

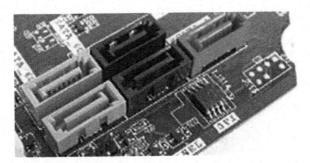

Figure 1-7   SATA

Integrated Drive Electronics (IDE), shown in Figure 1-8, is an older standard interface for connecting disk drives to the motherboard. IDE uses a 40-pin connector. Each IDE interface supports a maximum of two devices.

Figure 1-8   IDE

A 19-pin connector, shown in Figure 1-9, is used to connect the external USB 3 ports on the computer case to the motherboard. USB 1.1 and USB 2 connectors have nine pins.

Figure 1-9   Internal USB

Motherboard Chipset (1.2.2.3)

Figure 1-10 illustrates how a motherboard connects various components.

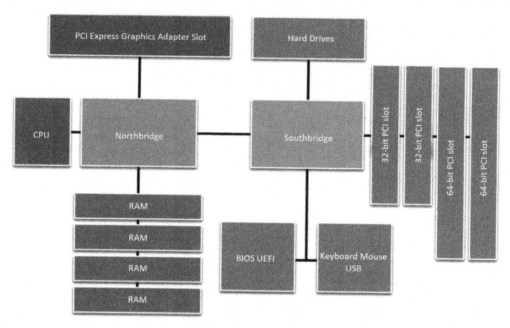

Figure 1-10   Motherboard Component Connections

Most chipsets consist of the following two types:

- *Northbridge*: This chipset controls high-speed access to the RAM and video card. It also controls the speed at which the CPU communicates with all the other components in the computer. Video capability is sometimes integrated into the Northbridge.

- *Southbridge*: This chipset allows the CPU to communicate with slower-speed devices, including hard drives, Universal Serial Bus (USB) ports, and expansion slots.

Motherboard Form Factors (1.2.2.4)

The form factor of motherboards pertains to the size and shape of the board. It also describes the physical layout of the different components and devices on the motherboard.

Many variations of motherboards have been developed over the years. There are three common motherboard form factors:

- **Advanced Technology Extended (ATX):** This is the most common motherboard form factor. The ATX case accommodates the integrated I/O ports on the standard ATX motherboard. The ATX power supply connects to the motherboard via a single 20-pin connector.

- **Micro-ATX:** This is a smaller form factor designed to be backward compatible with ATX. Micro-ATX boards often use the same Northbridge and Southbridge chipsets and power connectors as full-size ATX boards and therefore can use many of the same components. Generally, Micro-ATX boards can fit in standard ATX cases. However, Micro-ATX motherboards are much smaller than ATX motherboards and have fewer expansion slots.

- **ITX:** The ITX form factor has gained popularity because of its very small size. There are many types of ITX motherboards; Mini-ITX is one of the most popular. The Mini-ITX form factor uses very little power, and fans are not needed to keep it cool. A Mini-ITX motherboard has only one PCI slot for expansion cards. A computer based on a Mini-ITX form factor can be used in places where it is inconvenient to have a large or noisy computer.

Table 1-2 highlights these and other form factor variations.

Note

It is important to distinguish between form factors. The choice of motherboard form factor determines how individual components attach to it, the type of power supply required, and the shape of the computer case. Some manufacturers also have proprietary form factors based on the ATX design. For this reason, some motherboards, power supplies, and other components are incompatible with standard ATX cases.

Table 1-2   Motherboard Form Factors

Form Factor	Description
ATX	- Most popular form factor - 12 in. × 9.6 in. (30.5 cm × 24.4 cm)
Micro-ATX	- Smaller footprint than ATX - Popular in desktop and small form factor computers - 9.6 in. × 9.6 in. (24.4 cm × 24.4 cm)
Mini-ITX	- Designed for small devices such as thin clients and set-top boxes - 6.7 in. × 6.7 in. (17 cm × 17 cm)
ITX	- Comparable form factor to Micro-ATX - 8.5 in. × 7.5 in. (21.5 cm × 19.1 cm)

Check Your Understanding 1.2.2.5: Motherboards

Refer to the online course to complete this activity.

CPUs and Cooling Systems (1.2.3)

Whereas the motherboard is considered to be the backbone of the computer, the central processing unit (CPU) is considered to be the brain. In terms of computing power, the CPU, sometimes referred to as the processor, is the most important element of a computer system. Most calculations take place in the CPU, and the CPU therefore generates a significant amount of heat. It is important to have a proper cooling system to effectively keep the CPU as well as other computer components at safe operating temperatures to prevent damage or performance degradation.

What Is a CPU? (1.2.3.1)

The *central processing unit (CPU)* is responsible for interpreting and executing commands. It handles instructions from the computer's other hardware, such as a keyboard, and software. The CPU interprets the instructions and outputs the information to the monitor or performs the requested tasks.

The CPU is a small microchip that resides within a CPU package. The CPU package is often referred to as the CPU. CPU packages come in different form factors, and each style requires a particular socket on the motherboard. Common CPU manufacturers include Intel and AMD.

The CPU socket is the connection between the motherboard and the processor. Modern CPU sockets and processor packages are built around the following architectures:

- *Pin grid array (PGA)* (see Figure 1-11): With PGA architecture, the pins are on the underside of the processor package, and the pins are inserted into the motherboard CPU socket using *zero insertion force (ZIF)*. ZIF refers to the amount of force needed to install a CPU into the motherboard socket or slot.

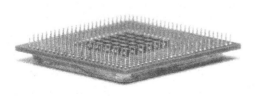

Figure 1-11   PGA CPU and Socket

- *Land grid array (LGA)* (see **Figure 1-12**): In an LGA architecture, the pins are in the socket instead of on the processor.

Figure 1-12   LGA CPU and Socket

Cooling Systems (1.2.3.2)

The flow of current between electronic components generates heat. Computer components perform better when kept cool. If the heat is not removed, the computer may run more slowly. If too much heat builds up, the computer could crash, or components can be damaged. Therefore, it is imperative that computers be kept cool.

Computers are kept cool using active and passive cooling solutions. Active solutions require power, and passive solutions do not. Passive solutions for cooling usually involve reducing the speed at which a component is operating or adding heat sinks to computer chips. A case fan is considered active cooling. Figure 1-13 shows examples of passive and active cooling solutions.

Figure 1-13   Cooling Systems

Interactive Graphic

Check Your Understanding 1.2.3.3: CPUs and Cooling Systems

Refer to the online course to complete this activity.

Memory (1.2.4)

Computers have different types of memory, which comes in different form factors and chip types. Computer memory components can be volatile and nonvolatile, and they can store information temporarily, as RAM (random access memory) does, or permanently, as ROM (read-only memory) does.

Types of Memory (1.2.4.1)

A computer might use different types of memory chips. However, all memory chips store data in the form of bytes. A byte is a grouping of digital information and represents information such as letters, numbers, and symbols. Specifically, a byte is a block of 8 bits stored as either 0 or 1 in the memory chip.

Read-Only Memory

An essential computer chip is the *read-only memory (ROM)* chip. ROM chips are located on the motherboard and other circuit boards and contain instructions that can be directly accessed by a CPU. The instructions stored in ROM include basic operation instructions such as for booting the computer and loading the operating system.

ROM is *nonvolatile memory*, which means the contents are not erased when the computer is powered off.

Random Access Memory

Random access memory (RAM) is temporary working storage for data and programs being accessed by the CPU. Unlike ROM, RAM is *volatile memory*, which means the contents are erased every time the computer is powered off.

Adding more RAM in a computer enhances the system performance. For instance, more RAM increases the memory capacity of the computer to hold and process programs and files. With less RAM, a computer must swap data between RAM and the much slower hard drive. The maximum amount of RAM that can be installed is limited by the motherboard.

Types of ROM (1.2.4.2)

The list that follows describes the types of ROM:

- **ROM:** Information is written to a ROM chip when it is manufactured (see Figure 1-14). ROM chips that cannot be erased or rewritten are now obsolete. The term ROM still tends to be used generically for any read-only memory chip type.

Figure 1-14   ROM

- **PROM:** Information on a *programmable read-only memory (PROM)* chip (see Figure 1-15) is written after the chip is manufactured. PROMs are manufactured blank and can be programmed by a PROM programmer when needed. Generally, these chips cannot be erased and can be programmed only once.

Figure 1-15   PROM

■ **EPROM:** *Erasable programmable read-only memory (EPROM)* (see Figure 1-16) is nonvolatile but can be erased by being exposed to strong ultraviolet light. EPROM usually has a transparent quartz window on the top of the chip. Constant erasing and reprogramming could eventually render the chip useless.

Figure 1-16   EPROM

■ **EEPROM:** Information is written to an *electrically erasable programmable read-only memory (EEPROM)* chip after it is manufactured and without needing to be removed from the device. EEPROM chips (see Figure 1-17) are also called flash ROMs because the contents can be "flashed" for deletion. EEPROMs are often used to store a computer system's BIOS.

Figure 1-17   EEPROM

Types of RAM (1.2.4.3)

Table 1-3 lists the different types of RAM.

Table 1-3   Types of RAM

Type	Description
Dynamic RAM (DRAM)	■ Older technology, popular until the mid-1990s ■ Used for main memory ■ DRAM gradually discharges energy, and it must be constantly refreshed with pulses of electricity in order to maintain the stored data in the chip
Static RAM (SRAM)	■ Requires constant power to function ■ Often used for cache memory ■ Consumes less power ■ Much faster than DRAM ■ More expensive than DRAM
Synchronous Dynamic RAM (SDRAM)	■ DRAM that operates in synchronization with the memory bus ■ Able to process overlapping instructions in parallel (for example, can process a read before a write has been completed) ■ Higher transfer rates
Double Data Rate Synchronous Dynamic RAM (DDR SDRAM)	■ Transfers data twice as fast as SDRAM ■ Able to support two writes and two reads per CPU clock cycle ■ Connector has 184 pins and a single notch ■ Uses lower standard voltage (2.5V) ■ Family: DDR2, DDR3, DDR4
Double Data Rate 2 Synchronous Dynamic RAM (DDR2 SDRAM)	■ Transfers data twice as fast as SDRAM ■ Runs at higher clock speeds than DDR (553 MHz vs. DDR at 200 MHz) ■ Improves performance by decreasing noise and cross-talk between signal wires ■ Connector has 240 pins ■ Uses lower standard voltage (1.8V)

Type	Description
Double Data Rate 3 Synchronous Dynamic RAM (DDR3 SDRAM)	■ Expands memory bandwidth by doubling the clock rate of DDR2 ■ Consumes less power than DDR2 (1.5V) ■ Generates less heat ■ Runs at higher clock speeds (up to 800 MHz) ■ Connector has 240 pins
Double Data Rate 4 Synchronous Dynamic RAM (DDR4 SDRAM)	■ Quadruples the maximum storage capacity compared to DDR3 ■ Consumes less power than DDR3 (1.2V) ■ Runs at higher clock speeds (up to 1600 MHz) ■ Connector has 288 pins ■ Advanced error correction features
Graphics Double Data Rate Synchronous Dynamic RAM (GDDR)	■ RAM specifically designed for video graphics ■ Used in conjunction with a dedicated GPU ■ Family: GDDR, GDDR2, GDDR3, GDDR4, GDDR5 ■ Each higher family member improves performance ■ Each higher family member lowers power consumption ■ GDDR SDRAM processes massive amounts of data but not necessarily at the fastest speeds
Double Data Rate 5 Synchronous Dynamic RAM (DDR5 SDRAM)	■ More than double the speed of the fastest DDR4 modules ■ Quadruples the maximum storage capacity of DDR4 ■ Consumes slightly less power than DDR4 (1.1V) ■ Connector has 288 pins but a different pattern than DDR4, so they are not compatible ■ Maximum module size is 128 GB

Memory Modules (1.2.4.4)

Early computers had RAM installed on the motherboard as individual chips. The individual memory chips, called *dual inline package* (*DIP*) chips, were difficult to install and often became loose. To solve this problem, designers soldered the memory chips to a circuit board to create a *memory module* that would then be placed into a memory slot on the motherboard.

The different types of memory modules are as follows:

- A *dual inline package (DIP)* (see Figure 1-18) is an individual memory chip. A DIP has dual rows of pins used to attach it to the motherboard.

Figure 1-18   DIP

- A *single inline memory module (SIMM)* (see Figure 1-19) is a small circuit board that holds several memory chips. SIMMs have 30-pin or 72-pin configurations.

Figure 1-19   SIMM

- A *dual inline memory module (DIMM)* (see Figure 1-20) is a circuit board that holds SDRAM, DDR SDRAM, DDR2 SDRAM, DDR3 SDRAM, and DDR4 SDRAM chips. There are 168-pin SDRAM DIMMs, 184-pin DDR DIMMs, 240-pin DDR2 and DDR3 DIMMs, and 288-pin DDR4 DIMMs.

Figure 1-20   DIMM

- A *small outline DIMM (SODIMM)* (see Figure 1-21) has 72-pin and 100-pin configurations for support of 32-bit transfers and 144-pin, 200-pin, 204-pin, and 260-pin configurations for support of 64-bit transfers. This smaller, more condensed version of DIMM provides random-access data storage that is ideal for use in laptops, printers, and other devices where conserving space is desirable.

Figure 1-21   SODIMM

Memory modules can be single-sided or double-sided. Single-sided memory modules contain RAM on only one side of the module. Double-sided memory modules contain RAM on both sides.

The speed of memory has a direct impact on how much data a processor can process in a given period of time. As processor speed increases, memory speed must also increase. Memory throughput has also been increased through multichannel technology. Standard RAM is *single channel*, meaning all the RAM slots are addressed at the same time. *Dual channel* RAM adds a second channel to make it possible to access a second module at the same time.

Triple channel technology provides yet another channel, so three modules can be accessed at the same time. Quadruple channel adds another channel to the memory controller for even higher bandwidth. To use triple and quadruple channel memory controllers for the most bandwidth, the chipset architecture must support it and will only be able to use the channels that have memory slots populated. In many cases, memory slots can only be populated in a certain order in order to ensure that all memory channels are used.

The fastest memory is typically static RAM (SRAM), which is cache memory for storing the most recently used data and CPU instructions. SRAM provides the processor with faster access to the data than retrieving it from the slower dynamic RAM (DRAM) or main memory.

Cache memory comes in three types:

- *L1 cache* is internal cache and is integrated into the CPU. A CPU can have various models, each with a different amount of L1 cache.

- *L2 cache* is external cache and was originally mounted on the motherboard near the CPU. L2 cache is now integrated into the CPU.

- *L3 cache* is used on some high-end workstations and server CPUs.

Memory errors occur when data is not stored correctly in the chips. The computer uses different methods to detect and correct data errors in memory. There are three types of memory error checking and correction:

- *Nonparity memory* does not check for errors in memory. Nonparity RAM is the most common RAM used for home and business workstations.

- *Parity memory* contains 8 bits for data and 1 bit for error checking. The error-checking bit is called a *parity bit*.

- *Error-correcting code (ECC) memory* can detect multiple bit errors in memory and correct single bit errors in memory. Servers used for financial or data analytics may require ECC memory modules.

Interactive Graphic

Check Your Understanding 1.2.4.5: Memory

Refer to the online course to complete this activity.

Adapter Cards and Expansion Slots (1.2.5)

Adapter cards are the peripheral hardware used in computers to improve the performance and compatibility of systems. On the motherboard, there are different kinds of *expansion slots* that provide connections to the system bus for the various types of adapter cards, allowing expansion of system performance. There are different kinds of adapter cards and expansion slots available.

Adapter Cards (1.2.5.1)

Adapter cards increase the functionality of a computer by adding controllers for specific devices or by replacing malfunctioning ports.

A variety of adapter cards are available to expand and customize the capability of a computer:

- *Sound adapter*: Sound adapters provide audio capability.
- *Network interface card (NIC)*: A NIC connects a computer to a network using a network cable.
- *Wireless NIC*: A wireless NIC connects a computer to a network using radio frequencies.
- *Video adapter*: Video adapters provide video capability.
- *Capture card*: Capture cards send video signals to a computer so the signals can be recorded to a storage drive with video capture software.
- *TV tuner card*: These cards provide the ability to watch and record television signals on a PC by connecting cable television, satellite, or antenna to the installed tuner card.
- *Universal Serial Bus (USB) controller card*: These cards provide additional USB ports to connect a computer to peripheral devices.
- *eSATA card*: These cards add additional internal and external SATA ports to a computer through a single PCI Express slot.

Figure 1-22 shows some of these adapter cards. It should be noted that some of these adapter cards can be integrated onto the motherboard.

Note

An older computer may also have a modem adapter, an Accelerated Graphics Port (AGP), a Small Computer System Interface (SCSI) adapter, and more.

Computers have expansion slots on the motherboard for installing adapter cards. The type of adapter card connector must match the expansion slot. Table 1-4 describes expansion slots.

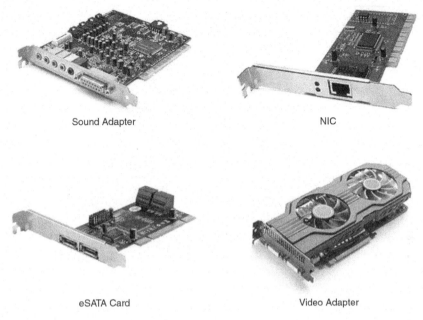

Sound Adapter

NIC

eSATA Card

Video Adapter

Figure 1-22   Adapter Cards

Table 1-4   Expansion Slots

Type	Example Image	Description
Peripheral Component Interconnect (PCI)		This is a 32-bit or 64-bit expansion slot. It is currently found in few computers. PCI expansion slots have become mostly obsolete.
Mini PCI		This is a smaller version of PCI found in some laptops. Mini PCI has three different form factors: Type I, Type II, and Type III.

Type	Example Image	Description
PCI-Extended (PCI-X)		This is an updated version of the standard PCI. It uses a 32-bit bus with higher bandwidth than the PCI bus. PCI-X can operate up to four times faster than PCI. PCI-X expansion slots have become mostly obsolete.
PCI Express (PCIe)		PCI Express is a 64-bit parallel interface that is backward compatible with 32-bit PCI devices. PCIe is a serial point-to-point connection with a different physical interface that was designed to supersede both PCI and PCI-X. There are four sizes (lengths): PCI Express x1, PCI Express x4 (with 4 data lanes), PCI Express x8 (with 8 data lanes), and PCI Express x16 (with 16 data lanes).
Riser card		A riser card can be added to a computer to provide additional expansion slots for more expansion cards.
Accelerated Graphics Port (AGP)		This was a high-speed slot for attaching an AGP video card. The AGP has been superseded by PCI. Few motherboards today use this technology.

Table 1-5 shows the speeds, in gigabytes per second (GB/s), for different versions of PCIe x1 and x16 slots.

Table 1-5 PCIe Versions

Version	GB/s for x1	GB/s for x16
2	0.5	8
3	0.985	15.754
4	1.969	31.508
5	3.938	63.015

Every version of PCIe is backward compatible with all other versions. For example, if you have a motherboard that supports version 4, you can still use version 3 PCIe components. The speed of the bus is determined by the lowest version component installed.

PCIe can supply up to 25 watts of power to each slot. For a graphics card, it can supply up to 75 watts. For very powerful graphics cards, an additional 75 watts can be supplied by a PCIe power connector from the power supply.

Interactive Graphic

Check Your Understanding 1.2.5.2: Adapter Cards and Expansion Slots

Refer to the online course to complete this activity.

Hard Disk Drives and SSDs (1.2.6)

Storage drives read information from or write information to magnetic, optical, or semiconductor storage media. The drives can be used to store data permanently or to retrieve information from a media disk.

Types of Storage Devices (1.2.6.1)

A number of different types of devices are available for data storage on a PC, as shown in Figure 1-23. Data drives provide nonvolatile storage of data, meaning when the drive loses power, the data is retained and available the next time the drive is powered on. Some drives have fixed media, and other drives have removable media. Some offer the ability to read and write data, while others only allow data to be accessed but not written. Data storage devices can be classified according to the media on which the data is stored: magnetic (such as hard disk drives and tape drives), solid state, or optical.

Hard Disk Drive

Optical Drive

Solid State Drive

Tape Drive

Figure 1-23   Data Storage Drives

Storage Device Interfaces (1.2.6.2)

Internal storage devices often connect to the motherboard using *Serial AT Attachment (SATA)* connections. The SATA standards define the way data is transferred, the transfer rates, and physical characteristics of the cables and connectors.

There are three main versions of the SATA standard: SATA 1, SATA 2, and SATA 3, as shown in Table 1-6. The cables and connectors for these versions are the same, but the data transfer speeds are different. SATA 1 allows for a maximum data transfer rate of 1.5 Gb/s, while SATA 2 can reach up to 3 Gb/s. SATA 3 is the fastest, with speeds up to 6 Gb/s.

Table 1-6   Storage Device Interfaces

ATA	Parallel (PATA)	IDE	8.3 Mbps
		EIDE	16.6 Mbps
	Serial (SATA)	SATA 1	1.5 Gbps
		SATA 2	3.0 Gbps
		SATA 3	6.0 Gbps

Note

Legacy internal drive connection methods include the Parallel ATA standards known as Integrated Drive Electronics (IDE) and Enhanced Integrated Drive Electronics (EIDE).

Small Computer System Interface (SCSI) is another interface between motherboards and data storage devices. It is an older standard that originally used parallel, rather than serial, data transfers. A new version of SCSI, known as Serial Attached SCSI (SAS), has been developed. SAS is a popular interface used for server storage.

Magnetic Media Storage (1.2.6.3)

One type of storage represents binary values as magnetized or non-magnetized physical areas of magnetic media. Mechanical systems are used to position and read the media. The following are common types of magnetic media storage drives:

- *Hard disk drive (HDD)*: HDDs are the traditional magnetic disk devices that have been used for years. Their storage capacity ranges from gigabytes (GB) to terabytes (TB). Their speed is measured in revolutions per minute (RPM). This indicates how fast the spindle turns the platters that hold the data. The faster the spindle speed, the more quickly a hard drive can find data on the platters. This can correspond to faster transfer speeds. Common hard drive spindle speeds include 5400, 7200, 10,000, and 15,000 RPM. HDDs come in 1.8-, 2.5-, and 3.5-inch form factors. The 3.5-inch form factor is standard for personal computers. 2.5-inch HDDs are typically used in mobile devices. 1.8-inch HDDs were used in portable media players and other mobile applications but are seldom used in new devices.

- *Tape drive*: Magnetic tapes are most often used for archiving data. At one time, they were useful for backing up PCs. However, the price of HDDs has dropped, and external HDDs are now frequently used for this purpose. However, tape backups are still used in enterprise networks. A tape drive uses a magnetic read/write head and removable tape cartridge. Although data retrieval using a tape drive can be fast, locating specific data is slow because the tape must be wound on a reel until the data is found. Common tape storage capacities vary between a few gigabytes and many terabytes.

Note

Older computers may still incorporate legacy storage devices, including floppy disk drives.

Semiconductor Storage (1.2.6.4)

Solid-state drives (SSD) store data as electrical charges in semiconductor *flash memory*. This makes SSDs much faster than magnetic HDDs. SSD storage capacity ranges from around 120 GB to many terabytes. SSDs have no moving parts, make no noise, are more energy efficient, and produce less heat than HDDs. Because SSDs have no moving parts to fail, they are considered to be more reliable than HDDs.

SSDs come in three form factors:

- **Disk drive form factor:** With this form factor, the semiconductor memory is in a closed package that can be mounted in computer cases like an HDD. It can be 2.5, 3.5, or 1.8 inches (although 1.8-inch form factors are rare).

- **Expansion card:** This plugs directly into the motherboard and mounts in the computer case like other expansion cards.

- *mSATA or M.2 module*: These packages may use a special socket. M.2 is a standard for computer expansion cards. It is a family of standards that specify physical aspects of expansion cards such as connectors and dimension.

Figure 1-24 shows these form factors.

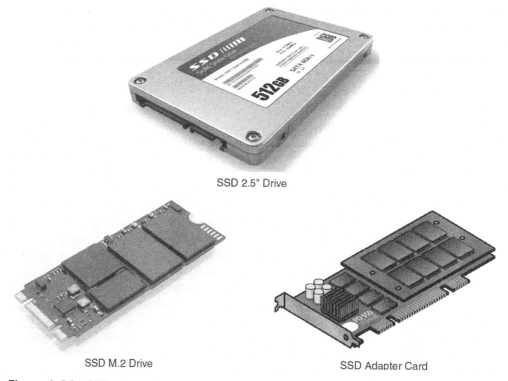

SSD 2.5" Drive

SSD M.2 Drive

SSD Adapter Card

Figure 1-24   SSD Form Factors

Figure 1-25 shows the 2.5-inch and M.2 form factors in comparison to a 3.5-inch magnetic HDD.

Figure 1-25   Data Storage Device Form Factors

The *Non-Volatile Memory Express (NVMe)* specification was developed specifically to allow computers to take greater advantage of the features of SSDs by providing a standard interface between SSDs, the PCIe bus, and operating systems. NVMe allows compliant SSDs to attach to the PCIe bus without requiring special drivers, in much the same way USB flash drives can be used in multiple computers without requiring installation on each.

Finally, a *solid-state hybrid drive (SSHD)* is a compromise between a magnetic HDD and an SSD. An SSHD is faster than an HDD but less expensive than an SSD. It combines a magnetic HDD with onboard flash memory that serves as a nonvolatile cache. An SSHD drive automatically caches data that is frequently accessed, which can speed up certain operations, such as operating system startup.

Interactive Graphic

Check Your Understanding 1.2.6.5: Data Storage Devices

Refer to the online course to complete this activity.

Optical Storage Devices (1.2.7)

An *optical storage device* is a peripheral computer component that can read CD-ROMs or other optical discs using a laser to store and retrieve saved data.

Types of Optical Storage Devices (1.2.7.1)

Using lasers to read and write data on *optical media*, optical drives provide another storage option in a computer system. They were developed to overcome the storage capacity limitations of removable magnetic media such as floppy disks and magnetic storage cartridges. Figure 1-26 shows an internal optical drive.

Figure 1-26   Internal Optical Drive

There are three types of optical drives:

- **Compact disc (CD):** Stores audio and data
- **Digital versatile disc (DVD):** Stores digital video and data
- **Blu-ray disc (BD):** Stores HD digital video and data

CD, DVD, and BD media can be prerecorded (read-only), recordable (write-once), or rerecordable (read and write multiple times). DVD and BD media can also be single layer (SL) or dual layer (DL). Dual layer media roughly doubles the capacity of a single disc.

Table 1-7 describes the various types of optical media and their approximate storage capacities.

Table 1-7   Types of Optical Media

Optical Media	Description	Storage Capacity
CD-ROM	CD read-only memory media that is prerecorded	700 MB
CD-R	CD recordable media that can be recorded one time	
CD-RW	CD rewritable media that can be recorded, erased, and rerecorded	
DVD-ROM	DVD read-only memory media that is prerecorded	4.7 GB (single layer) and 8.5 GB (dual layer)
DVD-RAM	DVD rewritable media that can be recorded, erased, and rerecorded	
DVD+/-R	DVD recordable media that can be recorded one time	
DVD+/-RW	DVD rewritable media that can be recorded, erased, and rerecorded	
BD-ROM	Blu-ray read-only media that is prerecorded with movies, games, or software	25 GB (single layer) and 50 GB (dual layer)
BD-R	Blu-ray recordable media that can be recorded one time	
BD-RE	Blu-ray rewritable media that can be recorded, erased, and rerecorded	

Interactive Graphic

Check Your Understanding 1.2.7.2: Types of Optical Media

Refer to the online course to complete this activity.

Ports, Cables, and Adapters (1.2.8)

This section describes and identifies common cables and ports used for connecting peripherals internally and externally on computers.

Video Ports and Cables (1.2.8.1)

A *video port* connects a monitor cable to a computer. Video ports and monitor cables transfer analog signals, digital signals, or both. Computers are digital devices that create digital signals. The digital signals are sent to the graphics card, where they are transmitted through a cable to a display.

Digital Visual Interface (DVI)

A *Digital Visual Interface (DVI)* connector, shown in Figure 1-27, is usually white and consists of as many as 24 pins (three rows of 8 pins) for digital signals, up to 4 pins for analog signals, and a flat pin called a ground bar.

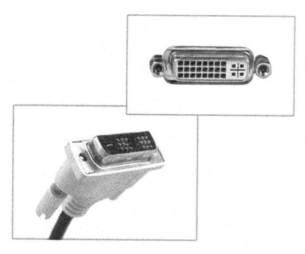

Figure 1-27   DVI

Five types of DVI are available for digital and analog output and also for single link and dual link, which offers extra bandwidth. DVI-D supports only digital devices and outputs. DVI-A supports only analog outputs. DVI-I supports digital outputs and analog devices.

There are currently two main types of DVI connectors: DVI-I and DVI-D. DVI-D provides a digital-only signal, whereas DVI-I can support digital and analog signals. DVI is disappearing as quickly as it appeared. It's still seen in some monitors alongside VGA, which is finally starting to fade in favor of HDMI.

DisplayPort

DisplayPort (see Figure 1-28) is an interface technology designed to connect high-end graphics-capable PCs and displays, as well as home theater equipment and displays.

Figure 1-28   DisplayPort

High-Definition Multimedia Interface (HDMI)

High-Definition Multimedia Interface (HDMI) (see Figure 1-29) was developed specifically for high-definition televisions. However, its digital features also make it a good candidate for computers.

Figure 1-29   HDMI

Thunderbolt 1 or 2

Thunderbolt (see Figure 1-30) allows for high-speed connection of peripherals such as hard drives, RAID arrays, and network interfaces, and it can transmit high-definition video using the DisplayPort protocol.

Figure 1-30   Thunderbolt 1 or 2

Thunderbolt 3

Thunderbolt 3 (see Figure 1-31) uses the same connector as USB-C. It has twice the bandwidth of Thunderbolt 2, uses less power, and can provide two 4K monitors with video.

Figure 1-31   Thunderbolt 3

Video Graphics Array (VGA)

Video Graphics Array (VGA), shown in Figure 1-32, is a connector for analog video. It has three rows and 15 pins. It is also sometimes referred to as a DE-15 or HD-15 connector.

Figure 1-32   VGA

Radio Corporation of America (RCA)

As shown in Figure 1-33, a *Radio Corporation of America (RCA)* connector has a central plug with a ring around it. RCA connectors, which are used to carry audio or video, are often found in groups of three, where a yellow connector carries video and a pair of red and white connectors carries left and right audio channels.

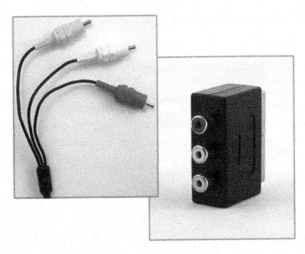

Figure 1-33   RCA

Other Ports and Cables (1.2.8.2)

Input/output (I/O) ports on a computer connect peripheral devices such as printers, scanners, and portable drives. In addition to the ports and interfaces previously discussed, a computer might also have other ports.

Personal System 2 (PS/2)

A *PS/2 port* (see Figure 1-34) connects a keyboard or a mouse to a computer. A PS/2 port is a 6-pin mini-DIN female connector. The connectors for the keyboard and mouse are often colored differently. If the ports are not color-coded, look for a small figure of a mouse or keyboard next to each port.

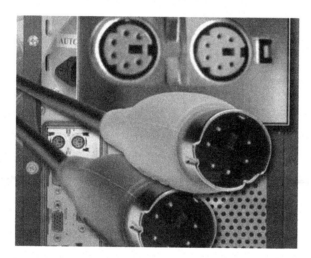

Figure 1-34   PS/2

Audio and Game Port

Figure 1-35 shows audio and game ports. *Audio ports* connect audio devices to the computer. Analog ports typically include a line-in port to connect to an external source (for example, a stereo system), a microphone port, and line-out ports to connect speakers or headphones. The *game port* connects to a joystick or MIDI-interfaced device.

Figure 1-35   Audio and Game Ports

Network

A *network port* (see Figure 1-36), also known as an RJ-45 or 8P8C port, has 8 pins and connects devices to a network. The connection speed depends on the type of network port. The maximum length of the Ethernet network cable is 100 m (328 ft.).

Figure 1-36   Network Port

Serial AT Attachment (SATA)

The Serial AT Attachment (SATA) cable connects SATA devices to the SATA interface using a 7-pin data cable, as shown in Figure 1-37. SATA connectors have an L-shaped slot so the cable fits in only one orientation. This cable does not supply any power to the SATA device. A separate power cable provides power to the drive.

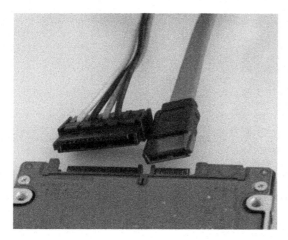

Figure 1-37   Drive Power Cable and SATA (red cable)

Integrated Drive Electronics (IDE)

An *Integrated Drive Electronics (IDE)* cable is a ribbon cable used to connect storage drives inside a computer. The two most common types of IDE ribbon cables are the 34-pin cable used for floppy drives and the 40-pin cable for hard drives and optical drives.

IDE cables are keyed so the cable inserts into the connector only one way, as shown in Figure 1-38.

Figure 1-38   IDE

The Universal Serial Bus (USB)

Universal Serial Bus (USB) is a standard interface that connects peripheral devices to a computer, as shown in Figure 1-39. USB devices are hot swappable, which means users can connect and disconnect the devices while the computer is powered on.

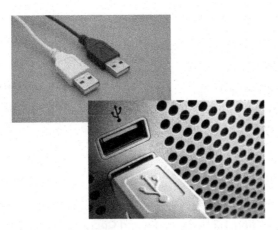

Figure 1-39   USB

Adapters and Converters (1.2.8.3)

There are many connection standards in use today. A number of them are interoperable but require specialized components, called adapters and converters:

- *Adapter*: This is a component that physically connects one technology to another (for example, a DVI-to-HDMI adapter). An adapter could be one component or a cable with different ends.

- *Converter*: This performs the same function as an adapter but also translates the signals from one technology to the other. For example, a USB 3.0-to-SATA converter enables a hard disk drive to be used as a flash drive.

Figure 1-40 shows some common adapters and converters.

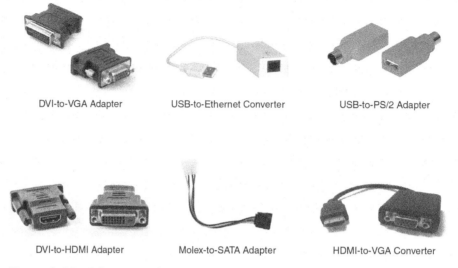

DVI-to-VGA Adapter   USB-to-Ethernet Converter   USB-to-PS/2 Adapter

DVI-to-HDMI Adapter   Molex-to-SATA Adapter   HDMI-to-VGA Converter

Figure 1-40   Adapters and Converters

Check Your Understanding 1.2.8.4: Cables and Connectors

Refer to the online course to complete this activity.

Input Devices (1.2.9)

Input devices are hardware devices (usually outside the computer case) that allow input of raw data for a computer to process, allowing users to interact with and control the computer.

The Original Input Devices (1.2.9.1)

Input devices allow the user to communicate with a computer. Some of the first input devices are as follows:

- **Keyboard and mouse:** These are the two most commonly used input devices. Keyboards are typically used for creating text documents and emails. The mouse is used to navigate the graphical user interface (GUI). Laptops also have touch-pads to provide built-in keyboard and mouse features. The keyboard was the very first type of input device.

- **ADF/flatbed scanner:** Figure 1-41 shows an example of a flatbed scanner. A scanner is a device that digitizes images and documents. A photograph or document is placed on the flat glass surface, and the scan head then moves under the glass. The digitized image is stored as a file that can be displayed, printed, emailed, or altered. Some of these scanners have automatic document feeders (ADFs) to support multiple-page input.

Figure 1-41   Flatbed Scanner

- **Joystick and gamepad:** Figure 1-42 shows a joystick and gamepad. These are input devices for playing games. Gamepads allow the player to control movement and views with small sticks and multiple buttons. Many gamepads also have triggers that register the amount of pressure the player puts on them. Joysticks are often used to play flight simulation-style games.

Figure 1-42   Joystick and Gamepad

- *KVM switch*: A keyboard, video, and mouse (KVM) switch, shown in Figure 1-43, is a hardware device that can be used to control more than one computer while using a single keyboard, monitor, and mouse. For businesses, KVM switches provide cost-efficient access to multiple servers. Home users can save space using a KVM switch to connect multiple computers to one keyboard, monitor, and mouse. Some KVM switches have the capability to share USB devices and speakers with multiple computers.

Figure 1-43   KVM Switch

New Input Devices (1.2.9.2)

Some relatively new input devices include the touchscreen, stylus, magnetic stripe reader, and barcode scanner:

■ **Touchscreen:** Touchscreens (see Figure 1-44) are input devices that have touch- or pressure-sensitive screens. The computer receives instructions specific to the place on the screen the user touches.

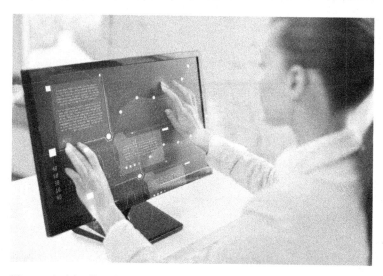

Figure 1-44   Touchscreen

- **Stylus:** A *stylus* (see Figure 1-45) is a type of digitizer that allows a designer or an artist to create blueprints, images, or other artwork by using a pen-like tool called a stylus on a surface that senses where the tip is touching it. Some digitizers have more than one surface, or sensor, and allow the user to create 3D models by performing actions with the stylus in mid-air.

Figure 1-45   Digitizer/Stylus

- **Magnetic stripe reader:** A *magnetic stripe reader* (see Figure 1-46), also called a magstripe reader, is a device that reads information that is magnetically encoded on the back of plastic cards, such as identification badges or credit cards. Also shown on the device in Figure 1-46 is a chip reader. For cards with chips, the card is inserted into the device, and the device reads the chip. Chip reading provides much more security of the user's data because each transaction generates a unique code that cannot be used again.

Figure 1-46   Magnetic Stripe Reader

- **Barcode scanner:** A *barcode scanner* (see Figure 1-47), also called a price scanner, reads the information contained in the barcodes affixed to many products. Barcode scanners can be handheld, wireless, or stationary. The light source on the reader captures the barcode image and translates the image into computer-readable content. This device is typically used at checkout counters in stores or for determining inventory levels. The barcode often is only a number that is used to look up information. Libraries, for instance, affix a barcode to a book so that when it is checked out, the number gets recorded to a library cardholder's record. Manufacturing facilities use barcodes to track inventory and equipment.

Figure 1-47   Barcode Scanner

More New Input Devices (1.2.9.3)

Some additional newer input devices are as follows:

- **Digital camera:** *Digital cameras* (see Figure 1-48) are input devices that capture images and videos that can be stored, displayed, printed, or altered.

Figure 1-48   Digital Camera

■ **Webcam:** A *webcam* is a video camera that can be integrated into a computer or that can be external, as shown in Figure 1-49. Webcams are typically used for video conferencing or to stream live video onto the Internet.

Figure 1-49   Webcam

■ **Signature pad:** A *signature pad*, shown in Figure 1-50, is a device that electronically captures a person's signature. A person uses a stylus to sign on the screen. Electronic signatures, which are legal signatures, are typically used to establish receipt of deliveries and to sign agreements or contracts.

Figure 1-50   Signature Pad

■ **Smart card reader:** *Smart card readers* are input devices typically used on a computer to authenticate the user, as shown in Figure 1-51. A smart card might be the size of a credit card with an embedded integrated circuit that is typically under a gold contact pad on one side of the card.

Figure 1-51   Smart Card Reader

- **Microphone:** This device is a type of digitizer that allows users to speak into a computer and have their voices digitized. Voice, music, or sounds can be stored on the computer to be played back, uploaded, or emailed. This device can also be used as input for games and communication software. Figure 1-52 shows an example of a microphone headset.

Figure 1-52   Microphone Headset

Most Recent Input Devices (1.2.9.4)

The newest input devices include NFC devices and terminals, facial recognition scanners, fingerprint scanners, voice recognition scanners, and virtual reality headsets, which are further described in the list that follows:

- *NFC devices and terminals*: Near field communication (NFC) tap-to-pay devices (see Figure 1-53), such as credit cards or smartphones, are able to read and write to NFC chips. An NFC-powered terminal can subtract money from the balance on a debit card or charge money to a credit card. Two NFC-capable devices can also transfer data such as photographs, links, or contacts between them.

Figure 1-53   NFC Devices and Terminals

- **Facial recognition scanners:** *Facial recognition scanners*, shown in Figure 1-54, are biometric input devices used to identify a person based on their unique facial features. Many laptops and smartphones have facial recognition scanners to automate logging in to the device. Facial recognition is becoming popular in many smartphones and even some computers and tablets. Microsoft promotes "Windows Hello" as using facial recognition or fingerprint readers as biometric input. These devices are typically used to provide secure access to devices or locations.

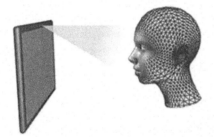

Figure 1-54   Facial Recognition Scanner

- **Fingerprint scanners:** A *fingerprint scanner*, shown in Figure 1-55, is a biometric input device used to identify a person based on their fingerprint. Many laptops and smart devices have fingerprint readers to automate logging in to the device. These devices are typically used to provide secure access to devices or locations.

Figure 1-55   Fingerprint Scanner

■ **Voice recognition scanners:** A voice recognition scanner, shown in Figure 1-56, is a biometric input device used to identify a person based on their unique voice. These devices are often used to provide secure access to locations. Voice recognition is also being used for input into personal assistant applications such as Apple's Siri and Amazon's Alexa.

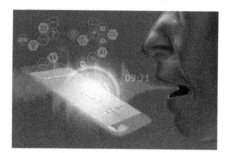

Figure 1-56   Voice Recognition Scanner

■ **Virtual reality headset:** *Virtual reality headsets*, shown in Figure 1-57, are devices typically used with computer games, simulators, and training applications. They are head-mounted devices that provide a separate image for each eye. Most headsets include head-motion and eye-motion tracking sensors. These devices are also output devices that deliver video and audio to the wearer.

Figure 1-57   Virtual Reality Headset

Interactive Graphic

Check Your Understanding 1.2.9.5: Input Devices

Refer to the online course to complete this activity.

Output Devices (1.2.10)

Output devices are hardware devices that take the data processed from input and pass on the information for use. Output devices are needed for a user to get processed data in a usable format.

What Are Output Devices? (1.2.10.1)

An output device takes binary information (ones and zeros) from a computer and converts it into a form easily understood by the user. Figure 1-58 shows a variety of output devices.

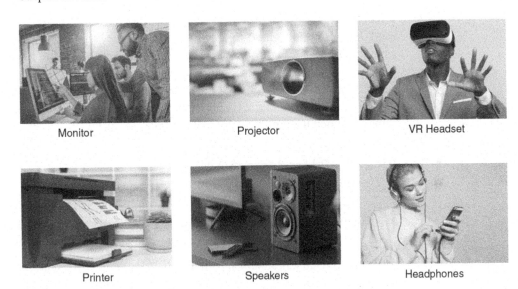

Monitor   Projector   VR Headset

Printer   Speakers   Headphones

Figure 1-58   Output Devices

Monitors and projectors are output devices that create visual and audio signals for the user. Virtual reality (VR) headsets are another type of output device. Televisions may also be output devices. Printers are visual output devices that create hard copies of computer files.

Speakers and headphones are output devices that produce only audio signals. Output devices make it possible for users to interact with computers.

Monitors and Projectors (1.2.10.2)

Most monitors use one of three types of technology: LCD, LED, or OLED. *Liquid crystal display (LCD)* has two polarizing filters with a liquid crystal solution between them. An electronic current aligns the crystals so light can pass through or not pass through, creating the image. *Light-emitting diode (LED)* is an LCD display that uses LED backlighting. LED has lower power consumption than standard LCD backlighting. The panel is thinner, lighter, and brighter and has better contrast than LCD. *Organic LED (OLED)* is a type of LED display that uses a layer of organic material that responds to electrical stimulus to emit light. Each *pixel* lights individually, resulting in much deeper black levels than are available with LED.

Most video projectors use LCD or DLP technology. *Digital light processing (DLP)* uses a spinning color wheel with an array of mirrors. Each mirror corresponds to a pixel and reflects light toward or away from the projector optics, creating an image of up to 1024 shades of gray. The color wheel then adds the color data to complete the projected image. Different projectors have different numbers of lumens, which affects the level of brightness of the projected image. LCD projectors typically have more lumens (are brighter) than DLP projectors. ANSI has a standardized procedure for testing projectors. Projectors tested with this procedure are quoted in "ANSI lumens." Projectors can be compared easily on the basis of their brightness specifications. Brightness (white light output) indicates the total amount of light projected, in lumens. The color brightness specification measures red, green, and blue using the same approach used to measure brightness.

VR and AR Headsets (1.2.10.3)

Virtual reality headsets can have specific hardware and software platforms. They may be tethered to a controller, standalone, or mobile. They may have a variety of sensors, including motion, external visual positioning, camera, motion tracking, accelerometer, gyroscope, and magnetometer sensors. Resolution and refresh rates vary.

Augmented reality headsets and smart glasses come with a wide array of features. Most have a camera, motion sensors, GPS, a CPU, battery power, and a controller. Many also have storage, Bluetooth, speakers, and voice control. The Microsoft HoloLens is a headset with an integrated holographic processing unit.

Virtual reality (VR) uses computer technology to create a simulated three-dimensional environment. The user feels immersed in this virtual world and can manipulate it. A VR headset completely encases the upper portion of the user's face, not allowing in any ambient light from the physical surroundings. Most VR experiences have three-dimensional images that seem life sized to the user. VR experiences also track a user's motions and adjust the images on the user's display accordingly.

Augmented reality (AR) uses similar technology to VR but superimposes images and audio over the real world in real time. AR can provide users with immediate access to information about their real surroundings. An AR headset, shown in Figure 1-59, usually does not close off ambient light to users, allowing them to see their real-life surroundings. Not all AR requires a headset. Some AR can simply be downloaded onto a smartphone. Pokémon Go is an early version of an AR game using a player's smartphone to "see and capture" virtual objects in the real world. Smart glasses are also AR devices. They weigh much less than AR headsets and are often designed for a specific audience, such as cyclists.

Figure 1-59   AR Headset

Printers (1.2.10.4)

Printers are output devices that create hard copies of files. A hard copy might be on a sheet of paper. It could also be a plastic form created by a 3D printer.

Figure 1-60 shows a variety of printer types. Today's printers can be wired, wireless, or both. They use different technologies to create the images you see. All printers require printing material (such as ink, toner, liquid plastic, and so on) and a method to place it accurately on the paper or extrude it into the desired shape. All printers have hardware that must be maintained. Most printers also have software, in the form of drivers, that must be kept up to date.

Inkjet Printer

Impact Printer

3D Printer

Thermal Printer

Figure 1-60   Printers

Speakers and Headphones (1.2.10.5)

Speakers are a type of auditory output device. Most computers and mobile devices have audio support either integrated into the motherboard or on an adapter card. Audio support includes ports that allow input and output of audio signals. The audio card has an amplifier to power headphones and external speakers.

Headphones, earbuds, and the earphones found in headsets are all auditory output devices. These can be wired or wireless. Some are Wi-Fi or Bluetooth enabled.

Interactive Graphic

Check Your Understanding 1.2.10.6: Visual and Auditory Output Device Characteristics

Refer to the online course to complete this activity.

Computer Disassembly (1.3)

In this section, you will explore in detail the steps used to disassemble a computer as well as the tools to complete the task properly, including ESD-specific tools to keep you and your computer safe.

The Technician's Toolkit (1.3.1)

An organized and well-stocked toolkit will help a technician complete work in a safe and efficient way. Having the right tools makes a job safer and can prevent damage from being done in the repair process. A toolkit is an important part of doing a job properly. As you become more experienced or as your role changes, you will find that your toolkit will continue to grow and change to meet your needs.

Video

Video Explanation 1.3.1.1: Technician's Toolkit

Interactive Graphic

Check Your Understanding 1.3.1.2: Technician's Toolkit

Refer to the online course to complete this activity.

Computer Disassembly (1.3.2)

Disassembling a computer system is a pretty straightforward task. Gathering documentation (if available), planning the process, having the right tools, and taking care to follow safety precautions such as powering down the computer and unplugging the PSU as well as using antistatic equipment will aid in making it a successful undertaking.

Lab 1.3.2.1: Safety

In this lab, you will use common safety procedures while building and/or servicing computer hardware.

Video Demonstration 1.3.2.2: Computer Disassembly

Lab 1.3.2.3: Disassemble a Computer

In this lab, you will disassemble a computer.

Summary (1.4)

At the beginning of this chapter, you were introduced to the contents of a computer and safety guidelines that can prevent electrical fires and injuries while working inside a computer. You also learned about ESD and how it can damage computer equipment if not discharged properly.

Next, you learned about all the components that make up a PC, starting with the case, which houses all the internal components. You learned about the various form factors of cases and power supplies and how they have evolved over time. Next, you learned about the various types of connectors used to power various internal components, such as the motherboard and storage drives. Serial AT Attachment (SATA), Molex, and PCIe were discussed, as were the voltages provided by the connectors.

You also learned about the motherboard, the backbone of the computer, which contains buses, or electrical pathways used to connect electronic components. These components include the CPU, RAM, expansion slots, chipset, and BIOS and UEFI chips.

Different types of storage devices, such as hard disk drives, optical drives, and solid-state drives, were also discussed, along with the different versions of PATA and SATA interfaces that connect them to the motherboard.

The commonly used tools were explained, and the computer disassembly process was demonstrated. At the end of the chapter, you disassembled a computer as part of a hands-on lab.

Practice

The following activities provide practice with the topics introduced in this chapter. The labs are available in the companion *IT Essentials v8 Labs & Study Guide* (ISBN 9780138166304).

Labs

Lab 1.3.2.1: Safety

Lab 1.3.2.3: Disassemble a Computer

Check Your Understanding Questions

Complete all the review questions listed here to test your understanding of the topics and concepts in this chapter. Appendix A, "Answers to 'Check Your Understanding' Questions," lists the answers.

1. Which two PC components communicate with the CPU through the Southbridge chipset? (Choose two.)

   A. hard drive

   B. 64-bit Gigabit Ethernet adapter

   C. video card

   D. RAM

2. A technician wants to replace a failing power supply on a high-end gaming computer. Which form factor should the technician be looking for?

   A. ATX 12V

   B. ATX

   C. EPS 12V

   D. AT

3. Which statement describes augmented reality (AR) technology?

   A. It always requires a headset.

   B. It does not provide users with immediate access to information about their real surroundings.

   C. It superimposes images and audio over the real world in real time.

   D. The headset closes off any ambient light to users.

4. Which type of input device can identify users based on their voice?

   A. scanner

   B. KVM switch

   C. digitizer

   D. biometric identification device

5. Which motherboard form factor has the smallest footprint for use in thin client devices?

   A. Micro-ATX

   B. ATX

   C. ITX

   D. Mini-ATX

6. How is the 6/8-pin PCIe power connector used in a PC?

   A. to connect disk drives

   B. to connect optical drives

   C. to connect legacy floppy drives

   D. to supply power to various internal components

7. Which expansion slot is used by an NVMe-compliant device?

   A. PCI

   B. PCIe

   C. SATA

   D. USB-C

8. How does a technician protect the internal components of a computer against ESD?

   A. by unplugging the computer after use

   B. by using multiple fans to move warm air through the case

   C. by grounding the internal components via attachment to the case

   D. by using computer cases made out of plastic or aluminum

9. A network administrator currently has three servers and needs to add a fourth but does not have enough room for an additional monitor and keyboard. Which device allows the administrator to connect all the servers to a single monitor and keyboard?

   A. touchscreen monitor

   B. UPS

   C. USB switch

   D. PS/2 hub

   E. KVM switch

10. What type of connecter is used to convert digital signals to analog signals?

    A. Molex-to-SATA adapter

    B. USB-to-PS/2 adapter

    C. HDMI-to-VGA converter

    D. DVI-to-HDMI adapter

11. Which action can reduce the risk of ESD damage when computer equipment is being worked on?

    A. moving cordless phones away from the work area

    B. keeping the computer plugged into a surge protector

    C. lowering the humidity level in the work area

    D. working on a grounded antistatic mat

12. Which port allows for the transmission of high-definition video using the DisplayPort protocol?

    A. DVI

    B. VGA

    C. Thunderbolt

    D. RCA

13. Which two PC components communicate with the CPU through the Northbridge chipset? (Choose two.)

    A. hard drive

    B. 64-bit Gigabit Ethernet adapter

    C. video card

    D. RAM

14. Which three devices are considered output devices? (Choose three.)

    A. headphones

    B. printer

    C. mouse

    D. fingerprint scanner

    E. keyboard

    F. monitor

15. Which disk drive type contains a magnetic HDD with onboard flash memory and serves as a nonvolatile cache?

    A. SSHD

    B. NVMe

    C. SCSI

    D. SSD

16. Which two of these devices are considered to be the most common input devices? (Choose two.)

A. headphones

B. printer

C. mouse

D. fingerprint scanner

E. keyboard

F. monitor

CHAPTER 2

PC Assembly

Objectives

Upon completion of this chapter, you will be able to answer the following questions:

- How do you connect the power supply?
- How do you install the motherboard components?
- How do you install internal drives?
- How do you install adapter cards?
- How do you select additional storage?
- How do you connect computer components with appropriate cables?

Key Terms

This chapter uses the following key terms. You can find the definitions in the glossary at the end of the book.

32-bit bus   page 72

64-bit bus   page 72

adapter card   page 81

address bus   page 72

audio   page 92

buffered memory   page 75

bus   page 72

capture card   page 82

clock multiplier   page 74

clock speed   page 72

CompactFlash   page 88

data bus   page 72

digital signal processor (DSP)   page 84

drive activity LEDs   page 91

FireWire   page 93

front-side bus (FSB)   page 74

graphics card   page 81

I/O card   page 81

maximum speed rating   page 74

Memory Stick   page 88

MicroSD   page 87

MiniSD   page 87

NIC   page 82

Northbridge   page 74

parallel bus   page 73

PCI Express (PCIe)   page 82

Peripheral Component Interconnect (PCI)   page 82

power button   page 91

power supply   page 70

processor chip   page 74

RAM   page 71

Introduction to PC Assembly (2.0)

Assembling computers is often a large part of an IT technician's job. You must work in a logical, methodical manner when working with computer components. At times, you might have to determine whether a component for a customer's computer needs to be upgraded or replaced. It is important that you develop skills in installation procedures, troubleshooting techniques, and diagnostic methods. This chapter discusses the importance of component compatibility. It also covers the need for adequate system resources to efficiently run the customer's hardware and software. Computers, computer components, and computer peripherals all contain hazards that can cause severe injury. Therefore, this chapter begins with general and fire safety guidelines to follow when working with computer components.

In this chapter, you will learn about PC power supplies and the voltages they provide to other computer components. You will learn about the components that are installed on the motherboard: the CPU, RAM, and various adapter cards. You will learn about different CPU architectures and how to select RAM that is compatible with the motherboard and the chipset. You will also learn about various types of storage drives and the factors to consider when selecting the appropriate drive.

It is important to not only learn about assembling computer components but also to build hands-on skills. This chapter includes several labs in which you will assemble a computer. Each of the labs has you progressively install components such as the power supply, CPU, RAM, drives, adapter cards, and cables until computer assembly is complete.

Assemble the Computer (2.1)

Choosing the right computer components when assembling a computer is important. It is also important to properly prepare the work area for the build. Whether you are building a computer with all new components or doing an upgrade, following recommended safety procedures, having the needed tools ready, and understanding how to work within the case are critical.

General and Fire Safety (2.1.1)

Follow general safety and fire safety guidelines to prevent cuts, burns, electrical shock, and damage to eyesight. As a best practice, make sure that a fire extinguisher and first-aid kit are available. Poorly placed or unsecured cables can cause tripping hazards in a network installation. Using safe cable management techniques such as installation of cables in conduit or cable trays helps prevent hazards. Knowing and using these and other safety techniques can help prevent injury to people and damage to computer equipment.

Video

Video Explanation 2.1.1.1: General and Fire Safety

Open the Case and Connect the Power Supply (2.1.2)

Video

Video Demonstration 2.1.2.1: Install the Power Supply

When building or repairing a computer, it is important that you prepare the workspace before opening the computer case. You want adequate lighting, good ventilation, and a comfortable room temperature. The workbench or table should be accessible from all sides. Avoid cluttering the surface of the work area with tools and computer components. Place an antistatic mat on the table to help prevent ESD damage to electronics. It is helpful to use small containers to hold screws and other parts as you remove them.

A technician might be required to replace or install a power supply. Most power supplies can fit only one way in the computer case. Always follow the power supply installation directions in the case and power supply manuals.

Interactive Graphic

Check Your Understanding 2.1.2.2: Install the Power Supply

Refer to the online course to complete this activity.

Select the Case and Fans (2.1.2.3)

The choice of motherboard and external components influences the selection of the case and power supply. The motherboard form factor must be matched with the correct type of computer case and power supply. For example, an ATX motherboard requires both an ATX-compatible case and power supply.

You can select a large computer case to accommodate additional components that may be required in the future. Or you might select a smaller case that requires minimal space. In general, the computer case should be durable and easy to service, and it should have enough room for expansion.

Various factors affecting the choice of a computer case are described in Table 2-1.

Table 2-1   Choosing a Computer Case

Factor	Rationale
Model type	The type of motherboard you choose determines the type of case that can be used. The size and shape must match exactly.
Size	If a computer has many components, it needs more room for airflow to keep the system cool.
Power supply	You must match the power rating and connection type of the power supply to the type of motherboard you have chosen.

Factor	Rationale
Appearance	For some people, how the case looks doesn't matter at all. For others, it is critical. There are many case designs to choose from, and it is possible to find a case that is attractive.
Status display	What is going on inside the case can be very important. LED indicators that are mounted on the outside of the case can tell you if the system is receiving power, when the hard drive is being used, and when the computer is in sleep or hibernate mode.
Vents	Every case has a vent on the power supply, and a case may have another vent on the back to help draw air into or out of the system. Some cases are designed with more vents in the event that the system needs a way to dissipate an unusual amount of heat. This situation may occur when many devices are installed close together in the case.

A case may come with a power supply preinstalled. In this situation, you still need to verify that the power supply provides enough power to operate all the components that will be installed in the case.

A computer has many internal components that generate heat while the computer is running. A case fan should be installed to move cooler air into the computer case while moving heat out of the case. When choosing a case fan, there are several factors to consider, as described in Table 2-2.

Table 2-2   Factors to Consider when Choosing a Case Fan

Factor	Considerations
Case size	Larger cases often require larger fans because smaller fans cannot create enough airflow.
Fan speed	Larger fans can spin more slowly than smaller fans, which reduces fan noise.
Number of components	Multiple components in a computer create additional heat, which requires more fans, larger fans, or faster fans.
Physical environment	The case fans must be able to disperse enough heat to keep the interior of the case cool.
Number of mounting places available	Different cases have different numbers of mounting places for fans.
Location of mounting places available	Different cases have different locations for mounting fans.
Electrical connections	Some case fans are connected directly to the motherboard, while others are connected directly to the power supply.

Note

All the fans in a case must work together to inject cooler air and expel hotter air by properly directing the airflow. Installing a fan backward or using fans with the incorrect size or speed for the case can lead to the airflows working against each other.

Select a Power Supply (2.1.2.4)

Power supplies convert AC input to DC output voltages. Power supplies typically provide voltages of 3.3V, 5V, and 12V and are measured in wattage. A power supply must provide enough power for the installed components and allow for other components that may be added at a later time. If you choose a power supply that powers only the current components, you might need to replace the power supply when other components are upgraded.

Table 2-3 describes various factors to consider when selecting a power supply.

Table 2-3   Choosing a Power Supply

Factor	Considerations
Type of motherboard	The power supply must be compatible with the motherboard.
Required wattage	Add enough wattage for each component. If the wattage is not listed on a component, calculate it by multiplying its voltage by its amperage. If a component requires various levels of wattage, use the higher requirement.
Number of components	Make sure the power supply provides enough wattage to support the number and types of components plus at least another 25%.
Types of components	Make sure the power supply provides the right types of power connectors.
Type of case	Make sure the power supply can be mounted in the desired case.

Be careful when connecting power supply cables to other components. If you have a difficult time inserting a connector, try repositioning it or check to make sure there are no bent pins or foreign objects in the way. If it is difficult to plug in a cable or another part, something is wrong. Cables, connectors, and components are designed to fit together snugly. Never force a connector or component. If a connector is plugged in incorrectly, it can damage the plug and the connector. Take your time and make sure you are connecting the hardware correctly.

Note

Make sure to select a power supply with the proper connectors for the types of devices to be powered.

Lab 2.1.2.5: Install the Power Supply

In this lab, you will install a power supply in a computer case.

Install the Motherboard Components (2.1.3)

This section examines the installation of many of the components that are directly installed on a motherboard and the installation of the motherboard itself into a computer case. As you will see throughout this chapter, all components in your computer system are in some way attached to your motherboard.

The CPU and the heat sink and fan assembly should be installed on the motherboard before the motherboard is placed in the computer case. This allows for extra room to see and maneuver components during installation. Before installing a CPU on a motherboard, verify that it is compatible with the CPU socket.

RAM provides fast, temporary data storage for the CPU while the computer is operating. RAM is volatile memory, which means its contents are lost every time the computer is powered off.

RAM may be installed on the motherboard before the motherboard is installed in the computer case. Before installation, consult the motherboard documentation or the website of the motherboard manufacturer to ensure that the RAM is compatible with the motherboard.

Like the CPU, RAM is also highly sensitive to ESD. Therefore, always work on an antistatic mat and wear a wrist strap or antistatic gloves when installing and removing RAM.

Video Demonstration 2.1.3.1: Install the CPU

Refer to the online course to view this video.

Check Your Understanding 2.1.3.2: Install the CPU

Refer to the online course to complete this activity.

Video Demonstration 2.1.3.3: Install the RAM

Refer to the online course to view this video.

Interactive Graphic

Check Your Understanding 2.1.3.4: Install the RAM

Refer to the online course to complete this activity.

Video

Video Demonstration 2.1.3.5: Install the Motherboard

Refer to the online course to view this video.

Interactive Graphic

Check Your Understanding 2.1.3.6: Install the Motherboard

Refer to the online course to complete this activity.

Select the Motherboard (2.1.3.7)

New motherboards often have new features or standards, which may be incompatible with older components. When you select a replacement motherboard, make sure it supports the CPU, RAM, video adapter, and other adapter cards. The socket and chipset on the motherboard must be compatible with the CPU. When you reuse the CPU, the motherboard must also accommodate the existing heat sink and fan assembly. Pay particular attention to the number and type of expansion slots. Make sure they match the existing adapter cards and allow for new cards that will be used. The existing power supply must have connections that fit the new motherboard. Finally, the new motherboard must physically fit into the current computer case.

When building a computer, choose a chipset that provides the capabilities you need. For example, you can purchase a motherboard with a chipset that enables multiple USB ports, eSATA connections, surround sound, and video.

The CPU package must match the CPU socket type. A CPU package contains the CPU, connection points, and materials surrounding the CPU that dissipate heat.

Data travels from one part of a computer to another through a collection of wires known as the *bus*. The bus has two parts. The data portion of the bus, known as the *data bus*, carries data between the computer components. The address portion, known as the *address bus*, carries the memory addresses of the locations where data is read or written by the CPU.

The bus size determines how much data can be transmitted at one time. A *32-bit bus* transmits 32 bits of data at one time from the processor to RAM or to other motherboard components, and a *64-bit bus* transmits 64 bits of data at one time. The speed at which data travels through the bus is determined by the *clock speed*, measured in MHz or GHz.

PCI expansion slots connect to a *parallel bus*, which sends multiple bits over multiple wires simultaneously. PCI expansion slots are being replaced with PCIe expansion slots that connect to a *serial bus*, which sends a bit at a time at a much faster rate.

When building a computer, choose a motherboard that has slots to meet your current and future needs.

Select the CPU and CPU Cooling (2.1.3.8)

Before you buy a CPU, make sure that it is compatible with the existing motherboard. Manufacturers' websites are a good resource when you're investigating compatibility between CPUs and other devices. Table 2-4 lists the various Intel sockets available and their supported processors.

Table 2-4   Intel Sockets

Intel Socket	Architecture
775	Land grid array (LGA)
1155	LGA
1156	LGA
1150	LGA
1366	LGA
2011	LGA

Table 2-5 lists the various AMD sockets available and their supported processors.

Table 2-5   AMD Sockets

AMD Socket	Architecture
AM3	Pin grid array (PGA)
AM3+	PGA
FM1	PGA
FM2	PGA
FM2+	PGA

The speed of a modern processor is measured in GHz. The *maximum speed rating* refers to the maximum speed at which a processor can function without errors. Two primary factors can limit the speed of a processor:

- **Processor chip:** The *processor chip* is a collection of *transistors* interconnected by wires. Transmitting data through the transistors and wires creates delays. As the transistors change state from on to off or off to on, a small amount of heat is generated. The amount of heat generated increases as the speed of the processor increases. When the processor becomes too hot, it begins to produce errors.

- **Front-side bus:** The *front-side bus (FSB)* is the path between the CPU and the *Northbridge*. It is used to connect various components, such as the chipset, expansion cards, and RAM. Data can travel in both directions across the FSB. The frequency of the bus is measured in MHz. The frequency at which a CPU operates is determined by applying a *clock multiplier* to the FSB speed. For example, a processor running at 3200 MHz might be using a 400 MHz FSB. 3200 MHz divided by 400 MHz is 8, so in this case, the CPU is eight times faster than the FSB.

Processors are further classified as 32-bit and 64-bit. The primary difference is the number of instructions that the processor can handle at one time. A 64-bit processor processes more instructions per clock cycle than a 32-bit processor. A 64-bit processor can also support more memory. To utilize the 64-bit processor capabilities, ensure that the operating system and applications installed support a 64-bit processor.

The CPU is one of the most expensive and sensitive components in the computer case. The CPU can become very hot; therefore, most CPUs require an air-cooled or liquid-cooled heat sink, combined with a fan for cooling.

Table 2-6 lists several factors to consider when choosing a CPU cooling system.

Table 2-6 CPU Cooling System Considerations

Factor	Considerations
Socket type	The heat sink or fan type must match the socket type of the motherboard.
Motherboard physical specifications	The heat sink or fan must not interfere with any components attached to the motherboard.
Case size	The heat sink or fan must fit within the case.
Physical environment	The heat sink or fan must be able to disperse enough heat to keep the CPU cool in warm environments.

Select the RAM (2.1.3.9)

New RAM may be needed when an application locks up or when the computer displays frequent error messages. When selecting new RAM, you must ensure that it is compatible with the current motherboard. Memory modules are commonly purchased in matched capacity pairs to support dual channel RAM that can be accessed at the same time. Also, the speed of the new RAM must be supported by the chipset. It may be helpful to take written notes about the original memory module when you shop for replacement RAM.

Memory can also be categorized as unbuffered or buffered:

- *Unbuffered memory*: This is regular memory for computers. With unbuffered memory, the computer reads data directly from the memory banks, which makes it faster than buffered memory. However, there is a limit on the amount of RAM that can be installed.

- *Buffered memory*: This is specialized memory for servers and high-end workstations that use a large amount of RAM. A buffered memory chip has a control chip built into the module. The control chip assists the memory controller in managing large quantities of RAM. Avoid buffered RAM for gaming computers and average workstations because the extra controller chip reduces RAM speed.

Lab 2.1.3.10: Install the Motherboard in a Computer

In this lab, you will install a CPU, a heat sink/fan assembly, and RAM module(s) on the motherboard. You will then install the motherboard in the computer case.

Install Internal Drives (2.1.4)

In this section, you will learn the steps to install a variety of drives in internal bays with external connections. This is a fairly straightforward process, and the overall procedures for installation are similar, but the exact steps vary depending on the type of drive you are installing.

Video Demonstration 2.1.4.1: Install the Drives

Refer to the online course to view this video.

Select Hard Drives (2.1.4.2)

You might need to replace an internal storage device when it no longer meets your customer's needs or if it fails. Signs that an internal storage device is failing include unusual noises, unusual vibrations, error messages, and corrupt data or applications that do not load.

Figure 2-1 shows an example of a hard disk drive.

Figure 2-1   A Hard Disk Drive

Consider these factors when purchasing a new hard disk drive:

- Whether it is internal or external
- Whether it is an HDD, SSD, or SSHD
- Whether it is hot swappable
- Heat generation
- Noise generation
- Power requirements

Internal drives usually connect to the motherboard with SATA, while external drives connect with USB, eSATA, or Thunderbolt. Legacy motherboards might offer only the IDE or EIDE interface. When selecting an HDD, it is important to choose one that is compatible with the interfaces offered by the motherboard.

Most internal HDDs are available in the 3.5-inch (8.9 cm) form factor; however, 2.5-inch (6.4 cm) drives are becoming popular. SSDs are generally available in the 2.5-inch (6.4 cm) form factor.

Note

SATA and eSATA cables are similar but not interchangeable.

Select Optical Drives (2.1.4.3)

Figure 2-2 shows an optical drive.

Figure 2-2   An Optical Drive

Consider these factors when purchasing an optical drive:

- Connector type

- Reading capability

- Writing capability

- Optical media type

Table 2-7 summarizes optical device capabilities.

Table 2-7   Optical Device Capabilities

Optical Device	Read CD	Write CD	Read DVD	Write DVD	Read Blu-ray	Write Blu-ray	Rewrite Blu-ray
CD-ROM	Yes	No	No	No	No	No	No
CD-RW	Yes	Yes	No	No	No	No	No
DVD-ROM	Yes	No	Yes	No	No	No	No
DVD-RW	Yes	Yes	Yes	Yes	No	No	No
BD-ROM	Yes	No	Yes	No	Yes	No	No
BD-R	Yes	Yes	Yes	Yes	Yes	Yes	No
BD-RE	Yes	Yes	Yes	Yes	Yes	Yes	Yes

DVDs hold significantly more data than CDs. Blu-ray discs (BDs) store significantly more data than DVDs. DVDs and BDs can also have dual layers for recording data, essentially doubling the amount of data that can be recorded on the media.

Install the Hard Drive (2.1.4.4)

A computer case holds drives in drive bays. Table 2-8 describes the three most common types of drive bays.

Table 2-8   Types of Drive Bays

Drive Bay Width	Description
5.25 in. (13.34 cm)	■ Commonly used for optical drives. ■ Most full-size tower cases have two or more bays.
3.5 in. (8.9 cm)	■ Commonly used for 3.5-inch HDDs. ■ Provide additional USB ports or smart card readers. ■ Most full-size tower cases have two or more internal bays.
2.5 in. (6.35 cm)	■ Intended for smaller 2.5-inch HDDs and SSDs. ■ Smallest width bay. ■ Becoming increasingly popular in newer cases.

To install an HDD, find an empty hard drive bay in the case that will accommodate the width of the drive. Smaller drives can often be installed in wider drive bays using special trays or adapters.

When installing multiple drives in a case, it is recommended to maintain some space between the drives to aid airflow and enhance cooling. Also, mount the drive with the metal side face up, as shown in Figure 2-3. This metal face helps to dissipate heat from the hard drive.

Screw Hole in Case

Screw Hole on HDD

Figure 2-3   Inserting the HDD into the Bay

Installation Tip

Slightly hand-tighten all the screws before tightening any of them with a screwdriver. This will make it easier to tighten the last two screws, as shown in Figure 2-4.

Figure 2-4   Securing the HDD

Install the Optical Drive (2.1.4.5)

Optical drives are installed in 5.25-inch (13.34 cm) drive bays that are accessed from the front of the case. The bays allow access to the media without requiring the case to be opened. In new installations, the bays are covered with a plastic insert that keeps dust from entering the case. Remove the plastic cover prior to mounting a drive.

To install an optical drive, follow these steps:

Step 1.   From the front of the case, choose the drive bay that you want to hold the drive. Remove the faceplate from that bay, if necessary.

Step 2.   Position the optical drive so that it aligns with the 5.25-inch (13.34 cm) drive bay opening at the front of the case, as shown in Figure 2-5.

Step 3.   Insert the optical drive into the drive bay so that the optical drive screw holes align with the screw holes in the case.

Step 4.   Secure the optical drive to the case by using the proper screws.

Figure 2-5   Optical Drive Installation

Installation Tip

Slightly hand-tighten all the screws before tightening any of them with a screwdriver. This will make it easier to tighten the last two screws.

Interactive Graphic

Check Your Understanding 2.1.4.6: Installing Drives

Refer to the online course to complete this activity.

Lab 2.1.4.7: Install the Drives

In this lab, you will install a hard drive and an optical drive in a computer case.

Install the Adapter Cards (2.1.5)

In this section, you will go through the steps of installing different types of adapter cards into their compatible expansion slots on the motherboard.

Video

Video Demonstration 2.1.5.1: Install the Adapter Cards

Refer to the online course to view this video.

Select Adapter Cards (2.1.5.2)

Many of the functions of the hardware of a computer, such as audio, USB, and network connections, are found on the motherboard. *Adapter cards*, also called *expansion cards* or *add-on cards*, are designed for specific tasks and add extra functionality to a computer. They can also be installed when an onboard function has failed. A variety of adapter cards are available to expand and customize the capability of a computer.

The following list provides an overview of expansion cards that can be upgraded:

- *Graphics card*: The type of graphics card installed affects the overall performance of a computer. For example, a graphics card that needs to support intensive graphics could be RAM intensive, CPU intensive, or both. The computer must have the slots, RAM, and CPU to support the full functionality of an upgraded graphics card. Choose the graphics card based on current and future needs. For example, to play 3D games, the graphics card must meet or exceed the minimum requirements. Some GPUs are integrated into the CPU. When the GPU is integrated into the CPU, there is no need to purchase a graphics card unless advanced video features, such as 3D graphics or very high resolution, are required.

- *Sound card*: The type of sound card installed determines the sound quality of the computer. A computer system must have quality speakers and a subwoofer to support the full functionality of an upgraded sound card. Choose the correct sound card based on your customer's current and future needs. For example, if a customer wants to hear a specific type of surround sound, the sound card must have the correct hardware decoder to reproduce it. In addition, the customer can get improved sound accuracy with a sound card that has a higher sample rate.

- *Storage controller*: Storage controllers can be integrated or added as expansion cards. They allow for the expansion of internal and external drives for a computer system. Storage controllers, such as RAID controllers, can also provide fault tolerance or increased speed. The amount of data and the level of data protection needed for the customer influences the type of storage controller required. Choose the correct storage controller based on your customer's current and future needs. For example, if a customer wants to implement RAID 5, a RAID storage controller with at least three drives is needed.

- *I/O card*: Installing an I/O card in a computer is a fast and easy way to add I/O ports. USB ports are some of the most common ports to install on a computer. Choose the correct I/O card based on your customer's current and future needs. For example, if a customer wants to add an internal card reader, and the motherboard has no internal USB connection, a USB I/O card with an internal USB connection is needed.

- **NIC**: Customers often upgrade a network interface card (NIC) to get wireless connectivity or to increase bandwidth.

- **Capture card**: A capture card imports video into a computer and records it on a hard drive. The addition of a capture card with a television tuner means you can view and record television programming. The computer system must have enough CPU power, adequate RAM, and a high-speed storage system to support the capture, recording, and editing demands of the customer. Choose the correct capture card based on your customer's current and future needs. For example, if a customer wants to record one program while watching another, either multiple capture cards or a capture card with multiple TV tuners must be installed.

Adapter cards are inserted into two types of expansion slots on a motherboard:

- **Peripheral Component Interconnect (PCI)**: PCI is commonly available to support older expansion cards.

- **PCI Express (PCIe)**: PCIe has four types of slots; x1, x4, x8, and x16. These PCIe slots vary in length from x1 (shortest) to x16 (longest).

Figure 2-6 shows the different types of expansion slots.

Note

If a motherboard does not have a compatible expansion slot, using an external device may be an option.

Figure 2-6   Types of Expansion Slots

Other Factors for Adapter Card Selection (2.1.5.3)

Before purchasing an adapter card, consider the following questions:

- What are the user's current and future needs?
- Is there an open and compatible expansion slot available?
- What are the possible configuration options?

Figure 2-7 shows a graphics card.

Figure 2-7 Graphics Card

Consider the following factors when purchasing a graphics card:

- Slot type
- Amount and speed of video RAM (VRAM)
- Graphics processing unit (GPU)
- Maximum resolution

Figure 2-8 shows a sound card.

Figure 2-8 Sound Card

Consider the following factors when purchasing a sound card:

- Slot type

- *Digital signal processor (DSP)*

- Port and connection types

- Signal-to-noise ratio (SNR)

Figure 2-9 shows a storage controller card.

Figure 2-9   Storage Controller Card

Consider the following factors when purchasing a storage controller card:

- Slot type

- Connector quantity

- Internal or external connectors

- Card size

- Controller card RAM

- Controller card processor

- RAID type

Figure 2-10 shows an I/O card.

Figure 2-10   I/O Card

Consider the following factors when purchasing an I/O card:

- Slot ratio
- I/O port type
- I/O port quantity
- Additional power requirements

Figure 2-11 shows a NIC.

Figure 2-11   NIC

Consider the following factors when purchasing a NIC:

- Slot type
- Speed
- Connector type

- Wired or wireless connection
- Standards compatibility

Figure 2-12 shows a capture card.

Figure 2-12   Capture Card

Consider the following factors when purchasing a capture card:

- Storage
- Resolution and frame rate
- I/O port
- Format standards

Install the Adapter Cards (2.1.5.4)

An expansion card is installed into an appropriate empty slot on a computer mother-board. For example, a wireless NIC enables a computer to connect to a wireless (Wi-Fi) network. Wireless NICs can be integrated into the motherboard, connected using a USB connector, or installed using PCI or PCIe expansion slots on the motherboard.

Many video adapter cards require separate power from the power supply using a 6-pin or 8-pin power connector. Some cards might need two of these connectors. If possible, provide some space between the video adapter and other expansion cards. Video adapters create excessive heat, which is often moved away from the card with a fan.

Installation Tip

Research the length of the video card (and other adapter cards) before purchase. Longer cards might not be compatible with certain motherboards. Chips and other electronics might stand in the way of the adapter card when you're trying to seat them in the expansion slot. Some cases might also limit the size of adapter cards that can be installed. Some adapter cards might come with mounting brackets of different heights to accommodate these cases.

Installation Tip

Some cases have small slots at the bottom of the hole where the cover was removed. Slide the bottom of the mounting bracket into this slot before seating the card.

Interactive Graphic

Check Your Understanding 2.1.5.5: Installing Adapter Cards

Refer to the online course to complete this activity.

Lab 2.1.5.6: Install Adapter Card

In this lab, you will install a NIC, a wireless NIC, and a video adapter card.

Select Additional Storage (2.1.6)

It is not uncommon to discover after purchasing or building a computer that storage is running low. Data maintenance and handling are critical to the user and to computer operation. Not having enough storage on a computer is not just an inconvenience but can affect computer performance. Selecting the best additional storage device for storing data as well as distributing it is important. Choose the correct type of external storage to supplement the user's digital needs.

Select a Media Reader (2.1.6.1)

Many digital devices, such as cameras, smartphones, and tablets, use media cards to store information, music, pictures, videos, data, and more.

Several media card formats have been developed over the years, including these:

- *Secure Digital (SD)*: SD cards are designed for use in portable devices such as cameras, MP3 players, and laptops. SD cards can hold as much as 2 TB of data.

- *MicroSD*: This is a much smaller version of SD, commonly used in smartphones and tablets.

- *MiniSD*: This is a version of SD between the size of an SD card and a microSD card. The format was developed for mobile phones.

- *CompactFlash*: CompactFlash is an older format but is still in wide use because of its high speed and high capacity (up to 128 GB is common). CompactFlash is often used as storage for video cameras.

- *Memory Stick*: Created by Sony Corporation, Memory Stick is a proprietary flash memory used in cameras, MP3 players, handheld video game systems, mobile phones, cameras, and other portable electronics.

- *xD*: Also known as Picture Card, this format was used in some digital cameras.

Figure 2-13 shows some of these media cards.

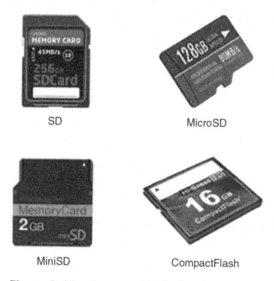

SD   MicroSD

MiniSD   CompactFlash

Figure 2-13   Common Media Cards

It is useful to have an internal or external device that can be used to read or write to media cards. When purchasing or replacing a media reader, ensure that it supports the types of media cards that will be used.

Figure 2-14 shows an external media card reader.

Consider the following factors when purchasing a media reader:

- Media cards supported
- Internal or external
- Size
- Connector type

Figure 2-14   Media Reader

Choose the correct media reader based on your customer's current and future needs. For example, if a customer needs to use multiple types of media cards, a multiple-format media reader is needed.

Select External Storage (2.1.6.2)

External storage offers portability and convenience when working with multiple computers. External USB flash drives, sometimes called *thumb drives*, are commonly used as removable external storage. External storage devices connect to external USB, eSATA, or Thunderbolt ports.

Figure 2-15 shows an external flash drive.

Figure 2-15   External Storage Device

Consider the following when purchasing an external storage device:

- Port type
- Storage capacity
- Speed
- Portability
- Power requirements

Choose the correct type of external storage for your customer's needs. For example, if your customer needs to transfer a small amount of data, such as a single presentation, an external flash drive is a good choice. If your customer needs to back up or transfer large amounts of data, choose an external hard drive.

Interactive Graphic

Check Your Understanding 2.1.6.3: Media Cards

Refer to the online course to complete this activity.

Install the Cables (2.1.7)

Computers use cables for different purposes. There are two main types of computer cables: data and power. Data cables provide a means for communication between two devices. A SATA data cable connects a storage device like a hard drive to the motherboard and carries data to and from the drive and other computer components. A power cable is a cable that provides power to a device. An AC power cable is an example of a power cable used for a computer. The power supply uses this AC power and converts it into DC power to give the motherboard the power it needs to operate. In this section, you will learn about the many cables and connections that you need to attach to your motherboard to provide data and power to the internal components.

Video

Video Demonstration 2.1.7.1: Connect the Internal Power Cables

Refer to the online course to view this video.

Interactive Graphic

Check Your Understanding 2.1.7.2: Identify the Power Connectors

Refer to the online course to complete this activity.

Video

Video Demonstration 2.1.7.3: Connect the Internal Data Cables

Refer to the online course to view this video.

Lab 2.1.7.4: Install Internal Cables

This modeling activity asks you to install the internal power and data cables in a computer.

Video

Video Demonstration 2.1.7.5: Install the Front Panel Cables

Refer to the online course to view this video.

Install the Front Panel Cables (2.1.7.6)

A computer case typically has a power button and visible activity lights on the front of the case. The case includes front panel cables that must be connected to a common system panel connector on a motherboard, as shown in Figure 2-16. Writing on the motherboard near the system panel connector shows where each cable is connected.

Front Panel Connectors   System Panel Connector

Figure 2-16   System Panel Connectors

System panel connectors include the following:

- *Power button*: The power button turns the computer on or off. If the power button fails to turn off the computer, hold down the power button for several (i.e., 5 or more) seconds.

- *Reset button*: The reset button (if available) restarts the computer without turning it off.

- **Power LED**: The power LED remains lit when the computer is on and may blink when the computer is in sleep mode.

- *Drive activity LEDs*: The drive activity LEDs remain lit or blink when the system is reading or writing to hard drives.

- *System speaker*: The motherboard uses a case speaker (if available) to indicate the computer's status. For example, one beep indicates that the computer started without problems. If there is a hardware problem, a series of diagnostic beeps is issued to indicate the type of problem. It is important to note that the system speaker is not the same as the speakers the computer uses to play music and other audio. The system speaker cable typically uses four pins on the system panel connector.

- *Audio*: Some cases have audio ports and jacks on the outside to connect microphones and external audio equipment such as signal processors, mixing boards, and instruments. Special audio panels can also be purchased and connected directly to the motherboard. These panels can be installed into one or more external drive bays, or they can be standalone panels.

System panel connectors are not keyed; however, each front panel cable usually has a small arrow indicating pin 1, and each pair of LED pins on the motherboard system panel connector has pin 1 marked with a plus sign (+), as shown in Figure 2-17.

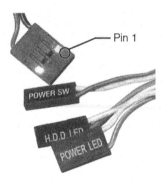
Pin 1 Arrow Indicator

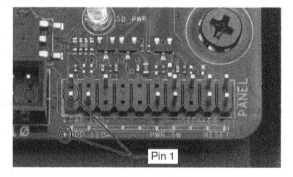
System Panel Connector Pin 1 Indicator

Figure 2-17   System Panel Connector Pin 1 Indicator

Note

The markings on your front panel cables and system panel connectors may be different from those shown in Figure 2-17 as no standards for labeling the case cables or the system panel connectors are defined. Always consult the motherboard manual for diagrams and additional information about connecting front panel cables.

New cases and motherboards have USB 3.0 or may even have USB 3.1 capabilities. A *USB 3.0 motherboard connector* or *USB 3.1 motherboard connector* is similar in design to a USB connector but has additional pins. USB connector cables often have 9 or 10 pins, arranged in two rows. These cables connect to USB motherboard connectors, as shown in Figure 2-18. This arrangement allows for two USB connections, so USB connectors are often in pairs. Sometimes the two connectors are together in one piece, as shown in the figure, and can be connected to the entire USB motherboard connector. USB connectors can also have 4 or 5 pins or individual groups of 4 or 5 pins. Most USB devices only require the connection of 4 pins. The fifth pin is used to ground the shielding of some USB cables.

USB Motherboard Connectors

Internal USB Connector

Figure 2-18   USB Motherboard Connectors

Caution

Make sure the motherboard connector is marked USB. *FireWire* connectors are very similar. Connecting a USB cable to a FireWire connector will cause damage.

Table 2-9 provides connection notes on various front panel connections.

Table 2-9   Front Panel Connection Notes

Front Panel	Connection Specifics
Power button	Align pin 1 of the 2-pin front panel power button cable with the power button pins on the motherboard.
Reset button	Align pin 1 of the 2-pin front panel reset button cable with the reset button pins on the motherboard.
Power LED	Align pin 1 of the front panel power LED cable with the power LED pins on the motherboard.
Drive activity LED	Align pin 1 of the front panel drive activity cable with the drive activity pins on the motherboard.
System speaker	Align pin 1 of the front panel system speaker cable with the system speaker pins on the motherboard.

Front Panel	Connection Specifics
Audio cables	Due to the specialized function and variety of the hardware, consult the motherboard, case, and audio panel documentation for specific instructions.
USB	Align pin 1 of the USB cable with the USB pins on the motherboard.

Generally, if a button or an LED does not function, the connector is incorrectly oriented. To correct this, shut down the computer and unplug it, open the case, and turn around the connector for the button or LED that does not function. To avoid wiring incorrectly, some manufacturers include a keyed pin extender that combines multiple front panel cable (that is, power and reset LED) connectors into one connector.

Installation Tip

The panel connector and case cable ends are very small. Take pictures of them to locate pin 1. Because space in the case can be limited at the end of assembly, a part retriever can be used to plug the cables into the connectors.

Check Your Understanding 2.1.7.7: Identify the Front Panel Cables

Refer to the online course to complete this activity.

Lab 2.1.7.8: Install the Front Panel Cables

In this lab, you will install the front panel cables in the computer.

Video Demonstration 2.1.7.9: Complete the Computer Assembly

Refer to the online course to view this video.

Check Your Understanding 2.1.7.10: Identify the External Connectors

Refer to the online course to complete this activity.

Lab 2.1.7.11: Complete the Computer Assembly

In this lab, you will install the side panels and the external cables on the computer.

Summary (2.2)

In this chapter, you learned that assembling computers is often a large part of a technician's job and that as a technician, you must work in a logical, methodical manner when working with computer components. For example, the choice of motherboard and external components influences the selection of the case and power supply, and the motherboard form factor must be matched with the correct type of computer case and power supply.

You learned that PC power supplies convert AC input to DC output voltages. Power supplies typically provide voltages of 3.3V, 5V, and 12V to power the various internal components of the computer, and the power supply must have the proper connectors for the motherboard and the various types of devices to be powered.

After learning about power supplies, you installed a power supply as well as other internal components, including a CPU and RAM. You learned that when you select a motherboard, it must support the CPU, RAM, video adapter, and other adapter cards and that the socket and chipset on the motherboard must be compatible with the CPU. The motherboard sockets may be designed to support Intel CPUs, which support an LGA architecture, or AMD CPUs, which support a PGA architecture.

In addition to learning about CPU architectures, you also learned that when selecting new RAM, it must be compatible with the motherboard and that the speed of the RAM must be supported by the chipset. You performed labs in which you installed a CPU, a heat sink/fan assembly, and RAM modules on the motherboard. You also installed the motherboard assembly into the computer case.

Next, you learned about the various types of storage drives, such as internal drives, external drives, hard disk drives, solid-state drives, and optical drives, and the factors to consider when selecting the appropriate drive. You also installed drives in the computer case.

Finally, you learned about adapter cards, which are also called expansion cards or add-on cards. There are many types of adapter cards, and each is designed for a specific task and is meant to add extra functionality to a computer. In this chapter you learned about graphics cards, sound cards, storage controllers, I/O cards, and NICs. These adapter cards are inserted into two types of expansion slots on a motherboard: PCI and PCIe. At the end of the chapter, there were labs in which you installed an adapter card, connected the appropriate internal power cables and front panel connectors, and performed final computer assembly.

Practice

The following activities provide practice with the topics introduced in this chapter. The labs are available in the companion *IT Essentials v8 Labs & Study Guide* (ISBN 9780138166304).

Labs

Lab 2.1.2.5: Install the Power Supply

Lab 2.1.3.10: Install the Motherboard in a Computer

Lab 2.1.4.7: Install the Drives

Lab 2.1.5.6: Install Adapter Card

Lab 2.1.7.4: Install Internal Cables

Lab 2.1.7.8: Install the Front Panel Cables

Lab 2.1.7.11: Complete the Computer Assembly

Check Your Understanding Questions

Complete all the review questions listed here to test your understanding of the topics and concepts in this chapter. Appendix A, "Answers to 'Check Your Understanding' Questions," lists the answers.

1. What are two reasons someone might upgrade a NIC? (Choose two.)
   A. to import videos
   B. to have wireless connectivity
   C. to implement a RAID
   D. to have a higher sample rate
   E. to increase bandwidth

2. The following parts were ordered by someone building a personal computer:

   AMD 3.7 GHz

   Gigawhiz GA-A239VM (does not include USB 3.1 front panel connectors)

   HorseAir DDR3 8 GB

ATX with up to three 3.5-inch drive bays

Eastern Divide 1TB 7200 RPM

Zoltz 550W

What is the significance of the 550W in the final item (Zoltz 550W)?

A. RAM speed

B. motherboard speed

C. input power

D. output power

3. Which SATA internal hard drive form factor is most often used in a tower computer?

A. 2.5 inch (6.4 cm)

B. 5.25 inch (13.3 cm)

C. 3.5 inch (8.9 cm)

D. 2.25 inch (5.7 cm)

4. A technician is being asked to move a heavy industrial printer. Which safety technique is recommended for this situation?

A. Use a pulley.

B. Remove paper and all sources of ink before moving.

C. Bend at the knees when lifting.

D. Wear safety goggles.

5. What should a technician do before working on a computer?

A. Ensure that the computer is free of viruses.

B. Remove all cables except the power cable.

C. Remove any watch and jewelry.

D. Check the surrounding area for trip hazards.

6. Which adapter card in a PC would provide data fault tolerance?

A. I/O card

B. SD card

C. capture card

D. RAID card

7. The bus is a collection of wires thorough which data travels from one part of a computer to another. What are the two parts of the bus? (Choose two.)

   A. data bus

   B. control bus

   C. expansion bus

   D. address bus

8. A technician needs to buy a replacement adapter for a department computer. Which type of adapter requires the technician to consider a DSP?

   A. sound

   B. capture

   C. storage

   D. graphics

9. Which type of media card is an older format but is still used in video cameras?

   A. xD

   B. CompactFlash

   C. miniSD

   D. microSD

10. Which two pieces of information are needed before selecting a power supply? (Choose two.)

    A. the total wattage of all components

    B. the form factor of the case

    C. the voltage requirements of peripheral devices

    D. the type of CPU

    E. the installed operating system

11. What should be done prior to the installation of RAM onto the motherboard?

    A. Consult the motherboard documentation or website of the manufacturer to ensure that the RAM is compatible with the motherboard.

    B. Populate the center memory slots first before inserting the new RAM.

    C. Change the voltage selector to meet the voltage specification of the RAM.

    D. Ensure that the memory expansion slot tabs are in the locked position before inserting the RAM module.

12. True or false: When installing a hard drive, it is recommended that you hand-tighten drive mounting screws prior to using a screwdriver.

13. What is a possible hardware upgrade that can be used to add more storage space to a modern smartphone?

    A. USB flash drive
    B. hard disk
    C. microSD
    D. CompactFlash

14. The front-side bus (FSB) is the path between the CPU and the _____?

    A. Northbridge
    B. power button
    C. Southbridge
    D. system clock

15. What is the name for the specialized memory chips with a control chip built into the module that is used for servers and high-end workstations that use a large amount of RAM?

    A. unbuffered memory
    B. buffered memory
    C. ECC memory
    D. nonvolatile memory

CHAPTER 3

Advanced Computer Hardware

Objectives

Upon completion of this chapter, you will be able to answer the following questions:

- What are general and fire safety standards?

- What are safe working conditions and procedures?

- What procedures help protect equipment and data?

- What procedures help to properly dispose of hazardous computer components and related material?

- What tools and software are used with personal computer components, and what is their purpose?

- What is the proper way to use tools?

- What should you expect the first time you boot a computer?

- What is the BIOS setup program?

- How do you use beep codes?

Key Terms

This chapter uses the following key terms. You can find the definitions in the glossary at the end of the book.

aspect ratio   *page 144*

audio port   *page 128*

basic input/output system (BIOS)   *page 105*

beep code   *page 106*

blackout   *page 115*

boot loader program   *page 105*

boot order   *page 110*

booting   *page 104*

brightness   *page 143*

brownout   *page 115*

case fan   *page 119*

Centronics connector   *page 140*

CGA   *page 144*

coaxial (coax) cable   *page 138*

complementary metal-oxide semiconductor (CMOS)   *page 105*

Complex Instruction Set Computer (CISC)   *page 117*

connectivity   *page 106*

contrast ratio   *page 143*

CPU fan   *page 120*

CPU throttling   *page 118*

CPU virtualization   *page 118*

DisplayPort   *page 130*

Introduction to Advanced Computer Hardware (3.0)

A technician's knowledge must extend beyond knowing how to assemble a computer. You need to have in-depth knowledge of computer system architecture and how each component operates and interacts with other components. This depth of knowledge is necessary when you have to upgrade a computer with new components that must be compatible with existing components and also when you build computers for very specialized applications. This chapter covers the computer boot process, protecting the computer from power fluctuations, multicore processors, redundancy through multiple storage drives, and protecting the environment from hazardous materials found inside computer components.

You will learn about the computer boot process, including the power-on self-test (POST) conducted by the BIOS. You will explore various BIOS and UEFI settings and how they impact this process. You will explore basic electrical theory and Ohm's law and calculate voltage, current, resistance, and power. Power fluctuations can damage computer components, and you will learn how to mitigate the risk of power fluctuations with surge protectors, uninterruptible power supplies (UPSs), and standby power supplies (SPSs). You will learn how to provide storage redundancy and load balancing using redundant arrays of independent disks (RAID). You will also learn how to upgrade computer components and configure specialized computers. Finally, after upgrading a computer, technicians must dispose of the old parts properly. Many computer components contain hazardous materials, such as mercury and rare earth metals in batteries and deadly voltage levels in power supplies. You will learn the risks posed by these components and how to dispose of them properly.

This chapter includes a lab in which you will research hardware upgrades to a computer system. You will use several sources to gather information about the computer hardware components and make recommendations for upgraded components. You will also discuss your recommended upgrade choices.

Boot the Computer (3.1)

Booting a computer refers to turning it on and beginning the startup sequence, verifying hardware, and loading operating system software. ROM BIOS is an integral part of the boot process. Once power is supplied to the computer, diagnostics are run, and BIOS takes control of the boot and searches for the master boot loader (MBL). The master boot loader reads the *master boot record (MBR)* and runs the code. At this point, the BIOS stops controlling the system, and control is passed to the boot loader program. The *boot loader program* is configured to locate and load an operating system from the boot device.

POST, BIOS, CMOS, and UEFI (3.1.1)

A *power-on self-test (POST)* is a self-diagnostic testing system in which the computer produces codes to signal problems to help identify hardware issues with the computer. The codes generated indicate the causes of different problems. The POST program is stored in the BIOS memory.

The *basic input/output system (BIOS)* is firmware that is built into the motherboard that initializes the computer's hardware as the computer is being booted. The BIOS can't be rewritten; it is read-only memory (ROM). BIOS and CMOS work together, but they do different things.

Complementary metal-oxide semiconductor (CMOS) is RAM that is volatile memory. In order for the CMOS to maintain its settings when no power is applied to the system or when it is in standby, there is a CMOS battery on the motherboard. The CMOS battery provides low voltage to the system so the CMOS keeps its settings. A CMOS editor program is used because BIOS ROM cannot be rewritten to access and make changes to programs stored in the BIOS. The custom settings configured in the BIOS—such as date and time, the boot sequence, or hardware settings—are made and stored in CMOS.

Unified Extensible Firmware Interface (UEFI) is a newer type of BIOS that has many advantages, including a GUI that is user friendly compared to older BIOS versions, the ability to recognize larger hard drives, and a built-in feature called secure boot. Secure boot stops any digitally unsigned drivers from loading and also helps stop malicious software.

Video

Video Demonstration 3.1.1.1: BIOS - UEFI Menus

Refer to the online course to view this video.

POST (3.1.1.2)

When a computer is booted, the basic input/output system (BIOS) performs a hardware check on the main components of the computer. This check is called a power-on self-test (POST).

For instance, Figure 3-1 displays a screen capture of a sample POST being performed. Notice that the computer checks whether the computer hardware is operating correctly.

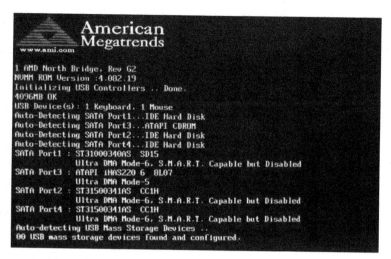

Figure 3-1 POST

If a device is malfunctioning, an error code or *beep code* alerts the technician of the problem. If there is a hardware problem, a blank screen might appear at bootup, and the computer may emit a series of beeps.

BIOS manufacturers use different codes to indicate hardware problems. Table 3-1 shows a chart of common beep codes. However, motherboard manufacturers may use different beep codes. Always consult the motherboard documentation to get the beep codes for your computer.

Table 3-1 Common Beep Codes

Beep Code	Meaning	Cause
1 beep (no video)	Memory refresh failure	Bad memory
2 beeps	Memory parity error	Bad memory
3 beeps	Base 64 memory failure	Bad memory
4 beeps	Timer not operational	Bad motherboard
5 beeps	Processor error	Bad processor
6 beeps	8042 Gate A2.0 failure	Bad CPU or motherboard
7 beeps	Processor exception	Bad processor
8 beeps	Video memory error	Bad video card or memory
9 beeps	ROM checksum error	Bad BIOS
10 beeps	CMOS checksum error	Bad motherboard
11 beeps	Cache memory bad	Bad CPU or motherboard

Installation Tip

To determine whether POST is working properly, remove all the RAM modules from the computer and power it on. The computer should emit the beep code for a computer with no RAM installed. Doing this will not harm the computer.

BIOS and CMOS (3.1.1.3)

All motherboards need BIOS to operate. BIOS is a ROM chip on the motherboard that contains a small program. This program controls the communication between the operating system and the hardware.

Along with the POST, BIOS also identifies the following:

- Which drives are available
- Which drives are bootable
- How the memory is configured and when it can be used
- How PCIe and PCI expansion slots are configured
- How SATA and USB ports are configured
- Motherboard power management features

The motherboard manufacturer saves the motherboard BIOS settings in a CMOS memory chip such as the one shown in Figure 3-2.

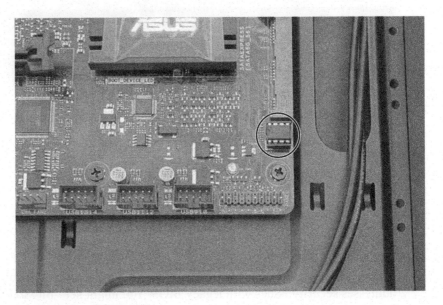

Figure 3-2   CMOS Chip

When a computer boots, the BIOS software reads the configured settings stored in CMOS to determine how to configure the hardware.

The BIOS settings are retained by CMOS using a battery, such as the one shown in Figure 3-3. If the battery fails, important settings can be lost. Therefore, it is recommended that BIOS settings be documented.

Note

An easy way to document BIOS settings is to take pictures of the various settings available to record them for later use.

Figure 3-3   CMOS Battery

Installation Tip

If the computer's time and date are incorrect, the CMOS battery might be dead or getting very low.

UEFI (3.1.1.4)

Most computers today run UEFI. Figure 3-4 shows an example.

All new computers come with UEFI, which provides additional features and addresses security issues with legacy BIOS. You might see "BIOS/UEFI" when booting into your BIOS settings. This is because Intel chips currently support backward compatibility with legacy BIOS systems. However, in 2020, Intel ended support for legacy BIOS. For more information, do an Internet search for "Intel removed legacy BIOS."

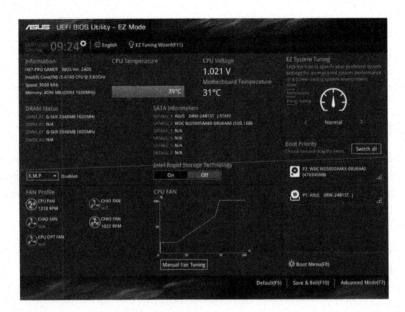

Figure 3-4   UEFI BIOS Utility Program

Note

This section uses the terms *BIOS*, *UEFI*, and *BIOS/UEFI* interchangeably. In addition, manufacturers may continue to label their UEFI programs with "BIOS" so that users know the programs support the same functions.

UEFI includes the same settings as traditional BIOS and also provides additional options. For example, UEFI can provide a mouse-enabled software interface instead of the traditional BIOS screens. However, most systems have text-based interfaces, similar to those of legacy BIOS systems.

UEFI can run on 32-bit and 64-bit systems, supports larger boot drives, and includes additional features, such as secure boot. Secure boot ensures that your computer boots to your specified operating system. This helps prevent rootkits from taking over the system. For more information, do an Internet search for "Secure boot and rootkits."

Note

The UEFI setup screens in this section are for reference only and most likely will not look the same as yours. Please consider them as a guide and refer to your motherboard manufacturer's documents.

Check Your Understanding 3.1.1.5: BIOS and UEFI Terminology

Refer to the online course to complete this activity.

Lab 3.1.1.6: Investigate BIOS or UEFI Settings

In this lab, you will boot the computer, explore the firmware setup utility program, and change the *boot order* sequence.

BIOS/UEFI Configuration (3.1.2)

Both UEFI and BIOS are low-level software that starts when you boot your PC before booting your operating system, but UEFI has a more modern approach to accessing settings, using a mouse and graphics. It also supports larger hard drives, faster boot times, more security features, and other options.

Video Demonstration 3.1.2.1: Configure BIOS - UEFI Settings

Refer to the online course to view this video.

BIOS and UEFI Security (3.1.2.2)

The legacy BIOS supports some security features to protect the BIOS setting. UEFI adds additional security features. These are some common security features found in BIOS/UEFI systems:

- **Passwords:** Passwords allow for different levels of access to the BIOS settings. Usually, there are two password settings that can be altered: the supervisor password and the user password. The *supervisor password* can access all user-access passwords and all BIOS screens and settings. The *user password* gives access to the BIOS based on a defined level. Table 3-2 lists common levels of user access to BIOS. The supervisor password must be set before the user password can be configured.

Table 3-2   Access Levels

Access Level	Level Description
Full access	All screens and settings are available except for the supervisor password setting.
Limited access	Changes can be made to certain settings only, such as the time and date.

Access Level	Level Description
View-only access	All screens are available, but no settings can be changed.
No access	No access is provided to the BIOS setup utility.

- *Drive encryption*: A hard drive can be encrypted to prevent data theft. Encryption changes the data on the drive into code. Without the correct password, the computer cannot boot, and data read from the hard drive cannot be understood. Even if the hard drive is placed in another computer, the data remains encrypted.

- *LoJack*: This is a security feature that consists of two programs: the persistence module and the application agent. The persistence module is embedded in the BIOS, and the application agent is installed by the user. When installed, the persistence module in the BIOS is activated and cannot be turned off. The application agent routinely contacts a monitoring center over the Internet to report device information and location. The owner can perform the following functions:

  o Locate the device using Wi-Fi or IP geolocation to see the last location.

  o Lock the device remotely to prevent access to personal information. Display a customized message on the screen.

  o Delete all files on the device to protect personal information and prevent identity theft.

- *Trusted Platform Module (TPM)*: This is a chip designed to secure hardware by storing encryption keys, digital certificates, passwords, and data. TPM is used by Windows to support BitLocker full-disk encryption.

- *Secure boot*: Secure boot is a UEFI security standard that ensures that a computer only boots an OS that is trusted by the motherboard manufacturer. Secure boot prevents an "unauthorized" OS from loading during startup.

Update the Firmware (3.1.2.3)

Motherboard manufacturers may publish updated BIOS versions to provide enhancements to system stability, compatibility, and performance. However, updating the firmware is risky. The release notes, such as those shown in Figure 3-5, describe the upgrade to the product, compatibility improvements, and the known bugs that have been addressed. Some newer devices operate properly only with an updated BIOS version installed. You can usually find the current version on the main screen of the BIOS/UEFI interface.

Figure 3-5   BIOS Release Notes

Before updating motherboard firmware, record the manufacturer of the BIOS and the motherboard model. Use this information to identify the exact files to download from the motherboard manufacturer's site. Update the firmware only if there are problems with the system hardware or to add functionality to the system.

Early computer BIOS information was contained in ROM chips. To upgrade the BIOS information, the ROM chip had to be physically replaced, which was not always possible. Modern BIOS chips are electrically erasable programmable read-only memory (EEPROM), which the user can upgrade without opening the computer case. This process is called *flashing the BIOS*.

To download a new BIOS, consult the manufacturer's website and follow the recommended installation procedures. Installing BIOS software online may involve downloading a new BIOS file, copying or extracting files to removable media, and then booting from the removable media. An installation program prompts the user for information to complete the process.

Many motherboard manufacturers now provide software to flash the BIOS from within an operating system. For example, the ASUS EZ Update utility automatically updates a motherboard's software, drivers, and the BIOS version. It also enables a user to manually update a saved BIOS and select a boot logo when the system goes into POST. The utility is included with the motherboard, or it can be downloaded from the ASUS website.

Caution

An improperly installed or aborted BIOS update can cause the computer to become unusable.

Check Your Understanding 3.1.2.4: BIOS and UEFI Configuration Terminology

Refer to the online course to complete this activity.

Lab 3.1.2.5: Search for BIOS or UEFI Firmware Updates

In this lab, you will identify the current BIOS or UEFI version and then search for BIOS or UEFI update files.

Lab 3.1.2.6: Install Windows

In this lab, you will perform a basic installation of Windows.

Lab 3.1.2.7: Install Third-Party Software in Windows

In this lab, you will install third-party software.

Electrical Power (3.2)

Electrical power is the rate at which electrical energy is being transferred.

Wattage and Voltage (3.2.1)

Electrical power is the product of voltage, which is electrical pressure, and current, which is the flow of electricity, measured in wattage.

Wattage and Voltage (3.2.1.1)

Power supply specifications are typically expressed in *watts (W)*. To understand what a watt is, refer to the interactive image in the online course, which describes the four basic units of electricity that a computer technician must know.

The basic equation known as Ohm's law indicates that voltage is equal to the current multiplied by the resistance: $V = IR$. In an electrical system, power is equal to the voltage multiplied by the current: $P = VI$. The following are definitions of power-related terminology:

- *Voltage*, measured in volts (V)

    o This is a measure of work required to move a charge from one location to another.

    o A computer power supply usually produces several different voltages.

- *Resistance*, measured in Ohms (O)
  - ○ This refers to the opposition to the flow of current in a circuit.
  - ○ Lower resistance allows more current to flow through a circuit.
  - ○ A good fuse has low resistance, or almost 0 ohms.
- Current, measured in amperes, or amps (A)
  - ○ This is a measure of the number of electrons moving through a circuit per second.
  - ○ Computer power supplies deliver different amperages for each output voltage.
- Power, measured in watts (W)
  - ○ This is a measure of the work required to move electrons through a circuit (voltage), multiplied by the number of electrons going through that circuit per second (current).
  - ○ Computer power supplies are rated in watts.

Power Supply Voltage Setting (3.2.1.2)

On the back of some power supplies is a small switch called the *voltage selector switch*, as shown in Figure 3-6.

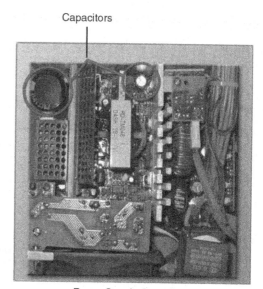

Capacitors

Power Supply Capacitors

Switch

Dual Voltage Power Supply

Figure 3-6 Power Supply Voltage Setting and Capacitors

This switch allows you to set the input voltage to the power supply to either 110V/115V or 220V/230V. A power supply with this switch is called a *dual voltage power supply*. The correct voltage setting depends on the country where the power supply is used. Setting the voltage switch to the incorrect input voltage could damage the power supply and other parts of the computer. If a power supply does not have this switch, it automatically detects and sets the correct voltage.

Caution

Do not open a power supply. Electronic capacitors located inside a power supply can hold a charge for extended periods of time.

For more information about power supplies, refer to https://www.newegg.com/insider/how-to-choose-a-pc-power-supply-buying-guide/.

 Lab 3.2.1.3: Ohm's Law

In this lab, you will answer questions based on electricity and Ohm's law.

Power Fluctuation and Protection (3.2.2)

Power fluctuations occur commonly almost everywhere. Happenings such as lightning, power line outages, accidental power interruptions, and simple line voltage variance can affect your computer. As important as electronic device usage has become in business and personal life, it is important to take steps to ensure the safety of all devices so that no damage is done to them in the event of a power fluctuation.

Power Fluctuation Types (3.2.2.1)

Voltage is a measure of energy required to move a charge from one location to another. The movement of electrons is called *current*. Computer circuits need voltage and current to operate electronic components. When the voltage in a computer is not accurate or steady, computer components might not operate correctly. Unsteady voltages are called *power fluctuations*.

The following types of AC power fluctuations can cause data loss or hardware failure:

- *Blackout*: Complete loss of AC power. A blown fuse, damaged transformer, or downed power line can cause a blackout.

- *Brownout*: A reduced voltage level of AC power that lasts for a period of time. Brownouts occur when the power line voltage drops below 80% of the normal voltage level and when electrical circuits are overloaded.

- *Noise*: Interference from generators and lightning. Noise results in poor-quality power, which can cause errors in a computer system.

- *Spike*: A sudden increase in voltage that lasts for a short period and exceeds 100% of the normal voltage on a line. Spikes can be caused by lightning strikes but can also occur when the electrical system comes back on after a blackout.

- *Power surge*: A dramatic increase in voltage above the normal flow of electrical current. A power surge lasts for a few nanoseconds. (A nanosecond is one-billionth of a second.)

Power Protection Devices (3.2.2.2)

To help shield against power fluctuation problems, use devices to protect the data and computer equipment:

- *Surge protector*: Helps protect against damage from surges and spikes. A surge suppressor diverts extra electrical voltage that is on the line to the ground. The amount of protection offered by a surge protector is measured in joules. The higher the joule rating, the more energy the surge protector can absorb over time. Once the number of joules is reached, the surge protector no longer provides protection and needs to be replaced.

- *Uninterruptible power supply (UPS)*: Helps protect against potential electrical power problems by supplying a consistent level of electrical power to a computer or other device. The battery is constantly recharging while the UPS is in use. The UPS provides a consistent quality of power when brownouts and blackouts occur. Many UPS devices can communicate directly with the computer operating system. This communication allows the UPS to safely shut down the computer and save data prior to the UPS losing all battery power.

- *Standby power supply (SPS)*: Helps protect against potential electrical power problems by providing a backup battery to supply power when the incoming voltage drops below the normal level. The battery is on standby during normal operation. When the voltage decreases, the battery provides DC power to a power inverter, which converts it to AC power for the computer. This device is not as reliable as a UPS because of the time it takes to switch over to the battery. If the switching device fails, the battery cannot supply power to the computer.

Caution

UPS manufacturers suggest never plugging a laser printer into a UPS because the printer could overload the UPS.

Check Your Understanding 3.2.2.3: Power Fluctuation Terms

Refer to the online course to complete this activity.

Advanced Computer Functionality (3.3)

A technician's knowledge must extend beyond knowing how to assemble a computer. You need to have in-depth knowledge of computer system architecture and how each component operates and interacts with other components. This depth of knowledge is necessary when you have to upgrade a computer with new components that must be compatible with existing components and also when you build computers for very specialized applications. This chapter covers the computer boot process, how to protect a computer from power fluctuations, multicore processors, redundancy through multiple storage drives, and how to protect the environment from hazardous materials found inside of computer components.

CPU Architectures and Operation (3.3.1)

The CPU is the computer component where calculations and operations take place. Its pins connect it to the buses on the motherboard, which is how instructions can be transferred between the CPU and other components. The CPU follows a set of instructions to perform some operation or calculation. CPUs are built to understand and execute instructions based on an instruction set architecture (ISA).

CPU Architectures (3.3.1.1)

A program is a sequence of stored instructions. A CPU executes these instructions by following a specific instruction set.

CPUs may use two distinct types of instruction sets:

- *Reduced Instruction Set Computer (RISC)*: This architecture uses a relatively small set of instructions. RISC chips are designed to execute these instructions very rapidly. Some well-known CPUs using RISC are PowerPC and ARM.

- *Complex Instruction Set Computer (CISC)*: This architecture uses a broad set of instructions, resulting in fewer steps per operation. Intel x86 and Motorola 68k are some well-known CPUs using CISC.

While the CPU is executing one step of a program, the remaining instructions and the data are stored nearby in a special high-speed memory, called *cache*.

Enhancing CPU Operation (3.3.1.2)

Various CPU manufacturers complement their CPUs with performance-enhancing features. For instance, Intel incorporates Hyper-Threading to enhance the performance of some of its CPUs. With *Hyper-Threading*, multiple pieces of code (threads) are executed simultaneously in the CPU. To an operating system, a single CPU with Hyper-Threading performs as though there are two CPUs when multiple threads are being processed. AMD processors use *HyperTransport* to enhance CPU performance. HyperTransport is a high-speed connection between the CPU and the Northbridge chip.

The power of a CPU is measured by the speed and the amount of data that it can process. The speed of a CPU is rated in cycles per second, such as millions of cycles per second, called megahertz (MHz), or billions of cycles per second, called gigahertz (GHz). The amount of data that a CPU can process at one time depends on the size of the front-side bus (FSB). This is also called the CPU bus or the processor data bus. Higher performance can be achieved when the width of the FSB increases, much as a roadway can carry more cars when it has many lanes. The width of the FSB is measured in bits. A bit is the smallest unit of data in a computer. Current processors use a 32-bit or 64-bit FSB.

Overclocking is a technique used to make a processor work at a faster speed than its original specification. Overclocking is not a recommended way to improve computer performance and can result in damage to the CPU. The opposite of overclocking is CPU throttling. *CPU throttling* is a technique used when the processor runs at less than the rated speed to conserve power or produce less heat. Throttling is commonly used on laptops and other mobile devices.

CPU virtualization is a hardware feature supported by AMD and Intel CPUs that enables a single processor to act as multiple processors. This hardware virtualization technology allows the operating system to support virtualization more effectively and efficiently than is possible through software emulation. With CPU virtualization, multiple operating systems can run in parallel on their own virtual machines as if they were running on completely independent computers. CPU virtualization is sometimes disabled by default in the BIOS and needs to be enabled.

Multicore Processors (3.3.1.3)

CPU manufacturers have found ways to incorporate more than one CPU core into a single chip. A *multicore CPU* has two or more processors on the same integrated circuit. In some architectures, the cores have separate L2 and L3 cache resources, while in other architectures, cache is shared among the different cores for better performance and resource allocation. Table 3-3 describes the various types of multicore processors.

Table 3-3   CPU Core Counts

Number of Cores	Description
Single-core CPU	One core inside a single CPU that handles all the processing. A motherboard may have sockets for more than a single processor, providing the ability to build a powerful multiprocessor computer.
Dual-core CPU	Two cores inside a single CPU, in which the two cores can process information at the same time.

Number of Cores	Description
Triple-core CPU	Three cores inside a single CPU. This is a quad-core processor with one of the cores disabled.
Quad-core CPU	Four cores inside a single CPU.
Hexa-core CPU	Six cores inside a single CPU.
Octa-core CPU	Eight cores inside a single CPU.

Integrating the processors on the same chip creates a very fast connection between them. Multicore processors execute instructions more quickly than do single-core processors. Instructions can be distributed to all the processors at the same time. RAM is shared between the processors because the cores reside on the same chip. A multicore processor is recommended for applications such as video editing, gaming, and photo manipulation.

High power consumption creates more heat in the computer case. Multicore processors conserve power and produce less heat than multiple single-core processors, thus increasing performance and efficiency.

Another feature found in some CPUs is an *integrated graphics processing unit (GPU)*. The GPU is a chip that performs the rapid mathematical calculations required to render graphics. A GPU can be integrated or dedicated. Integrated GPUs are often directly embedded on the CPU and are dependent on system RAM; a dedicated GPU is a separate chip with its own video memory dedicated exclusively to graphical processing. The benefit of integrated GPUs is cost and less heat dissipation. GPUs make it possible to create less expensive computers and smaller form factors. The trade-off is performance. Integrated GPUs are good for less complex tasks such as playing videos and processing graphical documents but are not best suited for intense gaming applications.

CPUs have also been enhanced using the *execute disable (NX) bit*. This feature, when supported and enabled in the operating system, can protect areas of memory that contain operating system files from malicious attacks by malware.

CPU Cooling Mechanisms (3.3.1.4)

Several mechanisms are used to cool a computer:

- *Case fan*: Increasing the airflow in the computer case allows more heat to be removed. An active cooling solution uses fans inside a computer case, as shown in Figure 3-7, to blow out hot air. For increased airflow, some cases have multiple fans to bring in cool air and also blow out hot air.

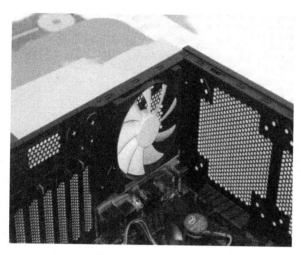

Figure 3-7   Case Fan

■ **CPU heat sink:** The CPU generates a lot of heat inside the case. To draw heat away from the CPU core, a *heat sink* (see Figure 3-8) is installed on top of it. The heat sink has a large surface area with metal fins to dissipate heat into the surrounding air. This is known as *passive cooling*. Between the heat sink and the CPU is a special *thermal compound*, which increases the efficiency of heat transfer from the CPU to the heat sink by filling any tiny gaps between the two.

Figure 3-8   CPU Heat Sink

■ *CPU fan:* CPUs that are overclocked or running multiple cores tend to generate excessive heat. It is a very common practice to install a fan (see Figure 3-9) on top of the heat sink. The fan moves heat away from the metal fins of the heat sink. This is known as *active cooling*.

Figure 3-9   CPU Fan

- *Graphics card cooling system*: Other components are also susceptible to heat damage and are often equipped with fans. Video adapter cards have their own processor, called a graphics processing unit (GPU), which generates excessive heat. Video adapter cards also come equipped with one or more fans, as shown in Figure 3-10.

Figure 3-10   Graphics Card Cooling System

- *Water cooling system*: Computers with extremely fast CPUs and GPUs might use a water cooling system like the one shown in Figure 3-11. A metal plate is placed over the processor, and water is pumped over the top to collect the heat that the processor generates. The water is pumped to a radiator to disperse the heat into the air, and the water is then recirculated. CPU fans make noise and can be annoying at high speeds. An alternative to cooling a CPU with a fan is a method that uses heat pipes. A heat pipe contains liquid that is permanently sealed at the factory and uses a system of cyclical evaporation and condensation.

Figure 3-11   Water Cooling System

Check Your Understanding 3.3.1.5: CPU Architectures and Operation

Refer to the online course to complete this activity.

RAID (3.3.2)

Redundant array of independent disks (RAID) can help improve a combination of fault tolerance, storage management, and performance. Different RAID levels have various characteristics that represent different configurations aimed at providing performance/fault tolerance.

What Do You Already Know? RAID (3.3.2.1)

What do you already know about RAID? These are the characteristics of RAID:

- Availability
- Capacity
- Economy
- Performance
- Redundancy
- Reliability

Scenarios

See if you can select the RAID characteristic that would solve the problem described in each of the following six scenarios.

Scenario 1: A user is concerned that the failure of an HDD will cause the loss of important data. What is the correct solution?

Scenario 2: A manager wants to be sure that employees can access the data they need when they need it.

Scenario 3: HDD data transfer rates have been identified as the cause of work delays.

Scenario 4: A small business has recently grown and is running out of data storage space.

Scenario 5: A company is shopping for larger HDDs and finds them to be too expensive.

Scenario 6: Corrupted data has been causing problems with applications.

Answers

Scenario 1 Answer: Redundancy. This involves having backup resources that can rapidly replace failed devices and lost data or connectivity.

Scenario 2 Answer: Availability. This means IT resources that can be accessed by those who need them at all times.

Scenario 3 Answer: Performance. This is the rate at which tasks can be performed. For storage devices, it is usually the read and write rates, in Mbps.

Scenario 4 Answer: Capacity. This is the amount of data that can be stored.

Scenario 5 Answer: Economy. This is the relative cost of a solution, based on its benefit. Economical things cost less than other things for the capabilities that they offer.

Scenario 6 Answer: Reliability. This is when devices function as intended for a predictable amount of time.

RAID Concepts (3.3.2.2)

With RAID, storage devices can be grouped and managed to create large storage volumes with redundancy. RAID provides a way to store data across multiple storage devices for availability, reliability, capacity, and redundancy and/or performance improvement. In addition, it may be more economical to create an array of smaller devices than it is to purchase a single device with the combined capacity provided by the RAID, especially for very large drives. To the operating system, a RAID array appears as one drive.

The following terms describe how RAID stores data on the various disks:

- *Striping*: This RAID type enables data to be distributed across multiple drives, which provides a significant performance increase. However, because the data is distributed across multiple drives, the failure of a single drive means that all data is lost.

- *Mirroring*: This RAID type stores duplicate data on one or more other drives. This provides redundancy so that the failure of a drive does not cause the loss of data. The mirror can be re-created by replacing the drive and restoring the data from the good drive.

- *Parity*: This RAID type provides basic error checking and fault tolerance by storing checksums separately from data. This enables the reconstruction of lost data without sacrificing speed and capacity, which is a problem with mirroring.

- *Double parity*: This RAID type provides fault tolerance for up to two failed drives.

A large drive enclosure can be used in a data center with one or more RAID implementations. Drive enclosures are specialized enclosures designed to hold and provide power to disk drives while allowing the drives within to communicate to one or more separate computers. Drive enclosures can use hot swappable drives. This means that a drive that fails can be replaced without powering down the entire RAID. Powering down the RAID may make the data on the RAID unavailable to users for an extended period of time. Not all drives and RAID types support hot swapping.

RAID Levels (3.3.2.3)

There are several levels of RAID available. These levels use mirroring, striping, and parity in different ways. Higher levels of RAID, such as RAID 5 or 6, use striping and parity in combination to provide speed and to create large volumes. Table 3-4 provides details about the RAID levels. RAID levels from 10 up combine lower RAID levels. For example, RAID 10 combines RAID 1 and RAID 0 functionalities.

Table 3-4   RAID Levels

RAID Level	Minimum Number of Drives	Features	Advantages	Disadvantages
0	2	Striping	Performance and capacity.	All data is lost if one drive fails.
1	2	Mirroring	Performance and reliability.	Capacity is half of total drive size.

RAID Level	Minimum Number of Drives	Features	Advantages	Disadvantages
5	3	Striping with parity	Performance, reliability, and capacity.	It takes time to rebuild the array if a drive fails.
6	3	Striping with double parity	Same as RAID 5 but can tolerate the loss of two drives.	It takes time to rebuild the array if one or more drives fail.
10 (0+1)	4	Mirroring and striping	Performance, capacity, and high reliability.	Capacity is half of total drive size.

Interactive Graphic

Check Your Understanding 3.3.2.4: RAID Levels

Refer to the online course to complete this activity.

Ports, Connectors, and Cables (3.3.3)

Many kinds of ports, connectors, and cables are used to attach devices to a computer so they can share data for communication. The main function of a computer port is to act as a point of attachment, where the cable from the peripheral can be connected to allow data to flow to and from the device.

Legacy Ports (3.3.3.1)

Computers have many different types of ports used to connect external peripheral devices. As computer technology has evolved, so have the types of ports used to connect peripheral devices. Legacy ports are typically found on older computers and have been mostly replaced by newer technologies such as USB. The sections that follow describes the various legacy ports.

Serial Ports

Serial ports were used to connect various peripherals such as printers, scanners, and modems. Today, serial ports are sometimes used for making console connections to network devices to perform initial configuration. There are two form factors of serial ports: a 9-pin DB-9 port and a 25-pin port. Figure 3-12 shows a 9-pin DB-9 port.

Figure 3-12 Serial Port

Parallel Ports

A *parallel port* has a 25-pin receptacle used to connect various peripheral devices, as shown in Figure 3-13. As the name implies, parallel ports send data in multiple bits at once, in parallel communication. Because these ports were often used to connect printers, they are often called *printer ports*.

Figure 3-13 Parallel Port

Game Ports

The 15-pin *game port* (see Figure 3-14) was used as a connector for joystick input. Game ports were originally located on a dedicated game controller expansion card and then later integrated with sound cards and on PC motherboards.

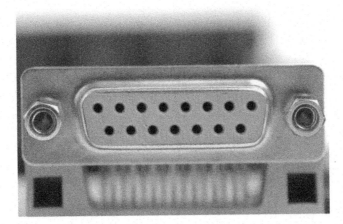

Figure 3-14   Game Port

PS/2 Ports

The *PS/2* is a 6-pin DIN connector used for connecting a keyboard and mouse. Figure 3-15 shows two color-coded PS/2 ports: purple for the keyboard and green for the mouse. In this figure, the green mouse port is at the top.

Figure 3-15   PS/2 Ports

Audio Ports

Audio ports (see Figure 3-16) connect audio devices to the computer. Analog ports typically include a line in port to connect to an external source (for example, a stereo system), a microphone port, and line out ports to connect speakers or headphones.

Figure 3-16   Audio Ports

Video and Graphic Ports (3.3.3.2)

Graphic ports are used to connect monitors and external video displays to desktop computers and laptops. The sections that follow describe these ports in greater detail.

VGA Ports

A *VGA* port (see Figure 3-17) is an analog port and is the oldest graphics port likely still used on some PCs, although it is quickly becoming a legacy technology. A VGA port is colored blue and accepts a 15-pin connector, with the pins arranged in three rows.

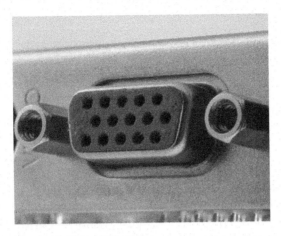

Figure 3-17   VGA Port

DVI Ports

The emergence of digital displays such as LCD monitors and TVs led to the development of *DVI* for transmitting uncompressed digital video. Variants of the DVI interface are configured to support multiple transmission modes. DVI-A (analog) supports analog only, DVI-D (digital) supports digital only, and DVI-I (integrated) supports both digital and analog. Figure 3-18 shows DVI-I. Two forms of DVI connections exist:

- Single-link connections that use a single Transition Minimized Differential Signaling (TMDS) transmitter

- Dual-link connections that use two TMDS transmitters to provide higher resolutions to larger monitors

Figure 3-18   DVI-I Port

HDMI Ports

HDMI (see Figure 3-19) carries the same video information as DVI but is also capable of providing digital audio and control signals. HDMI uses a 19-pin connector. Smaller portable electronic devices have a smaller 19-pin mini-HDMI port. HDMI is capable of very high resolutions. It is also capable of changing the refresh rate of a monitor to match the rate of the source device output.

There are two categories of HDMI: 1 (Standard) and 2 (High Speed). There are also many versions of the HDMI standard, such as Version 1.4. Newer versions of the standard support the latest features, such as high refresh rates and 4K and 8K resolutions. Versions 2.0 and 2.1 can achieve very high speeds. Version 2.0 supports Premium High Speed (up to 18 Gbps), and Version 2.1 supports Ultra High Speed (up to 48 Gbps). A high-speed HDMI cable that supports at least HDMI 1.4 is required for supporting 4K signals.

HDMI connectors are available in three sizes: standard, mini, and micro. The majority of HDMI connectors in use today are the Type A (standard), Type C (mini), and Type D (micro).

Figure 3-19   HDMI Port

DisplayPort

DisplayPort (see Figure 3-20) is a newer technology designed to replace both DVI and VGA for connecting computer monitors. DisplayPort uses a 20-pin connector for delivering high-bandwidth video and audio signals. As with HDMI, there is a miniaturized version of DisplayPort called Mini DisplayPort; it is primarily used on Apple computers.

DisplayPort can handle up to 20 Gbps with Version 2.0. It is also capable of connecting multiple monitors to the same video source with a single cable.

Figure 3-20   DisplayPort

USB Cables and Connectors (3.3.3.3)

The USB protocol has evolved over the years, and the various standards can be confusing. USB 1.0 provided a low-speed transfer rate at 1.5 Mbps for keyboards and mice and a full-speed channel at 12 Mbps. USB 2.0 made a significant leap, increasing transfer rates up to High Speed at 480 Mbps. USB 3.0 increased the transfer rate to SuperSpeed, at 5 Gbps, and USB 3.2, the latest USB-C specification, supports speeds of up to SuperSpeed+, or 20 Gbps. The sections that follow describe and show the various USB cables and connectors.

USB Type-A

USB Type-A, shown in Figure 3-21, is a rectangular connector found on nearly every desktop PC and laptop, as well as TVs, game consoles, and media players. USB 1.1, 2.0, and 3.0 Type-A connectors and receptacles are physically compatible.

Figure 3-21   USB Type-A

USB Mini-B

The *USB Mini-B* connector, shown in Figure 3-22, is rectangular with a small indention on each side. The USB Mini-B, also known as mini-USB, form factor is being phased out and replaced by the micro-USB connector.

Figure 3-22   Mini-USB

Micro-USB

The *micro-USB* connector, shown in Figure 3-23, is found on smartphones, tablets, and other devices. Except for Apple, most manufacturers have adopted the micro-USB interface. The USB 2.0 Micro-B connector has two corners pushed in at an angle.

Figure 3-23   Micro-USB

USB Type-B

The *USB Type-B* connector, shown in Figure 3-24, is commonly used to connect printer and external hard drives. It has a square shape with beveled exterior corners and an extra notch at the top.

Figure 3-24   USB Type-B

USB Type-C

USB Type-C, shown in Figure 3-25, is the newest USB interface. A USB Type-C connector is smaller than a Type-A connector and is rectangular, with four rounded corners. Both Thunderbolt 3 and USB Type-C are examples of multipurpose cables that can be used to attach different kinds of peripheral devices to a PC. USB Type-C refers to the shape of the port. Thunderbolt 3 combines the functionality of USB, Thunderbolt, and DisplayPort, and it provides the ability to deliver power to devices through the cable.

Figure 3-25   USB Type-C

Lightning

The *Lightning* connector, shown in Figure 3-26, is a small, proprietary 8-pin connector used by Apple mobile devices such as iPhones, iPads, and iPods for both power charging and data transfer. It is similar in appearance to a USB Type-C connector.

Figure 3-26   Lightning Cable

SATA Cables and Connectors (3.3.3.4)

SATA is an interface type used to connect SATA hard drives and other storage devices to the motherboard inside the computer. SATA cables are long (up to 1 meter) and thin, with a flat and thin 7-pin connector on each end. The sections that follow describe the characteristics and types of SATA cables and connectors.

SATA Cables and Connectors

Figure 3-27 shows a *SATA cable*. One end plugs into a SATA port on the motherboard, and the other end plugs into the back of an internal storage device such as a SATA hard drive. The SATA connecter has an L-shaped key so that it can be installed only one way.

Figure 3-27   SATA Cable

SATA Data and Power Cables

A *SATA data cable* does not provide power, and an additional cable is needed to supply power to SATA drives, as shown in Figure 3-28.

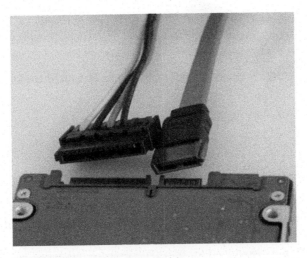

Figure 3-28   SATA Data Cable

eSATA Cables

An *eSATA cable*, shown in Figure 3-29, is used to connect an external SATA drive. Unlike a SATA connector, an eSATA connector does not have an L-shaped key. However, an eSATA port does have a key feature to prevent inadvertent insertion of a USB connector, which is similar in size and shape.

Figure 3-29   eSATA Cable

eSATA Adapter Card

Often, an *eSATA adapter card* (see Figure 3-30) is installed in a computer to provide eSATA ports.

Figure 3-30   eSATA Adapter

Twisted-Pair Cables and Connectors (3.3.3.5)

Twisted-pair cable is used in wired Ethernet networks and in older telephone networks. Twisted-pair cabling gets its name from the fact that pairs of wires inside the cable are twisted together. The twisting of wire pairs helps reduce crosstalk and electromagnetic induction. The sections that follow describe the characteristics and types of twisted-pair cables and connectors.

RJ-45 Connectors

Each end of a UTP cable must be terminated with a connector. In the case of Ethernet networks, an *RJ-45 connector* (see Figure 3-31) terminates the cable and is plugged into an Ethernet port.

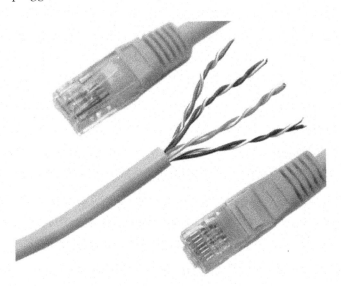

Figure 3-31   RJ-45 Connectors

Twisted-Pair Cables

There are basically two types of twisted-pair cables: *unshielded twisted-pair (UTP)* cabling and *shielded twisted-pair (STP)*. The most commonly used form of twisted-pair cabling is UTP, shown in Figure 3-31. It consists of color-coded insulated copper wires without the foil or braiding found in STP.

RJ-11 Connectors

Older telephone networks used a four-wire UTP cable with two wire pairs terminated with a 6-pin *RJ-11 connector*, shown in Figure 3-32. The RJ-11 connector looks very similar to the RJ-45 connector but is smaller.

Figure 3-32   RJ-11 Connector

Coax Cables and Connectors (3.3.3.6)

Coaxial (coax) cable has an inner center conductor, usually made from copper or copper-clad steel, which is surrounded by a nonconductive dielectric insulating material. The dielectric is surrounded by a foil shield, which forms the outer conductor and shields against electromagnetic interference (EMI). The outer conductor/shield is encased in a PVC outer jacket. The sections that follow describe the characteristics and types of coax cables and connectors.

Coax Cable Construction

The coax cable in Figure 3-33 has the outer jacket pulled back to reveal the braided shielding and copper core conductor.

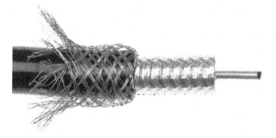

Figure 3-33   Coax Cable

RG-6

An *RG-6 cable* (see Figure 3-34) cable is heavy gauge and has insulation and shielding tuned for high-bandwidth, high-frequency applications such as Internet, cable TV, and satellite TV signals.

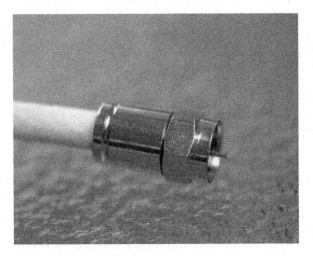

Figure 3-34   RG-6 Cable

RG-59

RG-59 cable is thinner and is recommended in low-bandwidth and lower-frequency applications, such as analog video and CCTV applications, such as for the camera in Figure 3-35.

Figure 3-35   RG-59 Cable

BNC

A BNC (Bayonet Neill–Concelman) connector, shown in Figure 3-36, connects coaxial cables to devices using a quarter-turn connection scheme. BNC is used with digital or analog audio or video.

Figure 3-36   BNC Connector

SCSI and IDE Cables and Connectors (3.3.3.7)

Small Computer System Interface (SCSI) is a standard for connecting peripheral and storage devices. SCSI is a bus technology, meaning that all devices connect to a central bus and are "daisy-chained" together. The cabling/connector requirements depend on the location of the SCSI bus.

Integrated Drive Electronics (IDE) is a standard type of interface used to connect some hard drives and optical drives to each other and to the motherboard.

The sections that follow describe the characteristics and types of SCSI and IDE cables and connectors.

External SCSI Cables

A *Centronics connector* (see Figure 3-37) is used for connecting older external SCSI devices such as scanners and printers. This connector comes in 36-pin and 50-pin versions, with the pins arranged in two rows and a plastic bar through the center that holds the contact pins. Squeeze latches or bail locks located on the sides of the connector are used to hold it in place.

Figure 3-37   External SCSI Cable

Internal SCSI Cables

A common SCSI connector for internal hard drives is the *internal 50-pin SCSI*, which has 50 pins arranged in two rows and is attached to a ribbon cable, as shown in Figure 3-38.

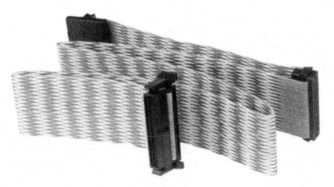

Figure 3-38   Internal SCSI Cable

IDE Cables

IDE ribbon cables, shown in Figure 3-39, look very similar to internal SCSI cables; however, IDE uses 40-pin connectors. There are typically three connectors on the cable: one to connect to the IDE port on the motherboard and two for attachment of IDE drives.

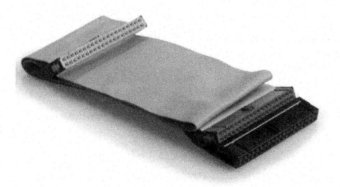

Figure 3-39   IDE Cable

Interactive Graphic

Check Your Understanding 3.3.3.8: Identify the External Connectors

Refer to the online course to complete this activity.

Monitors (3.3.4)

A monitor is an output device that connects by cable to a port on the graphics card. It displays the results of user input. There are different types of monitors, and the two primary types are liquid crystal display (LCD) and Light Emitting Diode (LED).

Monitor Characteristics (3.3.4.1)

There are many types of computer monitors available. Some are designed for casual use, and others are for specific requirements, such as those used by architects, graphic designers, or gamers.

Monitors vary by use, size, quality, clarity, brightness, and other factors. Therefore, it is useful to understand the various terms used when discussing monitors.

Computer monitors are usually described in terms of the following:

- *Screen size*: This is the diagonal measurement of the screen (such as from top left to bottom right), in inches. Common sizes include 19 to 24 inches, to ultrawide monitors that are 30 or more inches wide. Larger monitors are usually better but are more expensive and require more desk space.

- *Resolution*: Resolution is measured by the number of horizontal and vertical pixels. For example, 1920×1080 (called 1080p) is a common resolution. It means the monitor has 1920 horizontal pixels and 1080 vertical pixels.

- *Monitor resolution*: This relates to the amount of information that can be displayed on a screen. A higher-resolution monitor displays more information on a screen than a lower-resolution monitor does. This is true even with monitors that have the same screen size.

- *Native resolution*: This identifies the best monitor resolution for the specific monitor. In Windows 10, the native resolution of a monitor is identified by the keyword (Recommended) beside the monitor resolution. For example, in Figure 3-40, the native resolution of the monitor is 1920×1080.

- *Native mode*: This term describes the image sent to the monitor by the video adapter card matching the native resolution of the monitor.

- *Connectivity*: Older monitors used VGA or DVI connectors, and newer monitors support HDMI and DisplayPort ports. DisplayPort is a connection found on newer monitors. It supports higher resolutions and high refresh rates.

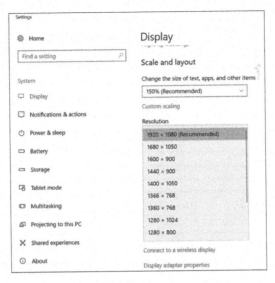

Figure 3-40   Native Resolution

Note

If you want to display more things on the screen, select a higher-resolution monitor. If you just want things to appear bigger, select a larger screen size.

Monitor Terms (3.3.4.2)

Table 3-5 lists the most common monitor-related terms.

Table 3-5   Technical Monitor Terms

Monitor Term	Description
Pixel	Abbreviation for "picture element," a tiny dot capable of displaying the shades red, green, and blue (RGB). With more pixels, a monitor can display more detail.
Dot pitch	The distance between pixels on the screen. A lower dot pitch (that is, a smaller distance between dots) produces a better image.
Brightness	The luminance of a monitor, measured in candelas per square meter (cd/m^2). Brightness up to 250 cd/m^2 is typically recommended, but in well-lit rooms, you may use up to 350 cd/m^2. Keep in mind that too much brightness may cause eyestrain.
Contrast ratio	A measurement of how white and how black a monitor can get. A contrast ratio of 1000:1 displays dimmer whites and more pale blacks than 4500:1.

Monitor Term	Description
Aspect ratio	The horizontal-to-vertical measurement of the viewing area of a monitor. For example, QSXGA measures 2560 pixels horizontally by 2048 pixels vertically, which creates an aspect ratio of 5:4. If a viewing area is 16 inches wide by 12 inches high, the aspect ratio is 4:3. A viewing area that is 24 inches wide by 18 inches high also has an aspect ratio of 4:3.
Refresh rate	How many times per second the monitor can redraw the screen, expressed in Hertz (Hz).
Response time	The amount in time for a pixel to change properties (such as color or brightness). Fast response times display a smooth image when displaying fast action.
Frames per second (fps)	How many times the computer creates each frame. The higher the FPS, the better, but the monitor must be able to display the frames at a high rate.
Interlaced/ non-interlaced	The type of scanning a monitor uses. Interlaced monitors create an image by scanning the screen two times. The first scan covers the odd lines, top to bottom, and the second scan covers the even lines. Non-interlaced monitors create an image by scanning the screen, one line at a time, from top to bottom.

Display Standards (3.3.4.3)

Over the years, many different display standards have been developed, as shown in Table 3-6.

Table 3-6 Legacy and Common Monitor Display Standards

Monitor Standard	Resolution	Aspect Ratio	Comments
CGA	320×200	16:10	■ Color Graphics Adapter ■ Introduced by IBM in 1981 ■ Obsolete
VGA	640×480	4:3	■ Video Graphics Array ■ Introduced in 1987 ■ Legacy
SVGA	800×600	4:3	■ Super Video Graphics Array ■ Introduced in 1989 ■ Still supported on some platforms
HD	1280×720	16:9	■ High-Definition ■ Also known as 720p

Monitor Standard	Resolution	Aspect Ratio	Comments
FHD	1920×1080	16:9	■ Full High-Definition ■ Also known as 1080p ■ Good setting for typical users
QHD	2560×1440	16:9	■ Quad High-Definition ■ Also known as 1440p ■ Suggested resolution for high-end users and gamers
UHD	3840×2160	16:9	■ Ultra High-Definition ■ Also known as 4K

Using Multiple Monitors (3.3.4.4)

Adding monitors can increase your visual desktop area and improve productivity. The added monitors enable you to expand the size of the monitor or duplicate the desktop so you can view additional windows. For example, the person in Figure 3-41 is using multiple displays. They are using the monitor on the right to make changes to a website and the monitor on the left to display the resulting changes. They are also using a laptop to display a library of images they are considering for inclusion in the website.

Figure 3-41   Using Multiple Monitors

Many computers have built-in support for multiple monitors. To connect multiple monitors to a computer, you need the supporting cables. You also need to enable your computer to support multiple monitors.

For example, on a Windows 10 host, right-click anywhere on the Desktop and choose **Display settings**. Windows should open the Display window, as shown in Figure 3-42. In the example, the user has two monitors connected in the configuration displayed. The current monitor selected is highlighted and has a resolution of 1920×1080. It is also the main display monitor. By clicking on monitor 1 or 2 you could see the resolution of that monitor.

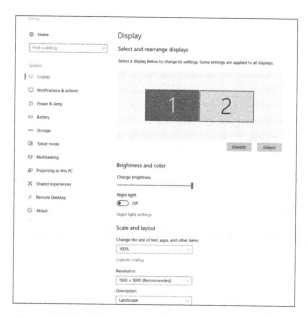

Figure 3-42   Enabling Dual Monitors on a Windows Host

<table>
<tr><td>Interactive
Graphic</td><td>**Check Your Understanding 3.3.4.5: Monitor Terminology**
Refer to the online course to complete this activity.</td></tr>
</table>

Computer Configuration (3.4)

Necessary changes to a computer may require an upgrade or replacement of components and peripherals. Research the effectiveness and cost for both upgrading and replacing. As a technician, it is important to understand the system usage and user needs as well as how computer components work together to upgrade or build a functioning PC with the right purpose.

Upgrade Computer Hardware (3.4.1)

When upgrading a computer, component compatibility is important. When you are adding new or additional components to an existing build, to ensure that the system continues to run efficiently after the upgrade, you need to choose the right components. Software upgrade compatibility is just as necessary as hardware compatibility.

Motherboard Upgrade (3.4.1.1)

Computers need periodic upgrades for various reasons:

- User requirements change.
- Upgraded software packages require new hardware.
- New hardware offers enhanced performance.

Changes to a computer may lead you to upgrade or replace components and peripherals. Research the effectiveness and cost of both upgrading and replacing.

If you upgrade or replace a motherboard, consider that you might have to replace other components, including the CPU, the heat sink and fan assembly, and RAM. A new motherboard must also fit into the old computer case, and the power supply must support it.

When upgrading the motherboard, if the CPU and the heat sink and fan assembly are to be reused, move them to the new motherboard. These items are much easier to work with when they are outside the case. Work on an antistatic mat and wear antistatic gloves or an antistatic wrist strap to avoid damaging the CPU. If the new motherboard requires a different CPU and RAM, install them at this time. Clean the thermal compound from the CPU and heat sink. Remember to reapply thermal compound between the CPU and the heat sink.

Steps to Upgrade a Motherboard (3.4.1.2)

Before beginning an upgrade, ensure that you know where and how everything is connected. Always make notes in a journal to record how the computer is originally set up. A quick way is to use a cell phone to take pictures of important items, such as how components connect to the motherboard. These pictures may be very helpful during reassembly.

To upgrade a motherboard from a computer case, follow these steps:

Step 1.   Record how the power supply, case fans, case LEDs, and case buttons attach to the old motherboard.

Step 2.   Disconnect the cables from the old motherboard.

Step 3.   Disconnect the expansion cards from the case. Remove each expansion card and place all the cards in antistatic bags or on an antistatic mat.

Step 4.   Carefully record how the old motherboard is secured to the case. Some mounting screws provide support, and some provide an important grounding connection between the motherboard and the chassis. In particular, pay attention to screws and *standoffs* that are non-metallic because they may be insulators. Replacing insulating screws and supports with metal hardware that conducts electricity might damage electrical components.

Step 5.   Remove the old motherboard from the case.

Step 6.   Examine the new motherboard and identify where all the connectors are, such as power, SATA, fan, USB, audio, front panel connector, and any others.

Step 7.   Examine the I/O shield located at the back of the computer case. Replace the old I/O shield with the I/O shield that comes with the new motherboard.

Step 8.   Insert and secure the motherboard into the case. Be sure to consult the case and motherboard manufacturer's user guides. Use the proper types of screws. Do not swap threaded screws with self-tapping metal screws, which would damage the threaded screw holes and might not be secure. Make sure the threaded screws are the correct length and have the same number of threads per inch. If the thread of screws is correct, they fit easily. If you force a screw to fit, you can damage the threaded hole, and it will not hold the motherboard securely. Using the wrong screw can also produce metal shavings that can cause short circuits.

Step 9.   Connect the power supply, case fans, case LEDs, front panel, and any other required cables. If the ATX power connectors are not the same size (some have more pins than others), you might need to use an adapter. Refer to the motherboard documentation for the layout of these connections.

Step 10. After the new motherboard is in place and the cables are connected, install and secure the expansion cards.

It is now time to check your work. Make sure that there are no loose parts or unconnected cables. Connect the keyboard, mouse, monitor, and power. If a problem is detected, shut off the power supply immediately.

CPU Upgrade (3.4.1.3)

One way to increase the power of a computer is to increase the processing speed. You can do this by upgrading the CPU (see Figure 3-43). The CPU must meet the following requirements:

- The new CPU must fit into the existing CPU socket.

- The new CPU must be compatible with the motherboard chipset.

- The new CPU must operate with the existing motherboard and power supply.

Figure 3-43   Installing a New CPU

The new CPU might require a different heat sink and fan assembly. The assembly must physically fit the CPU and must be compatible with the CPU socket. It must also be adequate to remove the heat of the faster CPU.

Caution

You must apply thermal compound between the new CPU and the heat sink and fan assembly.

View thermal settings in the BIOS to determine if there are any problems with the CPU and the heat sink and fan assembly. Third-party software applications can also report CPU temperature information in an easy-to-read format. Refer to the motherboard or CPU user documentation to determine if the chip is operating in the correct temperature range.

To install additional fans in the case to help cool the computer, follow these steps:

Step 1.   Align each fan so that it faces the correct direction to either draw air in or blow air out.

Step 2.   Mount each fan using the predrilled holes in the case. It is common to mount fans near the top of the case to blow hot air out and near the bottom of the case to bring air in. Avoid mounting two fans close together if they are moving air in opposite directions.

Step 3.   Connect the fan to the power supply or the motherboard, depending on the case fan plug type.

Storage Device Upgrade (3.4.1.4)

Instead of purchasing a new computer to get faster speed and more storage space, you might consider adding another hard drive (see Figure 3-44).

Figure 3-44   Installing a New Drive

There are several reasons for installing an additional drive, including the following:

- To increase storage space
- To increase hard drive speed
- To install a second operating system
- To store the system swap file
- To provide fault tolerance
- To back up the original hard drive

After selecting the appropriate hard drive for the computer, follow these general guidelines for installation:

Step 1.   Place the hard drive in an empty drive bay and tighten the screws to secure the hard drive.

Step 2.   Connect the drive to the motherboard, using the correct cable.

Step 3.   Attach the power cable to the drive.

Peripheral Upgrades (3.4.1.5)

Peripheral devices periodically need to be upgraded. For example, if a device stops operating or if you wish to improve performance and productivity, an upgrade might be necessary.

These are a few reasons for upgrading a keyboard and/or a mouse:

- You might want to use a keyboard and mouse with an ergonomic design, such as those shown in Figure 3-45. Ergonomic devices are made to be more comfortable to use and to help prevent repetitive motion injuries.

- You might want to reconfigure the keyboard to accommodate a special task, such as typing in a second language with additional characters.

- You might need to accommodate users with disabilities.

Figure 3-45   Ergonomic Keyboard and Mouse

Sometimes, however, it is not possible to perform an upgrade using the existing expansion slots or sockets. In this case, you might be able to accomplish the upgrade by using a USB connection. If the computer does not have an extra USB connection, you must install a USB adapter card or purchase a USB hub, such as the one shown in Figure 3-46.

Figure 3-46 USB Hub

Power Supply Upgrade (3.4.1.6)

Upgrading your computer hardware will most likely also change its power needs. If so, you might need to upgrade your power supply. You can find calculators on the Internet to help you determine whether you need to upgrade the power supply. Search for "power supply wattage calculator."

In addition to upgrading for additional power, a computer may be capable of having two power supplies, with one acting as a redundant power supply in case of failure. A special motherboard must be used to take advantage of this configuration. This configuration is not often found with desktop computers but is more commonly used in servers. When a computer has two power supplies, both power supplies are hot swappable. A faulty power supply can be replaced without losing power to the computer.

Lab 3.4.1.7: Research a Hardware Upgrade

In this lab, you will gather information about hardware components so you can upgrade a computer's hardware so the customer can play advanced video games.

Protecting the Environment (3.5)

There are multiple reasons you need be aware of how to protect your environment as a computer technician, such as complying with local, state, and federal government disposal regulations to avoid receiving serious fines and aiding in the prevention of harm to the ecosystem.

Safe Disposal of Equipment and Supplies (3.5.1)

Proper disposal of equipment and supplies is important to the health of an organization and the planet. Be aware of current local, regional, and national laws. Find reputable recyclers but be sure to wipe the data off a device before you recycle it and investigate the best method of disposal for all equipment. Improper disposal not only harms the environment but could pose other serious consequences to your business.

Safe Disposal Methods (3.5.1.1)

After upgrading a computer or replacing a broken device, what do you do with the leftover parts? If the parts are still good, they can be donated or sold. Parts that no longer work must be disposed of, but they must be disposed of responsibly.

The proper disposal or recycling of hazardous computer components is a global issue. Make sure to follow regulations that govern how to dispose of specific items. Organizations that violate these regulations can be fined or may face expensive legal battles. Regulations for the disposal of the items listed in the following sections vary from state to state and from country to country. Check with your local environmental regulatory agency.

Batteries

Batteries often contain rare earth metals that can be harmful to the environment. These metals do not decay and remain in the environment for many years. Mercury is commonly used in the manufacturing of batteries and is extremely harmful to humans.

Recycling batteries should be standard practice. All batteries are subject to disposal procedures that comply with local environmental regulations.

Monitors

Handle CRT monitors with care. Extremely high voltage can be stored in CRT monitors, even the monitors that have been disconnected from a power source.

Monitors contain glass, metal, plastics, lead, barium, and rare earth metals. According to the U.S. Environmental Protection Agency (EPA), monitors can contain approximately 4 pounds of lead. Monitors must be disposed of in compliance with environmental regulations.

Toner Kits, Cartridges, and Developers

Used printer toner kits and printer cartridges must be disposed of properly, in compliance with environmental regulations. They can also be recycled. Some toner cartridge suppliers and manufacturers take empty cartridges for refilling. Kits to refill inkjet printer cartridges are available but are not recommended because the ink might leak into the printer, causing irreparable damage. Using refilled inkjet cartridges might also void the inkjet printer warranty.

Chemical Solvents and Aerosol Cans

Contact the local sanitation company to learn how and where to dispose of the chemicals and solvents used to clean computers. Never dump chemicals or solvents down a sink or dispose of them in a drain that connects to public sewers.

Cell Phones and Tablets

The EPA recommends that individuals check with local health and sanitation agencies for their preferred way to dispose of electronics such as cell phones, tablets, and computers. Most computer equipment and mobile devices contain hazardous materials, such as heavy metals, that do not belong in a landfill because they contaminate the earth. Local communities may also have recycling programs.

Safety Data Sheets (3.5.1.2)

Hazardous materials are sometimes called *toxic waste*. These materials can contain high concentrations of heavy metals such as cadmium, lead, or mercury. The regulations for the disposal of hazardous materials vary by state or country. Contact the local recycling or waste removal authorities in your community for information about disposal procedures and services.

A *safety data sheet (SDS)*, formerly known as a material safety and data sheet (MSDS), is a fact sheet that summarizes information about material identification, including hazardous ingredients that can affect personal health, fire hazards, and first-aid requirements. An SDS contains chemical reactivity and incompatibility information. It also includes protective measures for the safe handling and storage of materials and spill, leak, and disposal procedures. To determine whether a material is classified as hazardous, consult the manufacturer's SDS, which in the Unites States is required by OSHA when the material is transferred to a new owner.

The SDS explains how to dispose of potentially hazardous materials in the safest manner. Always check local regulations concerning acceptable disposal methods before disposing of any electronic equipment.

In the European Union, the regulation Registration, Evaluation, Authorization and Restriction of Chemicals (REACH) came into effect in 2007, replacing various directives and regulations with a single system.

Interactive Graphic

Check Your Understanding 3.5.1.3: Safe Disposal

Refer to the online course to complete this activity.

Summary (3.6)

In this chapter, you learned about the computer boot process and the role played by the BIOS, which performs the POST on the main components of the computer. You also learned that the motherboard BIOS settings are saved in a CMOS memory chip. When a computer boots, the BIOS software reads the configured settings stored in CMOS to determine how to configure the hardware. In a lab, you installed Microsoft Windows operating system and third-party software.

After installing Windows, you learned about wattage and voltage and Ohm's law, which expresses the idea that voltage is equal to the current multiplied by the resistance ($V = IR$) and that power is equal to the voltage multiplied by the current ($P = VI$). You learned about the types of AC power fluctuations that can cause data loss or hardware failures such as blackouts, brownouts, noise, spikes, and power surges. You also learned about the devices that help shield against power fluctuation problems and protect the data and computer equipment. These devices include surge protectors, UPSs, and SPSs.

Next, you learned about multicore processors ranging from dual-core CPUs with two cores inside a single CPU, to octa-core CPUs with eight cores inside a single CPU, and different types of CPU cooling mechanisms, including fans, heat sinks, and water cooling systems. You also learned how multiple drives can be logically grouped and managed to create large storage volumes with redundancy using RAID technology. Striping, mirroring, parity, and double parity types of RAID were covered.

You learned about many different types of computer ports and connectors, starting with legacy ports that are typically found on older computers, such as serial, parallel, game, PS/2, and audio ports—most of which have been replaced by newer technologies, such as USB. You also learned about various video and game ports that are used to connect monitors and external video displays, including VGA, DVI, HDMI, and DisplayPort. You learned about the evolution of USB ports, including USB Type-A, mini-USB, micro-USB, USB Type-B, USB Type-C, and Lightning connectors.

You learned about the characteristics that define computer monitors. You learned that monitors vary in terms of use, size, quality, clarity, and brightness. You also learned that monitors are described by their screen size, as measured diagonally, and screen resolution, as measured by the number of pixels. The display standards CGA, VGA, SVGA, HD, FHD, QHD, and UHD were all defined as well.

The chapter concluded with a discussion of protecting the environment by using safe disposal methods for computer components. You learned that there are regulations for the disposal of many of these components, such as batteries, toner, printer cartridges, cell phones, and tablets. You also learned about the SDS, which explains how to dispose of potentially hazardous materials in the safest manner. Always check local regulations concerning acceptable disposal methods before disposing of any electronic equipment.

Practice

The following activities provide practice with the topics introduced in this chapter. The labs are available in the companion *IT Essentials v8 Labs & Study Guide* (ISBN 9780138166304).

Labs

Lab 3.1.1.6: Investigate BIOS or UEFI Settings

Lab 3.1.2.5: Search for BIOS or UEFI Firmware Updates

Lab 3.1.2.6: Install Windows

Lab 3.1.2.7: Install Third-Party Software in Windows

Lab 3.2.1.3: Ohm's Law

Lab 3.4.1.7: Research a Hardware Upgrade

Check Your Understanding Questions

Complete all the review questions listed here to test your understanding of the topics and concepts in this chapter. Appendix A, "Answers to 'Check Your Understanding' Questions," lists the answers.

1. Which device can protect computer equipment from brownouts by providing a consistent quality of electrical power?

    A. SPS

    B. surge suppressor

    C. AC adapter

    D. UPS

2. What unit is used to measure the amount of resistance to the flow of current in a circuit?

    A. Ohms

    B. volts

    C. watts

    D. amps

3. Where is the saved BIOS configuration data stored?

A. CMOS

B. hard drive

C. cache

D. RAM

4. A network administrator is setting up a web server for a small advertising office and is concerned about data availability. The administrator wishes to implement disk fault tolerance using the minimum number of disks required. Which RAID level should the administrator choose?

A. RAID 0

B. RAID 6

C. RAID 5

D. RAID 1

5. Which specialized computer component would be most important for a workstation built for audio and video editing?

A. a high-speed wireless adapter

B. a liquid CPU cooling system

C. a TV tuner card

D. a specialized video card

6. Which term refers to the technique of increasing the speed of a processor compared to the specified value of its manufacturer?

A. multitasking

B. overclocking

C. throttling

D. Hyper-Threading

7. When a dual-core CPU with Hyper-Threading features is installed on a motherboard, how many instructions can the CPU simultaneously process?

A. 4

B. 8

C. 6

D. 2

8. Which hardware upgrade would allow the processor in a gaming PC to provide the optimal gaming performance?

   A. large amounts of fast RAM

   B. high-capacity external hard drive

   C. liquid cooling

   D. fast EIDE drive

9. Which of the following can be modified in the BIOS setup program? (Choose two.)

   A. boot order

   B. drive partition size

   C. swap file size

   D. device drivers

   E. enabling and disabling devices

10. A technician accidentally spills a cleaning solution on the floor of the workshop. Where would the technician find instructions on how to properly clean up and dispose of the product?

    A. the insurance policy of the company

    B. the safety data sheet

    C. the regulations provided by the local occupational health and safety office

    D. the local hazardous materials team

11. Which of the following indicates that the charge on the CMOS battery could be getting low?

    A. Performance while accessing files on the hard drive is slow.

    B. A beep error code occurs during POST.

    C. The computer fails to boot.

    D. The computer time and date are incorrect.

12. Which website should a technician consult to find instructions for updating the BIOS on a computer?

    A. CPU manufacturer's website

    B. operating system developer's website

    C. case manufacturer's website

    D. motherboard manufacturer's website

13. Which term is used to describe the best monitor resolution for a specific monitor?

    A. native mode

    B. screen resolution

    C. monitor resolution

    D. native resolution

14. When upgrading the CPU, which of the following requirements must the replacement CPU meet? (Choose two.)

    A. The new CPU must be compatible with the motherboard chipset.

    B. The new CPU must use new cables to connect.

    C. The new CPU must have a different heat sink and fan assembly.

    D. The new CPU must operate with the existing motherboard and power supply.

15. Which connector is a small, proprietary 8-pin connector used by Apple mobile devices such as iPhones, iPads, and iPods for both power charging and data transfer?

    A. USB Type-C

    B. DisplayPort

    C. Thunderbolt

    D. Lightning

Objectives

Upon completion of this chapter, you will be able to answer the following questions:

- What are the benefits of preventive maintenance?

- What are the most common preventive maintenance tasks?

- What are the elements of the troubleshooting process?

- What are common problems and solutions when troubleshooting a PC?

Key Terms

This chapter uses the following key terms. You can find the definitions in the glossary at the end of the book.

Introduction (4.0)

Preventive maintenance is often overlooked, but good IT professionals understand the importance of regular and systematic inspection, cleaning, and replacement of worn parts, materials, and systems. Effective preventive maintenance reduces part, material, and system faults and keeps hardware and software in good working condition.

Preventive maintenance doesn't just apply to hardware. Performing basic tasks such as checking what programs run on startup, scanning for malware, and removing unused programs helps a computer function more efficiently and can keep it from slowing down. Good IT professionals also understand the importance of troubleshooting, which requires an organized and logical approach to problems with computers and other components.

In this chapter, you will learn general guidelines for creating preventive maintenance programs and troubleshooting procedures. These guidelines are a starting point to help you develop your preventive maintenance and troubleshooting skills. You will also learn the importance of maintaining an optimal operating environment for computer systems that are clean, free of potential contaminants, and within the temperature and humidity ranges specified by the manufacturer.

At the end of the chapter, you will learn the six-step troubleshooting processes and common problems and solutions for different computer components.

Preventive Maintenance (4.1)

Preventive maintenance can be the key to keeping computer systems from experiencing serious problems, such as data loss and hardware failures, and it also helps systems have a longer life span. In this section, you study the need for preventive maintenance of a computer system. Following a good preventive maintenance plan can keep computer problems from being too troublesome.

PC Preventive Maintenance Overview (4.1.1)

Preventive maintenance is the regular and systematic inspection, cleaning, and replacement of worn parts, materials, and systems. Effective preventive maintenance reduces part, material, and system faults and keeps hardware and software in good working condition.

Benefits to Preventive Maintenance (4.1.1.1)

Preventive maintenance plans are developed based on at least two factors:

- **Computer location or environment:** Dusty environments, such as construction sites, require more attention than an office environment.

- **Computer use:** High-traffic networks, such as a school network, might require additional scanning and removal of malicious software and unwanted files.

Regular preventive maintenance reduces potential hardware and software problems, computer downtime, repair costs, and the number of equipment failures. It also improves data protection, equipment life, and stability and saves money.

Preventive Maintenance - Dust (4.1.1.2)

The following are considerations to keep dust from damaging computer components:

- Clean/replace building air filters regularly to reduce the amount of dust in the air.
- Use a cloth or a duster to clean the outside of the computer case. If using a cleaning product, put a small amount onto a cleaning cloth and then wipe the outside of the case.
- Dust on the outside of a computer can travel through cooling fans to the inside.
- Accumulated dust prevents the flow of air and reduces the cooling of components.
- Hot computer components are more likely to break down.
- Remove dust from the inside of a computer using a combination of compressed air, a low-air-flow ESD vacuum cleaner, and a small lint-free cloth.
- Keep the can of compressed air upright to prevent the fluid from leaking onto computer components.
- Keep the compressed air can a safe distance from sensitive devices and components.
- Use the lint-free cloth to remove any dust left behind on the component.

Caution

When you clean a fan with compressed air, hold the fan blades in place. This prevents overspinning the rotor or moving the fan in the wrong direction.

Preventive Maintenance - Internal Components (4.1.1.3)

This is a basic list of components to inspect for dust and damage:

- **CPU heat sink and fan assembly:** The fan should spin freely, the fan power cable should be secure, and the fan should turn when the power is on.
- **RAM modules:** The modules must be seated securely in the RAM slots. Ensure that the retaining clips are not loose.

- **Storage devices:** All cables should be firmly connected. Check for loose, missing, or incorrectly set jumpers. A drive should not produce rattling, knocking, or grinding sounds.

- **Screws:** A loose screw inside the case can cause a short circuit.

- **Adapter cards:** Ensure that adapter cards are seated properly and secured with the retaining screws in their expansion slots. Loose cards can cause short circuits. Missing expansion slot covers can let dust, dirt, or living pests inside the computer.

- **Cables:** Examine all cable connections. Ensure that pins are not bent or broken and that cables are not crimped, pinched, or severely bent. Retaining screws should be finger-tightened.

- **Power devices:** Inspect power strips, surge suppressors (surge protectors), and UPS devices. Make sure the devices work properly and that there is clear ventilation.

- **Keyboard and mouse:** Use compressed air to clean the keyboard, mouse, and mouse sensor.

Preventive Maintenance - Environmental Concerns (4.1.1.4)

An optimal operating environment for a computer is clean, free of potential contaminants, and within the temperature and humidity ranges specified by the manufacturer, as shown in Figure 4-1 and defined in the list that follows.

Figure 4-1 Temperature and Humidity

Follow these guidelines to help ensure optimal computer operating performance:

- Do not obstruct vents or airflow to the internal components.

- Keep the room temperature between 45 and 90 degrees Fahrenheit (between 7 and 32 degrees Celsius).

- Keep the humidity level between 10% and 80%.

- Temperature and humidity recommendations vary by computer manufacturer. Research the recommended values for computers used in extreme conditions.

Preventive Maintenance - Software (4.1.1.5)

Verify that installed software is current and follow the policies of the organization when installing security updates, operating system, and program updates.

Create a software maintenance schedule to:

- Review and install the appropriate security, software, and driver updates.

- Update the virus definition files and scan for viruses and spyware.

- Remove unwanted or unused programs.

- Scan hard drives for errors and defragment hard drives.

Interactive Graphic

Check Your Understanding 4.1.1.6: Preventive Maintenance

Refer to the online course to complete this activity.

Troubleshooting Process (4.2)

Troubleshooting is a systematic process used to locate the cause of a fault in a computer system and correct the relevant hardware and software issues. Approaching problem solving using a logical and methodical approach is essential to successful resolution. Although experience is very useful to problem solving, following a troubleshooting model will enhance effectiveness and speed.

Troubleshooting Process Steps (4.2.1)

In this section, you will learn that to troubleshoot a problem quickly and effectively, you need to understand how to approach the issue. Troubleshooting is a way of discovering what is causing a problem and fixing it.

Introduction to Troubleshooting (4.2.1.1)

Troubleshooting requires an organized and logical approach to problems with computers and other components. Sometimes issues arise during preventive maintenance. At other times, customers may contact you with problems. Taking a logical approach to troubleshooting allows you to eliminate variables and identify causes of problems in a systematic order. Asking the right questions, testing the right hardware, and examining the right data helps you understand the problem and form a proposed solution.

Troubleshooting is a skill that you refine over time. Each time you solve a problem, you increase your troubleshooting skills by gaining more experience. You learn how and when to combine steps or skip steps to reach a solution quickly. The troubleshooting process is a guideline that is modified to fit your needs.

This section presents an approach to problem solving that you can apply to both hardware and software.

Note

The term *customer*, as used in this book, refers to any user who requires technical computer assistance.

Before you begin troubleshooting problems, always follow the necessary precautions to protect data on a computer. Some repairs, such as replacing a hard drive or reinstalling an operating system, might put the data on the computer at risk. Make sure you do everything possible to prevent data loss while attempting repairs. If your work results in data loss for the customer, you or your company could be held liable.

Data Backup

A *data backup* is a copy of the data on a computer hard drive that is saved to another storage device or to cloud storage. *Cloud storage* is online storage that is accessed via the Internet. In an organization, backups may be performed on a daily, weekly, or monthly basis.

If you are unsure about whether a backup has been done, do not attempt any troubleshooting activities until you check with the customer. Here is a list of items to verify with the customer regarding whether a backup has been performed:

- Date of the last backup
- Contents of the backup
- Data integrity of the backup
- Availability of all backup media for a data restore

If the customer does not have a current backup and you are not able to create one, ask the customer to sign a liability release form. A liability release form contains at least the following information:

- Permission to work on the computer without having a current backup available

- Release from liability if data is lost or corrupted
- Description of the work to be performed

Troubleshooting Process Steps (4.2.1.2)

The *troubleshooting process steps* are as follows:

Step 1.   Identify the problem.

Step 2.   Establish a theory of probable cause.

Step 3.   Test the theory to determine the cause.

Step 4.   Establish a plan of action to resolve the problem and implement the solution.

Step 5.   Verify full system functionality and, if applicable, implement preventive measures.

Step 6.   Document findings, actions, and outcomes.

Identify the Problem (4.2.1.3)

The first step in the troubleshooting process is to identify the problem. During this step, gather as much information as possible from the customer and from the computer.

Conversation Etiquette

When you are talking to a customer, follow these guidelines:

- Ask direct questions to gather information.
- Do not use industry jargon.
- Do not talk down to the customer.
- Do not insult the customer.
- Do not accuse the customer of causing the problem.

Table 4-1 lists some of the information to gather from the customer.

Table 4-1   Step 1: Identify the Problem

Customer information	■ Company name
	■ Contact name
	■ Address
	■ Phone number

Computer configuration	■ Manufacturer and model
	■ Operating system
	■ Network environment
	■ Connection type
Problem description	■ Open-ended questions
	■ Closed-ended questions
Error messages	
Beep sequences	
LEDs	
POST	

Open-Ended and Closed-Ended Questions

Open-ended questions allow customers to explain the details of the problem in their own words. Use open-ended question to obtain general information.

Based on the information from the customer, you can proceed with *closed-ended questions*. A closed-ended question generally requires a yes or no answer.

Documenting Responses

Document the information from the customer in the work order, in the repair log, and in your repair journal. Write down anything that you think might be important for you or another technician. The small details often lead to the solution of a difficult or complicated problem.

Beep Codes

Each BIOS manufacturer has a unique beep sequence—a combination of long and short beeps—for hardware failures. When troubleshooting, power on the computer and listen. As the system proceeds through the POST, most computers emit one beep to indicate that the system is booting properly. If there is an error, you might hear multiple beeps. Document the beep code sequence and research the code to determine the specific problem.

BIOS Information

If the computer boots and stops after the POST, investigate the BIOS settings. A device might not be detected or configured properly. Refer to the motherboard documentation to ensure that the BIOS settings are correct.

Event Viewer

When system, user, or software errors occur on a computer running Windows, the Event Viewer is updated with information about the errors. The *Event Viewer*, shown in Figure 4-2, records the following information about the problem:

- What problem occurred

- The date and time of the problem

- The severity of the problem

- The source of the problem

- The event ID number

- Which user was logged in when the problem occurred

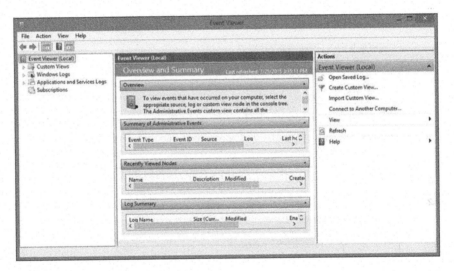

Figure 4-2   Event Viewer

Although the Event Viewer lists details about an error, you might need to further research the problem to determine a solution.

Device Manager

The *Device Manager*, shown in Figure 4-3, displays all the devices that are configured on a computer. The operating system flags the devices that are not operating correctly with an error icon. A yellow triangle with an exclamation point indicates that the device is in a problem state. A red X means that the device is disabled or removed or that Windows can't locate the device. An downward-pointing arrow means the device has been disabled. A yellow question mark indicates that the system does not know which driver to install for the hardware.

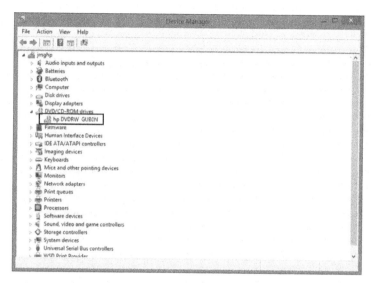

Figure 4-3   Device Manager

Task Manager

Task Manager, shown in Figure 4-4, displays the applications and background processes that are currently running. You can use Task Manager to close applications that have stopped responding. You can also use Task Manager to monitor the performance of the CPU and virtual memory, view all processes that are currently running, and view information about the network connections.

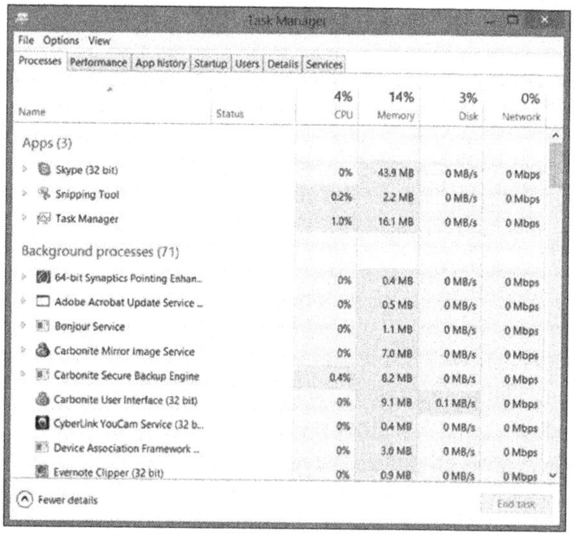

Figure 4-4   Task Manager

Diagnostic Tools

Conduct research to determine what software is available to help diagnose and solve problems. Many programs can help you troubleshoot hardware. Manufacturers of system hardware usually provide diagnostic tools of their own. For instance, a hard drive manufacturer might provide a tool to boot the computer and diagnose why the hard drive does not start the operating system.

Interactive Graphic

Check Your Understanding 4.2.1.4: Identify the Problem

Refer to the online course to complete this activity.

Establish a Theory of Probable Cause (4.2.1.5)

The second step in the troubleshooting process is to establish a theory of probable cause. First, create a list of the most common reasons for the error. Even if the customer thinks there is a major problem, start with the obvious issues before moving to more complex diagnoses, as outlined here:

1. Check whether the device is powered off.

2. Determine whether the power switch for an outlet is turned off.

3. Check whether the surge protector is turned off.

4. Ensure that there are no loose external cable connections.

5. Check whether there is a non-bootable disk in the designated boot drive.

6. Look for the incorrect boot order in the BIOS setup.

List the easiest or most obvious causes at the top. List the more complex causes at the bottom. If necessary, conduct internal (logs, journal) or external (internet) research based on the symptoms. The next steps of the troubleshooting process involve testing each possible cause.

Test the Theory to Determine the Cause (4.2.1.6)

You can determine an exact cause of an issue by testing your theories of probable causes one at a time, starting with the quickest and easiest. Some common steps to determine the cause of the problem are as follows:

1. Ensure that the device is powered on.

2. Ensure that the power switch for an outlet is turned on.

3. Ensure that the surge protector is turned on.

4. Ensure that external cable connections are secure.

5. Ensure that the designated boot drive is bootable.

6. Verify the boot order in the BIOS setup.

Once the theory is confirmed, you can determine the steps to resolve the problem. As you become more experienced at troubleshooting computers, you will work through the steps in the process faster. For now, practice each step to better understand the troubleshooting process.

If you cannot determine the exact cause of a problem after testing all your theories, establish a new theory of probable cause and test it. If necessary, escalate the problem to a technician who has more experience. Before you escalate, document each test that you tried, as shown in Figure 4-5.

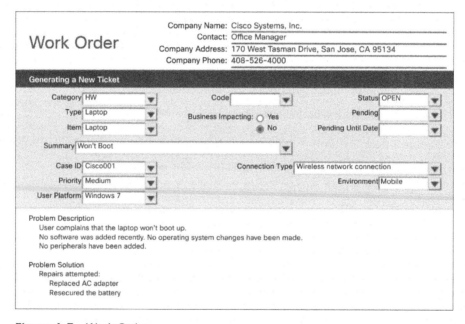

Figure 4-5   Work Order

Establish a Plan of Action to Resolve the Problem and Implement the Solution (4.2.1.7)

After you have determined the exact cause of the problem, establish a plan of action to resolve the problem and implement the solution. Sometimes quick procedures can correct the problem. If a quick procedure does correct the problem, verify full system functionality and, if applicable, implement preventive measures. If a quick procedure does not correct the problem, research the problem further and then return to Step 2 to establish a new theory of the probable cause.

Note

Always consider corporate policies, procedures, and impacts before implementing any changes.

After you have established a plan of action, you should research possible solutions by consulting sources such as the following:

- Help desk repair logs
- Other technicians
- Manufacturer FAQs
- Technical websites
- News groups
- Computer manuals
- Device manuals
- Online forums
- Internet search

Divide large problems into smaller problems that can be analyzed and solved individually. Prioritize solutions starting with the easiest and fastest to implement. Create a list of possible solutions and implement them one at a time. If you implement a possible solution and it does not correct the problem, reverse the action you just took and then try another solution. Continue this process until you have found the appropriate solution.

Verify Full Functionality and, if Applicable, Implement Preventive Measures (4.2.1.8)

After the repairs to the computer have been completed, continue the troubleshooting process by verifying full system functionality and implementing the preventive measures needed, as outlined here:

1. Reboot the computer.
2. Ensure that multiple applications work properly.
3. Verify network and Internet connections.
4. Print a document from one application.
5. Ensure that all attached devices work properly.
6. Ensure that no error messages are received.

Verifying full system functionality confirms that you have solved the original problem and ensures that you have not created another problem while repairing the computer. Whenever possible, have the customer verify the solution and system functionality.

Document Findings, Actions, and Outcomes (4.2.1.9)

After the repairs to the computer have been completed, finish the troubleshooting process with the customer. Explain the problem and the solution to the customer verbally and in writing. The steps to take when you have finished a repair are as follows:

1. Discuss the solution implemented with the customer.

2. Have the customer verify that the problem has been solved.

3. Provide the customer with all paperwork.

4. Document the steps taken to solve the problem in the work order and in the technician's journal.

5. Document any components used in the repair.

6. Document the amount of time spent on resolving the problem.

Verify the solution with the customer. If the customer is available, demonstrate how the solution has corrected the computer problem. Have the customer test the solution and try to reproduce the problem. When the customer can verify that the problem has been resolved, you can complete the documentation for the repair in the work order and in your journal. Include the following information in the documentation:

- Description of the problem

- Steps to resolve the problem

- Components used in the repair

Interactive Graphic

Check Your Understanding 4.2.1.10: Number the Steps

Refer to the online course to complete this activity.

Common Problems and Solutions for PCs (4.2.2)

As a technician, you will run into technical problems in your day-to-day routine that need your attention. As the issues arise, take the time to better understand the causes of problems and work through possible fixes. Be sure to document all that you do. This section discusses several common PC problems and suggested solutions.

PC Common Problems and Solutions (4.2.2.1)

Computer problems can be attributed to hardware, software, networks, or some combination of the three. You will resolve some types of problems more often than others.

Some common hardware problems are as follows:

- **Storage device:** Storage device problems are often related to loose or incorrect cable connections, incorrect drive and media formats, and incorrect jumper and BIOS settings.

- **Motherboard and internal components:** Motherboard and internal component problems are often caused by incorrect or loose cables, failed components, incorrect drivers, and corrupted updates.

- **Power supply:** Power problems are often caused by a faulty power supply, loose connections, and inadequate wattage.

- **CPU and memory:** Processor and memory problems are often caused by faulty installations, incorrect BIOS settings, inadequate cooling and ventilation, and compatibility issues.

- **Displays:** Display problems are often caused by incorrect settings, loose connections, and incorrect or corrupted drivers.

Common Problems and Solutions for Storage Devices (4.2.2.2)

Table 4-2 shows the probable causes and possible solutions for storage devices.

Table 4-2   Common Problems and Solutions for Storage Devices

Identify the Problem	Probable Causes	Possible Solutions
The computer does not recognize a storage device.	The power cable is loose.	Secure the power cable.
	The data cable is loose.	Secure the data cable.
	The jumpers are set incorrectly.	Reset the jumpers.
	A storage device failed.	Replace the storage device.
	The storage device settings in BIOS are incorrect.	Reset the storage device settings in BIOS.

Identify the Problem	Probable Causes	Possible Solutions
The computer does not recognize an optical disc.	The disc is inserted upside down.	Insert the disc correctly.
	There is more than one disc inserted in the drive.	Ensure that there is only one disc inserted in the drive.
	The disc is damaged.	Replace the disc.
	A disc is the wrong format.	Use the correct type of disc.
	The optical drive is faulty.	Replace the optical drive.
The computer will not eject an optical disc.	The optical drive is jammed.	Insert a pin in the small hole next to the eject button on the drive to open the drive.
	The optical drive has been locked by software.	Reboot the computer.
	The optical drive is faulty.	Replace the optical drive.
The computer does not recognize a removable external drive.	The removable external drive cable is not seated properly.	Remove and reinsert the drive cable.
	The external ports are disabled in the BIOS settings.	Enable the ports in the BIOS settings.
	The removable external drive is faulty.	Replace the removable external drive.
A media reader cannot read a memory card that works properly.	The media reader does not support the memory card type.	Use a different memory card type.
	The media reader is not connected correctly.	Ensure that the media reader is connected correctly in the computer.
	The media reader is not configured properly in the BIOS settings.	Reconfigure the media reader in the BIOS settings.
	The media reader is faulty.	Install a known good media reader.
Retrieving or saving data from the USB flash drive is slow.	The motherboard does not support USB 3.0 or 3.1.	Replace the motherboard with a USB 3.0-capable motherboard or add a USB 3.0 expansion card.
	The USB flash drive might be connected to a USB port rated slower or not configured properly.	Set the port to full speed in the BIOS settings.

Common Problems and Solutions for Motherboards and Internal Components (4.2.2.3)

Table 4-3 shows common problems and solutions for motherboards and internal components.

Table 4-3   Common Problems and Solutions for Motherboards and Internal Components

Identify the Problem	Probable Causes	Possible Solutions
The clock on the computer is no longer keeping the correct time or the BIOS settings are changing when the computer is rebooted.	The CMOS battery may be loose.	Secure the battery.
	The CMOS battery may be drained.	Replace the battery.
After updating the BIOS firmware, the computer will not start.	The BIOS firmware update did not install correctly.	Contact the motherboard manufacturer to obtain a new BIOS chip. (If the motherboard has two BIOS chips, the second BIOS chip can be used.)
The computer displays incorrect CPU information when the computer boots.	The CPU settings are not correct in the advanced BIOS settings.	Set the advanced BIOS settings correctly for the CPU.
	BIOS does not properly recognize the CPU.	Update the BIOS.
The hard drive LED on the front of the computer does not light.	The hard drive LED cable is not connected or is loose.	Reconnect the hard drive LED cable to the motherboard.
	The hard drive LED cable is incorrectly oriented to the front case panel connections.	Correctly orient the hard drive LED cable to the front case panel connection and reconnect it.
The built-in NIC has stopped working.	The NIC hardware has failed.	Add a new NIC to an open expansion slot.
The computer does not display any video after a new PCIe video card is installed.	BIOS settings are set to use the built-in video.	Disable the built-in video in the BIOS settings.
	The monitor cable is still connected to the built-in video.	Connect the monitor cable to the new video card.
	The new video card needs auxiliary power.	Connect any required power connectors to the video card.
	The new video card is faulty.	Install a known good video card.

Identify the Problem	Probable Causes	Possible Solutions
The new sound card does not work.	The speakers are not connected to the correct jack.	Connect the speakers to the correct jack.
	The audio is muted.	Unmute the audio.
	The sound card is faulty.	Install a known good sound card.
	BIOS settings are set to use the onboard sound device.	Disable the onboard audio device in the BIOS settings.
System attempts to boot to an incorrect device.	Media was left in a removable drive.	Check that the removable drives do not contain media that is interfering with the boot process and ensure that the boot order is configured correctly.
	Boot order configured incorrectly.	Check that the removable drives do not contain media that is interfering with the boot process and ensure that the boot order is configured correctly.
User can hear fans spinning, but the computer does not start, and there are no beeps from the speaker.	POST procedure is not executing.	Faulty cabling or damaged or mis-seated CPU or other motherboard component needs to be replaced.
Motherboard capacitors are distended, swollen, emitting residue, or bulging.	Damage has occurred due to heat, ESP, power surge, or spike.	Replace the motherboard.

Common Problems and Solutions for Power Supplies (4.2.2.4)

Table 4-4 lists common problems and solutions for power supplies.

Table 4-4   Common Problems and Solutions for Power Supplies

Identify the Problem	Probable Causes	Possible Solutions
The computer will not turn on.	The computer is not plugged into the AC outlet.	Plug the computer into a known good AC outlet.
	The AC outlet is faulty.	Plug the computer into a known good AC outlet.
	The power cord is faulty.	Use a known good power cord.

Identify the Problem	Probable Causes	Possible Solutions
	The power supply switch is not turned on.	Turn on the power supply switch.
	The power supply switch is set to the incorrect voltage.	Set the power supply switch to the correct voltage setting.
	The power button is not connected correctly to the front panel connector.	Correctly orient the power button to the front case panel connector and reconnect.
	The power supply has failed.	Install a known good power supply.
The computer reboots and turns off unexpectedly or there is smoke or the smell of burning electronics.	The power supply is starting to fail.	Replace the power supply.

Common Problems and Solutions for CPUs and Memory (4.2.2.5)

Table 4-5 lists common problems and solutions for CPUs and memory.

Table 4-5   Common Problems and Solutions for CPUs and Memory

Identify the Problem	Probable Causes	Possible Solutions
The computer will not boot or it locks up.	The CPU has overheated.	Reinstall the CPU.
	The CPU fan is failing.	Replace the CPU fan.
	The CPU has failed.	Add fan(s) to the case. Replace the CPU fan. Replace the CPU.
The CPU fan is making an unusual noise.	The CPU fan is failing.	Replace the CPU fan.
The computer reboots without warning, locks up, or displays error messages.	The front-side bus is set too high.	Reset to the factory default settings for the motherboard. Lower the front-side bus settings.
	The CPU multiplier is set too high.	Lower the multiplier settings.
	The CPU voltage is set too high.	Lower the CPU voltage settings.

Identify the Problem	Probable Causes	Possible Solutions
After upgrading from a single-core CPU to a dual-core CPU, the computer runs more slowly and shows only one CPU graph in the Task Manager.	The BIOS does not recognize the dual-core CPU.	Update the BIOS firmware to support the dual-core CPU.
A CPU does not install onto the motherboard.	The CPU is the incorrect type.	Replace the CPU with a CPU that matches the motherboard socket type.
The computer does not recognize the RAM that was added.	The new RAM is faulty.	Replace the RAM.
	The incorrect type of RAM was installed.	Install the correct type of RAM.
	The RAM that has been added is not the same type of RAM that was already installed.	Install the correct type of RAM.
	The new RAM is loose in the memory slot.	Secure the RAM in the memory slot.
After upgrading Windows, the computer runs very slowly.	The computer does not have enough RAM.	Install additional RAM.
	The video card does not have enough memory.	Install a video card that has more memory.

Common Problems and Solutions for Displays (4.2.2.6)

Table 4-6 lists common problems and solutions for displays

Table 4-6   Common Problems and Solutions for Displays

Identify the Problem	Probable Causes	Possible Solutions
Display has power but no image on the screen.	The video cable is loose or damaged.	Reconnect or replace the video cable.
	The computer is not sending a video signal to the external display.	Use the Fn key along with the multipurpose key to toggle to the external display.
The display is flickering.	Images on the screen are not refreshing fast enough.	Adjust the screen refresh rate.
	The display inverter is damaged or malfunctioning.	Disassemble the display unit and replace the inverter.

Identify the Problem	Probable Causes	Possible Solutions
The image on the display looks dim.	The LCD backlight is not properly adjusted.	Check the repair manual for instructions about calibrating the LCD backlight. Adjust the LCD backlight properly.
Pixels on the screen are dead or not generating color.	Power to the pixels has been cut off.	Contact the manufacturer.
The image on the screen appears to flash lines or patterns of different color and size (artifacts).	The display is not properly connected.	Disassemble the display and check the connections.
	The GPU is overheating.	Disassemble and clean the computer, checking for dust and debris.
	The GPU is faulty or malfunctioning.	Replace the GPU.
Color patterns on a screen are incorrect.	The display is not properly connected.	Disassemble the display and check the connections.
	The GPU is overheating.	Disassemble and clean the computer, checking for dust and debris.
	The GPU is faulty or malfunctioning.	Replace the GPU.
Images on a display screen are distorted.	Display settings have been changed.	Restore the display settings to the original factory settings.
	The display is not properly connected.	Disassemble the display to a point where you can check the display connections.
	The GPU is overheating.	Disassemble and clean the computer, checking for dust and debris.
	The GPU is faulty or malfunctioning.	Replace the GPU.
The display has a "ghost" image.	The display is experiencing burn-in.	Power off the display and unplug it from the power source for a few hours.
		Use the degauss feature, if it is available.
		Replace the display.

Identify the Problem	Probable Causes	Possible Solutions
The images on the display have distorted geometry.	The driver has become corrupted.	Update or reinstall the driver in safe mode.
	The display settings are incorrect.	Use the display's settings to correct the geometry.
The monitor has oversized images and icons.	The driver has become corrupted.	Update or reinstall the driver in safe mode.
	The display settings are incorrect.	Use the display's settings to correct the geometry.
The projector overheats and shuts down.	The fan has failed.	Replace the fan.
	The vents are clogged.	Clean the vents.
	The projector is in an enclosure.	Remove the enclosure or ensure proper ventilation.
In a multiple-monitor setup, the displays are not aligned or are incorrectly oriented.	The settings for multiple monitors are not correct.	Use the display control panel to identify each display and set the alignment and orientation.
	The driver has become corrupted.	Update or reinstall the driver in safe mode.
The display is in VGA mode.	The computer is in safe mode.	Reboot the computer.
	The driver has become corrupted.	Update or reinstall the driver in safe mode.

Apply Troubleshooting Process to Computer Components and Peripherals (4.2.3)

Troubleshooting requires that you always have a plan of action. Asking the right questions, narrowing down the cause, re-creating the problem, and attempting to fix the issue based on your plan is a good process for both internal and peripheral components. Once you start troubleshooting, write down each step you take for your future use and that of other technicians.

Personal Reference Tools (4.2.3.1)

Good customer service includes providing the customer with a detailed description of the problem and the solution. It is important for a technician to document all services and repairs and that this documentation be available to all other technicians. The documentation can then be used as reference material for similar problems.

Personal reference tools include troubleshooting guides, manufacturer manuals, quick reference guides, and repair journals. In addition to an invoice, a technician keeps a journal of upgrades and repairs:

- **Notes:** Make notes as you go through the troubleshooting and repair process. Refer to these notes to avoid repeating steps and to determine what needs to be done next.

- **Journal:** Include descriptions of the problem, possible solutions that have been tried to correct the problem, and the steps taken to repair the problem. Note any configuration changes made to the equipment and any replacement parts used in the repair. Your journal, along with your notes, can be valuable when you encounter similar situations in the future.

- **History of repairs:** Make a detailed list of problems and repairs, including the date, replacement parts, and customer information. The history allows a technician to determine what work has been performed on a specific computer in the past.

Internet Reference Tools (4.2.3.2)

The Internet is an excellent source of information about specific hardware problems and possible solutions. Visit the following for helpful information:

- Internet search engines
- News groups
- Manufacturer FAQs
- Online computer manuals
- Online forums and chat
- Technical websites

Check Your Understanding 4.2.3.3: Reference Tools

Refer to the online course to complete this activity.

Advanced Problems and Solutions for Hardware (4.2.3.4)

Table 4-7 lists advanced problems and solutions for hardware.

Table 4-7   Advanced Problems and Solutions for Hardware

Identify the Problem	Probable Causes	Possible Solutions
RAID cannot be found.	The external RAID controller is not receiving power.	Check the power connection to the RAID controller.
	The BIOS settings are incorrect.	Reconfigure the BIOS settings for the RAID controller.
	The RAID controller has failed.	Replace the RAID controller.
RAID stops working.	The external RAID controller is not receiving power.	Check the power connection to the RAID controller.
	The RAID controller has failed.	Replace the RAID controller.
The computer exhibits slow performance.	The computer does not have enough RAM.	Install additional RAM.
	The computer is overheating.	Clean the fans or install additional fans.
The computer does not recognize a removable external drive.	The OS does not have the correct drivers for the removable external drive.	Download the correct drivers for the drive.
	The USB port has too many attached devices to supply adequate power.	Attach external power to the device or remove some of the USB devices.
After updating the BIOS firmware, the computer will not start.	The BIOS firmware update did not install correctly.	Restore the original firmware from the onboard backup, if one is available.
		If the motherboard has two BIOS chips, use the second BIOS chip.
		Contact the motherboard manufacturer to obtain a new BIOS chip.

Identify the Problem	Probable Causes	Possible Solutions
The computer reboots without warning, locks up, or displays error messages or the BSOD.	RAM is failing.	Test each RAM module to determine if the modules are operating correctly.
	The front-side bus is set too high.	Reset to the factory default settings of the motherboard. Lower the FSB settings.
	The CPU multiplier is set too high.	Lower the multiplier settings. Lower the CPU voltage settings.
After upgrading from a single-core CPU to a multi-core CPU, the computer runs more slowly and shows only one CPU graph in Task Manager.	The BIOS does not recognize the multi-core CPU.	Update the BIOS firmware to support the multi-core CPU.

Lab 4.2.3.5: Use a Multimeter and a Power Supply Tester

In this lab, you will learn how to use and handle a multimeter and a power supply tester.

Lab 4.2.3.6: Troubleshoot Hardware Problems

In this lab, you will diagnose the causes of various hardware problems and solve them.

Summary (4.3)

In this chapter, you learned that there are many benefits of conducting preventive maintenance, such as fewer potential hardware and software problems, less computer downtime, lower repair costs, and less frequent equipment failures. You learned how to keep dust from damaging computer components by keeping air filters clean, cleaning the outside of the computer case, and using compressed air to remove dust from the inside of the computer.

You learned that there are components that should be regularly inspected for dust and damage. These components include the CPU heat sink and fan, RAM modules, storage devices, adapter cards, cables and power devices, and keyboards and mice. You also learned about guidelines for ensuring optimal computer operating performance, such as not obstructing vents or airflow and maintaining proper room temperature and humidity.

In addition to learning how to maintain the hardware of a computer, you learned that it is important to perform regular maintenance on computer software. This is best accomplished with a software maintenance schedule that covers security software, virus definition files, unwanted and unused programs, and hard drive defragmenting.

At the end of the chapter, you learned the six steps in the troubleshooting process as they pertain to preventive maintenance.

Practice

The following activities provide practice with the topics introduced in this chapter. The labs are available in the companion *IT Essentials v8 Labs & Study Guide* (ISBN 9780138166304).

Labs

Lab 4.2.3.5: Use a Multimeter and a Power Supply Tester

Lab 4.2.3.6: Troubleshoot Hardware Problems

Check Your Understanding Questions

Complete all the review questions listed here to test your understanding of the topics and concepts in this chapter. Appendix A, "Answers to 'Check Your Understanding' Questions," lists the answers.

1. A user has noticed that the hard drive LED on the front of the computer has stopped working. However, the computer seems to be functioning normally. What is the most likely cause of the problem?

   A. The motherboard BIOS needs to be updated.

   B. The power supply is not providing enough voltage to the motherboard.

   C. The hard drive LED cable has come loose from the motherboard.

   D. The hard drive data cable is malfunctioning.

2. After a problem is identified, what is the next step for the troubleshooter?

   A. Document the findings.

   B. Establish a theory of probable causes.

   C. Implement a solution.

   D. Verify the solution.

   E. Determine the exact cause.

3. What is the best way to determine if a CPU fan is spinning properly?

   A. Visually inspect the fan when the power is on to ensure that it is spinning.

   B. Spin the blades of the fan quickly with a finger.

   C. Spray compressed air on the fan to make the blades spin.

   D. Listen for the sound of the fan spinning when the power is on.

4. Which of the following is a symptom of a failing power supply?

   A. The power cord will not attach properly to either the power supply, the wall outlet, or both.

   B. The computer sometimes does not turn on.

   C. The computer displays a POST error code.

   D. The display has only a blinking cursor.

5. In which step of the troubleshooting process would a technician have to do more research on the Internet or using the computer manual in order to solve a problem?

   A. Document findings, actions, and outcomes.

   B. Identify the problem.

   C. Establish a plan of action to resolve the problem and implement the solution.

   D. Verify full system functionality and, if applicable, implement preventive measures.

   E. Test the theory to determine the cause.

6. A user has opened a ticket that indicates that the computer clock keeps losing the correct time. What is the most likely cause of the problem?

   A. The operating system needs to be patched.

   B. The CPU needs to be overclocked.

   C. The CMOS battery is loose or failing.

   D. The motherboard clocking crystal is damaged.

7. Members of a scientific expedition team are using laptops for their work. The temperatures where the scientists are working range from –13 degrees Fahrenheit (–25 degrees Celsius) to 80 degrees Fahrenheit (27 degrees Celsius). The humidity level is around 40%. Noise levels are low, but the terrain is rough, and winds can reach 45 miles per hour (72 kilometers per hour). When needed, the scientists stop walking and enter the data using the laptop. Which condition is most likely to adversely affect a laptop that is used in this environment?

   A. wind

   B. humidity

   C. rough terrain

   D. temperature

8. What is the most important reason for a company to ensure that computer preventive maintenance is done?

   A. Preventive maintenance enables the IT manager to check on the location and state of the computer assets.

   B. Preventive maintenance allows the IT department to regularly monitor the contents of user hard drives to ensure that computer use policies are being followed.

   C. Preventive maintenance helps protect computer equipment against future problems.

   D. Preventive maintenance provides an opportunity for junior technicians to obtain more experience in a nonthreatening or problem environment.

9. Which cleaning tool should be used to remove dust from components inside a computer case?

   A. compressed air

   B. damp cloth

   C. cotton swabs

   D. duster

10. What task should be completed before escalating a problem to a higher-level technician?

    A. Redo each test to ensure the accuracy of the results.

    B. Document each test that was tried.

    C. Ask the customer to open a new support request.

    D. Replace all hardware components with components that are known to work.

11. What are two effects of not having a preventive maintenance plan for users and organizations? (Choose two.)

    A. increased number of regular updates

    B. increased management tasks

    C. increased downtime

    D. increased repair costs

    E. increased documentation needs

12. Which procedure is recommended when cleaning inside a computer?

    A. Clean the hard drive heads with a cotton swab.

    B. Hold the CPU fan to prevent it from spinning and blow it with compressed air.

    C. Invert the can of compressed air while spraying.

    D. Remove the CPU before cleaning.

13. Which task should be performed on a hard drive as part of a preventive maintenance plan?

    A. Blow out the inside of the drive with compressed air to remove dust.

    B. Ensure that the disk spins freely.

    C. Ensure that cables are firmly connected.

    D. Clean the read and write heads with a cotton swab.

14. A customer reports that recently several files cannot be accessed. The service technician decides to check the hard disk status and the file system structure. The technician asks the customer if a backup has been performed on the disk, and the customer replies that the backup was done a week ago, and it was stored to a different logical partition on the disk. What should the technician do before performing diagnostic procedures on the disk?

    A. Perform a file restore from the existing backup copy at the logical partition.

    B. Install a new hard disk as the primary disk and then make the current disk a secondary drive.

    C. Run the CHKDSK utility.

    D. Back up the user data to a removable drive.

15. Which of these tasks should be part of a hardware maintenance routine?

    A. Review security updates.

    B. Update virus definition files.

    C. Remove dust from inside the hard drive.

    D. Check for and secure any loose cables.

    E. Adjust the monitor for optimum resolution.

16. During what step in the troubleshooting process does a technician demonstrate to the customer how the solution corrected the problem?

    A. Document the findings, actions, and outcomes.

    B. Establish a theory of probable cause.

    C. Verify full system functionality.

    D. Establish a plan of action to resolve the problem.

CHAPTER 5

Networking Concepts

Objectives

Upon completion of this chapter, you will be able to answer the following questions:

- What are the different types of transmission media used in networking?

- What are the different types of network devices?

- What are some common communication protocols and standards?

- What is the TCP/IP model?

- What are TCP and UDP protocols, what ports do they use, and what are their purposes?

- What are the various Wi-Fi networking standards?

- What are the different network types and their characteristics?

- What are TCP/IP services?

- What are the most common TCP/IP ports?

- What are ISP broadband technologies?

- What are cloud computing technologies?

Key Terms

This chapter uses the following key terms. You can find the definitions in the glossary at the end of the book.

1G/2G   page 221

2.5G   page 221

3G   page 221

3.5G   page 221

4G   page 222

5G   page 222

6G   page 222

802.11 collective group   page 217

access point (AP)   page 196

AFP   page 215

analog telephone   page 203

authentication, authorization, and accounting (AAA) services   page 231

Bluetooth   page 218

bridge   page 236

broadband   page 203

buffer   page 260

cable Internet   page 204

cable modem   page 204

cable tester   page 251

cellular   page 221

cladding   page 260

client   page 223

Introduction (5.0)

Computer networks allow users to share resources and to communicate. Can you imagine a world without email, online newspapers, blogs, websites, and the other services that depend on the Internet? Networks also allow users to share resources such as printers, applications, files, directories, and storage drives. This chapter provides an overview of network principles, standards, and purposes. IT professionals must be familiar with networking concepts to meet the expectations and needs of customers and network users.

You will learn the basics of network design and how devices on a network impact the flow of data. These devices include hubs, switches, access points, routers, and firewalls. Different Internet connection types, such as DSL, cable, cellular, and satellite, are also covered. You will learn about the four layers of the TCP/IP model and the functions and protocols associated with each layer. You will also learn about many wireless networks and protocols, including IEEE 802.11 wireless LAN protocols; wireless protocols for close proximity, such as radio frequency identification (RFID) and near field communication (NFC); and smart home protocol standards such as Zigbee and Z-Wave. This knowledge will help you successfully design, implement, and troubleshoot networks. The chapter concludes with discussions of network cable types, including twisted-pair, fiber-optic, and coaxial. You will learn how each type of cable is constructed, how the cables carry data signals, and appropriate use cases for each.

It is important to not only learn about computer network operation and components but also to build hands-on skills. In this chapter, you will build and test a straight-through unshielded twisted-pair (UTP) Ethernet network cable.

Network Components and Types (5.1)

Computer networks enable computers and other devices to communicate, and they share resources, data, and applications. Different network types share common components, functions, and features. One way to classify different computer network types is based on their scope or scale.

Types of Networks (5.1.1)

Networks are classified in many different ways, such as size, geographical scope, and purpose. This section examines the various network types and the icons used to symbolize them.

Network Icons (5.1.1.1)

Networks are systems that are formed by links. Computer networks connect devices and users to one another. A variety of networking icons are used to represent different parts of a computer network.

Host Devices

The network devices that people are most familiar with are called *end devices*, or host devices (see Figure 5-1). They are called end devices because they are at the end or edge of a network. They are called host devices because they typically host network applications, such as web browsers and email clients, that use the network to provide services to the user.

Figure 5-1   Host Device Icons

Intermediary Devices

Computer networks contain many devices that exist in between the host devices. These *intermediary devices* ensure that data flows from one host device to another host device. As shown in Figure 5-2, these are the most common intermediary devices:

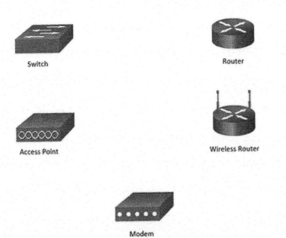

Figure 5-2   Intermediary Device Icons

- **Switch:** Connects multiple devices to a network.

- **Router:** Forwards traffic between networks.

- *Wireless router*: Connects multiple wireless devices to a network and may include a switch to connect wired hosts.

- *Access point (AP)*: Connects to a wireless router and is used to extend the reach of a wireless network.

- *Modem*: Connects a home or small office to the Internet.

Network Media

Communication across a network is carried on a medium. The medium provides the channel over which the message travels from source to destination. The plural for medium is media. The icons in Figure 5-3 represent different types of *network media*. Local area networks (LANs), wide area networks (WANs), and wireless networks are discussed further in this chapter. The cloud is typically used in network topologies to represent connections to the Internet. The Internet is often the medium for communications between one network and another network.

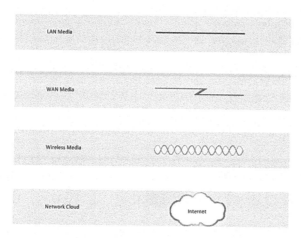

Figure 5-3   Network Media Icons

Network Topologies and Description (5.1.1.2)

Networks can be represented in a variety of configurations, such as the topologies described in the sections that follow.

PAN

A *personal area network (PAN)*, as shown in Figure 5-4, is a network that connects devices, such as mice, keyboards, printers, smartphones, and tablets, within the range of an individual person. These devices are most often connected using Bluetooth technology. Bluetooth is a wireless technology that enables devices to communicate over short distances.

Figure 5-4   PAN

LAN

Traditionally, a *local area network (LAN)*, as shown in Figure 5-5, is defined as a network that connects devices using wire cables in a small geographical area. The distinguishing characteristic for LANs today, however, is that they are typically owned by an individual, such as in a home or small business, or wholly managed by an IT department, such as in a school or corporation.

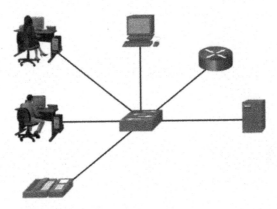

Figure 5-5   LAN

VLAN

Virtual LANs (VLANs) allow an administrator to segment the ports on a single switch as if it were multiple switches, as shown in Figure 5-6. This provides more efficient forwarding of data by isolating traffic to only those ports where it is required.

VLANs also allow end devices to be grouped together for administrative purposes. In Figure 5-6, VLAN 2 creates a virtual LAN for IT's computers, even on different floors, and its network permissions can be different from those of the other VLANs.

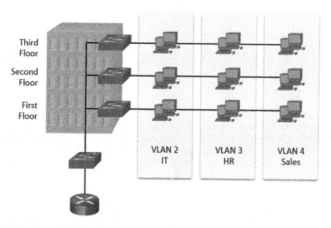

Figure 5-6   VLAN

WLAN

A *wireless LAN (WLAN)* is similar to a LAN but wirelessly connects users and devices in a small geographical area instead of using a wired connection, as shown in Figure 5-7. A WLAN uses radio waves to transmit data between wireless devices.

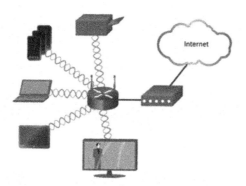

Figure 5-7   WLAN

WMN

A *wireless mesh network (WMN)* uses multiple access points to extend the WLAN. The topology in Figure 5-8 shows a wireless router. The two wireless APs extend the reach of the WLAN within the home. Similarly, businesses and municipalities can use WMNs to quickly add new areas of coverage.

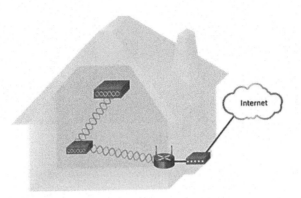

Figure 5-8   WMN

MAN

A *metropolitan area network (MAN)* is a network that spans a large campus or a city, as shown in Figure 5-9. The network consists of various buildings connected through wireless or fiber-optic media.

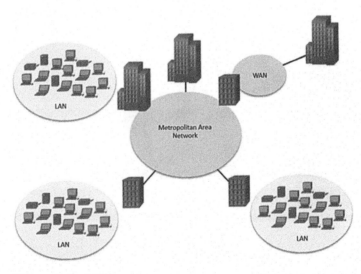

Figure 5-9   MAN

WAN

A *wide area network (WAN)* connects multiple networks that are in geographically separated locations. Individuals and organizations contract for WAN access from a service provider. Your service provider for your home or mobile device connects you to the largest WAN, the Internet. In Figure 5-10, the Tokyo and Moscow networks are connected through the Internet.

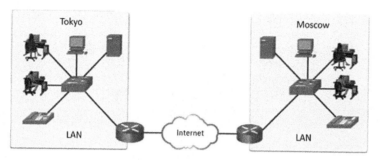

Figure 5-10   WAN

VPN

A *virtual private network (VPN)* is used to securely connect to another network over an insecure network, such as the Internet. The most common type of VPN is used by teleworkers to access a corporate private network. Teleworkers are network users who are offsite or remote. In Figure 5-11, the fat links between Teleworker 1 and the router at the company headquarters represent a VPN connection. Teleworker 1 uses VPN software to securely log into the company's network. Teleworker 2 is not securely connected and will not be able to access internal company resources.

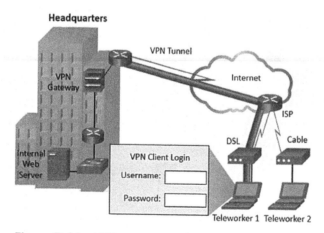

Figure 5-11   VPN

Interactive Graphic

Check Your Understanding 5.1.1.3: Types of Networks

Refer to the online course to complete this activity.

5.1.1.4 VLANs

Virtual LANs (VLANs) provide segmentation and organizational flexibility in a switched network. A group of devices within a VLAN communicate as if each device was attached to the same switch. VLANs are based on logical connections, instead of physical connections. An administrator can segment VLANs based on factors such as function, team, or application, without regard for the physical location of the users or devices.

In the figure, for example, a faculty member computer (PC1) is connected to S2 on VLAN 10. PC1 could communicate with another faculty member using PC4 connected to S3. Notice how both hosts are configured on network address 192.168.10.0/24.

VLAN Topology Example

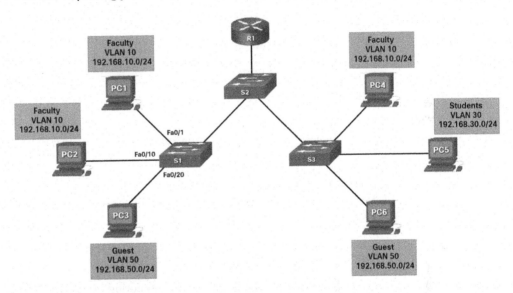

By default, all switch ports are assigned to VLAN 1. However, you can assign the PCs to different VLANs by configuring their interconnecting port.

For example, the command syntax below displays a sample configuration of switch S2. Notice that we first create the VLANs and assign them names. This makes it easier to work with the VLANs. Next, we configure the ports connecting to the PCs to the corresponding VLANs.

```
S2(config)# vlan 10
S2(config-vlan)# name Faculty
S2(config-vlan)# exit
S2(config)#
S2(config)# vlan 30
S2(config-vlan)# name Students
S2(config-vlan)# exit
S2(config)#
S2(config)# vlan 50
S2(config-vlan)# name Guest
S2(config-vlan)# exit
```

```
S2(config)#
S2(config)# interface fastethernet 0/1
S2(config-if)# switchport mode access
S2(config-if)# switchport access vlan 10
S2(config-if)# exit
S2(config)#
S2(config)# interface range fa0/10
S2(config-if)# switchport mode access
S2(config-if)# switchport access vlan 20
S2(config-if)# exit
S2(config)#
S2(config)# interface range fa0/20
S2(config-if)# switchport mode access
S2(config-if)# switchport access vlan 50
S2(config-if)# exit
S2(config)#
```

Once the VLAN information is configured on the other switches, the faculty member using PC1 would be able to communicate with PC4 because they are on the same VLANs. If the faculty member wanted to send something to PC5, which is assigned to VLAN 30, then the services of a router would be required.

VLANs help reduce excessive broadcast traffic and implement access and security policies between groups of users.

Internet Connection Types (5.1.2)

Several WAN solutions are available for connecting between sites or to the Internet. WAN connection services provide different speeds and levels of service. You should understand how users connect to the Internet and the advantages and disadvantages of different connection types.

Brief History of Connection Technologies (5.1.2.1)

In the 1990s, Internet speeds were slow compared to today; we now have the bandwidth to transmit voice and video as well as data. A dialup connection requires either an internal modem installed in the computer or an external modem connected by USB. The modem dialup port is connected to a phone socket using an RJ-11 connector. Once the modem is physically installed, it must be connected to one of the computer's software COM ports. The modem must also be configured with local dialing properties such as the prefix for an outside line and the area code.

In Windows, the Set Up a Connection or Network Wizard is used to configure a link to the ISP server. Connecting to the Internet has evolved from analog telephone to broadband.

Analog Telephone

Analog telephone Internet access can transmit data over standard voice telephone lines. This type of service uses an analog modem to place a telephone call to another modem at a remote site. This method of connection is known as *dialup*.

Integrated Services Digital Network

Integrated Services Digital Network (ISDN) uses multiple channels and can carry different types of services; therefore, it is considered a type of broadband. ISDN is a standard that uses multiple channels to send voice, video, and data over normal telephone wires. ISDN bandwidth is larger than that of traditional dialup.

Broadband

Broadband uses different frequencies to send multiple signals over the same medium. For example, the coaxial cables used to bring cable television to a home can carry computer network transmissions at the same time as hundreds of TV channels. Your cell phone can receive voice calls while also using a web browser.

Some common broadband network connections include cable, Digital Subscriber Line (DSL), ISDN, satellite, and cellular. Figure 5-12 shows equipment used to connect to or transmit broadband signals.

Satellite Receiver

Cable Modem

DSL Modem

Figure 5-12 Broadband Technologies

DSL, Cable, and Fiber (5.1.2.2)

Both *DSL* and cable use a modem to connect to the Internet through an Internet service provider (ISP), as shown in Figure 5-13. A DSL modem connects a user's network directly to the digital infrastructure of the phone company. A *cable modem* connects the user's network to a cable service provider.

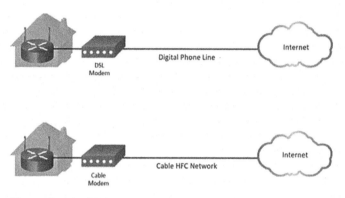

Figure 5-13   DSL and Cable Modems

DSL

DSL is an always-on service, which means there is no need to dial up each time you want to connect to the Internet. Voice and data signals are carried on different frequencies on the copper telephone wires. A filter prevents DSL signals from interfering with phone signals.

Very high-speed DSL (VDSL) attains much higher bit rates than DSL. A symmetric link can carry as much as 26 Mbps in both directions, while an asymmetric link can carry as much as 52 Mbps download and 6 Mbps upload. VDSL2 can carry as much as 100 Mbps in both directions.

Cable

A *cable Internet* connection does not use telephone lines. Cable uses coaxial cable lines originally designed to carry cable television. A cable modem connects your computer to the cable company. You can plug your computer directly into the cable modem; however, connecting a routing device to the modem allows multiple computers to share the connection to the Internet.

Fiber

Fiber-optic cables are made of glass or plastic and use light to transmit data. They have a very high bandwidth, which enables them to carry large amounts of data. At some point in your connection to the Internet, your data will cross a fiber network.

Fiber is used in backbone networks, large enterprise environments, and large data centers. The Internet backbone consists of many networks owned by numerous companies. Optical fiber trunk lines (the main core of the Internet backbone) consist of many fiber cables bundled to increase capacity, or bandwidth.

Older copper cabling infrastructures closer to homes and businesses are increasingly being replaced with fiber. For example, in Figure 5-13, the cable connection includes a hybrid fiber coaxial (HFC) network in which fiber is used in the last mile to the user's home. At the user's home, the network switches back to copper coaxial cable. This is known as *fiber to the curb (FTTC)*.

Fiber to the premises (FTTP) brings the fiber to the customer's building. A splitter in the street cabinet has an optical line terminal (OLT). The OLT has connections for each customer being supplied in the area. The building is connected to the optical network terminal (ONT) inside the customer's building. The optical signals are converted to electrical signals and connect to a router using a standard Ethernet patch cord.

The choice of connection varies depending on geographical location and service provider availability.

Line of Sight Wireless Internet Service (5.1.2.3)

Line of sight wireless Internet is an always-on service that uses radio signals for transmitting Internet access, as shown in Figure 5-14.

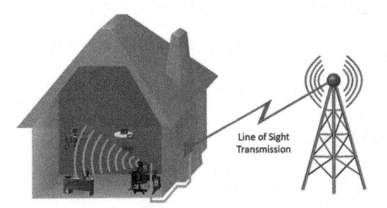

Line of Sight
Transmission

Figure 5-14   Line of Sight Wireless

Radio signals are sent from a tower to a receiver, which the customer connects to a computer or network device. A clear path between the transmission tower and customer is required. The tower may connect to other towers or directly to an Internet backbone connection. The distance the radio signal can travel and still be strong enough to provide a clear signal depends on the frequency of the signal. A lower frequency of 900 MHz can travel up to 40 miles (65 km), while a higher frequency of

5.7 GHz can travel only 2 miles (3 km). Extreme weather conditions, trees, and tall buildings can affect signal strength and performance.

Satellite (5.1.2.4)

Satellite broadband is an alternative for customers who cannot get cable or DSL connections. A satellite connection does not require a phone line or cable but uses a satellite dish for two-way communication. The satellite dish transmits and receives signals to and from a satellite, which relays these signals back to a service provider, as shown in Figure 5-15. Download speeds can reach up to 10 Mbps or more, and upload speeds are about one-tenth of the download speeds. It takes time for the signal from the satellite dish to relay to your ISP through the satellite orbiting the Earth. Due to this latency, it is difficult to use time-sensitive applications, such as video gaming, voice over Internet Protocol (VoIP), and video conferencing.

A new type of satellite service has far more satellites orbiting the Earth in *low Earth orbit (LEO)*. The service can support up to approximately 100 Mbps with much lower latency than standard satellite—between 100 and 200 ms. The satellite dish contains a motor so that it can realign with the satellites as they move relative to the surface of the Earth.

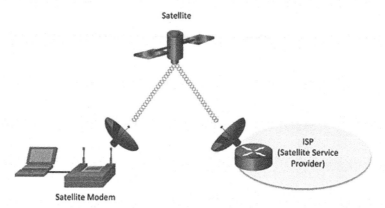

Figure 5-15   Satellite Connection

Cellular (5.1.2.5)

Cell phone technology relies on cell towers distributed throughout the user's coverage area to provide seamless access to cell phone services and the Internet, as shown in Figure 5-16. With the advent of the third generation (3G) of cellular technology, smartphones could access the Internet. Download and upload speeds continue to improve with each iteration of cell phone technology.

Figure 5-16   Cell Technology for Internet Access

In some regions of the world, the only way users can access the Internet is by using smartphones. In the United States, users are increasingly relying on smartphones for Internet access. According to the Pew Research Center, in 2021 23% of adults in the United States did not use broadband at home. Instead, they used smartphones for personal Internet access. Search for "Pew Internet research" for more interesting statistics.

Mobile Hotspot and Tethering (5.1.2.6)

Many cell phones provide the ability to connect other devices, as shown in Figure 5-17. Such a connection, known as *tethering*, can be made using Wi-Fi, Bluetooth, or a USB cable. Once a device is connected, it is able to use the phone's cellular connection to access the Internet. When a cellular phone allows Wi-Fi devices to connect and use the mobile data network, it is called a *mobile hotspot*.

Figure 5-17   Mobile Hotspot

Check Your Understanding 5.1.2.7: Internet Connection Types

Refer to the online course to complete this activity.

Networking Protocols, Standards, and Services (5.2)

Hundreds of different computer network *protocols* have been developed, each designed for specific purposes and environments. A protocol defines how two devices on a network communicate with one another. The devices use these rules to agree on how to send and receive data so they can be networked together effectively. Standardized network protocols provide a common language for network devices. Standards are guidelines for how a particular protocol should operate. Everyone being aware of the common standards and adhering to them for a protocol allows for interoperability between vendors and communication to be established even if devices are running different operating systems. Network end users rely on network protocols for connectivity and services for productivity.

Transport Layer Protocols (5.2.1)

Ports and protocols are used in networking to allow communications between devices, applications, and networks. Protocols define how this communication occurs, and *ports* are used to track various communications. This section explains common transport layer protocols and ports used in data networks. The transport layer is responsible for establishing a temporary communication session between two applications and delivering data between them. The transport layer is the link between the application layer and the lower layers, which are responsible for network transmission.

Video Explanation 5.2.1.1: Transport Layer Protocols

Refer to the online course to view this video.

Activity 5.2.1.2: Transport Layer Protocols

Refer to the online course to complete this activity.

The TCP/IP Model (5.2.1.3)

The *TCP/IP model* consists of layers that perform functions necessary to prepare data for transmission over a network. The model gets its name from the two important protocols in the model: Transmission Control Protocol (TCP) and Internet Protocol (IP). TCP is responsible for tracking all the network connections between a user's device and multiple destinations. IP is responsible for adding addressing so that data can be routed to the intended destination.

The two protocols that operate at the transport layer are TCP and User Datagram Protocol (UDP), as shown in Figure 5-18. TCP is considered a reliable, full-featured transport layer protocol; it ensures that all the data arrives at the destination. In contrast, UDP is a very simple transport layer protocol that does not provide for any reliability.

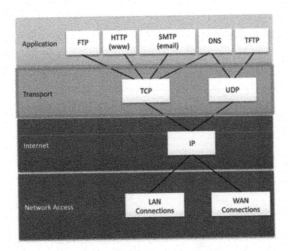

Figure 5-18   Two Transport Layer Protocols

Figure 5-19 highlights the properties of TCP and UDP.

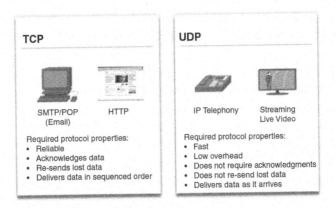

Figure 5-19   TCP and UDP Properties

TCP (5.2.1.4)

TCP transport is analogous to sending packages that are tracked from source to destination. If a shipping order is broken up into several packages, a customer can check online to see the order of the delivery.

With TCP, there are three basic operations of reliability:

- Numbering and tracking data segments transmitted to a specific device from a specific application

- Acknowledging received data

- Retransmitting any unacknowledged data after a certain period of time

Figures 5-20 through 5-23 demonstrate how TCP segments and acknowledgments are transmitted between sender and receiver.

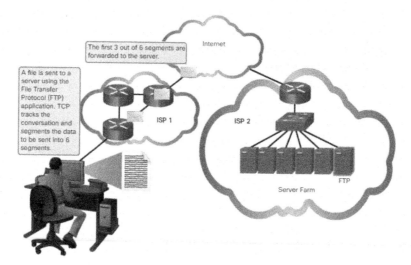

Figure 5-20   Sending Data Using a TCP Application: FTP

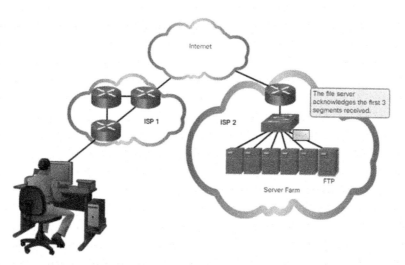

Figure 5-21   Acknowledging Receipt of TCP Application Data

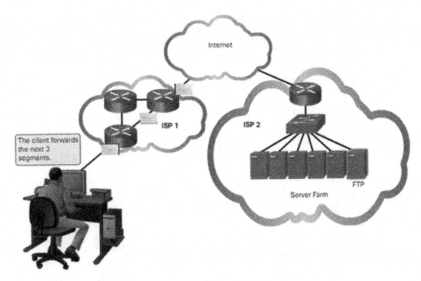

Figure 5-22   Sending More Data Using TCP

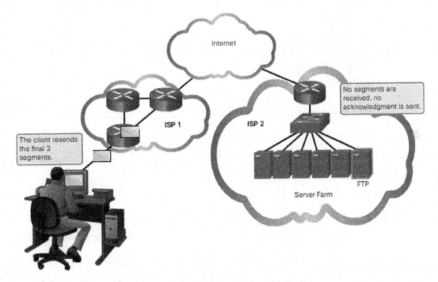

Figure 5-23   No Segments Received at Destination

UDP (5.2.1.5)

UDP works much like placing a regular, non-registered letter in the mail. The sender of the letter is not aware of the availability of the receiver to receive the letter. The post office is not responsible for tracking the letter or informing the sender if the letter does not arrive at the final destination.

UDP provides the basic functions for delivering data segments between the appropriate applications, with very little overhead and data checking. UDP is known as a *best-effort* delivery protocol. In the context of networking, best-effort delivery is referred to as *unreliable* because there is no acknowledgment that the data is received at the destination.

Figures 5-24 and 5-25 demonstrate how UDP segments are transmitted from sender to receiver.

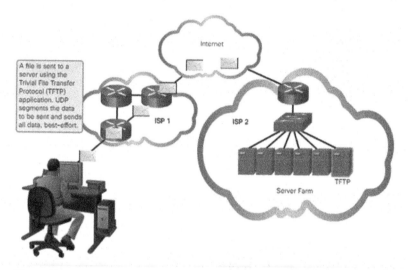

Figure 5-24 Sending Data Using a UDP Application: TFTP

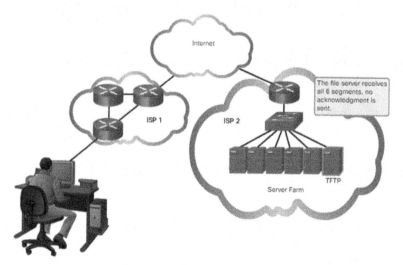

Figure 5-25 No Acknowledgments Sent by Destination

Check Your Understanding 5.2.1.6: Transport Layer Protocols

Refer to the online course to complete this activity.

Application Port Numbers (5.2.2)

Application port numbers are part of the addressing information used to identify the senders and receivers of messages. They allow different applications on the same computer to share network resources simultaneously. They are logical ports, unlike the physical ports that would be used for plugging in cables and connecting hardware devices.

Video Explanation 5.2.2.1: Application Port Numbers

Refer to the online course to view this video.

Classify Application Port Numbers (5.2.2.2)

TCP and UDP use a source port number and a destination port number to keep track of application conversations. The *source port number* is associated with the originating application on the local device. The *destination port number* is associated with the destination application on the remote device. These are not physical ports. They are numbers that are used by TCP and UDP to identify the applications that should handle the data.

The source port number is dynamically generated by the sending device. This process allows multiple conversations to occur at the same time for the same application. For example, when you use a web browser, you can have more than one tab open at a time. The destination port number is 80 for regular web traffic or 443 for secure web traffic. These are called well-known port numbers because they are consistently used by most web servers on the Internet. Source port numbers are different for each tab opened. This is how your computer knows which browser tab to deliver the web content to. Similarly, other network applications, such as email and file transfer, have their own assigned port numbers.

A number of different types of application layer protocols are identified by TCP or UDP port numbers at the transport layer:

- World Wide Web–related protocols (see Table 5-1)
- Email and identity management protocols (see Table 5-2)
- File transport and management protocols (see Table 5-3)
- Remote access protocols (see Table 5-4)
- Network operations protocols (see Table 5-5)

Table 5-1 World Wide Web–Related Protocols

Port	Transport Protocol	Application Protocol	Description
53	TCP, UDP	DNS	Domain Name System finds the IP address associated with a registered Internet domain for web, email, and other Internet services. It uses UDP for requests and information transfer between DNS servers. TCP is used for DNS responses, if required.
80	TCP	HTTP	Hypertext Transfer Protocol provides a set of rules for exchanging text, graphic images, sound, video, and other multimedia files on the World Wide Web.
443	TCP, UDP	HTTPS	A browser uses encryption and authenticates your connection with the web server.

Table 5-2 Email and Identity Management Protocols

Port	Transport Protocol	Application Protocol	Description
25	TCP	SMTP	Simple Mail Transfer Protocol is used to send email from clients to an email server. It may also be used to relay email messages from source to destination email servers.
110	TCP	POP3	Post Office Protocol 3 is used by email clients to retrieve messages from an email server.
143	TCP	IMAP	Internet Message Access Protocol is used to retrieve email messages from a server. It is more advanced than POP3 and offers a number of advantages.
389	TCP, UDP	LDAP	Lightweight Directory Access Protocol is used to maintain user identity directory information that can be shared across networks and systems. It can be used to manage information about users and network resources. It can be used to authenticate users on multiple computers.

Table 5-3 File Transport and Management Protocols

Port	Transport Protocol	Application Protocol	Description
20	TCP	FTP	File Transfer Protocol is used to transfer files between computers. FTP is considered insecure, and SSH File Transfer Protocol (SFTP; TCP port 22) should be used instead.

Port	Transport Protocol	Application Protocol	Description
21	TCP	FTP	FTP uses TCP port 21 to establish a connection between the client and the FTP server in order to start a data transfer session.
69	UDP	*TFTP*	Trivial File Transfer Protocol utilizes less overhead than FTP.
445	TCP	*SMB/CIFS*	Server Message Block and Common Internet File System allow for sharing of files, printers, and other resources between nodes on a network.
548	TCP, UDP	*AFP*	Apple Filing Protocol is a proprietary protocol developed by Apple to enable file services for macOS and classic Mac OS.

Table 5-4   Remote Access Protocols

Port	Transport Protocol	Application Protocol	Description
22	TCP	*SSH*	Secure Shell or Secure Socket Shell provides a strong authentication and encrypted data transport between a client and a remote computer. Like Telnet, it provides a command line on the remote computer.
23	TCP	*Telnet*	Telnet is an insecure remote access protocol that provides a command line on a remote computer. SSH is preferred for security reasons.
3389	TCP, UDP	*RDP*	Remote Desktop Protocol was developed by Microsoft to provide remote access to the graphical desktop of a remote machine. It is useful for tech support situations, but it should be used with caution because it provides a remote user with complete control of the destination computer.

Table 5-5   Network Operations Protocols

Port	Transport Protocol	Application Protocol	Description
67/68	UDP	*DHCP*	Dynamic Host Configuration Protocol automatically provides IP addresses to network hosts and provides a way to manage those addresses. The DHCP server uses UDP port 67, and the client host uses UDP port 68.

Port	Transport Protocol	Application Protocol	Description
137–139	UDP, TCP	*NetBIOS (NetBT)*	NetBIOS over TCP/IP provides a system through which older computer applications can communicate over large TCP/IP networks. Different NetBT functions use different protocols and ports in this range.
161/162	UDP	*SNMP*	Simple Network Management Protocol enables network administrators to monitor network operations from centralized monitoring stations.
427	UDP, TCP	*SLP*	Service Location Protocol allows computers and other devices to locate services on a LAN without previous configuration. Usually uses UDP but can use TCP.

Table 5-6 shows a summary table of all these application protocols, listed in port number order.

Table 5-6 Application Protocols in Port Number Order

Port Number	Protocol	Application
20	TCP	FTP (data)
21	TCP	FTP (control)
22	TCP	SSH
23	TCP	Telnet
25	TCP	SMTP
53	TCP, UDP	DNS
67	UDP	DHCP (server)
68	UDP	DHCP (client)
69	UDP	TFTP
80	TCP	HTTP
110	TCP	POP3
137–139	TCP, UDP	NetBIOS (NetBT)
143	TCP	IMAP
161/162	UDP	SNMP

Port Number	Protocol	Application
389	TCP, UDP	LDAP
427	TCP, UDP	SLP
443	TCP	HTTPS
445	TCP	SMB/CIFS
548	TCP	AFP
3389	TCP, UDP	RDP

Interactive Graphic

Check Your Understanding 5.2.2.3: Application Port Numbers

Refer to the online course to complete this activity.

Wireless Protocols (5.2.3)

Wireless signals are some of the most widely used communication options. Networks support different protocols because no single protocol provides an optimal solution for all of the different wireless technologies. Wireless protocols vary in speed, distance, reliability, and optimization for mobile devices to support different user needs. Wireless protocols and technologies are constantly changing and affecting how we communicate.

WLAN Protocols (5.2.3.1)

The *Institute of Electrical and Electronic Engineers (IEEE) standards* for Wi-Fi, as specified in the *802.11 collective group* of standards, specify the radio frequencies, speeds, and other capabilities for WLANs. Various implementations of the IEEE 802.11 standards have been developed over the years, as shown in Table 5-7, which compares the characteristics of the various 802.11 standards.

The 802.11a, 802.11b, and 802.11g standards are considered legacy. New WLANs should implement 802.11ac devices. Existing WLAN implementations should upgrade to 802.11ac when purchasing new devices.

Table 5-7   802.11 Standards Comparison

IEEE Standard	Maximum Speed	Maximum Indoor Range	Frequency	Backward Compatible with...
802.11a(Wi-Fi 2)	54 Mbps	115 ft (35 m)	5 GHz	—
802.11b(Wi-Fi 1)	11 Mbps	115 ft (35 m)	2.4 GHz	—
802.11g(Wi-Fi 3)	54 Mbps	125 ft (38 m)	2.4 GHz	802.11b

IEEE Standard	Maximum Speed	Maximum Indoor Range	Frequency	Backward Compatible with...
802.11n(Wi-Fi 4)	600 Mbps	230 ft (70 m)	2.4 GHz, 5 GHz	802.11a/b/g
802.11ac(Wi-Fi 5)	1.3 Gbps (1300 Mbps)	115 ft (35 m)	5 GHz	802.11a/n
802.11ax(Wi-Fi 6)	9.6 Gbps	150 ft (46m)	2.4 GHz, 5 GHz	802.11a/b/g/n/ac
802.11ax(Wi-Fi 6e)	9.6 Gbps	150 ft (46m)	1 GHz, 6 GHz	802.11a/b/g/n/ac

Bluetooth, NFC, and RFID (5.2.3.2)

Wireless protocols for close proximity connectivity include Bluetooth, radio frequency identification (RFID), and near field communication (NFC).

Bluetooth

A *Bluetooth* device can connect up to seven other Bluetooth devices, as shown in Figure 5-26. As described in the IEEE standard 802.15.1, Bluetooth operates in the 2.4 to 2.485 GHz radio frequency range and is typically used for PANs. The Bluetooth standard incorporates adaptive frequency hopping (AFH). AFH allows signals to "hop" around using different frequencies within the 2.4 to 2.485 GHz range, thereby reducing the chance of interference when multiple Bluetooth devices are present.

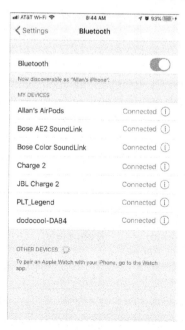

Figure 5-26   iPhone Bluetooth Settings

RFID

RFID uses the frequencies within the 125 MHz to 960 MHz range to uniquely identify items, such as in a shipping department, as shown in Figure 5-27. An active RFID tag that contains a battery can broadcast its ID up to 330 feet (100 m). Passive RFID tags rely on the RFID reader to use radio waves to activate and read the tag. Passive RFID tags are typically used for close scanning but have a range of up to 82 feet (25 m).

Figure 5-27   RFID Barcode Reader

NFC

NFC uses the frequency 13.56 MHz and is a subset of the RFID standards. NFC is designed to be a secure method to complete transactions. For example, a consumer can pay for goods or services by waving a smartphone near the payment system, as shown in Figure 5-28. Based on a unique ID, the payment is charged directly against a prepaid account or bank account. NFC is also used in mass-transportation services, the public parking sector, and many more consumer areas.

Figure 5-28   NFC Payment

Zigbee and Z-Wave (5.2.3.3)

Zigbee and Z-Wave are two smart home standards that allow users to connect multiple devices in a wireless mesh network. Typically, the devices are then managed from a smartphone app.

Zigbee

Zigbee uses low-power digital radios based on the IEEE 802.15.4 wireless standard for low-rate wireless personal area networks (LR-WPANs) and is meant to be used by low-cost, low-speed devices. Zigbee operates within frequencies from 868 MHz to 2.4 GHz and is limited to 10 to 20 meters. Zigbee has data rates from 40 to 250 Kbps and can support approximately 65,000 devices.

The Zigbee specification relies on a main device called a Zigbee coordinator. Tasked with managing all Zigbee client devices, the Zigbee coordinator is responsible for the creation and maintenance of the Zigbee network.

Although Zigbee is an open standard, software developers must be paid members of the Zigbee Alliance to use and contribute to the standard.

Z-Wave

Z-Wave technology is a proprietary standard that is now owned by Silicon Labs. However, a public version of the interoperability layer of Z-Wave was open sourced in 2016. These open source Z-Wave standards include Z-Wave's S2 security, Z/IP for transporting Z-Wave signals over IP networks, and Z-Ware middleware.

Z-Wave operates within a variety of frequencies, depending on the country, from 865.2 MHz in India to 922 to 926 MHz in Japan. It operates at 908.42 MHz in North America. Z-Wave can transmit data up to 100 meters but has slower data rates than Zigbee, at 9.6 to 100 Kbps. Z-Wave can support up to 232 devices in one wireless mesh network.

Search the Internet for "Zigbee and Z-Wave" to learn the latest information about these two smart home standards.

The Smart Home Market

The market for smart home products continues to grow. According to Statista.com, the number of smart homes was 258.54 million in 2021. The smart home market will continue to provide economic opportunities for individuals and companies.

Cellular Generations (5.2.3.4)

Cellular technology involves using a cell phone network to connect to the Internet. Performance is limited by the capabilities of the phone and the cell tower to which it is connected. Cellular technology has evolved through multiple generations (the "G" in the abbreviation), as shown in Table 5-8.

Table 5-8   Cellular Generations

Cell Technology	Description
1G/2G	■ The first generation (1G) of cell phones handled analog voice calls only. ■ 2G introduced digital voice, conference calls, and caller ID. ■ Speed: less than 9.6 Kbps.
2.5G	■ 2.5G supports web browsing, short audio and video clips, games, and application and ring tone downloads. ■ Speed: 9.6 to 237 Kbps.
3G	■ 3G supports faster data speeds as well as full-motion video, streaming music, 3D gaming, and faster web browsing. ■ Speed: 144 Kbps to 2 Mbps.
3.5G	■ 3.5G supports high-quality streaming video, high-quality video conferencing, and VoIP. ■ *Voice over IP (VoIP)* is a technology that applies Internet addressing to voice data. ■ Speed: 400 Kbps to 16 Mbps.

Cell Technology	Description
4G	■ 4G supports IP-based voice, gaming services, high-quality streamed multimedia, and Internet Protocol version 6 (IPv6) (the newest version of Internet addressing). ■ No cell phone carriers could meet the 4G speed standards when 4G was first announced in 2008. ■ Speed: 5.8 to 672 Mbps.
LTE	■ Long Term Evolution (LTE) is a designation for a 4G technology that meets the 4G speed standards. ■ An advanced version of LTE significantly improves speeds while the user is moving at high speeds, such as in a car on the highway. ■ Speed: 50 to 100 Mbps when mobile and up to 1 Gbps when stationary.
5G	■ The 5G standard was ratified in June 2018 and is currently being implemented in many markets around the world. ■ 5G supports a wide variety of applications, including augmented reality (AR), virtual reality (VR), smart homes, smart cars, and any scenario where data transfer occurs between devices. ■ Speed: 400 Mbps to 3 Gbps download; 500 Mbps to 1.5 Gbps upload.
6G	■ 6G is currently in development. As of early 2023, no standard yet exists. ■ 6G will support even faster speeds required for AR/VR applications, artificial intelligence (AI) applications, and instantaneous communications. ■ Speed: Current projections are 1 terabit per second (Tbps).

Interactive Graphic

Check Your Understanding 5.2.3.5: Wireless Protocols

Refer to the online course to complete this activity.

Network Services (5.2.4)

Network servers are components that provide clients with requested services. A *network service* is a service provided using the protocols agreed upon according to the type of service requested. There are many types of network services provided at a user's request, such as accessing the Internet, email, file sharing, and more.

Video

Video Explanation 5.2.4.1: Network Services

Refer to the online course to view this video.

Client–Server Roles (5.2.4.2)

Every computer connected to a network that participates directly in network communication is classified as a host. Hosts are also called *end devices*. Hosts on networks perform certain roles. Some network hosts perform security tasks, and others provide web services. There are also many legacy or embedded systems that perform specific tasks, such as file or print services. Hosts that provide services are called *servers*. Hosts that use these services are called *clients*.

Each service requires separate server software. For example, a server requires web server software in order to provide web services to the network. A computer with server software can provide services simultaneously to one or many clients. In addition, a single computer can run multiple types of server software. In a home or small business, it may be necessary for one computer to act as a file server, a web server, and an email server.

Clients need software installed in order to request and display the information obtained from the server. An example of client software is a web browser, like Chrome or Firefox. A single computer can also run multiple types of client software. For example, a user can check email and view a web page while instant messaging and listening to Internet radio.

Common client and server roles include the following:

- **File and client server:** Shown in Figure 5-29, the file server stores corporate and user files in a central location. The client devices access these files with client software such as Windows Explorer.

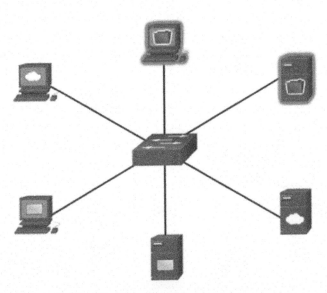

Figure 5-29   File Client and Server

- **Web client and server:** Shown in Figure 5-30, the web server runs web server software, and clients use their browser software, such as Windows Internet Explorer, to access web pages on the server.

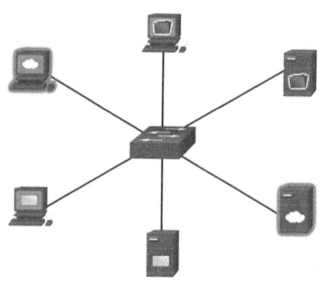

Figure 5-30   Web Client and Server

- **Email client and server:** Shown in Figure 5-31, an email server runs email server software, and clients use their mail client software, such as Microsoft Outlook, to access email on the server.

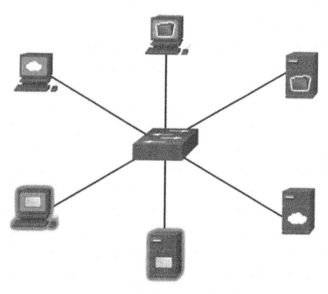

Figure 5-31   Email Client and Server

DHCP Server (5.2.4.3)

A host needs IP address information before it can send data on the network. Two important IP address services are Dynamic Host Configuration Protocol (DHCP) and Domain Name System (DNS).

DHCP is the service used by ISPs, network administrators, and wireless routers to automatically assign IP addressing information to hosts, as shown in Figure 5-32.

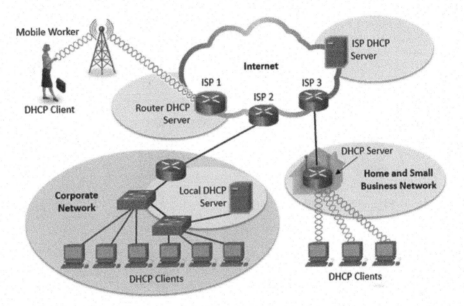

Figure 5-32   Types of DHCP Servers

DNS Server (5.2.4.4)

Computers use DNS to translate domain names into IP addresses. On the Internet, domain names, such as http://www.cisco.com, are much easier for people to remember than 72.163.4.185, which is the numeric IP address for the http://www.cisco.com server at the time of this writing. If Cisco decides to change the numeric IP address of www.cisco.com, the user will probably not know because the domain name remains the same. The new address is simply linked to the existing domain name, and connectivity is maintained.

Figures 5-33 through 5-37 show the steps involved in DNS resolution.

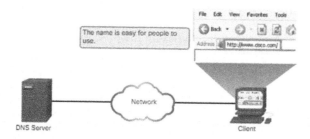

Figure 5-33   Resolving DNS Addresses, Step 1

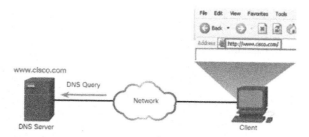

Figure 5-34   Resolving DNS Addresses, Step 2

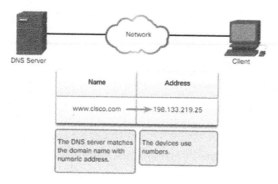

Figure 5-35   Resolving DNS Addresses, Step 3

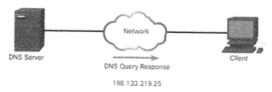

Figure 5-36   Resolving DNS Addresses, Step 4

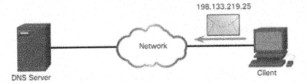

Figure 5-37   Resolving DNS Addresses, Step 5

Print Server (5.2.4.5)

A *print server* enables multiple computer users to access a single printer. A print server has three functions:

- Provide client access to print resources.

- Administer print jobs by storing them in a queue until the print device is ready for them and then feeding or spooling the print information to the printer.

- Provide feedback to users.

File Server (5.2.4.6)

File Transfer Protocol (FTP) provides the ability to transfer files between a client and a server. An FTP client is an application that runs on a computer that is used to push and pull files from a server running FTP as a service.

As Figure 5-38 illustrates, to successfully transfer files, FTP requires two connections between the client and the server: one for commands and replies and another for the actual file transfer.

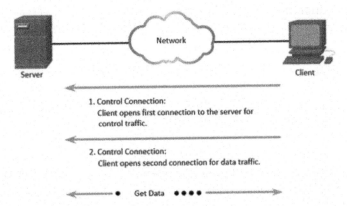

Figure 5-38   FTP Process

FTP has many security weaknesses. Therefore, a more secure file transfer service should be used, such as one of the following:

- *File Transfer Protocol Secure (FTPS)*: An FTP client can request that the file transfer session be encrypted. The file server can accept or deny the request.

- *SSH File Transfer Protocol (SFTP)*: As an extension to the Secure Shell (SSH) protocol, SFTP can be used to establish a more secure file transfer session.

- **Secure Copy (SCP)**: SCP also uses SSH to secure file transfers.

Web Server (5.2.4.7)

Web resources are provided by a ***web server***. The host accesses the web resources using Hypertext Transfer Protocol (HTTP) or Secure HTTP (HTTPS). HTTP is a set of rules for exchanging text, graphic images, sound, and video on the World Wide Web. HTTPS adds encryption and authentication services, using Secure Sockets Layer (SSL) or the newer Transport Layer Security (TLS). HTTP operates on port 80. HTTPS operates on port 443.

To better understand how a web browser and web server interact, we can examine how a web page is opened in a browser. For this example, use the URL http://www.cisco.com/index.html.

First, as shown in Figure 5-39, the browser interprets the three parts of the URL:

1. **http** (the protocol or scheme)

2. **www.cisco.com** (the server name)

3. **index.html** (the specific filename requested)

Figure 5-39   HTTP Example Topology

The browser then checks with a DNS server to convert www.cisco.com into a numeric address, which it uses to connect to the server. Using HTTP requirements, the browser sends a GET request to the server and asks for the index.html file, as shown in Figure 5-40.

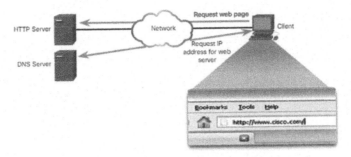

Figure 5-40   HTTP Process, Step 1

The server sends the HTML code for this web page back to the client's browser, as shown in Figure 5-41.

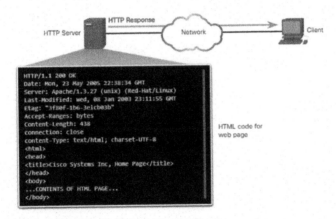

Figure 5-41   HTTP Process, Step 2

Finally, as shown in Figure 5-42, the browser interprets the HTML code and formats the page for the browser window.

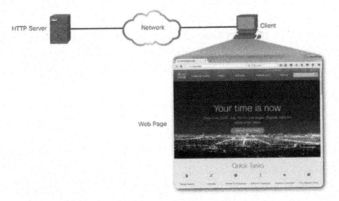

Figure 5-42   HTTP Process, Step 3

Mail Server (5.2.4.8)

Email requires several applications and services, as shown in Figure 5-43. *Email* is a store-and-forward method of sending, storing, and retrieving electronic messages across a network. Email messages are stored in databases on mail servers.

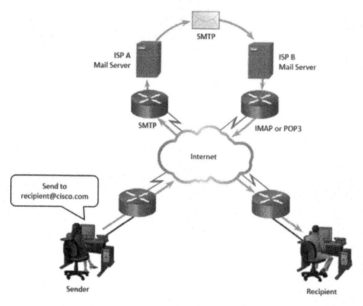

Figure 5-43   Email Process

Email clients communicate with mail servers to send and receive email. Mail servers communicate with other mail servers to transport messages from one domain to another. An email client does not communicate directly with another email client when sending email. Instead, both clients rely on the mail server to transport messages.

Email supports three separate protocols for operation: Simple Mail Transfer Protocol (SMTP), Post Office Protocol (POP), and Internet Message Access Protocol (IMAP). The application layer process that sends mail uses SMTP. A client retrieves email using one of the two application layer protocols: POP or IMAP.

Proxy Server (5.2.4.9)

A *proxy server* has the authority to act as another computer. A popular use for proxy servers is to act as storage or cache for web pages that are frequently accessed by devices on the internal network. For example, the proxy server in Figure 5-44 is storing web pages for www.cisco.com.

When any internal host sends an HTTP GET request to www.cisco.com, the proxy server completes the following steps:

1. It intercepts the requests.

2. It checks to see if the website content has changed.

3. If the content has not changed, the proxy server responds to the host with the web page.

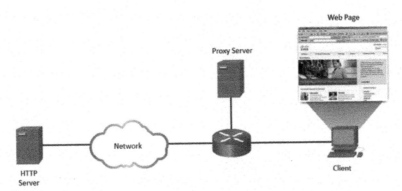

Figure 5-44   Proxy Server Caching Web Pages

In addition, a proxy server can effectively hide the IP addresses of internal hosts because all requests going out to the Internet are sourced from the proxy server's IP address.

Authentication Server (5.2.4.10)

Access to network devices is typically controlled through *authentication, authorization, and accounting (AAA) services*. AAA, or "triple A," services provide the primary framework to set up access control on a network device. AAA provides a way to control who is permitted to access a network (authenticate), control what users can do while they are there (authorize), and track what actions users perform while accessing the network (accounting).

In Figure 5-45, the remote client goes through a four-step process to authenticate with a AAA server and gain access to the network.

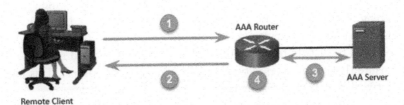

Figure 5-45   AAA Authentication Process

The steps illustrated in Figure 5-45 are as follows:

1. The client establishes a connection with the router.

2. The AAA router prompts the user for a username and password.

3. The router authenticates the username and password using a remote AAA server.

4. The user is provided access to the network, based on information in the remote AAA server.

Syslog Server (5.2.4.11)

Many networking devices support *syslog*, including routers, switches, application servers, firewalls, and other network appliances, as shown in Figure 5-46. The syslog protocol allows networking devices to send their system messages across the network to syslog servers.

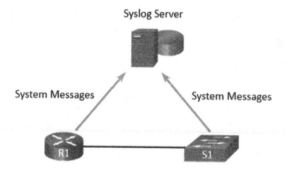

Figure 5-46 Syslog Example

The syslog logging service provides three primary functions:

- The ability to gather logging information for monitoring and troubleshooting
- The ability to select the type of logging information that is captured
- The ability to specify the destinations of captured syslog messages

Load Balancer (5.2.4.12)

Some network servers can experience very heavy loads. Some examples include streaming media servers, web servers, and email servers. Often, multiple servers are providing one service in order to provide timely content. A *load balancer* can be used to distribute the demand of requests. It is placed in front of the servers to ensure that each server is being used as much as the others. This prevents issues like network timeouts and slow responses.

SCADA (5.2.4.13)

A *Supervisory Control and Data Acquisition (SCADA)* system is used in an industrial control system (ICS). This type of system provides automation for critical services such as national security, water treatment plants, or power suppliers. SCADA software runs on a computer to gather data from the devices used by the ICS. The SCADA system manages the devices remotely, typically through the use of satellite or cellular communications.

Interactive Graphic

Check Your Understanding 5.2.4.14: Network Services

Refer to the online course to complete this activity.

Network Devices (5.3)

IT technicians must understand the purposes and characteristics of common network devices. Network devices are hardware components used to connect computers or other electronic devices together so that they can share files or resources. Network devices are used to transfer data in a secure manner over local or remote networks. This section discusses a variety of devices.

Basic Network Devices (5.3.1)

Many different types of devices are used in computer networks, and each plays a different role. Basic network components are physical components such as network cables, NICs, switches, hub, routers, and other components that allow the interconnection of devices and end systems.

Video

Video Explanation 5.3.1.1: Basic Network Devices

Refer to the online course to view this video.

Network Interface Card (5.3.1.2)

A *network interface card (NIC)* provides a physical connection to the network at a PC or other end device. As shown in Figure 5-47, there are different types of NICs. Ethernet NICs are used to connect to Ethernet networks, and wireless NICs are used to connect to 802.11 wireless networks. Most NICs in desktop computers are integrated into the motherboard or connected to an expansion slot. NICs are also available in a USB form factor.

Ethernet NIC   Wireless NIC

USB NIC

Figure 5-47   Types of NICs

A NIC also performs the important function of addressing data with the NIC's Media Access Control (MAC) address and sending the data out as bits on the network. NICs found on most computers today are Gigabit Ethernet (1000 Mbps) capable.

Note

Today's computers and motherboards typically have built-in NICs that include wireless capability. Refer to the manufacturer's specifications for more information.

Repeaters, Bridges, and Hubs (5.3.1.3)

In the early days of networking, solutions like using repeaters, hubs, and bridges were used to add more devices to the network.

Repeater

Regenerating weak signals is the primary purpose of a *repeater*, as shown in Figure 5-48. Repeaters are also called *extenders* because they extend the distance a signal can travel. In today's networks, repeaters are most often used to regenerate signals in fiber-optic cables. Also, every networking device that receives and sends data regenerates the signal.

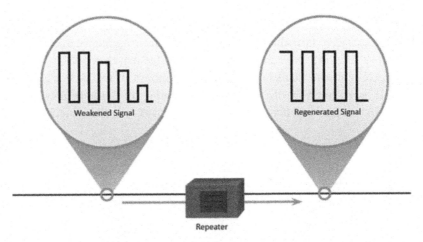

Figure 5-48   Repeaters Regenerate Signals

Hub

Hubs, as shown in Figure 5-49, receive data on one port and then send it out to all other ports. A *hub* extends the reach of a network by regenerating the electrical signal. A hub can also connect to another networking device, such as a switch or router, which connects to other sections of the network.

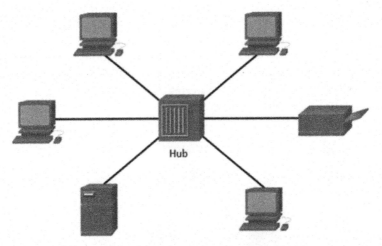

Figure 5-49   Hubs Connect Devices in a LAN

Hubs are legacy devices and should not be used in today's networks. Hubs do not segment network traffic. When one device sends traffic, the hub floods that traffic to all other devices connected to the hub, and the devices share the bandwidth.

Bridge

Bridges were introduced to divide LANs into segments. A *bridge* keeps a record of all the devices on each segment. The bridge can then filter network traffic between LAN segments. This helps reduce the amount of traffic between devices. For example, in Figure 5-50, if PC-A needs to send a job to the printer, the traffic will not be forwarded to Segment 2; however, the server will also receive this print job traffic.

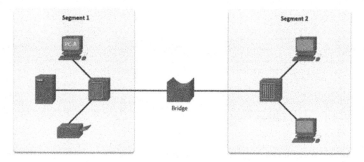

Figure 5-50   Bridges Segment a LAN

Switches (5.3.1.4)

Bridges and hubs are now considered legacy devices because of the benefits and low cost of switches. As shown in Figure 5-51, a switch microsegments a LAN. Microsegmenting means that *switches* filter and segment network traffic by sending data only to the device to which it is sent. This provides higher dedicated bandwidth to each device on the network. When PC-A sends a job to the printer, only the printer receives the traffic. Both switches and legacy bridges perform microsegmentation; however, switches perform this filtering and forwarding operation in hardware and also include additional features.

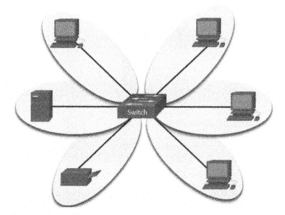

Figure 5-51   Switches Microsegment a LAN

Switch Operation

Every device on a network has a unique Media Access Control (MAC) address. This address is hardcoded by the manufacturer of the NIC. As devices send data, switches enter the device's MAC address into a switching table that records the MAC address for each device connected to the switch and records which switch port can be used to reach a device with a given MAC address. When traffic arrives that is destined for a particular MAC address, the switch uses the switching table to determine which port to use to reach the MAC address. The traffic is forwarded out the port to the destination. By sending traffic out only one port to the destination, other ports are not affected.

Managed and Unmanaged Switches

In larger networks, network administrators typically install managed switches. Managed switches come with additional features that the network administrator can configure to improve the functionality and security of the network. For example, a managed switch can be configured with VLANs and port security.

In a home or small business network, you probably do not need the added complexity and expense of a managed switch. Instead, you might consider installing an unmanaged switch. These switches typically have no management interface. You simply plug them into the network and attach network devices to benefit from their microsegmentation features.

Wireless Access Points (5.3.1.5)

Wireless access points (APs), as shown in Figure 5-52, provide network access to wireless devices, such as laptops and tablets. A wireless AP uses radio waves to communicate with the wireless NIC in the devices and other wireless access points. An access point has a limited range of coverage. Large networks require several access points to provide adequate wireless coverage. A wireless access point provides connectivity only to the network, while a wireless router provides additional features.

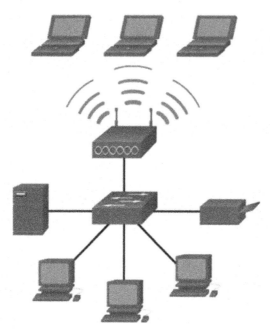

Figure 5-52   Wireless Access Points

Routers (5.3.1.6)

Switches and wireless APs forward data within a network segment. A *router* can have all the functionality of a switch or a wireless AP. However, routers connect networks, as shown in Figure 5-53. Switches use MAC addresses to forward traffic within a single network. Routers use IP addresses to forward traffic to other networks. In larger networks, routers connect to switches, which then connect to LANs, like the router on the right in Figure 5-53. The router serves as the gateway to outside networks.

The router on the left in the figure is also known as a *multipurpose device* or an *integrated router*. It includes a switch and a wireless access point. For some networks, it is more convenient to purchase and configure one device that serves all needs than to purchase a separate device for each function. This is especially true for a home or small office. A multipurpose device may also include a modem for connecting to the Internet.

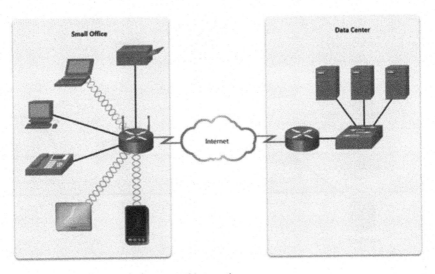

Figure 5-53   Routers Connect Networks

Interactive
Graphic

Check Your Understanding 5.3.1.7: Basic Network Devices

Refer to the online course to complete this activity.

Security Devices (5.3.2)

Network security devices defend a network by focusing on network device interaction and the connections between them. This protects against unauthorized access, misuse, or damage to the infrastructure. Endpoint security focuses on locking down individual systems or endpoints. Using the proper devices and solutions can help you defend your network. This section examines some of the most common types of network security devices that can help secure a network against external attacks.

Video

Video Explanation 5.3.2.1: Security Devices

Refer to the online course to view this video.

Firewalls (5.3.2.2)

An integrated router typically contains a switch, a router, and a firewall, as shown in Figure 5-54. *Firewalls* protect data and equipment on a network from unauthorized access. A firewall resides between two or more networks. It does not use the resources of the computers it is protecting, so there is no impact on processing performance.

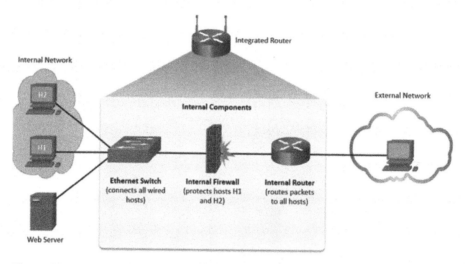

Figure 5-54   Features of an Integrated Router

Firewalls use various techniques, such as using an access control list (ACL), for determining what is permitted or denied access to a network segment. An ACL is a file that contains rules about data traffic between networks.

Note

On a secure network, if computer performance is not an issue, enable the internal operating system firewall for additional security. For example, in Windows 10, the firewall is called Windows Defender Firewall. Some applications might not operate properly unless the firewall is configured correctly for them.

IDS and IPS (5.3.2.3)

Intrusion detection systems (IDSs) passively monitor traffic on the network. Standalone IDSs have largely disappeared, and today *intrusion prevention systems (IPSs)* are more common. However, the detection feature of an IDS is still part of any IPS implementation. Figure 5-55 shows that an IDS-enabled device copies the traffic stream and analyzes the copied traffic rather than the actual forwarded packets. Working offline, it compares the captured traffic stream with known malicious signatures, much like software that checks for viruses.

An IPS builds upon IDS technology; however, an IPS device is implemented in inline mode. This means that all inbound and outbound traffic must flow through it for processing. As shown in Figure 5-56, an IPS does not allow packets to enter the target system without first being analyzed.

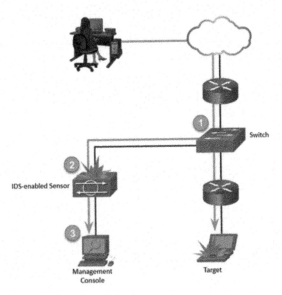

Figure 5-55   IDS Operation

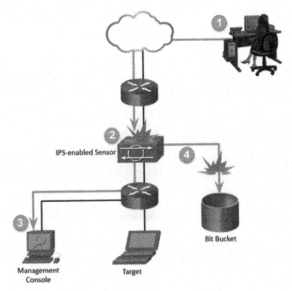

Figure 5-56   IPS Operation

The biggest difference between IDSs and IPSs is that an IPS responds immediately and does not allow any malicious traffic to pass, whereas an IDS allows malicious traffic to pass before it is addressed. However, a poorly configured IPS can negatively affect the flow of traffic in the network.

UTMs (5.3.2.4)

Unified threat management (UTM) is a generic name for an all-in-one security appliance. UTMs include all the functionality of an IDS/IPS as well as stateful firewall services. Stateful firewalls provide stateful packet filtering by using connection information maintained in a state table. A stateful firewall tracks each connection by logging the source and destination addresses, as well as source and destination port numbers.

In addition to IDS/IPS and stateful firewall services, UTMs also typically provide additional security services, such as the following:

- Zero-day protection
- Denial of service (DoS) and distributed denial of service (DDoS) protection
- Proxy filtering of applications
- Email filtering for spam and phishing attacks
- Antispyware
- Network access control
- VPN services

These features can vary significantly, depending on the UTM vendor.

In the firewall market today, UTMs are now typically called *next-generation firewalls*. For example, the Cisco Adaptive Security Appliance (ASA) in Figure 5-57 offers the latest in next-generation firewall features.

Figure 5-57   Cisco ASA 5506-X with Firepower Services

Endpoint Management Server (5.3.2.5)

An *endpoint management server* is typically responsible for monitoring all the end devices in a network, including desktops, laptops, servers, tablets, and any other device connected to the network. An endpoint management server can restrict an end device's connection to the network if the device does not meet certain predetermined requirements. For example, it can verify that devices have the latest operating system and antivirus updates.

Cisco's Digital Network Architecture (DNA) Center is an example of a solution that provides endpoint management. However, Cisco DNA Center is much more: It is a comprehensive management solution for managing all devices connected to the network so that the network administrator can optimize network performance to deliver the best possible user and application experience. Figure 5-58 shows the Cisco DNA Center tools available for managing a network.

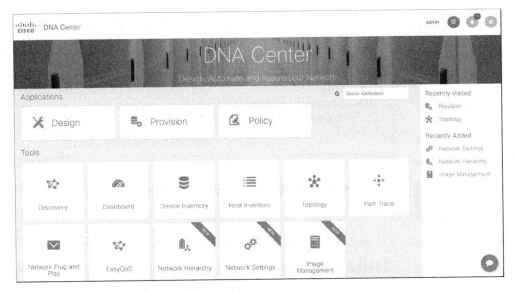

Figure 5-58   DNA Center Interface

Spam Management (5.3.2.6)

The DNS service is commonly abused by threat actors to assist in their SPAM email campaigns. For this reason, DNS servers now use TXT resource records to implement the anti-spam security features detailed in the following table.

DNS SPAM Management Feature	Description
Sender Policy Framework (SPF)	▪ The SPF is a special TXT resource record that identifies SMTP email servers authorized to send emails for an organization.
	▪ The RR includes the IP address and email server domain name that receiving servers use to determine legitimacy of emails.
	▪ There can be only one SPF RR per domain.
	▪ The SPF can also indicate how to process unknown servers, including rejecting them, flagging them, or accepting them.

DNS SPAM Management Feature	Description
DomainKeys Identified Mail (DKIM)	▪ DKIM is more advanced than SPF because it leverages cryptographic authentication using digital signatures instead of a list of authorized SMTP servers.
	▪ The TXT RR contains the public encryption key of the sending domain that external email servers use to validate the authenticity of the sending email server.
	▪ DKIM can replace or be used with SPF.
Domain-based Message Authentication, Reporting, and Conformance (DMARC)	▪ DMARC is a TXT RR that further enhances SPF and DKIM.
	▪ It specifies additional policy information for noncompliant SPF and DKIM DNS queries.

Interactive Graphic

Check Your Understanding 5.3.2.7: Security Devices

Refer to the online course to complete this activity.

Other Network Devices (5.3.3)

In addition to the network devices discussed in the previous section, other network components may be necessary to complete the network infrastructure to assure connectivity and content delivery.

Legacy and Embedded Systems (5.3.3.1)

Legacy systems are computer and networking systems that are no longer supported but that are still in operation in today's networks. Legacy systems range from industrial control systems (ICSs) to computer mainframe systems and include a wide variety of networking devices, such as hubs and bridges. Legacy systems are inherently vulnerable to security breaches because they cannot be upgraded or patched. One solution to alleviate some of the security risk is to air gap these systems. Air gapping is the process of physically isolating legacy systems from other networks, particularly the Internet.

Embedded systems are related to legacy systems in that many legacy systems have embedded microchips. These embedded microchips are typically programmed to provide dedicated input and output instructions to a specialized device. Examples of embedded systems in the home are things such as a thermostat, refrigerator, cooking range, dishwasher, washing machine, video game consoles, and smart TVs. Embedded systems are increasingly becoming connected to the Internet. Security should be top of mind when a technician recommends and installs embedded systems.

Patch Panel (5.3.3.2)

A *patch panel*, like the one shown in Figure 5-59, is commonly used as a place to collect incoming cable runs from the various networking devices throughout a facility. It provides a connection point between PCs and the switches or routers. A patch panel can be unpowered or powered. A powered patch panel can regenerate weak signals before sending them on to the next device.

Figure 5-59   Example of a Patch Panel

For safety, ensure that all cables are secured using cable ties or cable management products and are not crossing walkways or running under desks, where they can be kicked.

Power over Ethernet and Ethernet over Power (5.3.3.3)

Power over Ethernet (PoE) is a method for powering devices that do not have a battery or access to a power outlet. For example, a PoE switch (see Figure 5-60) transfers small amounts of DC current over an Ethernet cable, along with the data, to power PoE devices.

Figure 5-60   A Cisco PoE Managed Switch

Low-voltage devices that support PoE, such as wireless access points, surveillance video devices, and IP phones, can be powered from remote locations. Devices that support PoE can receive power over an Ethernet connection at distances up to 330 feet (100 m) away.

PoE devices like PoE switches, PoE injectors, IP cameras, voice over IP (VoIP) phones, and wireless access points (APs) are the five most popular devices. Power can also be inserted in the middle of a cable run using a PoE injector, as shown in Figure 5-61.

There are several IEEE standards for PoE:

- **802.3af:** Can supply up to 13 watts as 350mA at 48 volts.

- **802.3at (PoE+):** Can supply up to 25 watts as 600 mA.

- **802.3bt (PoE++ or 4PPoE):** Can supply 51 watts (Type 3) or 73 watts (Type 4).

Figure 5-61   PoE Injector

Ethernet over Power, more commonly called *powerline networking*, uses existing electrical wiring to connect devices, as shown in Figure 5-62.

Figure 5-62   Ethernet over Power

The concept of "no new wires" involves connecting a device to the network wherever there is an electrical outlet. This saves the cost of installing data cables and does not add any additional cost to the electrical bill. Using the same wiring that delivers electricity, powerline networking sends information by sending data on certain frequencies. Figure 5-62 shows a powerline networking adapter plugged into an electrical outlet.

Cloud-Based Network Controller (5.3.3.4)

A *cloud-based network controller* is a device in the cloud that allows network administrators to manage network devices. For example, a medium-sized company with multiple locations might have hundreds of wireless APs. Managing these devices can be cumbersome without the use of some type of controller.

For example, Cisco Meraki provides cloud-based networking that centralizes the management, visibility, and control of all Meraki devices into one dashboard interface, as shown in Figure 5-63. The network administrator is able to manage the wireless devices in multiple locations with the click of a mouse button.

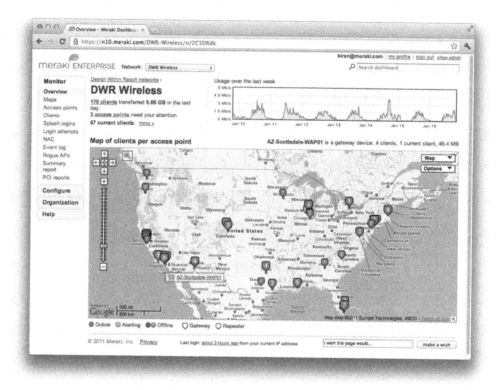

Figure 5-63   Meraki Enterprise Dashboard Interface

Check Your Understanding 5.3.3.5: Other Network Devices

Refer to the online course to complete this activity.

Network Cables (5.4)

The purpose of network cables is to connect devices to the network. Determining the network speed, range, and performance requirements is a good starting point in choosing the correct cable for installation. Different types of network cables, such as coaxial cable, fiber-optic cable, and twisted-pair cable, are used depending on the network's physical layer, topology, and size.

Network Tools (5.4.1)

It is important to purchase quality tools that will be used to create and maintain your wired and wireless network. Having the right tool for the job is essential for tasks such as cable testing, cable repair, and making cables.

Video Explanation 5.4.1.1: Network Cable Tools

Video

Refer to the online course to view this video.

Network Tools and Descriptions (5.4.1.2)

Network engineers and technicians use a variety of tools to install, test, and troubleshoot network implementations, as described and illustrated in the sections that follow.

Wire Cutters

Wire cutters are used to cut wires. Also known as *side-cutters*, the wire cutters shown in Figure 5-64 are specifically designed to snip aluminum and copper wire.

Figure 5-64   Wire Cutter

Wire Strippers

Wire strippers (see Figure 5-65) are used to remove the insulation from wire so that it can be twisted to other wires or crimped to connectors to make a cable. Wire strippers typically come with a variety of notches for different wire gauges.

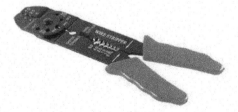

Figure 5-65   Wire Stripper

Crimper

A *crimper* is used to attach connectors to wires. The crimper tool shown in Figure 5-66 can attach RJ-45 connectors to networking cables used for Ethernet and RJ-11 connectors to telephone cables used for land lines.

Figure 5-66   Crimper

Punchdown Tool

A *punchdown tool* (see Figure 5-67) is used to terminate wire into termination blocks.

Figure 5-67   Punchdown Tool

Multimeter

A *multimeter* (see Figure 5-68) is a device that can take many types of measurements. It measures AC/DC voltage, electric current, and other electrical characteristics to test the integrity of circuits and the quality of electricity in computer components.

Figure 5-68   Multimeter

Cable Tester

A *cable tester* (see Figure 5-69) is used to check for wiring shorts and faults and for wires connected to the wrong pins.

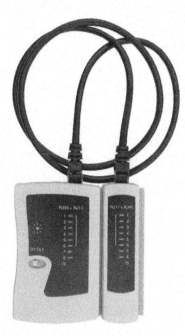

Figure 5-69   Cable Tester

Loopback Adapter

A *loopback adapter* (see Figure 5-70), also called a *loopback plug*, tests the basic functionality of computer ports. The adapter is specific to the port that you want to test. In networking, a loopback plug can be inserted in a computer NIC to test the send and receive functionality of the port.

Figure 5-70   Loopback

Tone Generator and Probe

The *tone generator and probe* (see Figure 5-71) is a two-part tool used to trace the remote end of a cable for testing and troubleshooting. The tone generator applies a tone to the wire to be tested. On the remote end, the probe is used to identify the test wire. When the probe is in near proximity to the cable to which the toner is attached, the tone can be heard through a speaker in the probe.

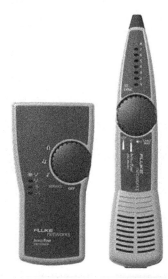

Figure 5-71 Tone Generator and Probe

Wi-Fi Analyzer

Wi-Fi analyzers, such as the one in Figure 5-72, are mobile tools for auditing and troubleshooting wireless networks.

Figure 5-72 Wi-Fi Analyzer

Many Wi-Fi analyzers, like the Cisco Spectrum Expert Wi-Fi application, are robust tools designed for enterprise network planning, security, compliance, and maintenance. But Wi-Fi analyzers can also be used for smaller wireless LANs. Technicians can use a Wi-Fi analyzer to see all available wireless networks in a given area, determine signal strengths, and position access points to adjust wireless coverage.

Some Wi-Fi analyzers can help troubleshoot a wireless network by detecting misconfigurations, access point failures, and radio frequency interference (RFI) problems.

Network Taps (5.4.1.3)

Sometimes it is necessary to capture network traffic to analyze it. This can often be done with software such as Wireshark. If this is not possible, a network tap can be used to capture the cable signals and send them to analyzing software. A network tap can be passive or active (powered):

- **Passive test access point (TAP):** This type of TAP is a box with network ports to carry signals in and out. Inside, an inductor or optical splitter is used to copy the signal and send it out to a monitor port. The monitor port receives all the traffic from the cable.

- **Active TAP:** This type of TAP regenerates the signal. Due to the complexity of gigabit signaling, a passive TAP is unable to be used. Also, some fiber links may become corrupt when using an optical splitter, so an active TAP is used instead.

Network sniffing can also be completed using a special port on a network switch. This is known as a switched port analyzer (SPAN)/mirror port. A mirror receives a copy of the traffic that is addressed to a specific port or to all other ports.

Interactive Graphic

Check Your Understanding 5.4.1.4: Network Tools

Refer to the online course to complete this activity.

Copper Cables and Connectors (5.4.2)

This section describes cables that are used in computers and networks to carry data or power to a device. It also covers the connectors, which are the parts of cables that plug into ports to connect devices to each other. There are different types of cables and various form factors of connectors.

Cable Types (5.4.2.1)

A wide variety of networking cables are available, as shown in Figure 5-73. Coaxial and twisted-pair cables use electrical signals over copper to transmit data. Fiber-optic cables use light signals to transmit data. These cables differ in bandwidth, size, and cost.

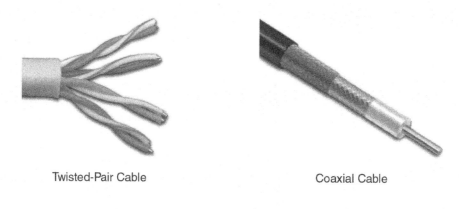

Twisted-Pair Cable   Coaxial Cable

Fiber-Optic Cable

Figure 5-73   Network Cables

Coaxial Cables (5.4.2.2)

Coaxial cable is usually constructed of either copper or aluminum. It is used by both cable television companies and satellite communication systems. Coaxial cable is enclosed in a sheath or jacket and can be terminated with a variety of connectors, as shown in Figure 5-74.

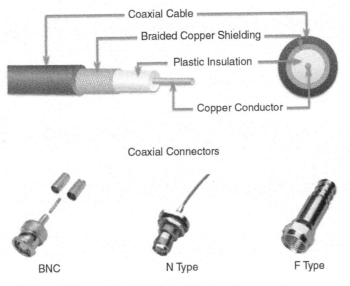

Figure 5-74   Coaxial Cable and Connectors

Coaxial cable (or coax) carries data in the form of electrical signals. It provides improved shielding compared to unshielded twisted-pair (UTP), so it has a higher signal-to-noise ratio, allowing it to carry more data. However, twisted-pair cabling has replaced coax in LANs because, compared to UTP, coax is physically harder to install, more expensive, and harder to troubleshoot.

Twisted-Pair Cables (5.4.2.3)

Twisted-pair is a type of copper cabling used for telephone communications and most Ethernet networks. The pair is twisted to provide protection against crosstalk, which is the noise generated by adjacent pairs of wires in the cable. *Unshielded twisted-pair (UTP)* cabling is the most common variety of twisted-pair cabling.

As shown in Figure 5-75, UTP cable consists of four pairs of color-coded wires that have been twisted together and then encased in a flexible plastic sheath that protects against minor physical damage. UTP does not protect against electromagnetic interference (EMI) or radio frequency interference (RFI). EMI and RFI can be caused by a variety of sources, including electric motors and fluorescent lights.

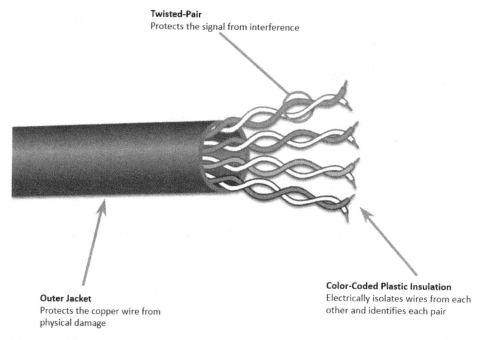

Twisted-Pair
Protects the signal from interference

Outer Jacket
Protects the copper wire from
physical damage

Color-Coded Plastic Insulation
Electrically isolates wires from each
other and identifies each pair

Figure 5-75   UTP Cable

Shielded twisted-pair (STP) was designed to provide better protection against EMI
and RFI. As shown in Figure 5-76, each twisted pair is wrapped in a foil shield. The
four pairs are then wrapped together in a metallic braid or foil.

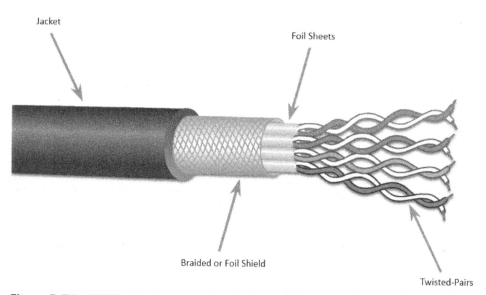

Jacket

Foil Sheets

Braided or Foil Shield

Twisted-Pairs

Figure 5-76   STP Cable

Both UTP and STP cables are terminated with an RJ-45 connector and plug into RJ-45 sockets, as shown in Figure 5-77. Compared to UTP cable, STP cable is significantly more expensive and difficult to install. To gain the full benefit of the shielding, STP cables are terminated with special shielded STP RJ-45 data connectors (not shown in Figure 5-77). If the cable is improperly grounded, the shield may act as an antenna and pick up unwanted signals.

RJ-45 UTP Connectors

RJ-45 UTP Sockets

Figure 5-77   RJ-45 Connectors and Sockets

Twisted-Pair Category Ratings (5.4.2.4)

New or renovated office buildings often have some type of UTP cabling that connects all the offices. The distance limitation of UTP cabling used for data is 100 meters.

Each category also comes in plenum-rated versions, which are installed inside plenum areas of buildings. Plenum is in any area that is used for ventilation, such as the area between the ceiling and a dropped ceiling. *Plenum-rated cables* are made from a special plastic that retards fire and produces less smoke than other cable types.

Table 5-9 lists details for Cat 5, Cat 5e, and Cat 6.

Table 5-9   Twisted-Pair Category Ratings

Category	Speed	Features
Cat 5 UTP	100 Mbps at 100 MHz	■ The first widely adopted 4-pair UTP that replaced Cat 3 UTP in Ethernet LANs.
		■ Manufactured with higher standards than Cat 3 to allow for higher data transfer rates.
Cat 5e UTP	1 Gbps at 100 MHz	■ Manufactured with higher standards than Cat 5 to allow for higher data transfer rates.
		■ More twists per foot than Cat 5 to better prevent EMI and RFI from outside sources.

Category	Speed	Features
Cat 6 UTP	1 Gbps at 250 MHz (Cat 6a: 500 MHz)	■ Manufactured with higher standards than Cat 5e to allow for higher data transfer rates. ■ More twists per foot than Cat 5e to better prevent EMI and RFI from outside sources. ■ May have a plastic divider to separate pairs of wires inside the cable to better prevent EMI and RFI. ■ Good choice for customers using applications that require large amounts of bandwidth, such as video conferencing or gaming. ■ Cat 6a has better insulation and performance than Cat 6.

Twisted-Pair Wire Schemes (5.4.2.5)

There are two different patterns, or wiring schemes, called *T568A and T568B*. Each wiring scheme defines the pinout, or order of wire connections, on the end of the cable. Only the orange pair and green pair are reversed between T568A and T568B, as shown in Figures 5-78 and 5-79.

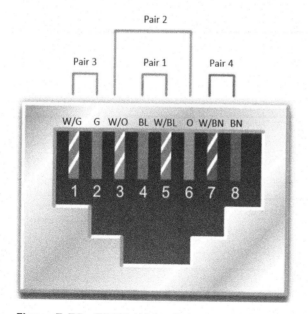

Color Labels	
W/G	Green with white stripe
G	Green
W/O	Orange with white stripe
BL	Blue
W/BL	Blue with white stripe
O	Orange
W/BN	Brown with white stripe
BN	Brown

Figure 5-78   T568A Wiring Scheme

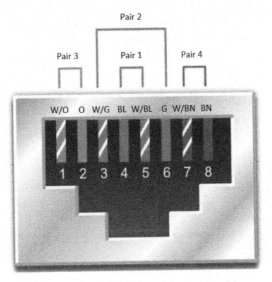

Color Labels	
W/O	Orange with white stripe
O	Orange
W/G	Green with white stripe
BL	Blue
W/BL	Blue with white stripe
G	Green
W/BN	Brown with white stripe
BN	Brown

Figure 5-79   T568B Wiring Scheme

On a network installation, one of the two wiring schemes, T568A or T568B, should be chosen and followed. It is important that the same wiring scheme be used for every termination in a project. If working on an existing network, use the wiring scheme that already exists.

Interactive Graphic

Activity 5.4.2.6: Cable Pinouts

Refer to the online course to complete this activity.

Video

Video Demonstration 5.4.2.7: Build and Test a Network Cable

Refer to the online course to view this video.

Lab 5.4.2.8: Build and Test a Network Cable

In this lab, you will build and test a straight-through UTP Ethernet network cable.

Fiber Cables and Connectors (5.4.3)

A fiber-optic cable contains strands of glass and is surrounded by insulating material. These network cables provide long-distance and high-bandwidth data networking. An optical fiber connector terminates the end of an optical fiber. A variety of optical fiber connectors are available. The main differences among the types of connectors are dimensions and methods of coupling. Businesses decide on the types of connectors that will be used, based on their equipment.

Fiber-Optic Cables (5.4.3.1)

Optical fiber is composed of two kinds of glass (core and cladding) and a protective outer shield (jacket), as shown in Figure 5-80.

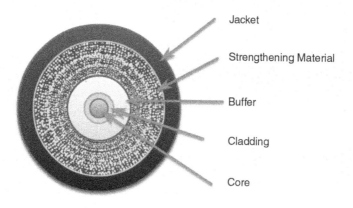

Jacket

Strengthening Material

Buffer

Cladding

Core

RJ-45 UTP Sockets

Figure 5-80   Structure of a Fiber-Optic Cable

The list that follows describes the different components of a fiber-optic cable:

- *Jacket*: Typically a PVC jacket that protects the fiber against abrasion, moisture, and other contaminants. The composition of the outer jacket varies depending on the cable usage.

- *Strengthening material*: Surrounds the buffer and prevents the fiber cable from being stretched when it is being pulled. The material used is often the same material used to produce bulletproof vests.

- *Buffer*: Used to help shield the core and cladding from damage.

- *Cladding*: Made from slightly different chemicals than those used to create the core. It tends to act like a mirror, reflecting light back into the core of the fiber. This keeps light in the core as it travels down the fiber.

- *Core*: The light transmission element at the center of the optical fiber. Light pulses travel through the fiber core, which is typically silica or glass.

Because it uses light to transmit signals, fiber-optic cable is not affected by EMI or RFI. All signals are converted to light pulses as they enter the cable, and they are converted back into electrical signals when they leave it. This means that fiber-optic cable can deliver signals that are clearer, can go farther, and have greater bandwidth than cable made of copper or other metals. Although the optical fiber is very thin and susceptible to breakage when it is bent sharply, the properties of the core and cladding make it very strong. Optical fiber is durable and is deployed in harsh environmental conditions in networks all around the world.

Types of Fiber Media (5.4.3.2)

Fiber-optic cables are broadly classified into two types:

- *Single-mode fiber (SMF)*: Consists of a very small core and uses laser technology to send a single ray of light (see Figure 5-81). Popular in long-distance situations spanning hundreds of kilometers, such as those required in long-haul telephony and cable TV applications.

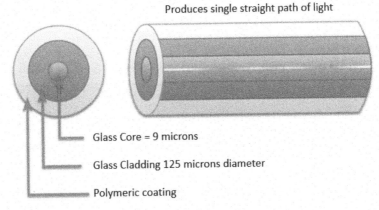

Figure 5-81   Single-Mode Fiber

The characteristics of SMF are as follows:

- Small core
- Less dispersion
- Suited for long-distance applications
- Uses lasers as the light source
- Commonly used with campus backbones for distances of several thousand meters

- *Multimode fiber (MMF)*: Consists of a larger core and uses LED emitters to send light pulses. Specifically, light from an LED enters the multimode fiber at different angles (see Figure 5-82). MMF is popular in LANs because it can be powered by low-cost LEDs. It provides bandwidth up to 10 Gbps over link lengths of up to 550 meters.

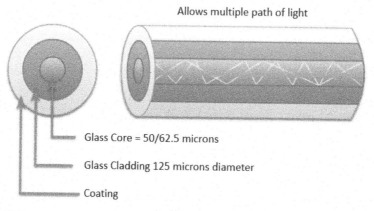

Figure 5-82   Multimode Fiber

The characteristics of MMF are as follows:

o Larger core than in single-mode cable

o Allows greater dispersion and, therefore, loss of signal

o Suited for long-distance applications but shorter than single mode

o Uses LEDs as the light source

o Commonly used with LANs or distances of a couple hundred meters within a campus network

Fiber-Optic Connectors (5.4.3.3)

An *optical fiber connector* terminates the end of an optical fiber. A variety of optical fiber connectors are available. The main differences among the types of connectors are the dimensions and methods of coupling. Businesses decide on the types of connectors that will be used, based on their equipment.

For fiber standards with FX and SX in the name, light travels in one direction over optical fiber. Therefore, two fibers are required to support full-duplex operation. Fiber-optic patch cables bundle together two optical fiber cables and are terminated with a pair of standard single-fiber connectors.

For fiber standards with BX in the name, light travels in both directions on a single strand of fiber. It does this through a process called Wave Division Multiplexing (WDM). WDM is a technology that separates the transmit and receive signals inside the fiber.

For more information on fiber standards, search online for "Gigabit Ethernet fiber-optic standards."

Straight-Tip (ST) Connectors

The straight-tip (ST) connector, shown in Figure 5-83, was one of the first connector types used. The connector locks securely with a "twist-on/twist-off" bayonet-style mechanism.

Figure 5-83   ST Connectors

Subscriber Connectors (SCs)

Subscriber connectors (SCs) (see Figure 5-84) are sometimes referred to as *square connectors* or *standard connectors*. SC connectors are widely adopted LAN and WAN connectors that use a push/pull mechanism to ensure positive insertion. This connector type is used with multimode and single-mode fiber.

Figure 5-84   SC Connectors

Lucent Connectors (LCs)

A *Lucent connector (LC)* (see Figure 5-85) is a smaller version of a fiber-optic SC connector. It is sometimes called a *little* or *local connector*. This type of connector has grown in popularity due to its smaller size.

Figure 5-85 Lucent Connector

Duplex Multimode LCs

Some fiber connectors accept both the transmitting and receiving fibers in a single connector known as a duplex connector (see Figure 5-86). A *duplex multimode LC* is similar to an LC simplex connector but uses a duplex connector.

Figure 5-86 Duplex Multimode LC

Interactive Graphic

Check Your Understanding 5.4.3.4: Fiber Cables and Connectors

Refer to the online course to complete this activity.

Summary (5.5)

In this chapter, you learned about the different types of components, devices, services, and protocols that comprise a network. All these elements are arranged to form different network topologies, such as PANs, LANs, VLANs, WLANs, and VPNs. There are also different ways in which computers and networks are connected to the Internet. For example, there are wired connections like DSL, cable, and fiber optics, and wireless connections, such as satellite and cellular services. It is even possible to connect network devices to the Internet through a cell phone using tethering.

You learned about the four layers of the TCP/IP model: network access, Internet, transport, and application. Each layer performs the functions necessary for data transmission over a network. Each layer also has specific protocols that are used for communication between peers.

The chapter covered different wireless technologies and standards, beginning with a comparison of the WLAN protocols and IEEE 802.11 standards. These standards use two radio frequency bands of 5 GHz (802.11a and 802.11ac) and 2.4 GHz (802.11b, 802.11g, and 802.11n). Other wireless protocols for close proximity connectivity, like Bluetooth and NFC, were discussed, along with standards for smart home applications, such as Zigbee, which is an open standard based on IEEE 802.15.4, and Z-Wave, which is a proprietary standard. You also learned about the evolution of the cellular generations from 1G, which supported only analog voice, through 6G, which has enough bandwidth to support AR, VR, and much higher speeds than 5G.

Many types of network hardware devices were discussed in this chapter. NICs provide physical connectivity for end devices, can be wired or wireless, and are installed inside a computer in an expansion slot or outside via USB. You learned that repeaters and hubs operate at Layer 1 and repeat network signals and that switches and routers operate at Layers 2 and 3, respectively, with switches forwarding frames based on MAC address and routers forwarding packets based on IP address.

Networks also include security devices such as firewalls, IDSs, IPSs, and UTMs. Firewalls protect data and equipment on a network against unauthorized access. IDSs passively monitor traffic on the network, and IPSs actively monitor traffic and respond immediately, not allowing any malicious traffic to pass. UTMs are all-in-one security appliances and include all the functionality of an IDS/IPS as well as stateful firewall services.

Finally, in this chapter, you learned about network cables and connectors and the tools network technicians use to test and repair them. Cables come in different sizes and costs and differ in the maximum bandwidth and distances that they support. Coax and twisted-pair cables carry data in the form of electrical signals, and fiber-optic cables use light. Twisted-pair cables use two different wiring schemes, T568A and T568B, which define the order of the individual wire connections at the end of the cable. You built and tested a straight-through UTP Ethernet network cable using either the T568A or T568B standards.

Practice

The following activities provide practice with the topics introduced in this chapter. The labs are available in the companion *IT Essentials v8 Labs & Study Guide* (ISBN 9780138166304).

Lab

Lab 5.4.2.8: Build and Test a Network Cable

Check Your Understanding Questions

Complete all the review questions listed here to test your understanding of the topics and concepts in this chapter. Appendix A, "Answers to 'Check Your Understanding' Questions," lists the answers.

1. A technician has been asked to assist with some LAN cabling. What are two standards that the technician should research before this project begins? (Choose two.)

   A. T568A

   B. T568B

   C. 802.11n

   D. Z-Wave

   E. Zigbee

   F. 802.11c

2. Which type of network extends a short distance and connects printers, mice, and keyboards to an individual host?

   A. MAN

   B. PAN

   C. LAN

   D. WLAN

3. A company is expanding its business to other countries. All branch offices must remain connected to corporate headquarters at all times. Which network technology is required to support this scenario?

   A. WLAN

   B. MAN

   C. LAN

   D. WAN

4. Which three Wi-Fi standards operate in the 2.4 GHz range of frequencies? (Choose three.)

   A. 802.11g

   B. 802.11ac

   C. 802.11a

   D. 802.11b

   E. 802.11n

5. Which smart home technology requires the use of a device, known as a coordinator, to create a wireless PAN?

   A. 802.11ac

   B. Zigbee

   C. 802.11n

   D. Z-Wave

6. Which network device regenerates the data signal without segmenting the network?

   A. hub

   B. switch

   C. modem

   D. router

7. Which security technology is used to passively monitor network traffic with the objective of detecting a possible attack?

   A. proxy server

   B. IDS

   C. firewall

   D. IPS

8. Which network service automatically assigns IP addresses to devices on the network?

   A. DHCP

   B. traceroute

   C. Telnet

   D. DNS

9. Which two protocols operate at the transport layer of the TCP/IP model? (Choose two.)

   A. IP

   B. UDP

   C. FTP

   D. ICMP

   E. TCP

10. A technician has captured packets on a network that has been running slowly when accessing the Internet. Which port number should the technician look for within the captured material to locate HTTP packets?

   A. 80

   B. 21

   C. 110

   D. 53

   E. 20

11. What are two common media used in networks? (Choose two.)

   A. water

   B. fiber

   C. nylon

   D. copper

   E. wood

12. A switch is a networking device that records _____ addresses by inspecting every incoming data frame.

   A. IP

   B. TCP/IP

    C. MAC

    D. SVI

    E. switch

13. What type of networking cable do television companies use to carry data as electrical signals?

    A. fiber optic

    B. unshielded twisted-pair

    C. shielded twisted-pair

    D. coaxial

CHAPTER 6

Applied Networking

Objectives

Upon completion of this chapter, you will be able to answer the following questions:

- What are MAC addressing and IP addressing for computer networks?

- How do you configure NICs for wired and wireless networks?

- How do you configure wireless networking in a small LAN?

- How do you configure firewall settings?

- How do you configure IoT devices?

- What are the six steps of the troubleshooting process for networks?

- How do you troubleshoot common and advanced problems related to networks?

Key Terms

This chapter uses the following key terms. You can find the definitions in the glossary at the end of the book.

Introduction (6.0)

Virtually all computers and mobile devices today are connected to some type of network and to the Internet. This means that configuring and troubleshooting computer networks is now a critical skill for IT professionals. This chapter focuses on applied networking with a discussion on the format and architecture of Media Access Control (MAC) addresses and Internet Protocol (IP) addresses, both IPv4 and IPv6, that are used to connect computers to a network. Examples of how to configure static and dynamic addressing on computers are included. This chapter also covers the configuration of both wired and wireless networks, firewalls, and IoT devices.

You will learn how to configure network interface cards (NICs), connect devices to a wireless router, and configure a wireless router for network connectivity. You will learn how to configure wireless networks, including using basic wireless settings, Network Address Translation (NAT), firewall settings, and quality of service (QoS). You will also learn about firewalls, Internet of Things (IoT) devices, and network troubleshooting. At the end of the chapter, you will learn the six-step troubleshooting process and common problems and solutions for computer networks.

Your networking skills should include the ability to configure wireless networks so that hosts can communicate, configure firewalls to filter traffic, verify network connectivity, and solve network connectivity problems. This chapter includes four labs in which you will build these skills. In these labs, you will configure basic settings on a wireless router and connect a PC to a wireless network; configure firewall settings to implement MAC address filtering, a DMZ, and single port forwarding; and diagnose and solve network problems.

Device to Network Connection (6.1)

Network devices, media, and configurations make a network connection possible. In this section, you will learn about the components that comprise a network, including both hardware and software. Having a solid understanding of the types of network devices available and proper configuration can help you build and maintain a network that serves your organization well.

Network Addressing (6.1.1)

Network devices rely on two sets of addresses to deliver messages quickly and efficiently. *Media Access Control (MAC) addresses* and *Internet Protocol (IP) addresses* are both key components of networking, but they have different purposes. MAC addresses are hardware addresses, whereas IP addresses are assigned as part of connecting to a network. It is common for a computer to have two versions of IP addresses, IPv4 and IPv6. This section discusses network equipment addressing.

Video **Video Explanation 6.1.1.1: MAC Addressing**

Refer to the online course to view this video.

Video **Video Explanation 6.1.1.2: IPv4 Addressing**

Refer to the online course to view this video.

Video **Video Explanation 6.1.1.3: IPv6 Addressing**

Refer to the online course to view this video.

Two Network Addresses (6.1.1.4)

Your fingerprint and mailing address both make it possible to identify you and locate you. Your fingerprint usually does not change. Your fingerprint can be used to uniquely identify you, wherever your location. Your mailing address is different. It is your location. Unlike your fingerprint, your mailing address can change.

Devices that are attached to a network have two addresses that are similar to your fingerprint and mailing address, as shown in Figure 6-1. These two types of addresses are the Media Access Control (MAC) address and the Internet Protocol (IP) address.

A Fingerprint Is Like a MAC Address   A Mailing Address Is Like an IP Address

Figure 6-1   Two Network Addresses

The MAC address is hard-coded onto the Ethernet or wireless network interface card (NIC) by the manufacturer. The address stays with the device, regardless of what network the device is connected to. A MAC address is 48 bits and can be represented in one of the three hexadecimal formats shown in Table 6-1.

Table 6-1   MAC Address Format

Address Format	Description
00-50-56-BE-D7-87	Two hexadecimal digits separated by hyphens
00:50:56:BE:D7:87	Two hexadecimal digits separated by colons
0050.56BE.D787	Four hexadecimal digits separated by periods

IP addresses are assigned by network administrators based on the location within the network. When a device moves from one network to another, its IP address is likely to change. An IP version 4 (IPv4) address is 32 bits and represented in dotted-decimal notation. An IP version 6 (IPv6) address is 128 bits and represented in hexadecimal format, as shown in Table 6-2.

Table 6-2   IP Address Format

Address Format	Description	Example
IPv4	32 bits in dotted-decimal notation	192.168.200.9
IPv6	128 bits in hexadecimal format	2001:0db8:cafe:0200:0000:0000:0000:0008
IPv6	128 bits in compressed format	2001:db8:cafe:200::8

Figure 6-2 shows a topology with two local area networks (LANs). This topology demonstrates that MAC addresses do not change when a device is moved, but IP addresses do change. The laptop was moved to LAN 2. Notice that the laptop's MAC address did not change, but its IP addresses did change.

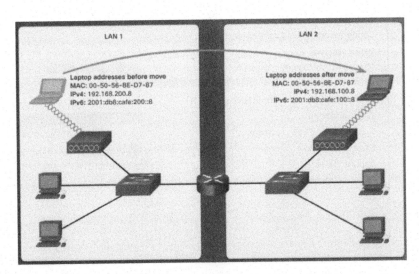

Figure 6-2   Topology with Two LANs

> **Note**
>
> Converting between decimal, binary, and hexadecimal numbering systems is beyond the scope
> of this course. Search the Internet to learn more about these numbering systems.

Displaying the Addresses (6.1.1.5)

Today, your computer probably has an IPv4 address and an IPv6 address, as shown
for the laptop in Figure 6-2. In the early 1990s, out of concern about running out of
IPv4 network addresses, the Internet Engineering Task Force (IETF) began to look
for a replacement. This led to the development of IPv6. Currently, IPv6 is operating
alongside IPv4 and is beginning to replace it.

Example 6-1 shows output for the command **ipconfig /all** on the laptop in Figure 6-2.
The output is highlighted to show the MAC address and two IP addresses.

Example 6-1   Laptop Addressing Information

```
C:\> ipconfig /all


Windows IP Configuration


  Host Name. . . . . . . . . . . . . . : ITEuser
  Primary Dns Suffix . . . . . . . . . :
  Node Type. . . . . . . . . . . . . . : Hybrid
  IP Routing Enabled . . . . . . . . . : No
  WINS Proxy Enabled . . . . . . . . . : No


Ethernet adapter Local Area Connection:


  Connection-specific DNS Suffix . . . :
  Description . . . . . . . . . . . . . : Intel(R) PRO/1000 MT Network Connection
  Physical Address . . . . . . . . . . : 00-50-56-BE-D7-87
  DHCP Enabled . . . . . . . . . . . . : No
  Autoconfiguration Enabled . . . . . . : Yes
  IPv6 Address . . . . . . . . . . . . : 2001:db8:cafe:200::8(Preferred)
  Link-local IPv6 Address . . . . . . . : fe80::8cbf:a682:d2e0:98a%11(Preferred)
  IPv4 Address . . . . . . . . . . . . : 192.168.200.8(Preferred)
  Subnet Mask . . . . . . . . . . . . . : 255.255.255.0
  Default Gateway . . . . . . . . : . . : 2001:db8:cafe:200::1
  192.168.200.1


C:\>
```

Note

Windows OS calls a NIC an *Ethernet adapter* and a MAC address a *physical address*.

IPv4 Address Format (6.1.1.6)

When you manually configure a device with an **IPv4 address**, you enter it in dotted-decimal format, as shown for a Windows computer in Figure 6-3. Each number separated by a period is called an *octet* because it represents 8 bits. Therefore, the 32-bit address 192.168.200.8 has four octets.

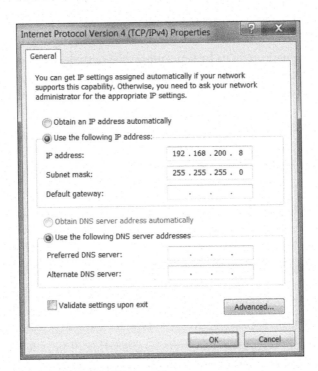

Figure 6-3   IPv4 Properties

An IPv4 address is composed of two parts. The first part identifies the network. The second part identifies this device on the network. A device uses the subnet mask to determine the network. For example, the computer in Figure 6-3 uses the subnet mask 255.255.255.0 to determine that the IPv4 address 192.168.200.8 belongs to the 192.168.200.0 network. The .8 portion is this device's unique host portion on the 192.168.200 network. Any other device with the same 192.168.200 prefix will be on the same network but have a different value for the host portion. Devices with a different prefix will be on a different network.

To see this at the binary level, you can convert the 32-bit IPv4 address and subnet mask to their binary equivalents, as shown in Table 6-3. A 1 bit in the subnet mask means that bit is part of the network portion. So, the first 24 bits of the 192.168.200.8 address are network bits. The last 8 bits are host bits.

Table 6-3   The Role of the Subnet Mask

Address	Network Portion		Host Portion
192.168.200.8	11000000.10101000.11001000	.	00001000
255.255.255.0	11111111.11111111.11111111	.	00000000
192.168.200.0	11000000.10101000.11001000	.	00000000

When a device prepares data to be sent out on the network, it must first determine whether to send data directly to the intended receiver or to a router. It sends it directly to the receiver if the receiver is on the same network. Otherwise, it sends the data to a router. A router then uses the network portion of the IP address to route traffic between different networks.

For example, if the Windows computer in Figure 6-3 has data to send to a host at 192.168.200.25, it sends the data directly to that host because it has the same prefix, 192.168.200. If the destination's IPv4 address is 192.168.201.25, the Windows computer sends the data to a router.

IPv6 Address Formats (6.1.1.7)

IPv6 overcomes the address space limitations of IPv4. The 32-bit IPv4 address space provides approximately 4,294,967,296 unique addresses. The 128-bit IPv6 address space provides 340,282,366,920,938,463,463,374,607,431,768,211,456 addresses, or 340 undecillion addresses.

The 128 bits of an *IPv6 address* are written as a string of hexadecimal values, with letters expressed in lowercase. Every 4 bits is represented by a single hexadecimal digit, for a total of 32 hexadecimal values. The following examples are fully expanded IPv6 addresses:

2001:0db8:0000:1111:0000:0000:0000:0200

fe80:0000:0000:0000:0123:4567:89ab:cdef

ff02:0000:0000:0000:0000:0000:0000:0001

Two rules help reduce the number of digits needed to represent an IPv6 address, as described in the sections that follow.

Rule 1: Omit Leading 0s

The first rule to help reduce the notation of IPv6 addresses is to omit any leading 0s (zeros) in any 16-bit section. For example, from the previous IPv6 address examples:

0db8 can be represented as **db8** in the first IPv6 address.

0123 can be represented as **123** in the second IPv6 address.

0001 can be represented as **1** in the third IPv6 address.

Note

IPv6 addresses must be represented using lowercase letters, but you might often see them as uppercase.

Rule 2: Omit All 0 Segments

The second rule to help reduce the notation of IPv6 addresses is that a double colon (::) can replace any group of consecutive zeros. The double colon (::) can be used only once within an address; otherwise, there would be more than one possible resulting address.

Tables 6-4 to 6-6 show examples of how to use the two rules to compress the IPv6 addresses.

Table 6-4   Compressing an IPv6 Address to Help Reduce the Notation of IPv6 Addresses

Fully expanded	2001:0db8:0000:1111:0000:0000:0000:0200
No leading 0s	2001: db8: 0:1111: 0: 0: 0: 200
Compressed	2001:db8:0:1111::200

Table 6-5   Example 2 of Compressing an IPv6 Address

Fully expanded	fe80:0000:0000:0000:0123:4567:89ab:cdef
No leading 0s	fe80: 0: 0: 0: 123:4567:89ab:cdef
Compressed	fe80::123:4567:89ab:cdef

Table 6-6   Example 3 of Compressing an IPv6 Address

Fully expanded	ff02:0000:0000:0000:0000:0000:0000:0001
No leading 0s	ff02: 0: 0: 0: 0: 0: 0: 1
Compressed	ff02::1

Static Addressing (6.1.1.8)

In a small network, you can manually configure each device with proper IP addressing. You assign a unique IP address to each host within the same network. This is known as *static IP addressing*.

On a Windows computer, as shown in Figure 6-4, you can assign the following IPv4 address configuration information to a host:

- *IP address*: Identifies this device on the network

- *Subnet mask*: Used to identify the network on which this device is connected

- *Default gateway*: Identifies the router that this device uses to access the Internet or another network

- **Optional values:** The preferred Domain Name System (DNS) server address and the alternate DNS server address

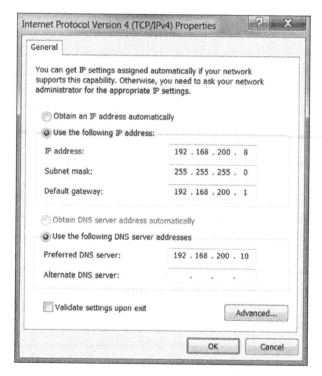

Figure 6-4 Static IPv4 Addressing

Figure 6-5 shows similar configuration information for IPv6 addressing.

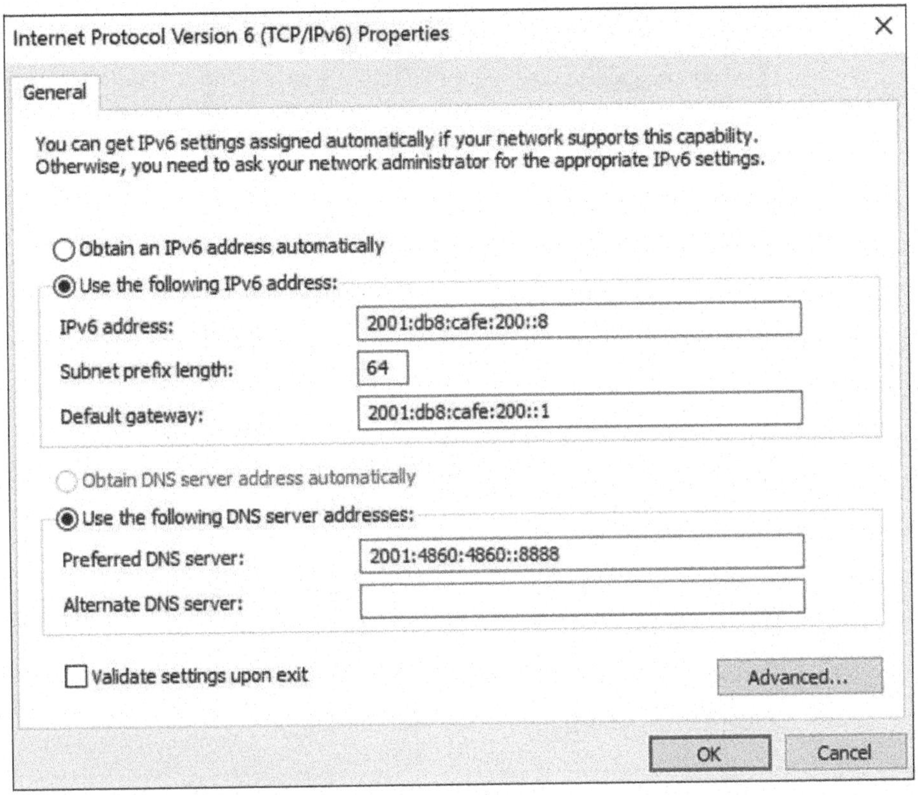

Figure 6-5   Static IPv6 Addressing

Dynamic Addressing (6.1.1.9)

Rather than manually configure every device, you can take advantage of dynamic addressing by using a *Dynamic Host Configuration Protocol (DHCP)* server. A DHCP server automatically assigns IP addresses, which simplifies the addressing process. Automatically configuring some of the IP addressing parameters also reduces the possibility of assigning duplicate or invalid IP addresses.

By default, most host devices are configured to request IP addressing from a DHCP server. Figure 6-6 shows the default setting for a Windows computer. When a computer is set to obtain an IP address automatically, all other IP addressing configuration boxes are not available. This process is the same for wired and wireless NICs.

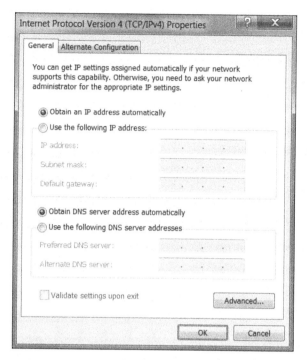

Figure 6-6   Configuring DHCP Addressing

A DHCP server can automatically assign the following IPv4 address configuration information to a host:

- IPv4 address
- Subnet mask
- Default gateway
- Optional values, such as a DNS server address

DHCP is also available for automatically assigning IPv6 addressing information.

Note

The steps to configure a Windows computer are beyond the scope of this course.

DNS (6.1.1.10)

DNS Records

When a client does not know the IP address of a web domain or an email domain name, it sends a DNS query to the DNS server identified in its IP configuration.

The DNS query may ask the DNS server:

- What is the IPv4 address for the xyz.com domain name?

- What is the IPv6 address for the xyz.com domain name?

- What is the IP address for emails forwarded to the @xyz.com domain name?

- Do you have additional information about the @xyz.com email domain?

To answer these types of questions, a DNS server keeps a list of domain names and IP addresses information in resource records (RRs). This list of RRs is stored on a DNS server in a DNS zone database.

When a server receives a DNS name query, it looks in its zone database for a matching RR to resolve the query. If it finds a match, it replies to the requesting host with the RR information. If there is no match, it queries a higher-level DNS server.

There are many types of DNS RRs. Table 6-7 lists some common types.

Table 6-7   Common DNS RR Types

RR	Description
A	An address (A) record is used to resolve a domain name to an IPv4 address.
AAAA	This RR is used to resolve a domain name to an IPv6 address.
MX	A Mail Exchange (MX) resource record identifies one or more email exchange servers that are responsible for accepting email messages on behalf of a domain name. MX records include a priority value (with the lowest integer preferred) when multiple email servers are available for redundancy.
TXT	A Text (TXT) record is used to provide textual information about a host, server, network, and more. This type of record is useful in distinguishing legitimate email servers from spam-generating servers.

Spam Management

Threat actors commonly abuse DNS to assist in their spam email campaigns. For this reason, DNS servers now implement anti-spam security features using TXT resource records (see Table 6-8).

Table 6-8   DNS Server Spam-Management Features

DNS Spam-Management Feature	Description
Sender Policy Framework (SPF)	The SPF is a special TXT resource record that identifies SMTP email servers authorized to send emails for an organization.
	The RR includes the IP address and email server domain name that receiving servers use to determine legitimacy of emails.
	There can only be one SPF RR per domain.
	The SPF can also indicate how to process unknown servers, including rejecting them, flagging them, or accepting them.
DomainKeys Identified Mail (DKIM)	DKIM is more advanced than SPF because it leverages cryptographic authentication using digital signatures instead of a list of authorized SMTP servers.
	The TXT RR contains the public encryption key of the sending domain that external email servers use to validate the authenticity of the sending email server.

DHCP Operation (6.1.1.11)

Dynamic Host Configuration Protocol (DHCP) works in client/server mode, where DHCP clients request available IP configurations from a DHCP server. A DHCP server is configured with a scope (that is, a pool or a range) of addresses that it can lease to requesting DHCP clients.

Note

A DHCP server can be a dedicated server or a router configured to provide DHCP services. The DHCP scope should not include manually assigned or reserved IP addresses such as the default gateway address, switch management address, or printer address.

As shown in Figure 6-7, when the DHCP client boots (or otherwise wants to join a network), it initiates the following four-step process to obtain a lease:

Step 1.   The DHCP client broadcasts a DHCPDISCOVER message to request an IP configuration from a DHCP server.

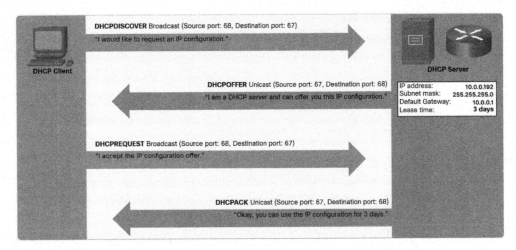

Figure 6-7   DHCP Four-Step Process to Obtain a Lease

Step 2.   The DHCP server chooses an available IP configuration from its configured scope and sends a DHCPOFFER unicast message to the client MAC address. The IP configuration can contain the IP address, subnet mask, default gateway, DNS servers, and period of time (i.e., the lease) that the host can use the IP configuration.

Step 3.   The client officially requests the IP configuration by sending a broadcast DHCPREQUEST message to the DHCP server.

Step 4.   The server removes the IP configuration from its pool of available IP configurations and sends a unicast acknowledgement (DHCPACK) to the DHCP client to confirm that it can use the address until the lease expires.

Note

DHCP messages are sent using UDP port 67 (servers) and UDP port 68 (clients). DHCP servers listen for client messages on UDP port 67, and DHCP clients listen for messages from servers on UDP port 68.

Figure 6-8 displays the DHCP process in Wireshark.

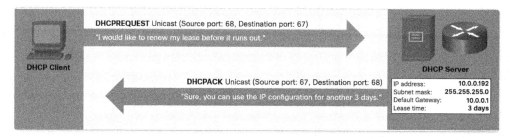

Figure 6-8 DHCP Process Captured by Wireshark

Once a client receives the DHCPACK from the server, it sends out an Address Resolution Protocol (ARP) message to the provided IP address to make sure it is not already assigned on the network. ARP is a network protocol that is used to discover the MAC address of a device using an IP address. If there is no response to the ARP request, the host can use the IP configuration. If the host receives an ARP reply, it restarts the DHCP process to obtain a different IP configuration.

DHCP Lease

A client must contact the DHCP server periodically to extend the lease, as shown in Figure 6-9. This lease mechanism ensures that moved or powered-off clients do not keep addresses that they no longer need. When a lease expires, the DHCP server returns the address to the pool, and it can be reallocated as necessary.

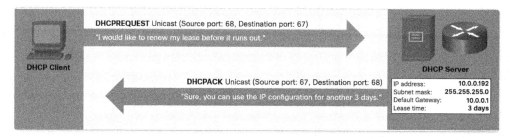

Figure 6-9 DHCP Address Renewal Process

DHCP Reservations

It is possible to ensure that a host, such as a particular server or printer, is always assigned the same IP address when it connects. To reserve IP addresses for hosts in this way, an administrator configures a DHCP server with a list of reserved IP addresses based on the requesting DHCP client's MAC address. Then, when a host sends a DHCPDISCOVER message, the DHCP server looks in its DHCP reserved address list for a matching MAC address. If it finds a match, it sends a DHCPOFFER message with the reserved IP address.

VLAN (6.1.1.12)

Virtual LANs (VLANs) provide segmentation and organizational flexibility in a switched network. A group of devices within a VLAN communicate as if all the devices were attached to the same switch. VLANs are based on logical connections instead of physical connections. An administrator can segment VLANs based on factors such as function, team, or application, without regard for the physical location of the users or devices.

In Figure 6-10, for example, a faculty member computer (PC1) is connected to S2 on VLAN 10. PC1 could communicate with another faculty member using PC4 connected to S3. Notice that both hosts are configured on network address 192.168.10.0/24.

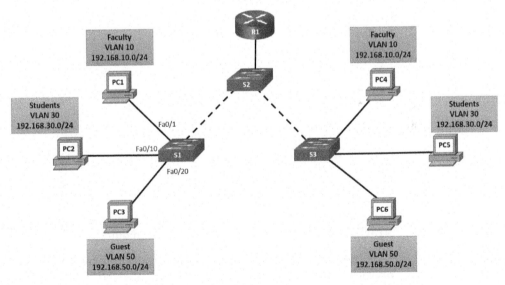

Figure 6-10   Example of a VLAN Topology

By default, all switch ports are assigned to VLAN 1. However, you can assign PCs to different VLANs by configuring their interconnecting port.

Example 6-2 shows a sample configuration of switch S2. Notice that you first create the VLANs and assign them names. This makes it easier to work with the VLANs. Next, you configure the ports connecting the PCs to the corresponding VLANs.

Example 6-2 VLAN Configuration for Switch S2

```
S2(config)# vlan 10
S2(config-vlan)# name Faculty
S2(config-vlan)# exit
S2(config)#
S2(config)# vlan 30
S2(config-vlan)# name Students
S2(config-vlan)# exit
S2(config)#
S2(config)# vlan 50
S2(config-vlan)# name Guest
S2(config-vlan)# exit
S2(config)#
S2(config)# interface fastethernet 0/1
S2(config-if)# switchport mode access
S2(config-if)# switchport access vlan 10
S2(config-if)# exit
S2(config)#
S2(config)# interface fa0/10
S2(config-if)# switchport mode access
S2(config-if)# switchport access vlan 20
S2(config-if)# exit
S2(config)#
S2(config)# interface fa0/20
S2(config-if)# switchport mode access
S2(config-if)# switchport access vlan 50
S2(config-if)# exit
S2(config)#
```

Once the VLAN information is configured on the other switches, the faculty member using PC1 would be able to communicate with PC4 because they are on the same VLAN. If the faculty member wanted to send something to PC5, which is assigned to VLAN 30, the services of a router would be required.

VLANs help reduce excessive broadcast traffic and implement access and security policies between groups of users.

Link-Local IPv4 and IPv6 Addresses (6.1.1.13)

A device uses *link-local addresses* for IPv4 and IPv6 to communicate with other computers connected to the same network within the same IP address range. This is the major difference between IPv4 and IPv6 link-local addresses:

- An IPv4 device uses the link-local address if the device cannot obtain an IPv4 address.

■ An IPv6 device must always be dynamically or manually configured with a link-local IPv6 address.

IPv4 Link-Local Address

If your Windows computer cannot communicate with a DHCP server to obtain an IPv4 address, Windows automatically uses *Automatic Private IP Addressing (APIPA)* to assign an address. This link-local address is in the range 169.254.0.0 to 169.254.255.255.

IPv6 Link-Local Address

Like an IPv4 link-local address, an IPv6 link-local address enables a device to communicate with other IPv6-enabled devices on the same network and only on that network. Unlike with IPv4, every IPv6-enabled device is required to have a link-local address. IPv6 link-local addresses are in the range fe80:: to febf::. For example, in Figure 6-11, the links to other networks are down (not connected), as indicated by the red Xs. However, all the devices on the LAN can still use link-local IPv6 addresses to communicate with each other.

Note

Unlike IPv4 link-local addresses, IPv6 link-local addresses are used in a variety of processes, including with network discovery protocols and routing protocols. However, these concepts are beyond the scope of this course.

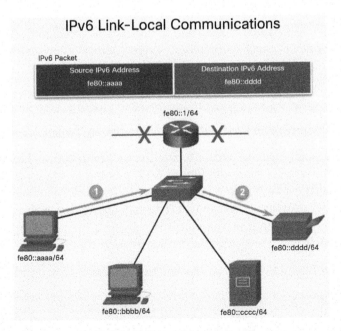

Figure 6-11   IPv6 Link-Local Communications

Check Your Understanding 6.1.1.14: Network Addressing

Refer to the online course to complete this activity.

Configure a NIC (6.1.2)

A network interface card (*NIC*) is computer hardware that contains the electronic circuitry required to communicate using a wired connection or a wireless connection. A network interface card is also known as a network interface controller, network adapter, or local area network (LAN) adapter. It needs to be configured with TCP/IP and other settings, such as DHCP or static addressing, in order to provide connectivity between network devices.

Packet Tracer
☐ Activity

Packet Tracer 6.1.2.1: Add Computers to an Existing Network

Cisco Packet Tracer is a network simulation program used to facilitate learning about networking technology. In this Packet Tracer activity, you will configure computers to use DHCP, configure static addressing, use **ipconfig** to retrieve host IPv4 information, and use **ping** to verify connectivity.

Network Design (6.1.2.2)

As a computer technician, you must be able to support the networking needs of your customers. Therefore, you must be familiar with:

- *Network components*: You need to understand wired and wireless NICs and network devices such as switches, wireless access points (APs), routers, multipurpose devices, and more.

- *Network design*: You need to know how networks are interconnected to support the needs of a business. For instance, the needs of a small business differ greatly from the needs of a large business.

Consider a small business with 10 employees. The business has contracted you to connect its users. As shown in Figure 6-12, a home or small office wireless router could be used for such a small number of users. Such routers are multipurpose and typically provide router, switch, firewall, and access point capabilities. In addition, these wireless routers often provide a variety of other services, including DHCP.

In small businesses and homes, wireless routers perform the role of access point, Ethernet switch, and router.

Figure 6-12 Typical Home Network

If the business were much larger, you would not use a wireless router. Instead, you would consult with a network architect to design a network of dedicated switches, access points (APs), firewall appliances, and routers.

Regardless of the network design, you must know how to install network cards, connect wired and wireless devices, and configure basic network equipment.

Note

This chapter focuses on connecting and configuring a small office or home wireless router. The configurations are demonstrated using Packet Tracer. However, the same functionality and similar graphical user interface (GUI) elements exist in all wireless routers. You can purchase a variety of low-cost wireless routers online and from consumer electronics stores. Search the Internet for "wireless router reviews" to research current recommendations.

Selecting a NIC (6.1.2.3)

A NIC is required to connect to a network. As shown in Figure 6-13, there are different types of NICs. Ethernet NICs are used to connect to Ethernet networks, and wireless NICs are used to connect to 802.11 wireless networks. Most NICs in desktop computers are integrated into the motherboard or connected to expansion slots. NICs are also available in a USB form factor.

Figure 6-13   Selecting a NIC

Many computers purchased today come with a wired and wireless NIC integrated on the motherboard.

Installing and Updating a NIC (6.1.2.4)

Read the user's guide and follow the steps to install the adapter card if you are installing a NIC inside the computer. A wireless NIC for a desktop device has an external antenna connected to the back of the card or attached with a cable so that it can be positioned for the best signal reception. You must connect and position the antenna.

Sometimes a manufacturer publishes new driver software for a NIC. A new driver might enhance the functionality of the NIC, or it might be needed for operating system compatibility. The latest drivers for all supported operating systems are available for download from the manufacturer's website.

When installing a new driver, disable virus protection software to ensure that the driver installs correctly. Some virus scanners detect a driver update as a possible virus attack. Install only one driver at a time; otherwise, some updating processes might conflict. A best practice is to close all applications that are running so that they are not using any files associated with the driver update.

Note

Figure 6-14 shows an example of Windows Device Manager and the place to update a NIC's driver; however, details of how to update drivers for specific devices and operating systems are beyond the scope of this course.

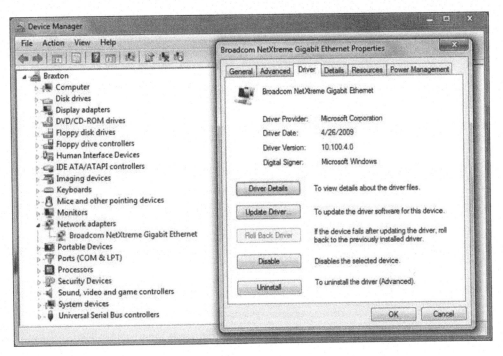

Figure 6-14   NIC Driver Management

Configure a NIC (6.1.2.5)

After a NIC driver is installed, the IP address settings must be configured. For Windows computers, IP addressing is dynamic by default. After you physically connect a Windows computer to the network, it automatically sends out a request for IPv4 addressing from the DHCP server. If a DHCP server is available, the computer receives a message with all its IPv4 addressing information.

Note

Dynamic addressing for IPv6 can also use DHCP but is beyond the scope of this course.

This dynamic default behavior is also typical for smartphones, tablets, gaming consoles, and other end-user devices. Static configuration is normally the job of a network administrator. However, you should be familiar with how to access the IP addressing configuration for any device you are asked to manage.

To find IP addressing configuration information, search the Internet for "IP address configuration for *device*," replacing *device* with your device, such as iPhone. For example, Figure 6-15 shows the dialog box for viewing and changing a Windows computer's IPv6 configuration.

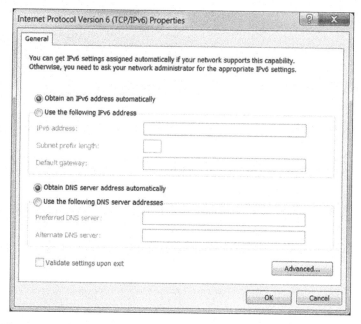

Figure 6-15 Configuring Automatic and Manual IPv4 Address Settings

Figure 6-16 shows the setting screens for automatic and manual IPv4 configuration on an iPhone.

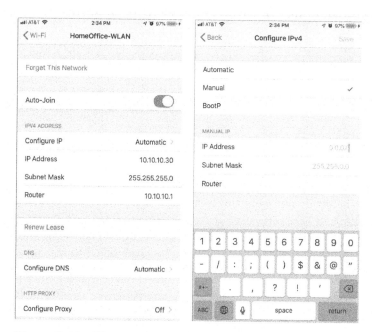

Figure 6-16 iPhone IP Address Settings

ICMP (6.1.2.6)

Devices on a network use *Internet Control Message Protocol (ICMP)* to send control and error messages. There are several different uses for ICMP, such as announcing network errors, announcing network congestion, and troubleshooting.

The *ping* command is commonly used to test connections between computers. To see a list of options that you can use with the **ping** command, type **ping /?** in the command prompt window, as shown in Example 6-3.

Example 6-3   Displaying **ping** Help Information

```
C:\> ping /?

Usage: ping [-t] [-a] [-n count] [-l size] [-f] [-i TTL] [-v TOS]
            [-r count] [-s count] [[-j host-list] | [-k host-list]]
            [-w timeout] [-R] [-S srcaddr] [-4] [-6] target_name

Options:
    -t              Ping the specified host until stopped.
                    To see statistics and continue - type Control-Break;
                    To stop - type Control-C.
    -a              Resolve addresses to hostnames.
   n count          Number of echo requests to send.
   -l size          Send buffer size.
   -f Set           Don't Fragment flag in packet (IPv4-only).
   -i TTL           Time To Live.
   -v TOS           Type Of Service (IPv4-only. This setting has been deprecated
                    and has no effect on the type of service field in the IP
                    Header).
   -r count         Record route for count hops (IPv4-only).
   -s count         Timestamp for count hops (IPv4-only).
   -j host-list     Loose source route along host-list (IPv4-only).
   -k host-list     Strict source route along host-list (IPv4-only).
   -w timeout       Timeout in milliseconds to wait for each reply.
   -R               Use routing header to test reverse route also (IPv6-only).
   -S srcaddr       Source address to use.
   -4               Force using IPv4.
   -6               Force using IPv6.

C:\>
```

ping works by sending an ICMP echo request to the IP address you entered. If the IP address is accessible, the receiving device sends back an ICMP echo reply message to confirm connectivity.

You can also use the **ping** command to test connectivity to a website by entering the website's domain name. For example, if you enter **ping cisco.com**, your computer first uses DNS to find the IP address and then sends the ICMP echo request to that IP address, as shown in Example 6-4.

Example 6-4   Testing Connectivity with **ping**

```
>C:\> ping cisco.com

Pinging e144.dscb.akamaiedge.net [23.200.16.170] with 32 bytes of data:
Reply from 23.200.16.170: bytes=32 time=25ms TTL=54
Reply from 23.200.16.170: bytes=32 time=26ms TTL=54
Reply from 23.200.16.170: bytes=32 time=25ms TTL=54
Reply from 23.200.16.170: bytes=32 time=25ms TTL=54

Ping statistics for 23.200.16.170:
    Packets: Sent = 4, Received = 4, Lost = 0 (0% loss),
Approximate round trip times in milli-seconds:
    Minimum = 25ms, Maximum = 26ms, Average = 25ms

C:\>
```

Lab 6.1.2.7: Configure a NIC to Use DHCP in Windows

In this lab, you will configure an Ethernet NIC to use DHCP to obtain an IP address and test connectivity between two computers.

Configure a Wired and Wireless Network (6.1.3)

Wired and wireless networks allow computers and other devices to communicate with each other so that users can connect to the Internet and share files, software, printers, and various other devices. Networks can be either wired, wireless, or a combination of the two types.

A *wired network* is a network that uses physical media such as copper cables to transfer data between connected devices. A *wireless network* uses radio signal frequencies for communication between network devices. It is also called a *Wi-Fi network* or a *WLAN*.

Wireless networks provide convenience in network access and mobility. Wireless setup can be easier than with a wired network, and advances in wireless network technology have reduced the speed and security differences between wired and wireless networks.

Video Explanation 6.1.3.1: Configure a Wired and Wireless Network

Refer to the online course to view this video.

Video

Connecting Wired Devices to the Internet (6.1.3.2)

The steps to connect a wired device to the Internet in a home or small office are as follows:

Step 1.   Connect a network cable to the device. To connect to a wired network, attach an Ethernet cable to the NIC port, as shown in Figure 6-17.

Figure 6-17   Connecting a Network Cable to the Device

Step 2.   Connect the device to a switch port. Connect the other end of the cable to an Ethernet port on the wireless router, such as one of the four yellow switch ports shown in Figure 6-18. In a SOHO network, the laptop would most likely connect to a wall jack, which in turn would connect to a network switch.

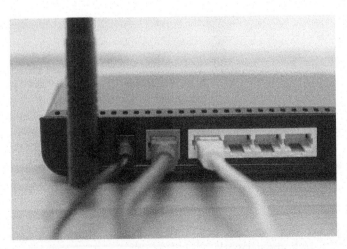

Figure 6-18   Connecting the Device to a Switch Port

Step 3.   Connect a network cable to the wireless router Internet port. On the wireless router, connect an Ethernet cable to the port labeled Internet (the blue port in Figure 6-18). This port might also be labeled WAN.

Step 4.   Connect the wireless router to the modem. The blue port in Figure 6-18 is an Ethernet port that is used to connect the router to a service provider device such as a DSL or cable modem (see Figure 6-19).

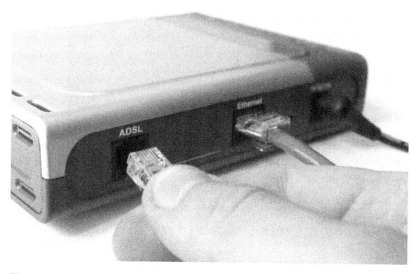

Figure 6-19   Connecting the Wireless Router to the Modem

Step 5.   Connect to the service provider's network.

Note

A separate modem isn't necessary if the wireless router is a router/modem combination.

Step 6.   Power all devices and verify physical connections. Turn on the broadband modem and plug in the power cord to the router. After the modem establishes a connection to the ISP, it begins communicating with the router. The laptop, router, and modem LEDs light up, indicating communication. The modem enables the router to receive the network information necessary to gain access to the Internet from the ISP. This information includes public IPv4 addresses, subnet mask, and DNS server addresses. With the depletion of public IPv4 addresses, many ISPs are providing IPv6 addressing information as well.

Figure 6-20 shows a topology depicting the physical connection of a wired laptop in a small office or home network.

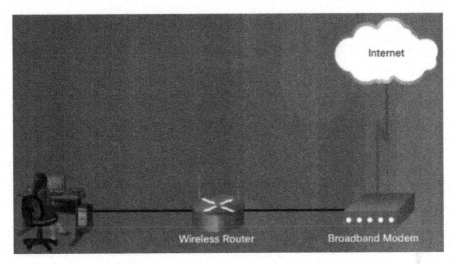

Figure 6-20   Small Office or Home Wired Network

Note

Cable or DSL modem configuration is usually done by the service provider's representative either on site or remotely through a walkthrough with you on the phone. If you buy a modem, it will come with documentation for how to connect it to your service provider, which will most likely include contacting your service provider for more information.

Logging in to the Router (6.1.3.3)

Most home and small office wireless routers are ready for service out of the box and are preconfigured to be connected to the network and provide service. For example, a wireless router uses DHCP to automatically provide addressing information to connected devices. However, wireless router default IP addresses, usernames, and passwords can easily be found on the Internet. Just enter the search phrase "default wireless router IP address" or "default wireless router passwords" to see a list of many websites that provide this information. For security reasons, your first priority should be to change these defaults.

To gain access to a wireless router's configuration GUI, open a web browser. In the address field, enter the default IP address for your wireless router. The default IP address can be found in the documentation that came with the wireless router, or you can search the Internet. Figure 6-21 shows the IPv4 address 192.168.0.1, which is a common default for many manufacturers. A security window prompts for authorization to access the router GUI. The word admin is commonly used as the default username and password. Again, check your wireless router's documentation or search the Internet.

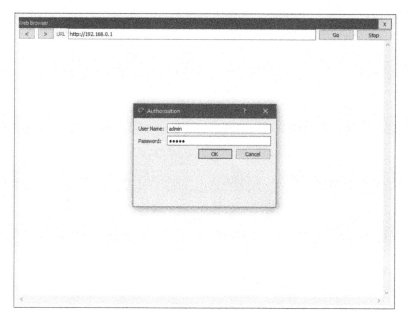

Figure 6-21   Logging into a Router

Basic Network Setup (6.1.3.4)

The basic setup of a network is performed using the following six steps:

Step 1.   Log in to the router from a web browser. You now see a GUI that has tabs or menus to help you navigate to various router configuration tasks (see Figure 6-22). It is often necessary to save the settings changed in one window before proceeding to another window. It is a best practice to make changes to the default settings.

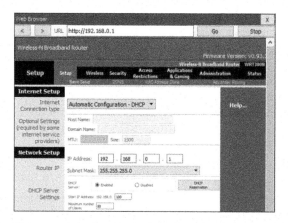

Figure 6-22   Logging into a Router Using a Browser

Step 2.   Change the default administrative password. To change the default login password, find the administration portion of the router's GUI. In the example in Figure 6-23, the Administration tab is selected. This is where the router password can be changed. On some devices, such as the one in the example, you can only change the password, and the username remains admin or whatever the default username is for the router you are configuring.

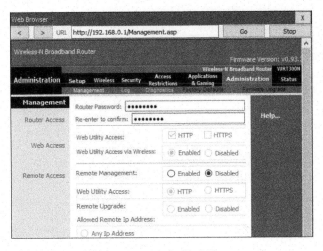

Figure 6-23   Changing the Default Password

Step 3.   Log in with the new password. After you save the new password, the wireless router requests authorization again. Enter the username and new password, as shown in Figure 6-24.

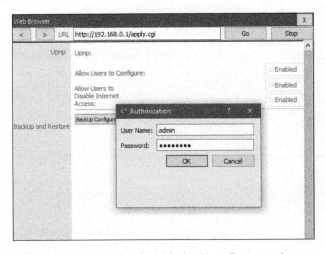

Figure 6-24   Logging in with the New Password

Step 4.   Change the default DHCP IPv4 addresses. It is a best practice to use private IPv4 addressing inside your network. The IPv4 address 10.10.10.1 is used in the example in Figure 6-25, but it could be any private IPv4 address you choose. Search the Internet for "private IP addressing" to learn more.

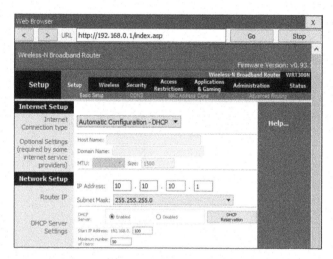

Figure 6-25   Changing the DHCP IPv4 Addresses

Step 5.   When you click Save, you temporarily lose access to the wireless router, so renew the IP address. To do so, open a command window and renew your IP address with the **ipconfig /renew** command, as shown in Figure 6-26.

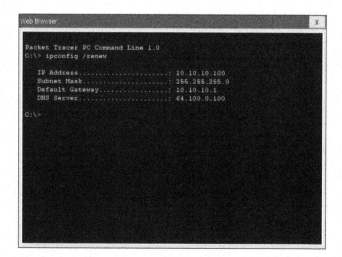

Figure 6-26   Renewing the IP Address

Step 6.   Log in at the new IP address by entering the router's new IP address to regain access to the router configuration GUI, as shown in Figure 6-27. You are now ready to continue configuring the router for wireless access.

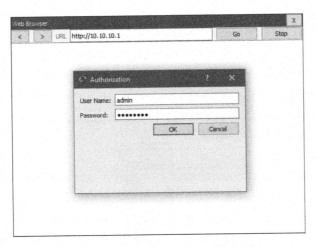

Figure 6-27   Logging in at the New IP Address

Basic Wireless Settings (6.1.3.5)

The basic wireless setup of a network is performed using the following six steps:

Step 1.   View the WLAN defaults. Out of the box, a wireless router provides wireless access to devices using a default wireless network name and password. The network name is the *service set identifier (SSID)*. Locate the basic wireless settings for your router to change these defaults, as shown in Figure 6-28.

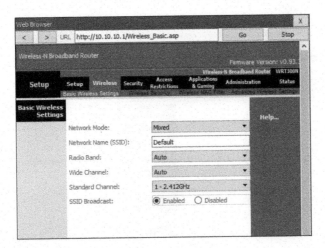

Figure 6-28   Viewing the WLAN Defaults

Step 2.   Change the network mode. Some wireless routers allow you to select which *802.11 standard* to implement. The example in Figure 6-29 shows that Mixed has been selected. This means wireless devices connecting to the wireless router can have a variety of wireless radios installed. Today's wireless routers that are configured for mixed mode most likely support 802.11a, 802.11n, and 802.11ac NICs.

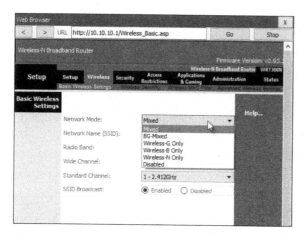

Figure 6-29   Changing the Network Mode

Step 3.   Assign an SSID to the wireless LAN (WLAN), as shown in Figure 6-30. OfficeNet is used in this example. The wireless router announces its presence by sending broadcasts advertising its SSID. This allows wireless hosts to automatically discover the name of the wireless network. If the SSID broadcast is disabled, you must manually enter the SSID on each wireless device that connects to the WLAN.

Figure 6-30   Configuring the SSID

Step 4.   Configure the channel, as shown in Figure 6-31. Devices configured with the same channel within the 2.4 GHz band may overlap and cause distortion, slowing down the wireless performance and potentially breaking network connections. The solution to avoid interference is to configure non-overlapping channels on the wireless routers and access points that are near each other. Specifically, channels 1, 6, and 11 are non-overlapping. In the example in Figure 6-31, the wireless router is configured to use channel 6.

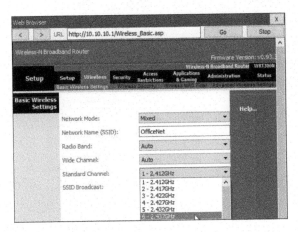

Figure 6-31   Configuring the Channel

Step 5.   Configure the security mode. Out of the box, a wireless router may have no WLAN security configured. In the example shown in Figure 6-32, the personal version of Wi-Fi Protected Access version 2 (WPA2 Personal) is selected. WPA2 with Advanced Encryption Standard (AES) is currently the strongest security mode.

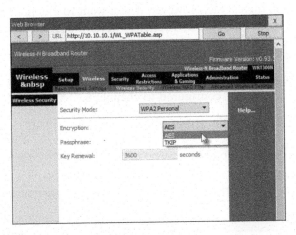

Figure 6-32   Configuring the Security Mode

Step 6.   Configure the passphrase, as shown in Figure 6-33. WPA2 Personal uses a passphrase to authenticate wireless clients. WPA2 Personal is easier to use in a small office or home environment because it does not require an authentication server. Larger organizations implement WPA2 Enterprise and require wireless clients to authenticate with a username and password.

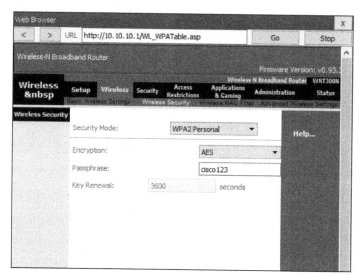

Figure 6-33   Configuring the Passphrase

Configure a Wireless Mesh Network (6.1.3.6)

In a small office or home network, one wireless router may suffice to provide wireless access to all the clients. However, if you want to extend the range beyond approximately 45 meters indoors or 90 meters outdoors, you can add wireless access points. In the wireless mesh network in Figure 6-34, two access points are configured with the same WLAN settings from our previous example. Notice that the channels selected are 1 and 11 so that the access points do not interfere with the wireless router, which was previously configured to channel 6.

Extending a WLAN in a small office or home has become increasingly easy. Manufacturers have made creating a *wireless mesh network (WMN)* simple through smartphone apps. You buy a system, disperse the access points, plug them in, download the app, and configure your WMN in a few steps. Search the Internet for "best Wi-Fi mesh network system" to find reviews of current offerings.

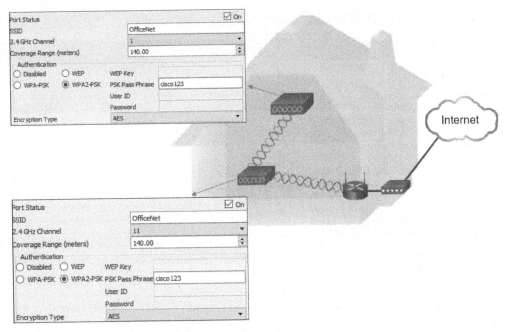

Figure 6-34   Wireless Mesh Network in a Home

NAT for IPv4 (6.1.3.7)

On a wireless router, if you look for a page like the Status page shown in Figure 6-35, you will find the IPv4 addressing information that the router uses to send data to the Internet. Notice that the IPv4 address 209.165.201.11 is a different network than the 10.10.10.1 address assigned to the router's LAN interface. All the devices on the router's LAN will be assigned addresses with the 10.10.10 prefix.

The 209.165.201.11 IPv4 address is publicly routable on the Internet. Any address with 10 in the first octet is a private IPv4 address and cannot be routed on the Internet. With the 10.10.10.1 address, the router will use a process called *Network Address Translation (NAT)* to convert private IPv4 addresses to Internet-routable IPv4 addresses. With NAT, a private (local) source IPv4 address is translated to a public (global) address. The process is reversed for incoming packets. The router is able to translate many internal IPv4 addresses into public addresses by using NAT.

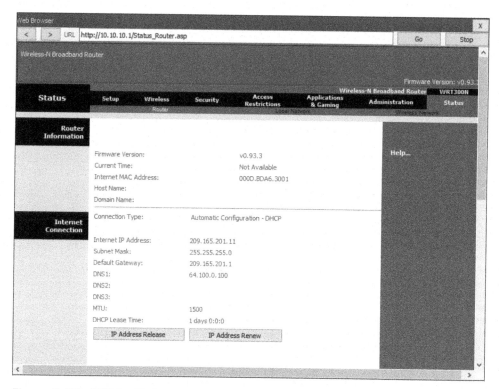

Figure 6-35   NAT for IPv4

Some ISPs use private addressing to connect to customer devices. However, eventually, your traffic will leave the provider's network and be routed on the Internet. To see the IP addresses for your devices, search the Internet for "what is my IP address." Do this for other devices on the same network, and you will see that they all share the same public IPv4 address. NAT makes this possible by tracking the source port numbers for every session established by a device. If your ISP has IPv6 enabled, you will see a unique IPv6 address for each device.

Quality of Service (6.1.3.8)

Many home and small office routers have an option for configuring *quality of service (QoS)*. By configuring QoS, you can guarantee that certain traffic types, such as voice and video, are prioritized over traffic that is not as time sensitive, such as email and web browsing. On some wireless routers, traffic can also be prioritized on specific ports.

Figure 6-36 is a simplified mockup of a QoS interface based on a Netgear GUI. You usually find the QoS settings in the advanced menus. If you have a wireless router available, investigate the QoS settings. Sometimes they are listed under "bandwidth control" or something similar. Consult the wireless router's documentation or search the Internet for "QoS settings" for your router's make and model.

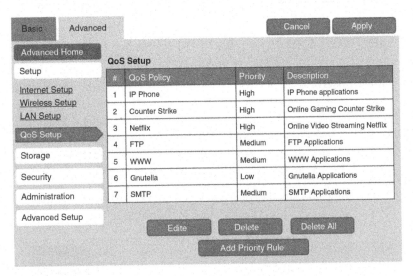

QoS Setup

#	QoS Policy	Priority	Description
1	IP Phone	High	IP Phone applications
2	Counter Strike	High	Online Gaming Counter Strike
3	Netflix	High	Online Video Streaming Netflix
4	FTP	Medium	FTP Applications
5	WWW	Medium	WWW Applications
6	Gnutella	Low	Gnutella Applications
7	SMTP	Medium	SMTP Applications

Figure 6-36   Typical Wireless Router QoS Interface

Packet Tracer 6.1.3.9: Connect to a Wireless Network

In this Packet Tracer activity, you will configure a wireless router and an access point to accept wireless clients and route IP packets.

Lab 6.1.3.10: Configure a Wireless Network

In this lab, you will configure basic settings on a wireless router and connect a PC to a router wirelessly.

Firewall Settings (6.1.4)

In most network infrastructures, firewalls provide an essential layer of security. A *firewall* is an important security application. One of its roles is to block unauthorized access to your network, and another role is to permit authorized data communications to and from your computer. Firewalls can be either network firewalls or host-based firewalls.

Network firewalls filter traffic between two or more networks and run on network hardware. Host-based firewalls run on host computers and control network traffic into and out of those machines. They are configured with rules and exceptions that are applied to both inbound and outbound traffic, and the rules are applied based on several conditions.

Video Explanation 6.1.4.1: Firewall Settings

Refer to the online course to view this video.

UPnP (6.1.4.2)

Universal Plug and Play (UPnP) is a protocol that enables devices to dynamically add themselves to a network without the need for user intervention or configuration. Although convenient, UPnP is not secure. The UPnP protocol has no method for authenticating devices, and it considers every device trustworthy. In addition, the UPnP protocol has numerous security vulnerabilities. For example, malware can use the UPnP protocol to redirect traffic to different IP addresses outside the network, potentially sending sensitive information to a hacker.

Many home and small office wireless routers have UPnP enabled by default. Therefore, you should check this configuration and disable it, as shown in Figure 6-37.

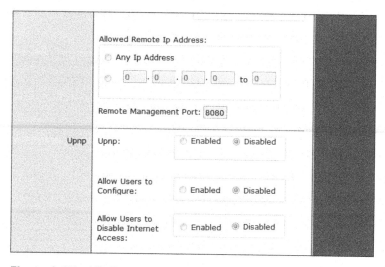

Figure 6-37   UPnP

Search the Internet for "vulnerability profiling tools" to determine whether your wireless router is exposed to UPnP vulnerabilities.

DMZ (6.1.4.3)

A *demilitarized zone (DMZ)* is a network that provides services to an untrusted network. An email, web, or FTP server is often placed into the DMZ so that the traffic using the server does not come inside the local network. This protects the internal network from attacks by this traffic but does not protect the servers in the DMZ in any way. It is common for a firewall to manage traffic to and from the DMZ.

On a wireless router, you can create a DMZ for one device by forwarding all traffic ports from the Internet to a specific IP address or MAC address. A server, game machine, or web camera can be in the DMZ so that the device can be accessed by anyone. For example, the web server in Figure 6-38 is in the DMZ and is statically assigned the IPv4 address 10.10.10.50.

Figure 6-38   Simple DMZ Scenario

Figure 6-39 shows a typical configuration in which any traffic sources from the Internet will be redirected to the web server's IPv4 address 10.10.10.50. However, the web server is exposed to attacks from hackers on the Internet and should have firewall software installed.

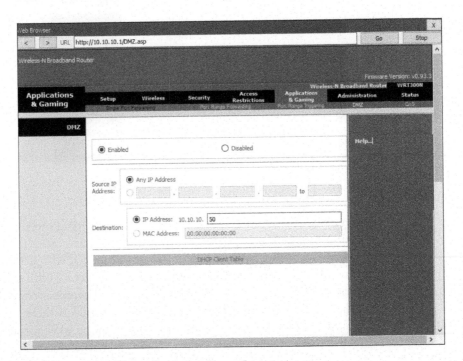

Figure 6-39   DMZ Configuration Example

Port Forwarding (6.1.4.4)

Hardware firewalls can be used to block TCP and UDP ports to prevent unauthorized access into and out of a LAN. However, there are situations when specific ports must be opened so that certain programs and applications can communicate with devices on different networks. *Port forwarding* is a rule-based method of directing traffic between devices on different networks.

When traffic reaches a router, the router determines if the traffic should be forwarded to a certain device based on the port number found with the traffic. *Port numbers* are associated with specific services, such as FTP, HTTP, HTTPS, and POP3. The rules determine which traffic is sent on to the LAN. For example, a router might be configured to forward port 80, which is associated with HTTP. When the router receives a packet with the destination port 80, the router forwards the traffic to the server inside the network that serves web pages. In Figure 6-40, port forwarding is enabled for port 80 and is associated with the web server at IPv4 address 10.10.10.50.

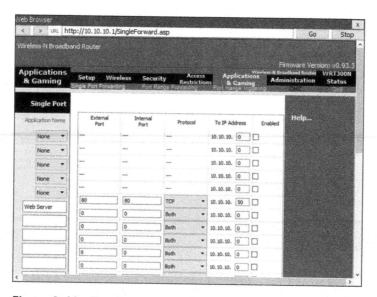

Figure 6-40   Port Forwarding to a Web Server

Port triggering allows a router to temporarily forward data through inbound ports to a specific device. You can use port triggering to forward data to a computer only when a designated port range is used to make an outbound request. For example, a video game might use ports 27000 to 27100 for connecting with other players. These are the trigger ports. A chat client might use port 56 for connecting the same players so that they can interact with each other. In this instance, if there is gaming traffic on an outbound port within the triggered port range, inbound chat traffic on port 56 is forwarded to the computer that is being used to play the video game and chat with friends. When the game is over and the triggered ports are no longer in use, port 56 is no longer allowed to send traffic of any type to this computer.

MAC Address Filtering (6.1.4.5)

MAC address filtering specifies exactly which MAC addresses are allowed or blocked from sending data on a network. Many wireless routers only give you the option of allowing or blocking MAC addresses—and not both. Technicians typically configure allowed MAC addresses. You can find the MAC address for your Windows computer by using the **ipconfig /all** command, as shown in Example 6-5.

Example 6-5   Laptop Addressing Information

```
C:\> ipconfig /all

Windows IP Configuration

    Host Name . . . . . . . . . . . . : ITEuser
    Primary Dns Suffix . . . . . . . :
    Node Type . . . . . . . . . . . . : Hybrid
    IP Routing Enabled. . . . . . . . : No
    WINS Proxy Enabled. . . . . . . . : No


Ethernet adapter Local Area Connection:

    Connection-specific DNS Suffix . :
    Description . . . . . . . . . . . : Intel(R) PRO/1000 MT Network Connection
Physical Address. . . . . . . . . : 00-50-56-BE-D7-87
    DHCP Enabled. . . . . . . . . . . : No
    Autoconfiguration Enabled . . . . : Yes
IPv6 Address. . . . . . . . . . . :  2001:db8:cafe:200::8(Preferred)
    Link-local IPv6 Address . . . . . : fe80::8cbf:a682:d2e0:98a%11(Preferred)
IPv4 Address. . . . . . . . . . . :  192.168.200.8(Preferred)
    Subnet Mask . . . . . . . . . . . : 255.255.255.0
    Default Gateway . . . . . . . . . : 2001:db8:cafe:200::1
                                        192.168.200.1

C:\
```

You might need to search the Internet for where to find the MAC address on a specific device. Finding the MAC address is not always straightforward because not all devices call it a MAC address. For example, Windows calls it a *physical address*, as shown in Example 6-5. On an iPhone, it is called the *Wi-Fi address*, and on an Android, it is called the *Wi-Fi MAC address*, as shown in Figure 6-41.

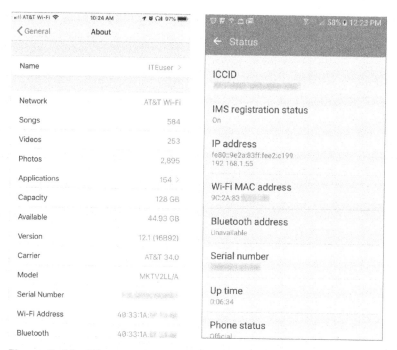

Figure 6-41   iPhone and Android MAC Addresses

In addition, a device might have two or more MAC addresses. For example, the PlayStation 4 in Figure 6-42 has two MAC addresses: one for wired networks and one for wireless networks.

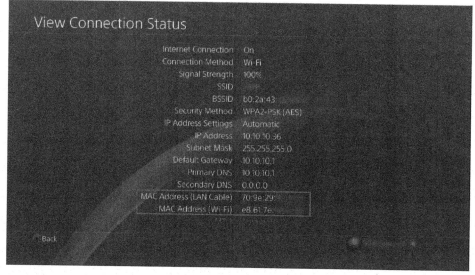

Figure 6-42   MAC Addresses on a PlayStation 4

Similarly, a Windows PC might have multiple MAC addresses. For example, the PC in Example 6-6 has three MAC addresses: wired, wireless, and virtual.

Example 6-6   Multiple MAC Addresses on a Windows PC

```
C:\> ipconfig /all

Windows IP Configuration
<output omitted>


Ethernet adapter Ethernet:

<output omitted>
    Physical Address. . . . . . . . . : 44-A8-42-XX-XX-XX
    DHCP Enabled. . . . . . . . . . .  : Yes
    Autoconfiguration Enabled . . . . : Yes

Ethernet adapter VirtualBox Host-Only Network:

    Connection-specific DNS Suffix .    :
    Description . . . . . . . . . . .    : VirtualBox Host-Only Ethernet Adapter
    Physical Address. . . . . . . . . : 0A-00-27-XX-XX-XX
<output omitted>

Wireless LAN adapter Wi-Fi:

    Connection-specific DNS Suffix . : lan
    Description . . . . . . . . . . .: Intel(R) Dual Band Wireless-AC 3165
    Physical Address. . . . . . . . . : E0-94-67-XX-XX-XX
<output omitted>

C:\>
```

Note

The last half of the MAC addresses and other identifying information is blurred out in Figures 6-41 and 6-42. The last six hexadecimal numbers are replaced with Xs in Example 6-6.

Finally, new devices might be added to the network at any time. You can see that a technician responsible for manually configuring all these MAC addresses might be overwhelmed. Imagine having to manually enter and maintain dozens of MAC addresses in an interface such as the one shown in Figure 6-43.

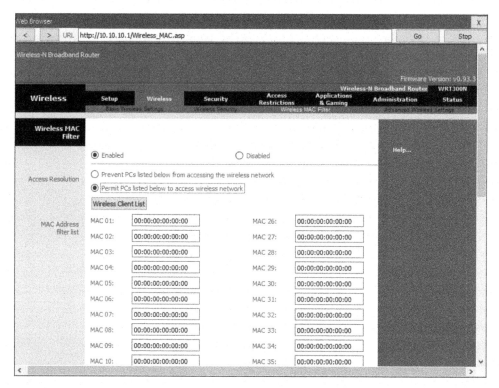

Figure 6-43   MAC Address Filter Configuration GUI

However, MAC address filtering may be your only option. Better solutions, such as port security, require a more expensive router or a separate firewall device and are beyond the scope of this course.

Whitelisting and Blacklisting (6.1.4.6)

Whitelisting and *blacklisting* involve specifying which IP addresses are allowed or denied on a network. Much as with MAC address filtering, you can manually configure specific IP addresses to be allowed or denied on your network. On a wireless router, this is typically done using an access list or access policy, as shown in Figure 6-44. Refer to your wireless router's documentation for specific steps or search the Internet for a tutorial.

Whitelisting is a good tool for allowing users, such as children or employees, access to IP addresses that you approve. You can also blacklist, or explicitly block, known sites. However, much like MAC address filtering, this can become burdensome. Better solutions exist. Search the Internet for "parental control software" and "content filters."

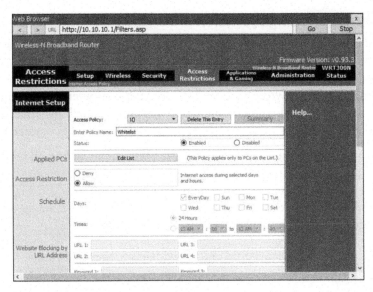

Figure 6-44   Whitelist Configuration

Packet Tracer 6.1.4.7: Configure Firewall Settings

In this Packet Tracer activity, you will configure a wireless router to rely on MAC filtering, allow access to a server in the DMZ, and disable the DMZ and configure support for single port forwarding.

Lab 6.1.4.8: Configure Firewall Settings

In this lab, you will configure firewall settings to use MAC address filtering, a DMZ, and single port forwarding on a wireless router to manage connections and traffic through the wireless router.

IoT Device Configuration (6.1.5)

Thanks to the Internet of Things (*IoT*), common everyday devices have become part of the Internet. The IoT extends connectivity beyond standard devices, like computers and smartphones, to include devices such as refrigerators and TVs that are embedded with sensors and other technology to allow them to become part of the network. The "things" can be common objects, but the possibilities are limitless in terms of what can become a device that is able to be connected. Connectivity and usage of IoT devices can provide insights into how consumers and businesses interact with the devices, services, and applications they provide. IoT devices provide real-time communication of data associated with users and their environment by connecting all the things to the Internet.

Internet of Things (6.1.5.1)

The Internet today is significantly different from the Internet of past decades. The Internet of today is more than email, web pages, and file transfers between computers. The evolving Internet is becoming an Internet of Things (IoT). No longer are the only devices accessing the Internet computers, tablets, and smartphones. Sensor-equipped, Internet-ready devices include everything from automobiles and biomedical devices to household appliances and natural ecosystems.

You may have some IoT devices in your home. You can buy all kinds of connected devices, including thermostats, light switches, security cameras, door locks, and voice-enabled digital assistants (such as Amazon Alexis and Google Home). These devices can all be connected to your network. In addition, many of them can be directly managed from a smartphone app (see Figure 6-45).

Figure 6-45   Internet of Things

IoT Devices in Packet Tracer (6.1.5.2)

At this point in its infancy, the IoT market has not yet agreed upon a set of standards for IoT device installation and configuration. Configuring IoT devices is very much device specific. Consult the manufacturer's documentation or website for configuration guides.

In this course, you will use Packet Tracer to explore a basic IoT device configuration. Figure 6-46 shows all the IoT devices in Packet Tracer. Packet Tracer also includes a number of sensors and actuators. In Figure 6-46, the sensors are shown in the bottom panel of the Packet Tracer interface.

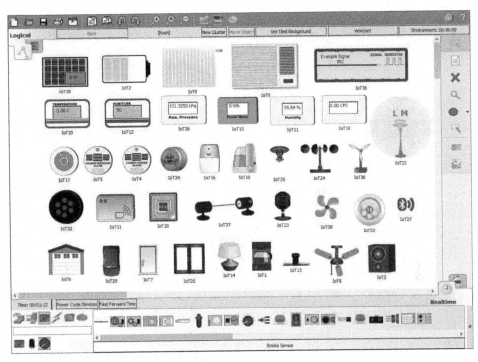

Figure 6-46   IoT Devices in Packet Tracer

Packet Tracer
☐ Activity

Packet Tracer 6.1.5.3: Control IoT Devices

In this Packet Tracer activity, you have just installed various IoT devices around the house and wish to configure them as a home security system. You will configure the home gateway to use a motion sensor, test and reset security features, and set the air conditioning.

The Basic Networking Troubleshooting Process (6.2)

Network problems can be simple or complex, and they can result from a combination of hardware, software, and connectivity issues.

Applying the Troubleshooting Process to Networking (6.2.1)

To repair a network issue, computer technicians must be able to analyze the problem and determine the cause of the error. This process is called *troubleshooting*.

The Six Steps of the Troubleshooting Process (6.2.1.1)

The troubleshooting process involves six steps:

Step 1. Identify the problem.

Step 2. Establish a theory of probable cause.

Step 3. Test the theory to determine the cause.

Step 4. Establish a plan of action to resolve the problem and implement the solution.

Step 5. Verify full system functionality and, if applicable, implement preventive measures.

Step 6. Document findings, actions, and outcomes.

Identify the Problem (6.2.1.2)

As a technician, you should develop a logical and consistent method for diagnosing network problems by eliminating one problem at a time.

For example, to assess a problem, you need to determine how many devices are experiencing the problem. If there is a problem with one device, start with that device. If the problem involves multiple devices, start the troubleshooting process in the network room where all the devices are connected.

The first step in the troubleshooting process is to identify the problem. Use the list of open-ended and closed-ended questions in Table 6-9 as a starting point to gather information from the customer.

Table 6-9 Step 1: Identify the Problem

Open-ended questions	■ What problems are you experiencing with your device?
	■ What software has been installed on your device recently?
	■ What were you doing when the problem was identified?
	■ What error message have you received?
	■ What type of network connection is the device using?
Closed-ended questions	■ Has anyone else used your device recently?
	■ Can you see any shared files or printers?
	■ Have you changed your password recently?
	■ Can you access the Internet?

- Are you currently logged into the network?

- Is anyone else having this problem?

- Have there been any environmental or infrastructure changes to the network?

Establish a Theory of Probable Cause (6.2.1.3)

After you have talked to the customer, you can establish a theory of probable cause. The list in Table 6-10 provides some common probable causes for network problems.

Table 6-10   Step 2: Establish a Theory of Probable Cause

Common causes of network problems	■ Loose cable connections
	■ Improperly installed NIC
	■ ISP down
	■ Low wireless signal strength
	■ Invalid IP address
	■ DNS server issue
	■ DHCP server issue

Test the Theory to Determine the Cause (6.2.1.4)

After you have developed some theories about what is wrong, test your theories to determine the cause of the problem. Once a theory is confirmed, determine the next steps to resolve the problem. Table 6-11 shows some procedures that you can use to quickly determine the cause of a problem or even to correct the problem. If one of these procedures corrects the problem, you can then verify full system functionality. You might also need to research the problem further to establish the exact cause.

Table 6-11   Step 3: Test the Theory to Determine the Cause

Common steps to determine cause	■ Check that all cables are connected to the proper locations.
	■ Unseat and then reconnect cables and connectors.
	■ Reboot the computer or network device.
	■ Log in as a different user.
	■ Repair or reenable the network connection.
	■ Contact the network administrator.
	■ Ping the device's default gateway.
	■ Access a remote web page, such as http://www.cisco.com.

Establish a Plan of Action to Resolve the Problem and Implement the Solution (6.2.1.5)

After you have determined the exact cause of the problem, establish a plan of action to resolve the problem and implement the solution. The list in Table 6-12 shows some sources you can use to gather additional information to resolve an issue.

Table 6-12   Step 4: Establish a Plan of Action to Resolve the Problem and Implement the Solution

If no solution is achieved in the previous step, further research is needed to implement the solution.	■ Help desk repair logs ■ Other technicians ■ Manufacturer FAQ websites ■ Technical websites ■ Newsgroups ■ Computer manuals ■ Device manuals ■ Online forums ■ Internet search

Verify Full Functionality and, if Applicable, Implement Preventive Measures (6.2.1.6)

After you have corrected the problem, verify full functionality and, if applicable, implement preventive measures. Table 6-13 shows a few steps to verify a solution.

Table 6-13   Step 5: Verify Full Functionality and, if Applicable, Implement Preventive Measures

Verify full system functionality and, if applicable, implement preventive measures.	■ Use the **ipconfig /all** command to display IP address information for all network adapters. ■ Use **ping** to check network connectivity by sending a packet to the specified address and getting response information. ■ Verify that the device can access authorized resources such as company email servers and the Internet. ■ Research additional commands or ask a supervisor for help with other testing utilities.

Document Findings, Actions, and Outcomes (6.2.1.7)

In the final step of the troubleshooting process, document your findings, actions, and outcomes, as shown in Table 6-14.

Table 6-14   Step 6: Document Findings, Actions, and Outcomes

Document findings, actions, and outcomes.	■ Discuss the solution implemented with the customer. ■ Have the customer verify that the problem has been solved. ■ Provide the customer with all paperwork. ■ Document the steps taken to solve the problem in the work order and technician's journal. ■ Document any components used in the repair. ■ Document the time spent to solve the problem.

Interactive Graphic

Check Your Understanding 6.2.1.8: Network Troubleshooting Process

Refer to the online course to complete this activity.

Network Problems and Solutions (6.2.2)

Applied networking involves the practical application of networking principles and technologies and considers various troubleshooting examples to address real-world problems.

Common Problems and Solutions for Networking (6.2.2.1)

Network problems can be attributed to hardware, software, or configuration issues or to some combination of the three. You will resolve some types of network problems more often than others. Table 6-15 lists some common networking problems and solutions.

Table 6-15   Common Networking Problems and Solutions

Problem	Probable Causes	Possible Solutions
NIC LED lights are not lit.	The network cable is unplugged or damaged.	Reconnect or replace the network connection to the computer.
	The NIC is damaged.	Replace the NIC.
User cannot use Secure Shell (SSH) to access a remote device.	The remote device is not configured for SSH access.	Configure the remote device for SSH access.
	SSH is not allowed from the user or a particular network.	Allow SSH access from the user or the network.

Problem	Probable Causes	Possible Solutions
Device cannot detect the wireless router.	The wireless router/access point is configured with a different 802.11 protocol.	Configure the wireless router with a compatible protocol for the device.
	The SSID is not being broadcast.	Configure the wireless router to broadcast the SSID.
	The wireless NIC in the device is disabled.	Enable the wireless NIC in the device.
Windows computer has IPv4 address 169.254.x.x.	The network cable is unplugged.	Reconnect the network cable.
	The router is powered off or the connection is faulty.	Ensure that the router is powered on and is properly connected to the network. Then release and renew the IPv4 address on the computer.
	The NIC is damaged.	Replace the NIC.
Remote device does not respond to a **ping** request.	Windows firewall disables **ping** by default.	Set the firewall to enable **ping**.
	The remote device is configured to not respond to **ping** requests.	Configure the remote device to respond to the **ping** request.
A user can access the local network but cannot access the Internet.	The gateway address is incorrect or not configured.	Ensure that the correct gateway address is assigned to the NIC.
	The ISP is down.	Call the ISP to report an outage.
The network is fully functional, but the wireless device cannot connect to the network.	The wireless capability of the device is turned off.	Enable wireless capability of the device.
	The device is out of wireless range.	Move closer to the wireless router/access point.
	There is interference from other wireless devices using the same frequency range.	Change the wireless router to a different channel.
Local resources such as file shares or printers are unavailable.	Could be a number of issues: bad cabling, switch or router not functioning, firewall blocking traffic, DNS name resolution not working, or service failed.	Establish the scope of the problem such as trying to connect from a different host.

Advanced Problems and Solutions for Network Connections (6.2.2.2)

Table 6-16 shows some advanced network connection problems and solutions.

Table 6-16 Advanced Network Connection Problems and Solutions

Problem	Probable Causes	Possible Solutions
A device can connect to a network device by the IP address but not by the hostname.	Incorrect hostname.	Reenter the hostname.
	Incorrect DNS settings.	Reenter the IP address of the DNS server.
	DNS server is not operational.	Restart the DNS server.
The device does not obtain or renew the IP address on the network.	The computer is using a static IP address from a different network.	Enable the computer to obtain an IP address automatically.
	Firewall is blocking DHCP.	Change the firewall settings to allow DHCP traffic.
	DHCP server is not operational.	Restart the DHCP server.
	Wireless NIC is disabled.	Enable the wireless NIC.
An IP address conflict message appears when connecting a new device to the network.	The same IP address is assigned to two devices on the network.	Configure each device with a unique IP address.
	Another computer has been configured with a static IP address that was already assigned by the DHCP server.	Configure the DHCP server to exclude the static IP address from assignments and reboot all affected devices.
A device has network access but does not have Internet access.	The gateway IP address is incorrect.	Configure the correct gateway IP address on the device or on the DHCP server.
	A router is configured incorrectly.	Reconfigure the router settings.
	The DNS server is not operational.	Restart the DNS server.
Users are experiencing slow transfer speeds, weak signal strength, and intermittent connectivity on the wireless network.	Wireless security has not been implemented, and unauthorized users are allowed access.	Implement a wireless security plan.
	There are too many users connected to the access point.	Add another access point or a repeater to increase the strengthen signal.
	User is too far away from access point.	Move the access point and ensure that it is centrally located.
	The wireless signal is experiencing interference from outside sources.	Change the channels on the wireless network.

Advanced Problems and Solutions for FTP and Secure Internet Connections (6.2.2.3)

Table 6-17 shows some advanced problems and solutions for FTP and secure Internet connections.

Table 6-17   Advanced Problems and Solutions for FTP and Secure Internet Connections

Problem	Probable Causes	Possible Solutions
A user cannot access the FTP server.	FTP is being blocked by the firewall at the router.	Ensure that ports 20 and 21 are allowed through the router's outbound firewall.
	FTP is being blocked by the Windows firewall.	Ensure that ports 20 and 21 are allowed through the Windows outbound firewall.
	The maximum number of users has been reached.	Increase the maximum number of simultaneous FTP users on the FTP server.
The FTP client software cannot find the FTP server.	The FTP client has an incorrect server/domain name or port setting.	Enter the correct server/domain name and port settings in the FTP client.
	The FTP server is not operational or is offline.	Restart the FTP server.
	The DNS server is not operational and not resolving names.	Restart the DNS server.
	The FTP client has an incorrect server/domain name or port setting.	Enter the correct server/domain name and port settings in the FTP client.
A device cannot access a specific HTTPS site.	The site is not on that computer's browser's list of trusted sites.	Decide whether to add the security certificate to the browser's list of trusted sites.

Advanced Problems and Solutions Using Network Tools (6.2.2.4)

Table 6-18 shows some advanced problems and solutions for using network tools.

Table 6-18 Advanced Problems and Solutions for Using Network Tools

Problem	Probable Causes	Possible Solutions
A device on one network cannot ping a device on another network.	There is a broken link between the two networks.	Use **tracert** to locate which link is down and fix the broken link.
	ICMP is blocked at the router.	Configure the router to allow ICMP echo requests and echo replies.
	ICMP is blocked at the Windows firewall.	Configure the Windows firewall to allow ICMP echo requests and echo replies.
The computer cannot Telnet into a remote computer.	The remote computer has not been configured to accept Telnet connections.	Configure the remote computer to accept Telnet connections.
	The Telnet service is not started on the remote computer.	Start the Telnet service on the remote computer.
The **nslookup** command reports "Can't find server name for address {*ip-address*}: timed out," where *ip-address* can be any IP address.	The DNS server is not responding.	Resolve connectivity issues to the DNS server and/or restart the DNS server.
	The DNS records are incorrect.	Configure the DNS server with the correct records.
The **ipconfig /release** or **ipconfig /renew** command results in the following message: "No operation can be performed on the adapter while the media is disconnected."	The network cable is unplugged.	Reconnect the network cable.
	The computer has been configured with a static IP address.	Reconfigure the NIC to obtain IP addressing automatically.
The **ipconfig /release** or **ipconfig /renew** command results in the following message: "The operation failed as no adapter is in the state permissible for this operation."	The computer has been configured with a static IP address.	Reconfigure the NIC to obtain IP addressing automatically.

Lab 6.2.2.5: Troubleshoot Network Problems

In this lab, you will diagnose the causes of and solve the network problems.

Summary (6.3)

In this chapter, you learned how to configure NICs, connect devices to a wireless router, and configure a wireless router for network connectivity. You also learned about firewalls, IoT devices, and network troubleshooting. You learned about 48-bit MAC addresses that identify devices connected to an Ethernet LAN and the two types of IP addresses, IPv4 and IPv6. IPv4 addresses are 32 bits in length and are written in dotted-decimal format; IPv6 addresses are 128 bits in length and written in hexadecimal format.

Configuring an IP address on a device can be done manually or dynamically by using DHCP. You learned that manual, or static, addressing is appropriate for small networks, while DHCP is best suited for larger networks. In addition to an IP address, DHCP can also automatically assign the subnet mask, default gateway, and address of DNS servers. You configured a NIC to use DHCP on a Windows computer in a lab exercise. You verified network configuration by using the **ipconfig /all** command in Windows and tested connectivity by using **ping**.

You then learned how to configure a wireless network, including the configuration of a wireless router with basic wireless settings, NAT, firewall settings, and QoS. You then completed two labs: one about configuring a wireless network and one on configuring firewall settings. In the wireless network lab, you configured basic wireless settings on a wireless host and an access point and then tested connectivity. In the firewall lab, you configured MAC filtering, a DMZ, and port forwarding.

The Internet today includes more than just computers, tablets, and smartphones. The IoT also includes sensor-equipped, Internet-ready devices that include automobiles, biomedical devices, household appliances, and natural ecosystems. You used Packet Tracer to explore IoT devices and their basic configuration.

At the end of the chapter, you learned the six steps in the troubleshooting process as they pertain to networks.

Practice

The following activities provide practice with the topics introduced in this chapter. The labs are available in the companion *IT Essentials v8 Labs & Study Guide* (ISBN 9780138166304).

Labs

Lab 6.1.2.7: Configure a NIC to Use DHCP in Windows

Lab 6.1.3.10: Configure a Wireless Network

Lab 6.1.4.8: Configure Firewall Settings

Lab 6.2.2.5: Troubleshoot Network Problems

Packet Tracer Activities

Packet Tracer 6.1.2.1: Add Computers to an Existing Network

Packet Tracer 6.1.3.9: Connect to a Wireless Network

Packet Tracer 6.1.4.7: Configure Firewall Settings

Check Your Understanding Questions

Complete all the review questions listed here to test your understanding of the topics and concepts in this chapter. Appendix A, "Answers to 'Check Your Understanding' Questions," lists the answers.

1. A user reports that the corporate web server cannot be accessed. A technician verifies that the web server can be accessed by using its IP address. What are two possible causes of the problem? (Choose two.)

   A. The default gateway address is misconfigured on the workstation.

   B. The web server information is misconfigured on the DNS server.

   C. The DNS server address is misconfigured on the workstation.

   D. The network connection is down.

   E. The web server is misconfigured.

2. A computer is assigned IP address 169.254.33.16. What can be said about the computer, based on the assigned address?

   A. It cannot communicate outside its own network.

   B. It can communicate on the local network as well as on the Internet.

   C. It has a public IP address that has been translated to a private IP address.

   D. It can communicate with networks inside a particular company with subnets.

3. A computer has been assigned IP address 169.254.33.16. What command initiates the process of requesting a new IP address?

   A. net computer

   B. ipconfig

   C. tracert

   D. nslookup

4. A customer has a web server for a small business. The business uses both wired and wireless networking. A Linksys WRT300N wireless router provides wireless and wired connectivity. What firewall option may be enabled in order for customers to gain access to the web server from their remote locations?

   A. WPA2

   B. port forwarding

   C. port triggering

   D. WEP

   E. MAC address filtering

5. A wireless router is displaying the IP address 192.168.0.1. What could this mean?

   A. The NAT function is not working on the wireless router.

   B. The wireless router still has the factory default IP address.

   C. The wireless router has been configured to use the frequencies on channel 1.

   D. Dynamic IP address allocation has been configured on the router and is functioning correctly.

6. Which filtering method uses IP addresses to specify what devices are allowed on a network?

   A. port forwarding

   B. MAC address filtering

   C. blacklisting

   D. port triggering

   E. whitelisting

7. Which protocol does the **ping** command use to test connectivity between network hosts?

   A. TCP

   B. ARP

   C. DHCP

   D. ICMP

8. What is the problem if a computer automatically configures an IP address in the 169.254.x.x address range?

   A. The DHCP server is unreachable.

   B. The computer is configured with an incorrect default gateway.

   C. The DNS server is unreachable.

   D. The computer's NIC is disabled.

9. A technician wishes to update the NIC driver for a computer. What is the best location for finding new drivers for the NIC?

   A. the website for the manufacturer of the NIC

   B. the installation media for Windows

   C. the website for Microsoft

   D. the installation media that came with the NIC

   E. Windows Update

10. Which network service automatically assigns IP addresses to devices on the network?

   A. Telnet

   B. **traceroute**

   C. DNS

   D. DHCP

11. What is a result when the DHCP servers are not operational in a network?

   A. Workstations are assigned IP addresses in the 169.254.0.0/16 network.

   B. Workstations are assigned the IP address 127.0.0.1.

   C. Workstations are assigned IP addresses in the 10.0.0.0/8 network.

   D. Workstations are assigned the IP address 0.0.0.0.

12. The process that a wireless router uses to translate a private IP address on internal traffic to a routable address for the Internet is called

   _____.

   A. NAP

   B. NAT

   C. TCP handshake

   D. Private Address Changing

13. A device has been assigned the IPv6 address 2001:0db8:cafe:4500:1000:00d8:
    0058:00ab/64. What is the network identifier of the device?

    A. 2001:0db8:cafe:4500:1000

    B. 2001

    C. 2001:0db8:cafe:4500

    D. 2001:0db8:cafe:4500:1000:00d8:0058:00ab

    E. 1000:00d8:0058:00ab

14. What command can be used to troubleshoot domain name resolution issues?

    A. tracert

    B. nslookup

    C. net

    D. ipconfig /displaydns

15. A new computer workstation has been installed in a small office. The user of the
    workstation can print a document by using a network printer on the LAN but
    cannot access the Internet. What is a possible cause of the problem?

    A. The TCP/IP stack is not functional.

    B. The DHCP server IP address is misconfigured.

    C. The workstation is configured with a static IP address.

    D. The gateway IP address is misconfigured.

CHAPTER 7

Laptops and Other Mobile Devices

Objectives

Upon completion of this chapter, you will be able to answer the following questions:

- What are the features of laptop components?
- What are the types of laptop displays?
- How do you configure power settings on laptops?
- How do you configure wireless communication on laptops?
- How do you remove and install laptop memory and adapter modules?
- How do you remove and install laptop hardware?
- What are some examples of common mobile device hardware?
- What are the hardware components of specialty mobile devices?

- How do you configure wireless and cellular data settings?
- How do you pair Bluetooth devices?
- How do you configure email settings?
- How do you synchronize data?
- How do you schedule and perform laptop and mobile device maintenance?
- What are the six steps of troubleshooting laptops and other mobile devices?
- What are some common problems and solutions related to laptops and other mobile devices?

Key Terms

This chapter uses the following key terms. You can find the definitions in the glossary at the end of the book.

1G page 380

2G page 380

3G page 380

4G page 380

5G page 380

account credentials page 389

Advanced Configuration and Power Interface (ACPI) page 353

Airplane mode page 380

Apple ID page 391

augmented reality (AR) page 342

backlight page 351

Backup page 394

backup storage location page 394

backup straight from an iOS device page 394

Introduction (7.0)

The first laptops were used primarily by businesspeople who needed to access and enter data when they were away from the office. The use of laptops was limited due to their expense, weight, and limited capabilities compared to desktops. Improvements in technology have allowed laptops to become lightweight, powerful, and much more affordable. Because of this, laptops are found in just about every setting today. Laptops run the same operating systems as desktop computers, and most come with built-in Wi-Fi, webcam, microphone, speakers, and ports to attach external components.

A *mobile device* is any device that is handheld and lightweight; in addition, mobile devices typically have touchscreens for input. Like a desktop or laptop computer, a mobile device uses an operating system to run applications (apps), games, and movies and music. The CPU architecture of mobile devices is designed for a reduced instruction set compared to laptop and desktop processors. With the increase in demand for mobility, the popularity of laptops and other mobile devices continues to grow. This chapter focuses on many features and capabilities of laptops and other mobile devices.

You will learn the features and functionality of laptops and other mobile devices, such as smartphones and tablets, as well as how to remove and install internal and external components. At the end of the chapter, you will learn the importance of having a preventive maintenance program for laptops and other mobile devices and apply the six steps in the troubleshooting process to laptops and other mobile devices.

It is important to not only learn about laptops and mobile devices and their components but also to build hands-on skills. In this chapter, you will research and gather information about Android and iOS mobile devices. In labs, you will research laptop screens, drives, and specifications. As an IT technician, asking the right questions is critical to solving customer problems. You need to be able to ask questions that will be recorded on a work order. You will create closed-ended and open-ended questions to ask a customer about a computer problem.

Characteristics of Laptops and Other Mobile Devices (7.1)

Laptops provide mobility and can easily be moved from location to location. They often replace desktops because of this convenience, but they are bigger and heavier than other mobile devices. Laptops are used for tasks that other mobile devices cannot easily accomplish due to their restricted operating systems. Compared to other mobile devices, laptops have increased storage capacity, ability to expand functionality with external devices more easily, bigger screens and displays, more powerful software, and more handy input devices.

Mobile devices can be used while on the move, and they are now the primary devices used for online access and web-related communication. The smaller size of handheld devices and their increasing video capabilities with multiple cameras make them increasingly popular, too. Laptops and other mobile devices serve different purposes for various user segments and complement each other.

Mobile Device Overview (7.1.1)

Mobile devices come in many forms, and the choice of mobile device depends greatly on its planned usage. Basically, mobile devices are handheld computers with wireless communications capability. Many users have more than one type of mobile device, such as smartphone, smartwatch, laptop, and so on. Mobile devices have become regular fixtures in businesses, as the devices in BYOD programs. Wherever they are, mobile device users can be connected thanks to wireless connectivity capabilities and productive thanks to apps. Long battery life and small form factor allow easy mobility.

What Do You Already Know? - Mobile Devices (7.1.1.1)

What do you already know about mobile devices? See if you can select the mobile device that is most appropriate for each of the following five scenarios from among these devices:

- Smartwatch
- Laptop
- Tablet
- Smartphone
- E-reader

Scenarios

Scenario 1: You are offline but need to work with full copies of a spreadsheet and word processing program.

Scenario 2: Someone is hiking in the park and does not have a smartwatch but wants to upload data from their fitness tracker to the Internet.

Scenario 3: A parent wants to keep their child entertained with a game while they talk to a friend on their smartphone.

Scenario 4: You want to read a book while you are at the beach but don't want to bring your more expensive computing devices.

Scenario 5: A sports fan leaves their smartphone at home but still wants to be alerted to the scores of some football games while they are out jogging.

Answers

Scenario 1 Answer: A laptop usually runs a full version of an operating system and can run full commercial office applications.

Scenario 2 Answer: A smartphone can act as a gateway to the Internet for devices that can connect to the phone over Bluetooth.

Scenario 3 Answer: Because they are small and have touchscreens, tablets are a favorite of children. Many children's games and educational apps exist for tablets.

Scenario 4 Answer: E-readers are optimized for reading text such as books and newspapers.

Scenario 5 Answer: A smartwatch is the best alternative for this. It can receive the updates, and the jogger can easily view them on the watch without needing to take out their phone.

Mobility (7.1.1.2)

Mobility in information technology refers to the ability to access information electronically from different locations outside the home or office. Mobile connectivity is limited only by the availability of cellular or data networks. Mobile devices have self-contained power in the form of rechargeable batteries, are generally small and lightweight, and do not rely on other connected peripheral devices, such as a mouse and keyboard, to operate.

Examples of mobile devices are laptops, tablets, smartphones, smartwatches, and wearables.

Laptops (7.1.1.3)

Laptops are portable computers. They usually run full versions of operating systems such as Microsoft Windows, macOS, or Linux.

Laptops often have the same computing power and memory resources as desktop computers. As shown in Figure 7-1, a laptop integrates a screen, a keyboard, and a pointing device, such as a touchpad, in one portable device. Laptops can be run from an internal battery or from an electrical outlet. They offer connectivity options such as wired or wireless Ethernet networking and Bluetooth.

Laptops offer device connection options such as USB and HDMI. Laptops frequently have speaker and microphone connections as well. Some laptops offer graphic connectivity using different types of graphics standards, much like desktops. However, in order to make laptops more portable, some peripheral connection options may require additional hardware, such as a dock or port replicator.

Figure 7-1   Laptop

In order to increase portability, laptops may sacrifice some of the advantages that are offered by desktop computers. For example, laptops may not use the fastest processors available due to cooling concerns and high power consumption. Laptop memory upgrades may be limited, and some types of laptop memory are more expensive than comparable desktop memory. Laptops lack the expansion capability of desktops as well. Special-purpose expansion cards and large-volume storage often cannot be installed in laptops. For example, upgrading the graphics subsystem in a laptop is likely to be impossible.

Smartphone Characteristics (7.1.1.4)

Smartphones differ from laptops in that they run special operating systems that are designed for mobile devices. Examples of these operating systems are Google's Android and Apple's iOS. Smartphones may have limited OS upgradability, and they can become out of date and require purchase of a new phone to take advantage of new features of the OS and apps that require a higher OS version. Software for smartphones is usually limited to apps that can be downloaded from stores such as Google Play or the Apple App Store.

Smartphones are very compact and quite powerful. They have small touchscreens with no physical keyboard. The keyboard is displayed on the screen. Because they are so small, they are usually limited to only one or two types of physical connection, such as USB and headphones.

Smartphones use cellular connectivity options for voice, text, and data services. Other data connections include Bluetooth and Wi-Fi.

Smartphone Features (7.1.1.5)

An additional feature of smartphones is location services. Most phones include *Global Positioning System (GPS)* functionality. A GPS receiver in a phone uses satellites to determine the geographic location of the device. This allows the device location to be used by apps for various purposes, such as social media updates and receiving offers from nearby businesses. Some apps allow a smartphone to act as a navigational GPS that provides guidance for driving, biking, or walking. If the GPS is off, most smartphones can still determine the location, in a less precise way, by using information coming from nearby mobile service antennas or nearby Wi-Fi access points.

Another feature of some smartphones is the ability to *tether*, or share, the cellular data connection with other devices, as shown in Figure 7-2. A smartphone can be configured to act as a modem that enables other devices to access the cellular data network over USB, Bluetooth, or Wi-Fi. Not all smartphone carriers permit tethering.

Figure 7-2 Tethered Smartphone

Tablets and E-readers (7.1.1.6)

Tablets (see Figure 7-3) are similar to smartphones in that they use special mobile operating systems, such as Android or iOS. Although many tablets do not have the ability to access cellular networks, some higher-end models do allow access to cellular services.

Figure 7-3   Tablet

Compared to smartphones, tablets normally have larger touchscreen displays. The displays are often quite vivid in their graphic rendering. Tablets usually offer Wi-Fi and Bluetooth connectivity, and most have USB and audio ports. In addition, some tablets include GPS receivers that can be activated to provide location services, much like smartphones. Most of the apps that work on phones are also available for tablets.

E-readers, such as the Amazon Kindle, are special-purpose devices with black-and-white or color displays that have been optimized for reading text. Although they resemble tablets, they lack many of the features and functions that tablets provide. Web access is limited to e-book stores that may be operated by the e-reader manufacturer. Many e-readers have touch displays that make it easy to turn pages, change settings, and access e-books online. Many e-readers can store 1000 or more books. For connectivity, some offer free cellular data connections for downloading books from a specific store, but most rely on Wi-Fi. Bluetooth is also available and supports headphones for audio books. The battery life of e-readers is usually longer than that of tablets—upto 15 to 20 hours of reading time or more.

Wearables: Smartwatches and Fitness Trackers (7.1.1.7)

Wearables are smart devices that are meant to be worn on the body or attached to clothing. Two popular types of wearables are smartwatches and fitness trackers.

Smartwatches

A *smartwatch* is a type of wearable that includes a microprocessor, a special operating system, and apps. Sensors in the smartwatch can gather data about various aspects of the body, such as heart rate, and use Bluetooth to report this information to another device, such as a smartphone. The smartphone then forwards the information to an application over the Internet for storage and analysis. Some smartwatches can also connect directly to a cellular network, serve as convenient displays for notifications from apps, include GPS location services, and store and play music and playlists.

Fitness Trackers

Fitness trackers (see Figure 7-4) are similar to smartwatches but are limited to monitoring the body, tracking physical activity, sleep, and exercise. Fitbit is a popular example that monitors heart rate and the number of steps taken. Similar to fitness trackers are more sophisticated *health monitoring devices* that can detect heart attacks, monitor air quality, and detect oxygen levels in the blood. These devices can deliver hospital-quality data to healthcare practitioners.

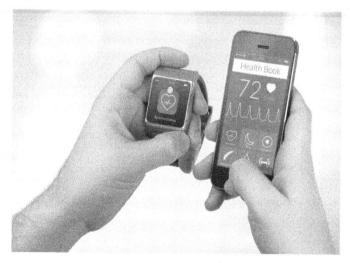

Figure 7-4   Fitness Tracker Syncing with a Smartphone

Wearables: Augmented and Virtual Realities (7.1.1.8)

In *augmented reality (AR)*, computer graphics are integrated with what is seen in the real world, usually through the device camera, as shown for the tablet in Figure 7-5.

The graphics overlays can range from cartoon characters in a game application to information for emergency management training for first responders. There are many potential uses for AR, and it is one of the most promising areas for future product development.

Figure 7-5   Augmented Reality

Related to AR is *virtual reality (VR)*. With VR, a user wears a special headset that displays graphics from a separate computer, as shown in Figure 7-6. The graphics are immersive 3D and create very realistic worlds. The VR user's motions are detected by sensors that allow the user to interact with and move around in the virtual environment. VR is very popular in games and also has applications in other fields, such as education and training.

Figure 7-6   Virtual Reality Headset

Interactive Graphic

Check Your Understanding 7.1.1.9: Laptops and Other Mobile Devices

Refer to the online course to complete this activity.

Lab 7.1.1.10: Mobile Device Information

In this lab, you will gather information about an Android device and an iOS device.

Laptop Components (7.1.2)

This section looks closely at both internal and external laptop components. Components can be located in different places on different laptop models. It is important to know each component to make informed decisions on the selection of components for purchases and upgrades. Understanding laptop components is necessary for troubleshooting when components malfunction or fail.

Video

Video Explanation 7.1.2.1: External Features Unique to Laptops

Refer to the online course to view this video.

Video

Video Explanation 7.1.2.2: Common Input Devices and LEDs in Laptops

Refer to the online course to view this video.

Motherboards (7.1.2.3)

The compact nature of laptops requires a number of internal components to fit in a small amount of space. The size restrictions result in a variety of form factors for a number of laptop components, such as the motherboard, RAM, CPU, and storage devices. Some laptop components, such as the CPU, may be designed to use less power to ensure that the system can operate for a longer period of time when using a battery source.

Desktop motherboards have standard form factors. The standard size and shape allow motherboards from different manufacturers to fit into common desktop cases. In contrast, laptop motherboards vary by manufacturer and are proprietary. When you repair a laptop, you must often obtain a replacement motherboard from the laptop manufacturer. Figure 7-7 shows a comparison between a desktop motherboard and a laptop motherboard.

Because laptop motherboards and desktop motherboards are designed differently, components designed for a laptop generally cannot be used in a desktop.

Desktop Motherboard   Laptop Motherboard

Component	Desktop	Laptop
Motherboard Form Factor	ATX, Micro-ATX, Mini-ITX, ITX	Proprietary
Expansion Slot	PCI, PCI-X, PCIe, miniPCI	Mini-PCI
RAM Slot Type	DIMM	SODIMM

Figure 7-7   Laptop and Desktop Motherboard Comparison

Internal Components (7.1.2.4)

Laptop internal components, including the following, are designed to fit into the confined spaces of the laptop form factor:

- RAM
- CPUs
- SATA drives
- Solid-state drives

RAM

Because of the limited amount of space in laptops, memory modules in laptops are much smaller than those used in desktops. Laptops use small outline dual in-line memory modules (SODIMMs), as shown in Figure 7-8.

CPUs

An example of a laptop CPU is shown in Figure 7-9. Laptop processors are designed to use less power and create less heat than desktop processors. As a result, laptop processors do not require cooling devices that are as large as those found in desktops. Laptop processors also use CPU throttling to modify the clock speed as needed to reduce power consumption and heat. This results in a slight decrease in performance. These specially designed processors allow laptops to operate for a longer period of time when using a battery.

Figure 7-8   Laptop RAM

Note

Refer to the laptop manual for compatible processors and for replacement instructions.

Figure 7-9   Laptop CPU

SATA Drive

Laptop storage devices are 1.8 inches (4.57 cm) or 2.5 inches (6.35 cm) in width, and desktop storage devices are typically 3.5 inches (8.9 cm). The 1.8-inch drives are mostly found in ultraportable laptops because they are smaller and lighter, and they consume less power. However, their spin rate is usually slower than that of 2.5-inch drives, which have spin rates of up to 10000 RPM.

Several storage drive form factors and technologies are used in laptops due to their compact size. An example is shown in Figure 7-10. SATA 2.5 is a specification of SATA hard drive with a compact casing that encloses a 2.5-inch drive platter.

Figure 7-10   SATA Drive

Solid-State Drives

M.2, shown in Figure 7-11, is a very small solid-state drive form factor; it is about the size of a stick of gum. It is very fast and designed for high performance in small, power-constrained devices. Another very fast and compact solid-state drive standard is NVMe, which has read and write speeds many times faster than those of SATA drives.

Figure 7-11   M.2 SSD

Special Function Keys (7.1.2.5)

The purpose of the *Function (Fn) key* is to activate a second function on a dual-purpose key. The feature that is accessed by pressing the Fn key in combination with another key is printed on the key in a smaller font or different color. Function keys vary on different laptop models, but these are some examples of functions that can be accessed:

- Dual displays
- Volume settings
- Media options such as fast forward or rewind
- Keyboard backlight
- Screen orientation
- Screen brightness
- Wi-Fi, cellular, and Bluetooth on or off
- Media options such as play or rewind
- Touchpad on or off
- GPS on or off
- Airplane mode

Note

Some laptops have dedicated function keys that perform functions without requiring users to press the Fn key.

A laptop monitor is a built-in LCD or LED screen. You cannot adjust the laptop monitor for height and distance because it is integrated into the lid of the case. You can often connect an external monitor or projector to a laptop. Pressing the Fn key with the appropriate function key on the keyboard toggles between the built-in display and the external display.

The Fn key acts as a modifier and does something only when used in conjunction with another key; it is usually used with icons on keys that are the same color as Fn. It is typically used in conjunction with the icons found on the F1 through F12 keys. Do not confuse the Fn key with function keys F1 through F12 that are typically located in a row across the top of the keyboard. Their function depends on the OS and the application that is running when they are pressed. Each key can perform up to seven different operations if pressed with one or more combinations of keys such as Shift, Ctrl, and Alt.

Video Explanation 7.1.2.6: Docking Station Versus Port Replicator

Refer to the online course to view this video.

Lab 7.1.2.7: Research Docking Stations and Port Replicators

In this lab, you will use the Internet, a newspaper, or a local store to gather information and then record the specifications for laptop docking stations and port replicators.

Laptop Display Components (7.1.3)

A *laptop display* is an output device that shows all the onscreen content. It is one of the most expensive components of a laptop. There are three different display types, and they come in various sizes and resolutions. Understanding the screen display types and the internal display components of a laptop is important when purchasing or repairing a system. Laptop displays are similar to desktop monitors in that you can adjust the resolution, brightness, and contrast by using software or button controls. You can connect a desktop monitor to a laptop to provide the user with multiple screens and increased functionality.

This section describes the different types of displays and the internal components for each type.

LCD, LED, and OLED Display Technologies (7.1.3.1)

There are three types of laptop displays:

- *Liquid-crystal display (LCD):* The three most common technologies used in the manufacturing of LCD displays are twisted nematic (TN), in-plane switching (IPS), and vertical alignment (VA). TN displays offer high brightness, use less power than IPS, and are inexpensive to manufacture. IPS displays offer better color reproduction and better viewing angles but have low contrast and slow response time. Manufacturers are now producing Super-IPS (S-IPS) panels, at reasonable prices, that have improved response times and contrast. VA uses tilting crystals to provide a much higher contrast ratio than other types. Contrast ratio is the difference in shade between a black pixel and a white pixel. The downside of a VA display is that it has a lower viewing angle and slower response time, and it may exhibit ghosting or motion blur.

- *Light-emitting diode (LED):* LED displays use less power and have a longer life span than LCD displays, making them the display choice for many laptop manufacturers.

■ *Organic light-emitting diode (OLED)*: OLED technology is commonly used for mobile devices and digital cameras but can also be found in some laptops. Whereas LCD and LED screens use backlights to illuminate their pixels, OLED pixels produce their own light.

Laptop Display Features (7.1.3.2)

Some common laptop display features are discussed in this section.

Detachable Screens

A laptop may come with a *detachable touchscreen* (see Figure 7-12) that can be used like a tablet when the display is detached. Other laptops permit the keyboard to fold back behind the display to allow the laptop to function like a tablet. To accommodate these types of laptops, Windows rotates the display 90, 180, or 270 degrees automatically, or you can rotate manually by pressing Ctrl+Alt simultaneously with the arrow key that points the way you want the laptop to face.

Figure 7-12   Detaching a Screen

Touchscreens

A laptop with a *touchscreen* (see Figure 7-13) has a special glass piece known as a digitizer attached to the front of the screen. The digitizer converts the touch actions (press, swipe, and so on) into digital signals that are processed by the laptop.

Figure 7-13   Using a Touchscreen

Cutoff Switch

On many laptops, a small pin on the laptop cover contacts a switch when the case is closed (see Figure 7-14); this is called a *cutoff switch*. The cutoff switch helps conserve power by turning off the display. If this switch breaks or is dirty, the display remains dark while the laptop is open. Carefully clean this switch to restore normal operation.

Figure 7-14   Shutting a Laptop to Activate the Cutoff Switch

Backlights and Inverters (7.1.3.3)

LCDs do not produce any light by themselves. A *backlight* shines through the screen and illuminates the display. Two common types of backlights are cold cathode fluorescent lamp (CCFL) and LED. With CCFL, fluorescent tubes are connected to an inverter and are used to convert direct current (DC) to alternating current (AC).

Fluorescent Backlight

A *fluorescent backlight* is behind the LCD screen. To replace the backlight, you must completely disassemble the display.

Inverter

An *inverter* is behind the screen panel and close to the LCD.

LED Backlights

LED monitors use *LED-based backlights* and do not have fluorescent tubes or inverters. LED technology increases the longevity of the display because it consumes less power. Also, LED technology is safer for the environment because LEDs do not contain mercury. Mercury is a key ingredient in fluorescent backlights used in LCDs.

Interactive Graphic

Check Your Understanding 7.1.3.4: Laptop Display Components

Refer to the online course to complete this activity.

Wi-Fi Antenna Connectors (7.1.3.5)

Wi-Fi antennas transmit and receive data carried over radio waves. In laptops, a Wi-Fi antenna is typically located above the screen and is connected to the wireless card by an antenna wire and antenna leads. The wires are fastened to the display unit by wire guides located on the sides of the screen.

Webcam and Microphone (7.1.3.6)

A laptop today is likely to have a webcam and microphone built in. The *webcam* is normally positioned at the center top of the display, as shown in Figure 7-15. The internal microphone can often be found next to the webcam. Some manufacturers place the microphone next to the keyboard or on the side of the laptop.

Figure 7-15 Close-up of a Laptop Camera and Microphones

Laptop Configuration (7.2)

Power conservation and management are important aspects to consider for laptops because they are intended for portable use. A laptop uses a battery as a power source when disconnected from an external power source.

Power Settings Configuration (7.2.1)

Software can be used to extend the life of a laptop battery and maximize battery usage. This section introduces methods of power management and settings for optimizing power management through software and the BIOS on a laptop.

Power Management (7.2.1.1)

Advances in power management and battery technology are increasing the amount of time a laptop can be powered from a battery. Many batteries can power a laptop for 10 hours or more. Configuring laptop power settings to better manage power usage is important to ensure that the battery is used efficiently.

Power management controls the flow of electricity to the components of a computer. The *Advanced Configuration and Power Interface (ACPI)* creates a bridge between the hardware and the operating system and allows technicians to create power management schemes to get the best performance from a laptop. The ACPI states shown Table 7-1 are applicable to most computers, and they are particularly important when managing power in laptops.

Table 7-1   ACPI Power States

State	Description
S0 state	The computer is on, and the CPU is running.
S1 state	The CPU and RAM are still receiving power, but unused devices are powered down.
S2 state	The CPU is off, but the RAM is refreshed. The system is in a lower mode than S1.
S3 state	The CPU is off, and the RAM is set to a slow refresh rate. This mode is often called "save to RAM." This state is known as suspend mode.
S4 state	The CPU and RAM are off. The contents of RAM have been saved to a temporary file on the hard disk. This mode is also called "save to disk." This state is known as hibernate mode.
S5 state	The computer is off.

Managing ACPI Settings in the BIOS (7.2.1.2)

Technicians are frequently required to configure power settings by changing the settings in the BIOS or UEFI setup. Configuring the power settings affects the following:

- System states
- Battery and AC modes
- Thermal management
- CPU PCI bus power management
- *Wake on LAN (WOL)*

Note

WOL might require a cable connection inside the computer from the network adapter to the motherboard.

The ACPI power management mode must be enabled in the BIOS or UEFI setup, as shown in Figure 7-16, to allow the OS to configure the power management states.

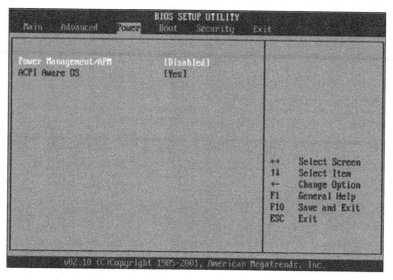

Figure 7-16   Power Settings in BIOS

To enable ACPI mode, follow these steps:

Step 1.   Enter BIOS or UEFI setup.

Step 2.   Locate and enter the Power Management settings menu item.

Step 3. Use the appropriate keys to enable ACPI mode.

Step 4. Save and exit.

Note

These steps are common to most laptops but be sure to check the laptop documentation for specific configuration settings. There is no standard name for each power management state. Different manufacturers might use different names for the same state.

Interactive Graphic

Check Your Understanding 7.2.1.3: Match ACPI Standards

Refer to the online course to complete this activity.

Video

Video Demonstration 7.2.1.4: Managing Laptop Power Options

Refer to the online course to view this video.

Wireless Configuration (7.2.2)

A major advantage of a laptop is that it is portable, and adding the use of wireless technologies increases the functionality of a laptop in any location. Laptop users can connect to the Internet, wireless peripheral devices, or other laptops through the use of wireless technologies. Most laptops have built-in wireless devices, adding to their flexibility and portability compared to desktop computers. This section takes a look at various wireless technologies.

Bluetooth (7.2.2.1)

The *Bluetooth* technical specification is described by the *Institute of Electrical and Electronics Engineers (IEEE) 802.15.1 standard*. Bluetooth devices are capable of handling voice, music, video, and data.

The distance of a Bluetooth personal area network (PAN) is limited by the amount of power used by the devices in the PAN. Bluetooth devices are broken into three classifications. The most common Bluetooth network is Class 2, which has a range of approximately 10 meters. Class specifications are shown in Table 7-2.

Table 7-2   Bluetooth Classifications

Class	Maximum Permitted Power mW	Approximate Distance
Bluetooth Class 1	100mW	~330 feet (100 meters)
Bluetooth Class 2	2.5mW	~33 feet (10 meters)
Bluetooth Class 3	1mW	~3 feet (1 meter)

Five specifications of Bluetooth technology are capable of different transfer rates, ranges, and power consumption levels, as shown in Table 7-3. Each subsequent version offers enhanced capabilities. For instance, Versions 1 through 3 are older technologies with limited capabilities and high power consumption. Later versions, such as Versions 4 and 5, are geared toward devices that have limited power and do not need high data transfer rates. Additionally, Version 5 has four different data rates to accommodate a variety of transmission ranges.

Security measures are included in the Bluetooth standard. The first time a Bluetooth device connects, the device is authenticated using a PIN. This is known as *pairing*. Bluetooth supports both 128-bit encryption and PIN authentication.

Table 7-3   Bluetooth Specifications

Specification	Version	Data Transfer Rate
Bluetooth Specification 1.0	v1.2	1 Mbps
Bluetooth Specification 2.0	v2.0 + EDR	3 Mbps
Bluetooth Specification 3.0	v3.0 + HS	24 Mbps
Bluetooth Specification 4.0	v4.0 + LE	1 Mbps
Bluetooth Specification 5.0	V5.0 + LE	125 Kbps, 500 Kbps, 1 Mbps, 2 Mbps

Bluetooth Laptop Connections (7.2.2.2)

Windows activates connections to Bluetooth devices by default. If a connection is not active, look for a switch on the front face or side of the laptop. Some laptops may have a special function key on the keyboard to enable the connection. If a laptop does not feature Bluetooth technology, you can purchase a Bluetooth adapter that plugs into a USB port.

Before installing and configuring a device, make sure Bluetooth is enabled in the BIOS.

Turn on the device and make it discoverable. Check the device documentation to learn how to make the device discoverable. Use the Bluetooth Wizard to search and discover Bluetooth devices that are in discoverable mode.

Video

Video Demonstration 7.2.2.3: Bluetooth Configuration

Refer to the online course to view this video.

Cellular WAN (7.2.2.4)

Laptops with integrated *cellular WAN* capabilities require no software installation and no additional antenna or accessories. When you turn on the laptop, the integrated WAN capabilities are ready to use. If the connection is not active, look for a switch on the front face or side of the laptop. Some laptops may have a special function key on the keyboard to enable the connection.

Many cell phones provide the ability to connect other devices. This connection, known as *tethering*, can be made using Wi-Fi, Bluetooth, or by using a USB cable. Once a device is connected, it is able to use the phone's cellular connection to access the Internet. When a cellular phone allows Wi-Fi devices to connect and use the mobile data network, this is called a *hotspot*.

You can also access a cellular network by using a cellular hotspot device.

Figure 7-17 shows the settings for a personal hotspot and a cellular hotspot device.

There are also wireless Mini-PCIe and M.2 adapters for laptops that can provide a combination of Wi-Fi, Bluetooth, and/or cellular data (5G/4G/LTE) connectivity. Some of these adapters require the installation of a new antenna kit that has wires that are usually routed around the screen in the laptop lid. When installing an adapter card with cellular functionality, a SIM card needs to be inserted as well.

Personal Hotspot

Cellular Hotspot Device

Figure 7-17 Hotspot Options

Wi-Fi (7.2.2.5)

Laptops usually access the Internet by using wireless adapters. *Wireless adapters* can be built in to the laptop or attached to the laptop through an expansion port. Three major types of wireless adapters are used in laptops:

- *Mini-PCI cards*: Have 124 pins and are capable of 802.11a, 802.11b, and 802.11g wireless LAN connection standards (see Figure 7-18).

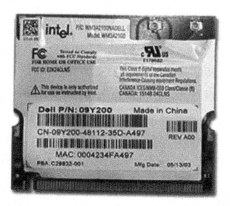

Figure 7-18   Mini-PCI

- *Mini-PCIe cards*: Have 54 pins and support the same standards as Mini-PCI with the addition of 802.11n and 802.11ac wireless LAN standards (see Figure 7-19).

Figure 7-19   Mini-PCIe

- *PCI Express Micro card*: Found in newer and smaller laptops, such as Ultrabooks, they are half the size of Mini-PCIe cards. PCI Express Micro cards (see Figure 7-20) have 54 pins and support the same standards as Mini-PCIe.

Figure 7-20   PCI Express Micro

Video Demonstration 7.2.2.6: Wi-Fi Configuration

Refer to the online course to view this video.

Video

Check Your Understanding 7.2.2.7: Wireless Configuration

Refer to the online course to complete this activity.

Interactive
Graphic

Laptop Hardware and Component Installation and Configuration (7.3)

Compactness and portability are two major reasons laptops are so popular. These two factors also cause the limitations in some areas of technology that users want to have available. This section discusses enhancing the functionality of a laptop through the installation and configuration of expansion devices.

Expansion Slots (7.3.1)

Expansion slots are different types of connection ports on a laptop that allow various types of peripheral devices to be connected to the system externally. There are many types, including USB ports and ExpressCard slots.

Expansion Cards (7.3.1.1)

One of the disadvantages of laptops in comparison to desktops is that their compact design might limit the availability of some functions. To address this problem, many laptops contain *expansion card* slots to add functionality. Figures 7-21 and 7-22 show a comparison of the two ExpressCard expansion card models: *ExpressCard/34* and *ExpressCard/54*. The models are 34 mm and 54 mm in width, respectively.

Figure 7-21   ExpressCard/34

The characteristics of ExpressCard/34 are as follows:

- **Express bus:** ExpressCard/34
- **Size:** 75 mm × 34 mm
- **Thickness:** 5 mm
- **Interface:** PCI Express, USB 2.0, or USB 3.0
- **Examples:** FireWire, TV tuner, wireless NIC

Figure 7-22   ExpressCard/54

The characteristics of the ExpressCard/54 are as follows:

- **Express bus:** ExpressCard/54
- **Size:** 75 mm × 54 mm
- **Thickness:** 5 mm
- **Interface:** PCI Express, USB 2.0, or USB 3.0
- **Examples:** Smart card reader, Compact Flash reader, 1.8-inch disk drive

Here are some examples of functionality that can be added when using ExpressCards:

- Additional memory card reader

- External hard drive access

- TV tuner cards

- USB and FireWire ports

- Wi-Fi connectivity

To install a card, insert the card into the slot and push it all the way in. To remove the card, press the eject button to release it.

If the ExpressCard is hot swappable, follow these steps to safely remove it:

Step 1.   Click the Safely Remove Hardware icon in the Windows system tray to ensure that the device is not in use.

Step 2.   Click the device that you want to remove. A message pops up to tell you that it is safe to remove the device.

Step 3.   Remove the hot swappable device from the laptop.

Caution

ExpressCards and USB devices are commonly hot swappable. However, removing a device that is not hot swappable while the computer is powered on can cause damage to data and devices.

Flash Memory (7.3.1.2)

You should be aware of the types of external flash memory and readers shown in Figure 7-23 and described in the list that follows:

- **External flash drive:** An *external flash drive* is a removable storage device that connects to an expansion port such as USB, eSATA, or FireWire. External flash drives can be SSD drives or smaller devices, such as the one shown in Figure 7-23. Flash drives provide fast access to data, high reliability, and reduced power usage. These drives are accessed by the operating system in the same way that other types of drives are accessed.

- **Flash cards:** A *flash card* is a data storage device that uses flash memory to store information. Flash cards are small and portable, and they require no power to maintain data. They are commonly used in laptops, mobile devices, and digital cameras. A large variety of flash card models are available, and they vary in size and shape.

- **Flash card readers:** Most modern laptops feature a *flash card reader* for Secure Digital (SD) and Secure Digital High Capacity (SDHC) flash cards.

Flash Drive   Flash Cards

MiniSD Card Reader

Figure 7-23   Flash Drive, Cards, and Reader

Note

Flash memory cards are hot swappable and should be removed by following the standard procedure for hot swappable device removal.

Smart Card Reader (7.3.1.3)

A *smart card* is similar to a credit card but has an embedded microprocessor that can be loaded with data. It can be used for telephone calling, electronic cash payments, and other applications. The microprocessor on a smart card provides security and can hold much more information than can the magnetic stripe on a credit card.

Smart card readers are used to read and write to smart cards and can be connected to a laptop using a USB port. There are two types of smart card readers:

- **Contact:** This type of reader requires a physical connection to the card, made by inserting the card into the reader, as shown in Figure 7-24.

- **Contactless:** This type of reader works using a radio frequency that communicates when the card comes close to the reader.

Figure 7-24   Smart Card Reader

Many smart card readers support contact and contactless read operations all in one device. These cards are identified by an oval logo that shows radio waves pointing to a hand holding a card.

SODIMM Memory (7.3.1.4)

The make and model of a laptop determines the type of RAM needed. It is important to select the memory type that is physically compatible with the laptop. Most desktop computers use memory that fits into a DIMM slot. Most laptops use a smaller-profile memory module that is called *SODIMM*. SODIMM has 72-pin and 100-pin configurations for support of 32-bit transfers and 144-pin, 200-pin, and 204-pin configurations for support of 64-bit transfers.

Note

SODIMMs can be further classified by DDR version. Different laptop models require different types of SODIMMs.

Before purchasing and installing additional RAM, consult the laptop documentation or the website of the manufacturer for form-factor specifications. Use the documentation to find where to install RAM on the laptop. On most laptops, RAM is inserted into slots behind a cover on the underside of the case, as shown in Figure 7-25. On some laptops, the keyboard must be removed to access the RAM slots.

Figure 7-25   SODIMM Installed in a Laptop

Consult the manufacturer of the laptop to confirm the maximum amount of RAM each slot can support. You can view the currently installed amount of RAM in the POST screen, BIOS, or System Properties window.

Figure 7-26 shows where the amount of RAM is displayed in the System utility.

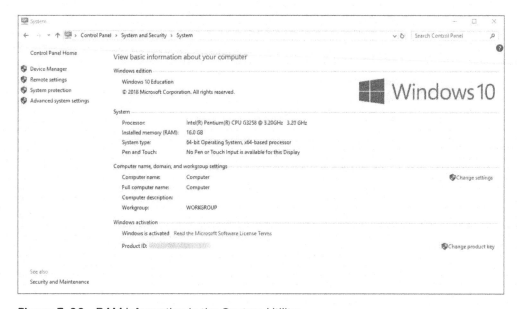

Figure 7-26   RAM Information in the System Utility

To replace or add memory, determine if the laptop has available slots and ensure that it supports the quantity and type of memory to be added. In some instances, there are no available slots for a new SODIMM.

Video

Video Demonstration 7.3.1.5: Install SODIMM

Refer to the online course to view this video.

Interactive Graphic

Check Your Understanding 7.3.1.6: Expansion Modules

Refer to the online course to complete this activity.

Replacing Laptop Components (7.3.2)

Some components of a laptop might need to be replaced or upgraded. Replacing or upgrading a laptop component is very different from replacing or upgrading a component in a desktop computer. Laptops tend to have custom cases and are small, with less room, by design. It's important to begin with the right tools and always remember to make sure you have the correct replacement component and documentation recommended by the manufacturer.

Overview of Hardware Replacement (7.3.2.1)

Some parts of a laptop, typically called *customer-replaceable units (CRUs)*, can be replaced by the customer. CRUs include components such as the laptop battery and RAM. Parts that should not be replaced by the customer are called *field-replaceable units (FRUs)*. FRUs include components such as the motherboard, LCD display, and keyboard. Replacing FRUs typically requires a considerable amount of technical skill. In many cases, the device may need to be returned to the place of purchase, a certified service center, or the manufacturer. In some special cases, such as with the video card, a user may be able to do a replacement; however, a repair center might be required in instances where there are additional power and cooling requirements and space limitations. When repairing a laptop or other portable device, it is important to keep parts organized and cables labeled to aid in reassembly.

A repair center might provide service on laptops made by different manufacturers or might specialize in a specific brand and be considered an authorized dealer for warranty work and repair. The following are common repairs performed at local repair centers:

- Hardware and software diagnostics
- Data transfer and recovery
- Keyboard and fan replacement
- Internal laptop cleaning
- Screen repair
- LCD inverter and backlight repair

Most repairs to displays must be performed in a repair center. The repairs include replacing the screen, the backlight, or the inverter.

If no local services are available, you might need to send a laptop to a regional repair center or to the manufacturer. If the laptop damage is severe or requires specialized software and tools, the manufacturer can decide to replace the laptop instead of attempting a repair.

Caution

Before attempting to repair a laptop or other portable device, check the warranty to see if repairs during the warranty period must be done at an authorized service center to avoid invalidating the warranty. If you repair a laptop yourself, always back up the data and disconnect the device from the power source before you begin the repair. Always consult the service manual before beginning a laptop repair.

Video Demonstration 7.3.2.2: Keyboard Replacement

Refer to the online course to view this video.

Video Demonstration 7.3.2.3: Screen Replacement

Refer to the online course to view this video.

Lab 7.3.2.4: Research Laptop Screens

In this activity, you will use the Internet, a newspaper, or a local store to gather information and then record the specifications for a laptop display onto a worksheet.

Power (7.3.2.5)

These are some signs that a laptop battery may need to be replaced:

- The battery does not hold a charge.
- The battery overheats.
- The battery is leaking.

If you experience problems that you suspect are battery related, exchange the battery with a known good battery that is compatible with the laptop, as shown in Figure 7-27. If a replacement battery cannot be located, take the battery to an authorized repair center for testing.

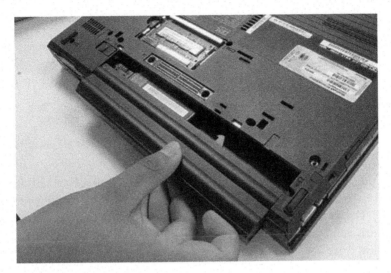

Figure 7-27 Removing a Laptop Battery

A replacement battery must meet or exceed the specifications of the laptop manufacturer. New batteries must use the same form factor as the original battery. Voltages, power ratings, and AC adapters must also meet manufacturer specifications.

Note

Always follow the instructions provided by the manufacturer when charging a new battery. A laptop can be used during an initial charge, but do not unplug the AC adapter.

Caution

Handle batteries with care. Batteries can explode if they are shorted, mishandled, or improperly charged. Be sure that the battery charger is designed for the chemistry, size, and voltage of your battery. Batteries are considered toxic waste and must be disposed of according to local laws.

Video

Video Demonstration 7.3.2.6: DC Jack Replacement

Refer to the online course to view this video.

Lab 7.3.2.7: Research Laptop Batteries

In this lab, you will use the Internet, a newspaper, or a local store to gather information and then record the specifications for a laptop battery.

Internal Storage and Optical Drive (7.3.2.8)

The form factor of an internal storage device is smaller for a laptop than for a desktop computer. Laptop drives are 1.8 inches (4.57 cm) or 2.5 inches (6.35 cm) in width. Most storage devices are CRUs unless a warranty requires technical assistance.

Before purchasing a new internal or external storage device, check the laptop documentation or the website of the manufacturer for compatibility requirements. Documentation often contains FAQs that may be helpful. It is also important to research known laptop component issues on the Internet.

On most laptops, the internal hard drive and the internal optical drive are inserted into bays that are protected by a removable cover on the case, as shown in Figure 7-28. On some laptops, the keyboard must be removed to access these drives. Optical drives might not be interchangeable in a laptop. Some laptops do not include optical drives at all.

Figure 7-28   Inserting an Optical Drive

To view the currently installed storage devices, check the POST screen or BIOS. If installing a second drive or an optical drive, confirm that there are no error icons next to the device in the Device Manager.

Video

Video Demonstration 7.3.2.9: Internal Storage and Optical Drive Replacement

Refer to the online course to view this video.

Lab 7.3.2.10: Research Laptop Drives

In this lab, you will use the Internet, a newspaper, or a local store to gather information about data drives for a laptop.

Video Demonstration 7.3.2.11: Wireless Card Replacement

Refer to the online course to view this video.

Video Demonstration 7.3.2.12: Speakers Replacement

Refer to the online course to view this video.

Video Demonstration 7.3.2.13: CPU Replacement

Refer to the online course to view this video.

Video Demonstration 7.3.2.14: Motherboard Replacement

Refer to the online course to view this video.

Video Demonstration 7.3.2.15: Plastic Frames

Refer to the online course to view this video.

Check Your Understanding 7.3.2.16: Replacing Laptop Components

Refer to the online course to complete this activity.

Other Mobile Device Hardware Overview (7.4)

With the increase in demand for mobility, the popularity of mobile devices continues to grow. Like a laptop computer, a mobile device uses an operating system to run applications (apps), games, and movies and music. Android and iOS are examples of mobile device operating systems.

Other Mobile Device Hardware (7.4.1)

Additional mobile phone hardware is usually not fundamental to the operation of a mobile device but adds extra functionality and customization options to the mobile device for optimal efficiency and convenience.

Cell Phone Parts (7.4.1.1)

Because of their small size, mobile devices usually do not have field-serviceable parts. Mobile devices consist of several compact components integrated into a single unit. When a mobile device malfunctions, it is usually sent to the manufacturer for repair or replacement.

A cell phone contains one or more of these field replaceable parts: memory, a SIM card, and a battery (see Figure 7-29).

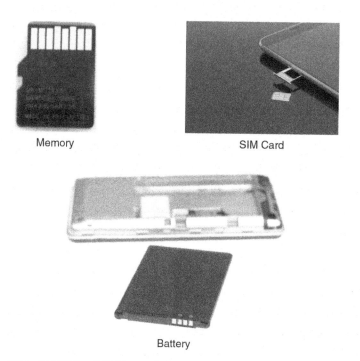

Memory   SIM Card

Battery

Figure 7-29   Cell Phone Parts

Secure Digital (SD) cards are used to add memory to many mobile devices.

A *SIM card* is a small card that contains information used to authenticate a device to mobile telephone and data providers. The card can also hold user data such as personal contacts and text messages. Some phones can have two SIM cards installed; such a device is called a dual SIM device. A dual SIM device allows a number for personal use and a number for professional use to be received and sent from the same phone, for example. The dual SIM device could also hold SIM cards from different vendors.

Some mobile device batteries can be replaced, such as the battery shown outside the cell phone in Figure 7-29. Be sure to check the battery for bulging and avoid placing a mobile device in direct sunlight.

Wired Connectivity (7.4.1.2)

Mobile devices use a variety of cables and connectors.

A mini-USB Cable

A *mini-USB cable* (see Figure 7-30) may be used to connect a mobile device to an electrical outlet charger or to connect to another device in order to charge and/or transfer data.

Figure 7-30 Mini-USB Cable

A USB-C Cable

A *USB-C cable* and port (see Figure 7-31) can be plugged in in either direction. A USB-C cable may be used with a mobile device to connect to an electrical outlet charger or to connect to another device, such as to connect a smartphone to a laptop, in order to charge and/or transfer data.

Figure 7-31 USB-C Cable

Micro-USB cable

A *micro-USB cable* (see Figure 7-32) is used to connect a mobile device to an electrical outlet charger or to connect to another device in order to charge and/or transfer data.

Figure 7-32 Micro-USB Cable

Lightning Cable and Port

A *Lightning cable* (see Figure 7-33) is used to connect an Apple device to a host computer or another peripheral, such as a USB battery charger, a monitor, or a camera.

Figure 7-33 Lightning Cable and Port

Proprietary Cables and Ports

Proprietary, or vendor-specific, cables (see Figure 7-34) and ports can be found on some mobile devices. These cables are not compatible with other vendors' ports but often are compatible with other products from the same vendor.

Figure 7-34   Proprietary Cable

Wireless Connections and Shared Internet Connections (7.4.1.3)

Besides Wi-Fi, mobile devices also use the following wireless connections:

- *Near field communication (NFC)*: NFC enables mobile devices to establish radio communications with other devices if the devices are close together or touching.

- *Infrared (IR)*: If a mobile device is IR enabled, it can be used to control other IR-controlled devices remotely, such as a TV, a set-top box, or audio equipment.

- **Bluetooth:** This wireless technology allows data exchange over a short distance between two Bluetooth-enabled devices or can connect Bluetooth-enabled peripheral devices, such as speakers or headphones.

A smartphone's Internet connection can be shared with other devices. There are two ways to share a smartphone's Internet connection:

- **Tethering:** Tethering involves using a cellular phone as a modem for another device, such as a tablet or laptop. The connection is made over a USB cable or Bluetooth.

- *Mobile hotspot*: With a hotspot, devices connect using Wi-Fi to share a cellular data connection.

The ability to share a connection depends on the cellular carrier and the plan with the carrier.

Interactive Graphic

Check Your Understanding 7.4.1.4: Identify Connection Types

Refer to the online course to complete this activity.

Specialty Mobile Devices (7.4.2)

Types of mobile devices are growing and changing. In general, the number of different types of devices is growing, and the size of some devices is shrinking. Specialty mobile devices are electronic devices that are able to connect, share, and interact with a user and other smart devices. Commonly they are connected to other devices or networks using wireless protocols such as Bluetooth, Zigbee, and NFC.

Smart devices include smart thermostats, smartwatches, smart bands, smart keychains, and smart speakers.

Wearable Devices (7.4.2.1)

Wearable devices are clothing or accessories that include miniature computing devices. Smartwatches, fitness monitors, and smart headsets are some examples.

Fitness Monitors

Fitness monitors (see Figure 7-35) are designed to clip onto clothing or be worn on the wrist and are used for tracking a person's daily activity and body metrics as they work toward their fitness goals. These devices measure and collect activity data and can connect with other Internet-connected devices to upload the data for later review. Some fitness monitors may also have basic smartwatch capabilities, such as displaying caller ID and text messages.

Figure 7-35   Fitness Monitor

Smartwatch

Smartwatches (see Figure 7-36) combine the functions of watches and some functions of mobile devices. Some smartwatches include sensors to measure body and environmental metrics, such as heart rate, body temperature, elevation, or air temperature. They have touchscreen displays, and they can function on their own or be paired with smartphones. These watches can display notifications of incoming messages, incoming phone calls, and social media updates. Some smartwatches can send and receive messages and phone calls. Smartwatches can run apps directly or via a smartphone. They may also allow users to control some functions, such as music and a camera, on a smartphone.

Figure 7-36   Smartwatch

VR/AR Headsets

A common misconception is that virtual reality (VR) and augmented reality (AR) are the same thing. However, they are very different concepts. VR headsets (see Figure 7-37) provide the wearer with a complete immersion experience, shutting out the physical world. When a VR headset is turned on, the viewing panels inside completely fill the wearer's field of vision. AR headsets overlay digital elements to a live view of the physical world, often using the camera of a smartphone. In other words, AR projects a digital image over the real world. Pokémon Go is an example of an AR experience. Beyond games, there are some very practical uses for AR, such as a neurosurgeon using an AR projection of a 3D brain to aid in performing a surgery.

Figure 7-37   VR Headset

Specialty Devices (7.4.2.2)

There are many other types of smart devices. These devices benefit from network connectivity and advanced functions.

Global Positioning System

Global Positioning System (GPS) is a satellite-based navigation system. GPS satellites are located in space and transmit signals back to Earth (see Figure 7-38).

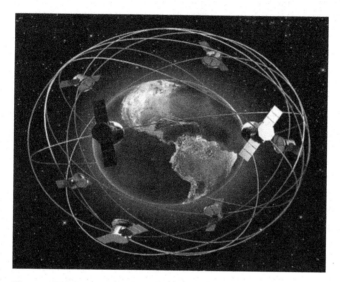

Figure 7-38   Global Positioning System

GPS Receiver

A *GPS receiver* (see Figure 7-39) locks onto GPS signals and constantly calculates its position relative to these satellites. After the position has been determined, the GPS receiver calculates other information, such as speed and time and distance to a programmed destination.

Figure 7-39   GPS Receiver

E-reader

An electronic reader, or e-reader, is a device optimized for reading electronic books, newspapers, magazines, and other documents, as shown in Figure 7-40. E-readers have Wi-Fi or cellular connectivity to download content. An e-reader has a similar form factor as a tablet, but the screen provides much better readability, especially in sunlight. E-readers are often lighter weight and have much longer battery life than an average tablet. This is made possible by using electronic paper technology, which makes text and images look similar to ink on paper.

Figure 7-40   E-reader

Network Connectivity and Email (7.5)

Network connectivity makes it possible to use many different hardware devices and software devices for communication. Connectivity happens using wired or wireless topologies and protocols. Different services are accessed when connected to a network; email is one such service, and it uses many protocols.

Wireless and Cellular Data Networks (7.5.1)

A cellular network and a wireless network basically let you do the same thing: connect to the network. Wireless makes use of radio waves in order to provide high-speed connections to users on a local area network (LAN), and Wi-Fi usually has no limit on the amount of data. Cellular networks cover large areas; access to these networks is typically based on paying for bandwidth through a mobile carrier. Cellular often provides slower connections than Wi-Fi.

Wireless Data Networks (7.5.1.1)

The ability of laptops, tablets, and cell phones to wirelessly connect to the Internet has provided people with the freedom to work, learn, communicate, and play wherever they want.

Mobile devices typically have two wireless Internet connectivity options:

- *Wi-Fi*: A wireless network connection involves local Wi-Fi settings.

- *Cellular*: Wireless network connection is provided for a fee using cellular data. Cellular networks require cellular towers and satellites to create a mesh of global coverage. A cellular data network connection can become expensive without an appropriate service plan.

You might need to register a device with a carrier or provide some kind of unique identifier to use a cellular network. Every mobile device has a unique 15-digit number called an *International Mobile Equipment Identity (IMEI)*. This number identifies the device to a carrier's network. The numbers come from a family of devices called the *Global System for Mobile Communications (GSM)*. The IMEI can often be found in the configuration settings of the device or in a battery compartment if the battery is removable.

The user of a device is also identified using a unique number called the International Mobile Subscriber Identity (IMSI). The IMSI is often programmed on the subscriber identity module (SIM) card, or it can be programmed on the phone itself, depending on the network type.

Wi-Fi is usually preferred over a cellular connection because it is usually free. Wi-Fi radios use less battery power than cellular radios, so the device battery should last longer using Wi-Fi.

Many businesses, organizations, and locations now also offer free Wi-Fi connections to attract customers. For example, coffee shops, restaurants, libraries, and even public transportation may offer free Wi-Fi access to users. Educational institutions also typically provide Wi-Fi connectivity. For instance, college campuses enable students to connect their mobile devices to the college network and sign up for classes, watch lectures, and submit assignments using the Wi-Fi.

It is important to secure home Wi-Fi networks. These precautions should be taken to protect Wi-Fi communications on mobile devices:

- Enable security on home networks. Always enable the highest Wi-Fi security framework possible. Currently, WPA2 security is the most secure.

- Never send login or password information using clear, unencrypted text.

- Use a secure VPN connection when possible.

Devices can connect to Wi-Fi networks automatically or manually. Use the following steps to connect to Wi-Fi on an Android device:

Step 1.   Select Settings > Add network.

Step 2.   Enter the network SSID.

Step 3.   Touch Security and select a security type.

Step 4.   Touch Password and enter the password.

Step 5.   Touch Save.

Use the following steps to connect to Wi-Fi on an iOS device:

Step 1.   Select Settings > Wi-Fi > Other.

Step 2.   Enter the network SSID.

Step 3.   Touch Security and select a security type.

Step 4.   Touch Other Network.

Step 5.   Touch Password and enter the password.

Step 6.   Touch Join.

Lab 7.5.1.2: Mobile Wi-Fi

In this lab, you will turn the Wi-Fi radio on and off, forget a found Wi-Fi network, and find and connect to a Wi-Fi network.

Cellular Communication Standards (7.5.1.3)

Cell phones were introduced in the mid-1980s. Back then, cell phones were big and bulky. It was difficult and expensive to call people on another cellular network because there were few industry standards for cellular technology. Without standards, interoperability between cell phone manufacturers was very difficult.

Industry standards have simplified interconnectivity between cell providers. These standards have also made it less expensive to use cellular technology. However, cellular standards have not been adopted uniformly around the world. Therefore, some cell phones may only work in one country and may not operate in other countries. Other cell phones are capable of using multiple standards and can operate in many countries.

Cellular technology has evolved to a new generation approximately every 10 years. The following are the major cellular standards:

- *1G*: Introduced in the 1980s, first-generation (1G) standards used analog standards. Analog systems were prone to noise and interference, which made it difficult to get a clear voice signal. Few 1G devices are in use today.

- *2G*: Introduced in the 1990s, the second-generation (2G) standards switched from analog to digital standards. 2G provided speeds up to 1 Mbps and supported higher call quality. 2G also introduced Short Message Service (SMS), which is used for text messaging, and Multimedia Message Service (MMS), which is used for sending and receiving photos and videos.

- *3G*: Introduced in the late 1990s, third-generation (3G) standards enabled speeds up to 2 Mbps to support mobile Internet access, web browsing, video calls, video streaming, and picture sharing.

- *4G*: Introduced in the late 2000s, 4G standards enable speeds of 100 Mbps and up to 1 Gb/s. 4G supports gaming services, high-quality video conferencing, and high-definition television. 4G technology is commonly available with Long Term Evolution (LTE). LTE adds improvements to 4G.

- *5G*: Introduced in 2019, 5G is more efficient than previous standards and may support speeds up to 20 Gb/s.

- 6G: This standard is currently under development at the time of this writing. It will likely support speeds significantly faster than 5G for advanced applications such as AR or VR that require more data throughput.

Many cell phones can also support multiple standards to enable backward compatibility. For instance, many cell phones support 4G and 5G standards. Such a phone uses 5G when available, and when the 5G network is no longer available, the phone automatically switches to 4G without losing connection.

Airplane Mode (7.5.1.4)

You might be required to disable your cellular access on occasion. For instance, airlines typically ask their passengers to disable cellular access. To simplify this process, most mobile devices have a setting called *Airplane mode*. This setting turns off all cellular as well as Wi-Fi and Bluetooth radios on the device.

Airplane mode is useful when traveling on an airplane or when located where accessing data is prohibited or expensive. Most mobile device functions are still usable, but communication is not possible.

Figure 7-41 displays the screen to turn Airplane mode on or off on an iOS device.

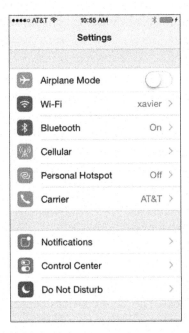

Figure 7-41   Airplane Mode Toggle on iOS

You can also enable or disable cellular access. Figure 7-42 shows the screen to enable or disable cellular access on an iOS device.

Figure 7-42   Cellular Data Toggle on iOS

Use the following steps to enable or disable cellular on an Android device:

Step 1.   Select Settings.

Step 2.   Touch More under Wireless and Networks.

Step 3.   Touch Mobile Networks.

Step 4.   Touch Data to enable or to disable it.

Use the following steps to enable or disable cellular on an iOS device:

Step 1.   Select Settings.

Step 2.   Touch General.

Step 3.   Touch Cellular Data to enable or to disable it.

Hotspot (7.5.1.5)

Another useful cellular feature is to use a cellular device as a *hotspot* to provide an Internet connection to other devices. The Wi-Fi devices could select the cellular device as its Wi-Fi connection. For instance, a user may need to connect a computer to the Internet when no Wi-Fi or wired connection is available. A cell phone can be used as a bridge to the Internet, through the cellular carrier's network.

To enable an iOS device to become a personal hotspot, touch Personal Hotspot, as shown at the bottom of Figure 7-43.

Figure 7-43   Personal Hotspot Toggle on iOS

This opens the Personal Hotspot screen shown in Figure 7-44. Notice that the iOS Personal Hotspot feature can also connect Bluetooth- or USB-connected devices to the Internet.

Figure 7-44   Personal Hotspot Settings on iOS

Note

Using a hotspot is sometimes referred to as tethering.

Finally, apps for mobile devices can be useful tools when diagnosing mobile device radio problems. For instance, a Wi-Fi analyzer can be used to display information about wireless networks, and a cell tower analyzer can be used on cellular networks.

Check Your Understanding 7.5.1.6: Wireless Technology

Refer to the online course to complete this activity.

Bluetooth (7.5.2)

Bluetooth is a low-power wireless technology standard that works using radio frequency to connect devices. It is a wireless short-range communications technology standard available in many products. Bluetooth devices automatically detect and connect to one another, and up to eight of them can communicate at any one time. They don't interfere with one another because each pair of devices uses a different channel of the 79 available channels. If two devices want to talk, they pick a channel randomly, and if that's already taken, they randomly switch to one of the others.

Bluetooth for Mobile Devices (7.5.2.1)

Bluetooth devices include wireless speakers, wireless headphones, wireless keyboards and mice, and wireless gaming controllers.

Wireless Speaker

Figure 7-45 shows an example of a portable mobile speaker that connects to mobile devices to provide high-quality audio without a stereo system.

Figure 7-45   Wireless Speaker

Wireless Headphones

Figure 7-46 shows high-quality Bluetooth headphones for listening to music. Some headphones also include a microphone and can be used as hands-free headsets for making and receiving telephone calls.

Figure 7-46   Wireless Headphones

Wireless Keyboard or Mouse

Some mobile devices can pair with a Bluetooth keyboard and mouse, as shown in Figure 7-47, to make input easier.

Figure 7-47   Wireless Keyboard and Mouse

Wireless Gaming Controller

Bluetooth game controllers, shown in Figure 7-48, can be paired to mobile devices.

Figure 7-48   Wireless Gaming Controller

Bluetooth Pairing (7.5.2.2)

Bluetooth is a networking standard that consists of two levels: the physical level and the protocol level. The physical level for Bluetooth is a radio frequency standard. Devices connect to other Bluetooth-enabled devices at the protocol level. This is referred to as Bluetooth pairing. At the protocol level, devices agree on when bits are sent and how they are sent, and they agree that what is received is the same as what was sent.

Specifically, with *Bluetooth pairing*, two Bluetooth devices establish a connection to share resources. In order for the devices to pair, the Bluetooth radios must be turned on, and one device begins searching for other devices. Other devices must be set to *discoverable mode*, also called *visible*, so that they can be detected.

When a Bluetooth device is in discoverable mode, it transmits Bluetooth and device information, such as device name, services that the device can use, Bluetooth class, and device name.

During the pairing process, a PIN may be requested to authenticate the pairing process, as shown in Figure 7-49. The PIN is often a number but can also be a numeric code or passkey. The PIN is stored using pairing services, so it does not have to be entered the next time the device tries to connect. This is convenient when using a headset with a smartphone because the phone and headset are paired automatically when the headset is turned on and within range.

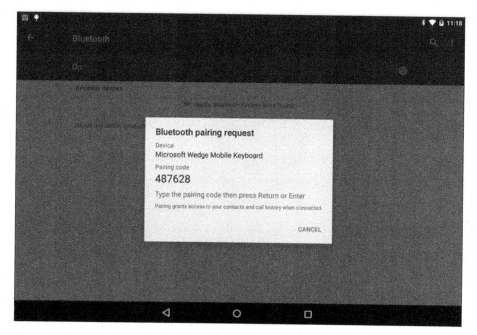

Figure 7-49   Bluetooth Pairing on Android

Use the following steps to pair a Bluetooth device with an Android device:

Step 1. Follow the instructions for your device to place it in discoverable mode.

Step 2. Check the instructions for your device to find the connection PIN.

Step 3. Select Settings > Bluetooth (under Wireless & Networks section).

Step 4. Touch the Bluetooth toggle to turn it on.

Step 5. Wait until Android scans and locates the Bluetooth device previously placed in discoverable mode.

Step 6. Touch the discovered device to select it.

Step 7. Enter the PIN.

Use the following steps to pair a Bluetooth device with an iOS device:

Step 1. Follow the instructions for your device to place it in discoverable mode.

Step 2. Check the instructions for your device to find the connection PIN.

Step 3. Select Settings > Bluetooth.

Step 4. Touch Bluetooth to turn it on.

Step 5. Touch the discovered device to select it.

Step 6. Enter the PIN.

Configuring Email (7.5.3)

Email consists of messages that are sent and received using the Internet. Many different email services allow you to create an email account and send and receive email and attachments, and many of them are free. The email communication basically uses three protocols—POP, SMTP, and IMAP—and a client/server network model. The user on the client system prepares and sends an email using an application called an *email client*. The server uses a server-side email protocol to forward the email to the appropriate devices and protocols until it reaches the intended recipient.

Introduction to Email (7.5.3.1)

We all use email, but most of us never really think about how email actually works. The email structure relies on the functions of email servers and email clients, as shown in Table 7-4.

Table 7-4   Email Servers and Clients

Servers	Clients
Responsible for forwarding email messages sent by their users.	Connect to the email servers to retrieve their emails.
Forward emails to other email servers.	Used to compose, read, and manage messages.
Store emails until retrieved by users.	Can be web-based or standalone applications. Standalone email clients are platform dependent.

Note

This section focuses on email clients for mobile devices.

Email clients and servers use various protocols and standards to exchange emails. The most common of them are described in Table 7-5.

Table 7-5   Email Protocols and Standards

Protocol or Standard	Description
Post Office Protocol 3 (POP3)	■ This is an email client protocol that is used to retrieve emails from a remote server over TCP/IP. ■ It enables a client to connect to an email server, download the user email from the server, and then disconnect. ■ POP3 typically does not leave a copy of the email on the server. ■ POP3 uses TCP port 110. ■ Compare with IMAP.
Internet Mail Access Protocol (IMAP)	■ This is an email client similar to POP3 except that it synchronizes email folders between the server and client and downloads copies of the email from the email server. ■ IMAP is faster than POP3 but requires more disk space and more CPU resources. ■ It is often used in large networks, such as a university campus. ■ The most recent version of IMAP is IMAP4, and it uses TCP port 143. ■ Compare with POP3.

Protocol or Standard	Description
Simple Mail Transfer Protocol (SMTP)	■ Email clients use SMTP to send emails to servers. ■ Email servers also use SMTP to send emails to other email servers. ■ A message is sent only after recipients are identified and verified. ■ SMTP is text based and uses only ASCII encoding and requires MIME to send all other file types. ■ SMTP uses TCP port 25.
Multipurpose Internet Mail Extensions (MIME)	■ MIME is normally used in conjunction with SMTP. ■ MIME extends the text-based email format to include other formats, such as pictures and word processor documents.
Secure Sockets Layer (SSL)	■ SSL was developed to transmit files securely. ■ Most email clients and servers support encryption of emails.

Email servers require email software such as *Microsoft Server Exchange*. Exchange is also a contact manager and calendaring software. It uses a proprietary messaging architecture called *Messaging Application Programming Interface (MAPI)*. MAPI is used by the Microsoft Office Outlook client to connect to Exchange servers to provide email, calendar, and contact management.

Email clients have to be installed on a mobile device. Many clients are configurable using a wizard. However, you need to know key information to set up an email account. Table 7-6 lists the type of information required when setting up an email account.

Table 7-6   Information Needed to Set Up an Email Account

Email Account Information	Description
Email address	This is the address people use in order to send email to you. An email address is a username followed by the @ symbol and the domain of the email server (for example, *user@ example*.net).
Display name	This can be your real name, a nickname, or any name that you want people to see.
Email protocols	The incoming mail server uses email protocols. Different protocols provide different email services.
Incoming and outgoing mail server names	These names are provided by the network administrator or ISP.
Account credentials	The credentials consist of the username that is used to log in to the mail server and the account password. Always use strong passwords.

Activity 7.5.3.2: Matching Email Protocols

Refer to the online course to complete this activity.

Android Email Configuration (7.5.3.3)

Android devices are capable of using advanced communication applications and data services. Many of these applications and features require the use of web services provided by Google.

When you configure an Android mobile device for the first time, you are prompted to sign in to your Google account with your Gmail email address and password. By signing in to your Gmail account, you gain access to the Google Play store, data and settings backup, and other Google services. The device synchronizes contacts, email messages, apps, downloaded content, and other information from Google services. If you do not have a Gmail account, you can use the Google account sign-in page to create one.

Use the following steps to add an email account on an Android device:

Step 1.   Touch the Email app icon or the Gmail app icon.

Step 2.   Choose the type of account (that is, Google/GMAIL, Personal, or Exchange) and tap Next.

Step 3.   Enter the device's passcode, if needed.

Step 4.   Enter the email address and password you want to use.

Step 5.   Tap Create New Account.

Step 6.   Enter your first name, last name, email address, and password.

Step 7.   Provide a phone number for account recovery purposes (optional).

Step 8.   Review the account information and tap Next.

> **Note**
>
> If you want to restore Android settings to a tablet that you have previously backed up, you must sign in to the account when setting up the tablet for the first time. You cannot restore your Android settings if you sign in after the initial setup.

After the initial setup, access your mailbox by touching the Gmail app icon. Android devices also have an email app for connecting to other email accounts, but it simply redirects the user to the Gmail app in later versions of Android.

iOS Email Configuration (7.5.3.4)

iOS devices ship with a stock Mail app that can handle multiple email accounts simultaneously. The Mail app also supports a number of different email account types, including iCloud, Yahoo, Gmail, Outlook, and Microsoft Exchange.

An *Apple ID* is required to set up an iOS device and is used to access the Apple App Store, the iTunes Store, and iCloud. iCloud provides email and the ability to store content on remote servers. iCloud email is free and comes with remote storage for backups, mail, and documents.

All your iOS devices, apps, and content are linked to your Apple ID. When an iOS device is turned on for the first time, the Setup Assistant guides you through the process of connecting the device and signing in with or creating an Apple ID. The Setup Assistant also allows you to create an iCloud email account. You can restore settings, content, and apps from a different iOS device from an iCloud backup during the setup process.

Use the following steps to set up an email account on an iOS device:

Step 1. Select Settings > Mail, Contacts, Calendars > Add Account.

Step 2. Tap the account type: iCloud, Exchange, Google, Yahoo, AOL, or Outlook.

Step 3. If the account type is not listed, touch Other.

Step 4. Enter the account information.

Step 5. Touch Save.

Internet Email (7.5.3.5)

Many people have multiple email addresses. For instance, you may have a personal email account and a school or work account.

The email service is provided using either:

- *Local email*: The email server is managed by a local IT department, such as a school network, business network, or organizational network.

- *Internet email*: The email service is hosted on the Internet and controlled by a service provider such as Gmail.

Users can access their online mailboxes by using any of the following:

- The default mobile email app included in the OS, such as iOS Mail.

- A browser-based email client, such as Mail, Outlook, Windows Live Mail, or Thunderbird.

- A mobile email client app, such as Gmail or Yahoo.

Email client apps provide a better user experience compared to the web interfaces.

Mobile Device Synchronization (7.5.4)

Mobile device synchronization involves making data available on different platforms and different devices and ensuring that all of them have the same data and settings and that there is no data loss. Synchronization is usually linked to a common account, and the data can include things like contacts and calendar data, as well as stored images, songs, movies, and business files.

Types of Data to Synchronize (7.5.4.1)

Many people use a combination of desktop, laptop, tablet, and smartphone devices to access and store information. It is helpful when specific information is the same across multiple devices. For example, without synchronization, when scheduling appointments using a calendar program, each new appointment would need to be entered in each device to ensure that each device is up to date. Data synchronization eliminates the need to make changes to every device.

Data synchronization involves the exchange of data between two or more devices while maintaining consistent data on those devices.

Synchronization methods include synchronization to the cloud, synchronization to a desktop, and synchronization to an automobile.

There are many different types of data to synchronize, including:

- Contacts
- Applications
- Email
- Pictures
- Music
- Videos
- Calendar
- Bookmarks
- Documents
- Location data
- Social media data
- E-books
- Passwords

Enabling Synchronization (7.5.4.2)

Sync typically means *data synchronization*. However, the meaning of sync varies slightly between Android and an iOS.

Android devices can synchronize your contacts and other data, including data from Facebook, Google, and Twitter. As a result, all devices using the same Google account will have access to the same data. This makes it easier to replace a damaged device without data loss. Android Sync also allows the user to choose the types of data to synchronize.

Android devices also support automatic synchronization with a feature called Auto Sync. This synchronizes the device with the service provider's servers automatically—without user intervention. To save on battery life, you can disable automatic synchronization for all or just some of the data.

Use the following steps to review what data to synchronize on an Android device:

Step 1.   Open your device's Settings app.

Step 2.   Tap Accounts. If you don't see Accounts, tap Users & accounts.

Step 3.   If you have more than one account on your device, tap the one you want.

Step 4.   Tap Account sync.

Step 5.   Review the data to be synchronized and when the data last synced. You can enable or disable which apps to sync.

Use the following steps to disable Auto Sync on an Android device:

Step 1.   Open your device's Settings app.

Step 2.   Tap Accounts. If you don't see Accounts, tap Users & accounts.

Step 3.   Disable Automatically sync data.

Use the following steps to manually sync an account on an Android device:

Step 1.   Open your device's Settings app.

Step 2.   Tap Accounts. If you don't see Accounts, tap Users & accounts. If you have more than one account on your device, tap the one you want.

Step 3.   Tap Account sync.

Step 4.   Tap More... and then Sync now.

Figure 7-50 displays a sample Sync screen on an Android device.

Figure 7-50 Specifying Types of Data to Back Up on Android

iOS devices support two types of synchronizing:

- *Backup*: Copies your personal data (application settings, text messages, voicemails, and other data types) from your phone to your computer. Backup saves a copy of all data created by the user and by apps.

- *Sync*: Copies new apps, music, video, or books from iTunes to your phone and from your phone to iTunes, resulting in full synchronization on your phone and iTunes. Sync copies only media downloaded via the iTunes Store mobile app, respecting what was specified through the iTunes Sync definitions. For example, a user can prevent movies from syncing to the phone if the user does not watch movies on the phone.

As a general rule, when connecting an iOS device to iTunes, always run Backup first and then run Sync. This order can be changed in the iTunes Preferences.

A few more useful options are available when performing Sync or Backup on iOS:

- *Backup storage location*: iTunes allows backups to be stored on the local computer hard drive or on the iCloud online service.

- *Backup straight from an iOS device*: In addition to backing up data from an iOS device to the local hard drive or iCloud through iTunes, users can configure the iOS device to upload a copy of the data directly to iCloud. This is useful as backups can be performed automatically, eliminating the need to connect to iTunes. As with Android, the user can specify what type of data is sent to the iCloud backup, as shown in Figure 7-51.

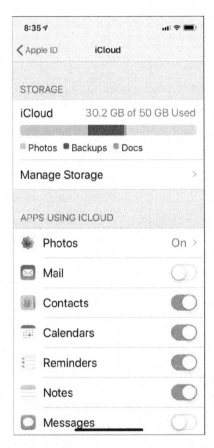

Figure 7-51   Specifying Types of Data to Back Up on iOS

- *Sync over Wi-Fi*: iTunes can scan and connect to iOS on the same Wi-Fi network. When connected, the backup process can be initiated automatically between iOS devices and iTunes. This is useful as backups can be performed automatically every time iTunes and the iOS device are on the same Wi-Fi, eliminating the need for a wired USB connection.

When a new iPhone is connected to the computer, iTunes offers to restore it using the most recent backup of data from another iOS device, if available. Figure 7-52 shows the iTunes window on a computer.

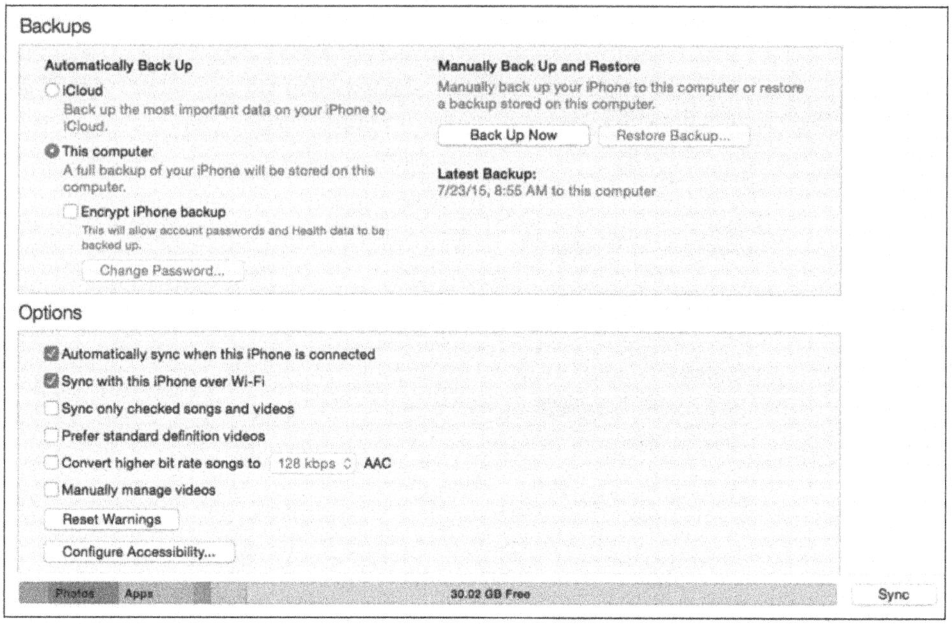

Figure 7-52   Syncing Data on iTunes

Synchronization Connection Types (7.5.4.3)

To synchronize data between devices, the devices use either USB or Wi-Fi connections.

Most Android devices do not have a desktop program for performing data synchronization, so most users sync with Google's different web services, even when synchronizing with a desktop or laptop computer. One benefit of synchronizing data using this method is that the data is accessible from any computer or mobile device at any time by signing in to a Google account. The disadvantage of this arrangement is that it can be difficult to synchronize data with programs that are installed locally on a computer, such as Outlook for email, calendar, and contacts.

iOS devices can also use Wi-Fi sync to synchronize with iTunes. To use Wi-Fi sync, the iOS device must first synchronize with iTunes using a USB cable. You must also turn on Sync over Wi-Fi Connection in the Summary pane of iTunes, as shown in Figure 7-53. After that, you can use Wi-Fi sync or a USB cable. When the iOS device is on the same wireless network as the computer running iTunes and is plugged into a power source, it automatically synchronizes with iTunes.

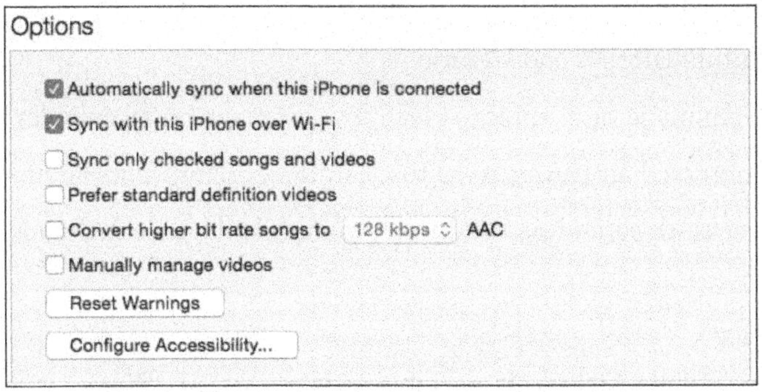

Figure 7-53   Syncing Data on iTunes over Wi-Fi

Microsoft also offers cloud storage for synchronizing data between devices through the use of OneDrive. OneDrive is also able to synchronize data between mobile devices and PCs.

Preventive Maintenance for Laptops and Other Mobile Devices (7.6)

Preventive maintenance should be scheduled at regular intervals to keep laptops and mobile devices running properly. It is important to keep them clean and to ensure that they are being used in an optimal environment. This section covers preventive maintenance techniques for laptops and mobile devices.

Scheduled Maintenance for Laptops and Other Mobile Devices (7.6.1)

The preventive maintenance schedule for a laptop may include practices that are unique to a particular organization but should also include these standard procedures: cleaning, hard drive maintenance, and software updates.

Mobile devices are prone to damage, and there should be a plan of care for any device before a problem arises. Preventive maintenance for mobile devices is necessary to ensure that they can be used safely and effectively and to make them last longer.

What Do You Already Know? - Preventive Maintenance (7.6.1.1)

What do you already know about preventive maintenance of laptops and other mobile devices? Choose whether the following statements are true or false.

1. Mobile devices are more likely than desktop computers to be exposed to harmful materials and situations.

2. Use ammonia or alcohol to clean touchscreens on mobile devices.

3. Compressed air can be used to clean the cooling vents and fan on a laptop.

4. A wet cloth should be used to clean mobile device touchpads.

Answers:

1. True. Mobile devices are portable and are used in different types of environments. They are also commonly carried in pockets and purses. They can be damaged by drops, excess moisture, heat, or cold.

2. False. Harsh chemicals such as alcohol or ammonia can damage mobile device components such as touchscreens. Instead, use cleaning solutions designed for touchscreens and lint-free cloths.

3. True. To clean out the dust from the vents and from the fan behind a vent, use compressed air or non-electrostatic vacuum.

4. False. To clean the touchpad, gently use a soft, lint-free cloth that is moistened with an approved cleaner.

The Reason for Maintenance (7.6.1.2)

Because laptops and mobile devices are portable, they are used in different types of environments. As a result, they are more likely than desktop computers to be exposed to harmful materials and situations, including dirt and contamination, spills, drops, excessive heat or cold, and excessive moisture. In a laptop, many components are placed in a very small area, directly beneath the keyboard. Spilling liquid on the keyboard can result in severe internal damage. It is important to keep a laptop clean. Proper care and maintenance can help laptop components run more efficiently and extend the life of the equipment.

Laptop Preventive Maintenance Program (7.6.1.3)

A *preventive maintenance program* is important in addressing issues such as dirt, contamination, drops, and other concerns related to laptops. It must include a routine schedule for maintenance. Maintenance should also be performed when usage demands it.

The preventive maintenance schedule for a laptop may include practices that are unique to a particular organization but should also include the standard procedures of cleaning, hard drive maintenance, and software updates.

To keep a laptop clean, be proactive, not reactive. Keep fluids and food away from the laptop. Close the laptop when it is not in use. When cleaning a laptop, never use harsh cleaners or solutions that contain ammonia. Use nonabrasive materials including compressed air, mild cleaning solutions, cotton swabs, and a soft, lint-free cloth.

Caution

Before you clean a laptop, disconnect it from all power sources and remove the battery.

Routine maintenance includes the monthly cleaning of these laptop components:

- **Exterior case:** Wipe the case with a soft, lint-free cloth that is lightly moistened with water or mild cleaning solution.

- **Cooling vents and I/O ports:** Use compressed air or a non-electrostatic vacuum to clean out the dust from the vents and from the fan behind the vent. Use tweezers to remove any debris.

- **Display:** Wipe the display with a soft, lint-free cloth that is lightly moistened with a computer screen cleaner.

- **Keyboard:** Wipe the keyboard with a soft, lint-free cloth that is lightly moistened with water or a mild cleaning solution.

- **Touchpad:** Wipe the surface of the touchpad gently with a soft, lint-free cloth that is moistened with an approved cleaner. Never use a wet cloth.

Note

If it is obvious that the laptop needs to be cleaned, clean it. Do not wait for the next scheduled maintenance.

Mobile Device Preventive Maintenance Program (7.6.1.4)

Mobile devices are often carried in pockets or purses. They can be damaged by drops, excess moisture, heat, or cold. Although mobile device screens are designed to prevent light scratching, the touchscreen should be protected using a screen protector if possible.

Preventive maintenance for mobile devices requires only three basic tasks:

- **Cleaning:** Use a soft, lint-free cloth and a cleaning solution designed for a touchscreen to keep the touchscreen clean. Do not use ammonia or alcohol to clean the touchscreen.

- **Backing up the data:** Keep a backup copy of the information on the mobile device (contacts, music, photos, video, apps, and any customized settings) somewhere else, such as in a cloud drive.

- **Updating the system and applications:** When a new version of the operating system or applications is available, the device should be updated to ensure that the device is working at its best. An update can include new features, fixes, or improvements to performance and stability.

Basic Troubleshooting Process for Laptops and Other Mobile Devices (7.7)

Troubleshooting is a skill that is developed with experience. Technicians can better develop their troubleshooting skills through gaining experience and using an organized approach to problem solving.

Applying the Troubleshooting Process to Laptops and Other Mobile Devices (7.7.1)

This section outlines a systematic approach that can be employed to properly troubleshoot and gives specifics on how to address issues that are particular to laptops and mobile devices.

The Six Steps of the Troubleshooting Process (7.7.1.1)

The troubleshooting process has six steps:

Step 1.   Identify the problem.

Step 2.   Establish a theory of probable cause.

Step 3.   Test the theory to determine the cause.

Step 4.   Establish a plan of action to resolve the problem and implement the solution.

Step 5.   Verify full system functionality and, if applicable, implement preventive measures.

Step 6.   Document findings, actions, and outcomes.

Identify the Problem (7.7.1.2)

Laptop and mobile device problems can result from a combination of hardware, software, and network issues. Technicians must be able to analyze a problem and determine the cause of the error to repair the device. This process is called *troubleshooting*.

The first step in the troubleshooting process is to identify the problem. Table 7-7 shows a list of open-ended and closed-ended questions to ask laptop and mobile device customers.

Table 7-7   Step 1: Identify the Problem

Identify the Problem for Laptops

Open-ended questions	▪ What problems are you experiencing with your laptop?
	▪ What software has been installed recently?
	▪ What were you doing when the problem was identified?
	▪ What error messages have you received?
Closed-ended questions	▪ Is the laptop under warranty?
	▪ Is the laptop currently using the battery?
	▪ Can the laptop operate using the AC adapter?
	▪ Can the laptop boot and show the operating system desktop?

Identify the Problem for Other Mobile Devices

Open-ended questions	▪ What is the problem you are experiencing?
	▪ What are the make and model of your mobile device?
	▪ What service provider do you have?
Closed-ended questions	▪ Has this problem happened before?
	▪ Has anyone else used the mobile device?
	▪ Is your mobile device under warranty?

Establish a Theory of Probable Cause (7.7.1.3)

After you have talked to the customer, you can establish a theory of probable cause. Table 7-8 lists some common probable causes of laptop and mobile device problems.

Table 7-8   Step 2: Establish a Theory of Probable Cause

Common causes of laptop problems	▪ Battery does not have a charge
	▪ Battery will not charge
	▪ Loose cable connections
	▪ Keyboard does not work
	▪ Num Lock key is on
	▪ Loose RAM module

Common causes of mobile device problems	<ul><li>The Power button is broken.</li><li>The battery can no longer hold a charge.</li><li>There is excessive dirt in the speaker, microphone, or charging port.</li><li>The mobile device has been dropped.</li><li>The mobile device has been submerged.</li></ul>

Test the Theory to Determine Cause (7.7.1.4)

After you have developed some theories about what is wrong, test your theories to determine the cause of the problem. Table 7-9 shows a list of quick procedures you can use to determine the exact cause of the problem or even correct the problem. If a quick procedure does not correct the problem, research the problem further to establish the exact cause.

Table 7-9   Step 3: Test the Theory to Determine Cause

Common steps to determine the cause for laptop problems	<ul><li>Use the AC adapter with the laptop.</li><li>Replace the battery.</li><li>Reboot the laptop.</li><li>Check the BIOS settings.</li><li>Disconnect and reconnect the cables.</li><li>Disconnect peripherals.</li><li>Toggle the Num Lock key.</li><li>Remove and reinstall RAM.</li><li>Check whether the caps lock key is on.</li><li>Check for non-bootable media in a boot device.</li></ul>
Common steps to determine the cause of mobile device problems	<ul><li>Restart the mobile device.</li><li>Plug the mobile device into an AC outlet.</li><li>Replace the mobile device battery.</li><li>Remove any removable battery and reinstall it.</li><li>Clean the speaker, microphone, charging port, or other connection ports.</li></ul>

Establish a Plan of Action to Resolve the Problem and Implement the Solution (7.7.1.5)

After you have determined the exact cause of the problem, establish a plan of action to resolve the problem and implement the solution. Table 7-10 shows some sources you can use to gather additional information to resolve an issue.

Table 7-10 Step 4: Establish a Plan of Action to Resolve the Problem and Implement the Solution

If no solution is achieved in the previous step, further research is needed to implement the solution.	■ Help desk repair logs ■ Other technicians ■ Manufacturer FAQ websites ■ Technical websites ■ News groups ■ Computer manuals ■ Device manuals ■ Online forums ■ Internet search

Verify Full System Functionality and, if Applicable, Implement Preventive Measures (7.7.1.6)

After you have established a plan of action to resolve the problem and implement the solution, the next step is to document your findings, actions, and outcomes. Table 7-11 shows a list of the tasks required to document the problem and the solution.

Table 7-11 Step 5: Verify Full System Functionality and, if Applicable, Implement Preventive Measures

Verify solution and full system functionality for laptops	■ Reboot the laptop. ■ Attach all peripherals. ■ Operate the laptop using only the battery. ■ Print a document from an application. ■ Type a sample document to test the keyboard. ■ Check Event Viewer for warnings or errors.

Verify solution and full system functionality for mobile devices	■ Reboot the mobile device.
	■ Browse the Internet using Wi-Fi.
	■ Browse the Internet using 4G, 3G, or another carrier network type.
	■ Make a phone call.
	■ Send a text message.
	■ Open different types of apps.
	■ Operate the mobile device using only the battery.

Document Findings, Actions, and Outcomes (7.7.1.7)

In the final step of the troubleshooting process, document your findings, actions, and outcomes. Table 7-12 shows a list of the tasks required to document the problem and the solution.

Table 7-12   Step 6: Document Findings, Actions, and Outcomes

Document your findings, actions, and outcomes	■ Discuss the solution implemented with the customer.
	■ Have the customer verify that the problem has been solved.
	■ Provide the customer with all paperwork.
	■ Document the steps taken to solve the problem in the work order and technician's journal.
	■ Document any components used in the repair.
	■ Document the time spent to solve the problem.

Common Problems and Solutions for Laptops and Other Mobile Devices (7.7.2)

In this section you will go through some of the symptoms and problems that you will possibly come across on your laptop or other mobile devices. To repair a device, a technician must be able to analyze the problems and determine the causes of the error.

Identify Common Problems and Solutions (7.7.2.1)

Problems with laptops and other mobile devices can be attributed to hardware, software, or networks or some combination of the three. You will resolve some types of problems more often than others.

Common Problems and Solutions for Laptops (7.7.2.2)

Table 7-13 lists common problems, probable causes, and possible solutions for laptops.

Table 7-13   Common Problems and Solutions for Laptops

Identify the Problem	Probable Causes	Possible Solutions
Laptop does not power on.	Laptop is not plugged in.	Plug the laptop into AC power.
	Battery is not charged.	Remove and reinstall the battery.
	Battery will not hold a charge.	Replace battery if it will not charge.
Laptop battery supports the system for a reduced period of time.	Proper battery charging and discharging practices have not been followed.	Follow the battery charging procedures described in the manual.
	Extra peripherals are draining the battery.	Remove unneeded peripherals and disable the wireless NIC, if possible.
	Power plan isn't configured correctly.	Modify the power plan to decrease battery usage.
	Battery is not holding a charge for very long.	Replace the battery.
External display has power but no image on the screen.	Video cable is loose or damaged.	Reconnect or replace video cable.
	The laptop is not sending a video signal to the external display.	Use the Fn key along with the multipurpose key to toggle to the external display.
Laptop is powered on but nothing appears on the display when the laptop lid is reopened.	The screen cutoff switch is dirty or damaged.	Check the laptop repair manual for instructions about cleaning or replacing the LCD cutoff switch.
	The laptop has gone into sleep mode.	Press a key on the keyboard to bring the computer out of sleep mode.
The image on a laptop screen looks dull and pale.	The LCD backlight is not properly adjusted.	Check the laptop repair manual for instructions about calibrating the LCD backlight.
The image on a laptop display is pixilated.	Display properties are incorrect.	Set the display to native resolution.
The laptop display is flickering.	Images on the screen are not refreshing fast enough.	Adjust the screen refresh rate.
	The inverter is damaged or malfunctioning.	Disassemble the display and replace the inverter.

Identify the Problem	Probable Causes	Possible Solutions
A user is experiencing a ghost cursor that moves on its own.	The track pad is dirty.	Clean the track pad.
	A track pad and mouse are being used at the same time.	Disconnect the mouse.
	A finger or hand has touched the track pad while typing.	Try not to touch the track pad while typing.
Pixels on the screen are dead or not generating color.	Power to the pixels has been cut off.	Contact the manufacturer.
The image on the screen appears to flash lines or patterns of different color and size (artifacts).	The display is not properly connected.	Disassemble the laptop and check the display connections.
	The GPU is overheating.	Disassemble and clean the computer, checking for dust and debris.
	The GPU is faulty or malfunctioning.	Replace the GPU.
Color patterns on a screen are incorrect.	The display is not properly connected.	Disassemble the laptop to check the display connections.
	The GPU is overheating.	Disassemble and clean the computer, checking for dust and debris.
	The GPU is faulty or malfunctioning.	Replace the GPU.
Images on a display are distorted.	Display settings have been changed.	Restore the display settings to the original factory settings.
	The display is not properly connected.	Disassemble the computer to a point where you can check the display connections.
	The GPU is overheating.	Disassemble and clean the computer, checking for dust and debris.
	The GPU is faulty or malfunctioning.	Replace the GPU.
The network is fully functional, and the wireless connection is enabled, but the laptop cannot connect to the network.	Wi-Fi is turned off.	Turn on Wi-Fi using the wireless NIC properties or the Fn key along with the appropriate multipurpose key.
	The laptop is out of wireless range.	Move the laptop closer to the wireless access point.

Identify the Problem	Probable Causes	Possible Solutions
Input devices connected with Bluetooth are not functioning properly.	Bluetooth is turned off.	Turn on Bluetooth by using the Bluetooth settings applet or the Fn key along with the appropriate multipurpose key.
	Batteries in the input device are dead.	Replace the batteries.
	The input device is out of range.	Move the input device closer to the laptop's Bluetooth receiver and verify that Bluetooth is turned on.
The keyboard is inserting numbers instead of letters.	Num Lock is enabled.	Turn off Num Lock by using the Num Lock key or the Fn key along with the appropriate multipurpose key.
The battery is swollen.	The battery has been overcharged. An incompatible charger has been used. The battery is defective.	Replace the battery with a new one from the manufacturer.

Common Problems and Solutions for Other Mobile Devices (7.7.2.3)

Table 7-14 lists common problems, probable causes, and possible solutions for other mobile devices.

Table 7-14   Common Problems and Solutions for Other Mobile Devices

Identify the Problem	Probable Causes	Possible Solutions
The mobile device will not connect to the Internet.	Wi-Fi is not available.	Move to within the boundaries of a Wi-Fi network.
	There is no carrier data network in range.	Move to within the boundaries of a carrier data network.
The mobile device will not turn on.	The battery is drained.	Charge the mobile device or replace the battery with a charged battery.
	The power button is broken. The device has failed.	Contact customer support to determine the next course of action.

Identify the Problem	Probable Causes	Possible Solutions
A tablet fails to charge or charges very slowly when connected to AC power.	The tablet is in use when charging.	Turn off the tablet when charging.
	The AC adapter does not have enough amperage.	Use the AC adapter that came with the tablet.
		Use an AC adapter that has the correct amount of amperage.
A smartphone cannot connect to the carrier's network.	The SIM card is not installed.	Install the SIM card.
The mobile device does not power on.	The battery is not charged.	Plug the device into AC power to charge the battery.
	The battery will not hold a charge.	Replace the battery with a known good one.
		Use an AC adapter with the correct amperage rating.
	The power button is broken.	Contact customer support to determine the next course of action.
The mobile device battery supports the system for a reduced period of time.	Device settings are incorrectly configured.	Modify the power plan to decrease the battery usage.
	The battery is not holding a charge.	Replace the battery.
The mobile device will not connect to the Internet.	Wi-Fi is not available.	Turn on Wi-Fi.
		Make sure Airplane mode is turned off.
	Wi-Fi is turned off.	Turn on Wi-Fi.
	Wi-Fi settings are incorrect.	Configure the correct Wi-Fi settings.
	There is no carrier data network in range.	Move to within the boundaries of a Wi-Fi network.

Identify the Problem	Probable Causes	Possible Solutions
The mobile device will not connect with Bluetooth.	Bluetooth is turned off.	Turn on Bluetooth.
	The devices are not paired.	Pair the devices.
	The device is not in range.	Bring the device into range.
The battery is swollen.	The battery has been overcharged.	Replace the battery with a new one from the manufacturer.
	An incompatible charger has been used.	
	The battery is defective.	
The touchscreen is not responsive.	The touchscreen is dirty.	Clean the touchscreen.
	The touchscreen has shorted out due to damage or water.	Replace the touchscreen.
	The touchscreen has failed.	
The device exhibits very short battery life.	The battery has been cycled so many times that it does not hold a high charge.	Replace the battery.
	The battery is defective.	
The device is overheating.	A power-intensive app is running while the device is charging.	Close any unnecessary apps or remove the device from the charger.
	Many radios are on while the device is charging.	Turn off any unnecessary radios or remove the device from the charger.
	The battery is defective.	Replace the battery.

Lab 7.7.2.4: Research Laptop Specifications

Laptops often use proprietary parts. To find information about the replacement parts, you may have to research the website of the laptop manufacturer.

Lab 7.7.2.5: Gather Information from the Customer

In this lab, you will act as a call center technician and create closed-ended and open-ended questions to ask a customer about a laptop problem.

Lab 7.7.2.6: Investigate Support Websites

In this lab, you will investigate the services provided by a local laptop repair company or a laptop manufacturer's support website. Use the Internet or a local phone directory to locate a local laptop repair company or laptop manufacturer's support website.

Summary (7.8)

In this chapter, you learned the features and functionality of laptops and other mobile devices, such as smartphones and tablets, as well as how to remove and install internal and external components. Laptops are portable computers and usually run full versions of operating systems such as Microsoft Windows, macOS, or Linux. Smartphones and tablets run special operating systems that are designed for mobile devices. Other small mobile devices that are popular are smartwatches, fitness trackers, and virtual and augmented reality headsets.

You learned that laptops use the same types of ports as desktop computers so that peripheral devices can be interchangeable. Mobile devices can also use some of the same peripheral devices. Essential input devices, such as a keyboard and track pad, are built into laptops to provide similar functionality to desktop computers. Some laptops and mobile devices use touchscreens as input devices. The internal components of laptops are typically smaller than desktop components because they are designed to fit into compact spaces and conserve energy. The internal components of mobile devices are usually connected to the circuit board to keep the device compact and lightweight.

Laptops feature function keys that can be pressed in combination with the Fn key. The functions performed by these keys are specific to the laptop model. Docking stations and port replicators can increase the functionality of laptops by providing the same types of ports that are featured on desktop computers. A mobile device may use a docking station to charge or may use peripheral devices. Laptops and mobile devices most commonly feature LCD or LED screens, many of which are touchscreens. Backlights illuminate LCD and LED laptop displays. OLED displays have no backlight.

Laptops and mobile devices can feature several wireless technologies, including Bluetooth, infrared, Wi-Fi, and the ability to access cellular WANs.

Laptops provide many expansion possibilities. Users can add memory to increase performance, make use of flash memory to increase storage capacity, or increase functionality by using expansion cards. Some mobile devices can add more storage capacity by upgrading or adding more flash memory, such as MicroSD cards.

At the end of the chapter, you learned the importance of having a preventive maintenance program for laptops and other mobile devices. Mobile devices are used in different types of environments, and as a result, they are more likely than desktop computers to be exposed to harmful materials and situations, including dirt and contamination, spills, drops, excessive heat or cold, and excessive moisture.

Finally, you learned the six steps in the troubleshooting process as they pertain to laptops and other mobile devices.

Practice

The following activities provide practice with the topics introduced in this chapter. The labs are available in the companion *IT Essentials v8 Labs & Study Guide* (ISBN 9780138166304).

Labs

Lab 7.1.1.10: Mobile Device Information

Lab 7.1.2.7: Research Docking Stations and Port Replicators

Lab 7.3.2.4: Research Laptop Screens

Lab 7.3.2.7: Research Laptop Batteries

Lab 7.3.2.10: Research Laptop Drives

Lab 7.5.1.2: Mobile Wi-Fi

Lab 7.7.2.4: Research Laptop Specifications

Lab 7.7.2.5: Gather Information from the Customer

Lab 7.7.2.6: Investigate Support Websites

Check Your Understanding Questions

Complete all the review questions listed here to test your understanding of the topics and concepts in this chapter. Appendix A, "Answers to 'Check Your Understanding' Questions," lists the answers.

1. At a conference, a presenter cannot get the laptop to display through the projector, and a technician is called. What should the technician try first?

   A. Replace the projector or provide an alternate one.

   B. Use the appropriate Fn key to output to the external display.

   C. Attach an AC adapter to the laptop.

   D. Reboot the laptop.

2. What is a CRU as it relates to a laptop?

    A. a network connector

    B. a type of processor

    C. a type of storage device

    D. a part a user can replace

3. Which wireless technology can be used to connect wireless headphones to a computer?

    A. Bluetooth

    B. NFC

    C. Wi-Fi

    D. 4G/LTE

4. A technician is trying to determine the cause of a laptop problem. Which of the listed activities is an example of the technician testing a theory?

    A. The technician uses an AC adapter to power the laptop.

    B. The technician suspects a loose cable.

    C. The technician determines that the keyboard does not work.

    D. The technician asks the user when they first noticed the problem.

5. Which type of media would be used with a card reader attached to a laptop?

    A. DVD

    B. CD-R

    C. Blu-ray

    D. SD

6. Which statement is true of laptop motherboards?

    A. Most of them use the ATX form factor.

    B. The form factor varies by manufacturer.

    C. They are interchangeable with most desktop motherboards.

    D. They follow standard form factors so they can be interchanged easily.

7. A traveling sales representative uses a cell phone to interact with the home office and customers, track samples, make sales calls, log mileage, and upload/download data while at a hotel. Which Internet connectivity method would be a preferred method to use on the mobile device due to the low cost?

    A. cable

    B. cellular

    C. Z-Wave

    D. Wi-Fi

    E. DSL

8. Which protocol enables mail to be downloaded from an email server to a client and then deletes the email from the server?

    A. SMTP

    B. IMAP

    C. POP3

    D. HTTP

9. Why are SODIMMs well suited for laptops?

    A. They do not produce heat.

    B. They connect to external ports.

    C. They have a small form factor.

    D. They are interchangeable with desktops.

10. Which type of laptop display has components that may contain mercury and uses either a CCFL or LED backlight?

    A. LED

    B. LCD

    C. plasma

    D. OLED

11. What is used to provide location information to smart devices?

    A. GPS

    B. smart hub

    C. Zigbee coordinator

    D. e-reader

12. Which laptop component makes use of throttling to reduce power consumption and heat?

    A. optical drive

    B. motherboard

    C. CPU

    D. hard drive

13. What two sources of information are used to enable geocaching, geotagging, and device tracking on Android and iOS devices? (Choose two.)

A. images of the environment from the integrated camera

B. the user profile

C. cellular or Wi-Fi network

D. GPS signals

14. Which ACPI power state provides power to the CPU and RAM but powers down unused devices?

A. S3

B. S0

C. S1

D. S2

E. S4

15. Which laptop part is removed by pressing outward on clips that hold it into place?

A. SODIMM

B. power supply

C. card reader

D. wireless antenna

CHAPTER 8

Printers

Objectives

Upon completion of this chapter, you will be able to answer the following questions:

- What are the characteristics and capabilities of printers?

- What are printer connectors and ports?

- What are the parts and characteristics of inkjet printers?

- What are the parts and characteristics of laser printers?

- How do laser printers operate?

- What are the characteristics of thermal printers and impact printers?

- What are the characteristics of virtual printers?

- What are the parts and characteristics of 3D printers?

- How do you install and update the device driver, firmware, and RAM for a printer?

- How do you configure settings on a printer?

- How do you optimize printing performance?

- How do you configure printer sharing?

- How do you configure printer sharing using a print server?

- What are vendor guidelines, and what is the importance of appropriate operational environments for printers?

- How do you perform preventive maintenance on an inkjet printer?

- How do you perform preventive maintenance on a laser printer?

- How do you perform preventive maintenance on a thermal printer?

- How do you perform preventive maintenance on an impact printer?

- How do you perform preventive maintenance on a 3D printer?

- What are the six steps of troubleshooting printers?

- What are common problems and solutions for printers?

Key Terms

This chapter uses the following key terms. You can find the definitions in the glossary at the end of the book.

3D printer   page 446

automatic document feeder (ADF)   page 420

axis   page 449

belt   page 430

carriage   page 430

charging   page 436

Introduction (8.0)

Printers produce paper copies of electronic files. Government regulations and business policies often require that physical records be kept. This makes paper copies of digital documents as important today as they were when the paperless revolution began several years ago. This chapter provides essential information about printers. You will learn how printers operate, what to consider when purchasing a printer, and how to connect printers to an individual computer or to a network. You will also learn the operation of various types of printers and how to install them and maintain them, as well as how to troubleshoot common problems that arise. At the end of the chapter you will learn the importance of a preventive maintenance program for printers and apply the six steps in the troubleshooting process as they pertain to printers.

It is important to not only learn about the different types of printers and their components but also to build hands-on skills. In this chapter you will complete labs performing preventive maintenance on an inkjet printer and a laser printer. You will also work labs on installing a printer and sharing a printer in Windows.

Common Printer Features (8.1)

Printers come in various models and types, and they are chosen to meet the different needs and necessities of an organization. Choosing printers requires an understanding of their individual features. Choosing the right model saves time, is cost-effective, and efficiently uses company resources. Different purchase choices will be made for high-volume document printing than for printing of digital pictures to create brochures.

Characteristics and Capabilities (8.1.1)

No matter what model, price range, and type of printer you purchase, you need to consider how the printer is going to be used. Printing speeds, monochrome or color, cost and availability of cartridges, driver compatibility, power consumption, network type, and total cost of ownership are some of the many factors that need to be considered when purchasing, repairing, and maintaining printers.

Characteristics of Printers (8.1.1.1)

Computer technicians are often required to select, purchase, and install printers for users. Technicians need to know how to configure, troubleshoot, and repair the most common types of printers. Most printers available today are either laser printers using imaging drums or inkjet printers using electrostatic spray technology.

Dot matrix printers using impact technology are used in applications that require carbon copies. Thermal printers, commonly found in retail environments, are typically used to print receipts. 3D printers are used in design and manufacturing. Figure 8-1 shows examples of these five types of printers.

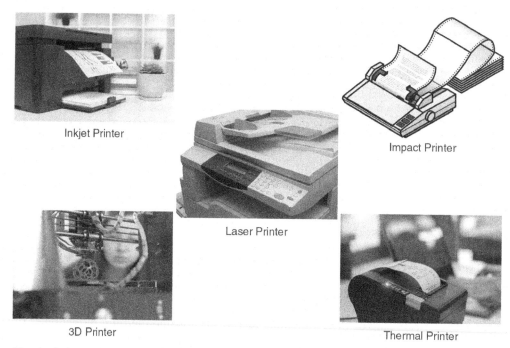

Inkjet Printer

Impact Printer

Laser Printer

3D Printer

Thermal Printer

Figure 8-1   Characteristics of Printers

Printer Speed, Quality, and Color (8.1.1.2)

Printer speed is a factor to consider when selecting a printer. The speed of a printer is measured in *pages per minute (PPM)*. Printer speed varies between makes and models. Speed is also affected by the complexity of the image and the quality desired by the user. The quality of printing is measured in *dots per inch (dpi)*. The larger the dpi number, the better the image resolution. When the resolution is higher, text and images are clearer. To produce the best high-resolution images, use high-quality ink or toner and high-quality paper.

The color printing process uses the primary colors cyan, magenta, and yellow (CMY). For inkjet printing, the color black serves as the base or key color. Thus, the acronym *CMYK* refers to the inkjet color printing process. Figure 8-2 shows a CMYK color wheel.

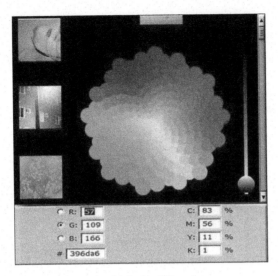

Figure 8-2 CMYK Color Wheel

Reliability and Total Cost of Ownership (8.1.1.3)

A printer should be reliable. Many types of printers are on the market, and it is important to research the specifications of several printers before selecting one. Here are some manufacturer options to consider:

- **Warranty:** Identify what is covered by the warranty.

- **Scheduled servicing:** Servicing is based on expected usage. Usage information is in the documentation or on the manufacturer's website.

- *Mean time between failures (MTBF)*: A printer should work without failing for an average length of time. Information about the MTBF is provided in the documentation or on the manufacturer's website.

When buying a printer, there is more than just the initial cost of the printer to consider. The *total cost of ownership (TCO)* includes a number of factors:

- Initial purchase price

- Cost of consumable supplies, such as paper and ink (see Figure 8-3)

- Pages per month

- Price per page

- Maintenance costs

- Warranty costs

Figure 8-3   Reliability and Total Cost of Ownership

When calculating the TCO, consider the amount of printing required and the expected lifetime of the printer.

Automatic Document Feeder and Network Scanning (8.1.1.4)

An *automatic document feeder (ADF)* can be found on some laser and inkjet printers that also have the capabilities of copy machines. These are called multifunction devices (MFDs). The ADF is a slot where an existing document can be placed, as shown in Figure 8-4. The machine is then set to make copies of this document.

Figure 8-4   ADF

When the print process is started, the ADF pulls one page of the document onto the glass surface of the *platen*, where it is scanned and copies are made. The page on the platen is then automatically removed, and the next page in the original document is pulled onto the platen. This process continues until the entire original document in the feeder has been pulled through. Some machines can make multiple copies. Usually these machines can also collate these copies.

Depending on the capabilities of the machine, the original document may be placed face up in the feeder or face down. The machine may have a limit as to how many pages can be put in the ADF at a time.

It is possible to configure an MFD as a device on the network, just like a networked printer, to provide scanning and copying to network locations rather than simply printing or copying to paper. There are three popular places to direct these scans:

- **Scan to cloud:** The scan is uploaded to a storage location in the cloud, such as Google Drive or Apple iCloud. The MFD may have specific cloud locations that are preconfigured or may allow you to configure your own. You log in using the scanning prompts either in the software or on the MFD screen, if it has one.

- **Scan to folder:** The scan is sent to a network folder on the LAN. The scanning prompts should ask for the path to the folder to which you wish the scan to be saved.

- **Scan to email:** The scan will be created as a file attachment in an email. The scanning prompts will ask for the hostname or IP address of the SMTP server and, often, the email account credentials.

Interactive Graphic

8.1.1.5 Check Your Understanding: Printer Capabilities and Characteristics

Refer to the online course to complete this activity.

Printer Connections (8.1.2)

Printers have many types of connection choices, which gives a technician a great deal of flexibility in choosing the type of printer and printer installation. For example, a printer can be connected to an individual PC for a single user or as a network printer to extend usage to many devices or even give remote access through the Internet.

Printer Connection Types (8.1.2.1)

A printer must have a compatible interface with the computer. Typically, a printer connects to a home computer using a USB or wireless interface. However, a printer may also connect directly to a network, using a network cable or a wireless interface, as shown in Figure 8-5.

Figure 8-5   Printer Connection Types

Serial Connectors

A *serial* connection can be used for dot matrix printers because the printers do not require high-speed data transfer. A serial connection, shown in Figure 8-6, for a printer is often referred to as COM. Serial ports are generally found on legacy computer systems.

Figure 8-6   Serial

Parallel Connectors

With a *parallel* connection, the data transfer path is wider than a serial data transfer path, allowing data to move more quickly to or from the printer.

IEEE 1284 is the standard for parallel printer ports. *Enhanced Parallel Port (EPP)* and *Enhanced Capabilities Port (ECP)* are two modes of operation within the IEEE 1284 standard that allow bidirectional communication. A parallel connection for a printer is often referred to as LPT. Parallel ports, shown in Figure 8-7, are generally found on legacy computer systems.

Figure 8-7   Parallel

USB Connectors

USB, shown in Figure 8-8, is a common interface for printers and other devices. When a USB device is added to a computer system that supports Plug and Play, the device is automatically detected and starts the driver installation process.

Figure 8-8   USB

FireWire Connectors

FireWire, also known as *i.LINK* or *IEEE 1394*, is a high-speed communication bus that is platform independent. FireWire, shown in Figure 8-9, connects digital devices such as printers, scanners, cameras, and hard drives.

Figure 8-9   FireWire

Ethernet Connectors

With an *Ethernet* connection, connecting a printer to the network requires cabling that is compatible with both the network and the network port installed in the printer. Most network printers use an RJ-45 interface to connect to a network (see Figure 8-10).

Figure 8-10   Ethernet

Wireless Connections

Many printers come with built-in wireless capability, which enables them to be connected to a Wi-Fi network (see Figure 8-11). Some printers come equipped with the ability to connect to devices through Bluetooth pairing.

Figure 8-11   Wireless

Interactive Graphic

8.1.2.2 Check Your Understanding: Printer Connections

Refer to the online course to complete this activity.

Printer Type Comparison (8.2)

This section describes the characteristics of two main printer categories: impact and non-impact. There are several types of printers in each of these categories. Not all printers can provide all the functions you may want, so understanding the features and characteristics of different printer types is necessary to make the best choice for the intended printer use. The intended use of the printer is also important in the purchasing decision. Considerations include whether a printer will be used for business or home use, whether it will be networked or local, and whether it is a special use printer.

Inkjet Printers (8.2.1)

An *inkjet printer* is a type of non-impact printer that creates output by spraying ink onto the material being printed on. This type of printer is commonly used for low-volume printing and is a strong choice for home users and small businesses.

Inkjet Printer Characteristics (8.2.1.1)

Inkjet printers are easy to use and usually less expensive than laser printers. Figure 8-12 shows an all-in-one device that contains an inkjet printer.

Figure 8-12   Inkjet Printer

Some advantages of an inkjet printer are the initial low cost, high resolution, and short warmup time. Some disadvantages of an inkjet printer are that the nozzles are prone to clogging, ink cartridges can be expensive, and the ink is wet for a few seconds after printing.

Inkjet Printer Parts (8.2.1.2)

The sections that follow illustrate and describe the main components of an inkjet printer.

Ink Cartridges/Paper

Paper and ink cartridges, shown in Figure 8-13, are the primary consumable items in an inkjet printer. Ink cartridges are designed for specific makes and models of inkjet printers. Most inkjet printers use plain paper for printing. Some can also print images on high-quality photo paper. Consult your printer's manual for the correct type of ink cartridges and paper to use.

Figure 8-13   Ink Cartridges

If inkjet printer quality degrades, check the printer calibration by using the printer software.

Print Head

Inkjet printers use ink cartridges that spray ink onto a page through tiny holes. The tiny holes are called *nozzles* and are located in the **print head**, shown in Figure 8-14.

Figure 8-14   Print Head

There are two types of inkjet nozzles:

- *Thermal*: A pulse of electrical current is applied to heating chambers around the nozzles. The heat creates a bubble of steam in the chamber. The steam forces ink out through the nozzle and onto the paper.

- *Piezoelectric*: Piezoelectric crystals are located in the ink reservoir at the back of each nozzle. A charge is applied to the crystals, causing them to vibrate. This vibration of the crystals controls the flow of ink onto the paper.

Roller

Rollers, shown in Figure 8-15, pull paper in from the feeder.

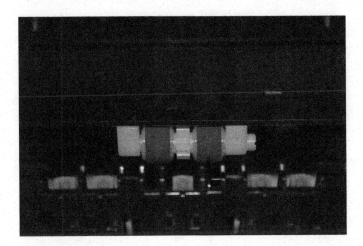

Figure 8-15   Rollers

Feeder

The *feeder*, shown in Figure 8-16, may hold blank paper in a tray or cassette. Some inkjet printers are also copiers. In addition, an inkjet printer may have an ADF. The ADF holds documents, which are fed page by page onto the scanner bed for copying.

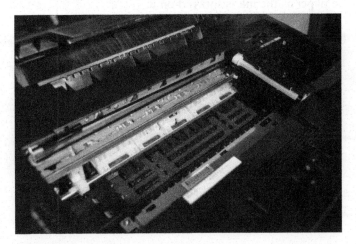

Figure 8-16   Feeder

Duplexing Assembly

Some inkjet printers can print on both sides of a page. This requires a *duplexing assembly*, shown in Figure 8-17, which turns a printed page over and feeds it back through the printer to be printed on the other side.

Figure 8-17   Duplexing Assembly

Carriage/Belt

The print head and ink cartridges are located on the *carriage*, which is attached to a *belt* and motor, as shown in Figure 8-18. The belt moves the carriage back and forth across the paper as the ink is sprayed on it.

Figure 8-18   Carriage/Belt

8.2.1.3 Check Your Understanding: Inkjet Printers

Refer to the online course to complete this activity.

Laser Printers (8.2.2)

Laser printers are non-impact printers that create output by using toner and lasers. Laser printers usually have an expensive up-front cost but offer a lower total cost of ownership.

Laser Printer Characteristics (8.2.2.1)

A *laser printer*, shown in Figure 8-19, is a high-quality, fast printer that uses a laser beam to create an image.

Figure 8-19   Laser Printer

Some advantages of a laser printer are low cost per page, high number of pages printed per minute, high capacity, and dry printed pages. Some disadvantages of a laser printer are high cost of startup and potentially expensive toner cartridges.

Laser Printer Parts (8.2.2.2)

The sections that follow illustrate and describe the main components of a laser printer.

Imaging Drum

The central part of a laser printer is its *imaging drum*, shown in Figure 8-20. The drum is a metal cylinder that is coated with a light-sensitive insulating material. When a beam of laser light strikes the drum, the drum becomes a conductor at the point where the light hits it.

Figure 8-20   Imaging Drum

Toner Cartridge/Paper

As the drum rotates, the laser beam draws an electrostatic image on the drum. This undeveloped image is passed by a supply of toner. The *toner* is a negatively charged combination of plastic and metal particles. The electrostatic charge attracts toner to the image. The drum turns and brings the exposed image in contact with the paper, which attracts the toner from the drum.

The toner cartridge (see Figure 8-21) and paper are the primary consumable items in a laser printer. Other parts may also be contained in the toner cartridge. Check your printer's manual for more information.

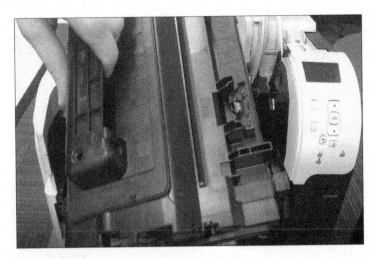

Figure 8-21   Toner Cartridge

Fuser Assembly

The paper is passed through a *fuser assembly*, shown in Figure 8-22, that is made up of hot rollers, which melt the toner into the paper.

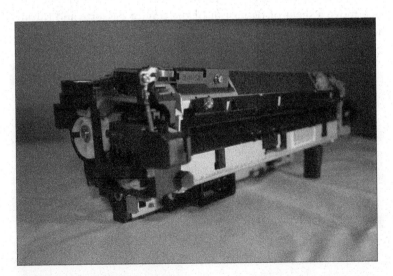

Figure 8-22   Fuser Assembly

Transfer Roller

The *transfer roller*, shown in Figure 8-23, assists in transferring the toner from the imaging drum to the paper.

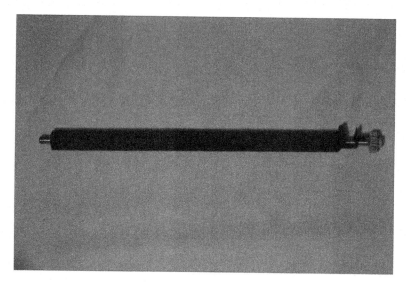

Figure 8-23   Transfer Roller

Pickup Rollers

Pickup rollers, shown in Figure 8-24, may be located in multiple areas of a printer. They move a sheet of paper out of the tray or cassette and through the printer during the printing process.

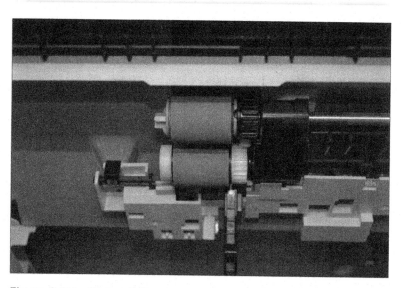

Figure 8-24   Pickup Rollers

Duplexing Assembly

The duplexing assembly, shown in Figure 8-25, turns a page that is already printed on one side so that it can be printed on the other side.

Figure 8-25   Duplexing Assembly

8.2.2.3 Check Your Understanding: Laser Printers

Refer to the online course to complete this activity.

Laser Printing Process (8.2.3)

A laser printer uses a laser to imprint an image onto a copier drum, and that image is then transferred onto paper. It sounds simple but is rather complex. Many moving parts and components inside a laser printer must work together to produce the final product. Each component has an important part to play. The key components of a printer are the toner cartridge, imaging drum, transfer roller, fuser, laser, and mirrors.

Laser printers are very efficient and cost-effective to use when you need to quickly print in large quantities.

How Laser Printing Works (8.2.3.1)

The laser printer process involves seven steps to print information onto a single sheet of paper:

Step 1.   *Processing* (see Figure 8-26): The data from the source must be converted into a printable form. The printer converts data from common languages, such as Adobe PostScript (PS) or HP Printer Command Language (PCL), to a bitmap image stored in the printer's memory. Some laser printers have built-in graphics device interface (GDI) support. Windows applications use GDI to display printed images on a monitor, so there is no need to convert the output to another format, such as PS or PCL.

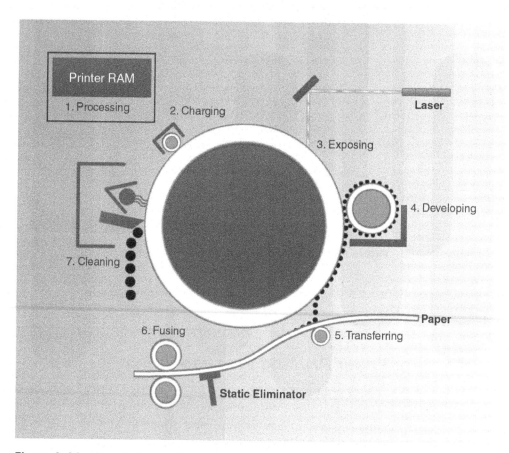

Figure 8-26   Step 1: Processing

Step 2.   *Charging* (see Figure 8-27): The image on the drum is removed, and the drum is conditioned for the new image. A wire, grid, or roller receives a charge of approximately −600 volts DC uniformly across the surface of the drum. The charged wire or grid is called the *primary corona*. The roller is called a *conditioning roller*.

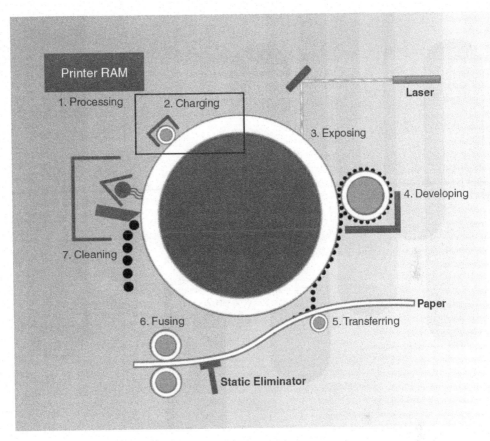

Figure 8-27   Step 2: Charging

Step 3.   *Exposing* (see Figure 8-28): To write the image, the photosensitive drum is exposed with the laser beam. Every portion of the drum that is scanned with the light has the surface charge reduced to about –100 volts DC. This electrical charge has a lower negative charge than the rest of the drum. As the drum turns, an invisible image is created on the drum.

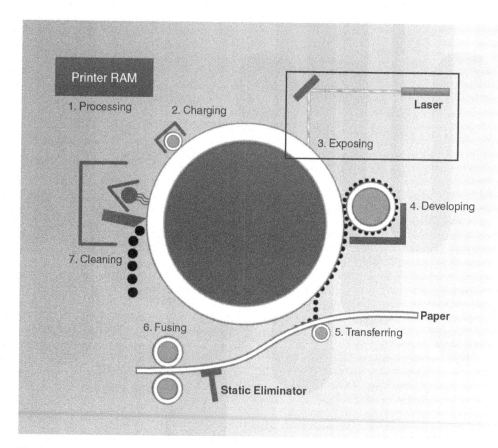

Figure 8-28   Step 3: Exposing

Step 4.   *Developing* (see Figure 8-29): The toner is applied to the image on the drum. A control blade holds the toner a microscopic distance from the drum. The toner then moves from the control blade to the more positively charged image on the drum.

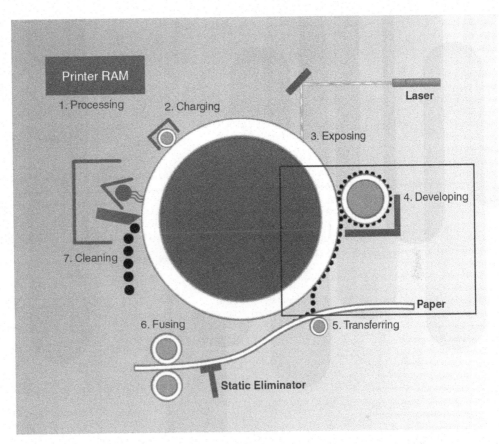

Figure 8-29 Step 4: Developing

Step 5. *Transferring* (see Figure 8-30): The toner, attached to the image, is transferred to the paper. The corona wire places a positive charge on the paper. Because the drum was charged negatively, the toner on the drum is now attracted to the paper. The image is now on the paper and is held in place by the positive charge. Because color printers have three cartridges of toner, a colored image must go through multiple transfers to be complete. To ensure precise images, some color printers write multiple times onto a transfer belt that transfers the complete image to paper.

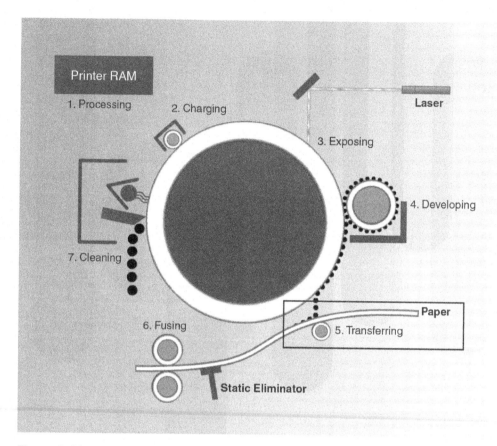

Figure 8-30   Step 5: Transferring

Step 6.   *Fusing* (see **Figure 8-31**): The toner is permanently fused to the paper. The printing paper is rolled between a heated roller and a pressure roller. As the paper moves through the rollers, the loose toner is melted and fused with the fibers in the paper. The paper is then moved to the output tray as a printed page. Laser printers with duplex assemblies can print on both sides of a sheet of paper.

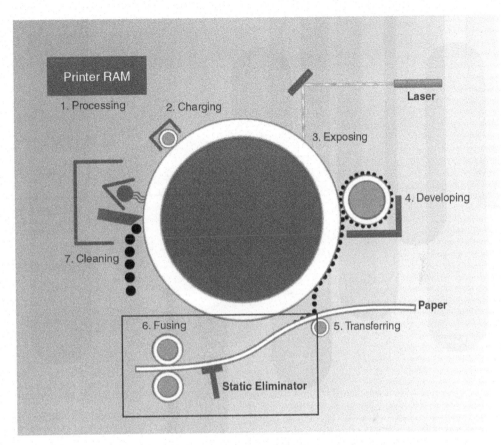

Figure 8-31   Step 6: Fusing

Step 7.   *Cleaning* (see Figure 8-32): When an image has been deposited on the paper and the drum has separated from the paper, the remaining toner must be removed from the drum. A printer might have a blade that scrapes the excess toner. Some printers use AC voltage on a wire to remove the charge from the drum surface and allow the excess toner to fall away from the drum. The excess toner is stored in a used toner container that is either emptied or discarded.

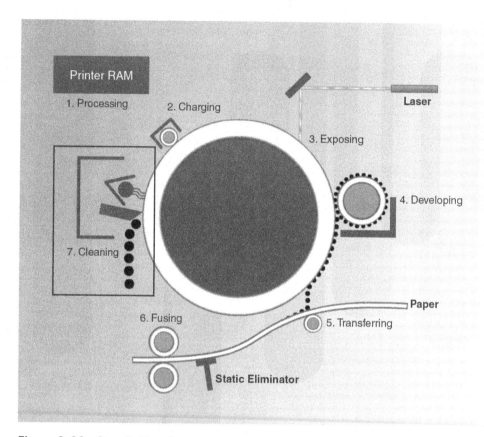

Figure 8-32   Step 7: Cleaning

8.2.3.2 Check Your Understanding: The Laser Printing Process

Refer to the online course to complete this activity.

Thermal Printers and Impact Printers (8.2.4)

Typically, businesses choose between two main types of receipt printers with their POS systems: thermal printers and dot matrix printers.

Impact printers are more reliable than thermal printers but are noisier and slower than thermal printers. Location for the usage of these printers can be particularly important. Because the paper that resides inside thermal printers is, by necessity, sensitive to heat, the performance of these printers suffers when exposed to the high temperatures and humidity levels; therefore, in an environment that is hot and humid, an impact printer is the better option. Knowing what the usage of a printer will be is critical in deciding on the type of printer.

Thermal Printer Characteristics (8.2.4.1)

Many retail cash registers and some older fax machines contain thermal printers (see Figure 8-33). Thermal paper is chemically treated, has a waxy quality, and becomes black when heated. After a roll of thermal paper is loaded, the feed assembly moves the paper through the printer. Electrical current is sent to the heating element in the print head to generate heat. The heated areas of the print head make the image on the paper.

Figure 8-33   Cash Receipt Thermal Printer

Some advantages of thermal printers are that they last a long time because there are few moving parts, their operation is quiet, and there is no cost for ink or toner. However, thermal paper is expensive, it must be stored at room temperature, and it can degrade over time. Thermal printer images are poor quality, and color printing is not available.

Impact Printer Characteristics (8.2.4.2)

Impact printers have print heads that strike an inked ribbon, causing characters to be imprinted on the paper. *Dot matrix* and *daisy wheel* are examples of impact printers.

An advantage of impact printers is that the ribbon is less expensive than inkjet cartridges or laser printer toner cartridges. In addition, these printers can use continuous-feed or normal sheets of paper and can print carbon copies. Disadvantages include the fact that they are noisy, the graphics are low resolution, and they have limited color printing capabilities.

A dot matrix printer (see Figure 8-34) has a print head containing pins that are surrounded by electromagnets. When energized, the pins push forward onto the ink ribbon, creating a character on the paper. The number of pins on a print head, 9 or 24, determines the quality of the print. The highest quality of print that is produced by a dot matrix printer is referred to as *near letter quality (NLQ)*.

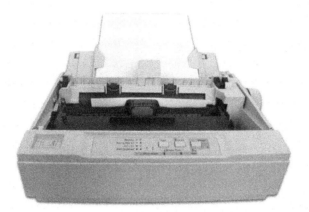

Figure 8-34   Impact Printer

Most dot matrix printers use continuous-feed paper, also known as *tractor feed*. The paper has perforations between sheets, and perforated strips on the side are used to feed the paper and to prevent skewing or shifting. Sheet feeders that print one page at a time are available for some higher-quality printers. A large roller, called the *platen*, applies pressure to keep the paper from slipping. If a multiple-copy paper is used, you can adjust the platen gap to the thickness of the paper.

Interactive Graphic

8.2.4.3 Check Your Understanding: Thermal Printers and Impact Printers

Refer to the online course to complete this activity.

Virtual Printers (8.2.5)

A *virtual printer* is not actually a printer; rather, it is software on the computer with an interface similar to a print driver that is coded to send the output to other applications rather than to a physical device. A virtual printer sends its output to a file, such as a PDF. It can help save resources by carrying out tasks that would otherwise involve actual printing but without wasting paper and ink.

Virtual Printer Characteristics (8.2.5.1)

Virtual printing does not involve sending a print job to a printer within your local network. Instead, the print software either sends the job to a file or transmits the information to a remote destination in the cloud for printing.

Typical methods for sending a print job to a file include the following:

- *Print to file*: Originally, print to file saved the data in a file with the .prn extension. The .prn file then could be quickly printed at any time without opening the original document. Print to file can now save in other formats, as shown in Figure 8-35.

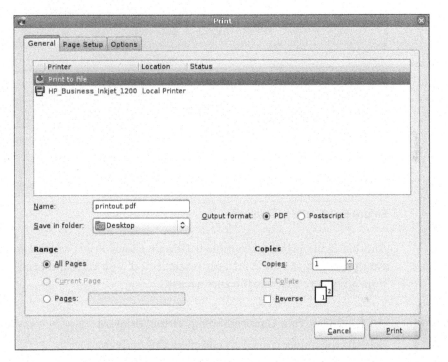

Figure 8-35   Printing to a File

- *Print to PDF*: Adobe's Portable Document Format (PDF) was released as an open standard in 2008.

- *Print to XPS*: Introduced by Microsoft in Windows Vista, the XML Paper Specification (XPS) format was meant to be an alternative to PDF.

- *Print to image*: To prevent others from easily copying the content in a document, you can choose to print to an image file format, such as JPG or TIFF.

Cloud Printing (8.2.5.2)

Cloud printing is the process of sending a print job to a remote printer, as shown in Figure 8-36. The printer could be at any location within your organization's network. Some printing companies provide software that you can install and use to send print jobs to their closest location for processing.

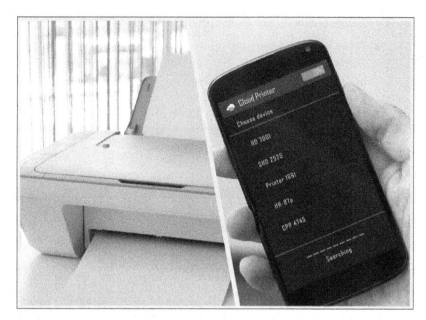

Figure 8-36   Cloud Printing

Another cloud printing example is Google Cloud Print, which allows you to connect your printer to the Web. After it is connected, you can send print jobs to your printer from anywhere that has Internet access.

Interactive Graphic

8.2.5.3 Check Your Understanding: Virtual Printers

Refer to the online course to complete this activity.

3D Printers (8.2.6)

3D printing is the process of making three-dimensional solid objects from digital files by putting down layer after layer of material, usually plastic, until the object is completed. 3D printing is being used in a variety of industries for many different applications, from dentures to models of dinosaur bones.

3D Printer Characteristics (8.2.6.1)

3D printers, shown in Figure 8-37, are used to create three-dimensional objects. These objects are first designed using a computer. A variety of media are now available to create these objects. For beginners, plastic filament is the most commonly used 3D printer medium. The plastic filament is added in layers to create the object that was programmed on the computer.

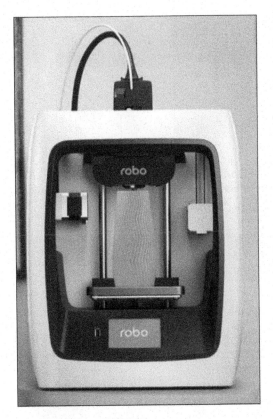

Figure 8-37   3D Printer

Traditionally, machines cut or drilled pieces out of raw material (such as stone, metal, or wood) to create an object. This is known as *subtractive manufacturing*. 3D printers add the material used to create objects in layers or even small bits; therefore, they are known as *additive manufacturing machines*.

3D Printer Parts (8.2.6.2)

The main parts of 3D printers are as follows:

- *Filament*: This is the material used in 3D printers to create objects. Common types of filament are plastic based: ABS, PLA, and PVA (see Figure 8-38). There are also filaments made of nylon, metal, or wood. Check your 3D printer's manual to determine which type(s) of filament to use.

Figure 8-38   Filament

- **Feeder:** The feeder (see Figure 8-39) takes filament from a feed tube that is placed into the extruder. The feeder pulls it down to be heated and then sends it through the hotend nozzle.

Figure 8-39   Feeder

- *Hotend nozzle:* When the filament is heated to the correct temperature, it is extruded from the hotend nozzle, shown in Figure 8-40.

Figure 8-40   Hotend Nozzle

■ *Axis*: An axis is one of several bars on which the hotend nozzle travels to dispense filament (see Figure 8-41). An axis is either vertical or horizontal so that the hotend nozzle can be located within a specified location in a 3D environment to "print" the object.

Figure 8-41   Axis

■ *Print bed*: The print bed, shown in Figure 8-42, is the platform onto which the heated filament forms the object.

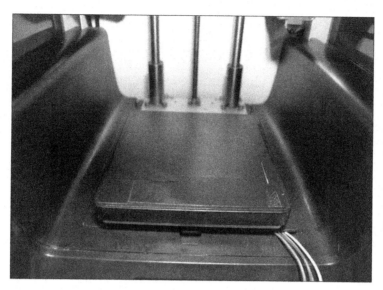

Figure 8-42   Print Bed

8.2.6.3 Check Your Understanding: 3D Printers

Refer to the online course to complete this activity.

Installing and Configuring Printers (8.3)

Installing and configuring a printer can be straightforward and is easiest when done by following the manufacturer's directions. Preparing the hardware for installation is the starting point, and the rest depends on how the operating system works with the print driver.

Installing and Updating a Printer (8.3.1)

In this section, you will learn about installing and upgrading a printer and how to set up the different features that printers offer.

Installing a Printer (8.3.1.1)

When you purchase a printer, the installation and configuration information is usually found on the manufacturer's website. Before you install a printer, remove all packing material. Remove anything that prevents moving parts from shifting during shipping. Keep the original packing material in case you need to return the printer to the manufacturer for warranty service.

Note

Before connecting the printer to the computer, read the installation instructions. In some cases, the printer driver needs to be installed before the printer is connected.

If the printer has a USB, FireWire, or parallel port, connect the corresponding cable to the printer port. Connect the other end of the data cable to the corresponding port on the back of the computer. If you are installing a network printer, connect the network cable to the network port.

After the data cable has been properly connected, attach the power cable to the printer. Connect the other end of the power cable to an available electrical outlet. When you turn on the power to the device, the computer determines the correct device driver to install.

Test Printer Functions (8.3.1.2)

The installation of any device is not complete until you have successfully tested all its functions. Depending on the printer you have, functions might include the following (see Figure 8-43):

- Printing double-sided documents
- Using different paper trays for different paper sizes
- Changing the settings of a color printer so that it prints in black and white or grayscale
- Printing in draft mode
- Using an optical character recognition (OCR) application
- Printing a collated document

Note

Collated printing is ideal when you need to print several copies of a multiple-page document. The Collate setting prints each set in turn. Some printers can even staple each printed set.

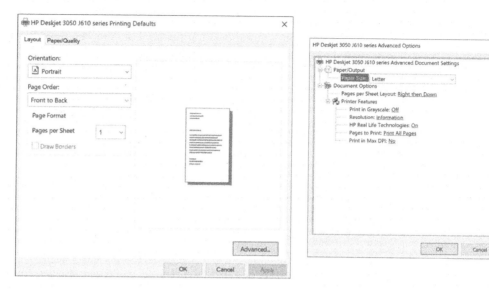

Figure 8-43   Collated Printing

Functions for an all-in-one printer include the following:

- Faxing to another known working fax

- Creating a copy of a document

- Scanning a document

- Printing a document

8.3.1.3 Lab: Install a Printer in Windows

In this lab, you will install a printer. You will find, download, and update the driver and the software for the printer.

Configuring Options and Default Settings (8.3.2)

Each printer may have different configurations and default options.

Common Configuration Settings (8.3.2.1)

Check the printer documentation for specific information about its configuration and default settings. Table 8-1 shows some common configuration options available for printers.

Table 8-1 Common Configuration Settings

Configuration Option	Details
Paper type	Standard, draft, gloss, or photo
Print quality	Draft, normal, or photo
Color printing	Multiple colors of ink are used
Black-and-white printing	Only black ink is used
Grayscale printing	Images printed using only black ink in different proportions to produce shades of gray
Paper size	Standard paper sizes, envelopes, and business cards
Paper orientation	Landscape or portrait
Print layout	Normal, banner, booklet, or poster
Duplex	Two-sided printing
Collate	Print sets of a document with multiple pages arranged in order

Common printer options that the user can configure include media control and printer output.

Media Control Options

These are some media control options specific to paper:

- Input paper tray selection
- Output path selection
- Media size and orientation
- Paper weight selection

Printer Output Options

These are two printer output options that manage how the ink or toner goes on the media:

- Color management
- Print speed

8.3.2.2 Check Your Understanding: Configuration Options

Refer to the online course to complete this activity.

Optimizing Printer Performance (8.3.3)

Output relies on many factors, such as settings that are configurable through software that comes with the printer, the paper used, and whether the printer is kept clean.

Software Optimization (8.3.3.1)

With printers, most optimization is completed through the software that comes with the drivers.

The following tools optimize performance:

- *Print spool settings*: Cancel or pause current print jobs in the printer queue.

- *Color calibration*: Adjust settings to match the colors on the screen to the colors on the printed sheet.

- *Paper orientation*: Select landscape or portrait image layout, as shown in Figure 8-44.

Figure 8-44 Changing the Paper Orientation to Landscape

Printers are calibrated using the printer driver software. Calibration ensures that the print heads are aligned and that they can print on different kinds of media, such as cardstock, photographic paper, and optical discs. Some inkjet print heads are fitted to the ink cartridge, and you might have to recalibrate the printer each time you change a cartridge.

Hardware Optimization (8.3.3.2)

It is possible to upgrade some printers to print faster and to accommodate more print jobs by adding hardware. The hardware may include additional paper trays, sheet feeders, network cards, and expansion memory.

The procedure to upgrade firmware is similar to the procedure to install printer drivers. Firmware updates do not take place automatically, so you can visit the home page of the printer manufacturer to check the availability of new firmware.

All printers have RAM, such as the chips shown in Figure 8-45. Printers usually arrive from the factory with enough memory to handle jobs that involve text. However, print jobs involving graphics, and especially photographs, run more efficiently if the printer memory is adequate to store the entire job before it starts. Upgrading the printer memory increases the printing speed and enhances complex print job performance.

Figure 8-45 Hardware Optimization

Print job buffering involves capturing a print job in the internal printer memory. Buffering is a common feature in laser printers and plotters, as well as in advanced inkjet and dot matrix printers.

Low memory errors can indicate that the printer is out of memory or has a memory overload. In such a case, you may need more memory.

8.3.3.3 Check Your Understanding: Printer Optimization
Refer to the online course to complete this activity.

Sharing Printers (8.4)

Sharing printers has many advantages for businesses. Sharing printers can provide savings in printer maintenance and purchases, it can provide options for placement and selections for printers used, computers running on multiple platforms can access the same network printers and send print jobs to the printers using drivers designed for each platform, plus many other advantages. This section discusses installation and use of shared printers.

Operating System Settings for Sharing Printers (8.4.1)

Shared printers can reduce resources needed in a business. You can enable multiple PCs to share a single printer by following the operating system steps for connecting the printer to the network and then configuring the PCs to connect and share the networked printer.

Configuring Printer Sharing (8.4.1.1)

Windows allows computer users to share their printers with other users on the network.

Users who cannot connect to a shared printer might not have the required drivers installed. They might also be using different operating systems than the computer that is hosting the shared printer. Windows can automatically download the correct drivers to these users. Accessing Printer properties will take the user to the Additional Drivers button to select operating systems that the other users are using. After the user clicks this button and selects their OS and then clicks OK, Windows asks to obtain those additional drivers and downloads them. If other users are also using the same Windows operating system, they will not need to click the Additional Drivers button.

Figure 8-46 and Figure 8-47 show how to begin the process of printer sharing in Windows 10.

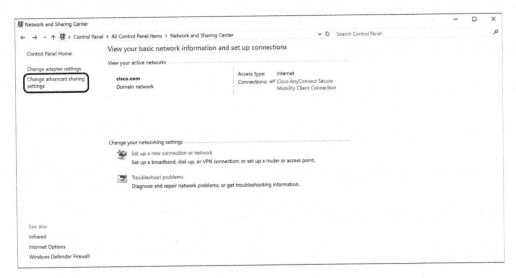

Figure 8-46   Changing Advanced Sharing Settings

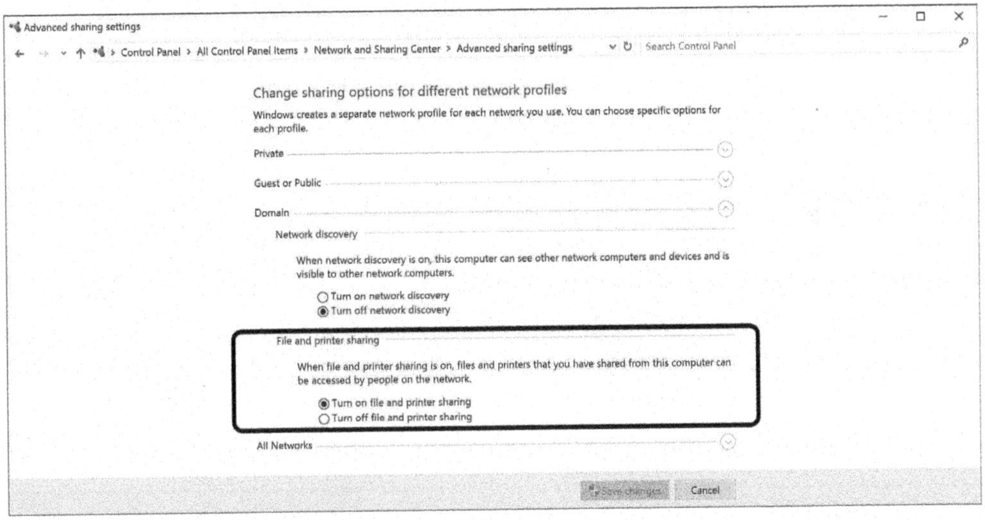

Figure 8-47   File and Printer Sharing

There are potential data privacy and security issues to consider when sharing printers:

- *Hard drive caching*: Cached print files pose privacy and security risks because someone with access to the device could recover files and then access confidential or personal information.

- **User authentication:** To prevent unauthorized use of a network or cloud-based printer, permissions and user authentication methods can be used to control access to the printer.

- **Data privacy:** Print jobs sent over a network could be intercepted and read, copied, or modified.

Wireless Printer Connections (8.4.1.2)

Wireless printers enable hosts to connect and print wirelessly using Bluetooth or a Wi-Fi connection. For a wireless printer to use Bluetooth, both the printer and the host device must have Bluetooth capabilities, and they must be paired. If necessary, you can add a Bluetooth adapter to a computer, usually in a USB port. Wireless Bluetooth printers also allow for printing from mobile devices.

Wireless printers that use Wi-Fi connect directly to a wireless router or an access point. Setup is completed by connecting the printer to the computer with the supplied software or by using the printer display panel to connect to the wireless router. The printer's wireless adapter supports an 802.11 standard. The devices connecting to the printer must also support the same standard.

In wireless infrastructure mode, the printer is configured to connect to an access point. Client connections to the printer go through the access point. In wireless ad hoc mode, client devices connect directly to the printer (see Figure 8-48).

Figure 8-48 Sharing a Printer Wirelessly

8.4.1.3 Lab: Share a Printer in Windows

In this lab, you will share a printer, configure the printer on a networked computer, and print a test page from the remote computer.

Print Servers (8.4.2)

A print server manages files in a user's printing queue and makes the status available to the user. It provides print resources to all connected print clients. It can manage printing requests for both your computer and the printing device.

Purposes of Print Servers (8.4.2.1)

A printer that does not have built-in network interfaces may require a separate print server to enable network connectivity. *Print servers* let multiple computer users, regardless of device or operating system, access a single printer (see Figure 8-49). A print server has three functions:

- Providing client access to print resources

- Administering print jobs by storing them in a queue until the print device is ready for them and then feeding or spooling the print information to the printer

- Providing feedback to users about the state of the printer

Figure 8-49   Serving Many Devices with a Print Server

Sharing a printer from a computer also has disadvantages. The computer sharing the printer uses its own resources to manage the print jobs coming to the printer. If the computer user on the desktop is working at the same time as a user on the network is printing, the desktop computer user might notice a performance slowdown. In addition, the printer is not available if the user reboots or powers off the computer that shares the printer.

Software Print Servers (8.4.2.2)

In some instances, the computer sharing a printer is running an operating system that is not Windows, such as macOS. In such a case, you can use print server software. One example is Apple's free Bonjour Printer Server, which is a built-in service in macOS. It is automatically installed on a Windows computer if you install the Apple Safari browser. You can also download Bonjour Print Services for Windows, as shown in Figure 8-50, for free from the Apple website.

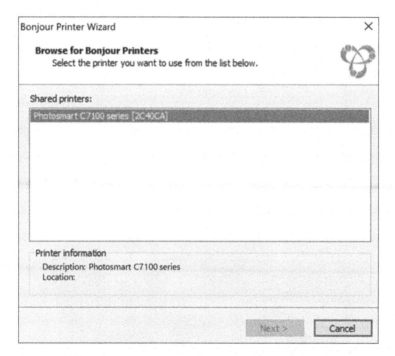

Figure 8-50   Bonjour Print Services

When it is downloaded and installed, Bonjour Print Services operates in the background, automatically detecting any compatible printers connected to the network.

Hardware Print Servers (8.4.2.3)

A hardware print server is a simple device with a network card and memory. It connects to the network and communicates with the printer to enable printer sharing. The print server in Figure 8-51 is connected to the printer by a USB cable.

A hardware print server may be integrated with another device, such as a wireless router. In this case, the printer would connect directly to the wireless router, most likely through a USB cable.

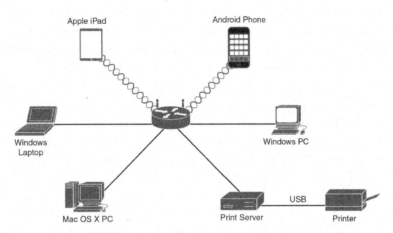

Figure 8-51   Hardware Print Servers

Apple's AirPort Extreme is a hardware print server. Through the AirPrint service, AirPort Extreme can share a printer with any device on the network.

A hardware print server can manage network printing through either wired or wireless connections. An advantage of using a hardware print server is that the server accepts incoming print jobs from devices, thereby freeing the computers for other tasks. A hardware print server is always available to users, unlike a printer shared from a user's computer.

Dedicated Print Servers (8.4.2.4)

For larger networking environments with multiple LANs and many users, a dedicated print server is needed to manage printing services (see Figure 8-52).

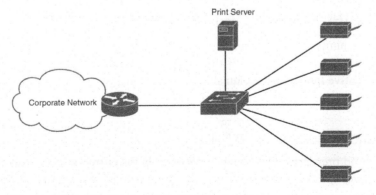

Figure 8-52   Dedicated Print Server

A dedicated print server is more powerful than a hardware print server. It handles client print jobs in the most efficient manner and can manage more than one printer at a time. A dedicated print server must have the following resources to meet the requests of print clients:

- **Powerful processor:** Because the dedicated print server uses its processor to manage and route printing information, it must be fast enough to handle all incoming requests.

- **Adequate storage space:** A dedicated print server captures print jobs from clients, places them in a print queue, and sends them to the printer in a timely manner. This process requires the computer to have enough storage space to hold these jobs until they are completed.

- **Adequate memory:** The processor and RAM handle the process of sending print jobs to a printer. If there is not enough memory to handle an entire print job, the document is stored on the drive in the print server and printed from there. This is generally slower than printing directly from memory.

Interactive Graphic

8.4.2.5 Check Your Understanding: Print Servers

Refer to the online course to complete this activity.

Maintaining and Troubleshooting Printers (8.5)

A printer is one of the most commonly used peripheral devices. There are many different types of printers and ways to connect them to a device or network, but doing maintenance is an important task no matter what type of printer. Troubleshooting specifics may vary, but it is a certainty that a technician will be required to troubleshoot printer issues, so it is important for a technician to understand the methodology and steps.

Printer Preventive Maintenance (8.5.1)

Performing preventive maintenance is a proactive way to decrease printer problems and increase the life span of the hardware. Using manufacturers' guidelines, a preventive maintenance plan should be established and implemented. This section examines preventive maintenance guidelines and best practices.

Vendor Guidelines (8.5.1.1)

A good preventive maintenance program helps ensure good-quality prints and uninterrupted operation. The printer documentation contains information on how to maintain and clean the equipment.

Read the information manuals that come with every new piece of equipment. Follow the recommended maintenance instructions. Use the supplies listed by the manufacturer. Less expensive supplies can save money but may produce poor results, damage the equipment, or void the warranty.

Most manufacturers sell maintenance kits for their printers (see Figure 8-53). If you do not know how to maintain printing equipment, consult with a manufacturer-certified technician. When servicing toner kits and cartridges, wear air filter masks to avoid breathing in harmful particles.

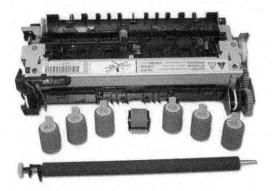

Figure 8-53 Maintenance Kit

What Do You Already Know? Printer Operating Environment (8.5.1.2)

Printers are affected by temperature, humidity, and electrical interference. In fact, laser printers tend to create a great deal of heat and must be operated in a well-ventilated area, or they will overheat.

Paper is also affected by its environment. Although paper can withstand warm and cool temperatures, it is easily affected by humidity. Paper can absorb moisture from the air, which can cause pieces to stick together and sometimes jam during printing.

Toner is also affected by its environment, especially humidity. High humidity can prevent the toner from attaching to the paper correctly. It is therefore best to keep toner cartridges in their original wrappers and store them in a cool, dust-free environment, until you are ready to use them.

Dust is an environmental problem for all printers. Dusty conditions in and around a printer's location, as well as dust from the printer paper, must be removed regularly. Use compressed air to blow dust away from the interior of a printer.

Inkjet Printer Preventive Maintenance (8.5.2)

Using a consistent preventive maintenance program can improve the performance and safety of the equipment in a home or an organization. Ensuring safety, properly locating a device, using the correct supplies, and keeping a printer clean can all help prolong the life of a printer.

Video

8.5.2.1 Video Demonstration: Inkjet Printer Preventive Maintenance

Refer to the online course to view this video.

Always consult the printer manual before performing maintenance tasks. The manual gives instructions that are specific to your inkjet printer.

The type and quality of paper and ink used can affect the life of a printer. The printer manufacturer might recommend a type of paper to use for best results. Some types of paper, especially photo paper, transparencies, and multilayered carbon paper, have a right and wrong side. Load the paper according to the manufacturer's instructions.

The manufacturer recommends the brand and type of ink to use. If the wrong type of ink is installed, the printer might not work, or the print quality might deteriorate. Avoid refilling ink cartridges because the ink can leak.

When an inkjet printer produces blank pages, the ink cartridges might be empty. Some inkjet printers may not print any pages if one of the ink cartridges is empty. You can set the printer software to draft quality to reduce the amount of ink that the printer uses. These settings also reduce the print quality and the time it takes to print a document.

Over time, printer parts collect dust, dirt, and other debris. If not cleaned regularly, a printer may not work well or could stop working completely. On inkjet printers, clean the paper-handling machinery with a damp cloth.

8.5.2.2 Lab: Perform Preventive Maintenance on an Inkjet Printer

In this lab, you will perform preventive maintenance on an inkjet printer.

Laser Printer Preventive Maintenance (8.5.3)

Preventive maintenance keeps a laser printer working at its greatest potential and at optimal quality.

Video

8.5.3.1 Video Demonstration: Laser Printer Preventive Maintenance

Refer to the online course to view this video.

Laser printers do not usually require much maintenance unless they are in a dusty area or are very old. When cleaning a laser printer, use only a vacuum cleaner with high-efficiency particulate air (HEPA) filtration. HEPA filtration catches microscopic particles within the filters.

Always consult the printer manual before performing maintenance tasks. The manual gives instructions that are specific to your laser printer. For some maintenance tasks done on a laser printer, you need to disconnect the printer from its power source. Consult your manual for specific information. If you do not know how to maintain printing equipment, consult a manufacturer-certified technician. Use caution when handling printer parts as some can become very hot and burn you.

Most manufacturers sell maintenance kits for their printers. For laser printers, such a kit might contain replacement parts that often break or wear out, such as a fuser assembly, transfer rollers, and pickup rollers.

When you install new parts or replace ink or toner cartridges, visually inspect all internal components, remove bits of paper and dust, clean spilled ink or toner, and look for worn gears, cracked plastic, or broken parts.

Laser printers do not produce blank pages. Instead, they begin to print poor-quality prints. Some printers have LCD message screens or LED lights that warn users when toner supplies are low. Some types of printers use more toner than others. For example, a photograph uses more toner than a letter. You can set the printer software to toner save or draft quality to reduce the amount of toner that the printer uses. These settings also reduce the quality of laser prints.

When maintenance is completed, reset the counters to allow the next maintenance to be completed at the correct time. On many types of printers, the page count is viewed through the LCD display or a counter located inside the main cover.

8.5.3.2 Lab: Perform Preventive Maintenance on a Laser Printer

In this lab, you will perform preventive maintenance on a laser printer.

Thermal Printer Preventive Maintenance (8.5.4)

Many factors can impact the performance of a thermal printer, such as heat, dust, wear on the printheads, and more. Properly maintaining a printer is critical to ensuring that the printer continues to generate high-quality images and text.

Preventive Maintenance on a Thermal Printer (8.5.4.1)

Always consult the thermal printer's manual before performing maintenance tasks. The manual gives instructions that are specific to your thermal printer on how to replace the paper roll. Figure 8-54 shows a thermal printer's paper being replaced.

Figure 8-54   Replacing the Paper

Thermal printers use heat to create an image on special paper. To extend the life of the printer, dampen a cotton swab with isopropyl alcohol and use it to clean the heating element. Do this on a regular basis. The heating element is located near the slot where the printed paper emerges (see Figure 8-55). While the printer is open, use compressed air or a lint-free cloth to remove any debris.

Figure 8-55   Heating Element

8.5.4.2 Check Your Understanding: Thermal Printer Preventive Maintenance

Refer to the online course to complete this activity.

Impact Printer Preventive Maintenance (8.5.5)

Regularly performing preventive maintenance is the best way to reduce printer problems. Impact printers have many moving parts, and doing scheduled checks of parts for cleanliness, lubrication, wear, and so on can add to the longevity of the device.

Preventive Maintenance of an Impact Printer (8.5.5.1)

Always consult the printer manual before performing maintenance tasks on an impact printer. The manual gives instructions that are specific to your impact printer. For safety reasons, it is important to pay attention to the components that the manual indicates may be hot as they can cause you physical harm.

An impact printer is similar to a typewriter in that the print head strikes an inked ribbon to transfer ink to the paper. When an impact printer produces faded or light characters, the ribbon (see Figure 8-56) is worn out and needs to be replaced. Consult your manual for instructions on how to replace the ribbon.

Figure 8-56 Impact Printer Ribbon

If a consistent flaw is produced in all characters, the print head (see Figure 8-57) is stuck or broken and needs to be cleaned or possibly replaced. Search online for procedures on dot matrix printhead cleaning to learn about this.

Figure 8-57 Print Head

Interactive
Graphic

8.5.5.2 Check Your Understanding: Impact Printer Preventive Maintenance

Refer to the online course to complete this activity.

3D Printer Preventive Maintenance (8.5.6)

Costly repairs can stem from neglect. Preventive maintenance helps avoid issues or failures that result from neglect. 3D printers are highly mechanical devices with moving parts that need attention.

Video

8.5.6.1 Video Demonstration: 3D Printer Preventive Maintenance

Refer to the online course to view this video.

Always consult the printer manual before performing maintenance tasks. The manual gives instructions that are specific to your 3D printer.

Video

8.5.6.2 Video Demonstration: 3D Printer Printing a Component

Refer to the online course to view this video.

Applying the Troubleshooting Process to Printers (8.5.7)

Knowing the troubleshooting steps to take when you have encountered a printing problem is critical to getting the printer problems diagnosed. This section outlines a systematic troubleshooting approach and offers specifics on how to address issues that are particular to printers.

The Six Steps of the Troubleshooting Process (8.5.7.1)

The six steps of the troubleshooting process are as follows:

Step 1.   Identify the problem.

Step 2.   Establish a theory of probable cause.

Step 3.   Test the theory to determine the cause.

Step 4.   Establish a plan of action to resolve the problem and implement the solution.

Step 5.   Verify full system functionality and, if applicable, implement preventive measures.

Step 6.   Document findings, actions, and outcomes.

Identify the Problem (8.5.7.2)

Printer problems can result from a combination of hardware, software, and connectivity issues. A technician must be able to determine if a problem exists with the device, a cable connection, or the computer to which the printer is connected. Computer technicians must be able to analyze the problem and determine the cause of the error to repair the printer issues.

The first step in the troubleshooting process is to identify the problem. Table 8-2 shows a list of open-ended and closed-ended questions to ask the customer.

Table 8-2   Step 1: Identify the Problem

Open-Ended Questions	Closed-Ended Questions
■ What problems are you experiencing with your printer?	■ Is the printer under warranty?
■ What software or hardware has been changed recently on your computer?	■ Can you print a test page?
	■ Is this a new printer?
■ What were you doing when the problem was identified?	■ Is the printer powered on?
■ What error messages have you received?	

Establish a Theory of Probable Cause (8.5.7.3)

After you have talked to the customer, you can establish a theory of probable cause. Table 8-3 lists some common probable causes for printer problems. If necessary, conduct internal and external research based on the symptoms of the problem.

Table 8-3   Step 2: Establish a Theory of Probable Cause

Common causes of printer problems	<ul><li>Loose cable connections</li><li>Paper jams</li><li>Equipment power</li><li>Low ink warning</li><li>Out of paper</li><li>Errors on equipment display</li><li>Errors on computer screen</li></ul>

Test the Theory to Determine Cause (8.5.7.4)

After you have developed some theories about what is wrong, test them to determine the cause of the problem. Once a theory is confirmed, you can determine the steps to resolve the problem. Table 8-4 lists some quick procedures that can help you determine the exact cause of a problem or even correct the problem. If a quick procedure does correct the problem, you can verify full system functionality. If a quick procedure does not correct the problem, you may need to research the problem further to determine the exact cause.

Table 8-4   Step 3: Test the Theory to Determine the Cause

Common steps to determine cause	<ul><li>Restart the printer or scanner.</li><li>Disconnect and reconnect the cables.</li><li>Restart the computer.</li><li>Check printer for paper jams.</li><li>Reseat paper in paper trays.</li><li>Open and close printer trays.</li><li>Ensure printer doors are closed.</li><li>Install a new ink or toner cartridge.</li></ul>

Establish a Plan of Action to Resolve the Problem and Implement the Solution (8.5.7.5)

After you have determined the exact cause of a problem, establish a plan of action to resolve the problem and implement the solution. Table 8-5 shows some sources you can use to gather additional information to resolve an issue.

Table 8-5   Step 4: Establish a Plan of Action to Resolve the Problem and Implement the Solution

If no solution is achieved in the previous step, further research is needed to implement the solution, using these sources.	■ Help desk repair logs ■ Other technicians ■ Manufacturer FAQs ■ Technical websites ■ Newsgroups ■ Computer manuals ■ Device manuals ■ Online forums ■ Internet search

Verify Full System Functionality and, if Applicable, Implement Preventive Measures (8.5.7.6)

After you have corrected the problem, verify full functionality and, if applicable, implement preventive measures. Table 8-6 lists the steps to verify the solution.

Table 8-6   Step 5: Verify Full Functionality and, if Applicable, Implement Preventive Measures

Verify full functionality.	■ Reboot the computer. ■ Reboot the printer. ■ Print a test page from the printer control panel. ■ Print a document from an application. ■ Reprint the customer's problem document.

Document Findings, Actions, and Outcomes (8.5.7.7)

In the final step of the troubleshooting process, document your findings, actions, and outcomes. Table 8-7 lists the tasks required to document a problem and its solution.

Table 8-7   Step 6: Document Findings, Actions, and Outcomes

Document your findings, actions, and outcomes.	■ Discuss with the customer the solution that was implemented.
	■ Have the customer verify that the problem has been solved.
	■ Provide the customer with all paperwork.
	■ Document the steps taken to solve the problem in the work order and the technician's journal.
	■ Document any components used in the repair.
	■ Document the time spent to resolve the problem.

Problems and Solutions (8.5.8)

Specific troubleshooting solutions vary depending on the printer, but when you understand some common issues, you can search and find fixes. Printer problems can stem from many sources, including the printer hardware, printer drivers, print server, or, in the case of a network printer, the network. Recognizing the source of a problem and identifying a solution are the topics of this section.

Identify Printer Problems and Solutions (8.5.8.1)

Printer problems can be attributed to hardware, software, networks, or some combination of the three. You will resolve some types of problems more often than others.

Common Problems and Solutions for Printers (8.5.8.2)

Table 8-8 documents some common printing problems and possible solutions.

Table 8-8   Common Problems and Solutions for Printers

Identify the Problem	Probable Causes	Possible Solutions
An application document does not print.	There is a document error in the print queue.	Manage the print jobs by canceling the document from the print queue and printing again.
Printer cannot be added or there is a print spooler error.	The printer service is stopped or not working properly.	Start the print spooler and, if necessary, reboot the computer.
Printer jobs are sent to the print queue but are not printed.	The printer has been installed on the wrong port.	Use printer properties and settings to configure the printer port.

Identify the Problem	Probable Causes	Possible Solutions
Print queue is functioning properly, but the printer does not print.	There is a bad cable connection.	Check for bent pins on the printer cable and check the printer cable connections to the printer and computer.
	The printer is in standby.	Manually resume the printer from standby or power cycle the printer.
	The printer has an error such as being out of paper, being out of toner, or having a paper jam.	Check the printer status and correct any errors.
Printer is printing unknown characters or does not print a test page.	Wrong or outdated printer driver is installed.	Uninstall the current print driver and install the correct print driver.
Printer prints unknown characters or does not print anything.	Printer may be plugged into a UPS.	Plug the printer directly into a wall outlet or surge protector.
	Incorrect print driver installed.	Uninstall incorrect print driver and install correct driver.
	Printer cables are loose.	Secure printer cables.
	No paper in printer.	Add paper to the printer.
Paper jams when printing.	Printer is dirty.	Clean the printer.
	The wrong paper type is being used.	Replace paper with the manufacturer's recommended paper type.
	Humidity causes the paper to stick together.	Insert new paper in the paper tray.
The print jobs are faded.	The toner cartridge is low or the toner cartridge is defective.	Replace the toner cartridge.
	The paper is incompatible with the printer.	Replace the paper.
The toner is not fusing to the paper.	The toner cartridge is empty or defective.	Replace the toner cartridge.
	The paper is incompatible with the printer.	Replace the paper.

Identify the Problem	Probable Causes	Possible Solutions
The paper is creased after printing.	The paper is defective.	Remove paper from printer, check for defects, and replace.
	The paper is loaded incorrectly.	Remove, align, and replace the paper.
The paper is not being fed into the printer.	The paper is wrinkled.	Remove the wrinkled paper from print tray.
		Check rollers for damage or need of replacement.
	Printer set to print to a different paper size than currently loaded.	Change paper size in print settings.
User receives a "Document failed to print" message.	A cable is loose or disconnected.	Check and reconnect the parallel, USB, or power cable.
	A printer is no longer shared.	Configure the printer for sharing.
User receives an "Access Denied" message when trying to install a printer.	User does not have administrative or power user privileges.	Log out and log in as an administrator or power user.
Printer is printing incorrect colors.	Print cartridge is empty or defective.	Replace the printer cartridge.
	Incorrect cartridge installed.	
	Print heads need to be cleaned and calibrated.	Clean and calibrate the printer using the supplied software.
The printer is printing blank pages.	The printer is out of ink or toner.	Replace the ink or toner cartridge.
	The print head is clogged.	Replace the ink cartridge.
	The corona wire has failed.	Replace the corona wire.
	The high-voltage power supply has failed.	Replace the high-voltage power supply.
The printer display has no image.	The printer is not turned on.	Turn on the printer.
	The contrast of the screen is set too low.	Increase the screen contrast.
	The display is broken.	Replace the display.

Advanced Problems and Solutions for Printers (8.5.8.3)

Table 8-9 documents some advanced printing problems and possible solutions.

Table 8-9   Advanced Problems and Solutions for Printers

Identify the Problem	Probable Causes	Possible Solutions
Printer prints unknown characters.	An incorrect print driver is installed.	Uninstall the incorrect print driver and install the correct driver.
	The printer cables are loose.	Secure the printer cables.
Printer will not print large or complex images.	The printer does not have enough memory.	Add more memory to the printer.
Laser printer prints vertical lines or streaks on every page.	The drum is damaged.	Replace the drum or replace the toner cartridge when it contains the drum.
	Toner is not evenly distributed in the cartridge.	Remove and shake the toner cartridge.
Printed pages show ghost images.	The drum is scratched or dirty.	Replace the drum or replace the toner cartridge when it contains the drum.
	The drum wiper blade is worn.	Replace the drum or replace the toner cartridge when it contains the drum.
The toner is not fusing to the paper.	The fuser is defective.	Replace the fuser.
Paper is creased after printing.	The pickup rollers are obstructed, damaged, or dirty.	Clean or replace the pickup rollers.
Paper is not being fed into the printer.	The pickup rollers are obstructed, damaged, or dirty.	Clean or replace the pickup rollers.
Each time a network printer is restarted, users receive a "Document failed to print" message.	The printer's IP configuration is set for DHCP.	Assign a static IP address to the printer.
	A device on the network has the same IP address as the network printer.	Assign a different static IP address to the printer.
There are multiple failed jobs in the printer logs.	The printer is off.	Turn on the printer.
	The printer is out of paper.	Add paper to the printer.
	The printer is out of toner or ink.	Replace the toner or ink cartridge(s).
	The print job is corrupt.	Restart or delete the print job.

Summary (8.6)

In this chapter, you learned how printers operate, what to consider when purchasing a printer, and how to connect printers to an individual computer or to a network. There are many different types and sizes of printers, each with different capabilities, speeds, and uses. Printers can be connected directly to computers or shared across a network. The chapter also introduced the different types of cables and interfaces available to connect a printer.

Some printers have low output and are adequate for home use, whereas other printers have high output and are designed for commercial use. Printers can have different speeds and print qualities. Older printers use parallel cables and ports. Newer printers typically use Wi-Fi, USB, or FireWire cables and connectors. With newer printers, the computer automatically installs the necessary drivers. If the device drivers are not automatically installed by the computer, download them from the manufacturer's website or use the supplied CD.

You learned about important characteristics and components of the various printer types. The primary components of an inkjet printer are the ink cartridges and the print head, roller, and feeder. A laser printer is a high-quality, fast printer that uses a laser beam to create an image. The central parts of a laser printer are the imaging drum, toner cartridge, fuser assembly, and rollers. Thermal printers use a special thermal paper that becomes black where heated. Impact printers have print heads that strike an inked ribbon, causing characters to be imprinted on the paper. Dot matrix and daisy wheel are examples of impact printers. 3D printers are used to create three-dimensional objects. These objects are first designed using a computer. A variety of media are now available to create these objects.

You also learned about virtual printing and cloud printing. With virtual printing the user does not send a print job to a physical printing device; rather, the print software sends the job to a file or transmits the information to a remote destination in the cloud for printing. Common virtual printing options are print to file, print to PDF, print to XPS, and print to image. Cloud printing involves sending a print job to a remote printer that could be at any location connected to the Internet.

You completed a lab installing a printer in Windows. In the lab, you installed a print driver, downloaded and installed an updated print driver, and, if all was configured correctly, were able to print a test page. After you set up the printer, you had a lab in which you shared the device in Windows with other users on the network.

At the end of the chapter, you learned the importance of following a preventive maintenance program for printers. A good preventive maintenance program extends the life of a printer and keeps it performing well. Always follow safety procedures when working with printers. Many parts inside printers contain high voltage or become very hot with use. In two labs, you performed preventive maintenance on inkjet and laser printers.

Finally, you learned the six steps in the troubleshooting process as they pertain to printers.

Practice

The following activities provide practice with the topics introduced in this chapter. The labs are available in the companion *IT Essentials v8 Labs & Study Guide* (ISBN 9780138166304).

Labs

8.3.1.3 Lab: Install a Printer in Windows

8.4.1.3 Lab: Share a Printer in Windows

8.5.2.2 Lab: Perform Preventive Maintenance on an Inkjet Printer

8.5.3.2 Lab: Perform Preventive Maintenance on a Laser Printer

Check Your Understanding Questions

Complete all the review questions listed here to test your understanding of the topics and concepts in this chapter. Appendix A, "Answers to 'Check Your Understanding' Questions," lists the answers.

1. Which type of document typically takes the longest time to print?

   A. a high-quality page of text

   B. a digital color photograph

   C. a draft photo–quality printout

   D. draft text

2. Which of the following are potential disadvantages of replacing printer consumables with parts or components that are not recommended by the manufacturer? (Choose two.)

   A. Nonrecommended parts might be more readily available.

   B. The printer may need to be cleaned more often.

   C. Print quality might be poor.

   D. The manufacturer warranty might be voided.

   E. Nonrecommended parts might be less expensive.

3. A small company is deciding whether a laser printer should be purchased to replace an inkjet printer. What are two disadvantages of a laser printer? (Choose two.)

A. It only prints black-and-white documents.
B. Toner cartridges are expensive.
C. The startup cost is high.
D. It cannot print in high resolution.
E. It uses expensive piezoelectric crystals to generate print images.

4. A technician wants to share a printer on the network, but according to the company policy, no PC should have a directly connected printer. Which device would the technician need?

A. a USB hub
B. a LAN switch
C. a hardware print server
D. a docking station

5. What term is used to describe dual-sided printing?

A. spooling
B. duplex printing
C. IR printing
D. buffering

6. While troubleshooting a printer problem, a technician discovers that the printer has been connected to the wrong computer port. Which printer problem would this mistake cause?

A. Blank pages are printed by the printer.
B. When a document is printed, there are unknown characters on the page.
C. The print spooler displays an error.
D. The print queue is functioning, but print jobs are not printed.

7. Which method is recommended for cleaning the print heads in an inkjet printer?

A. Use compressed air.
B. Wipe the print heads with isopropyl alcohol.
C. Wipe the print heads with a damp cloth.
D. Use the printer software utility.

8. A small business has connected several printers to the Web using Google Cloud Print. Mobile workers can therefore print job orders while they are on the road. This is an example of using what type of printer?

   A. thermal

   B. virtual

   C. laser

   D. inkjet

9. How could a user share a locally connected printer with other users on the same network?

   A. Enable print sharing.

   B. Install a USB hub.

   C. Install shared PCL drivers.

   D. Remove the PS drivers.

10. What is the first action that should be taken when performing preventive maintenance on a printer?

    A. Disconnect the printer from the network.

    B. Clean the print heads using the printer software utility.

    C. Remove the paper from the printer paper tray.

    D. Disconnect the printer from the power source.

11. What are two disadvantages of sharing a directly connected printer from a computer? (Choose two.)

    A. Only one computer at a time can use the printer.

    B. Other computers do not need to be cabled directly to the printer.

    C. The computer sharing the printer uses its own resources to manage all the print jobs coming to the printer.

    D. The computer directly connected to the printer always needs to be powered on, even if not in use.

    E. All the computers using the printer need to use the same operating system.

12. Which statement describes the print buffering process?

    A. Large documents are stored temporarily in internal printer memory while waiting for the printer to be available.

    B. A document is being prepared by the application to be printed.

    C. A document is being printed on the printer.

    D. A PC is encoding a photograph into a language that the printer understands.

13. Dots per inch is used as a measure for which characteristic of a printer?

   A. speed

   B. quality of printing

   C. cost of ownership

   D. reliability

14. What software enables users to set and change printer options?

   A. drivers

   B. firmware

   C. configuration software

   D. word processing applications

15. What are two closed-ended questions that a technician could ask a user when trying to identify the problem with a printer? (Choose two.)

   A. What error messages were displayed when the problem occurred?

   B. What were you doing when the problem occurred?

   C. Is the printer powered on?

   D. What recent software or hardware changes have been made to your computer?

   E. Can you print a test page on the printer?

16. Which method is recommended for cleaning the print heads in an inkjet printer?

   A. Use the printer software utility.

   B. Use compressed air.

   C. Wipe the print heads with a damp cloth.

   D. Wipe the print heads with isopropyl alcohol.

CHAPTER 9

Virtualization and Cloud Computing

Objectives

Upon completion of this chapter, you will be able to answer the following questions:

- What is server virtualization?
- How do you install virtualization software on a computer?
- What are the uses of the cloud?
- What are the characteristics of public, private, hybrid, and community cloud computing?

Key Terms

This chapter uses the following key terms. You can find the definitions in the glossary at the end of the book.

broad network access   page 495

client-side emulator   page 489

client-side virtualization   page 486

cloud computing   page 483

cloud computing services   page 491

cloud service provider   page 492

community cloud   page 494

guest operating system (guest OS)   page 487

host computer   page 487

host operating system (host OS)   page 487

hybrid cloud   page 494

hypervisor   page 488

Infrastructure as a Service (IaaS)   page 492

measured and metered service   page 495

memory support   page 489

National Institute of Standards and Technology (NIST)   page 492

network requirements   page 489

on-demand (self-service)   page 495

Platform as a Service (PaaS)   page 492

processor support   page 489

rapid elasticity   page 495

resource pooling   page 495

server virtualization   page 484

single point of failure   page 484

Software as a Service (SaaS)   page 492

software defined networking (SDN)   page 495

storage   page 489

Type 1 (native) hypervisor   page 488

Type 2 (hosted) hypervisor   page 488

virtual machine (VM)   page 483

virtual machine manager (VMM)   page 488

virtualization   page 483

Introduction (9.0)

Organizations both large and small are investing heavily in virtualization and cloud computing. It is therefore important for IT technicians and professionals to understand these two technologies. While the two technologies do overlap, they are, in fact, two different technologies. Virtualization software allows one physical server to run several individual computing environments. *Cloud computing* is a term used to describe the availability of shared computing resources—software or data—as a service and on demand over the Internet.

In this chapter, you will learn about the advantages of virtualization over dedicated servers, such as using fewer resources, requiring less space, reducing cost, and increasing server uptime. You will also learn the terms that are used when discussing client-side virtualization, such as *host computer*, which refers to a physical computer controlled by a user. The host OS is the OS on the host computer, and the guest OS is the OS running in the virtual machine on the host computer.

You will learn about the two types of hypervisors: Type 1 (native) hypervisor, also called bare-metal hypervisor, and Type 2 (hosted) hypervisor. You will also learn the minimum system requirements to run Windows Hyper-V, which is a Type 2 hypervisor, in Windows 7, Windows 8, and Windows 10.

It is important to not only learn about virtualization and cloud technology but to also build hands-on skills. In this chapter, you will complete a lab installing Linux in a virtual machine.

Virtualization (9.1)

Virtualization allows the use of one physical computer on which you install a virtualization software layer called a *hypervisor* for creating virtual machines; the virtual machines are independent of each other and use hardware resources of the physical machine for their operation. With virtualization, organizations can save money, reduce hardware, consolidate management and other system features, and realize many other benefits.

Virtualization (9.1.1)

Virtualization involves virtual (as opposed to physical) versions of components like hardware and software, such as server operating systems in network infrastructure. Virtualization can provide benefits such as cost savings, better performance, ease of management, and increased efficiency in a variety of environments, such as businesses and homes.

Video Explanation 9.1.1.1: What Is the Cloud?

Video

Refer to the online course to view this video.

Cloud Computing and Virtualization (9.1.1.2)

The terms *virtualization* and *cloud computing* are often used interchangeably, although they mean different things.

Virtualization enables a single computer to host multiple independent virtual computers that share the host computer hardware. Virtualization software separates the physical hardware from the *virtual machine (VM)* instances. VMs have their own operating systems and connect to hardware resources through software running on the host computer. An image of a VM can be saved as a file and can then be restarted when required.

It is important to remember that all the VMs share the resources of the host computer. Therefore, the factors that limit the number of VMs that can run at the same time are the processing power, memory, and storage.

Cloud computing separates the applications from the hardware. It provides organizations with on-demand delivery of computing services over the network. Service providers such as Amazon Web Services (AWS) own and manage the cloud infrastructure—including networking devices, servers, and storage devices—which is usually housed in a data center.

Virtualization is the foundation that supports cloud computing. Providers such as AWS offer cloud services using powerful servers that can dynamically provision virtual servers as required.

Without virtualization, cloud computing as it is most widely implemented would not be possible.

Traditional Server Deployment (9.1.1.3)

To fully appreciate virtualization, it is necessary to understand how servers are used in an organization.

Traditionally, organizations delivered applications and services to their users by using powerful dedicated servers, as shown in Figure 9-1. These Windows and Linux servers are high-end computers with large amounts of RAM, powerful processors, and multiple large storage devices. New servers are added if more users or new services are required.

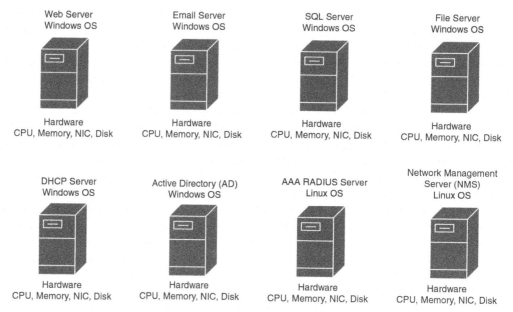

Figure 9-1 Dedicated Servers

Problems with the traditional server deployment approach include the following:

- **Wasted resources:** Dedicated servers may sit idle for long periods until they are needed to deliver their specific services. Meanwhile, these servers waste energy.

- *Single point of failure*: A dedicated server may fail or go offline, and there may be no backup servers to handle the failure.

- **Server sprawl:** When an organization does not have adequate space to physically house underutilized servers, the servers take up more space than is warranted by the services that they provide.

Virtualizing servers to use resources more efficiently addresses these problems.

Server Virtualization (9.1.1.4)

Server virtualization takes advantage of idle resources to reduce the number of servers required to provide services to users.

A special program called a *hypervisor* is used to manage computer resources and various VMs. It provides VMs access to all the hardware of the physical machine, such as CPUs, memory, disk controllers, and NICs. Each of the VMs runs a complete and separate operating system.

Virtualization enables an enterprise to reduce the number of servers. For example, it is not uncommon for 100 physical servers to be consolidated as virtual machines on top of 10 physical servers using hypervisors. In Figure 9-2, the previous 8 dedicated servers have been consolidated into 2 servers using hypervisors to support multiple virtual instances of the operating systems.

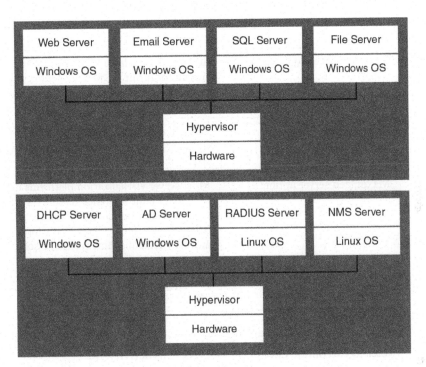

Figure 9-2   Hypervisor OS Installation

Advantages of Server Virtualization (9.1.1.5)

Virtualization offers major advantages, as shown in Table 9-1.

Table 9-1   Virtualization Advantages

Advantage	Description
Better use of resources	Virtualization reduces the number of physical servers, the number of networking devices, the supporting infrastructure requirements, and maintenance costs.
Reduced energy consumption	Consolidating servers lowers the monthly power and cooling costs. Reduced consumption helps enterprises to achieve a smaller carbon footprint.
Faster server provisioning	Creating a virtual server is far faster than provisioning a physical server.

Advantage	Description
Improved disaster recovery	Virtualization offers advanced solutions to keep business continuing during a disaster. VMs can be copied to other hardware platforms that may even be located in a different data center.
Reduced space requirement	Server consolidation with virtualization reduces the overall footprint of the data center. Having fewer servers, network devices, and racks reduces the amount of required floor space.
Reduced cost	Cost savings result from less equipment being required, less energy being consumed, and less space being required.
Maximized server uptime	Most server virtualization platforms now offer advanced redundant fault tolerance features, such as live migration, storage migration, high availability, and distributed resource scheduling. They also support the ability to move a virtual machine from one server to another.
Support for legacy systems	Virtualization can extend the life of OSs and applications, providing more time for organizations to migrate to newer solutions.

Interactive Graphic

9.1.1.6 Check Your Understanding: Match the Advantages of Virtualization

Refer to the online course to complete this activity.

Client-Side Virtualization (9.1.2)

Client-side virtualization, sometimes called *desktop virtualization*, provides a way to have multiple operating systems running on a single desktop, possibly running simultaneously (unlike with a dual-boot system). Each virtual machine is self-contained and has no awareness of the other virtual machines, but all the VMs are running on one single piece of hardware. On a desktop operating system, this is host-based virtualization.

Client-Side Virtualization (9.1.2.1)

Many organizations use server virtualization to optimize network resources and reduce equipment and maintenance costs. Organizations also use client-side virtualization to enable users with specific needs to run VMs on their local computer.

Client-side virtualization is beneficial for IT staff, IT support people, and software developers and testers, as well as for educational reasons. It provides users with resources to test new operating systems or software or to run older software. It can also be used to sandbox and create a secure isolated environment to open or run a suspicious file.

Some terms that are used when discussing client-side virtualization include the following:

- *Host computer*: This is the physical computer controlled by a user. VMs use the system resources of the host machine to boot and run an OS.

- *Host operating system (host OS)*: This is the operating system of the host computer. Users can use a virtualization emulator such as VirtualBox on the host OS to create and manage VMs.

- *Guest operating system (guest OS)*: This is the operating system that is running in the VM. Drivers are required to run the different OS version.

The guest OS is independent of the host OS. For example, the host OS could be Windows 10, and the VM could have Windows 7 installed. This guest of the VM would be Windows 7. In this example, the guest OS (Windows 7) does not interfere with the host OS (Windows 10) on the host computer.

Host and guest operating systems do not need to be of the same family. For example, the host OS could be Windows 10, while the guest OS could be Linux. This is beneficial for users who need to increase the functionality of their host computer by running multiple operating systems at the same time.

Figure 9-3 shows a logical virtual machine diagram. The bottom gray box represents the physical computer with its host OS (such as Windows 10). Hyper-V, Virtual PC, and VirtualBox are examples of virtualization software or emulators that could be used to create and manage the three VMs shown at the top of Figure 9-3.

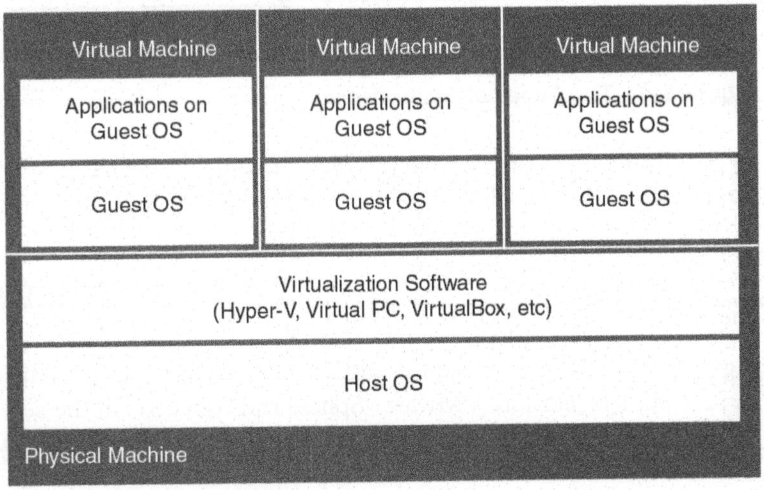

Figure 9-3   Logical Virtual Machine Diagram

Type 1 and Type 2 Hypervisors (9.1.2.2)

The hypervisor, also called the *virtual machine manager (VMM)*, is the brain in virtualization. The *hypervisor* is the software used on the host computer to create and manage VMs.

The hypervisor allocates physical system resources, such as CPU, RAM, and storage, to each VM as needed. This ensures that the operation of one virtual machine does not interfere with that of another.

There are two types of hypervisors, as shown in Figure 9-4:

- *Type 1 (native) hypervisor*: Also called a bare-metal hypervisor and typically used with server virtualization, this type of hypervisor runs directly on the hardware of a host and manages the allocation of system resources to virtual operating systems.

- *Type 2 (hosted) hypervisor*: This type of hypervisor is hosted by an OS and is commonly used with client-side virtualization. Virtualization software such as Windows Hyper-V and VMware Workstation are examples of Type 2 hypervisors.

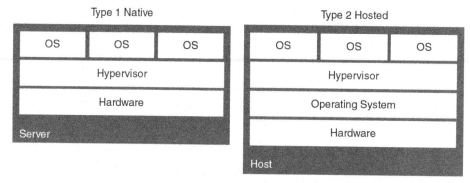

Figure 9-4   Two Types of Hypervisors

Type 1 hypervisors are common in data centers and in cloud computing. Examples of Type 1 hypervisors include VMware vSphere/ESXi, Xen, and Oracle VM Server.

Type 2 hypervisors such as VMware Workstation work with a host computer to create and use multiple VMs. Windows Hyper-V is also included in Windows 10 Pro and Windows Server (2012 and 2016).

Figure 9-5 shows sample Type 1 and a Type 2 hypervisor implementations. In the Type 1 implementation, VMware vSphere runs directly on the server hardware with no operating system. VMware vSphere has been used to create a Windows server VM and a Linux server VM. In the Type 2 implementation, the host OS on the

computer is Windows 10. Windows Hyper-V has been used to create and manage the
Windows 7 VM and a Linux VM.

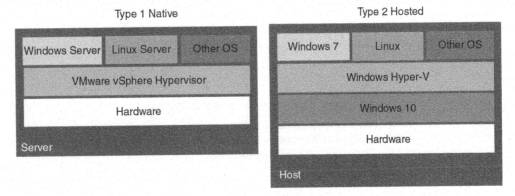

Figure 9-5   Hypervisor Implementation Examples

Client-side emulators can run software meant for a different guest OS or an OS
meant for different hardware. For example, if the host OS is Linux, you might create
a VM using Windows 7 to run an application that runs only in Windows 7. The Linux
host computer in essence pretends to be a Windows 7 computer.

Virtual Machine Requirements (9.1.2.3)

Virtual computing requires more powerful hardware configurations because each
installation needs its own resources.

All virtual machines share the following basic system requirements:

- *Processor support*: Processors such as Intel VT and AMD-V are specifically
  designed to support virtualization. The virtualization feature on these processors
  may need to be enabled. Processors with multiple cores are also recommended
  as the additional cores increase speed and responsiveness when running multiple
  VMs. The more cores a computer has, the more things it can do at once, including running more virtual machines simultaneously.

- *Memory support*: Consider that you need memory for your host OS and also
  need enough RAM to meet the requirements of each VM and its guest OS.

- *Storage*: Each VM creates very large files to store operating systems, applications, and all the VM data. You must also factor in that an active VM requires a
  few gigabytes of storage space. Therefore, large and fast drives are recommended.

- *Network requirements*: Network connection requirements depend on the type
  of VM. Some VMs do not require outside connections, and others do. VMs
  can be configured in a bridged, NAT, host-only, or special network to connect

only to other VMs. To connect to the Internet, a VM uses a virtual network adapter that simulates the real host adapter. The virtual network adapter connects through the physical NIC to establish a connection to the Internet.

The minimum system requirements for Windows Hyper-V for Windows 10 and Windows 8 and Windows Virtual PC for Windows 7 are displayed in Tables 9-2, 9-3, and 9-4, respectively.

VMs are susceptible to the same threats and malicious attacks as physical computers. Although VMs are isolated from the host, they can share resources (for example, NIC, folders, files). Users should exercise the same security considerations as on the host and install security software, enable firewall features, install patches, and update the operating system and programs. It is also important to keep the virtualization software updated.

Table 9-2   Windows Hyper-V Requirements for Windows 10

Host OS	Windows 10 Pro or Windows Server (2012 and 2016)
Processor	64-bit processor with second-level address translation (SLAT)
BIOS	CPU support for VM Monitor Mode Extension (VT-c on Intel CPUs)
Memory	Minimum 4 GB system RAM
Hard disk space	At least 15 GB per VM

Table 9-3   Windows Hyper-V Requirements in Windows 8

Host OS	Windows 8 Pro or Enterprise 64-bit operating system
Processor	64-bit processor with SLAT
BIOS	BIOS-level hardware virtualization support
Memory	At least 4 GB system RAM
Hard disk space	At least 15 GB per virtual OS

Table 9-4   Windows Virtual PC Requirements in Windows 7

Processor	1 GHz 32-bit or 64-bit processor
Memory	2 GB
Hard disk space	15 GB per virtual OS

Interactive Graphic

9.1.2.4 Check Your Understanding: Virtualization Terminology

Refer to the online course to complete this activity.

9.1.2.5 Lab: Install Linux in a Virtual Machine and Explore the GUI

In this lab, you will install a Linux OS in a virtual machine using a desktop virtualization application, such as VirtualBox. After completing the installation, you will explore the GUI interface.

Cloud Computing (9.2)

Cloud computing involves delivering services over the Internet. With cloud computing, you are not using local storage, networking resources, databases, and so on.

Cloud Computing Applications (9.2.1)

With cloud computing, the applications being used do not reside on the desktop or somewhere inside a company's network; rather, each application is provided as a service called a *cloud application*. Cloud applications are located on remote servers that are typically operated by third parties, but they can function offline and can be updated online. Cloud applications process on the remote computer, and storage and data access happen through a connection to the Internet. Cloud applications are platform independent.

How We Use the Cloud (9.2.1.1)

Cloud computing provides users with on-demand delivery of computing services over the Internet. *Cloud computing services* are owned and hosted by service providers. You use cloud services when you use social media applications, access online music libraries, or use online storage to save photos. Organizations typically pay cloud providers a usage fee based on user access and usage of services:

- **Virtual application streaming/cloud-based applications:** Organizations use cloud-based applications to provide on-demand software delivery. For example, Microsoft Office 365 provides online versions of applications such as Microsoft Word, Excel, and PowerPoint. When a user requests an application, minimal application code is forwarded to the client. The client pulls additional code from the cloud server as required. For offline use, the application may be saved locally on the host.

- **Cloud-based email:** Organizations use cloud-based solutions for their email requirements. Examples of cloud-based email applications include Office 365, Gmail, iCloud Mail, Outlook, Yahoo, and Exchange Online.

- **Cloud file storage solutions:** Organizations use cloud-based storage solutions for their corporate data. Examples of cloud storage solutions include Google Drive, OneDrive, iCloud Drive, Box, and Dropbox. Some of these solutions include synchronization applications that are either vendor-provided or commercially available applications.

- **Virtual desktop (infrastructure VDI):** An organization can use this technology to deploy entire desktop environments from a server in a data center to clients. The virtual desktops are created by a VM controlled by a hypervisor. However, all computing on the VDI is done on servers. VDIs can be persistent, providing the user with a customizable image that is saved for future use, or non-persistent, reverting the image to its initial state when a user logs out.

- **Windows Virtual Desktop (WVD):** This is a virtual desktop–enabled edition of Windows 10 that runs on modern or legacy computers or remotely on Azure virtual machines. It provides a virtualized Windows 10 experience that is always up to date and available on any device.

Cloud Services (9.2.2)

Cloud computing involves a number of evolving features, such as providing large storage space, powerful analytics tools, and applications and system infrastructure software; developing and testing applications; and delivering applications.

Cloud Services (9.2.2.1)

Cloud service providers can provide various services tailored to meet customer requirements. However, most cloud computing services can be categorized into three main cloud computing services, as defined by the *National Institute of Standards and Technology (NIST)* in Special Publication 800-145:

- *Software as a Service (SaaS)*: The cloud provider provides access to services, such as email, calendar, communication, and office tools over the Internet on a subscription basis. Users access the software by using a browser. Advantages include minimal up-front costs for customers and immediate application availability. SaaS providers include Salesforce customer relationship management (CRM) software, Microsoft Office 365, Microsoft SharePoint software, and Google G Suite.

- *Platform as a Service (PaaS)*: The cloud provider provides access to operating systems, development tools, programming languages, and libraries used to develop, test, and deliver applications. This is useful to application and software developers. The cloud provider manages the underlying network, servers, and cloud infrastructure. PaaS providers include Amazon Web Services, Oracle Cloud, Google Cloud Platform, and Microsoft Azure.

- *Infrastructure as a Service (IaaS)*: The cloud provider manages the network and provides organizations access to network equipment, virtualized network services, storage, software, and supporting network infrastructure. IaaS provides many advantages for organizations. For example, organizations do not need to invest in capital equipment and pay for usage on demand. In addition, the provider network includes redundancy, thus eliminating single points of failure in the provider network infrastructure. Also, the network can scale seamlessly, based on changing requirements. IaaS providers include Amazon Web Services, DigitalOcean, and Microsoft Azure.

Cloud service providers have extended the IaaS model to also provide IT as a service (ITaaS). ITaaS can extend the capability of IT without requiring investment in new infrastructure, training of new personnel, or licensing of new software. These services are available on demand and delivered economically to any device anywhere in the world without compromising security or function.

What Do You Already Know? - Cloud Models (9.2.2.2)

Four primary cloud models are used by people, organizations, and cloud service providers: private, public, community, and hybrid.

Read each scenario and select the cloud model that is used for each one.

Scenarios

Scenario 1: Bob uses Gmail to email his friend to tell him he will not be able to meet him after work because he is working late on a project.

Scenario 2: Bob arrives at his office in the Department of Transportation. He logs onto his computer and reviews his budget for the asphalt required for the extension of the road due to the proposed building of a new shopping mall.

Scenario 3: A resident of Smithtown needs information from the Department of Transportation website to better understand how the proposed new shopping mall will impact traffic in her community. After she learns that the traffic volume may double on her road, she leaves a public comment protesting the building.

Scenario 4: Andrea is a project manager for an asphalt company. She is submitting a bid to the Department of Transportation's vendor website to build the new road required for the development of a new shopping center.

Answers

Scenario 1 Answer: Public

Examples of the public cloud model are Gmail, Dropbox, Apple Music, Yahoo Mail, Box, and Netflix. These cloud-based applications and services are offered in a public cloud and made available to the general population. Services may be free or may be offered using a pay-per-use model, as with paying for online storage. The public cloud uses the Internet to provide services. Public clouds are the most common for users.

Public clouds:

- Use shared virtualized resources
- Support multiple customers
- Support Internet connectivity

Scenario 2 Answer: Private

A private cloud is dedicated to an organization or entity. Examples of organizations that use private clouds include service providers, financial institutions, and healthcare providers. A private cloud can be created using the organization's private network, but such a cloud can be expensive to build and maintain. A private cloud can also be managed by an outside organization with strict access security.

Private clouds:

- Use privately shared virtualized resources
- Each support a single customer (the organization)
- Secure highly sensitive information

Scenario 3 Answer: Hybrid

A *hybrid cloud* is made up of two or more different cloud types (such as part private and part public), where each part remains a distinctive object but the two are connected using a single architecture. Organizations may use a private cloud for confidential information and a public cloud for general, customer-facing content. In this example, the resident can access the private portion of the Department of Transportation's private cloud to gather research and can also access the public portion to leave feedback. Individuals on a hybrid cloud would be able to have degrees of access to various services, based on user access rights. An organization could use a hybrid cloud to provide services during short-term spikes.

Scenario 4 Answer: Community

A *community cloud* is created for exclusive use by specific entities or organizations. The differences between public clouds and community clouds are the functional needs that have been customized for the community. For example, healthcare organizations must remain compliant with policies and laws (such as HIPAA) that require special authentication and confidentiality. Community clouds are used by multiple organizations that have similar needs and concerns. Community clouds are similar to public clouds but with the set levels of security, privacy, and regulatory compliance of a private cloud.

`Interactive Graphic`

9.2.2.3 Check Your Understanding: Cloud Service and Cloud Model Terminology

Refer to the online course to complete this activity.

Cloud Computing Characteristics (9.2.2.4)

The cloud computing model is composed of five essential characteristics, as shown in Table 9-5.

Table 9-5 Cloud Computing Characteristics

Characteristic	Description
On-demand (self-service)	Individuals can provision or make changes to computing services as needed without the need for human interaction with the service provider.
Rapid elasticity	Services can be provisioned when needed and then released very quickly when no longer required. In some cases, the demand can be met and can scale automatically based on user demand.
Resource pooling	The provider's computing resources are pooled to serve multiple consumers using a multi-tenant model. In this model, each tenant (that is, customer) shares the different physical and virtual resources dynamically assigned and reassigned according to consumer demand. Examples of resources that can be pooled and shared include storage, processing, memory, and network bandwidth.
Measured and metered service	Cloud systems provide service performance measurements that can be used to automatically control and optimize resources using a metering mechanism. Metering can be used to set thresholds to ensure that a customer is always provided with satisfactory service levels. Measured and metered services also provide reports for both the provider and the service consumer.
Broad network access	Capabilities are available over the network and can be accessed using smartphones, tablets, laptops, and workstations.

Software Defined Networking (9.2.2.5)

To achieve efficient elasticity in the cloud, services must be provisioned and deprovisioned rapidly. This is done using scripting. *Software defined networking (SDN)* is often used to perform these operations. The SDN model has three layers: the application layer at the top, the control layer in the center, and the infrastructure layer at the bottom.

The application layer uses logic to decide how traffic is prioritized and where to switch it. The infrastructure layer is the physical and virtual devices that perform the routing and switching of traffic. The SDN controller is in the center and controls the application and infrastructure layers.

The control of the layers is performed by scripts through an application programming interface (API). The API between the SDN controller and the application layer is called the northbound API, and the API between the SDN controller and the infrastructure layer is called the southbound API, as shown in Figure 9-6.

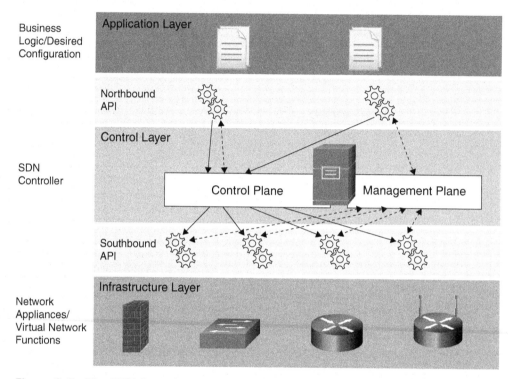

Figure 9-6   The SDN Controller Sits in the Management Plane, Between the Application and Infrastructure Layers

SD-WAN technologies make it possible to simplify an organization's network architecture, reducing it to a single orchestrated layer rather than a mixture of connected and integrated physical solutions. By virtualizing network architecture, organizations can better monitor and maintain their network organization, and they can even offload a significant amount of work through automated processes. SD-WAN solutions include built-in firewalls, artificially intelligent security solutions, and integrated security features such as encryption, sandboxing, and IPS. As businesses are operating increasingly outside brick-and-mortar locations, SD-WAN technology can help reduce their costs. Through SD-WAN technology, companies can better improve their consistency and reliability.

Interactive Graphic

9.2.2.6 Check Your Understanding: Match the Cloud Characteristics

Refer to the online course to complete this activity.

Summary (9.3)

In this chapter, you learned that the terms *virtualization* and *cloud computing* are often used interchangeably, although they actually mean different things. Virtualization is a technology that enables a single computer to host multiple virtual computers that share the same host computer hardware. Cloud computing is a technology that enables the separation of applications from hardware. Virtualization is the foundation that supports cloud computing.

You learned that the traditional way of delivering applications and services to users by using dedicated servers is inefficient, unreliable, and not scalable. Dedicated servers can sit idle for long periods, they create single points of failure, and they take up a lot of physical space. Virtualization solves these issues by consolidating many virtual servers onto a single physical server, taking advantage of idle resources, and reducing the number of servers required to provide services to users. You learned the many advantages that virtualization has over the traditional use of dedicated servers, such as better use of resources, lower space requirements, reduced cost, and increased server uptime.

Cloud computing provides users with on-demand delivery of computer services over the Internet. Most of us already use these services when we access online music services or online data storage. You learned about the types of cloud services offered by cloud service providers. SaaS provides access to services such as email, calendar, communication, and office tools over the Internet on a subscription basis. PaaS provides access to operating systems, development tools, programming languages, and libraries used to develop, test, and deliver applications. IaaS provides organizations access to network equipment, virtualized network services, storage, software, and supporting network infrastructure.

The chapter concluded with several exercises to test your understanding of cloud computing terminology and characteristics.

Practice

The following activities provide practice with the topics introduced in this chapter. The labs are available in the companion *IT Essentials v8 Labs & Study Guide* (ISBN 9780138166304).

Lab

9.1.2.5 Lab: Install Linux in a Virtual Machine and Explore the GUI

Check Your Understanding Questions

Complete all the review questions listed here to test your understanding of the topics and concepts in this chapter. Appendix A, "Answers to 'Check Your Understanding' Questions," lists the answers.

1. Which cloud computing opportunity would provide the use of network hardware such as routers and switches for a particular company?

   A. Software as a Service (SaaS)

   B. Wireless as a Service (WaaS)

   C. Browser as a Service (BaaS)

   D. Infrastructure as a Service (IaaS)

2. What is a characteristic of a virtual machine on a PC?

   A. The number of virtual machines that can be made available depends on the software resources of the host machine.

   B. A virtual machine is not susceptible to threats and malicious attacks.

   C. A virtual machine needs a physical network adapter to connect to the Internet.

   D. A virtual machine runs its own operating system.

3. To which category of hypervisor does Windows Virtual PC belong?

   A. Type 4

   B. Type 1

   C. Type 2

   D. Type 3

4. Which term is associated with cloud computing?

   A. virtualization

   B. wireless

   C. teleworkers

   D. tall servers

5. How does cloud computing improve the performance and user experience of an online version of office productivity tools?

   A. by ensuring a secure connection between the client and the service provider

   B. by providing application code, as needed

   C. by connecting local hardware devices, such as a printer, to the service provider

   D. by downloading the application package to the local storage

6. What is the minimum amount of system RAM that is required to run the Windows 8 Hyper-V virtualization platform?

   A. 512 MB

   B. 1 GB

   C. 8 GB

   D. 4 GB

7. A small advertising company is considering outsourcing information technology services to a cloud provider. The services would include user training, software licensing, and provisioning. What cloud service would the company consider purchasing?

   A. Platform as a Service (PaaS)

   B. IT as a Service (ITaaS)

   C. Software as a Service (SaaS)

   D. Infrastructure as a Service (IaaS)

8. For a large enterprise deploying virtualized servers, what are two benefits of using a bare-metal hypervisor solution instead of a hosted hypervisor solution? (Choose two.)

   A. direct access to hardware resources

   B. enhanced security

   C. elimination of the need for management console software

   D. increased efficiency

   E. addition of an extra layer of abstraction

9. A research and development group has members from different company locations. The group is looking for a central file storage solution to store research-related documents. What are two possible solutions? (Choose two.)

   A. OneDrive

   B. Exchange Online

   C. Gmail

   D. Google Drive

   E. virtual desktop

10. Which statement describes the concept of cloud computing?

   A. separation of the management plane from the control plane

   B. separation of the control plane from the data plane

   C. separation of the operating system from the hardware

   D. separation of the application from the hardware

11. The IT department in a company is looking for a solution to consolidate the functionality of several mission-critical server computers into VMs on a few high-performance host machines. Which two hypervisors should be considered? (Choose two.)

   A. Windows 10 Hyper-V

   B. VMWare Workstation

   C. VMWare vSphere

   D. Oracle VM Server

   E. Oracle VM VirtualBox

12. A college is exploring options to outsource the student email service to a cloud provider. Which two solutions would help the college to achieve the task? (Choose two.)

   A. Gmail

   B. Dropbox

   C. Exchange Online

   D. virtual desktop

   E. OneDrive

13. A company uses a cloud-based payroll system. Which cloud computing technology is this company using?

   A. Browser as a Service (BaaS)

   B. Infrastructure as a Service (IaaS)

   C. Wireless as a Service (WaaS)

   D. Software as a Service (SaaS)

14. Which statement describes a characteristic of cloud computing?

   A. Applications can be accessed over the Internet through a subscription.

   B. Investment in new infrastructure is required in order to access the cloud.

   C. Devices can connect to the Internet through existing electrical wiring.

   D. A business can connect directly to the Internet without the use of an ISP.

15. What is the difference between a data center and cloud computing?

    A. Cloud computing provides access to shared computing resources, while a data center is a facility that stores and processes data.

    B. Data centers require cloud computing, but cloud computing does not require data centers.

    C. Of the two, only cloud computing is located off-site.

    D. There is no difference. These terms can be used interchangeably.

    E. The data center makes use of more devices to process data.

CHAPTER 10

Windows Installation

Objectives

Upon completion of this chapter, you will be able to answer the following questions:

- What are the functions of operating systems?

- What are operating system software and hardware requirements?

- What is the process of upgrading an operating system?

- What is disk management?

- How do you install a Windows operating system?

- What are custom installation options?

- What are the boot sequence and Registry files?

Key Terms

This chapter uses the following key terms. You can find the definitions in the glossary at the end of the book.

Introduction (10.0)

IT technicians and professionals need to understand the general functions of any operating system (OS), such as controlling hardware access, managing files and folders, providing a user interface, and managing applications. To help determine the best OS for a customer and make an OS recommendation, a technician needs to understand budget constraints, how the computer will be used, and which types of applications will be installed. This chapter focuses on the Windows 10, Windows 8, and Windows 7 operating systems and explores the components, functions, system requirements, and terminology related to each one. The chapter also details the steps to install a Windows operating system and the Windows boot sequence.

You will learn how to prepare a hard drive for a Windows installation by formatting the drive into partitions. You will learn about the different types of partitions and logical drives as well as other terms related to hard drive setup. You will also learn about the different file systems that are supported by Windows, such as File Allocation Table (FAT), New Technology File System (NTFS), Compact Disc File System (CDFS), and Network File System (NFS).

It is important to not only learn about virtualization and cloud technology but to also build hands-on skills. In this chapter, you will complete a lab in which you create a FAT32 partition in Windows and then convert the partition to NTFS. You will also complete labs on installing Windows, performing basic Windows setup tasks, creating user accounts, and installing Windows updates.

Modern Operating Systems (10.1)

An operating system provides an interface for the user and manages how resources are allocated to the hardware and applications. The OS boots the computer and manages the file system. An operating system can support more than one user, task, or CPU.

Operating System Features (10.1.1)

To understand the capabilities of an operating system, it is important to first understand some basic terms and common features.

Terms (10.1.1.1)

An *operating system (OS)* has a number of functions. One of its main tasks is to act as an interface between the user and the hardware connected to the computer, as shown in Figure 10-1. The operating system also controls other functions:

- Software resources

- Memory allocation and all peripheral devices

- Common services to computer application software

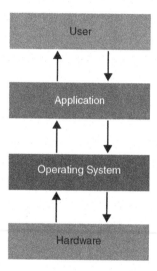

Figure 10-1   Operating System Diagram

Almost every computer, from a digital watch to a desktop computer, requires an operating system before it can be operated.

To understand the capabilities of an operating system, it is important to first understand some basic terms. The following terms are often used when describing operating systems:

- *Multi-user*: Two or more users have individual accounts that allow them to work with programs and peripheral devices at the same time.

- *Multitasking*: The computer is capable of operating multiple applications at the same time.

- *Multiprocessing*: The operating system can support two or more CPUs.

- *Multithreading*: A program can be broken into smaller parts that are loaded as needed by the operating system. Multithreading allows different parts of a program to be run at the same time.

The OS boots the computer and manages the file system. An operating system can support more than one user, task, or CPU.

Basic Functions of an Operating System (10.1.1.2)

Regardless of the size and complexity of the computer and the operating system, all operating systems perform the same four basic functions:

- Control *hardware access*
- Manage files and folders
- Provide a user interface
- Manage applications

Hardware Access

The OS manages the interaction between applications and the hardware, as shown in Figure 10-2. To access and communicate with each hardware component, the OS uses a program called a *device driver*. When a hardware device is installed, the OS locates and installs the device driver for that component. Assigning system resources and installing drivers are performed using a Plug and Play (PnP) process. The OS then configures the device and updates the Registry, which is a database that contains all the information about the computer.

Figure 10-2   Hardware Access

If the OS cannot locate a device driver, a technician must install the driver manually, either by using the media that came with the device or by downloading it from the manufacturer's website.

File and Folder Management

The OS creates a file structure on the hard disk drive to store data (see Figure 10-3). A *file* is a block of related data that is given a single name and treated as a single unit. Program and data files are grouped together in a *directory*. The files and directories are organized for easy retrieval and use. Directories can be kept inside other directories. These nested directories are referred to as *subdirectories*. In Windows, directories are called *folders*, and subdirectories are called *subfolders*.

Figure 10-3   File and Folder Management

User Interface

The OS enables the user to interact with the software and hardware. Operating systems include two types of *user interfaces*:

- *Command line interface (CLI)*: The user types commands at a prompt.

- *Graphical user interface (GUI)*: The user interacts with menus and icons, as shown in Figure 10-4.

Figure 10-4   User Interface

Application Management

The OS locates an application and loads it into the RAM of the computer. *Applications* are software programs, such as word processors, databases, spreadsheets, and games. The OS allocates available system resources to running applications.

To ensure that a new application is compatible with an OS, programmers follow a set of guidelines known as an *application programming interface (API)*. An API allows programs to access the resources managed by the operating system in a consistent and reliable manner. Here are some examples of APIs (see Figure 10-5):

- *Open Graphics Library (OpenGL)*: This is a cross-platform standard specification for multimedia graphics.

- *DirectX*: This is a collection of APIs related to multimedia tasks for Microsoft Windows.

- *Windows API*: The Windows API provides application developers with user interface controls, file management, and graphical elements, such as windows, scroll bars, and dialog boxes.

- *Java APIs*: This is a collection of APIs related to the development of Java programming.

Figure 10-5   Application Management

Windows Operating Systems (10.1.1.3)

Windows 10 is an update from the previous version of Windows that is designed for personal computers, tablets, embedded devices, and Internet of Things devices.

This version integrates the Cortana virtual assistant, a Windows 7–style start menu, and the Windows 8 live tiles in desktop mode, and it includes the new Microsoft Edge Web browser. There are 12 different editions of Windows 10, with varying feature sets and use cases to meet the needs of consumer, business, and education environments.

Like Windows 10, Windows 11 is an upgrade from the previous version. Most of the changes are superficial, like smaller taskbar icons that are placed in the center. There are also other visual additions, such as improved dark mode, transparency changes, and animation changes. Widgets have been expanded and are now more personalized. The Settings application has been redesigned with a menu on the left, making navigation easier. There are also minor convenience additions for Windows tablets running Windows 11, including better spacing of taskbar icons and a three-finger swipe to customize actions. Windows 11 is more energy efficient yet usually performs faster than previous versions. Finally, all versions of Windows 11 are 64-bit only, so it will not install on older, 32-bit computers.

Interactive Graphic

10.1.1.4 Check Your Understanding: Windows Terminology

Refer to the online course to complete this activity.

Customer Requirements for an Operating System (10.1.2)

Customer needs and preferences must be addressed when deciding on the best hardware and software solutions for the usage of a system. You need to gather information about the specific use of a computer to appropriately assess the user's technology requirements.

Compatible System Software and Hardware Requirements (10.1.2.1)

Understanding how a computer will be used is important when recommending an OS to a customer. The OS must be compatible with the existing hardware and the required applications.

To make an OS recommendation, a technician must review budget constraints, learn how the computer will be used, determine which types of applications will be installed, and decide whether a new computer may be purchased. These are some guidelines to help determine the best OS for a customer:

- **Does the customer use off-the-shelf applications for this computer?** An off-the-shelf application specifies a list of compatible operating systems on the application package, as shown in Figure 10-6.

Figure 10-6   Choosing the Correct OS

- **Does the customer use customized applications that were programmed specifically for the customer?** If the customer is using a customized application, the programmer of that application specifies which OS to use.

Minimum Hardware Requirements and Compatibility with OS (10.1.2.2)

Each operating system has minimum hardware requirements that must be met for the OS to be installed and function correctly.

Identify the equipment that your customer has in place. If hardware upgrades are necessary to meet the minimum requirements for an OS, conduct a cost analysis to determine the best course of action. In some cases, it might be less expensive for the customer to purchase a new computer than to upgrade the current system. In other cases, it might be cost-effective to upgrade one or more of the following components:

- RAM
- Hard disk drive
- CPU
- Video adapter card
- Motherboard

Note

If the application requirements exceed the hardware requirements of the OS, you must meet the additional requirements in order for the application to function properly.

Table 10-1 shows the minimum system requirements for Windows versions that Microsoft lists on its website.

Table 10-1   Windows Recommended Minimum System Requirements

Component	Windows 10	Windows 8.1	Windows 7
Processor	1 GHz or faster	1 GHz or faster	1 GHz or faster
RAM	1 GB for 32-bit or 2 GB for 64-bit	1 GB for 32-bit or 2 GB for 64-bit	1 GB for 32-bit or 2 GB for 64-bit
Hard drive space	16 GB for 32-bit or 20 GB for 64-bit	16 GB for 32-bit or 20 GB for 64-bit	16 GB for 32-bit or 20 GB for 64-bit
Graphics card	DirectX 9 or later with WDDM 1.0 driver	DirectX 9 or later with WDDM 1.0 driver	DirectX 9 or later with WDDM 1.0 driver
Display	800×600	1024×768	Not specified
Internet connection	Necessary to perform updates and some features	Necessary to perform updates and some features	Necessary to perform updates and some features

32-bit vs. 64-bit Processor Architecture (10.1.2.3)

The processor architecture of the CPU affects the performance of the computer.

The terms *32-bit* and *64-bit* refer to the amount of data a computer's CPU can manage. A 32-bit register can store 2^{32} different binary values. Therefore, a 32-bit processor can directly address 4,294,967,295 bytes. A 64-bit register can store 2^{64} different binary values. Therefore, a 64-bit processor can directly address 18,446,744,073,709,551,615 bytes.

Table 10-2 shows the main differences between the 32-bit and 64-bit architectures.

Table 10-2   32-bit vs. 64-bit Processor Architecture

Architecture	Description
32-bit (x86-32)	■ Processes multiple instructions using a 32-bit address space ■ Supports a maximum of 4 GB of RAM memory ■ Supports 32-bit operating systems only ■ Supports 32-bit applications only
64-bit (x86-64)	■ Adds additional registers specifically for instructions that use a 64-bit address space ■ Is backward compatible with 32-bit processors ■ Supports 32-bit and 64-bit operating systems ■ Supports 32-bit and 64-bit applications

What Do You Already Know? Choosing a Windows Edition (10.1.2.4)

Instructions

People and organizations use four primary Windows editions: Pro, Enterprise, Education, and Home.

Read the following scenarios and select the most appropriate edition for each of them.

Scenarios

Scenario 1: Robert is a school principal and needs an operating system for his school that is designed explicitly for academic purposes and is distributed through academic volume licensing.

Scenario 2: Bob is selecting a Windows operating system for use in his small business. Because Bob's business does not have an IT staff, the operating system needs to have built-in security, productivity, and management features. It must also provide an intuitive user experience and support tablet mode and touchscreens.

Scenario 3: Jane is selecting a Windows operating system for her personal computer. She will use the computer to complete school assignments, access email and the Internet, and play games in the Xbox community. Because her younger sister will also use the computer, it needs to have built-in family safety and parental controls. The price of the operating system must also fit into her budget.

Scenario 4: Sue is the IT director of a large organization and is selecting a Windows 10 operating system for a new regional office. The operating system must have customizable features and apps. It must also allow the IT staff to deploy, manage, and update devices remotely anywhere employees work. Windows Defender Advanced Threat Protection (ATP) with centralized detection and prevention management is also a requirement.

Scenario Answers

Scenario 1 Answer: Windows 10 Education

Windows 10 Education builds on Windows 10 Enterprise and is designed to meet the needs of schools, including staff, administrators, teachers, and students. This edition is available through academic volume licensing and has paths for schools and students using Windows 10 Home and Windows 10 Pro devices to upgrade to Windows 10 Education.

Scenario 2 Answer: Windows 10 Pro

Windows 10 Pro is a desktop edition for PCs, tablets, and 2-in-1s for small businesses that need built-in security, productivity, and management features. It builds on both the familiar and innovative features of Windows 10 Home and also has many extra features to meet the diverse needs of small businesses.

Scenario 3 Answer: Windows 10 Home

Windows 10 Home is the consumer-focused desktop edition. It offers a familiar and personal experience for PCs, tablets, and 2-in-1s. It is for individuals and households and includes consumer features such as Xbox One, Cortana, and Windows Hello.

Scenario 4 Answer: Windows 10 Enterprise

Windows 10 Enterprise is for large to mid-sized organizations with advanced security and management needs. It builds on Windows 10 Pro, adding advanced features designed to meet the demands of medium and large organizations. It also provides advanced capabilities to help protect against the ever-growing range of modern security threats targeting devices, identities, applications, and sensitive company information.

10.1.2.5 Check Your Understanding: Choosing an Operating System

Refer to the online course to complete this activity.

Operating System Upgrades (10.1.3)

Cost, compatibility, support, security, and performance issues are some of the factors to be considered when considering an operating system upgrade. Being well prepared when doing an upgrade is critical, and it involves backing up data and system information before beginning to upgrade. This section discusses methods that can help in this process.

Checking OS Compatibility (10.1.3.1)

An OS must be upgraded periodically to remain compatible with the latest hardware and software. It is also necessary to upgrade an OS when a manufacturer stops supporting it. Upgrading an OS can increase performance. New hardware products often require that the latest OS version be installed to operate correctly. While upgrading an OS may be expensive, you can gain enhanced functionality through new features and support for newer hardware.

> **Note**
>
> When newer versions of an OS are released, support for older versions is eventually withdrawn.
>
> Before upgrading an operating system, check the minimum hardware requirements of the new OS to ensure that it can be successfully installed on the computer.

Windows OS Upgrades (10.1.3.2)

The process of upgrading the OS can be quicker than the process of performing a new installation. The upgrade process varies depending on the version of Windows being upgraded.

The version of an OS determines available upgrade options. For example, a 32-bit OS cannot be upgraded to a 64-bit OS. Also, Windows 7 and Windows 8 can be upgraded to Windows 10, but Windows Vista and Windows XP cannot.

Note

Prior to performing an upgrade, back up all data in case there is a problem with the installation. Also, the version of Windows being upgraded must be activated.

To upgrade Windows 7 or Windows 8 to Windows 10, use the Windows 10 Update Assistant, available on the Download Windows 10 website (see Figure 10-7). The Windows 10 Update Assistant installs and runs directly on the computer being upgraded. The tool walks the user through all the steps in the Windows 10 setup process. It is designed to prepare your computer for upgrading by checking for compatibility issues and downloading all necessary files to start the installation.

Figure 10-7 Windows 10 Update Assistant

Computers running Windows XP or Windows Vista do not have an upgrade path to Windows 10 and require a clean installation. Windows 10 installation media can be created using the Create Windows 10 installation media tool. This tool creates installation media (USB flash, DVD, or ISO file) that can be used to perform a clean installation.

Data Migration (10.1.3.3)

When a new installation is required, user data must be migrated from the old OS to the new one. There are several tools available to transfer data and settings. The *data migration* tool you select depends on your level of experience and your requirements.

User State Migration Tool

The *User State Migration Tool (USMT)*, shown in Figure 10-8, is a command line utility developed by Microsoft that allows users who are comfortable with scripting languages to transfer files and settings between Windows PCs. USMT is one of many core assessment and deployment tools included in the Windows Assessment and Deployment Kit, which can be downloaded from the Microsoft website. You can use USMT version 10.0 to streamline and simplify user state migration during large deployments of Windows operating systems. USMT captures user accounts, user files, operating system settings, and application settings and then migrates them to a new Windows installation. You can use USMT for both PC replacement and PC refresh migrations.

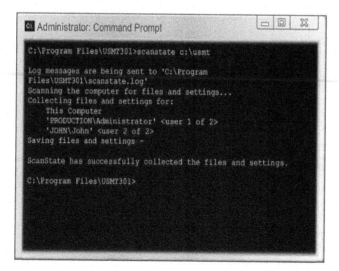

Figure 10-8   User State Migration Tool

Note

USMT version 10.0 supports data migration from Windows 7 through Windows 10.

Windows Easy Transfer

If a user is switching from an old computer to a new one, use *Windows Easy Transfer* to migrate personal files and settings, as shown in Figure 10-9. You can perform the file transfer using a USB cable, a CD or DVD, a USB flash drive, an external drive, or a network connection.

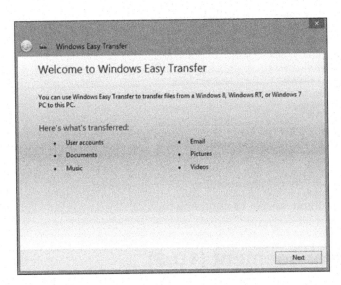

Figure 10-9   Windows Easy Transfer

Use Windows Easy Transfer to transfer information to a computer running Windows 8.1 from a computer with one of the following operating systems:

- Windows 8

- Windows 7

- Windows Vista

Windows Easy Transfer is not available in Windows 10 and has been replaced with PCmover Express.

PCmover Express

Microsoft has partnered with Laplink to provide *PCmover Express*, shown in Figure 10-10, which is a tool for transferring selected files, folders, profiles, and applications from an old Windows PC to a Windows 10 PC. Instead of repurchasing and manually installing programs on the new PC, a user can use PCmover to transfer selected applications to the new PC, and they will be installed and ready to use.

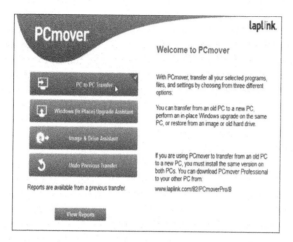

Figure 10-10 PCmover Express

10.1.3.4 Check Your Understanding: OS Upgrades

Refer to the online course to complete this activity.

Disk Management (10.2)

Disk management is the process of configuring and managing storage disks. It involves creating, deleting, and formatting partitions. It can also include tasks such as changing volume labels, reassigning drive letters, checking disks for errors, and backing up drives.

Disk Management (10.2.1)

This section examines terms related to disk management, various storage device types, file systems, and methods to ready disks for installing operating systems.

Storage Device Types (10.2.1.1)

As a technician, you might have to perform a clean installation of an OS. Perform a clean install in the following situations:

- When a computer is passed from one employee to another
- When the OS is corrupt
- When the primary hard drive in a computer is replaced

The installation and initial booting of the OS is called the *operating system setup*. Although it is possible to install an OS over a network from a server or from a local hard drive, the most common installation method for a home or small business is through external media such as DVDs or USB drives.

Note

If the hardware is not supported by the OS, you may need to install third-party drivers when performing a clean installation.

Before the operating system can be installed, a storage device must be chosen and prepared. Several types of storage devices are available and can be used to receive the new operating system, as shown in Figure 10-11. The two most common types of data storage devices used today are hard disk drives and flash memory–based drives such as solid-state hard drives and USB drives.

Hard Disk Drive

Flash Drive

Solid-State Drive

Figure 10-11   Storage Device Types

When the storage device type has been chosen, it must be prepared to receive the new operating system. Modern operating systems ship with an installer program. Installers usually prepare the disk to receive the operating system, but it is crucial for a technician to understand the terms and methods involved in this preparation.

Hard Drive Partitioning (10.2.1.2)

A hard drive is divided into areas called *partitions*. Each partition is a logical storage unit that can be formatted to store information, such as data files or applications. If you imagine a hard drive as a wooden cabinet, the partitions would be the shelves. During the installation process, most operating systems automatically partition and format available hard drive space.

Partitioning a drive is a simple process, but to ensure a successful boot, the firmware must know what disk and partition on that disk has an operating system installed. The partition scheme has a direct influence on the location of the operating systems on a disk. Finding and launching the operating system is one of the responsibilities of computer firmware. The partition scheme is very important to the firmware. Two of the most popular partition scheme standards are the *Master Boot Record (MBR)* and *globally unique identifier (GUID) partition table (GPT)*.

Master Boot Record

Publicly introduced in 1983, the MBR contains information on how the hard drive partitions are organized. The MBR is 512 bytes long and contains the boot loader, which is an executable program that allows a user to choose from multiple operating systems. The MBR has become the de facto standard but has limitations that have had to be addressed. The MBR is commonly used in computers with BIOS-based firmware.

GUID Partition Table

Also designed as a partition table scheme standard for hard drives, the GPT makes use of a number of modern techniques to expand on the older MBR partitioning scheme. GPT is commonly used in computers with UEFI firmware. Most modern operating systems support GPT.

Table 10-3 shows a comparison of MBR and GPT.

Table 10-3   MBR and GPT Comparison

MBR	GPT
Maximum of 4 primary partitions	Maximum of 128 partitions in Windows
Maximum partition size of 2 TB	Maximum partition size of 9.4 ZB (9.4×10^{21} bytes)
No partition table backup	Stores a partition table backup
Partition and boot data stored in one place	Partition and boot data stored in multiple locations across the disk
Any computer can boot from MBR	Computer must be UEFI-based and run a 64-bit OS

Partitions and Logical Drives (10.2.1.3)

A hard drive can be segmented into different types of partitions and logical drives. A technician should understand the process and terms related to hard drive setup.

Primary Partition

The *primary partition* contains the operating system files and is usually the first partition. A primary partition cannot be subdivided into smaller sections. On a GPT partitioned disk, all partitions are primary partitions. On an MBR partitioned disk, there can be a maximum of four partitions, with only one being primary.

Active Partition

On MBR disks, the *active partition* is the partition used to store and boot an operating system. Notice that only primary partitions can be marked active on MBR disks. Another limitation is that only one primary partition per disk can be marked active at one time. In most cases, the C: drive is the active partition and contains the boot and system files. Some users create additional partitions to organize files or in order to be able to dual-boot the computer. Active partitions are only found on drives with MBR partition tables.

Extended Partition

If more than four partitions are required on an MBR partitioned disk, one of the primary partitions can be designated an *extended partition*. After the extended partition is created, up to 23 logical drives (or *logical partitions*) can be created within this extended partition. A common setup is to create a primary partition for the OS (drive C:) and allow an extended partition to occupy the remaining free space on a hard drive, right after a primary partition. Any extra partitions can be created within the extended partition (drives D:, E:, and so on). While the logical drives can't be used to boot an OS, they are perfect for storing user data. Notice that there can be only one extended partition per MBR hard drive and that extended partitions are only found on drives with MBR partition tables.

Logical Drive

A *logical drive* is a section of an extended partition. It can be used to separate information for administrative purposes. Because GPT partitioned drives cannot have extended partitions, they do not have logical drives.

Basic Disk

A *basic disk* (the default) contains partitions such as primary and extended as well as logical drives that are formatted for data storage. More space can be added to a partition by extending it into adjacent, unallocated space, as long as it is contiguous. Either the MBR or GPT can be used as the underlying partition scheme for basic disks.

Dynamic Disk

Dynamic disks provide features not supported by basic disks. A dynamic disk has the ability to create volumes that span more than one disk. The sizes of the partitions can be changed after they have been set, even if the unallocated space is noncontiguous. Free space can be added from the same disk or a different disk, allowing a user to efficiently store large files. After a partition has been extended, it cannot be shrunk without deleting the entire partition. Either the MBR or GPT can be used as the partition scheme for dynamic disks.

Formatting

The *formatting* process creates a file system on a partition for storage of files.

Interactive Graphic

10.2.1.4 Check Your Understanding: Disk Terminology

Refer to the online course to complete this activity.

File Systems (10.2.1.5)

A new installation of an OS proceeds as if the disk were brand new. No information that is currently on the target partition is preserved. The first phase of the installation process involves partitioning and formatting the hard drive. This process prepares the disk to accept the new file system. The *file system* provides the directory structure that organizes the user's operating system, application, configuration, and data files. There are many different kinds of file systems, and each one has a unique structure and logic. Different file systems also differ in terms of speed, flexibility, security, size, and more. Here are five common file systems:

- *File Allocation Table, 32-bit (FAT32)*: FAT32 supports partition sizes up to 2 TB, or 2048 GB. The FAT32 file system is used by Windows XP and earlier OS versions.

- *New Technology File System (NTFS)*: NTFS, in theory, supports partition sizes up to 16 EB. NTFS incorporates file system security features and extended attributes. Windows 8.1, Windows 7, and Windows 10 automatically create a partition using the entire hard drive. If a user does not create custom partitions using the New option, the system formats the partition and begins installing Windows. If users create a partition, they can determine the size of the partition.

- *exFAT (FAT64)*: exFAT was created to address some of the limitations of FAT, FAT32, and NTFS when formatting USB flash drives, such as file size and directory size. One of the primary advantages of exFAT is that it can support files larger than 4GB.

- *Compact Disc File System (CDFS)*: CDFS was created specifically for optical disc media.

- *Network File System (NFS)*: NFS is a network-based file system that allows file access over the network. From the user's standpoint, there is no difference between accessing a file stored locally and accessing a file stored on another computer on the network. NFS is an open standard, which means anyone can implement it.

Quick Format vs. Full Format

Quick format removes files from the partition but does not scan the disk for bad sectors. Scanning a disk for bad sectors can prevent data loss in the future. For this reason, you should not use quick format for disks that have been formatted previously. Although it is possible to quick format a partition or a disk after the OS is installed, the quick format option is not available when installing Windows 8.1 and Windows 7.

Full format removes files from the partition while scanning the disk for bad sectors. It is required for all new hard drives. The full format option takes more time to complete than quick format.

Multiple Partitions During Windows 10 Installation

Figure 10-12 shows that two partitions were created as a result of selecting Drive 0 Unallocated Space and clicking New in the Windows Setup process before the OS is installed. The installer also allows the user to specify the size of the new partition.

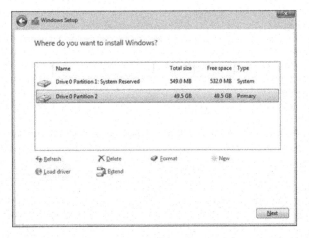

Figure 10-12   Creating Multiple Partitions

10.2.1.6 Video Demonstration: Disk Management Utility and Disk Partitioning

Refer to the online course to view this video.

10.2.1.7 Video Demonstration: Multiboot Procedures

Refer to the online course to view this video.

10.2.1.8 Lab: Create a Partition in Windows

In this lab, you will create a FAT32 formatted partition on a disk. You will convert the partition to NTFS. You will then identify the differences between the FAT32 format and the NTFS format.

Install Windows (10.3)

The steps to install Windows are similar between versions. The OS must be installed and configured to run on a specific device. When the installation is complete, the computer will be able to boot (start up) to the new operating system. During the boot process, the computer searches to find the location of the operating system files to boot from. The order in which the computer looks at devices for the boot information is known as the *boot sequence*.

Basic Windows Installation (10.3.1)

The installation process for Windows OS is similar across Windows 10, 8.x, and 7. The process involves installing the operating system on the device and configuring the necessary system settings so that the installed operating system can function properly with all hardware and other software components and users can log on.

10.3.1.1 Lab: Windows Installation

In this lab, you will install the Windows operating system.

Account Creation (10.3.1.2)

When users attempt to log onto a device or access system resources, Windows uses the process of authentication to verify the identity of the users. Authentication occurs when a user enters a username and password to access a user account. Windows uses *single sign-on (SSO)* authentication, which allows a user to log in once to access all system resources rather than log in each time they need to access an individual one.

User accounts allow multiple users to share a single computer with their own files and settings. Windows 10 offers two account types: Administrator and Standard User (see Figure 10-13). In previous versions of Windows, there was also a Guest account, but that was removed in Windows 10.

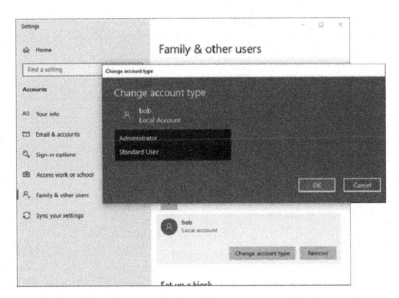

Figure 10-13   Account Creation

Administrator accounts have complete control over a computer. Users with this type of account can change settings globally, install programs, and run all applications by default with full administrative privileges, so such an account bypasses the use of User Account Control (UAC) when elevation to perform a task is required.

Standard User accounts have limited control over a computer. Users with this type of account can run applications, but they cannot install programs. A Standard User account can change system settings—but only settings that do not affect other user accounts.

Finalize the Installation (10.3.1.3)

To update the OS after the initial installation, *Microsoft Windows Update* is used to scan for new software and install service packs and patches.

After installation, verify that all hardware is installed correctly. Device Manager is used to locate device problems and install the correct or updated drivers in Windows.

Figure 10-14 shows the Windows Update and Device Manager utilities on Windows 10.

Figure 10-14   Finalizing the Installation

10.3.1.4 Lab: Finalize the Windows Installation

In this lab, you will add user accounts and finalize an installation of Windows 10.

Custom Installation Options (10.3.2)

A custom installation can save time and money in the process of deploying multiple systems with new operating system installations. Using a system image for installation can also be useful if you need to recover a system that has stopped working properly. As discussed in this section, one custom installation option is *disk cloning*, which involves copying the contents of an entire hard drive to another hard drive, thereby decreasing the time it takes to install drivers, applications, updates, and so forth on the second drive.

Disk Cloning (10.3.2.1)

Installing an OS on a single computer takes time. Imagine the time it would take to install operating systems on multiple computers, one at a time. To simplify this activity, administrators usually elect a computer to act as a base system and go through the regular operating system installation process. After the operating system is installed on the base computer, a specific program is used to duplicate all the information on its disk, sector by sector, to another disk. This new disk, usually an external device, then contains a fully deployed operating system and can be used to quickly deploy a fresh copy of the base operating system and any installed applications and data without the lengthy installation process or user involvement. Because the target disk now contains a sector-to-sector mapping of the original disk, the target disk contains an image of the original disk.

If an undesirable setting is accidentally included during the base installation, an administrator can use the *Microsoft System Preparation (Sysprep)* tool to remove it before creating the final image. Sysprep can be used to install and configure the same OS on multiple computers. Sysprep prepares the OS with different hardware configurations. With Sysprep, technicians can quickly install the OS, complete the last configuration steps, and then install applications.

To run Sysprep in Windows 10, open Windows Explorer and navigate to C:\Windows\System32\sysprep. You can also just type **sysprep** in the Run command box and click OK.

Figure 10-15 shows the Sysprep tool in Windows.

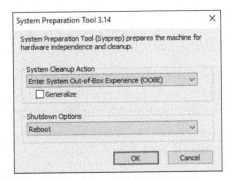

Figure 10-15   Disk Cloning

Other Installation Methods (10.3.2.2)

A standard installation of Windows is sufficient for most computers used in a home or small office environment, but there are cases when a custom installation process is required.

Take, for example, an IT support department; technicians in such environments must deploy hundreds or even thousands of Windows systems. Performing this many installations in the standard way is not feasible.

A standard installation is done via the installation medium (DVD or USB drive) provided by Microsoft, as shown in Figure 10-16, and is an interactive process; the installer prompts the user for settings such as time zone and system language.

Figure 10-16   Installation Methods

A custom installation of Windows can save time and provide consistent configuration across computers within a large organization. A popular technique to install Windows across many computers is to perform installation in one computer and use it as a reference installation. When the installation is complete, an image is created. An image is a file that contains all the data from a partition.

When the image is ready, technicians can perform a much shorter installation by simply replicating and deploying the image to all computers in the organization. If the new installation requires any adjustments, they can be made quickly after the image is deployed.

Windows has several different types of custom installations:

- *Network installation*: This includes *Preboot Execution Environment (PXE)* installation, unattended installation, and remote installation.

- *Image-based internal partition installation*: This is a Windows image stored on an internal (often hidden) partition that can be used to restore Windows to its original factory state.

- **Other types of custom installations**: This includes *Windows Advanced Startup Options*, refreshing the PC (Windows 8.x only), *System Restore*, upgrade, repair installation, remote network installation, recovery partition, and refresh/restore.

Remote Network Installation (10.3.2.3)

A popular method for OS installation in environments with many computers is a remote network installation. With this method, the operating system installation files are stored on a server so that a client computer can access the files remotely to begin the installation. A software package such as *Remote Installation Services (RIS)* is used to communicate with the client, store the setup files, and provide the necessary instructions for the client to access the setup files, download them, and begin the operating system installation.

Because the client computer does not have an operating system installed, a special environment must be used to boot the computer, connect to the network, and communicate with the server to begin the installation process. This special environment is known as the PXE. For the PXE to work, the NIC must be PXE enabled. This functionality may come from the BIOS or the firmware on the NIC. When the computer is started, the NIC listens for special instructions on the network to start the PXE.

Figure 10-17 shows the client loading setup files from the PXE server over TFTP.

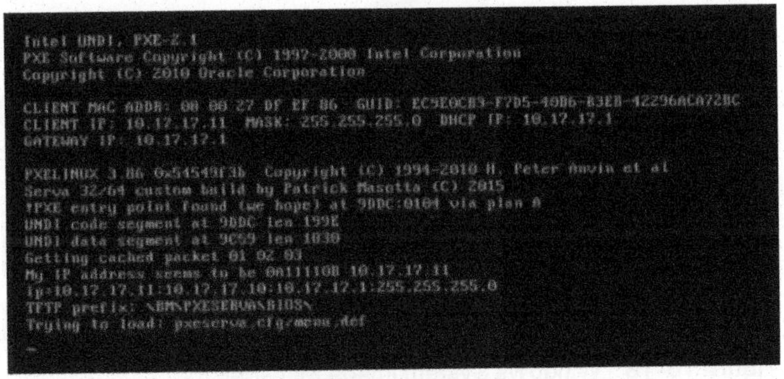

Figure 10-17   Windows PXE Installation

Note

If a NIC is not PXE enabled, third-party software may be used to load PXE from storage media.

Unattended Network Installation (10.3.2.4)

Unattended installation, another type of network-based installation, allows a Windows system to be installed or upgraded with little user intervention. The Windows unattended installation is based on an *answer file*. This file contains simple text that instructs Windows Setup how to configure and install the OS.

To perform a Windows unattended installation, setup.exe must be run with the user options in the answer file. The installation process begins as usual, but instead of prompting the user, Setup uses the answers listed in the answer file.

To customize a standard Windows 10 installation, the *System Image Manager (SIM)*, shown in Figure 10-18, is used to create the setup answer file. You can also add packages, such as applications or drivers, to answer files.

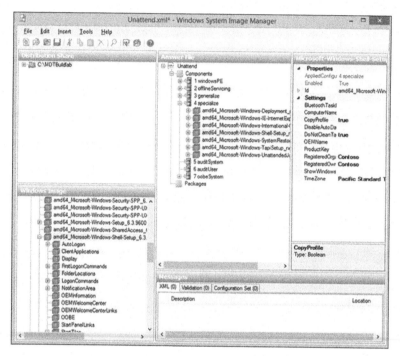

Figure 10-18   Windows System Image Manager

The answer file is copied to the distribution shared folder on a server. At this point, you can do one of two things:

- Run the *unattended.bat file* on the client machine to prepare the hard drive and install the OS from the server over the network.

- Create a boot disk that boots the computer and connects to the distribution shared folder on the server. You then run a batch file containing a set of instructions to install the OS over the network.

Note

Windows SIM is part of the *Windows Automated Installation Kit (AIK)* and can be downloaded from the Microsoft website.

10.3.2.5 Video Demonstration: Windows Restore and Recovery

Refer to the online course to view this video.

Recovery Partition (10.3.2.6)

Some computers that have Windows installed contain a section of the disk that is inaccessible to the user. This partition, called a *recovery partition* (see Figure 10-19), contains an image that can be used to restore the computer to its original configuration.

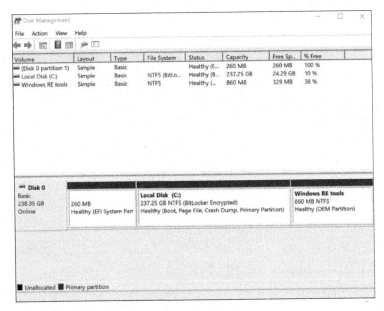

Figure 10-19   Recovery Partition in Disk Management

The recovery partition is often hidden to prevent it from being used for anything other than restoration. To restore the computer using the recovery partition, you often must use a special key or key combination when the computer is starting. Sometimes, the option to restore from the factory recovery partition is located in the BIOS or a program from the manufacturer that is accessed in Windows. Contact the computer manufacturer to find out how to access the partition and restore the original configuration of the computer.

Note

If the operating system has been damaged because of a faulty hard drive, the recovery partition may also be corrupt and may not be able to recover the operating system.

Upgrade Methods (10.3.2.7)

There are two methods for upgrading a PC running Windows, as described in the sections that follow.

In-Place Upgrade

The simplest path to upgrade a PC that is currently running Windows 7 or Windows 8.1 to Windows 10 is through an in-place upgrade. This type of upgrade updates the operating system and migrates apps and settings to the new OS. The *System Center Configuration Manager (Configuration Manager)* task sequence can be used to completely automate the process. Figure 10-20 shows the Configuration Manager upgrade task sequence for Windows 10.

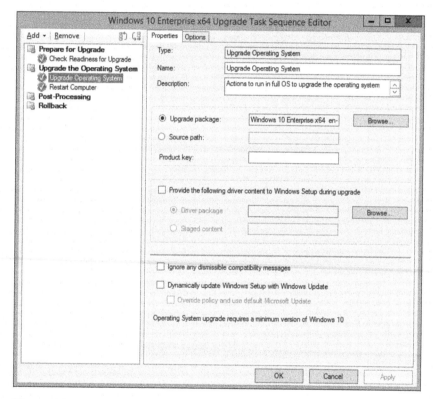

Figure 10-20   Windows 10 Enterprise x64 Upgrade Task Sequence Editor

When upgrading Windows 7 or Windows 8 to Windows 10, the Windows installation program (*Setup.exe*) performs an in-place upgrade, which automatically preserves all data, settings, applications, and drivers from the existing operating system version. This saves effort because there is no need for complex deployment infrastructure.

Note

Be sure to back up any user data before performing the upgrade.

Clean Install

Another way to upgrade to a newer version of Windows is to perform a clean install. Because a *clean install* wipes the drive completely, all files and data should be saved to some form of backup drive.

Before a clean install of Windows can be performed, the installation media needs to be created. This can be a disk or flash drive that the PC can boot from to run the setup. Windows 7, 8.1, and 10 can be downloaded directly from Microsoft. The Windows download website includes directions for creating the installation media.

> **Note**
>
> A valid product key is needed for the particular Windows version and edition in order to activate Windows after the installation process.

Interactive Graphic

10.3.2.8 Check Your Understanding: Identify OS Installation Terminology

Refer to the online course to complete this activity.

10.3.2.9 Lab: Operating System Upgrades

In this lab, you will explore the process of upgrading an operating system.

Windows Boot Sequence (10.3.3)

The boot sequence defines which devices a computer should check for the operating system's boot files and specifies the order in which those devices should be checked. Understanding the boot process in Windows can help a technician troubleshoot boot problems.

Windows Boot Sequence (10.3.3.1)

After POST (Power-On Self-Test), the BIOS locates and reads the configuration settings that are stored in the CMOS memory. The boot device priority, as shown in Figure 10-21, is the order in which devices are checked to locate the bootable partition. The boot device priority is set in the BIOS and can be arranged in any order. The BIOS boots the computer using the first drive that contains a valid boot sector. This sector contains the Master Boot Record (MBR). The MBR identifies the *Volume Boot Record (VBR)* and loads the boot manager, which for Windows is bootmgr.exe.

Hard drives, network drives, USB drives, and even removable media can be used in the boot order, depending on the capabilities of the motherboard. A BIOS may also have a boot device priority menu that is accessed with a special key during computer startup. You can use this menu to select the device to boot, as shown in Figure 10-21.

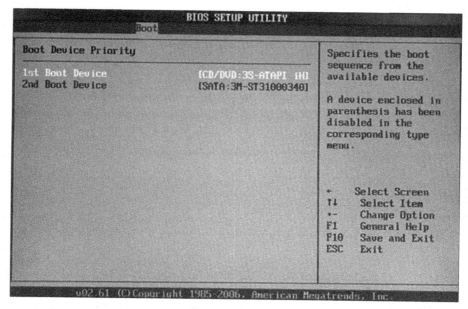

Figure 10-21 Boot Device Priority

Windows 7 Startup Modes (10.3.3.2)

Some problems prevent Windows from starting up. To troubleshoot and fix such problems, use one of the many Windows startup modes.

Pressing the *F8 key* during the boot process opens the *Windows Advanced Boot Options* menu, as shown in Figure 10-22. This allows users to select how they wish to boot Windows. These are four commonly used startup options:

- *Safe Mode*: This diagnostic mode is used to troubleshoot Windows and Windows startup issues. Functionality is limited as many device drivers are not loaded.

- *Safe Mode with Networking*: This option starts Windows in Safe Mode with networking support.

- *Safe Mode with Command Prompt*: This option starts Windows and loads the command prompt instead of the GUI.

- *Last Known Good Configuration*: This option loads the configuration settings that were used the last time that Windows started successfully. It does this by accessing a copy of the Registry that is created for this purpose.

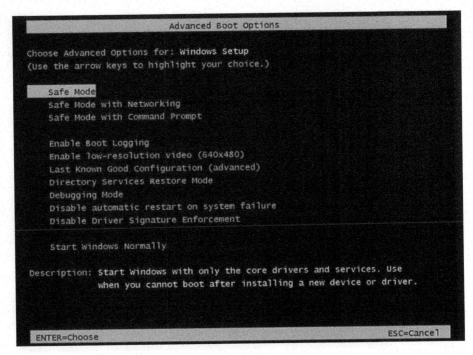

Figure 10-22   Advanced Boot Options

Note

Last Known Good Configuration is not useful unless it is applied immediately after a failure occurs. If the machine is restarted and manages to open Windows, the Registry is updated with the faulty information.

Windows 8 and 10 Startup Modes (10.3.3.3)

Both Windows 8 and Windows 10 boot too quickly to use F8 to access startup settings. Instead, press the Shift key and select the Restart option in the Power menu. Windows displays the Choose an Option screen. To get the startup settings, select Troubleshoot and then, from the next screen, select Advanced Options and then Startup Settings. On the next screen, select Restart. The computer restarts and displays the Startup Settings menu shown in Figure 10-23. To choose a startup option, use the number or function key (F1 through F9) that corresponds with the desired option.

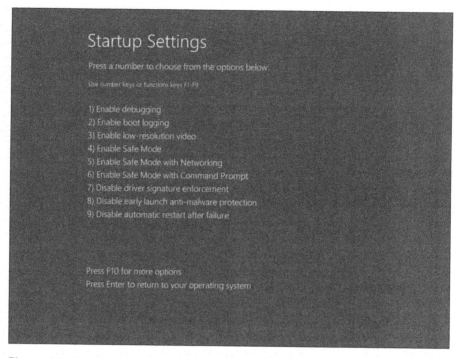

Figure 10-23   Startup Settings

10.3.3.4 Lab: Boot Methods

In this activity, you will investigate some of the available Windows installation boot methods and boot into another operating system using a bootable USB flash or optical media.

10.3.3.5 Check Your Understanding: Windows Boot Sequence

Refer to the online course to complete this activity.

Summary (10.4)

In this chapter, you learned that all operating systems perform the same four basic functions: control hardware access, manage files and folders, provide a user interface, and manage applications. You also learned that there are three commonly used desktop operating systems: Microsoft Windows, Apple macOS, and Linux. This chapter focused on Microsoft Windows operating systems, specifically Windows 7, Windows 8, and Windows 10. You learned about the minimum system requirements of each Windows operating system. These system requirements define the minimum amount of RAM, storage drive space, and CPU speed needed for the operating system to install and function properly.

Before the OS can be installed, a storage media device must be chosen and prepared to receive the operating system. You learned how to prepare a storage drive for a Windows installation by formatting the drive into partitions. You learned about the primary partition that contains the operating system files, the active partition that is used to store and boot the operating system, and extended partitions that can be created to hold logical drives. You completed a lab in which you created a FAT 32 partition in Windows and then converted the partition to NTFS.

You also performed a Windows operating system installation through two labs. In these labs, you installed Windows, performed basic setup tasks, created user accounts, and installed updates.

The chapter concluded with a review of the Windows boot sequence and the startup modes for Windows 7, Windows 8, and Windows 10.

Practice

The following activities provide practice with the topics introduced in this chapter. The labs are available in the companion *IT Essentials v8 Labs & Study Guide* (ISBN 9780138166304).

Labs

10.2.1.8 Lab: Create a Partition in Windows

10.3.1.1 Lab: Windows Installation

10.3.1.4 Lab: Finalize the Windows Installation

10.3.2.9 Lab: Operating System Upgrades

10.3.3.4 Lab: Boot Methods

Check Your Understanding Questions

Complete all the review questions listed here to test your understanding of the topics and concepts in this chapter. Appendix A, "Answers to 'Check Your Understanding' Questions," lists the answers.

1. A technician is asked to set up one hard drive that will support two operating systems and that will store data files in three separate drive locations. Which partition settings will support these requirements?

   A. 2 primary, 1 active, 1 extended, 3 logical

   B. 1 primary, 3 active, 1 extended, 2 logical

   C. 3 primary, 1 active, 2 extended

   D. 2 logical, 2 active, 3 extended

2. Which of the following contains information on how hard drive partitions are organized?

   A. BOOTMGR

   B. MBR

   C. CPU

   D. Windows Registry

3. Which location on a hard disk does the BIOS use to search for operating system instructions in order to boot a PC?

   A. the active partition

   B. the logical drive

   C. the extended partition

   D. the Windows partition

4. Which type of user account is created automatically during a Windows 8.1 installation?

   A. Administrator

   B. Standard User

   C. Guest

   D. Remote Desktop User

5. What term is used to describe a logical drive that can be formatted to store data?

   A. sector

   B. partition

   C. track

   D. cluster

   E. volume

6. A technician is attempting to create multiple partitions on a hard disk that is using the boot sector standard that supports a maximum partition size of 2 TB. What is the maximum number of primary partitions allowed per hard drive?

   A. 32

   B. 2

   C. 128

   D. 16

   E. 4

   F. 1

7. What type of file system allows the use of files larger than 5 GB and is mostly used on internal hard drives?

   A. NTFS

   B. CDFS

   C. FAT32

   D. FAT64

   E. exFAT

8. Which version of the OS can be upgraded to 64-bit Windows 10 Pro?

   A. 64-bit version of Windows 7 Home

   B. 64-bit version of Windows XP Pro

   C. 32-bit version of Windows 8 Pro

   D. 32-bit version of Windows 10 Pro

9. Which key or key sequence pressed during the boot process allows a user to start a Windows PC using the last known good configuration?

   A. F8

   B. F12

   C. Alt-Z

   D. Windows key

   E. F1

10. What is the maximum amount of physical RAM that can be addressed by a PC running 32-bit Windows 10 Pro?

A. 8 GB

B. 2 GB

C. 4 GB

D. 16 GB

11. Which user account should be used only to perform system management and not as the account for regular use?

A. Guest

B. Power User

C. Administrator

D. Standard User

12. Which of the following are advantages of NTFS compared with FAT32? (Choose two.)

A. NTFS allows the automatic detection of bad sectors.

B. NTFS supports larger partitions.

C. NTFS allows faster access to external peripherals such as a USB drive.

D. NTFS provides more security features.

E. NTFS allows faster formatting of drives.

F. NTFS is easier to configure.

13. Which file system is used to access files over a network?

A. CDFS

B. NTFS

C. NFS

D. FAT

14. Which of the following are types of computer user interfaces? (Choose two.)

A. API

B. OpenGL

C. CLI

D. GUI

E. PnP

Objectives

Upon completion of this chapter, you will be able to answer the following questions:

- What are the differences in Windows versions 7, 8, 8.1, and 10?

- How do you use features of the Windows desktop?

- How do you use Windows Task Manager to manage running processes and services?

- How do you use File Explorer to manage files, folders, and applications?

- How do you use Microsoft Windows Control Panel utilities?

- How do you configure user accounts with Control Panel utilities?

- How do you configure Internet and network connectivity using Control Panel utilities?

- How do you configure Windows display settings and personalization?

- How do you use the System and Power Options control panels?

- How do you use the Hardware and Sound control panels?

- How do you use the Clock, Region, and Language control panels or settings to configure a computer for a location?

- How do you use the Programs and Features control panel to manage Windows software?

- How is the Windows Troubleshooting control panel used to investigate system issues?

- How do you manage system resources with Microsoft Windows utilities?

- How do you use Microsoft Windows utilities to manage system operation?

- How do you manage system volume storage with Microsoft Windows utilities?

- How do you manage software applications?

- How do you use the Windows command window CLI?

- How do you use file system CLI commands to work with the Windows file system?

- How do you use disk CLI commands to work with Windows disks?

- How do you use task and system CLI commands to control Windows operation?

- How do you use other CLI commands to accomplish Windows tasks?

- How do you configure a Windows computer to share resources on a network?

- How do you configure local resources to be shared with other network users?

- How do you configure wired network interfaces in Windows?

- How do you configure wireless network interfaces in Windows?

- How do you use Windows applications to access remote computers?

- How do you use Windows Remote Desktop and Remote Assistance to work with remote computers?

- How do you perform preventive maintenance on a computer using Microsoft Windows tools?

- How do you perform system restore procedures?

- What are the six steps of troubleshooting a Microsoft Windows operating system?

- What are the common problems and solutions related to Microsoft Windows operating systems?

- How do you troubleshoot advanced Windows operating systems problems?

Key Terms

This chapter uses the following key terms. You can find the definitions in the glossary at the end of the book.

Introduction (11.0)

The first version of the Microsoft Windows operating system was released in 1985. Since then, more than 25 versions, sub-versions, and varieties have been released. As an IT technician and professional, you should understand the features of the most prevalent Windows versions in use today: Windows 7, Windows 8, and Windows 10.

In this chapter, you will learn about the different Windows versions and the editions of each that are most suited for corporate and home users. You will learn how to configure the Windows operating system and to perform administrative tasks using the Control Panel in the GUI and commands at the Windows command line interface (CLI) and in the PowerShell command line utility. You will have an opportunity to put into practice what you learn by working through several labs that involve working with file system commands, disk CLI commands, task and system CLI commands, and others.

You will learn about the two methods for organizing and managing Windows computers on a network—the domain and the workgroup—and how to share local computer resources, such as files, folders, and printers, on the network. You will also learn how to configure a wired network connection in Windows. You will perform labs creating and sharing folders on the network and setting access permissions. You will also connect a computer to a wireless router and test the wireless connection as well as configure Windows for remote access using the Remote Desktop and Remote Assistance tools.

You will learn how a preventive maintenance plan can decrease downtime, improve performance, improve reliability, and lower repair costs; you will also see that preventive maintenance should take place when it causes the least amount of disruption to users. Regular scans for viruses and malware are also an important part of preventive maintenance. You will perform several labs to schedule a task by using the GUI and the command line and to manage startup applications by using the Run key in the Registry.

At the end of the chapter, you will learn how the six steps in the troubleshooting process are applied to Windows operating systems.

Windows Desktop and File Explorer (11.1)

The Windows desktop is the screen that you see when the computer turns on, and it presents all the tools you need to manage and organize your files. File Explorer can also be used to navigate and manage the drives, folders, and files on your computer. It is a file browser available in every version of Microsoft Windows since Windows 95. In Windows 95, this file browser was called Windows Explorer, and it has been called File Explorer in all versions since Windows 8.

Comparing Windows Versions (11.1.1)

In some ways, Microsoft Windows versions differ greatly from their predecessors; for example, the appearance in the user interface and the computing power vary greatly. However, familiar elements have survived the different iterations. This section compares the similarities and differences in the many versions of Windows.

Windows Versions (11.1.1.1)

The first version of the Microsoft Windows operating system was released in 1985—nearly 40 years ago! Since then, more than 40 versions, sub-versions, and varieties have been released. In addition, each version can also have editions, such as Home, Pro, Ultimate, or Enterprise, in 32-bit and 64-bit versions. For example, 12 editions of Windows 10 have been developed and released. However, only 9 of them are currently offered.

Corporate and personal users of the Windows operating system have different needs. On a corporate network, it is usually necessary to manage user accounts and system policies centrally due to the number of devices on the network and higher security requirements. Centralized management is provided through joining an Active Directory domain, where the user accounts and security policies are configured on a domain controller. Windows Professional, Pro, Enterprise, Ultimate, and Education editions can join an Active Directory domain.

Other corporate features include:

- **BitLocker:** A feature that enables a user to encrypt all data on a disk drive or removable drive. It is available on Windows 7 Enterprise and Ultimate, Windows 8 Pro and Enterprise, and Windows 10 Pro, Enterprise, and Education editions.

- *Encrypting File System (EFS):* A feature found on Windows 7 Professional, Enterprise, and Ultimate, Windows 8 Pro and Enterprise, and Windows 10 Pro, Enterprise, and Education editions that allows the user to configure file- and folder-level encryption.

- *Branch cache:* A feature that allows remote computers to share access to a single cache of data from shared folders and files or document portals, such as SharePoint sites. This can reduce WAN traffic because the individual clients do not each need to download a copy of cache data. The branch cache is available on Windows 7 Enterprise and Ultimate, Windows 8 Enterprise, and Windows 10 Pro, Enterprise, and Education editions.

Some features of Windows are aimed at personal use, such as *Windows Media Center.* This is a Microsoft app that allows the computer to be used as a home entertainment appliance for playing DVDs. Windows Media Center was included in

Windows 7 Home Premium, Professional, Enterprise, and Ultimate editions. It was also a paid-for add-on to Windows 8 but was discontinued in Windows 10.

This chapter covers the various tools and applications that are available for configuring, maintaining, and troubleshooting Windows. The primary focus of this chapter is Windows 10. When relevant major differences exist between them and Windows 10, Windows 8 and Windows 7 are discussed.

Windows 10 (11.1.1.2)

Nine editions of *Windows 10* are currently offered. The examples used in this book are from the Windows 10 Professional edition.

The retail version of Windows 10 became available in July 2015. Windows 10 brought a return to the desktop computer-oriented interface that had been replaced in Windows 8. It supports an easy transition between a point-and-click interface and the touch interfaces of tablets, phones, and embedded systems like Internet of Things (IoT) single-board computers. Windows 10 includes support for universal apps that run on desktop and mobile devices. It also introduced the Microsoft Edge web browser. It offers enhanced security features, faster logons, and encryption of system files to save disk space. *Charms* were replaced with the Windows Action Center, which provides notifications and quick settings.

Windows 10 uses a new update model. Twice a year, Microsoft offers feature updates. These updates add new features to Windows and also improve existing features. The updates are numbered, and the description of each one is provided on the Microsoft website. It is entirely possible that you will notice changes to the interfaces of some *Windows apps* and tools after a feature update. Quality updates, or cumulative updates, usually install monthly. They contain patches to fix problems with Windows or security updates to address new threats and vulnerabilities.

Table 11-1 summarizes the important features of the Windows versions that are covered in this book.

Table 11-1   Overview of Windows Versions

Windows Version	Release Date	Important Features	End of Support
Windows 11	October 2021	Redesigned taskbar and icons. Increased energy efficiency. Integrated with Microsoft Teams. Improved Settings app.	October 2025

Windows Version	Release Date	Important Features	End of Support
Windows 10	July 2015	Improved desktop interface combines menu entries and *tiles* in the Start menu. Universal apps. Windows Action Center replaces charms.	Mainstream: October 2020 Extended: October 2025
Windows 8.1	October 2013	Start screen more similar to Windows 7. More interface configuration options.	January 2023
Windows 8.0	October 2012	Interface optimized for mobile devices. Antivirus included. File Explorer instead of Windows Explorer. Unpopular and considered hard to learn.	January 2016
Windows 7	October 2009	Improved interface. Improved taskbar. Libraries. HomeGroup file sharing.	January 2020

The Windows Desktop (11.1.2)

This section examines the Windows desktop, which is the main screen of the Windows graphical user interface (GUI) and allows users to organize icons on the screen in order to interact with the operating system applications and tools. The Microsoft Windows desktop has been included with every version of Windows since Windows 95. After the OS has been installed, you can customize the computer desktop to suit individual needs. The desktop has icons, toolbars, and menus that are used for a variety of purposes. You can add or change images, sounds, and colors to provide a more personalized look and feel, for example.

Personalizing the Windows Desktop (11.1.2.1)

Windows offers many settings that enable users to personalize the desktop and other aspects of the Windows GUI. The fastest way to get to these settings is to right-click an empty area of the desktop and select *Personalize*. Windows then shows the Background settings. Drag the right-hand border of the settings box to widen it and reveal the Personalization settings menu. The fastest way to change the look and feel of the Windows GUI is to select from the available themes, as shown in Figure 11-1. A theme is a preset combination of GUI settings that go together. You can also create themes from settings that you have made so that they can be used later. Themes beyond those that are provided can be downloaded from the Microsoft Store. Many other changes can be made to the Windows GUI from here.

Figure 11-1   Windows 10 Themes

In Windows 8, the apps environment is highly customizable. To rearrange the tiles, click and drag them. To rename a tile group, right-click on any empty area of the screen and select Name Groups. To add tiles to the main screen, right-click the desired Windows app after searching for it and select Pin to Start. To search for an app, click Search from the charms bar. Alternatively, you can start typing the name of the app in the Windows apps environment, and search starts. Figure 11-2 shows the Windows 8 apps environment and the charms bar.

In Windows 7 and 8.1, to customize the desktop, right-click anywhere on the desktop and choose Personalize. In the Personalization window, you can change the desktop appearance, display settings, and sound settings. Figure 11-3 shows the Windows 8 Personalization window. It is very similar to the Personalization window in Windows 7.

Figure 11-2   Windows 8 Start Screen

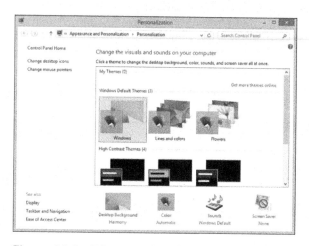

Figure 11-3   Windows 8 Personalization Menu

11.1.2.2 Video Demonstration: The Windows 10 Desktop

Refer to the online course to view this video.

Video

The Windows 10 Start Menu (11.1.2.3)

The Windows 10 *Start menu* consists of three main parts. To the left is a strip of shortcuts to common libraries, with a button that provides access to settings and the shutdown button. To the right of this is a menu of applications that are available, in alphabetical order, with areas for the most recently installed and most used applications at the top. To the right is an area containing tiles for apps that are arranged by category, such as games, creative software, and so on. The Windows 10 Start menu is shown in Figure 11-4.

Figure 11-4   The Windows 10 Start Menu

The Taskbar (11.1.2.4)

The *taskbar* provides easy access to many important and commonly used features of Windows. Applications, files, tools, and settings can all be accessed from this one place. Right-clicking the taskbar or opening the Taskbar and Navigation control panel leads you to a Settings screen that allows easy configuration of the taskbar's appearance, location, operation, and features. The Windows 10 Taskbar Settings screen is shown in Figure 11-5. It is available from the Taskbar option in the Personalization Settings window.

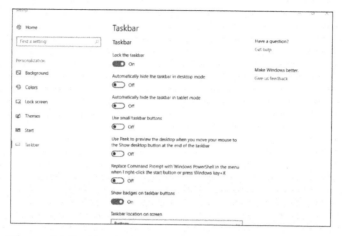

Figure 11-5 Windows 10 Taskbar Settings

These are some useful features of the taskbar:

- *Jump lists*: To display a list of tasks that are unique to the application, right-click the application's icon in the taskbar.

- *Pinned applications*: To add an application to the taskbar for easy access, right-click the icon of an application and select Pin to taskbar.

- *Thumbnail previews*: To view a thumbnail image of a running program, hover the mouse over the program icon on the taskbar.

Taskbar settings vary slightly between Windows versions.

Figure 11-6 shows the Windows 8.1 Taskbar and Navigation Properties dialog.

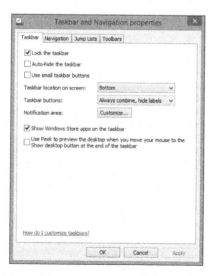

Figure 11-6 Windows 8.1 Taskbar and Navigation Properties

Figure 11-7 shows the Windows 7 Taskbar and Start Menu Properties dialog.

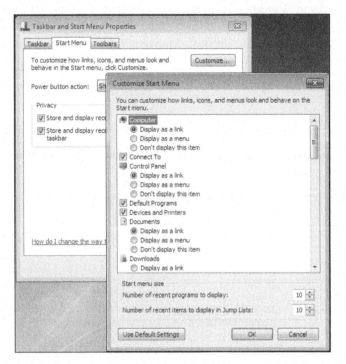

Figure 11-7   Windows 7 Taskbar and Start Menu Properties

 11.1.2.5 Lab: Explore the Windows Desktop

In this lab, you will explore the Windows desktop, Start menu, and taskbar.

Windows Task Manager (11.1.3)

The Windows Task Manager provides information about all the applications, processes, and services that are running on the computer. It can be used to monitor system resources and the programs that are using them. Task Manager can also be used to terminate processes that are causing system issues or that have stopped responding to user input. Care must be taken when terminating processes because they may be required for system operation. Task Manager is essentially the same in Windows 10 and Windows 8. The Windows 7 Task Manager has some essential differences.

11.1.3.1 Video Demonstration: Working with Task Manager

Video

Refer to the online course to view this video.

Windows 10 Task Manager Functions (11.1.3.2)

The seven tabs in Windows 10 Task Manager provide important information for monitoring the operation of Windows. You can open Task Manager by right-clicking on the taskbar and selecting the Task Manager entry or by pressing **Win+X** or **Ctrl+Shift+Esc** or **Ctrl+Alt+Del**.

Table 11-2 describes the seven tabs of the Windows 10 Task Manager.

Table 11-2   Windows 10 Task Manager Tabs

Tab	Description
Processes	This tab shows a list of processes currently running on the PC. A process is a set of instructions started by the user, a program, or the OS. Running processes are categorized as apps, background processes, and Windows system processes.
Performance	This tab contains dynamic system performance graphs. You can select any of the options—CPU, Memory, Disk, or Ethernet, and so on—to see graphs for it.
App History	This tab displays historical resource utilization, such as CPU time, network data usage, and data uploads and downloads. Information is shown by date. The data can be cleared and the date can be reset to the current date. This information is only available for installed apps, mostly from the Microsoft Store.
Startup	This tab shows what processes are automatically started during Windows startup. Windows also measures the relative impact each process has on the system's overall startup time. To keep a process from starting automatically, right-click on the process and disable its automatic startup.
Users	This tab shows the users who are currently connected to the PC and the system resources that they are currently using. The information displayed is much like the information on the Performance tab. Users can be disconnected on this tab as well.
Details	This tab improves on the Windows 7 Task Manager Process tab. From this tab, it is possible to tweak the level of CPU priority for a given process. It is also possible to specify which CPU a process will use to run (CPU affinity). Application icons are included as well.
Services	This tab displays all services that are available and the status of each one. It allows for easy stopping, starting, and restarting of services. Services are identified by process ID (PID).

Task Manager in Windows 7 (11.1.3.3)

Task Manager is different in Windows 7 than in Windows 10, as shown in Figure 11-8.

Figure 11-8   Task Manager in Windows 7

In many ways, the Windows 10 Task Manager is a significant upgrade from the Windows 7 Task Manager. The Windows 7 Task Manager has six tabs:

- **Applications:** This tab shows all running applications. From this tab, you can create, switch to, or close any applications that have stopped responding using the buttons at the bottom.

- **Processes:** This tab shows all running processes. From this tab, you can end processes or set process priorities.

- **Services:** This tab shows the available services, including the operational status of each one. Services are identified by PID.

- **Performance:** This tab shows the CPU and page file usage.

- **Networking:** This tab shows the usage of all network adapters.

- **Users:** This tab shows all users who are logged onto the computer.

Several major differences exist between Task Manager in Windows 7 and Windows 10:

- The Windows 7 Applications and Processes tabs are combined in Windows 10.

- The Windows 7 Networking tab is included with the Performance tab in Windows 10.

- The Windows 7 Users tab is enhanced in Windows 10 to show not only the users who are connected but also the resources they are using.

11.1.3.4 Lab: Work with Task Manager

In this lab, you will use Task Manager to monitor system performance.

Interactive
Graphic

11.1.3.5 Check Your Understanding: Compare Task Manager in Windows 7 and 10

Refer to the online course to complete this activity.

Windows File Explorer (11.1.4)

File Explorer is a centralized place where you can view, open, copy, move, and manage files and folders. It is a graphical representation of the file storage system to help users keep files organized.

File Explorer (11.1.4.1)

File Explorer is a file management application in Window 8 and Windows 10. It is used to navigate the file system and manage the folders, subfolders, and applications on storage media. You can also preview some types of files.

In File Explorer, common tasks, such as copying and moving files and creating new folders, can be done using the Ribbon. The tabs at the top of the window change as different types of items are selected. In Figure 11-9, the Home tab of the Ribbon is displayed for Quick Access. If the Ribbon is not displaying, click the Expand the Ribbon icon, represented by a down arrow, in the upper-right corner of the window.

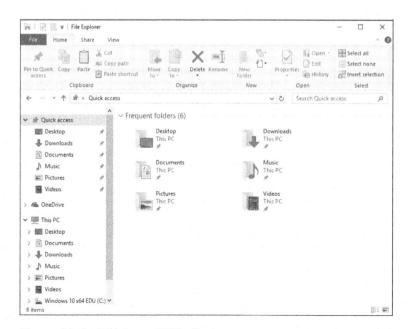

Figure 11-9 Windows 10 File Explorer

Windows Explorer is the name of the file management application in Windows 7 and earlier. Windows Explorer performs functions similar to those of File Explorer but lacks the Ribbon.

11.1.4.2 Video Demonstration: Working with File Explorer

Refer to the online course to view this video.

This PC (11.1.4.3)

In Windows versions 10 and 8.1, the This PC feature allows you to access the various devices and drives installed on the computer. In Windows 7, this feature is called Computer.

To open This PC, open File Explorer, and it displays This PC by default, as shown in Figure 11-10.

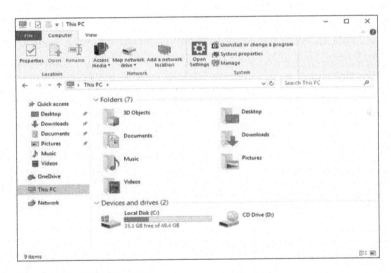

Figure 11-10   This PC

In Windows 8.0 or 7, click Start and select Computer. Figure 11-11 shows the Computer feature in Windows 7.

Figure 11-11   Computer in Windows Explorer

Run as Administrator (11.1.4.4)

Modern operating systems use a number of methods to improve security. One of these methods is file permissions. Only users with enough permission can access a file. System files, other user files, or files with elevated permissions are examples of files that could lead Windows to deny access to a user. To override this behavior and gain access to those files, you must open or execute them as the system administrator.

To open or execute a file using elevated permission, right-click the file and choose Run as Administrator, as shown in Figure 11-12. Choose Yes in the User Account Control (UAC) window (which is where administrators can manage user accounts). In some cases, software does not install properly unless the installer is run with Administrator privileges.

Note

An administrator password is required to use these features if the current user does not belong to the Administrator group.

Windows Libraries (11.1.4.5)

Windows libraries allow you to easily organize content from various storage devices on your local computer and network, including removable media, without actually moving the files. A library is a virtual folder that presents content from different locations in the same view. When Windows 10 is installed, each user has six default libraries, as shown in Figure 11-13.

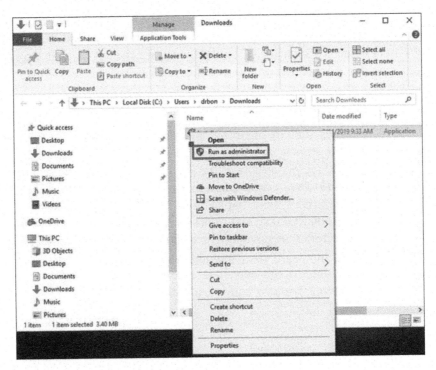

Figure 11-12 Run as Administrator

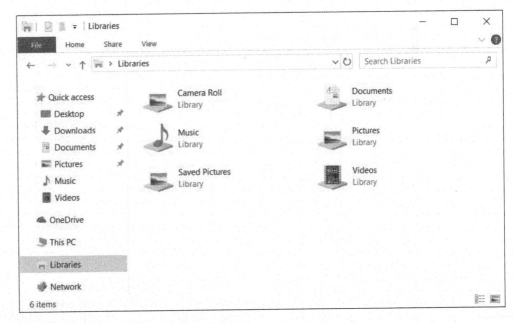

Figure 11-13 Windows 10 Libraries

You can search a library, and you can filter the content by using criteria such as filename, file type, or date modified. In Windows 10 and Windows 8.1, the libraries are hidden by default. The context menu for the left pane of the File Explorer window contains an option that shows the libraries.

Directory Structures (11.1.4.6)

In Windows, files are organized in a directory structure. A directory structure is designed to store system files, user files, and program files. The root level of the Windows directory structure, the partition, is usually labeled drive C:, as shown in Figure 11-14. The C: drive contains a set of standardized directories, called *folders*, for the operating system, applications, configuration information, and data files. Directories may contain additional directories, as shown in Figure 11-14. These additional directories are commonly called *subfolders*. The number of nested folders is essentially limited by the maximum length of the path to the folders. In Windows 10, the default limit is 260 characters. Figure 11-14 shows several nested folders in File Explorer, along with the equivalent path.

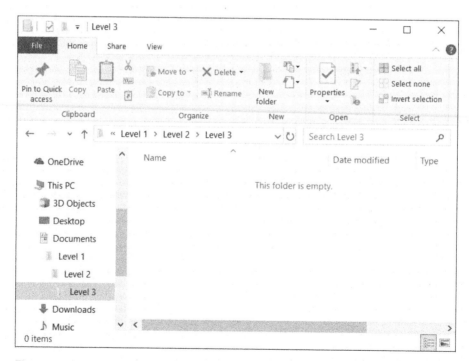

Figure 11-14   Nested Folders and Path in File Explorer

Windows creates a series of folders for each user account that is configured on the computer. These folders appear to be the same in File Explorer for each user, but they are actually unique to each user account. Users therefore cannot access each other's files, applications, or data.

Note

It is a best practice to store files in folders and subfolders rather than at the root level of a drive.

User and System File Locations (11.1.4.7)

User and System folders and files can be found in the following locations:

- **Users folder:** By default, Windows stores most of the files created by users in the Users folder, C:\Users*User_name*\\. Each user's folder contains folders for music, videos, websites, and pictures, among other things. Many programs also store specific user data here. If a single computer has many users, each user has their own folders containing favorites, desktop items, logs, and so on. Figure 11-15 shows the Admin user folder.

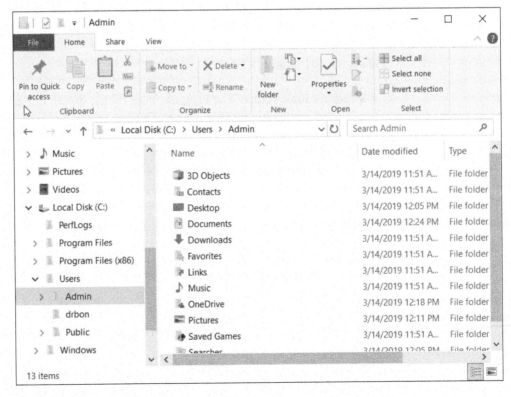

Figure 11-15   User Folders

- **System folder:** When the Windows OS is installed, most of the files that are used to run the computer are located in the folder C:\Windows\System32, as shown in Figure 11-16. Making changes to the contents of the System folder could cause problems with Windows operation.

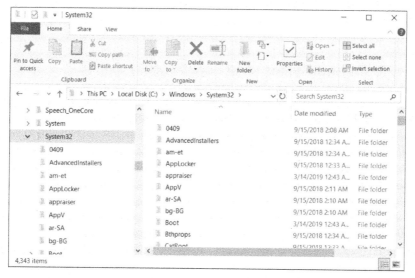

Figure 11-16 System Folder

- **Program Files folder:** The Program Files folder, shown in Figure 11-17, is used by most application installation programs to install software. In 32-bit versions of Windows, all programs are 32-bit and are installed in the folder C:\Program Files. In 64-bit systems, 64-bit programs are installed in the folder C:\Program Files, and 32-bit programs are installed in the folder C:\Program Files (x86).

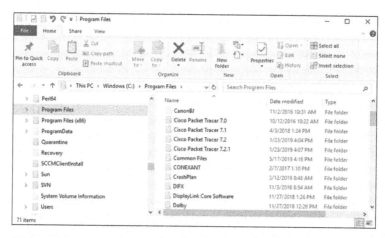

Figure 11-17 Program Files Folder

File Extensions (11.1.4.8)

Files in the directory structure adhere to the Windows naming conventions:

- A maximum of 255 characters is allowed.

- Characters such as slash and backslash (/ \) are not allowed.

- An extension of three or four letters is added to the filename to identify the file type.

- Filenames are not case sensitive.

By default, file extensions are hidden. To display them in Windows 10 and Windows 8.1, in the File Explorer ribbon, click the View tab and then select File Name Extensions, as shown in Figure 11-18.

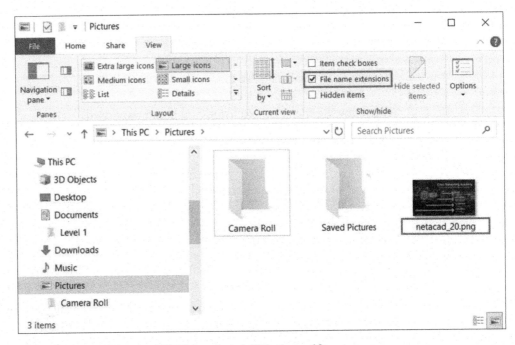

Figure 11-18   Showing File Extensions in Windows 10

To display file extensions in Windows 7, you must disable the Hide Extensions for Known File Types setting in the Folder Options control panel utility, as shown in Figure 11-19.

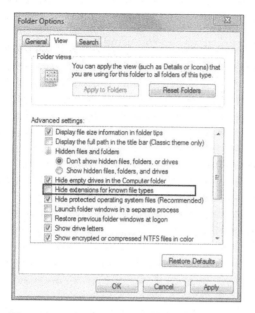

Figure 11-19   Showing File Extensions in Windows 7

The following filename extensions are commonly used:

- **.docx:** Microsoft Word (2007 and later)

- **.txt:** ASCII text only

- **.jpg:** Graphics format

- **.pptx:** Microsoft PowerPoint (2007 and later)

- **.zip:** Compressed format

File Attributes (11.1.4.9)

The directory structure maintains a set of attributes for each file that controls how the file can be viewed or altered. These are the most common file attributes:

- **R:** The file is read-only.

- **A:** The file will be archived the next time the disk is backed up.

- **S:** The file is marked as a system file, and a warning is given if an attempt is made to delete or modify the file.

- **H:** The file is hidden in the directory display.

Figure 11-20 shows the file properties dialog box in which attributes can be viewed or set.

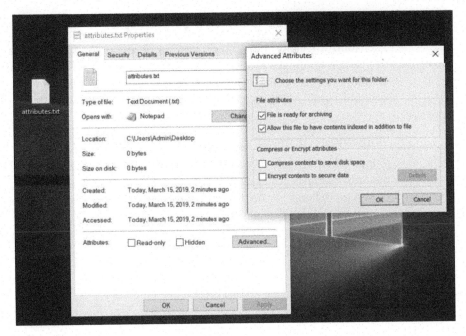

Figure 11-20   Setting File Attributes

Video

11.1.4.10 Video Demonstration: File and Folder Properties

Refer to the online course to view this video.

11.1.4.11 Lab: Working with File Explorer

In this lab, you will use File Explorer to work with files and folders.

Interactive Graphic

11.1.4.12 Check Your Understanding: File Explorer

Refer to the online course to complete this activity.

Configure Windows with Control Panels (11.2)

This section examines the *Control Panel*, which is a graphical centralized configuration area in Windows. By using Control Panel, you can modify the system in almost every aspect of the hardware and software, including OS functions. These settings are categorized in Control Panel applets. In the newest versions of Windows, you can adjust how the Control Panel is shown by using the View By option. This section gives an overview of what is available in the Windows Control Panel.

Control Panel Utilities (11.2.1)

The Control Panel is made up of a group of individual Control Panel applets or utilities. When you make changes in the Control Panel, you are making changes to the Windows Registry. The utilities available vary slightly, depending on the version of Windows you are running. This section examines Control Panel utilities.

Windows 10: Settings and Control Panels (11.2.1.1)

Windows 10 offers two ways to configure the operating system. The first is by using the *Settings app*. It has an interface that follows the modern Windows interface design guidelines. Figure 11-21 shows the Settings app menu, from which you can access many system settings.

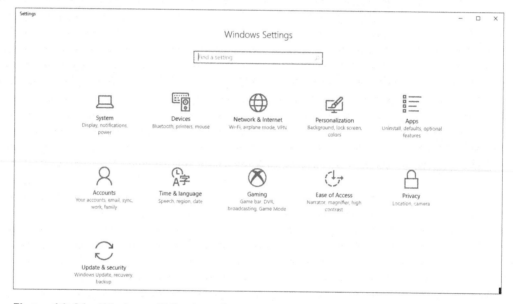

Figure 11-21   Windows 10 Settings App

The Settings app first appeared in Windows 8, where it looks as shown in Figure 11-22. It provides access to fewer settings than the Windows 10 version, which has now become robust. Note that a search field in both versions enables you to find settings without taking a lot of time clicking through menus.

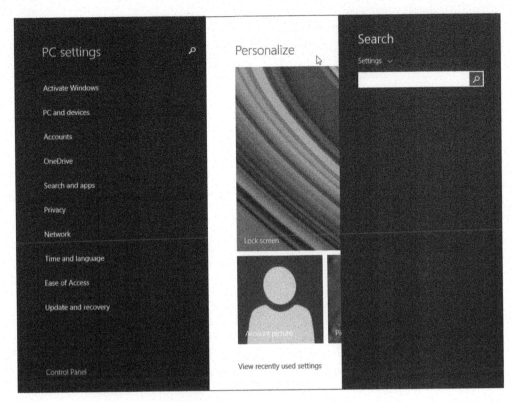

Figure 11-22   Windows 8 Settings with Search Box

Windows 7 does not have the Settings app. The most efficient way to make system configuration changes in Windows 7 is by using the Control Panel, as shown in Figure 11-23.

While it appears that Microsoft is moving more and more functionality to the Settings app, the Control Panel is still present in Windows 8 and 10, and using it is the only way to make changes to some configuration settings. In other cases, especially in regard to personalization, the Settings app provides more configuration options than does the Control Panel.

This book focuses on the Control Panel in Windows 10, and it mentions the Settings app where necessary. If important differences exist between the Windows 7 and 8 Control Panels and Windows 10, you will learn about those differences. The Control Panel window looks very similar between Windows versions, but some Control Panel items differ between the versions.

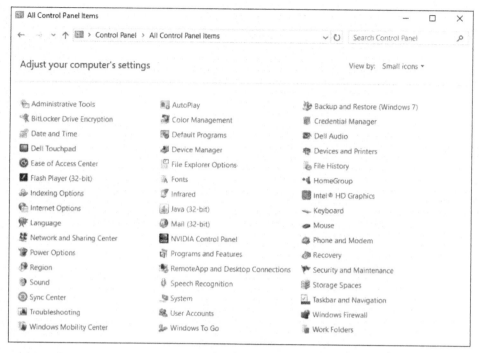

Figure 11-23   Windows 7 Control Panel

Introduction to Control Panel (11.2.1.2)

Windows 10 usually defaults to the Settings app for configuration changes. This is good for the casual user, but a PC technician frequently needs more configuration options than are available in the Settings app. The Control Panel offers many configuration tools, and many experienced Windows administrators prefer its interface. In fact, some Settings app items actually link to Control Panel items.

To start Control Panel, type **Control Panel** in the Search box and click the Control Panel desktop app that appears in the results, as shown in Figure 11-24. If you right-click on the result, you can pin it to the Start menu to make it easier to find. You can also open it from the command prompt by typing **control**.

In Windows 7, the Control Panel has an entry on the Start menu. In Windows 8.1, it can be accessed by right-clicking the Start button. In Windows 8, it can be opened by searching for **Control Panel** and clicking the result.

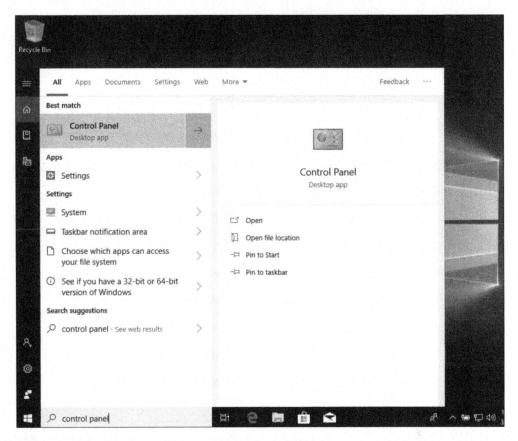

Figure 11-24 Windows 10 Control Panel Search Results

Control Panel Views (11.2.1.3)

The Windows 10 Control Panel opens to the Categories view by default, as shown in Figure 11-25. This helps to organize the 40 or more Control Panel items and makes them easier to find. This view also provides a search box that returns a list of Control Panel items that are relevant to a search term.

The classic view of Control Panel is reached by changing the setting in the View By dropdown menu to Small Icons, as shown in Figure 11-26. Note that there are variations in what is available in Control Panel depending on the features of an individual computer.

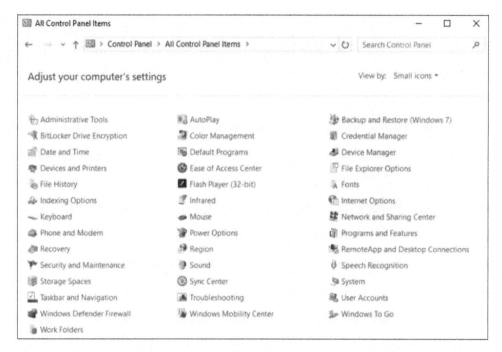

Figure 11-25   Control Panel Category View

Figure 11-26   Control Panel Small Icons View

Define Control Panel Categories (11.2.1.4)

The sections that follow show and describe each of the eight Control Panel categories.

System and Security

In the *System and Security control panel*, you can view and configure security settings such as Windows Defender Firewall, as shown in Figure 11-27. You can also access *administrative tools* that enable you to configure a wide range of system functions, such as general hardware, storage, and encryption settings and operations.

Figure 11-27   System and Security Category

Network and Internet

The Network and Internet category allows for configuration, verification, and troubleshooting of networking and file sharing, as shown in Figure 11-28. It also allows for configuration of the default Microsoft browser that is present on the system.

Figure 11-28   Network and Internet Category

Hardware and Sound

The *Hardware and Sound* category permits configuration of devices such as printers, media devices, power, and mobility, as shown in Figure 11-29.

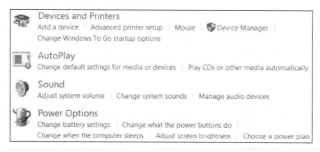

Figure 11-29   Hardware and Sound Category

Programs

The *Programs* category allows you to make changes to installed programs and Windows updates, including removal, as shown in Figure 11-30. Activation or deactivation of a wide range of Windows features can also be accomplished here.

Figure 11-30   Programs Category

User Accounts

The *User Accounts* category enables administration of Windows user accounts and User Account Control (UAC), as shown in Figure 11-31. You can also use this category to manage web and Windows credentials, including the file encryption certificates that are used to encrypt files stored on the computer.

Figure 11-31   User Accounts Category

Ease of Access

The *Ease of Access* category provides many options that make Windows easier to use, especially for people who require accommodations for physical or perceptual challenges, as shown in Figure 11-32. Configuration of speech recognition and text-to-speech services are also found here.

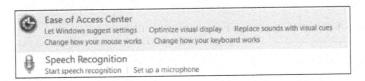

Figure 11-32   Ease of Access Category

Clock and Region

The *Clock and Region* category enables configuration of time and date settings and formats, as shown in Figure 11-33. Location and language can also be configured here in some Windows versions.

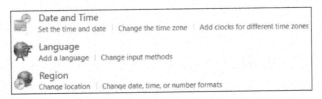

Figure 11-33   Clock and Region Category

Appearance and Personalization

The *Appearance and Personalization* category permits configuration of the taskbar and navigation (via Settings), File Explorer, and available fonts, as shown in Figure 11-34. More options are available through the Personalization Settings app.

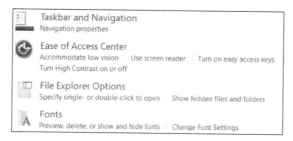

Figure 11-34   Appearance and Personalization Category

11.2.1.5 Lab: Explore Control Panel Categories

In this lab, you will investigate the options provided in the various commonly used Control Panel items.

11.2.1.6 Check Your Understanding: Control Panel Categories

Refer to the online course to complete this activity.

User and Account Control Panel Items (11.2.2)

Each user has a user account, which allows the user to sign onto a computer with a username and hopefully a password. A user account is stored information that Windows uses to determine which files and folders a user can access, what changes the user can make to the computer, and the user's personal preferences, such as the desktop background or screen saver. Thanks to user accounts, a computer can have several users, each with their own files and settings.

User Accounts (11.2.2.1)

An administrative account is created when Windows is installed. To create a user account later, open the User Accounts Control Panel item, as shown in Figure 11-35.

Administrator accounts have the ability to change all system settings and access all files and folders on the computer. For that reason, administrator accounts should be carefully controlled. Standard user accounts can manage most configuration settings that don't affect other users. They can only access their own files and folders.

The User Accounts Control Panel item provides options to help you create, change, and delete user accounts. It is very similar in various Windows versions.

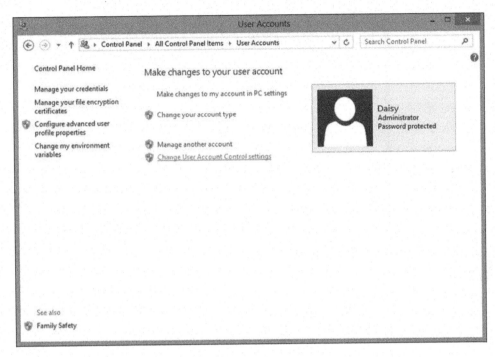

Figure 11-35   User Accounts Control Panel Options

User Account Control Settings (11.2.2.2)

User Account Control (UAC) monitors programs on a computer and warns users when an action might present a threat to the computer. In Windows versions 7 through 10, you can adjust the level of monitoring that the UAC performs. When Windows is installed, the UAC window for the primary account defaults to the setting Notify Me Only When Programs Try to Make Changes to My Computer, as shown in Figure 11-36. You are not notified when you make changes to these settings.

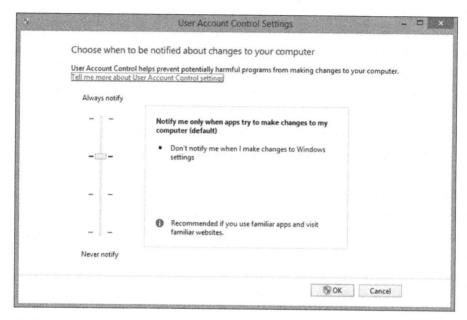

Figure 11-36   User Account Control Settings

To change when you are notified about changes that programs may make to your computer, adjust the level in the UAC window.

11.2.2.3 Lab: User Accounts

In this lab, you will work with the User Accounts Control Panel item to create and modify users.

11.2.2.4 Lab: Permissions

In this lab, you will work with permissions.

Credential Manager (11.2.2.5)

Credential Manager helps you manage passwords that are used for websites and Windows applications (see Figure 11-37). These passwords and usernames are stored in a secure location. Credentials are automatically updated as they are created or changed. You can view, add, edit, or delete the credentials that are stored by Credential Manager.

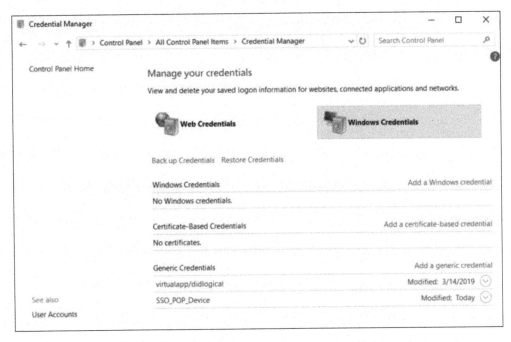

Figure 11-37   Credential Manager

Credential Manager has been enhanced since the Windows 7 version, although the interface is similar.

Note

Web credentials are not saved for sites accessed by browsers other than Internet Explorer and Edge. Credentials created with another browser must be managed from within that browser.

Sync Center (11.2.2.6)

Sync Center allows files to be edited from multiple Windows devices. While accessing networked files from multiple devices is nothing new, Sync Center allows a form of version control. This means that changes made to the networked files by one device will be made on all devices that are configured to synchronize those files. With this synchronization service, there is no need to physically copy a new version of a file from the device on which the changes were made to the device that you are currently working on. The updated file is on the networked storage location, and the local versions are updated to the latest version automatically. When changes are made on the local machine, those changes are made to networked files, too. All devices must be able to connect to the same networked storage location.

Another benefit of Sync Center is that users can work on files on a device that is offline, and the server copy can be updated over the network when the device reconnects.

Using Sync Center requires activation of the Offline Files feature. This sets up a local file location that stores the files to be synchronized. It also requires you to set up a sync partnership with the networked file location, as shown in Figure 11-38. Files can be synchronized manually, and synchronization can also be scheduled to occur automatically.

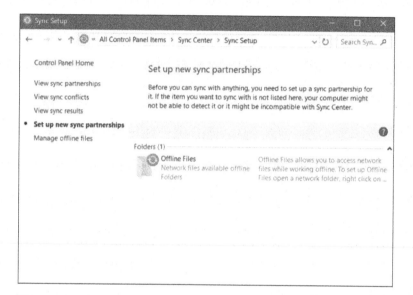

Figure 11-38   Sync Center

Microsoft OneDrive offers a similar service. OneDrive is a cloud storage service that is available to Microsoft Windows users. Since OneDrive is reachable over the Internet, work can be done on any device that can connect to OneDrive from any location with Internet access. Sync Center requires access to a network server that may not be reachable from networks in other locations.

11.2.2.7 Check Your Understanding: User and Account Control Panels

Refer to the online course to complete this activity.

Network and Internet Control Panels (11.2.3)

This section examines the Network and Internet control panels, which are important and useful Control Panel apps where a technician can see information about the network and make changes that can affect how resources are accessed on the network.

Network Settings (11.2.3.1)

Windows 10 has a new Settings app for network settings. It combines many different functions in one high-level app, as shown in Figure 11-39. The links in this app can point to new settings screens, Control Panel items, or even the Action Center. Some of the options, such as Airplane Mode, Mobile Hotspot, and Data Usage, are more relevant to mobile devices than to desktop computers.

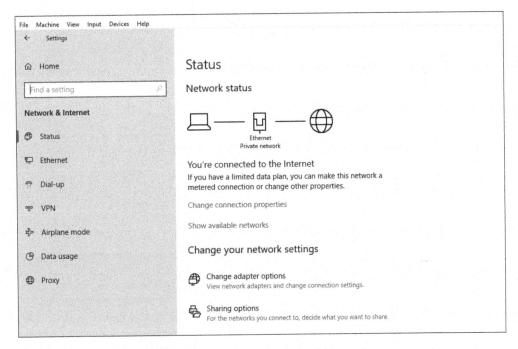

Figure 11-39   Network Status

Mobile devices use *wireless wide area network (WWAN)* or cellular Internet access technology. WWAN requires using an adapter to link to a cellular provider's network through the nearest base station or transmitter. WWAN adapters can be internal or external (connected by USB). The bandwidth available over WWAN connections is dependent on the technologies supported by the adapter and the transmitter, such as 3G or 4G. Connection to the WWAN is automatic after the adapter and adapter software are installed.

Internet Options (11.2.3.2)

Internet Options is used to configure Microsoft Internet Explorer. The sections that follow describe the available tabs.

General Tab

The General tab, shown in Figure 11-40, is used to configure basic Internet settings, such as selecting the default home page, viewing and deleting browsing history, adjusting search settings, and customizing the browser appearance.

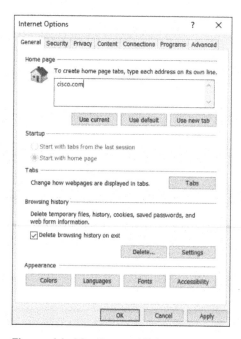

Figure 11-40   General Tab

Security Tab

The Security tab, shown in Figure 11-41, is used to adjust the security settings for the Internet, local intranet, trusted sites, and restricted sites. Security levels for each zone can range from low (minimal security) to high (maximum security).

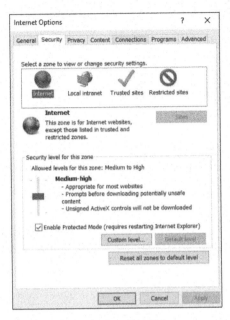

Figure 11-41 Security Tab

Privacy Tab

The Privacy tab, shown in Figure 11-42, is used to configure privacy settings for the Internet zone, manage location services, and enable Pop-up Blocker.

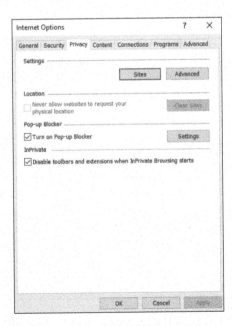

Figure 11-42 Privacy Tab

Content Tab

The Content tab, shown in Figure 11-43, is used to access parental controls, control content viewed on the computer, adjust AutoComplete settings, and configure the feeds and web slices that can be viewed in Internet Explorer. Web slices are specific content from websites that allow users to subscribe and view the updated content, such as current temperature and stock quotes.

Figure 11-43   Content Tab

Connections Tab

The Connections tab, shown in Figure 11-44, is used to set up an Internet connection and adjust network settings. Dial-up, VPN, and proxy server settings can be managed in this tab. Use of a proxy server can improve performance and security. Internet requests from the client are sent to the proxy server, which forwards the requests to the Internet. Return traffic is received by the proxy server, which then forwards the traffic to the client. The proxy server can cache pages and content that is frequently requested or that is requested by many clients, which can reduce bandwidth usage. Configure a proxy by selecting Internet Options > Connections > LAN Settings.

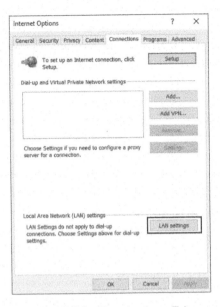

Figure 11-44   Connections Tab

Programs Tab

The Programs tab, shown in Figure 11-45, is used to make Internet Explorer the default web browser, enable browser add-ons, select the HTML editor for Internet Explorer, and select programs used for Internet services. Hypertext Markup Language (HTML) is a system that tags text files to affect the appearance of web pages.

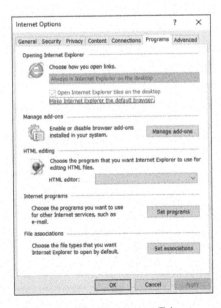

Figure 11-45   Programs Tab

Advanced Tab

The Advanced tab, shown in Figure 11-46, is used to adjust advanced settings and reset Internet Explorer's settings to the default state.

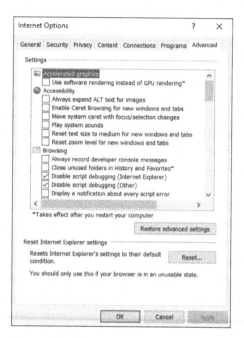

Figure 11-46   Advanced Tab

Network and Sharing Center (11.2.3.3)

Network and Sharing Center allows an administrator to configure and review nearly all network settings on a Windows computer. With it, you can do everything from view network status to change properties of the protocols and services that are running on a network adapter. Figures 11-47 through 11-49 show the Network and Sharing Center for Windows 10, 8, and 7. Note that although they look very similar, small differences exist between the versions.

Network and Sharing Center shows how a computer connects to a network. Internet connectivity, if present, is also displayed here. The window displays and allows the configuration of shared network resources. Some useful and common network-related tasks are displayed on the left pane of the window.

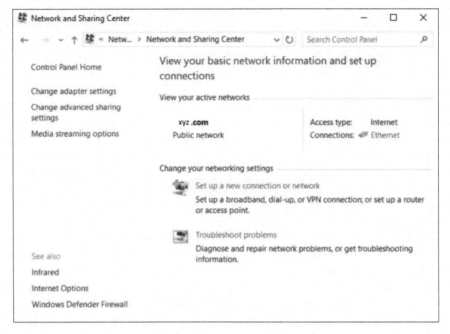

Figure 11-47   Windows 10 Network and Sharing Center

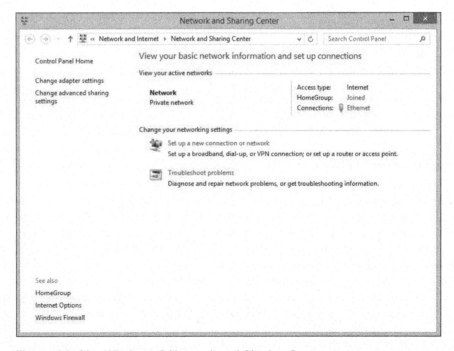

Figure 11-48   Windows 8 Network and Sharing Center

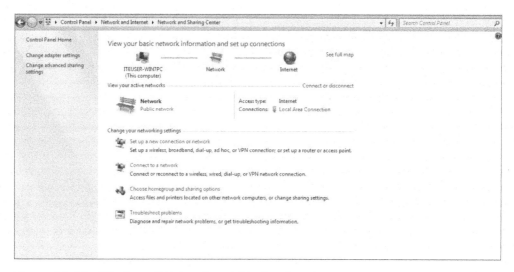

Figure 11-49   Windows 7 Network and Sharing Center

Network and Sharing Center allows the configuration of file and device sharing through the use of network profiles. The network profiles enable basic sharing settings to change, depending on whether you are attached to a private or public network. Sharing can be inactive on an insecure public network but active on a private secure network.

HomeGroup (11.2.3.4)

In Windows networking, a *HomeGroup* is a group of computers that are on the same network. HomeGroups simplify file sharing on simple networks. They are intended to make networking in the home easier by requiring minimal configuration. You can share your library folders on the network, making it easy for other devices to access your music, videos, photos, and documents. Devices that are attached to computers in the HomeGroup can also be shared. Users need the HomeGroup password in order to join the HomeGroup and access shared resources.

HomeGroups were used in Windows 7 and 8. Microsoft has been phasing out the HomeGroup functionality. In Windows 8.1, HomeGroups cannot be created, but Windows 8.1 computers can join existing HomeGroups. In newer versions of Windows 10 (version 1803 and higher), HomeGroup functionality is not available.

Figure 11-50 shows the Windows 8 HomeGroup configuration screen. In Windows 8, nothing is shared by default. Figure 11-51 shows the Windows 7 screen. Note that everything except for documents is shared by default.

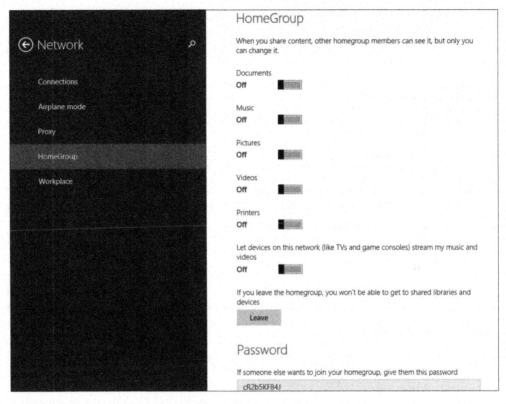

Figure 11-50   Windows 8 HomeGroup Configuration

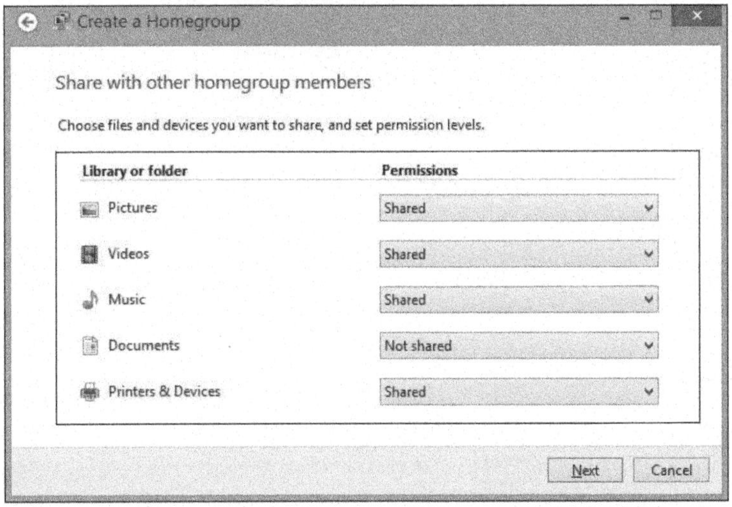

Figure 11-51   Windows 7 HomeGroup Configuration

11.2.3.5 Lab: Configure Browser Settings

In this lab, you will configure Internet settings in Internet Explorer.

11.2.3.6 Check Your Understanding: Network and Internet Control Panel

Refer to the online course to complete this activity.

Display Settings and Control Panel (11.2.4)

Most of the advanced display settings are made in the Display section of the Settings app. Display parameters such as background wallpaper, screen colors, and screen resolution are adjustable.

Display Settings and Configuration (11.2.4.1)

In Windows 10, much of the Appearance and Personalization configuration has been moved to the Settings app, as shown in Figure 11-52. The Windows 10 display settings are reached by right-clicking an empty area of the desktop and selecting Display Settings from the context menu. Alternatively, the Settings app can be opened. Display settings are available in the System category.

Figure 11-52   Display Settings in Windows 10

You can change the appearance of the desktop by modifying the resolution that is output by the graphics adapter. If the screen resolution is not set properly, you might get unexpected display results from different video cards and monitors. You can also change the magnification of the desktop and text size in Windows interface elements. Figure 11-53 shows the Windows 8.1 Display Control Panel item. In Windows 7 and 8, the Display Control Panel item is found in the Hardware and Sound category.

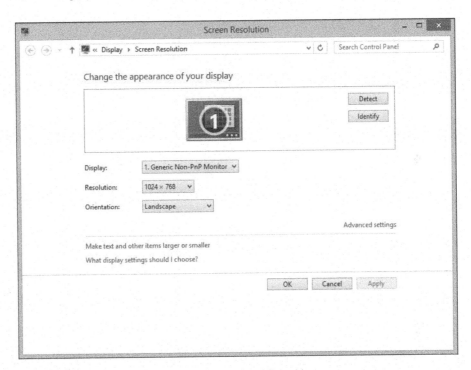

Figure 11-53   Windows 8.1 Display Control Panel Item

When using an LCD screen, set the resolution to the recommended setting. When you do, Windows sets the resolution to the native resolution, which sets the video output to the same number of pixels that the monitor has. If you do not use native resolution, the monitor does not produce the best picture.

Display Features (11.2.4.2)

Figure 11-54 shows how to adjust the screen resolution.

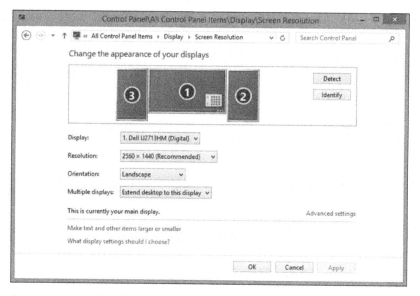

Figure 11-54   Display Features

You can adjust the following features in the Windows 8 and 7 Display Control Panel item:

- **Display:** A specific monitor can be configured when the user has more than one monitor.

- *Screen resolution:* This specifies the number of pixels horizontally and vertically. A higher number of pixels provides better resolution. Typically expressed as horizontal pixels by vertical pixels (for example, 1920×1080).

- *Orientation:* This determines whether the display appears in landscape, portrait, flipped landscape, or flipped portrait orientation.

- *Refresh rate:* This sets how often the image in the screen is redrawn. The refresh rate is in Hertz (Hz). 60 Hz means the screen is redrawn 60 times per second. The higher the refresh rate, the steadier the screen image appears. However, some monitors cannot handle all refresh rate settings.

- *Display colors:* In older systems, the number of colors to display, or the bit depth, needed to be set to a value that was compatible with the graphics adapter and monitor. The higher the bit depth, the greater the number of colors. For example, the 24-bit color (True Color) palette contains 16 million colors. The 32-bit color palette contains 24-bit color and 8 bits for other data, such as transparency.

- *Multiple displays:* Some computers or graphics cards permit the attachment of two or more monitors to the same computer. The desktop can be extended, meaning the displays combine to make one large display, or mirrored, meaning the same image is shown on all displays.

11.2.4.3 Check Your Understanding: Display Features

Refer to the online course to complete this activity.

Power and System Control Panels (11.2.5)

The Power Options window setting, which is used to regulate the computer's power plan settings, is accessed through the Power Options control panel. System information displays computer information such as the version of Windows, computer name, workgroup, Windows activation status, processor speed, RAM, and so on. This sections examines these Control Panels and settings.

Power Options (11.2.5.1)

The *Power Options control panel* allows you to change the power consumption of certain devices or the entire computer. Use Power Options to maximize battery performance or conserve energy by configuring a power plan. A power plan is a collection of hardware and system settings that manage the power usage of the computer. Figure 11-55 shows the Power Options control panel in Windows 10. It varies slightly in Windows 7 and 8. One important difference is that the setting that requires a password when the computer wakes has been moved from Power Options to User Accounts in Windows 10. This is an important setting for data security.

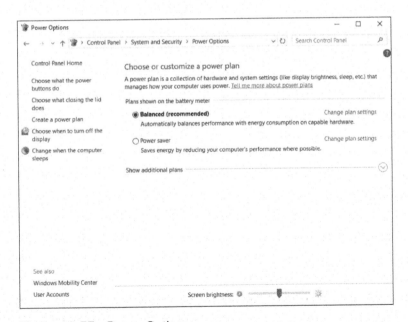

Figure 11-55   Power Options

Windows has preset power plans. These are default settings that were created when Windows was installed. You can use default settings or create your own customized plans based on specific work or device requirements.

Note

Windows automatically detects some devices that are part of the computer and creates power settings accordingly. Therefore, the Power Options settings vary depending on the hardware that is detected.

Power Options Settings (11.2.5.2)

The Power Options control panel is part of the System and Security Control Panel category. Figure 11-56 shows the Widows 8 Power Options control panel.

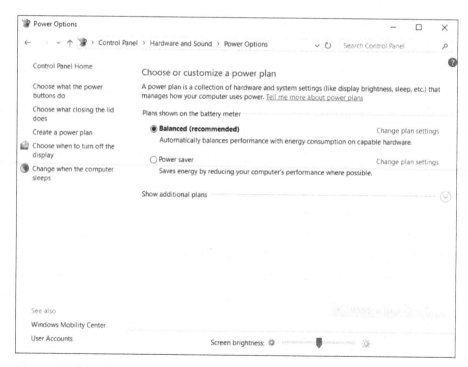

Figure 11-56   Power Options Settings

You can choose from the following options:

- Require a password on wakeup (Windows 7 and 8 only)

- Choose what the power buttons do

- Choose what closing the lid does (for laptops only)

- Create a power plan

- Choose when to turn off the display

- Change when the computer sleeps

Power Options Actions (11.2.5.3)

By selecting Choose What the Power Buttons Do or Choose What Closing the Lid Does, you can configure how a computer acts when power or sleep buttons are pressed or the lid is closed, as shown in Figure 11-57.

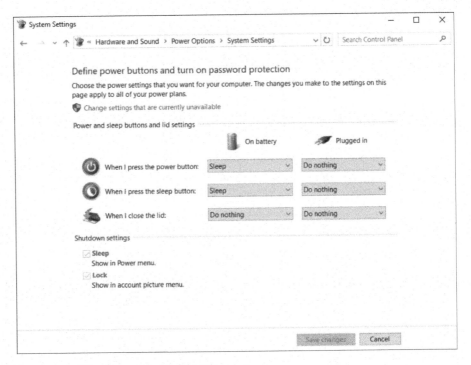

Figure 11-57   Power Options Actions

Some of these settings also appear as shutdown options for the Windows Start button or the Windows 10 Power button. If users do not want to completely shut down a computer, they might be able to use the following options:

- **Do nothing:** The computer continues to run at full power.

- *Sleep*: Documents, applications, and the state of the operating system are saved in RAM. This allows the computer to power on quickly but requires power to retain the information in RAM.

- *Hibernate*: Documents, applications, and the state of the operating system are saved to a temporary file on the hard drive. With this option, the computer takes a little longer to power on than with the Sleep state, but it does not use any power to retain the information on the hard drive.

- **Turn off the display:** The computer operates at full power. The display is turned off.

- **Shut down:** Shuts down the computer.

Interactive Graphic

11.2.5.4 Check Your Understanding: Power Options

Refer to the online course to complete this activity.

System Control Panel Item (11.2.5.5)

The *System control panel* allows all users to view basic system information, access tools, and configure advanced system settings. The System control panel is found under the System and Security category. The Windows 10 System control panel is shown in Figure 11-58. The System control panel is very similar in Windows 7 and 8.

The various settings can be accessed by clicking the links in the left panel.

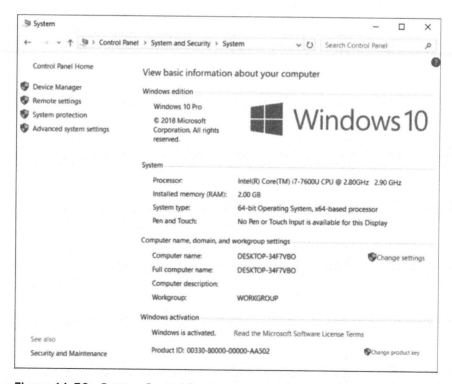

Figure 11-58   System Control Panel

System Properties (11.2.5.6)

When Remote Settings or System Protection is clicked, the System Properties utility appears, with the following tabs:

- **Computer Name:** Use this tab (see Figure 11-59) to view or modify the name and workgroup settings for a computer, as well as change the domain or workgroup.

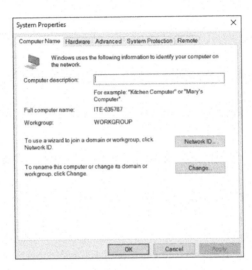

Figure 11-59   Computer Name Tab

- **Hardware:** Use this tab (see Figure 11-60) to access the Device Manager or adjust the device installation settings.

Figure 11-60   Hardware Tab

- **Advanced:** Use this tab (see Figure 11-61) to configure settings for performance, user profiles, startup, and recovery.

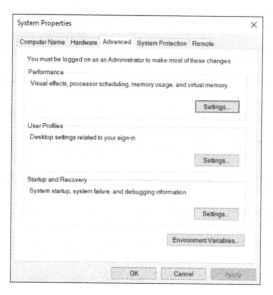

Figure 11-61   Advanced Tab

- *System Protection*: Use this tab (see Figure 11-62) to access System Restore, which returns a computer to an earlier configuration and allows you to configure settings to enable system restore points and the amount of disk space that is used for them.

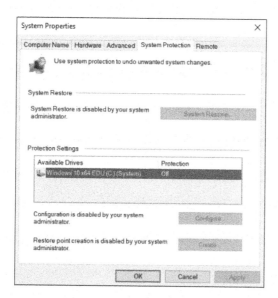

Figure 11-62   System Protection Tab

- *Remote*: Use this tab (see Figure 11-63) to adjust settings for Remote Assistance and Remote Desktop to allow other people to connect to a computer to view the screen or operate it remotely.

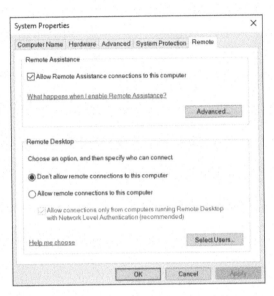

Figure 11-63   Remote Tab

Increasing Performance (11.2.5.7)

To enhance the performance of the OS, you can change the *virtual memory* configuration settings, as shown in Figure 11-64. When Windows determines that system RAM is insufficient, it creates a paging file on the hard drive that contains some of the data from RAM. When the data is required back in RAM, it is read from the paging file. This process is much slower than the process of accessing the RAM directly. If a computer has a small amount of RAM, consider purchasing additional RAM to reduce paging.

Another form of virtual memory is the use of an external flash device and *Windows ReadyBoost* to enhance system performance. Windows ReadyBoost enables Windows to treat an external flash device, such as a USB drive, as hard drive cache. ReadyBoost is not available if Windows determines that no performance improvement can be gained.

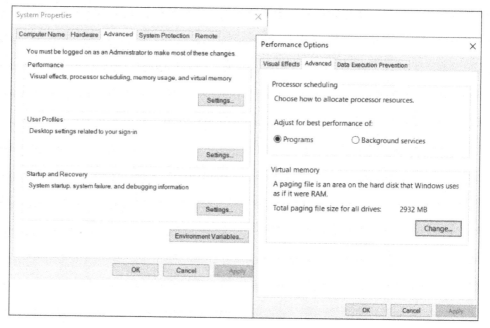

Figure 11-64 *Increasing Performance*

To activate Windows ReadyBoost, insert a flash device and right-click the drive in File Explorer. Click Properties and select the ReadyBoost tab.

11.2.5.8 Lab: Manage Virtual Memory

In this lab, you will use the System control panel to configure and manage virtual memory.

11.2.5.9 Check Your Understanding: Power Options and System Properties

Refer to the online course to complete this activity.

Hardware and Sound Control Panels (11.2.6)

The *Hardware control panel* contains tools that a technician can use to add and remove printers and other types of hardware, configure AutoPlay, manage power, update drivers, and more. The Sound control panel allows you to change system sounds settings.

Device Manager (11.2.6.1)

Device Manager, shown in Figure 11-65, displays a list of all the devices installed in the computer, allowing you to diagnose and resolve device problems.

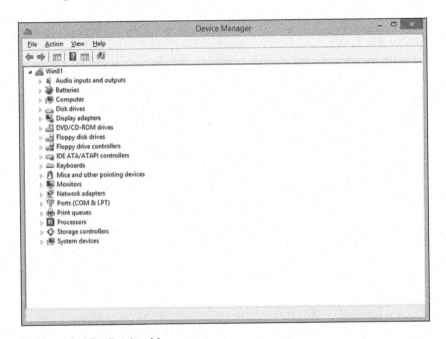

Figure 11-65   Device Manager

You can view details about the installed hardware and drivers, as well as perform the following functions:

- *Update a driver*: Change the currently installed driver.

- *Roll back a driver*: Change the currently installed driver to the previously installed driver.

- *Uninstall a driver*: Remove a driver.

- *Disable a device*: Disable a device.

Device Manager organizes devices by type. To view the devices, expand the appropriate category. You can view the properties of any device in the computer by double-clicking the device name.

The Device Manager utility uses icons to indicate the types of problems that might exist with a device, as indicated in Table 11-3.

Table 11-3 Device Manager Status Icons

Device Manager Icon	Meaning
⚠	The device has an error. It may be functioning, but it requires attention. Right-click on the item in Device Manager and select Properties to see the problem code in the Device Status Error of the Properties box. The code can be researched to determine the problem.
�	The device is disabled. The device is installed on the system, but no driver is loaded for it.
?	The device-specific driver for the device is not available. A compatible driver is in use.
ℹ	This is not a problem code. It means that a driver has been manually, rather than automatically, installed for the device.

The devices that are available in Device Manager vary from computer to computer. Device Manager is very similar in Windows versions 7, 8, and 10.

11.2.6.2 Lab: Use Device Manager

In this lab, you will investigate Device Manager.

Devices and Printers (11.2.6.3)

The *Devices and Printers control panel* provides a high-level view of the devices connected to a computer, as shown in Figure 11-66.

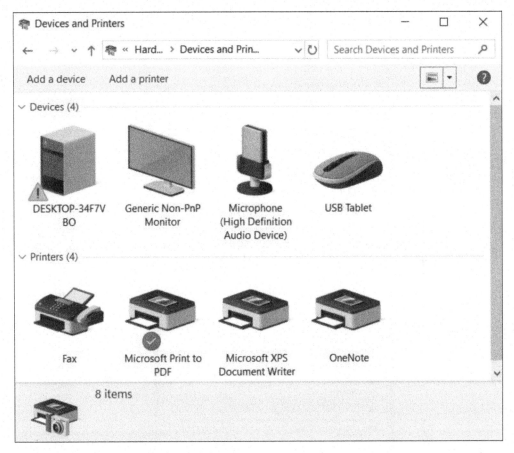

Figure 11-66 Devices and Printers in Windows 10

Devices displayed in the Devices and Printers control panel are typically external devices you can connect to your computer through a port such as USB or a network connection. Devices and Printers also allows you to quickly add a new device to the computer. In most cases, Windows automatically installs any drivers that are required by the device. Note that the desktop computer device in Figure 11-66 shows a yellow triangle alert, indicating that there is a problem with the driver. The green checkmark next to a device indicates that it is to be used as the default device. Right-click on a device to view its properties.

Devices typically shown in Devices and Printers include:

- Portable devices that you occasionally connect to your computer, such as mobile phones, personal fitness devices, and digital cameras

- Devices you plug into a USB port on your computer, such as external USB hard drives, flash drives, webcams, keyboards, and mice

- Printers connected to your computer or available on the network

- Wireless devices connected to your computer, such as Bluetooth and wireless USB devices

- Compatible network devices connected to your computer, such as network-enabled scanners, media extenders, or network attached storage (NAS) devices

The Devices and Printers control panel is very similar in Windows versions 7, 8, and 10.

Sound (11.2.6.4)

Use the *Sound control panel* (see Figure 11-67) to configure audio devices or change the sound scheme of the computer. For example, you can change the email notification sound from a beep to a chime. Sound also allows a user to choose which audio device is to be used for playback or recording.

The Sound control panel is largely unchanged between Windows 7, 8, and 10.

Figure 11-67   The Sound Control Panel

Clock, Region, and Language (11.2.7)

The categories view of the Clock, Region, and Language control panel shows areas where settings can be viewed and links to the subcategories where changes can be made for setting the clock, region, and language.

Clock (11.2.7.1)

Windows allows you to change the system time and date through the *Date and Time control panel*, as shown in Figure 11-68. You can also adjust your time zone. Windows automatically updates the time settings when time changes occur. The Windows clock automatically synchronizes with a time authority on the Internet to ensure that the time value is accurate.

Figure 11-68   Windows 10 Date and Time

Date and Time is accessed through the Clock and Region Control Panel category in Windows 10. In Windows 7 and 8, it is accessed through the Clock, Language, and Region Control Panel category.

Region (11.2.7.2)

Windows allows you to change the format of numbers, currencies, dates, and times by using the *Region control panel*. Windows 7 had tabs available for changing the system keyboard layout and language, as well as the computer location. In Windows 8, the tab for keyboard and language was removed. Windows 10 attempts to use location services to automatically detect the location of the computer. The location can also be set manually if the location can't be determined. Figure 11-69 shows the Windows 8 Region control panel, and Figure 11-70 shows the Windows 10 Region control panel.

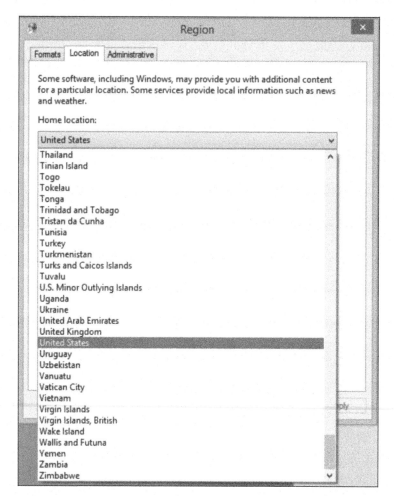

Figure 11-69   Windows 8 Region Control Panel Item with Location

Date and time setting formats can be changed by changing the display patterns available in the Date and Time formats area. Click Additional Settings to change number and currency formats and the measurement system used in the region. Additional date and time formats are also available.

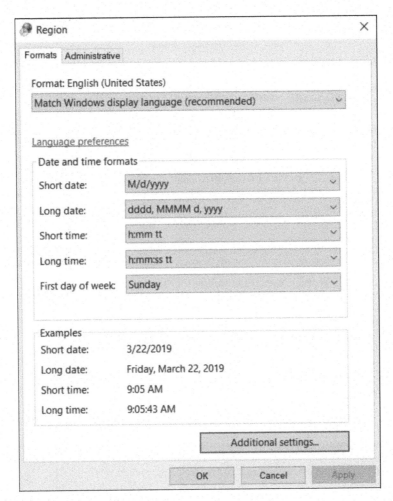

Figure 11-70   Windows 10 Region Control

Language (11.2.7.3)

In Windows 7 and Windows 8, as shown in Figure 11-71, language can be configured through Control Panel items. Users can install language packs that include fonts and other resources required by different languages.

In Windows 10, these settings were moved to the Language Settings app, as shown in Figure 11-72. When adding a language, you can choose to install Cortana support for voice commands in that language, if available.

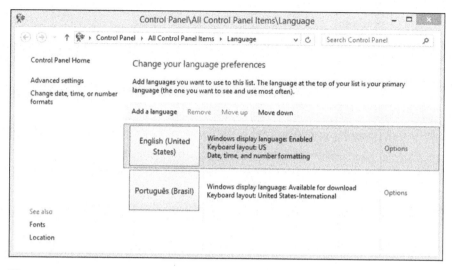

Figure 11-71   Windows 8 Language Configuration

Figure 11-72   Windows 10 Language Settings

11.2.7.4 Lab: Region and Language Options

In this lab, you will examine region and language options in Windows.

11.2.7.5 Check Your Understanding: Clock, Region, and Language

Refer to the online course to complete this activity.

Programs and Features Control Panels (11.2.8)

Uninstalling and managing software installed on a computer is a key concern of computer technicians. The Programs category in Control Panel provides access to the links that allow changes, repairs, and uninstallation of any program that is installed on the computer.

Programs (11.2.8.1)

Use the *Programs and Features control panel* to uninstall a program from your computer if you no longer use it or if you want to free up space on your hard disk, as shown in Figure 11-73. It is important that applications be uninstalled either through the Programs and Features control panel or from an uninstallation menu choice that is associated with the application in the Start menu.

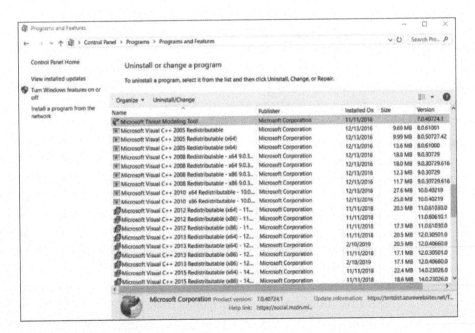

Figure 11-73   Uninstalling Programs

In addition, you can repair the installation of some programs that may have problems. You can also troubleshoot problems with programs that were made for older versions of Windows that are not running correctly.

Finally, you can choose to manually install software from the network. It is possible that your organization provides updates or patches that could require manual installation.

Windows Features and Updates (11.2.8.2)

You can activate or deactivate Windows features, as shown in Figure 11-74. Programs and Features also allows you to view the Windows updates that have been installed and to uninstall specific updates if they are causing problems and don't have dependencies with other installed updates or software.

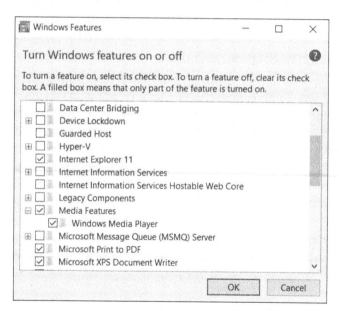

Figure 11-74   Configuring Windows Features

Default Programs (11.2.8.3)

The *Default Programs control panel* provides the means to configure the way that Windows handles files and the applications that are used to work with them, as shown in Figure 11-75. For example, if you have multiple web browsers installed, you can choose which web browser will open to view a link that you have clicked on in an email or another file. This can be done by choosing default applications or by choosing which application opens for a specific file type. For example, you configure a JPEG graphics file to open in a browser, for viewing, or in a graphics editor.

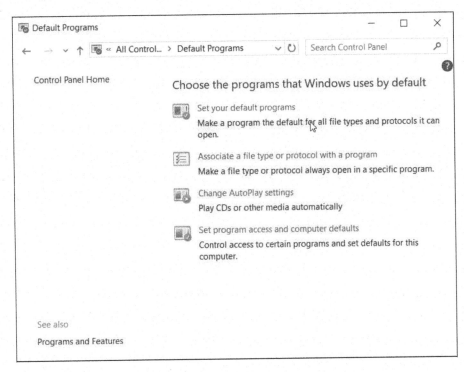

Figure 11-75   Default Programs Control Panel

Finally, you can choose how AutoPlay works. You can select how Windows will automatically open files of different types, depending on the type of removable storage media on which they are stored. You can select to have audio CDs open automatically in Windows Media Player or have a Windows File Explorer display a directory of the disk contents.

Windows 10 uses a settings app for all but the AutoPlay configuration. Windows 7 and 8 use Control Panel utilities.

11.2.8.4 Check Your Understanding: Programs and Features

Interactive
Graphic

Refer to the online course to complete this activity.

Other Control Panels (11.2.9)

Control Panel has many utilities that contain the settings and options for the various parts of Windows.

Troubleshooting (11.2.9.1)

The *Troubleshooting control panel* has a number of built-in scripts that are used to identify and solve common problems with many Windows components, as shown in Figure 11-76. The scripts run automatically and can be configured to automatically make the changes to fix the problems that are found. You can also view when the troubleshooting scripts have been run in the past by using the View History feature.

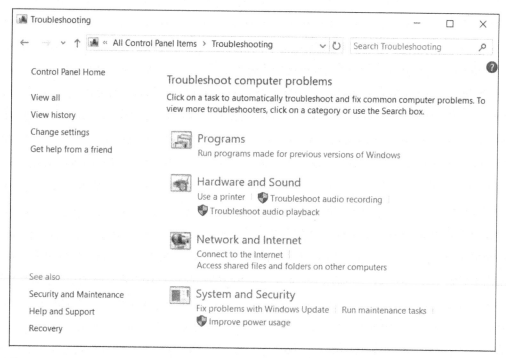

Figure 11-76   Windows 10 Troubleshooting Categories

BitLocker Drive Encryption (11.2.9.2)

BitLocker is a service provided with Windows to encrypt an entire volume of disk data so that it can't be read by unauthorized parties. Data can be lost if your computer or disk drives are stolen. In addition, when a computer is taken out of service, BitLocker can help ensure that the hard drive can't be read after it is removed from the computer and scrapped.

The BitLocker Drive Encryption control panel, shown in Figure 11-77, enables you to control the way BitLocker operates.

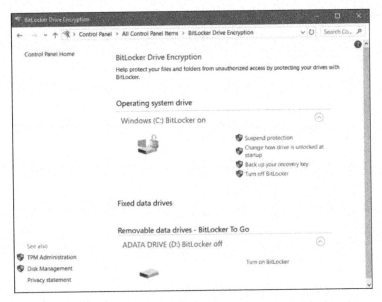

Figure 11-77   BitLocker Drive Encryption Control Panel Item

File Explorer and Folder Options (11.2.9.3)

The Folder Option control panel allows you to change a variety of settings related to the way files are displayed in Windows Explorer or File Explorer. This Control Panel item is called *File Explorer Options* in Windows 10 and *Folder Options* in Windows 7 and 8.1. The Windows 10 File Explorer Options control panel is shown in Figure 11-78. The Windows 7 and 8 versions are very similar. The Windows 8 version is shown in Figure 11-79.

Figure 11-78   Windows 10 File Explorer Folder Options

Figure 11-79   Folder Options in Windows 8.

In Windows 10, many of the most commonly used file and folder options can be found in the File Explorer ribbon. In Windows 8.1, some functions are present in the ribbon, but the selection is not as comprehensive as it is in Windows 10. In Windows 7, there is no ribbon, and the Control Panel must be used.

The functions of the tabs in Windows 10 are described below.

The General tab is used to adjust the following settings:

- **Browse Folders:** Configures how a folder is displayed when it is opened.

- **Click Items as Follows:** Specifies the number of clicks required to open an item.

- **Privacy:** Determines which files and folders are shown in Quick Access. Also allows File History to be cleared.

The View tab is used to adjust the following settings:

- **Folder Views:** Applies the view settings for a folder being viewed to all folders of the same type.

- **Advanced Settings:** Customizes the viewing experience, including the ability to view hidden files and file extensions.

The Search tab is used to adjust the following settings:

- **What to Search (Windows 7):** Configures search settings based on indexed and non-indexed locations to make files and folders easier to find.

- **How to Search:** Chooses whether an indexed search is used.

- **When Searching Non-indexed Locations:** Determines whether system directories, compressed files, and file contents are included when searching non-indexed locations.

11.2.9.4 Lab: Privacy and Gaming

In this lab, you will research the issue of privacy and gaming and configure Windows Privacy and Gaming settings.

11.2.9.5 Check Your Understanding: Other Control Panels

Refer to the online course to complete this activity.

System Administration (11.3)

System administration involves managing and maintaining hardware and software systems in a multi-user environment.

Administrative Tools (11.3.1)

Many tools are available from third-party vendors and in Microsoft Windows to help with system administration. Administrative Tools is a control panel that contains many system tools for use by advanced users, technicians, and system administration. Administrative Tools might be different depending on the version of Windows.

Administrative Tools Control Panel Item (11.3.1.1)

The *Administrative Tools control panel* is a collection of tools that are used to monitor and configure Windows operation. This Control Panel item has evolved over time. In Windows 7, it was somewhat limited. Microsoft added many different utilities in Windows 8.1. In Windows 10, the available tools changed slightly.

The Administrative Tools control panel is unusual in that it is a collection of shortcuts that open in File Explorer. Because each icon represents a shortcut to an application, you can investigate the properties of each shortcut to see the name of the application file that is run when the shortcut is clicked. You can start the same applications by typing the name of the application at the command prompt. When you become experienced with managing Windows, this may be the most efficient way for you to access the tools you need. Figure 11-80 shows the Administrative Tools control panel in Windows 10.

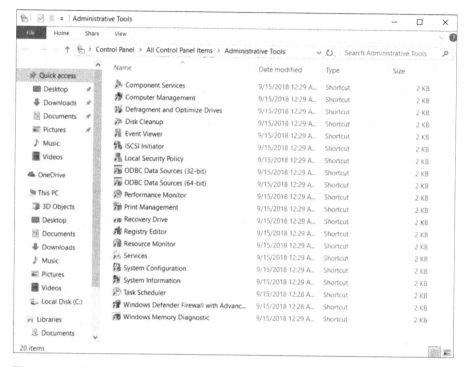

Figure 11-80   Administrative Tools Control Panel Item

Computer Management (11.3.1.2)

One of the Administrative Tools items is the *Computer Management console*, shown in Figure 11-81. It allows you to manage many aspects of your computer and remote computers in one tool.

The Computer Management console provides access to three groups of utilities. This section discusses the System Tools group.

Conveniently, the Computer Management console can be accessed by right-clicking This PC in Windows 8.1 or 10 or by right-clicking Computer in Windows 7 and 8 and selecting Manage. Administrator privileges are required to open the Computer Management console.

To view the Computer Management console for a remote computer, follow these steps:

Step 1.   In the console tree, click **Computer Management (Local)** and select **Connect to another computer.**

Step 2. Enter the name of the computer or click **Browse** and find the computer to manage on the network.

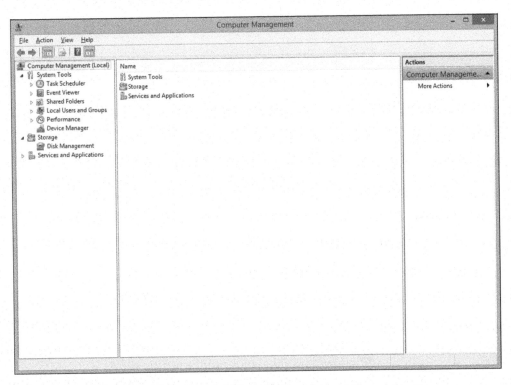

Figure 11-81 Computer Management Console

Event Viewer (11.3.1.3)

Event Viewer, shown in Figure 11-82, allows you to view the history of application, security, and Windows system events. These events are stored in log files. The log files are valuable troubleshooting tools because they provide information necessary to identify a problem. Event Viewer permits filtering and customization of log views to make it easier to find important information from the various log files that Windows compiles.

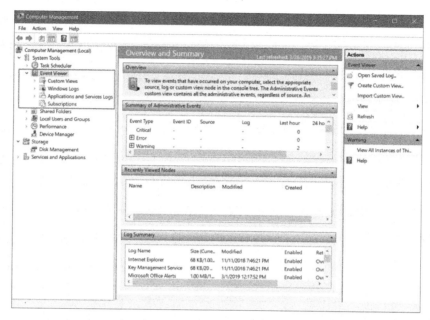

Figure 11-82 Event Viewer

Windows logs many events that can originate from applications, the Windows OS, application setup, and security events. Each message is identified by its type or level:

- *Information*: A successful event. A driver or program has executed successfully. Windows logs thousands of information events.

- *Warning*: There is a potential problem with a software component that is not functioning ideally.

- *Error*: A problem exists, but no immediate action is required.

- *Critical*: Immediate attention is required. Usually related to system or software crashes or lockups.

- *Success audit (security only)*: A security event has been successful. For example, a successful logon from a user will trigger an event with this level.

- *Failure audit (security only)*: A security event has not been successful. Failed attempts by someone attempting to log on to a computer will trigger this event.

Local Users and Groups (11.3.1.4)

Local Users and Groups, shown in Figure 11-83, provides an efficient way of managing users.

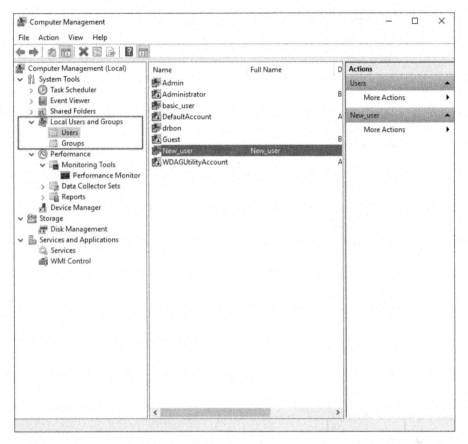

Figure 11-83 Local Users and Groups

You can create new users and assign those users to be members of groups. Groups have rights and permissions assigned that are suitable for different types of users. Rather than configuring rights and permissions for each individual user, you can assign a user to an appropriate group. Windows provides default user accounts and groups to make managing users easier:

- *Administrators*: Administrators have full control of the computer and access to all folders.

- *Guests*: Guests can access the computer through a temporary profile that is created at logon and deleted at logoff. Guest accounts are disabled by default.

- *Users*: Users can perform common tasks such as running applications and accessing local or network printers. A user profile is created and persists on the system.

Performance Monitor (11.3.1.5)

Performance Monitor allows customized performance graphs and reports to be created from a wide range of hardware and software components. Data collector sets are collections of metrics, called *performance counters*. Windows has a number of default data collector sets, and you can also create your own. A wide range of counters can be graphed against time, and reports can also be generated and read or printed. Data collection can be scheduled to occur at different times and for different durations. In addition, stop criteria for a monitoring session can also be set.

The information provided by Performance Monitor is different from the performance information that is available through Task Manager and Resource Monitor. The Performance Monitor administrative tool helps you create detailed custom reports from very specific counters. Figure 11-84 shows a graph derived from a selection of data counters available for the CPU.

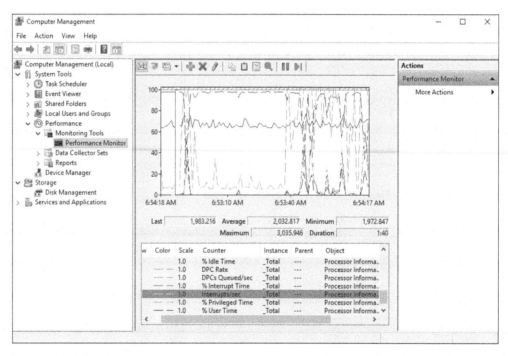

Figure 11-84   Performance Monitor

Component Services and Data Sources (11.3.1.6)

Component Services (see Figure 11-85) is an administrative tool that administrators and developers can use to deploy, configure, and manage Component Object Model (COM) components. COM is a way to allow the use of software components in distributed environments such as in enterprise, Internet, and intranet applications.

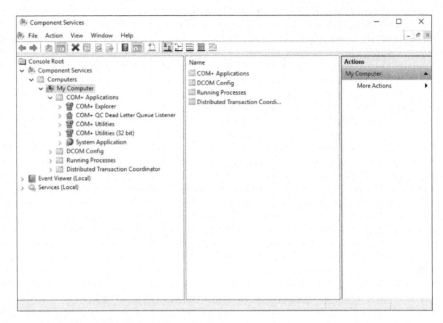

Figure 11-85   Component Services

Services (11.3.1.7)

The *Services console (services.msc)*, shown in Figure 11-86, allows you to manage all the services on your computer and remote computers.

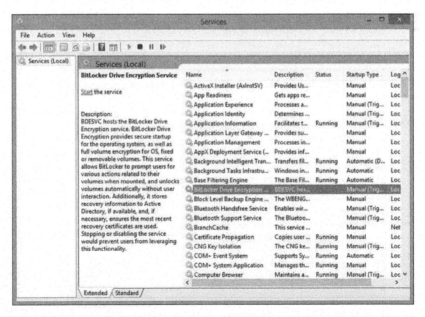

Figure 11-86   Services Console

A *service* is a type of application that runs in the background to achieve a specific goal or to wait for service requests. To reduce security risks, you should start only the necessary services. You can use the following settings, or states, to control a service:

- **Automatic:** The service starts when the computer is started. This prioritizes the most important services.

- **Automatic (Delayed):** The service starts after services that are set to Automatic have started. The Automatic (Delayed) setting is available only in Windows 7.

- **Manual:** The service must be started manually by the user or by a service or program that needs it.

- **Disabled:** The service cannot be started until it is enabled.

- **Stopped:** The service is not running.

To view the Services console for a remote computer, right-click on Services (Local) in the Computer Management window and select Connect to Another Computer. Enter the name for the computer or click Browse to allow Windows to scan the network for connected computers.

Data Sources (11.3.1.8)

Data Sources is a tool that administrators can use to add, remove, or manage data sources using *Open Database Connectivity (ODBC)*. ODBC is a technology that programs use to access a wide range of databases or data sources. Figure 11-87 shows the Data Sources tool.

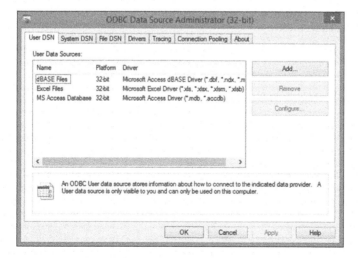

Figure 11-87   Data Sources

Print Management (11.3.1.9)

The *Print Management utility*, shown in Figure 11-88, provides a detailed view of all the printers that are available to a computer. It is not available in all Windows editions. It is available in Windows servers and in Pro, Enterprise, and Ultimate editions. It enables efficient configuration and monitoring of directly attached and network printers, including print queues for all printers to which it has access. It also allows the deployment of a printer configuration to multiple computers on a network through the use of Group Policy.

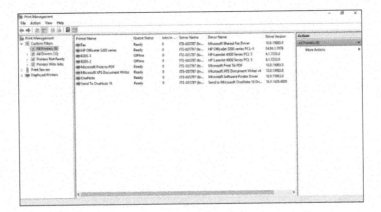

Figure 11-88   Print Management

Windows Memory Diagnostics (11.3.1.10)

The *Windows Memory Diagnostics* tool schedules a memory test that is executed when the computer starts. It can be configured to automatically restart the computer or execute the test the next time the computer starts. After the test is complete, Windows restarts. The type of diagnostics to be run can be configured by pressing **F1** as the tool runs, as shown in Figure 11-89. The results of the test can be viewed by finding the memory diagnostic test result in the Windows Log folder in Event Viewer.

11.3.1.11 Lab: Monitor and Manage System Resources

In this lab, you will use administrative tools to monitor and manage system resources.

11.3.1.12 Check Your Understanding: Administrative Tools

Refer to the online course to complete this activity.

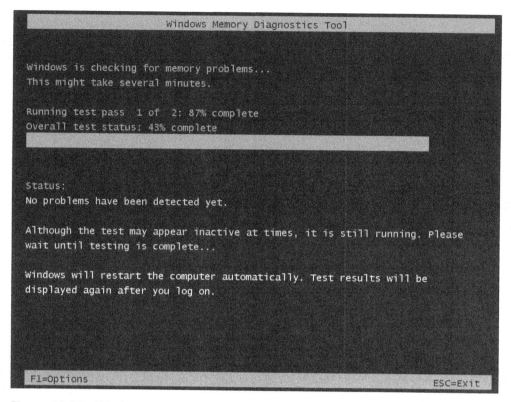

Figure 11-89   Windows Memory Diagnostics

System Utilities (11.3.2)

System utilities are designed for specific purposes, to carry out tasks that can optimize performance, monitor computer resources and usage, and generally customize a computer in ways that are not usually a part of daily OS operation. This section examines many Windows utilities, such as System Information, Registry Editor, and more.

System Information (11.3.2.1)

Administrators can use the *System Information* tool, as shown in Figure 11-90, to collect and display information about local and remote computers. The System Information tool is designed to quickly find information about software, drivers, hardware configurations, and computer components. Support personnel can use this information to diagnose and troubleshoot a computer.

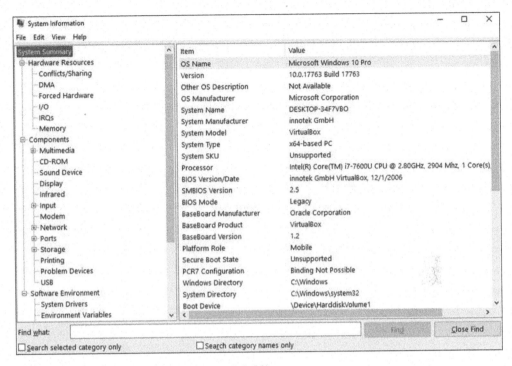

Figure 11-90   System Information (msinfo32)

You can also create a file containing all the information about the computer to send to someone. To export a System Information file, select File > Export, type the file-name, choose a location, and click Save. The System Information utility can also display the configuration of other machines on the network.

You can open the System Information tool from the command prompt by typing **msinfo32**, or you can find it in the Administrative Tools control panel.

System Configuration (11.3.2.2)

System Configuration (msconfig) is a tool used to identify problems that keep Windows from starting correctly. To help with isolating the issue, services and startup programs can be turned off and turned back on, one at a time. After you have determined the cause, permanently remove or disable the program or service or reinstall it.

The sections that follow show and describe the tabs available in the System Configuration utility.

General Tab

Use the *General* tab (see Figure 11-91) to display three startup selections to aid troubleshooting:

- **Normal startup:** Full startup as normal

- **Diagnostic startup:** Startup with basic services and drivers only

- **Selective startup:** Startup with basic services and drivers by default (but can be changed)

Figure 11-91   General Tab

Boot Tab

Use the *Boot* tab (see Figure 11-92) to choose the Windows OS version to boot if more than one is present. You can also choose to boot up in Safe boot (formerly Safe mode) with different options regarding the way that Windows starts.

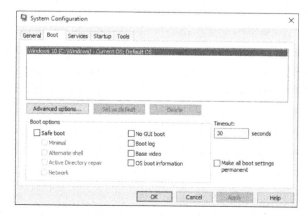

Figure 11-92   Boot Tab

Services Tab

Use the *Services* tab (see Figure 11-93) to display a list of services that are started with the operating system. You can specify that individual services not be loaded on boot for troubleshooting purposes.

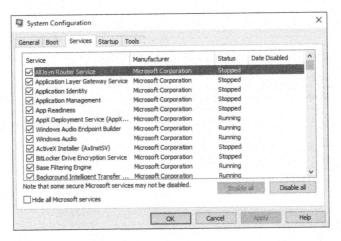

Figure 11-93   Services Tab

Startup Tab

Use the *Startup* tab for Startup settings. In Windows 7, this tab displays a list of all the applications that run automatically when Windows starts, and you can disable individual items. In Windows 8.1 and 10, these settings appear in Task Manager, as shown in Figure 11-94.

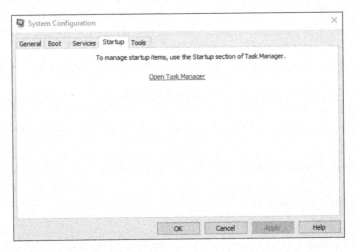

Figure 11-94   Startup Tab

Tools Tab

Use the *Tools* tab (see Figure 11-95) to display a compact and very comprehensive list of diagnostic tools that can be run to help with troubleshooting.

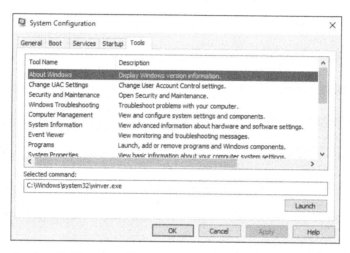

Figure 11-95 Tools Tab

The Registry (11.3.2.3)

The *Windows Registry* is a database that contains settings for Windows and for applications that use the Registry. The settings contained in the Registry are very low level, meaning there are many, many of them. Values in the Registry are created when new software is installed or new devices are added. Every setting in Windows, from the background of the desktop and the color of the screen buttons to the licensing of applications, is stored in the Registry. When a user makes changes to the Control Panel settings, file associations, system policies, or installed software, the changes are stored in the Registry.

The Registry consists of a hierarchical arrangement of *keys* and subkeys that are represented as a tree. Levels of the subkey tree can be deeply nested to a maximum of 512 levels. Locating the key for the value you want to see is a matter of working through the hierarchy of trees and subtrees. There are five top-level, or root, keys.

The Registry exists as multiple database files, called *hives*, that are associated with each of the top-level Registry keys. Each key has values. The values consist of the name of the value, its data type, and the setting or data that is associated with the value. The values tell Windows how to operate.

The Windows Registry keys are an important part of the Windows boot process. These keys are recognized by their distinctive names, which begin with HKEY_, as shown in Table 11-4. The words and letters that follow HKEY_ indicate the portion of the OS controlled by that key.

Table 11-4   The Registry

Root Key	Contents
HKEY_LOCAL_MACHINE	Information about the physical state of the computer, including hardware configuration, network logon and security information, Plug and Play information, and so on.
HKEY_CURRENT_USER	Data about the preferences of the currently logged on user, including Personalization settings, default devices, programs, and so on.
HKEY_CLASSES_ROOT	Settings about the file system, file associations, and shortcuts. Information here is used when you ask Windows to run a file or view a directory.
HKEY_USERS	All of the configuration settings for the hardware and software configured on the computer for all users.
HKEY_CURRENT_CONFIG	Information about the current hardware profile of the machine.

Regedit (11.3.2.4)

The *Registry Editor* allows an administrator to view or make changes to the Windows Registry. Using the Registry Editor utility incorrectly could cause hardware, application, or operating system problems, including problems that require you to reinstall the operating system.

The Registry Editor can only be opened from a search or command prompt. You can search for *regedit* and open it from the search results, or you can open a command or PowerShell prompt and type **regedit**.

Figure 11-96 shows the regedit utility with the value of the OneDrive subkey open for modification.

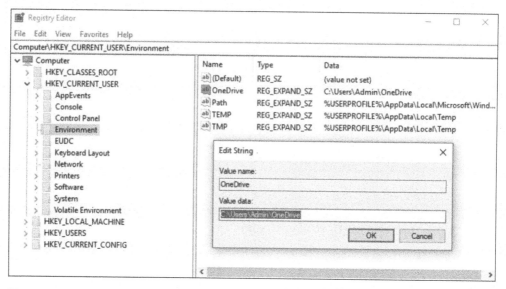

Figure 11-96   regedit

Microsoft Management Console (11.3.2.5)

Microsoft Management Console (MMC) is an application that allows the creation of custom management consoles for collections of utilities and tools from Microsoft or other sources. The Computer Management console, discussed earlier in this chapter, is a premade MMC. When initially opened, the MMC is empty. Utilities and tools, known as snap-ins, can be added to the console. You can also add web page links, tasks, ActiveX controls, and folders.

The MMC can then be saved and reopened when needed. You can construct management consoles for specific purposes. You can create as many customized MMCs as needed, each with a different name. This is useful when multiple administrators manage different aspects of the same computer. Each administrator can have an individualized console for monitoring and configuring computer settings.

Figure 11-97 shows a new empty console with the dialog box for selecting and adding snap-ins.

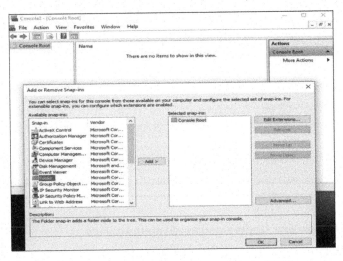

Figure 11-97   Creating an Empty Console in MMC

DxDiag (11.3.2.6)

The *DirectX Diagnostic Tool (DxDiag)* displays details for all DirectX components and drivers that are installed in a computer, as shown in Figure 11-98. DxDiag is run from a search or from the command line.

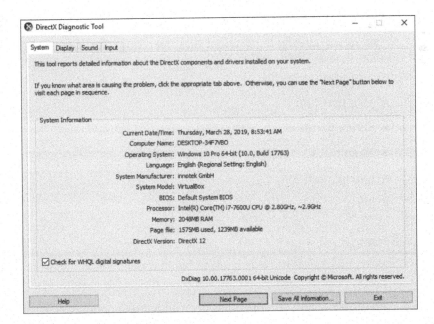

Figure 11-98   DxDiag

DirectX is a software environment and interface for multimedia applications, especially games. It defines interfaces for 2D and 3D graphics, audio, media encoders and decoders, and so on.

11.3.2.7 Lab: System Utilities

In this lab, you will use Windows utilities to configure operating system settings.

11.3.2.8 Lab: Manage System Files

In this lab, you will use Windows utilities to gather information about a computer.

11.3.2.9 Check Your Understanding: System Utilities

Refer to the online course to complete this activity.

Disk Management (11.3.3)

Disk Management allows full management of the disk drives installed in a computer, such as hard disk drives, optical disc drives, and flash drives. It can be used to partition drives, format drives, assign drive letters, and perform other disk-related tasks.

What Do You Already Know? Disk Operations (11.3.3.1)

What do you already know about disk operation? See if you can select the disk operation term that is most appropriate for each of the following five scenarios. The disk operation terms are:

- Split partition
- Shrink partition
- Mount disk
- Extend partition
- Initialize disk

Scenario

Scenario 1: A user has a disk image file that they would like to be able to browse like a disk volume in order to see the contents of the file system.

Scenario 2: A new disk drive has been added to a computer, but it is not formatted.

Scenario 3: A drive has a system partition and a data partition. The system partition is running out of space.

Scenario 4: A user's disk volume has a single partition. You want to create a new partition for data files on the user's computer.

Scenario 5: A new partition needs to be created on a disk in which the existing partitions take up the entire drive capacity.

Answers

Scenario 1 Answer: Mount disk; Mounting a volume means opening a disk image like a drive. This is useful with optical media image file formats such as ISO and BIN.

Scenario 2 Answer: Initialize disk; Disks that have not been formatted need to be initialized before they can be used in Windows. Initializing erases any data that might be on the drive.

Scenario 3 Answer: Extend partition; Extending a partition means adding space to a volume on a disk that has more than one volume. Space is taken from one volume and allocated to another.

Scenario 4 Answer: Split partition; Splitting a partition means creating a new partition from an existing one. There is no way in Disk Management to do this directly. Instead, you must shrink the existing partition and create a new partition from the unallocated space.

Scenario 5 Answer: Shrink partition; When a new partition needs to be created, the last partition on the drive (all the way to the right in Disk Manager) can be shrunk to create unallocated space that can be used to create a new partition.

Disk Management Utility (11.3.3.2)

The *Disk Management utility* is part of the Computer Management console. It can be opened by right-clicking on This PC or Computer and selecting Manage. It can also be opened through the Computer Management control panel or in its own Window by pressing **Win+X** and selecting Disk Management.

In addition to extending and shrinking partitions, as demonstrated in Chapter 10, "Windows Installation," you can also use the Disk Management utility to complete the following tasks:

- View drive status
- Assign or change drive letters
- Add drives
- Add arrays
- Designate the active partition

Figure 11-99 shows the Disk Management utility in Windows 10.

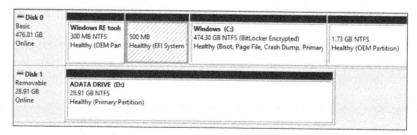

Figure 11-99   Disk Management Utility

Drive Status (11.3.3.3)

The Disk Management utility displays the *drive status* of each disk, as shown in Figure 11-100.

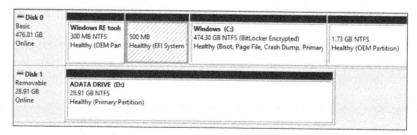

Figure 11-100   Disk Volumes

Each drive in the computer displays one of the following conditions:

- **Foreign:** A dynamic disk that has been moved to a computer from another computer running Windows

- *Healthy*: A volume that is functioning properly

- **Initializing:** A basic disk that is being converted into a dynamic disk

- **Missing:** A dynamic disk that is corrupted, turned off, or disconnected

- **Not Initialized:** A disk that does not contain a valid signature

- **Online:** A basic or dynamic disk that is accessible and shows no problems

- **Online (Errors):** A dynamic disk on which I/O errors have been detected

- **Offline:** A dynamic disk that is corrupted or unavailable

- **Unreadable:** A basic or dynamic disk that has experienced hardware failure, corruption, or I/O errors

Other drive status indicators might be displayed when using drives other than hard drives, such as an audio CD that is in the optical drive or a removable drive that is empty.

Mounting a Drive (11.3.3.4)

Mounting a drive refers to making a disk image file readable as a drive. A good example of this is an ISO file, as shown in Figure 11-101. It is the entire contents of the disk, represented as a single file. ISO images are used as archives of the contents of an optical disc. Disc writer software can write the contents of an ISO to the disc.

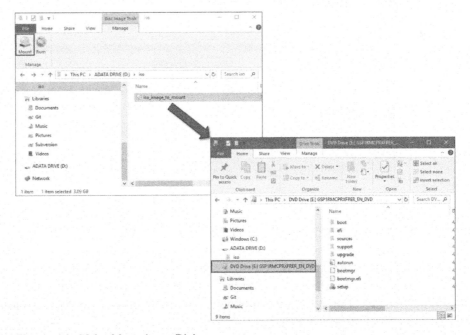

Figure 11-101   Mounting a Disk

These ISO files can also be mounted on virtual drives. To mount an image, open File Explorer and locate and select an ISO file. In the ribbon, select the Manage menu under Disk Image Tools. Select Mount. The ISO file is mounted as a removable media drive. The drive can be browsed, and files can be opened. However, there is actually no drive. The drive is an ISO image mounted as a volume.

You can also create a *mount point*, which is similar to a shortcut. You can create a mount point that makes an entire drive appear as a folder. This might provide an easy way for users to access files since the mounted folder can appear in their My Documents folder, for example.

Adding Arrays (11.3.3.5)

In Windows disk management, you can create mirrored, spanned, or RAID 5 arrays from multiple dynamic disks. This is done by right-clicking a volume and selecting the type of multidisk volume that you want to create, as shown in Figure 11-102. Note that there must be two or more initialized dynamic drives available on the computer.

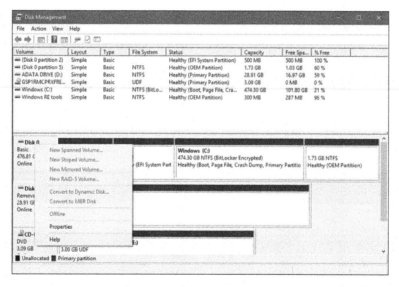

Figure 11-102   Arrays in Disk Management

Storage Spaces became available in Windows 8 and 10. Storage Spaces can be configured from a Control Panel item, as shown in Figure 11-103. Storage Spaces is the disk array technology that is recommended by Windows. It creates pools of physical hard drives from which virtual disks (storage spaces) can be created. Many different types of drives can be combined. Like other disk arrays, Storage Spaces offer mirrored, striped, and parity options.

Figure 11-103   Storage Spaces Control Panel Item

Disk Optimization (11.3.3.6)

To maintain and optimize disk storage, you can use various *disk optimization* tools in Windows, including hard drive defragmentation, which consolidates files for faster access.

As files increase in size, some data is written to the next available cluster on the disk. In time, data becomes fragmented and spread over non-adjacent clusters on the hard drive. As a result, it takes longer to locate and retrieve each section of the data. A disk defragmenter gathers the noncontiguous data into one place, making the OS run faster.

Note

It is not recommended to perform disk defragmentation on SSDs. SSDs are optimized by the controller and firmware they use. It should not be harmful to defragment hybrid SSDs (SSHDs) because they use hard disks rather than solid-state RAM to store data.

In Windows 8 and 10, the disk optimization option is called Optimize, and it can be accessed from the disk properties menu or from the File Explorer ribbon (see Figure 11-104). In Windows 7, the disk optimization option is called Defragment Now.

Figure 11-104   Disk Optimization

Figure 11-105 shows the Optimize Drives utility, which analyzes a drive prior to optimization and displays the degree of fragmentation of the drive.

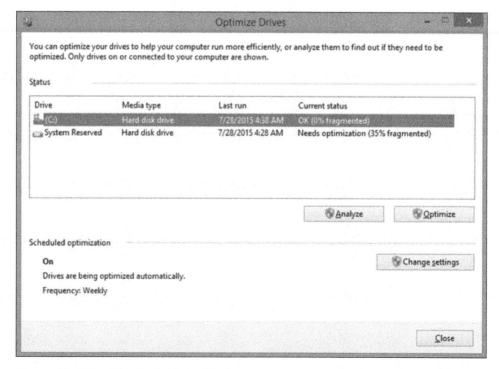

Figure 11-105   Disk Optimization Tool

You can also optimize the available space by doing a disk cleanup operation to remove unnecessary files from the drive.

Disk Error-Checking (11.3.3.7)

The *Disk Error-Checking* tool checks the integrity of files and folders by scanning the hard disk surface for physical errors.

If errors are detected, the tool attempts to repair them. In File Explorer or File Manager, right-click the drive and select Properties. Select the Tools tab and select Check or Check Now in Windows 7. In Windows 8, select Scan Drive to attempt to recover bad sectors. In Windows 7, select Scan For and Attempt Recovery of Bad Sectors and click Start. The tool fixes file system errors and checks the disk for bad sectors. It also attempts to recover data from bad sectors.

In Windows 8 and 10, if you want to see a detailed report of the results of the scan, click Check Results after the scan has completed. In the Event Viewer window that opens, you can view the log entry for the scan. In Windows 7, a report is displayed by the error-checking utility, as shown in Figure 11-106.

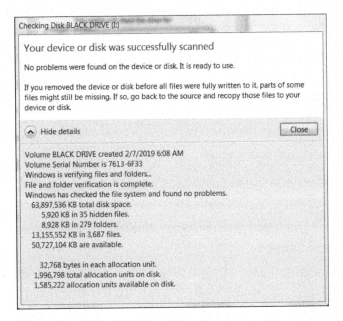

Figure 11-106   Disk Error-Checking

Note

Use the Disk Error-Checking tool whenever a sudden loss of power causes the system to shut down incorrectly.

11.3.3.8 Lab: Hard Drive Maintenance

In this lab, you will perform hard drive maintenance tasks, including defragmentation and error checking.

11.3.3.9 Check Your Understanding: Disk Management

Refer to the online course to complete this activity.

Application Installation and Configuration (11.3.4)

Installing an application means that a program is being set up to run on a computer, and it needs to be compatible with the system on which it is being installed. One way to check for compatibility is by verifying that a program meets system requirements. After an application is installed, it is then configured to be functional for the users of the system.

System Requirements (11.3.4.1)

Before purchasing or attempting to install an application, you should verify that the system requirements are met. System requirements are usually stated as minimum requirements. The recommended system requirements may also be stated, as shown in Table 11-5. The following requirements are normally defined in the software packaging or on the software download page:

- Processor type, which is 32-bit or 64-bit, x86, or other

- RAM, sometimes as minimum or recommended capacities

- Operating system and version

- Hard disk space available

- Software dependencies (Runtime and other frameworks or environments may be required to be present in order for the software to run.)

- Graphics and display

- Network access, if any

- Peripheral devices

Table 11-5   System Requirements

Requirement	Minimum	Recommended
Operating system	Windows 7, 8, or 10	Windows 8 or 10
	macOS X 10.5 and higher	macOS X 10.7 or higher

Requirement	Minimum	Recommended
Processor	1 GHz or above	Multicore 2GHz
Memory	2 GB	4 GB
Display resolution	1024×768	1024×768
Available HDD space	2 GB	8 GB
Network connection	High-speed Internet connection, 512 kbps	High-speed Internet connection, 1.5 Mbps
Java	Most recent version	Most recent version
Other	Adobe Flash for video playback	

Graphics Considerations (11.3.4.2)

Two popular types of graphic cards found on PCs are integrated and dedicated.

Integrated graphics chips are integrated on the motherboard or on the same die as the CPU. These graphics chips rely on the system RAM and share the same memory as the CPU.

For a graphics-intensive game or application, a dedicated graphics card with its own video RAM (VRAM) may be the better choice. A dedicated graphics card can simply be replaced when upgrading; however, these cards are usually more expensive and require more power, air circulation, and heat dissipation than the integrated version. Figure 11-107 shows an example of a dedicated GPU.

Figure 11-107   Dedicated Graphics Card

Installation Methods (11.3.4.3)

As a technician, you will be responsible for adding and removing software from your customers' computers. Most applications use an automatic installation process when the application disc is inserted in the optical drive. The user is required to click through the installation wizard and provide information when requested. Most Windows software installations are attended, meaning the user must be present to interact with the installer software to provide input about the options to use when installing the software. The various types of installations are defined in Table 11-6.

Table 11-6   Installation Methods

Method	Definition
Attended	A user must be present to respond to prompts from the installer software.
Silent, or *unattended*	No prompts or other information is displayed during installation.
Scheduled, or *automated*	Installation occurs without being started by a user. Preconfigured tasks that run according to conditions or timers can install software when appropriate.
Clean	All components of any previous version of the software have been removed prior to installation.
Network	The installation packages are available on a server, and the installation occurs across the network.

ISO Mountable (11.3.4.4)

An ISO image is a single file that represents all the data on an optical disc. An ISO is usually distributed via the Internet. For example, you can download the Windows 10 installation media from the official website of Microsoft, as shown in Figure 11-108. After the ISO image has been downloaded, its authenticity and integrity should be verified using a digital signature or a hash value provided by the source and scanned for malware.

The ISO image can be used to create installation media using a USB flash drive or optical media. Another option is to mount the ISO image directly on your PC as if it were an optical disc. Starting with Windows 10, no third-party tool is needed to mount an ISO image. Right-click the ISO file in File Explorer and select Mount, and the ISO file is assigned a drive letter. In Figure 11-109, the Windows 11 ISO is mounted as F:.

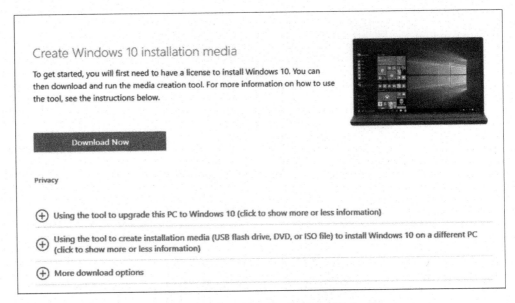

Figure 11-108 Windows 10 Installation Media Creation Dialog Box

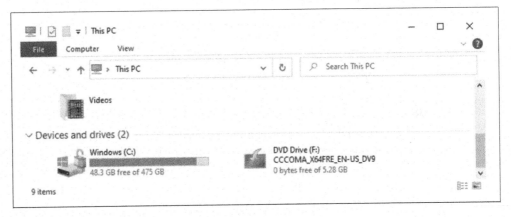

Figure 11-109 Devices and Drives in This PC

External Hardware Tokens (11.3.4.5)

An external hardware token is a portable security device that can be a smart card or a USB device. It provides a more secure multifactor authentication method when used in conjunction with a username and password. The hardware token stores cryptographic information that identifies the user. When the user requests access, the user presents the hardware token and supplies an authorization gesture, such as scanning a fingerprint (see Figure 11-110) or entering a PIN (see Figure 11-111) to gain access.

Figure 11-110   USB Fingerprint Scanner Hardware Token

Figure 11-111   PIN-Generating Hardware Token

Installing an Application (11.3.4.6)

Local installation can occur from the hard drive, CD, DVD, or USB media. To perform a local, attended installation, insert the media or drive or open the downloaded program file. Depending on the AutoPlay settings, the software installation process may not automatically start. If it doesn't, you need to browse the installation media in order to find and execute the installer. Installer software usually has an .exe or .msi (Microsoft Silent Installer) file extension.

Note that the user must have the appropriate permissions in order to install the software. The user must also not be blocked by a group policy that prevents software installation.

After the application is installed, you can run it from the Start menu or the application's shortcut icon on the desktop. Check the application to ensure that it is functioning properly. If there are problems, repair or uninstall the application. Some applications, such as Microsoft Office, provide a repair option within the installation program. In addition to the process described above, Windows 8 and 10 provide access to the Microsoft Store, where a user can search for and install apps on

Windows devices (see Figure 11-112). To open the Windows Store app, search from the Start screen taskbar by entering **Store**. Click the Store icon when it appears in the search results. The Windows Store app is not available in Windows 7.

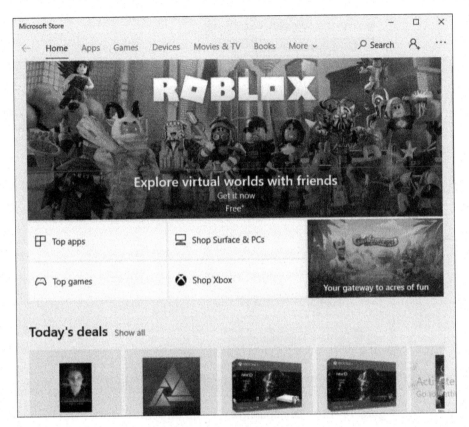

Figure 11-112   The Microsoft Store

Compatibility Mode (11.3.4.7)

Older applications may not run properly on newer Windows operating systems. Windows provides a way that these programs can be configured to run. If older software is not running properly, locate the executable file for the application. This can be done by right-clicking a shortcut for the application and selecting Open File Location. Right-click the executable file and choose Properties. From the Compatibility tab, shown in Figure 11-113, you can click Run Compatibility Troubleshooter or manually configure the environment for the application.

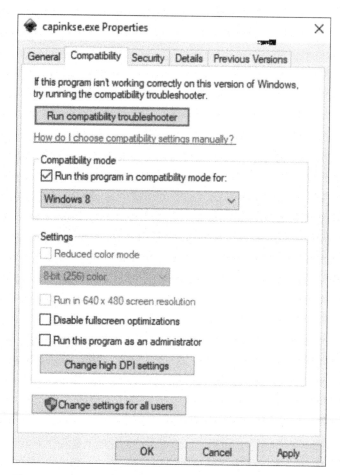

Figure 11-113   Configuring *Compatibility Mode*

Uninstalling or Changing a Program (11.3.4.8)

If an application is uninstalled incorrectly, you might be leaving files on the hard drive and unnecessary settings in the Registry, which wastes hard drive space and system resources. Unnecessary files might also reduce the speed at which the Registry is read. Microsoft recommends that you always use the Programs and Features Control Panel utility when removing, changing, or repairing applications. This utility guides you through the software removal process and removes every file that was installed, as shown in Figure 11-114.

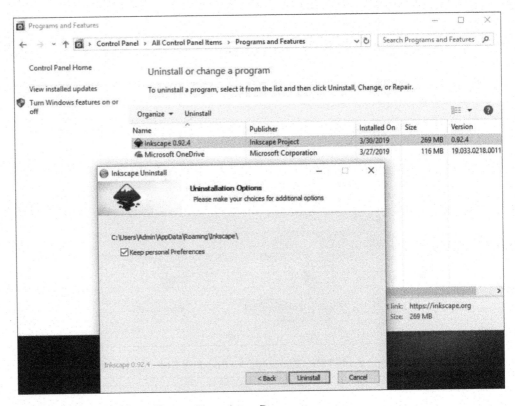

Figure 11-114   Uninstalling or Changing a Program

Some applications include an uninstall feature that is located in the Windows Start menu with the application.

11.3.4.9 Lab: Install Third-Party Software

In this lab, you will install and remove a third-party software application.

Security Considerations (11.3.4.10)

Allowing users to install software on computers that are owned by a business organization can be a security risk. Users can be tricked into downloading malicious software that can cause data loss, either through theft or destruction. Malicious software, known as malware, can infect all computers that are attached to a network and can cause widespread damage and loss. It is important for a technician to enforce policies regarding software installation and ensure that anti-malware software, such as *Windows Defender*, is active and up to date. Figure 11-115 shows the Windows 10 security dashboard.

Figure 11-115   Windows 10 Security Settings Dashboard

Other Considerations (11.3.4.11)

When deploying new third-party applications, potential impacts to operation and the business must be considered to maintain a secure computing environment.

Impacts to Operation

Deploying new applications to hundreds of workstations can be a time-consuming process. Automated deployment tools can save time by automatically deploying, updating, and supporting applications.

Organizations can use Windows deployment tools such as Group Policy to deploy applications to multiple workstations from a server. An administrator sets up the installer packages and copies the packages on the shared network folder for distribution. The administrator creates Group Policy Objects (GPOs) in the Group Policy Manager to deploy the application from the network shared folder to the eligible users without any further intervention from the administrator. When users power on the computers, the applications are installed and available.

By using deployment tools, the users are not required to log on with administrative privileges to install the applications. Users require only read and execute privileges, not full control, for the program's installation directory. Any custom settings or user files can be saved to the users' home folders instead of the program directory. This prevents users from accidentally modifying files related to the installed programs.

Impacts to the Business

Any application deployed in a business must be supported and maintained. These are some of the considerations:

- **Software licensing:** Software licensing establishes the number of devices that can have the software installed or the number of authorized users. Using unlicensed software can expose a business to legal and financial penalties.

- **Technical support:** Depending on the availability and technical expertise of the internal IT staff, some or all of the technical support may be outsourced to the software vendor. The vendor can provide paid technical support for updates and maintenance releases, monitor and fix security issues, and provide technical assistance. The impact to the business should be assessed for either support method.

- **User training:** Training on programs should be available to the users, if applicable. Training can be a recurring cost as the vendors deploy newer versions of the program or as part of the onboarding process for new employees. The program may also be supported by an internal team that requires more in-depth technical training to support and maintain the programs in a secure manner.

Interactive Graphic

11.3.4.12 Check Your Understanding: Application Installation and Configuration
Refer to the online course to complete this activity.

Command-Line Tools (11.4)

A number of command-line tools can be run using the Windows CLI. To use many of these tools, you must run the CLI as an administrator. This section examines the use of the Windows CLI and many command-line tools.

Using Windows CLI (11.4.1)

The command line is a text interface in Windows that can be used to enter commands, which the operating system then runs.

PowerShell (11.4.1.1)

The old Windows command line application was replaced in the Windows Power User menu **Win+X** with *PowerShell*. The original command line still exists in Windows 10 and can be opened by typing **cmd** into the search field on the taskbar. You can also change which command line is displayed in the menu by changing a taskbar setting.

PowerShell is a more powerful command line utility. It offers many advanced features, such as scripting and automation. It even comes with its own scripting development environment, called PowerShell ISE, to help with the task of writing scripts. PowerShell uses *cmdlets*, which are small applications that represent the commands that are available. PowerShell also allows naming of cmdlets with aliases, so the same cmdlet can be run at the command line with any name you choose to assign to it, as long as it adheres to the Microsoft naming conventions. Microsoft has created aliases for all of the old **cmd** commands so that PowerShell works much like the older command line.

Figure 11-116 shows Windows PowerShell ISE, with the PowerShell command line in the lower-left window. PowerShell can also be opened as the command line shell alone.

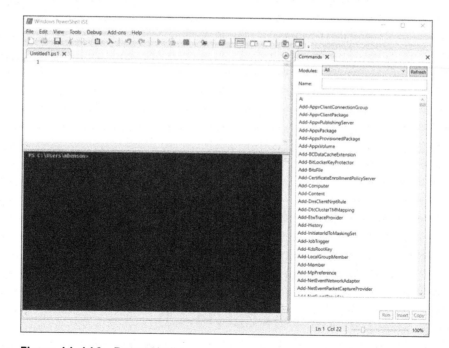

Figure 11-116   PowerShell

The Command Shell (11.4.1.2)

Windows has two command line utilities. One is the classic **command** application, known as *cmd*. This command line is a remnant of the very early days of Microsoft, when DOS was the only operating system that Microsoft had to offer. Many users were experienced with using **cmd**, so it was retained when Windows was developed. It persisted as the default command line for Windows until Windows 10 build 14791, when PowerShell became the default. To open the command shell, type **cmd** in the search box and click the app in the results. You can also press *Win+R* to open a run box. Type **cmd** in the run box and click OK. Press *Ctrl+Shift+Enter* to run the command prompt as an administrator. The title bar for the command window indicates that the command window is open in Administrator mode. Issuing the *whoami* command will display the computer name and the user account of the system where the command is being issued, as shown in Figure 11-117.

Figure 11-117   The Command Shell

The following sections focus on the **cmd** command line. All the commonly used commands are supported by Windows 7, 8, and 10.

Basic Commands (11.4.1.3)

This section lists basic Windows commands and keystrokes.

help

The *help* command, shown in Example 11-1, provides information on commands. Enter it by itself to see all available commands. Type **help** followed by a specific command to see information about that command.

Example 11-1   The **help** Command

```
Microsoft Windows [Version 10.0.18362.175]
(c) 2019 Microsoft Corporation. All rights reserved.


C:\Windows\System32> help
For more information on a specific command, type HELP command-name
ASSOC           Displays or modifies file extension associations.
ATTRIB          Displays or changes file attributes.
BREAK           Sets or clears extended CTRL+C checking.
BCDEDIT         Sets properties in boot database to control boot loading.
CACLS           Displays or modifies access control lists (ACLs) of files.
CALL            Calls one batch program from another.
CD              Displays the name of or changes the current directory.
CHCP            Displays or sets the active code page number.
CHDIR           Displays the name of or changes the current directory.
CHKDSK          Checks a disk and displays a status report.
CHKNTFS         Displays or modifies the checking of disk at boot time.
CLS             Clears the screen.
CMD             Starts a new instance of the Windows command interpreter.
COLOR           Sets the default console foreground and background colors.
COMP            Compares the contents of two files or sets of files.
COMPACT         Displays or alters the compression of files on NTFS partitions.
CONVERT         Converts FAT volumes to NTFS. You cannot convert the
                current drive.
COPY            Copies one or more files to another location.
DATE            Displays or sets the date.
(output omitted)
```

command /?

As an alternative to using the **help** command, get help on a specific command by using the command **/?**, as shown in Example 11-2. In this case, help is specified as a command option. All commands accept the **/?** option.

Example 11-2   Using **/?**

```
C:\Windows\System32> dir /?
Displays a list of files and subdirectories in a directory.

DIR [drive:][path][filename] [/A[[:]attributes]] [/B] [/C] [/D] [/L] [/N]
  [/O[[:]sortorder]] [/P] [/Q] [/R] [/S] [/T[[:]timefield]] [/W] [/X] [/4]
[drive:][path][filename]
```

```
                        Specifies drive, directory, and/or files to list.
/A                      Displays files with specified attributes.
attributes              D  Directories                 R    Read-only files
                        H  Hidden files                A    Files ready for archiving
                        S System files                 I    Not content indexed files
                        L Reparse Points               O    Offline files
                        - Prefix meaning not
/B                      Uses bare format (no heading information or summary).
/C                      Display the thousand separator in file sizes. This is the
                        default. Use /-C to disable display of separator.
/D                      Same as wide but files are list sorted by column.
/L                      Uses lowercase.
/N                      New long list format where filenames are on the far right.
/O                      List by files in sorted order.
sortorder               N  By name (alphabetic)        S By size (smallest first)
                        E By extension (alphabetic)    D By date/time (oldest first)
                        G Group directories first      - Prefix to reverse order
/P                      Pauses after each screenful of information.
/Q                      Display the owner of the file.
/R                      Display alternate data streams of the file.
/S                      Displays files in specified directory and all subdirectories.
/T                      Controls which time field displayed or used for sorting
(output omitted)
```

cls

Clear the screen with *cls*, as shown in Example 11-3. This command deletes all command output and moves the command prompt to the top of the command window.

Example 11-3   Clearing the Screen

```
C:\Windows\System32>cls /?
Clears the screen.

CLS

C:\Windows\System32>cls
```

Up-Arrow Key

Use the *up-arrow key* to move through previously entered commands. Previously entered commands are saved in the history buffer. The up-arrow key moves through the previously entered commands. If you type a command incorrectly, you can use the up-arrow key to recall it to the command line and edit it to correct it before executing.

F7 Key

You can also display command history in an overlay window by using the *F7 key*. As shown in Figure 11-118, it displays a list of the commands previously entered. Use the arrow keys to select a previously entered command and press **Enter** to execute it. Use **Esc** to hide the window.

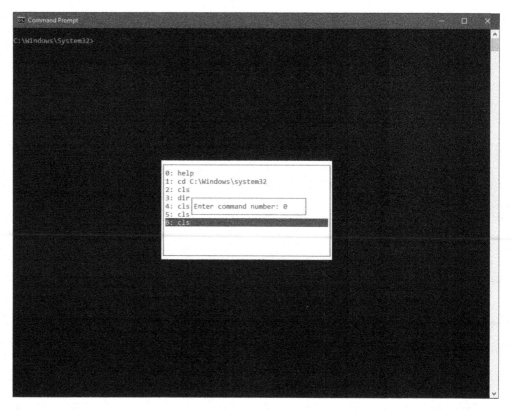

Figure 11-118   Using the F7 Key

Ctrl+C Key Combination

Use the key combination *Ctrl+C* to exit a running command process or script.

exit

Type *exit* to close the command window.

11.4.1.4 Video Demonstration: Managing CLI Sessions

Working at a command line might be new to some people. Refer to the online course to see a demonstration of how it is done.

11.4.1.5 Lab: Work in the Windows Command Shell

In this lab, you will practice techniques for working in the Windows command shell.

11.4.1.6 Check Your Understanding: Basic Command Line Commands

Refer to the online course to complete this activity.

File System CLI Commands (11.4.2)

CLI commands can be used to navigate the Windows file system. This section examines some of these commands.

Command Syntax Conventions (11.4.2.1)

It is important to be able to use technical resources to learn how to use CLI commands. Different software vendors and organizations use different conventions to indicate syntax for commands. Microsoft provides an online command reference. Table 11-7 summarizes many conventions used by Microsoft for CLI commands.

Table 11-7   Command Syntax Conventions

Notation	Description
Text without brackets or braces	Syntax that must be typed exactly as shown
<Text inside angle brackets>	A value that must be supplied
[Text inside square brackets]	Optional input
{Text inside braces}	A list of items from which one must be chosen
Vertical bar (|)	Mutually exclusive items
Ellipsis (…)	Repeatable input

Special characters called *wildcards* can be substituted for characters or groups of characters in filenames. You can use wildcards when you know only part of a filename that you are trying to find or when you want to perform a file operation on a group of files that share elements of a filename or an extension. The two wildcards that can be used at the Windows command line are:

- **The asterisk (*):** This character matches groups of characters, including entire filenames and file extensions. The asterisk (commonly called the star) matches any character that is permitted in a filename and also matches any group of characters. For example, myfile.* matches files that are called myfile with any file extension. The asterisk can be used with a pattern of characters, too. For example, my*.txt matches all filenames that start with my and have the .txt extension. Finally, *.* matches any filename with any extension.

- **The question mark (?):** This character stands for any single character. It does not stand for a group of characters. For example, to match myfile.txt using the question mark, you would need to use my????.txt, which matches filenames that start with my followed by any four characters and then a .txt file extension.

File System Navigation (11.4.2.2)

When working at the command line, there is no File Explorer to help you get to the files and folders that you want to work with. Instead, you need to move through the folder structure by using a combination of commands, normally displaying the contents of a drive or directory and changing directories until you find what you are looking for.

File System Navigation - Commands (11.4.2.3)

For file system navigation at the command line, you can change drives, list contents, and change directories.

<Drive>:

To change drives, simply type the drive letter followed by a colon at the command prompt. Example 11-4 shows directories displayed for the C: drive, and then the drive is changed, and a directory is displayed for the D: drive.

Example 11-4   Displaying Contents of a Different Drive

```
C:\myFolders> dir
Volume in drive C is Windows
Volume Serial Number is 9C9E-C3F4


 Directory of C:\myFolders


04/04/2019  04:34 PM    <DIR>              .
04/04/2019  04:34 PM    <DIR>              ..
04/04/2019  04:37 PM    <DIR>              newfolder_2
               0 File(s)              0 bytes
```

```
             3 Dir(s)    133,658,624,000 bytes free

C:\myFolders> d:
D:\> dir
 Volume in drive D is ADATA DRIVE
 Volume Serial Number is CCD9-AB77


Directory of D:\
03/28/2019  06:37 PM      <DIR>             iso
02/06/2019  04:52 PM       5,075,539,968 Win10_1809Oct_English_x64.iso
02/15/2019  02:23 PM       3,320,903,680 Win7_Pro_SP1_English_x64.iso
02/07/2019  10:57 AM       4,320,641,024 Win8.1_English_x64_no_reg.iso
               3 File(s)  12,717,084,672 bytes
               1 Dir(s)   14,903,140,352 bytes free
D:\>
-------
```

dir

The *dir* command has the following syntax:

```
dir [<drive>:] [<path>] [<filename>]
```

The **dir** command has the following options to display various file attributes and properties:

- /a: Displays files with attributes by including the attribute type

- /os: Sorts files by size

- /b: Lists file and folder names only

- /w: Displays wide view, with files and folders arranged in columns

Options also change how the file list is displayed. Type **dir /?** to obtain help with the **dir** command syntax.

Example 11-5 demonstrates output from the **dir** command.

Example 11-5 Displaying the Contents of the Current Drive

```
C:\myFolders> dir
 Volume in drive C is Windows
 Volume Serial Number is 9C9E-C3F4


 Directory of C:\myFolders
04/04/2019  05:10 PM      <DIR>          .
04/04/2019  05:10 PM      <DIR>          ..
04/04/2019  05:10 PM                   6 newfile1.txt
```

```
04/04/2019   05:10 PM     <DIR>              newFolder_1
04/04/2019   04:37 PM     <DIR>              newFolder_2
                1 File(s)             6 bytes
                4 Dir(s)   133,548,445,696 bytes free


C:\myFolders>
```

cd

Use the *cd* command to change the current directory to the path specified after the command. The **cd** command has the following syntax:

```
cd [/d] [<drive>:] [<path>]
```

The **cd** command can be used with the following options:

- **<*drive*>:** Displays the root directory of another drive
- **/d:** Changes the drive and directory
- **.:** Refers to the current path
- **.. (two dots):** Goes up the path one level
- **\:** Goes to the root of the drive

Example 11-6 shows the **cd** command in action.

Example 11-6   Changing Directory

```
C:\Users> dir
 Volume in drive C has no label.
 Volume Serial Number is 5A1B-98AA


 Directory of C:\Users


03/14/2019   01:53 PM     <DIR>              .
03/14/2019   01:53 PM     <DIR>              ..
04/04/2019   06:12 PM     <DIR>              Admin
04/04/2019   03:34 PM     <DIR>              basic_user
04/02/2019   03:18 PM     <DIR>              drbon
03/06/2019   11:08 AM     <DIR>              Public
                0 File(s)             0 bytes
                6 Dir(s)   36,035,579,904 bytes free


C:\Users> cd Admin
C:\Users\Admin> dir
 Volume in drive C has no label.
 Volume Serial Number is 5A1B-98AA
```

```
 Directory of C:\Users\Admin
04/04/2019  06:12 PM    <DIR>          .
04/04/2019  06:12 PM    <DIR>          ..
03/14/2019  11:51 AM    <DIR>          3D Objects
03/14/2019  11:51 AM    <DIR>          Contacts
04/02/2019  06:15 PM    <DIR>          data2
03/15/2019  01:08 PM    <DIR>          Desktop
04/03/2019  09:31 AM    <DIR>          Documents
04/02/2019  08:59 AM    <DIR>          Downloads
03/14/2019  11:51 AM    <DIR>          Favorites
04/02/2019  07:50 AM    <DIR>          Level_1
03/14/2019  11:51 AM    <DIR>          Links
04/03/2019  09:31 AM    <DIR>          Music
03/27/2019  12:17 PM    <DIR>          OneDrive
03/14/2019  03:11 PM    <DIR>          Pictures
03/14/2019  11:51 AM    <DIR>          Saved Games
03/14/2019  12:05 PM    <DIR>          Searches
04/03/2019  09:31 AM    <DIR>          Videos
               0 File(s)              0 bytes
              17 Dir(s)   36,035,579,904 bytes free

C:\Users\Admin>
```

Video

11.4.2.4 Video Demonstration: Working with Files and Folders

Refer to the online course to view this video.

Manipulating Folders - Commands (11.4.2.5)

You can create, move, and remove folders by using the command line.

md

Use *md* to create a new directory, as shown in Example 11-7. The syntax for **md** is as follows:

md [<*drive*>:]<*path*>

When you use **md**, you make a new directory at the location specified. If you don't provide a drive and path, the new directory is created at the current location. Example 11-7 shows output from the **md** command.

Example 11-7   The **md** Command

```
C:\myFolders> dir
  Volume in drive C is Windows
  Volume Serial Number is 9C9E-C3F4
```

```
       Directory of C:\myFolders

04/04/2019  03:56 PM      <DIR>              .
04/04/2019  03:56 PM      <DIR>              ..
                0 File(s)                0 bytes
                2 Dir(s)   133,642,625,024 bytes free

C:\myFolders> md New_Folder

C:\myFolders> dir
 Volume in drive C is Windows
 Volume Serial Number is 9C9E-C3F4

 Directory of C:\myFolders

04/04/2019  04:21 PM      <DIR>              .
04/04/2019  04:21 PM      <DIR>              ..
04/04/2019  04:21 PM      <DIR>              New_Folder
                0 File(s)                0 bytes
                3 Dir(s)   133,642,625,024 bytes free

C:\myFolders>
```

rd

Use the *rd* command to delete a directory. The syntax for the **rd** command is as follows:

```
rd [<drive>:]<path>
```

The **rd** command can be used with the following options:

- **/s:** Removes all subdirectories and files if the directory is empty. When using this option, use caution to be sure that all the subdirectories are intended to be deleted along with the parent.

- **/q:** Enters quiet mode, which means the command does not request user confirmation when deleting subdirectories and files. Use with caution!

Example 11-8 shows the **rd** command in action.

Example 11-8   The **rd** Command

```
C:\myFolders> dir
 Volume in drive C is Windows
 Volume Serial Number is 9C9E-C3F4

 Directory of C:\myFolders
04/04/2019  04:21 PM      <DIR>              .
```

```
04/04/2019  04:21 PM      <DIR>           ..
04/04/2019  04:21 PM      <DIR>           New_Folder
               0 File(s)               0 bytes
               3 Dir(s) 133,639,602,176 bytes free


C:\myFolders> rd New_folder

C:\myFolders> dir
 Volume in drive C is Windows
 Volume Serial Number is 9C9E-C3F4

 Directory of C:\myFolders


04/04/2019  04:27 PM      <DIR>           .
04/04/2019  04:27 PM      <DIR>           ..
               0 File(s)               0 bytes
               2 Dir(s) 133,639,602,176 bytes free


C:\myFolders>
```

move

Use the *move* command to move a file or directory from one directory to another. The syntax of the **move** command is as follows:

```
move [source][target]
```

The source can be in the current folder, but the destination must be another folder. Full paths, including different drives, can be supplied. Example 11-9 demonstrates the **move** command.

Example 11-9   The **move** Command

```
C:\myFolders> dir
 Volume in drive C is Windows
 Volume Serial Number is 9C9E-C3F4

 Directory of C:\myFolders


04/04/2019  04:33 PM      <DIR>           .
04/04/2019  04:33 PM      <DIR>           ..
04/04/2019  04:33 PM      <DIR>           newfolder_1
04/04/2019  04:33 PM      <DIR>           newfolder_2
               0 File(s)               0 bytes
               4 Dir(s)  133,645,930,496 bytes free
```

```
C:\myFolders> move newfolder_1 newfolder_2
         1 dir(s) moved.
C:\myFolders> cd newfolder_2

C:\myFolders\newfolder_2> dir
 Volume in drive C is Windows
 Volume Serial Number is 9C9E-C3F4

 Directory of C:\myFolders\newfolder_2

04/04/2019  04:34 PM    <DIR>             .
04/04/2019  04:34 PM    <DIR>             ..
04/04/2019  04:33 PM    <DIR>             newfolder_1
               0 File(s)              0 bytes
               3 Dir(s)   133,646,000,128 bytes free

C:\myFolders\newfolder_2>
```

ren

Use the *ren* command to rename a directory or file. The **ren** command uses the following syntax:

```
ren [path:old name] [new name]
```

When using **ren**, the renamed folder must appear in the same folder as the original. Example 11-10 demonstrates the **ren** command.

Example 11-10 The **ren** Command

```
C:\myFolders\newfolder_2> dir
 Volume in drive C is Windows
 Volume Serial Number is 9C9E-C3F4

 Directory of C:\myFolders\newfolder_2

04/04/2019  04:34 PM    <DIR>             .
04/04/2019  04:34 PM    <DIR>             ..
04/04/2019  04:33 PM    <DIR>             newfolder_1
               0 File(s)              0 bytes
               3 Dir(s)   133,540,413,440 bytes free

C:\myFolders\newfolder_2> ren newfolder_1 newfolder

C:\myFolders\newfolder_2> dir
 Volume in drive C is Windows
 Volume Serial Number is 9C9E-C3F4
```

```
 Directory of C:\myFolders\newfolder_2


04/04/2019  04:37 PM    <DIR>            .
04/04/2019  04:37 PM    <DIR>            ..
04/04/2019  04:33 PM    <DIR>            newfolder
               0 File(s)              0 bytes
               3 Dir(s)   133,540,274,176 bytes free


C:\myFolders\newfolder_2>
```

Manipulating Files - Commands (11.4.2.6)

You can manipulate files in a variety of ways, as described in the sections that follow.

> symbol

Use the **>** symbol to send the output of a command to a file. Because the output is redirected, it does not display on the screen, as shown in Example 11-11.

Example 11-11   Directing Output to a File

```
C:\Users\Admin\Documents> dir > directory.txt


C:\Users\Admin\Documents> dir
 Volume in drive C has no label.
 Volume Serial Number is 5A1B-98AA


 Directory of C:\Users\Admin\Documents


04/05/2019  10:23 AM    <DIR>            .
04/05/2019  10:23 AM    <DIR>            ..
04/05/2019  10:23 AM                761 directory.txt
03/27/2019  08:34 AM    <DIR>            Fax
04/02/2019  07:50 AM              5,740 help.txt
03/14/2019  12:24 PM    <DIR>            Level 1
03/29/2019  07:05 AM    <DIR>            mounted docs
04/02/2019  06:56 AM                 22 myfile.txt
03/27/2019  08:34 AM    <DIR>            Scanned Documents
04/03/2019  09:31 AM    <DIR>            Sound recordings
03/27/2019  02:20 PM          1,351,034 test.nfo
               4 File(s)      1,357,557 bytes
               7 Dir(s)   35,931,115,520 bytes free


C:\Users\Admin\Documents>
```

type

The *type* command displays the contents of a file. The syntax for **type** is as follows:

```
type [<drive>:][<path>] <filename>
```

The **type** command is a very simple command for displaying the contents of a text file, as shown in Example 11-12. If the filename has spaces in it, use quotes around it. Combine it with a pipe character (|) and **more** to display one screen at a time.

Example 11-12 The **type** Command

```
C:\Users\Admin\Documents> type directory.txt
 Volume in drive C has no label.
 Volume Serial Number is 5A1B-98AA

 Directory of C:\Users\Admin\Documents

04/05/2019  10:23 AM    <DIR>          .
04/05/2019  10:23 AM    <DIR>          ..
04/05/2019  10:23 AM                 0 directory.txt
03/27/2019  08:34 AM    <DIR>          Fax
04/02/2019  07:50 AM             5,740 help.txt
03/14/2019  12:24 PM    <DIR>          Level 1
03/29/2019  07:05 AM    <DIR>          mounted docs
04/02/2019  06:56 AM                22 myfile.txt
03/27/2019  08:34 AM    <DIR>          Scanned Documents
04/03/2019  09:31 AM    <DIR>          Sound recordings
03/27/2019  02:20 PM         1,351,034 test.nfo
               4 File(s)      1,356,796 bytes
               7 Dir(s)  35,931,115,520 bytes free

C:\Users\Admin\Documents>
```

more

The *more* command displays the contents of a file one screen at a time. The syntax for **more** is as follows:

```
more [<drive>:][<path>] <filename>
```

more can be used directly as a command to view a file one screen at a time, as shown in Example 11-13.

Example 11-13 The **more** Command

```
C:\Users\Admin\Documents> more help.txt
For more information on a specific command, type HELP command-name
ASSOC          Displays or modifies file extension associations.
```

```
ATTRIB           Displays or changes file attributes.
BREAK            Sets or clears extended CTRL+C checking.
BCDEDIT          Sets properties in boot database to control boot loading.
CACLS            Displays or modifies access control lists (ACLs) of files.
CALL             Calls one batch program from another.
CD               Displays the name of or changes the current directory.
CHCP             Displays or sets the active code page number.
CHDIR            Displays the name of or changes the current directory.
CHKDSK           Checks a disk and displays a status report.
CHKNTFS          Displays or modifies the checking of disk at boot time.
CLS              Clears the screen.
CMD              Starts a new instance of the Windows command interpreter.
COLOR            Sets the default console foreground and background colors.
COMP             Compares the contents of two files or sets of files.
COMPACT          Displays or alters the compression of files on NTFS partitions.
CONVERT          Converts FAT volumes to NTFS. You cannot convert the
                 current drive.
COPY             Copies one or more files to another location.
DATE             Displays or sets the date.
DEL              Deletes one or more files.
DIR              Displays a list of files and subdirectories in a directory.
DISKPART         Displays or configures Disk Partition properties.
DOSKEY           Edits command lines, recalls Windows commands, and
                 creates macros.
DRIVERQUERY      Displays current device driver status and properties.
ECHO             Displays messages, or turns command echoing on or off.
ENDLOCAL         Ends localization of environment changes in a batch file.
ERASE            Deletes one or more files.
EXIT             Quits the CMD.EXE program (command interpreter).
FC               Compares two files or sets of files, and displays the
                 differences between them.
-- More (35%) --
```

del

Use the *del* command to delete a file or folder. The syntax for **del** is as follows:

```
del <names>
```

The **del** command, shown in Example 11-14, can take a list of files or folders and wildcards. Files deleted with this command are not normally recoverable. Parameters allow deletion of files with specific attributes.

Example 11-14 The **del** Command

```
C:\Users\Admin\Documents> dir *.txt
 Volume in drive C has no label.
 Volume Serial Number is 5A1B-98AA

 Directory of C:\Users\Admin\Documents

04/05/2019  10:48 AM                    712 directory.txt
04/05/2019  10:48 AM                  5,740 help.txt
04/02/2019  06:56 AM                     22 myfile.txt
               3 File(s)          6,474 bytes
               0 Dir(s)  35,955,425,280 bytes free

C:\Users\Admin\Documents> del help.txt, directory.txt

C:\Users\Admin\Documents> dir *.txt
 Volume in drive C has no label.
 Volume Serial Number is 5A1B-98AA

 Directory of C:\Users\Admin\Documents

04/02/2019  06:56 AM                     22 myfile.txt
               1 File(s)             22 bytes
               0 Dir(s) 35,955,437,568 bytes free

C:\Users\Admin\Documents>
```

copy

The *copy* command makes a copy of a file. The syntax for **copy** is as follows:

```
copy <source> [<destination>]
```

You can use this command to copy a file to the destination filename and location.
The same folder as the source is the default if no path is specified, as shown in Example 11-15. Many parameters provide flexibility to the command.

Example 11-15 The **copy** Command

```
C:\Users\Admin\Documents> dir
 Volume in drive C has no label.
 Volume Serial Number is 5A1B-98AA

 Directory of C:\Users\Admin\Documents

04/05/2019  10:48 AM    <DIR>          .
04/05/2019  10:48 AM    <DIR>          ..
03/27/2019  08:34 AM    <DIR>          Fax
03/14/2019  12:24 PM    <DIR>          Level 1
03/29/2019  07:05 AM    <DIR>          mounted docs
```

```
04/02/2019  06:56 AM                      22 myfile.txt
03/27/2019  08:34 AM    <DIR>                Scanned Documents
04/03/2019  09:31 AM    <DIR>                Sound recordings
03/27/2019  02:20 PM              1,351,034 test.nfo
                 2 File(s)        1,351,056 bytes
                 7 Dir(s)    35,955,691,520 bytes free

C:\Users\Admin\Documents> copy myfile.txt myfile2.txt
 1 file(s) copied.

C:\Users\Admin\Documents> dir
 Volume in drive C has no label.
 Volume Serial Number is 5A1B-98AA

Directory of C:\Users\Admin\Documents

04/05/2019  10:51 AM    <DIR>                .
04/05/2019  10:51 AM    <DIR>                ..
03/27/2019  08:34 AM    <DIR>                Fax
03/14/2019  12:24 PM    <DIR>                Level 1
03/29/2019  07:05 AM    <DIR>                mounted docs
04/02/2019  06:56 AM                      22 myfile.txt
04/02/2019  06:56 AM                      22 myfile2.txt
03/27/2019  08:34 AM    <DIR>                Scanned Documents
04/03/2019  09:31 AM    <DIR>                Sound recordings
03/27/2019  02:20 PM              1,351,034 test.nfo
                 3 File(s)        1,351,078 bytes
                 7 Dir(s)    35,955,490,816 bytes free

C:\Users\Admin\Documents>
```

xcopy

Use the *xcopy* command to copy files or entire directory trees. The syntax for **xcopy** is as follows:

```
xcopy <source> <destination>
```

The **xcopy** command offers a powerful way to copy files and directories with many useful options, as shown in Example 11-16.

Example 11-16   The xcopy Command

```
C:\Users\Admin\Documents> xcopy /? | more
Copies files and directory trees.

XCOPY source [destination] [/A | /M] [/D[:date]] [/P] [/S [/E]] [/V] [/W]
                              [/C] [/I] [/Q] [/F] [/L] [/G] [/H] [/R] [/T] [/U]
```

```
                                [/K] [/N] [/O] [/X] [/Y] [/-Y] [/Z] [/B] [/J]
                                [/EXCLUDE:file1[+file2][+file3]...]

source         Specifies the file(s) to copy.
destination    Specifies the location and/or name of new files.
/A             Copies only files with the archive attribute set,
               doesn't change the attribute.
/M             Copies only files with the archive attribute set,
               turns off the archive attribute.
/D:m-d-y       Copies files changed on or after the specified date.
               If no date is given, copies only those files whose
               source time is newer than the destination time.
/EXCLUDE:file1[+file2][+file3]...
               Specifies a list of files containing strings. Each string
               should be in a separate line in the files. When any of the
               strings match any part of the absolute path of the file to be
               copied, that file will be excluded from being copied. For
               example, specifying a string like \obj\ or .obj will exclude
               all files underneath the directory obj or all files with the
               .obj extension respectively.
/P             Prompts you before creating each destination file.
/S             Copies directories and subdirectories except empty ones.
/E             Copies directories and subdirectories, including empty ones.
               Same as /S /E. May be used to modify /T.
/V             Verifies the size of each new file.
/W             Prompts you to press a key before copying.
/C             Continues copying even if errors occur.
/I             If destination does not exist and copying more than one file,
               assumes that destination must be a directory.
/Q             Does not display file names while copying.
/F             Displays full source and destination file names while copying.
/L             Displays files that would be copied.
/G             Allows the copying of encrypted files to destination that does
               not support encryption.
/H             Copies hidden and system files also.
/R             Overwrites read-only files.
/T             Creates directory structure, but does not copy files. Does not
               include empty directories or subdirectories. /T /E includes
               empty directories and subdirectories.
/U             Copies only files that already exist in destination.
-- More --
```

robocopy

Microsoft now recommends the use of *robocopy* instead of **xcopy**. The syntax for **robocopy** is as follows:

```
robocopy <source> <destination>
```

This command is extremely powerful, and you can use many options to specify how files are copied, the types of files to include in the copy action, and the file attributes to include for the destination files, as shown in Example 11-17.

Example 11-17   The **robocopy** Command

```
C:\Users\Admin\Documents> robocopy /? | more
-------------------------------------------------------------------------------
   ROBOCOPY     ::     Robust File Copy for Windows
-------------------------------------------------------------------------------

   Started : Friday, April 5, 2019 11:12:55 AM
               Usage :: ROBOCOPY source destination [file [file]...] [options]

             source :: Source Directory (drive:\path or \\server\share\path).
             destination :: Destination Dir (drive:\path or \\server\share\
   path).
                  file :: File(s) to copy (names/wildcards: default is "*.*").


::
:: Copy options :
::
                  /S :: copy Subdirectories, but not empty ones.
                  /E :: copy subdirectories, including Empty ones.
              /LEV:n :: only copy the top n LEVels of the source directory tree.

                  /Z :: copy files in restartable mode.
                  /B :: copy files in Backup mode.
                 /ZB :: use restartable mode; if access denied use Backup mode.
                  /J :: copy using unbuffered I/O (recommended for large files).
              /EFSRAW :: copy all encrypted files in EFS RAW mode.

   /COPY:copyflag[s] :: what to COPY for files (default is /COPY:DAT).
                        (copyflags : D=Data, A=Attributes, T=Timestamps).
                        (S=Security=NTFS ACLs, O=Owner info, U=aUditing info).

                /SEC :: copy files with SECurity (equivalent to /COPY:DATS).
             /COPYALL :: COPY ALL file info (equivalent to /COPY:DATSOU).
              /NOCOPY :: COPY NO file info (useful with /PURGE).
              /SECFIX :: FIX file SECurity on all files, even skipped files.

              /TIMFIX :: FIX file TIMes on all files, even skipped files.
               /PURGE :: delete dest files/dirs that no longer exist in source.
                 /MIR :: MIRror a directory tree (equivalent to /E plus /PURGE).

                 /MOV :: MOVe files (delete from source after copying).
                /MOVE :: MOVE files AND dirs (delete from source after copying).
-- More --
```

11.4.2.7 Lab: File System Commands

In this lab, you will work with file system commands.

Interactive Graphic

11.4.2.8 Check Your Understanding: File System CLI Commands

Refer to the online course to complete this activity.

Disk CLI Commands (11.4.3)

Using the CLI can be a good alternative to using GUI-based disk management tools. The CLI can be especially useful if Windows is experiencing boot problems.

Disk Operations - Commands (11.4.3.1)

The command line can be used to perform disk operations similar to those available in the Windows Disk Management utility.

chkdsk

The *chkdsk* command, which requires Administrator privileges, checks a file system for errors, including errors with physical media. It can repair some file system errors. The syntax for the **chkdsk** command is as follows:

```
chkdsk <volume> <path> <filename>
```

The **chkdsk** command can be used with the following options:

- **/f**: Fixes disk errors, recovers bad sectors, and recovers readable information

- **/r**: Does the same as **/f** but fixes physical errors, if possible

Example 11-18 shows an example of running the **chkdsk** command.

Example 11-18   The chkdsk Command

```
C:\Users\Admin\Documents> chkdsk e:
The type of the file system is NTFS.
Volume label is New Volume.

WARNING! /F parameter not specified.
Running CHKDSK in read-only mode.

Stage 1: Examining basic file system structure ...
  256 file records processed.
File verification completed.
  0 large file records processed.
```

```
    0 bad file records processed.

Stage 2: Examining file name linkage ...
  278 index entries processed.
Index verification completed.
  0 unindexed files scanned.
  0 unindexed files recovered to lost and found.
  0 reparse records processed.
  0 reparse records processed.

Stage 3: Examining security descriptors ...
Security descriptor verification completed.
  11 data files processed.


Windows has scanned the file system and found no problems.
No further action is required.

  10238975 KB total disk space.
     17472 KB in 7 files.
        72 KB in 13 indexes.
         0 KB in bad sectors.
     17371 KB in use by the system.
     16384 KB occupied by the log file.
  10204060 KB available on disk.
      4096 bytes in each allocation unit.
   2559743 total allocation units on disk.
   2551015 allocation units available on disk.

C:\Users\Admin\Documents>
```

format

The *format* command, which requires Administrator privileges, creates a new file system for a disk. It can also check for physical disk errors. The syntax for the **format** command is as follows:

```
format <volume>
```

The **format** command must be used on a new disk or a disk that was used with a different file system.

Options allow specification of various file system parameters:

- **/q:** Does a quick format, without scanning for bad areas

- **/v:** Specifies the volume name (label)

- **/fs:** Specifies the file system

Example 11-19 shows the results of running the **format** command.

Example 11-19 The **format** Command

```
C:\Users\Admin\Documents> format e:
The type of the file system is NTFS.
Enter current volume label for drive E: New Volume


WARNING, ALL DATA ON NON-REMOVABLE DISK
DRIVE E: WILL BE LOST!
Proceed with Format (Y/N)? y
Formatting 9.8 GB
Volume label (32 characters, ENTER for none)?
Creating file system structures.
Format complete.
          9.8 GB total disk space.
          9.7 GB are available.


C:\Users\Admin\Documents>
```

diskpart

The *diskpart* command, which requires Administrator privileges, starts a separate command interpreter with commands for working with disk partitions. This command opens its own command prompt, under which many of the functions of the Windows Disk Management utility can be performed. Use the **help** command to see all the available commands, as shown in Example 11-20.

Example 11-20 The **diskpart** Command

```
C:\Users\Admin\Documents> diskpart

Microsoft DiskPart version 10.0.17763.1

Copyright (C) Microsoft Corporation.
On computer: DESKTOP-34F7VBO

DISKPART> help

Microsoft DiskPart version 10.0.17763.1
```

```
ACTIVE        - Mark the selected partition as active.
ADD           - Add a mirror to a simple volume.
ASSIGN        - Assign a drive letter or mount point to the selected volume.
ATTRIBUTES    - Manipulate volume or disk attributes.
ATTACH        - Attaches a virtual disk file.
AUTOMOUNT     - Enable and disable automatic mounting of basic volumes.
BREAK         - Break a mirror set.
CLEAN         - Clear the configuration information, or all information, off the
                  disk.
COMPACT       - Attempts to reduce the physical size of the file.
CONVERT       - Convert between different disk formats.
CREATE        - Create a volume, partition or virtual disk.
DELETE        - Delete an object.
DETAIL        - Provide details about an object.
DETACH        - Detaches a virtual disk file.
EXIT          - Exit DiskPart.
EXTEND        - Extend a volume.
EXPAND        - Expands the maximum size available on a virtual disk.
FILESYSTEMS   - Display current and supported file systems on the volume.
FORMAT        - Format the volume or partition.
GPT           - Assign attributes to the selected GPT partition.
HELP          - Display a list of commands.
IMPORT        - Import a disk group.
INACTIVE      - Mark the selected partition as inactive.
LIST          - Display a list of objects.
MERGE         - Merges a child disk with its parents.
ONLINE        - Online an object that is currently marked as offline.
OFFLINE       - Offline an object that is currently marked as online.
RECOVER       - Refreshes the state of all disks in the selected pack.
                  Attempts recovery on disks in the invalid pack, and
                  resynchronizes mirrored volumes and RAID5 volumes
                  that have stale plex or parity data.
REM           - Does nothing. This is used to comment scripts.
REMOVE        - Remove a drive letter or mount point assignment.
REPAIR        - Repair a RAID-5 volume with a failed member.
RESCAN        - Rescan the computer looking for disks and volumes.
RETAIN        - Place a retained partition under a simple volume.
SAN           - Display or set the SAN policy for the currently booted OS.
SELECT        - Shift the focus to an object.
SETID         - Change the partition type.
SHRINK        - Reduce the size of the selected volume.
UNIQUEID      - Displays or sets the GUID partition table (GPT) identifier or
                  master boot record (MBR) signature of a disk.


DISKPART>
```

11.4.3.2 Lab: Disk CLI Commands

In this lab, you will work with disk CLI commands.

11.4.3.3 Check Your Understanding: Disk Operations Commands

Refer to the online course to complete this activity.

Task and System CLI Commands (11.4.4)

The commands examined in this section are used to do operating system tasks from a command line interface instead of the graphical Windows interface.

System CLI Commands (11.4.4.1)

Task operations commands provide functions similar to those found in Task Manager. System operation commands affect the Windows system.

tasklist

The *tasklist* command displays a list of the processes that are currently running on the local computer or a remote computer, as shown as Example 11-21.

Options concern the format and filtering of the output of the command and connecting to other PCs on the network.

Running processes are identified by their process IDs (PIDs).

Example 11-21   The **tasklist** Command

```
C:\Windows\System32> tasklist | more

Image Name                    PID   Session Name     Session#   Mem Usage
========================= ======== ================ ========== ===========
System Idle Process           0   Services           0          8 K
System                        4   Services           0       12,112 K
Registry                    120   Services           0       73,672 K
smss.exe                    476   Services           0          328 K
csrss.exe                   792   Services           0        2,100 K
csrss.exe                   912   Console            1        2,848 K
wininit.exe                 936   Services           0        1,032 K
winlogon.exe                980   Console            1        2,224 K
services.exe                344   Services           0        9,408 K
lsass.exe                   528   Services           0       16,428 K
svchost.exe                 908   Services           0        1,188 K
svchost.exe                 584   Services           0       31,500 K
```

```
fontdrvhost.exe              1032   Console             1      7,888 K
fontdrvhost.exe              1040   Services            0      1,128 K
svchost.exe                  1124   Services            0     21,480 K
svchost.exe                  1176   Services            0      3,100 K
dwm.exe                      1240   Console             1     90,168 K
svchost.exe                  1284   Services            0      2,096 K
svchost.exe                  1356   Services            0      2,276 K
svchost.exe                  1436   Services            0      1,552 K
svchost.exe                  1476   Services            0      4,648 K
svchost.exe                  1520   Services            0      4,912 K
-- More --
```

taskkill

The *taskkill* command, shown in Example 11-22, allows you to kill a running process. The syntax for the **taskkill** command is as follows:

```
taskkill [/pid <ProcessID> | /im <ImageName>]
```

Some options include the following:

- **/pid**: Specifies a task to kill by process ID
- **/im**: Specifies a task to kill by image name (name of the process)
- **/f**: Forcefully terminates a process
- **/t**: Terminates a process and any child processes started by it

Example 11-22   The **taskkill** Command

```
C:\Windows\System32> tasklist /fi "pid gt 45600" | more

Image Name                  PID Session Name      Session#   Mem Usage
=========================== ======== ================ =========== ============
plugin-container.exe        51092 Console              1      1,288 K
HPSupportSolutionsFramewo   55232 Services             0     26,720 K
iCloudServices.exe          50832 Console              1     16,660 K
APSDaemon.exe               50320 Console              1      9,312 K
ApplePhotoStreams.exe       55236 Console              1      9,876 K
secd.exe                    50836 Console              1      4,516 K
iTunesHelper.exe            54376 Console              1      2,384 K
filezilla.exe               53148 Console              1      4,028 K
iTunes.exe                  48672 Console              1     92,980 K
AppleMobileDeviceHelper.e   45740 Console              1      1,324 K
```

```
conhost.exe                      53724 Console            1         912 K
distnoted.exe                    56836 Console            1       1,032 K
SyncServer.exe                   56448 Console            1       1,224 K
conhost.exe                      47576 Console            1         904 K
CodeSetup-stable-0f3794b3        57948 Console            1       1,600 K
SystemSettingsBroker.exe         57560 Console            1       9,320 K
svchost.exe                      54424 Services           0       2,340 K
dllhost.exe                      65180 Console            1      15,776 K
OfficeClickToRun.exe             69496 Services           0      30,660 K
^C^C
C:\Windows\System32> taskkill /pid 50832
SUCCESS: Sent termination signal to the process with PID 50832.


C:\Windows\System32>
```

dism

The *dism* command is used to work with system images before they are deployed
(see Example 11-23). **dism** stands for Deployment Image Servicing and Management.
Use the **dism** command to create customized system image files that will be installed
on computers in the enterprise.

Example 11-23   The **dism** Command

```
C:\WINDOWS\system32> dism | more


Deployment Image Servicing and Management tool
Version: 10.0.18362.1


DISM.exe [dism_options] {Imaging_command} [<Imaging_arguments>]
DISM.exe {/Image:<path_to_offline_image> | /Online} [dism_options]
         {servicing_command} [<servicing_arguments>]


DESCRIPTION:


  DISM enumerates, installs, uninstalls, configures, and updates features
  and packages in Windows images. The commands that are available depend
  on the image being serviced and whether the image is offline or running.


GENERIC IMAGING COMMANDS:
  /Split-Image               - Splits an existing .wim file into multiple
                                 read-only split WIM (SWM) files.

  /Apply-Image               - Applies an image.
  /Get-MountedImageInfo      - Displays information about mounted WIM and VHD
                                 images.
```

```
    /Get-ImageInfo            - Displays information about images in a WIM, a VHD
                                or a FFU file.
    /Commit-Image             - Saves changes to a mounted WIM or VHD image.
    /Unmount-Image            - Unmounts a mounted WIM or VHD image.
    /Mount-Image              - Mounts an image from a WIM or VHD file.
    /Remount-Image            - Recovers an orphaned image mount directory.
    /Cleanup-Mountpoints      - Deletes resources associated with corrupted
                                mounted images.

WIM COMMANDS:
-- More --
```

sfc

The *sfc* command, which requires Administrator privileges, verifies and repairs Windows system files. It can scan important protected system files for changes and can make repairs. It can verify a single file or all files. Finally, **sfc** can restore files from cached versions. Some options include the following:

- **/scannow**: Scans and repairs, as shown in Example 11-24

- **/verifyonly**: Checks only, without repairing

Example 11-24   Scanning and Repairing with **sfc**

```
C:\WINDOWS\system32> sfc /scannow

Beginning system scan. This process will take some time.

Beginning verification phase of system scan.
Verification 95% complete.
```

shutdown

The *shutdown* command can be used to power off a local or remote computer. Options include naming a remote computer, using the **shutdown** mode, and messaging the user. This command requires shutdown permissions and Administrator privileges. Use the **/? | more** switch to see the variety of options for the **shutdown** command, as shown in Example 11-25. A few key options include:

- **/m ***ComputerName*: Specifies a remote computer

- **/s**: Shuts down the computer

- **/r**: Restarts the computer

- **/h:** Puts the local computer into hibernation

- **/f:** Forces running applications to close without warning the user

Example 11-25 The **shutdown** Command

```
C:\> shutdown /? | more
Usage: shutdown [/i | /l | /s | /sg | /r | /g | /a | /p | /h | /e | /o] [/hybrid]
    [/soft] [/fw] [/f] [/m \\computer][/t xxx][/d [p|u:]xx:yy [/c "comment"]]
 No args    Display help. This is the same as typing /?.
 /?         Display help. This is the same as not typing any options.
 /i         Display the graphical user interface (GUI).
            This must be the first option.
 /l         Log off. This cannot be used with /m or /d options.
 /s         Shutdown the computer.
 /sg        Shutdown the computer. On the next boot, if Automatic Restart
  Sign-On
            is enabled, automatically sign in and lock last interactive user.
            After sign in, restart any registered applications.
 /r         Full shutdown and restart the computer.
 /g         Full shutdown and restart the computer. After the system is
  rebooted,
            if Automatic Restart Sign-On is enabled, automatically sign in and
            lock last interactive user.
            After sign in, restart any registered applications.
 /a         Abort a system shutdown.
            This can only be used during the time-out period.
            Combine with /fw to clear any pending boots to firmware.
 /p         Turn off the local computer with no time-out or warning.
            Can be used with /d and /f options.
 /h         Hibernate the local computer.
            Can be used with the /f option.
 /hybrid    Performs a shutdown of the computer and prepares it for fast startup.
            Must be used with /s option.
 /fw        Combine with a shutdown option to cause the next boot to go to the
            firmware user interface.
 /e         Document the reason for an unexpected shutdown of a computer.
 /o         Go to the advanced boot options menu and restart the computer.
            Must be used with /r option.
 /m \\computer Specify the target computer.
 /t xxx     Set the time-out period before shutdown to xxx seconds.
            The valid range is 0-315360000 (10 years), with a default of 30.
            If the timeout period is greater than 0, the /f parameter is
-- More --
```

11.4.4.2 Lab: Task and System CLI Commands

In this lab, you will work with task and system CLI commands.

11.4.4.3 Check Your Understanding: Task and System Commands

Refer to the online course to complete this activity.

Other Useful CLI Commands (11.4.5)

A technician who is familiar with the right commands can carry out powerful and useful tasks with the Windows command prompt. This section continues to examine useful CLI commands.

Other Useful Commands (11.4.5.1)

A few other useful commands include **gpupdate**, **gpresult**, **net use**, and **net user**.

gpupdate

The *gpupdate* command can be used to do a Group Policy update. Group Policy can be set by an administrator and configured on all machines on a network from a central location. The **gpupdate** command is used to update a local machine and verify that the machine is getting Group Policy updates, as shown in Example 11-26. Some options include:

- **/target:***computer*: Forces the update of another computer

- **/force:** Forces updates even if Group Policy has not changed

- **/boot:** Restarts the computer after an update

Example 11-26   The **gpupdate** Command

```
C:\> gpupdate
Updating policy...

Computer Policy update has completed successfully.
User Policy update has completed successfully.


C:\>
```

gpresult

The *gpresult* command is used to display the Group Policy settings that are in effect for a currently logged in user. It works locally and for remote computers. It is good for checking that computers have received distributed Group Policy.

Options concern the system and system user for whom the policy will be viewed:

- **/s:** Indicates the system on which to view the result, by name or IP address

- **/r:** Displays summary data (though it is still lengthy)

The type of report to view is also configurable. Example 11-27 demonstrates the use of this command.

Example 11-27 The **gpresult** Command

```
C:\> gpresult /r | more


Microsoft (R) Windows (R) Operating System Group Policy Result tool v2.0
c 2018 Microsoft Corporation. All rights reserved.


Created on 4/8/2019 at 12:49:07 PM


RSOP data for DESKTOP-34F7VBO\Admin on DESKTOP-34F7VBO : Logging Mode
-------------------------------------------------------------------
OS Configuration:            Standalone Workstation
OS Version:                  10.0.17763
Site Name:                   N/A
Roaming Profile:             N/A
Local Profile:               C:\Users\Admin
Connected over a slow link?: No


COMPUTER SETTINGS
------------------


    Last time Group Policy was applied: 4/8/2019 at 12:31:43 PM
    Group Policy was applied from:     N/A
    Group Policy slow link threshold:  500 kbps
    Domain Name:                        DESKTOP-34F7VBO
    Domain Type:


    Applied Group Policy Objects
    -----------------------------
       N/A


    The following GPOs were not applied because they were filtered out
    -------------------------------------------------------------------
-- More --
```

net use

The *net use* command can be used to display and connect to network resources. It is one of a series of **net** commands that are used to configure how a computer works on a network. You can display the network resources that a computer is connected to and also connect the computer to resources such as shared drives. Example 11-28 shows the options for **net use**.

Example 11-28   The Options for the **net use** Command

```
C:\> net use /?
The syntax of this command is:


NET USE
[devicename | *] [\\computername\sharename[\volume] [password | *]]
            [/USER:[domainname\]username]
            [/USER:[dotted domain name\]username]
            [/USER:[username@dotted domain name]
            [/SMARTCARD]
            [/SAVECRED]
            [/REQUIREINTEGRITY]
            [/REQUIREPRIVACY]
            [/WRITETHROUGH]
            [[/DELETE] | [/PERSISTENT:{YES | NO}]]

NET USE {devicename | *} [password | *] /HOME

NET USE [/PERSISTENT:{YES | NO}]

C:\>
```

net user

The *net user* command can be used to display and change information about computer users. It displays information about all the user accounts on a computer. In addition, you can use it to change many settings for an account as well as to create new accounts.

Options include the following:

- *username*: Indicates the username that you want to work with
- /add (after *username*): Creates a new user
- /delete (after *username*): Deletes the user

Example 11-29 shows the **net user** command being used to view information about the guest user.

Example 11-29   The **net user** Command

```
C:\> net user
User accounts for \\DESKTOP-34F7VBO


-------------------------------------------------------------------------------
Admin                       Administrator              basic_user
DefaultAccount Guest        New_user
WDAGUtilityAccount
The command completed successfully.


C:\> net user guest
User name                   Guest
Full Name
Comment                     Built-in account for guest access to the computer/
                            domain
User's comment
Country/region code         000 (System Default)
Account active              No
Account expires             Never

Password last set           4/8/2019 1:16:19 PM
Password expires            Never
Password changeable         4/8/2019 1:16:19 PM
Password required           No
User may change password    No

Workstations allowed        All
Logon script
User profile
Home directory
Last logon                  Never

Logon hours allowed         All

Local Group Memberships     *Guests
Global Group memberships    *None
The command completed successfully.

C:\>
```

Running System Utilities (11.4.5.2)

The Windows Run utility can be opened by pressing the **Win+R** key combination
and entering **cmd** to open the Run window, as shown in Figure 11-119.

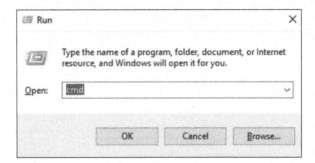

Figure 11-119 Running System Utilities

You can run a number of Windows utilities and tools by entering their commands in the Run utility:

- *EXPLORER*: Opens File Explorer or Windows Explorer.

- *MMC*: Opens Microsoft Management Console (MMC). Specify the path and .msc filename to open a saved console.

- *MSINFO32*: Opens the System Information window, which shows a summary of system components, including hardware components and software information.

- *MSTSC*: Opens the Remote Desktop utility.

- *NOTEPAD*: Opens the Notepad basic text editor.

11.4.5.3 Lab: Other Useful Commands

In this lab, you will work other useful commands.

11.4.5.4 Check Your Understanding: Other Useful CLI Commands

Refer to the online course to complete this activity.

Windows Networking (11.5)

Microsoft Windows has built-in networking capabilities for connecting two or more computers to share resources.

Network Sharing and Mapping Drives (11.5.1)

Resources such as files can be shared across a network. Creating a shortcut to a shared folder on a remote computer is known as a *mapping a drive*. A mapped drive is assigned a drive letter to identify it. Mapped drives are available only from the user account that has created them, and they are not available for all the users on the same Windows computer.

Domain and Workgroup (11.5.1.1)

You can organize and manage computers on a network by using domains and workgroups:

- *Domain*: A domain is a group of computers and electronic devices with a common set of rules and procedures administered as a unit. Computers in a domain can be in different locations in the world. A specialized server called a *domain controller* manages all security-related aspects of users and network resources, centralizing security and administration. For example, within a domain, Lightweight Directory Access Protocol (LDAP) is a protocol used to allow computers to access data directories that are distributed throughout the network.

- *Workgroup*: A workgroup is a collection of workstations and servers on a LAN that are designed to communicate and exchange data with one another. Each individual workstation controls its user accounts, security information, and access to data and resources.

All computers on a network must be part of either a domain or a workgroup. When Windows is first installed on a computer, it is automatically assigned to a workgroup, as shown in Figure 11-120.

Figure 11-120   Domain and Workgroup

HomeGroup (11.5.1.2)

The HomeGroup feature was introduced in Windows 7 (see Figure 11-121) and is also available in Windows 8 to simplify secure access to shared resources such as folders, pictures, music, videos, and printers on a home network. HomeGroups were removed from Windows 10 with the release of version 1803.

Figure 11-121   Creating a HomeGroup

All Windows computers that belong to the same workgroup can also belong to a HomeGroup. There can be only one HomeGroup per workgroup on a network. A computer can be a member of only one HomeGroup at a time. A HomeGroup is secured with a simple password. A HomeGroup can be a mix of Windows 7 and Windows 8 computers.

One user in a workgroup creates the HomeGroup. The other users can join the HomeGroup if they know the HomeGroup password. HomeGroup availability depends on the network location profile:

- *Home network*: Allowed to create or join a HomeGroup

- *Work network*: Not allowed to create or join a HomeGroup but allowed to view and share resources with other computers

- *Public network*: HomeGroup not available

When a computer joins a HomeGroup, all user accounts on the computer, except the Guest account, become members of the HomeGroup. Being part of a HomeGroup makes it easy to share pictures, music, videos, documents, libraries, and printers with other people in the same HomeGroup. Users control access to their own resources.

Note

If a computer belongs to a domain, you can join a HomeGroup and access files and resources on other HomeGroup computers. You are not allowed to create a new HomeGroup or share your own files and resources with a HomeGroup.

11.5.1.3 Video Demonstration: Connecting to a Workgroup or Domain

Refer to the online course to view this video.

Network Shares and Mapping Drives (11.5.1.4)

Network file sharing and mapping of network drives is a secure and convenient way to provide easy access to network resources. This is especially true when different versions of Windows require access to network resources. This section provides more information on network shares and mapping drives.

Mapped Drives

Mapping a local drive, as shown in Figure 11-122, is a useful way to access a single file, specific folders, or an entire drive between different operating systems over a network. Mapping a drive is done by assigning a letter (A to Z) to the resource on a remote drive. You can then use the remote *mapped drive* as if it were a local drive.

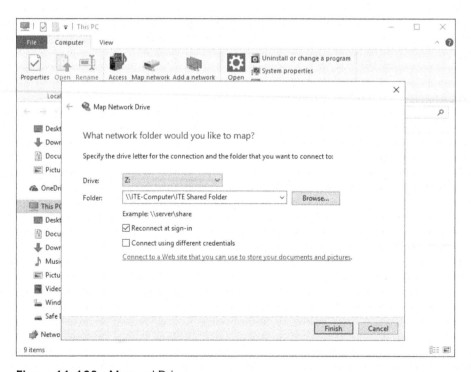

Figure 11-122   Mapped Drive

Network File Sharing

Figure 11-123 shows the dialog box progression for sharing a folder and setting permissions.

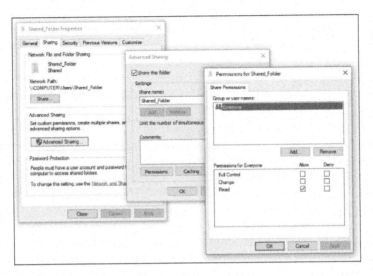

Figure 11-123   Network File Sharing

You can determine which resources will be shared over the network and the type of permissions users will have to the resources. Permissions define the type of access a user has to a file or folder:

- **Read:** The user can view the file and subfolder names, navigate to subfolders, view data in files, and run program files.

- **Change:** In addition to having Read permissions, the user can add files and subfolders, change the data in files, and delete subfolders and files.

- **Full Control:** In addition to having Change and Read permissions, the user can change the permission of files and folders in an NTFS partition and take ownership of files and folders.

Administrative Shares (11.5.1.5)

Administrative shares, also called hidden shares, are identified with a dollar sign ($) at the end of the share name. By default, Windows creates several hidden administrative shares, including the root folder of any local drives (C$), the system folder (ADMIN$), and the print driver folder (PRINT$). Administrative shares are hidden from users and are accessible only by members of the local Administrators group.

Figure 11-124 shows administrative shares on a Windows 10 PC. Note the $ after each share name.

Adding a $ sign to the end of any local share name causes it to become a hidden share. It will not be visible to a user who is browsing but can be accessed via the command line if a user maps a drive to the share name.

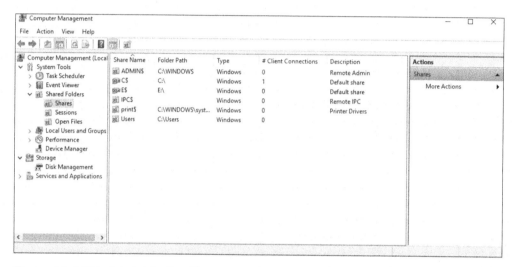

Figure 11-124   Administrative Shares

Sharing Local Resources with Others (11.5.2)

Windows 10 allows you to control which resources are shared and how they are shared by letting you turn specific sharing features on and off.

Sharing Local Resources (11.5.2.1)

Advanced Sharing Settings, located in the Network and Sharing Center, allows you to manage the sharing options for three different network profiles: Private, Guest or Public, and All Networks. Different options can be chosen for each profile. You can control the following:

- Network discovery
- File and printer sharing
- Public folder sharing
- Password protected sharing
- Media streaming

To access Advanced Sharing Settings, select Start > Control Panel > Network and Internet > Network and Sharing Center. To enable sharing of resources between computers connected to the same workgroup, you must turn on network discovery and file and printer sharing, as shown in Figure 11-125.

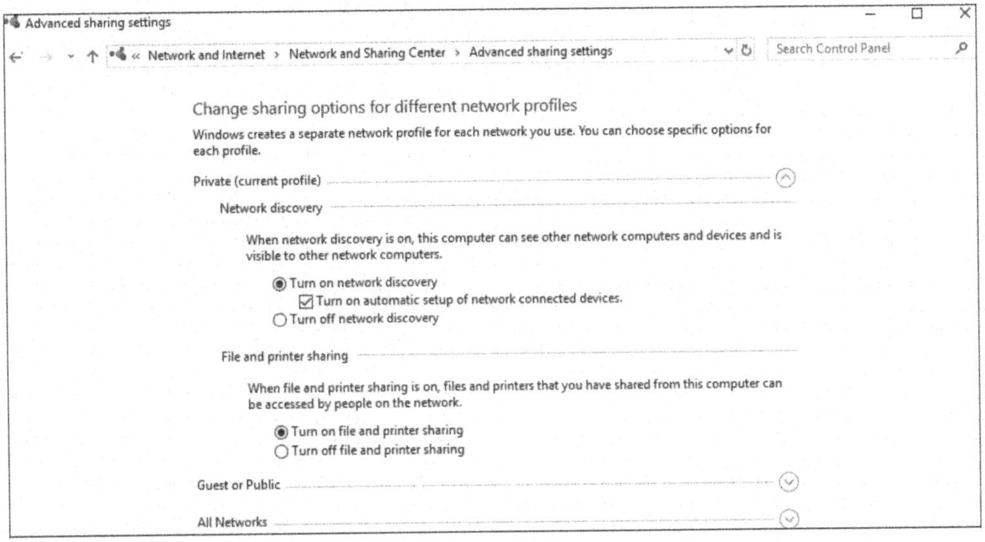

Figure 11-125 Sharing Local Resources

OS vendors have created simple file sharing mechanisms. Microsoft's file sharing mechanism is called *Nearby Sharing*. Nearby Sharing was introduced in Windows 10, partly to replace the previous HomeGroup feature. Nearby Sharing provides the ability to share content with a nearby device using either Wi-Fi or Bluetooth.

AirDrop, which is supported by Apple iOS and macOS, uses Bluetooth to establish a Wi-Fi direct connection between devices for the file transfer to take place.

There are also many third-party and open source file sharing alternatives, but they introduce the potential for security vulnerabilities that allow unsolicited transfers.

Printer Sharing vs. Network Printer Mapping (11.5.2.2)

Printing is one of the most common tasks for users in both home and business environments.

Printer Sharing

A print device can be directly attached to a computer via USB or direct network connection. This is considered a "local" printer, and the PC it is attached to acts as the print server. The local printer can be shared on the network via the Sharing tab on the printer Properties dialog box, as shown in Figure 11-126. When a printer is shared, users with the correct permissions can connect to the network shared printer. Drivers for the print device can also be installed on the local computer so that clients obtain the driver when they connect to the print share.

To find a network shared printer, users can browse through network resources by using the Network object in File Explorer, as shown in Figure 11-126.

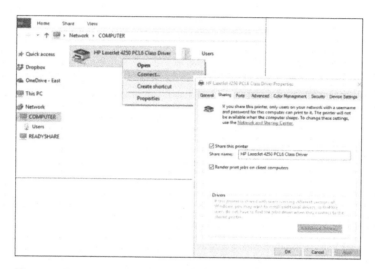

Figure 11-126   *Printer Sharing*

Network Printer Mapping

A print device can come with an integrated Ethernet or Wi-Fi adapter and connect directly to the network. Once the print device is connected to the network, it can be mapped using the Add Printer Wizard in the Devices and Printers window, as shown in Figure 11-127. Mapping a printer to a computer allows the user to print over the network without the need for a direct connection to the print device. Once mapped, the printer shows up in the list of available printers on the computer.

11.5.2.3 Video Demonstration: Sharing Files and Folders on a Local Network

Refer to the online course to view this video.

11.5.2.4 Lab: Share Resources

In this lab, you will work with another student. You will create and share a folder, and you will set permissions for the share so your partner will only have Read access.

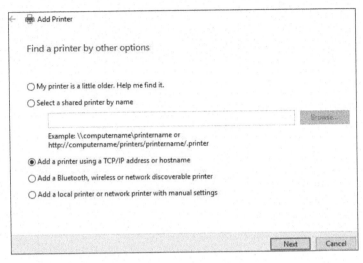

Figure 11-127   *Network Printer Mapping*

Configure a Wired Network Connection (11.5.3)

Windows OS is capable of networking and does most of the work during the configuration. Configuring a wired network connection is an excellent way to share resources and even a common Internet connection on a home or business network.

Configuring Wired Network Interfaces in Windows 10 (11.5.3.1)

Windows 10 network settings are managed through the Network & Internet section in the Settings app, shown in Figure 11-128. From the Network & Internet window, there are links to view network properties and to the Network and Sharing Center. To view available network connections, both wired and wireless, select the Change Adapter Options link. From there, you can configure each network connection.

Network card properties are configured in the Advanced tab of the adapter Properties window. Navigate to Device Manager. Locate and right-click the network adapter. Choose Properties > Advanced tab. A list of properties allows configuration of features such as speed, duplex, QoS, and Wake-on-LAN. Click the desired feature in the Property dropdown list. Each property has configurable values in the Value dropdown list.

The Windows Internet Protocol Version 4 (TCP/IPv4) Properties window includes an Alternate Configuration tab, which allows an administrator to configure an alternative IP address for the PC to use if it is unable to contact a DHCP server. Note that this tab is not visible if a static IPv4 address is configured in the General tab.

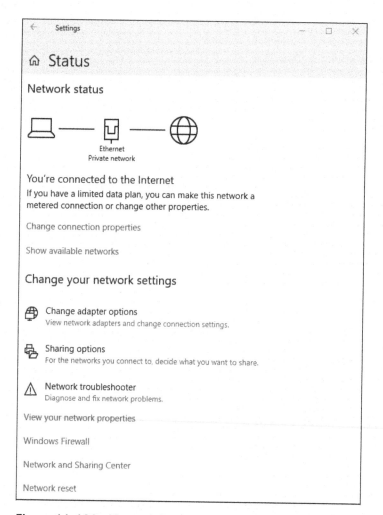

Figure 11-128 Network Status

Configuring a Wired NIC (11.5.3.2)

After a NIC driver is installed, the IP address settings must be configured. A computer can be assigned its IP configuration in one of two ways:

- **Manually:** The host is statically assigned a specific IP configuration.

- **Dynamically:** The host requests its IP address configuration from a DHCP server.

From the Properties window of the wired NIC, both IPv4 and IPv6 addresses and other options such as the default gateway and DNS server address can be configured, as shown in Figure 11-129.

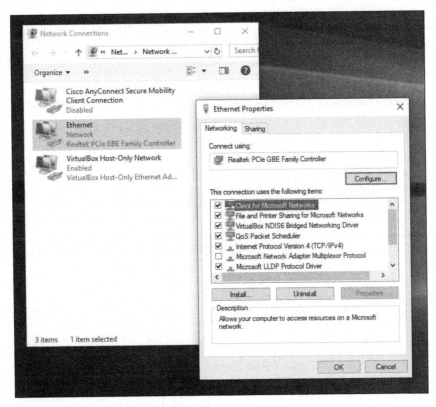

Figure 11-129   Configuring a Wired NIC

The default for both IPv4 and IPv6 is to obtain the IP settings automatically using DHCP in the case of IPv4 and stateless address autoconfiguration (SLAAC) in the case of IPv6.

Note

Most computers today come with an onboard NIC. If you are installing a new NIC, it is considered a best practice to disable the onboard NIC in the BIOS settings.

IPv4 Configuration

To configure IPv4 settings manually, click Use the Following IP Address and enter the appropriate IPv4 address, subnet mask, and default gateway, as shown in Figure 11-130. If a Windows machine fails to obtain an IPv4 address dynamically, it uses an Automatic Private IP Addressing (APIPA) address from a reserved range in the 169.254.x.y network space.

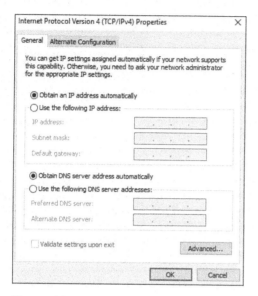

Figure 11-130   IPv4 Configuration

IPv4 Alternate Configuration

Windows 10 allows for an alternative IPv4 address configuration for a computer if it cannot access a DHCP server and if APIPA is unsuitable or not desired, as shown in Figure 11-131. This is useful for mobile devices that move between a network with DHCP and another network that needs a static IPv4 address.

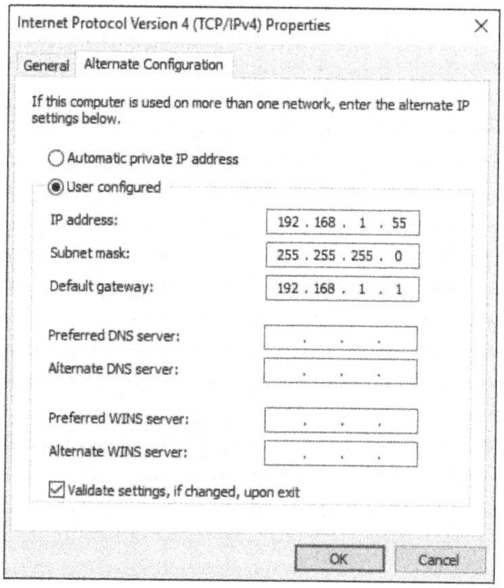

Figure 11-131   IPv4 Alternate Configuration

IPv6 Configuration

To configure IPv6 settings, click Internet Protocol Version 6 (TCP/IPv6) > Properties to open the Internet Protocol Version 6 (TCP/IPv6) Properties window. Click Use the Following IPv6 Address and enter the appropriate IPv6 address, prefix length, and default gateway, as shown in Figure 11-132.

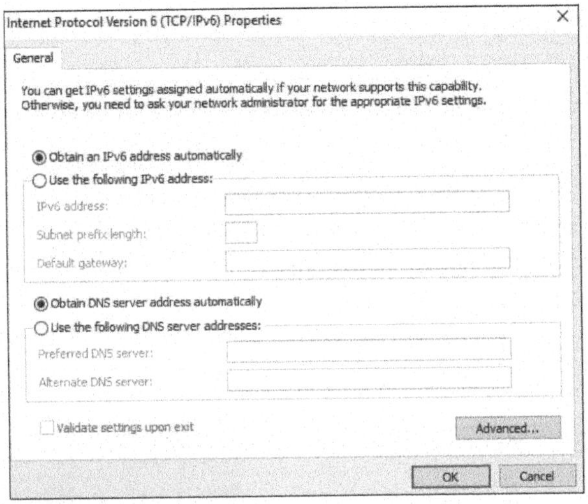

Figure 11-132   IPv6 Configuration

Setting a Network Profile (11.5.3.3)

The first time a computer with Windows 10 connects to a network, a network profile must be selected. Each network profile has unique default settings. Depending on the profile selected, file and printer sharing or network discovery can be turned off or on, and different firewall settings can be applied.

Windows 10 has two network profiles, as shown in Figure 11-133:

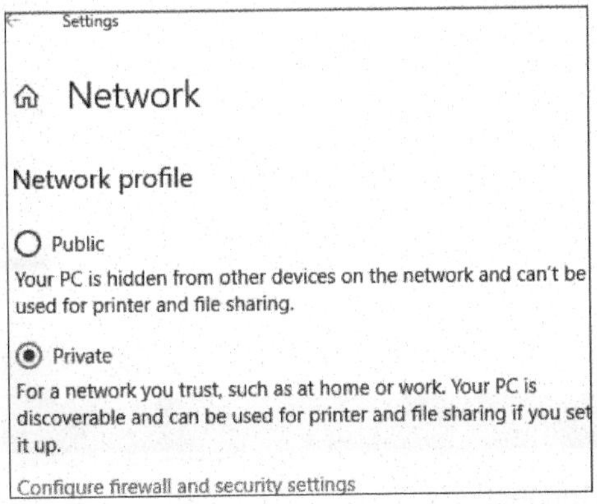

Figure 11-133   Network Profile Setting

- *Public*: The public profile disables file and printer sharing and network discovery on the link. The PC is hidden from other devices.

- *Private*: The private profile allows the user to customize the sharing options. This profile is for use on trusted networks as the PC is discoverable by other devices.

Verify Connectivity with the Windows GUI (11.5.3.4)

The easiest way to test for an Internet connection is to open a web browser and see if the Internet is available. To troubleshoot a connection, you can use the Windows GUI or CLI.

In Windows 10, the status of a network connection can be viewed on the General tab, as shown in Figure 11-134. Click the Details button to view IP addressing information, subnet mask, default gateway, MAC address, and other information. If the connection is not functioning correctly, close the Details window and click Diagnose to have the Windows Network Diagnostics troubleshooter attempt to troubleshoot and fix the issue.

Figure 11-134   Verifying Connectivity

ipconfig Command (11.5.3.5)

The *ipconfig* command displays basic IP configuration information, including the IP address, subnet mask, and default gateway for all network adapters to which TCP/IP is bound. Table 11-8 displays the available **ipconfig** command options. To use a command option, enter **ipconfig** /*option* (for example, **ipconfig** /**all**).

Table 11-8   ipconfig Command Options

ipconfig Argument	Description
ipconfig /all	Displays additional network configuration information, including DHCP and DNS servers, MAC address, NetBIOS status, and domain name.
ipconfig /release	Releases the IP address learned from the DHCP server, resulting in the network adapter(s) no longer having an IP address.
ipconfig /renew	Forces a DHCP client to renew its DHCP address lease from the DHCP server.
ipconfig /displaydns	Displays the DNS resolver cache, which contains host and domain names that have been recently queried.
ipconfig /flushdns	Clears the DNS resolver cache on the host.

Network CLI Commands (11.5.3.6)

Several CLI commands can be executed from the command prompt to test network connectivity:

- **ping:** This command tests basic connectivity between devices by using ICMP echo request and reply messages.

- **tracert:** This command traces the route that packets take from your computer to a destination host. At the command prompt, enter **tracert** *hostname*. The first listing in the results is your default gateway. Each listing after that is the router that packets are traveling through to reach the destination. **tracert** shows you where packets are stopping, indicating where a problem is occurring.

- **nslookup:** This command tests and troubleshoots DNS servers. It queries the DNS server to discover IP addresses or hostnames. At the command prompt, enter **nslookup** *hostname*. **nslookup** returns the IP address for the hostname entered. A reverse **nslookup** command, **nslookup** *IP_address*, returns the corresponding hostname for the IP address entered.

11.5.3.7 Video Demonstration: Network Testing and Verification with CLI Commands

Video

Refer to the online course to view this video.

Configure a Wireless Network Interface in Windows (11.5.4)

There are different types of wireless networks, and each has its own setup configuration and management necessities. This section examines Wi-Fi network configuration.

Wireless Settings (11.5.4.1)

Wireless networks can be added in Windows 10 by going to Settings > Network & Internet > Wi-Fi > Manage Known Networks (see Figure 11-135).

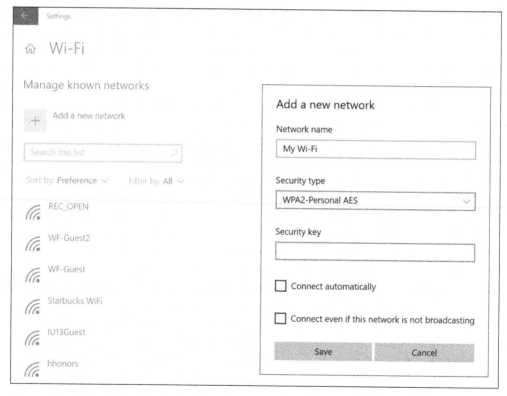

Figure 11-135   Wireless Settings

Enter the network name and select a security type that matches the configuration on the wireless router. There are four security type options:

- *No authentication (open)*: Data is sent unencrypted and with no authentication.

- *WEP*: Provides very weak security and should not be relied upon for confidentiality.

- **WPA2-Personal**: Uses the Advanced Encryption Standard (AES) cipher and Pre-Shared Key (PSK) to encrypt communications.

- **WPA2-Enterprise**: Authentication is passed from the access point to a centralized authentication server running Remote Authentication Dial-in User Service (RADIUS).

Remote authentication for wireless devices can be provided by a scalable authentication architecture by using *RADIUS* or *Terminal Controller Access Control System Plus (TACACS+)*. Both technologies use a separate server—an *authentication, authorization, and accounting (AAA) server*—that performs the authentication on behalf of network devices. The network devices do not store and validate user credentials directly; rather, they pass the request to the AAA server and forward the response to the user.

11.5.4.2 Lab: Connect and Test the Wireless Connection

In this lab, you and your partner will connect your computers to a wireless router and test the wireless connection.

Remote Access Protocols (11.5.5)

Remote access protocols enable systems to access each other when they are not directly connected to each other. Remote access is accomplished with a combination of software, hardware, and network connectivity. Windows has different remote protocol options to choose from, and which one is appropriate depends on many factors, such as functionality, security, and system configuration. This section provides information a technician can use in implementing remote access.

VPN Access in Windows (11.5.5.1)

To communicate and share resources over a network that is not secure, you can use a *virtual private network (VPN)*. A VPN is a private network that connects remote sites or users together over a public network, such as the Internet. VPNs are commonly used to access private corporate networks.

A VPN uses dedicated secure connections, routed through the Internet, from the private corporate network to the remote user. When connected to the private corporate network, users become part of that network and have access to all services and resources as if they were physically connected to it.

Remote-access users must install a VPN client on their computers to form secure connections with the private corporate network. Special routers can also be used to connect computers connected to it to the private corporate network. The VPN software encrypts data before sending it over the Internet to the VPN gateway at the private corporate network. VPN gateways establish, manage, and control VPN connections, also known as *VPN tunnels*. Figure 11-136 shows VPN client software.

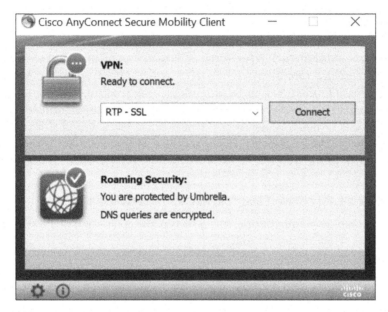

Figure 11-136   VPN Client Software

You can set up a VPN in Windows 10 from the Network and Sharing Center, as shown in Figure 11-137.

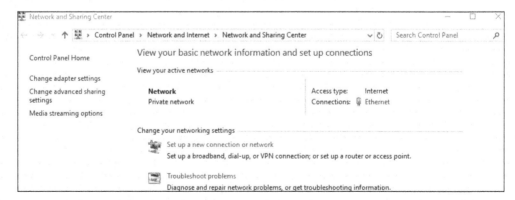

Figure 11-137   Setting Up VPN Access in Windows

Windows supports several VPN types; for some VPNs, third-party software may be required.

Telnet and SSH (11.5.5.2)

Telnet is a command-line terminal emulation protocol and program. The Telnet daemon listens for connections on TCP port 23. Telnet is sometimes used for trouble-shooting services and for connecting to routers and switches for entering configurations. Telnet is not installed in Windows by default but can be added using Programs and Features. In addition, third-party and free terminal emulation programs support Telnet. Telnet messages are sent in plaintext, so anyone with a packet sniffer can capture and see the contents of Telnet messages. It is therefore advisable to use a secure connection rather than Telnet.

Secure Shell (SSH) is a secure alternative to Telnet and other file copy programs, such as FTP. SSH communicates over TCP port 22 and uses encryption to protect the session. There are several methods in which a client can authenticate to an SSH server:

- **Username/password:** The client sends credentials to the SSH host, and the credentials are verified against a local user database or sent to a centralized authentication server.

- *Kerberos*: Networks that use the Kerberos authentication protocol, such as Windows Active Directory, allow for single sign-on (SSO). SSO allows users to sign in to multiple systems with only one username and password.

- *Host-based authentication*: The client requests authentication with a public key. The server generates a challenge with this key, and the client must decrypt it with the matching private key to complete the authentication.

- *Public key authentication*: This provides additional protection over host-based authentication. The user must enter a passphrase to access the private key, which helps prevent the private key from becoming compromised.

Packet Tracer
☐ Activity

11.5.5.3 Packet Tracer: Use Telnet and SSH

In this Packet Tracer activity, you will establish remote sessions to two routers, using Telnet and SSH. You may also install a third-party terminal emulation program and access a dedicated SSH server provided by your instructor.

Remote Desktop and Assistance (11.5.6)

Remote Desktop and Remote Assistance are different features in Windows OS, but they are both involved in remote access of computers. Remote Desktop is a tool for logging on to remote computers; with it, all processes run on the remote computer, and only one user is logged in at a time. Remote Assistance is a tool to allow remote technical support but only when it is requested; with it, both users use the same credentials.

Other operating systems can also perform these functions. For example, in macOS, remote access functionality is provided by the Screen Sharing feature, which is based on Virtual Network Computing (VNC). Any VNC client can connect to a Screen Sharing server. VNC is a freeware product that is similar in functionality to RDP and works over port 5900.

Video

11.5.6.1 Video Demonstration: Remote Desktop and Remote Assistance

Refer to the online course to view this video.

11.5.6.2 Lab: Windows Remote Desktop and Assistance

In this lab, you will partner with another student and then configure a Remote Desktop connection for your partner and invite your partner to provide assistance on your computer by using a Remote Assistance connection.

Interactive Graphic

11.5.6.3 Check Your Understanding: Remote Desktop and Assistance

Refer to the online course to complete this activity.

Common Preventive Maintenance Techniques for Operating Systems (11.6)

Preventive maintenance techniques should be planned and implemented to avoid preventable problems. A plan should be developed that focuses on areas that would affect productivity the most and should include detailed information about an organization's hardware and software and what needs to be done to ensure ongoing optimal operation of systems.

OS Preventive Maintenance Plan (11.6.1)

Accurate and updated documentation is a critical component in preventive maintenance plans.

Preventive Maintenance Plan Contents (11.6.1.1)

To ensure that an OS remains fully functional, you must implement a preventive maintenance plan. A *preventive maintenance plan* provides many benefits to users and organizations, such as decreased downtime, improved performance, improved reliability, and lower repair costs.

Preventive maintenance plans should include detailed information about the maintenance of all computers and network equipment. A plan should prioritize equipment that would affect the organization the most if that equipment were to fail. Preventive maintenance for an OS includes automating tasks to perform scheduled updates. Preventive maintenance also involves installing service packs that help keep the system up to date and compatible with new software and hardware. Preventive maintenance includes the following important tasks:

- Hard drive error checking, defragmentation, and backup

- Updates to the operating system, applications, antivirus, and other protective software

Perform preventive maintenance regularly and record all actions taken and observations made. A *repair log* helps you determine which equipment is the most reliable and which is least reliable. It also provides a history of when a computer was last fixed, how it was fixed, and what the problem was.

Preventive maintenance should take place when it causes the least amount of disruption to the users. This often means scheduling tasks at night, early in the morning, or over the weekend. Tools and techniques can be used to automate many preventive maintenance tasks.

Security

Security is an important aspect of a preventive maintenance program. Install antivirus and anti-malware software and perform regular scans on computers to help ensure that they remain free of malicious software. Use the *Windows Malicious Software Removal Tool* to check a computer for malicious software. If an infection is found, the tool removes it. Each time a new version of the tool is available from Microsoft, download it and scan your computer for new threats. This should be a standard item in your preventive maintenance program, along with regular updates to your antivirus and spyware removal tools.

Startup Programs

Some programs, such as antivirus scanners and spyware removal tools, do not automatically start when the computer boots. To ensure that these programs run each time the computer is booted, add them to the Startup folder of the Start menu. A program may have a switch to allow the program to perform a specific action, such as starting without being displayed. Check the documentation to determine if your programs allow the use of special switches.

11.6.1.2 Lab: Manage the Startup Folder

In this lab, you will learn how to manage the Startup folder.

Windows Updates (11.6.1.3)

Windows Update is a website located at update.microsoft.com. The site hosts maintenance updates, critical updates, and security patches, as well as optional software and hardware updates for Microsoft Windows versions 7, 8, and 10. There is also a program called Microsoft Update, which can keep Microsoft Office software patched at the same time. A control installed in Windows allows the OS to browse the update site and select updates for download and installation, using the *Background Intelligent Transfer Service (BITS)* protocol.

Microsoft releases updates on the second Tuesday of each month, unofficially known as *Patch Tuesday*.

Windows 10 automatically downloads and installs updates to make sure your device is secure and up to date. This means you receive the latest fixes and security updates to help your device run efficiently and securely. In most cases, the only user interaction required is the restarting of the device to complete the update.

You can manually check for updates in Windows 10 by selecting Settings > Update & Security, as shown Figure 11-138. You can then choose which updates to apply, and you can configure update settings.

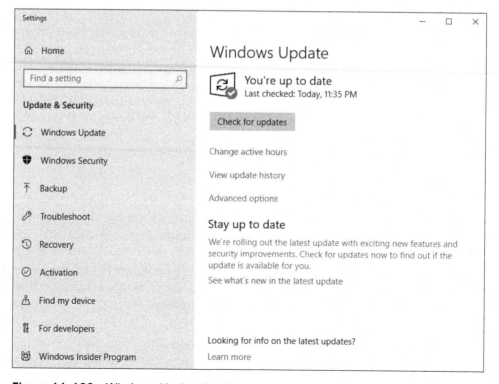

Figure 11-138   Windows Update Settings

A *windowsupdate.log* file, stored in the **%SystemRoot%** directory, contains records of update activity. If an update fails to install properly, you can check the log file for an error code that can be referenced in the Microsoft Knowledge Base. If an update causes problems, you can uninstall it by selecting Settings > Update and Security > View Update History.

Device Driver Updates

Manufacturers occasionally release new drivers to address issues with the current drivers. Check for updated drivers when your hardware does not work properly or to prevent future problems, as shown in Figure 11-139. It is also important to update drivers that patch or correct security problems. If a driver update does not work properly, use the Roll Back Driver feature to revert to the previously installed driver.

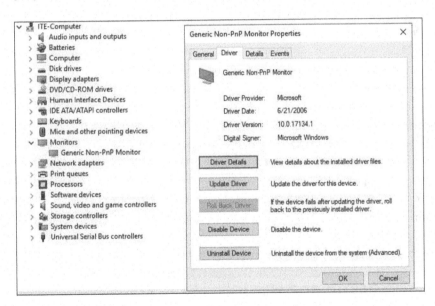

Figure 11-139   Device Driver Updates

Firmware Updates

Firmware updates are less common than driver updates. Manufacturers release new firmware updates to address issues that might not be fixed with driver updates. Firmware updates can increase the speed of certain types of hardware, enable new features, or increase the stability of a product. Follow the manufacturer's instructions carefully when performing a firmware update to avoid making the hardware unusable. Research the update completely because it might not be possible to revert to the original firmware. An example of updating firmware is shown in Figure 11-140.

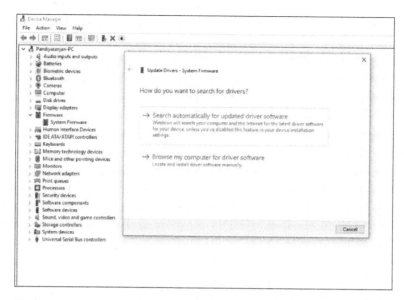

Figure 11-140   Firmware Updates

11.6.1.4 Video Demonstration: Scheduling Tasks

Refer to the online course to view this video.

11.6.1.5 Lab: Schedule a Task Using the GUI and the Command Line

In this lab, you will learn how to schedule a task using the GUI and the command line.

Backup and Restore (11.6.2)

Backup and restoration should be part of an overall disaster recovery plan. A backup is a copy of data that is stored in a separate location from the original and that helps protect data from being permanently lost. Data from an earlier time can be recovered only if it has been backed up.

A system restore usually occurs automatically on a computer's operating system. At scheduled or OS-determined times, a computer creates restore points of the computer configuration. Restore points can be used when a computer has a problem.

Restore Points (11.6.2.1)

Sometimes installing an application or a hardware driver can cause instability or create unexpected problems. Uninstalling the application or hardware driver usually corrects the problem. If it doesn't, you can restore the computer to a time before the installation by using the *System Restore utility*.

Restore points contain information about the operating system, installed programs, and Registry settings. If a computer crashes or if an update causes a problem, the computer can be rolled back to a previous configuration by using a restore point. System Restore does not back up personal data files, nor does it recover personal files that have been corrupted or deleted. Always use a dedicated backup system, such as a tape drive, an optical disc, or a USB storage device to back up personal files locally. Remote backup locations can also be used for backing up personal files.

A technician should create a restore point before making changes to a system in the following situations:

- When updating the OS
- When installing or upgrading hardware
- When installing an application
- When installing a driver

To open the System Restore utility in Windows 10, shown in Figure 11-141, open System Properties and click System Restore.

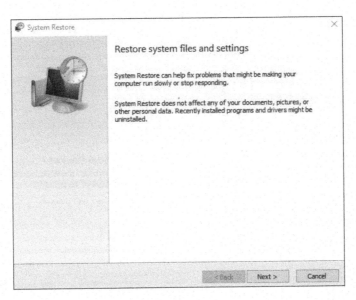

Figure 11-141 Restore Points

Hard Drive Backup (11.6.2.2)

It is important to establish a backup strategy that includes data recovery of personal files. You can use the *Microsoft Backup utility* to perform backups as required. How the computer system is used and organizational requirements determine how often the data must be backed up and the type of backup to perform.

It can take a long time to run a backup. If the backup strategy is followed carefully, it is not necessary to back up all files every time. Only the files that have changed since the last backup need to be backed up.

The backup tool included with Windows 7 allowed users to back up files or create and use a system image backup or repair disc. Windows 8 and Windows 10 ship with *File History*, which can be used to back up the files in the Documents, Music, Pictures, Videos, and Desktop folders. Over time, File History builds a history of your files, allowing you to go back and recover specific versions of a file. This is a helpful feature if there are damaged or lost files.

To open File History in Windows 10, select Settings > Update & Security > Backup (see Figure 11-142).

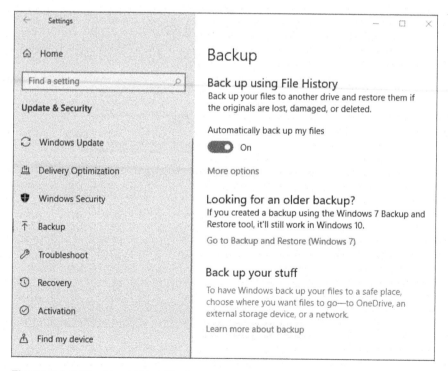

Figure 11-142   Hard Drive Backup

Video

11.6.2.3 Video Demonstration: Back Up and Restore

Refer to the online course to view this video.

11.6.2.4 Lab: System Restore and Hard Drive Backup

In this lab, you will create a restore point and use it to restore your computer. You will also configure a hard drive backup.

Basic Troubleshooting Process for Windows Operating Systems (11.7)

The troubleshooting process helps resolve problems with the operating system. OS problems can result from a combination of hardware, software, and network issues. These problems range from simple, such as a driver not operating properly, to complex, such as a system locking up.

Applying Troubleshooting Process to Windows Operating Systems (11.7.1)

This section explores the troubleshooting steps to guide a technician in how to accurately identify, repair, and document problems.

The Six Steps of the Troubleshooting Process (11.7.1.1)

The six steps for the troubleshooting process are:

Step 1.   Identify the problem.

Step 2.   Establish a theory of probable cause.

Step 3.   Test the theory to determine the cause.

Step 4.   Establish a plan of action to resolve the problem and implement the solution.

Step 5.   Verify full system functionality and, if applicable, implement preventive measures.

Step 6.   Document findings, actions, and outcomes.

Identify the Problem (11.7.1.2)

OS problems can result from a combination of hardware, software, and network issues. Computer technicians must be able to analyze a problem and determine the cause of the error to repair the computer. This process is called *troubleshooting*.

The first step in the troubleshooting process is to identify the problem. Table 11-9 provides examples of open-ended and closed-ended questions.

Table 11-9   Step 1: Identify the Problem

Open-Ended Questions	Closed-Ended Questions
■ What problems are you having?	■ Can you start the operating system?
■ What operating system is installed on the computer?	■ Can you start the operating system in Safe mode?
■ What updates have you performed lately?	■ Have you changed your password recently?
■ What programs have you installed recently?	■ Have you seen any error messages on the computer?
■ What were you doing when the problem was discovered?	■ Has anyone else used the computer recently?
	■ Has any hardware been added recently?

Establish a Theory of Probable Cause (11.7.1.3)

After you have talked to the customer, you can establish a theory of probable causes. Table 11-10 lists some common probable causes of OS problems.

Table 11-10   Step 2: Establish a Theory of Probable Cause

Common causes of operating system problems	
	■ Incorrect settings in BIOS
	■ Caps Lock key is set to on
	■ Non-bootable media during computer boot up
	■ Password has changed
	■ Incorrect monitor settings in Control Panel
	■ Operating system update failure
	■ Driver update failure
	■ Malware infection
	■ Hard drive failure
	■ Corrupt operating system files

Test the Theory to Determine the Cause (11.7.1.4)

After you have developed some theories about what is wrong, test your theories to determine the cause of the problem. Table 11-11 shows a list of quick procedures that can help you determine the exact cause of the problem or even correct the problem. If a quick procedure does correct the problem, you can jump to verifying the full system functionality. If a quick procedure does not correct the problem, you need to research the problem further to establish the exact cause.

Table 11-11 Step 3: Test the Theory to Determine Cause

Common steps to determine cause	
	■ Log in as a different user
	■ Use third-party diagnostic software
	■ Determine whether new software or software updates have just been installed
	■ Uninstall recently installed applications
	■ Boot into Safe mode to determine whether the problem is driver related
	■ Roll back newly updated drivers
	■ Examine Device Manager for device conflicts
	■ Examine event logs for warnings or errors
	■ Check the hard drive for errors and fix file system issues
	■ Use the System File Checker to recover corrupt system files
	■ Use System Restore if a system update or service pack has been installed

Establish a Plan of Action to Resolve the Problem and Implement the Solution (11.7.1.5)

After you have determined the exact cause of the problem, you can establish a plan of action to resolve the problem and implement the solution. Table 11-12 shows some sources you can use to gather additional information to resolve an issue.

Table 11-12   Step 4: Establish a Plan of Action to Resolve the Problem and Implement the Solution

If no solution is achieved in the previous step, further research is needed to implement the solution, using these sources	<ul><li>Help desk repair logs</li><li>Other technicians</li><li>Manufacturer FAQ websites</li><li>Technical websites</li><li>News groups</li><li>Computer manuals</li><li>Device manuals</li><li>Online forums</li><li>Internet search</li></ul>

Verify Full System Fuzctionality and, if Applicable, Implement Preventive Measures (11.7.1.6)

After you have corrected the problem, you can verify full system functionality and, if applicable, implement preventive measures. Table 11-13 lists the steps to verify full system functionality.

Table 11-13   Step 5: Verify Full System Functionality and, if Applicable, Implement Preventive Measures

Verify full functionality	<ul><li>Shut down the computer and restart it</li><li>Check event logs to make sure there are no new warnings or errors</li><li>Check Device Manager to see that there are no warnings or errors</li><li>Run DxDiag to make sure DirectX is running correctly</li><li>Make sure applications run properly</li><li>Make sure network shares are accessible</li><li>Make sure the Internet can be accessed</li><li>Rerun System File Checker to ensure that all files are correct</li><li>Check Task Manager to ensure that the status of all programs is Running</li><li>Rerun any third-party diagnostic tools</li></ul>

Document Findings, Actions, and Outcomes (11.7.1.7)

In the final step of the troubleshooting process, you must document your findings, actions, and outcomes. Table 11-14 lists the tasks required to document the problem and the solution.

Table 11-14   Step 6: Document Findings, Actions, and Outcomes

Document findings, actions, and outcomes	<ul><li>Discuss with the customer the solution that was implemented.</li><li>Have the customer verify that the problem has been solved.</li><li>Provide the customer with all paperwork.</li><li>Document the steps taken to solve the problem in the work order and the technician's journal.</li><li>Document any components used in the repair.</li><li>Document the time spent to resolve the problem.</li></ul>

Common Problems and Solutions for Windows Operating Systems (11.7.2)

Troubleshooting computer problems is a part of every PC technician's job. No computer performs perfectly all the time, and it is important to be aware of troubleshooting techniques, tools, and common issues.

Common Problems and Solutions for Windows Operating Systems (11.7.2.1)

Table 11-15 lists common problems, probable causes, and possible solutions for Windows operating systems.

Table 11-15   Common Problems and Solutions for Windows Operating Systems

Identify the Problem	Probable Causes	Possible Solutions
The OS locks up.	The computer is overheating.	Clean internal components. Check the fan connections to ensure that fans are operating properly. Address any events in the event log.
	An unknown event may have occurred and caused the OS to lock up.	Address any events in the event log.

Identify the Problem	Probable Causes	Possible Solutions
	Some of the operating system files may be corrupted.	Run the System File Checker (SFC) to replace corrupt operating system files.
	The power supply, RAM, hard drive, or motherboard may be defective.	Test the power supply, RAM, hard drive, or motherboard using third-party diagnostic software and replace as necessary.
	The BIOS settings may be incorrect.	Examine and adjust the BIOS settings.
	An incorrect driver may have been installed.	Install or roll back updated drivers.
The keyboard or mouse does not respond.	The computer has an incompatible or an out-of-date driver.	Reboot the computer. Install or roll back drivers.
	The cable has been damaged or disconnected.	Replace or reconnect the cable.
	The device is defective.	Replace the device.
	A KVM switch is being used, and the active computer is not being displayed.	Change the input on the KVM switch.
	The wireless keyboard or mouse has failed.	Replace the battery.
The operating system will not start.	A hardware device failed to initialize.	Reboot the computer.
	Some of the operating system files may be corrupted.	Restore Windows using the System Restore tool. Recover the system disk by using the System Image Recovery tool. Perform a repair installation on the operating system.
	The boot sector is corrupted.	Use the Recovery Environment to fix the boot sector.

Identify the Problem	Probable Causes	Possible Solutions
	The power supply, RAM, hard drive, or motherboard may be defective.	Replace the power supply, RAM, hard drive, or motherboard with one that works.
	New hardware drivers did not install properly.	Disconnect any newly connected devices and use the Last Known Good Configuration option to start the operating system.
	Windows updates have corrupted the operating system.	Boot the computer in Safe mode and address all events in the event log.
The computer displays an "Invalid Boot Disk" error after POST.	The boot order is not set correctly in BIOS.	Change the boot order in BIOS to start with the boot drive.
	The hard drive is not detected.	Reconnect the hard drive cables.
	The hard drive does not have an operating system installed.	Install an operating system.
	The MBR is corrupted.	Using a system repair disc, run **bootrec /FixMbr** to repair the MBR.
	The GPT is corrupted.	Using a system repair disc, run DISKPART to repair the GPT (or the MBR).
	The computer has a boot sector virus.	Run antivirus software.
	The hard drive is failing.	Replace the hard drive.
The computer displays a "BOOTMGR is missing" error after POST.	BOOTMGR is missing or damaged.	Restore BOOTMGR from installation media.
	Boot configuration data is missing or damaged.	Restore the boot configuration data from installation media.
	The boot order is not set correctly in BIOS.	Change the boot order in BIOS to start with the boot drive.
	The MBR is corrupted.	Run **bootrec /FixMbr** from the Recovery Environment.
	The hard drive is failing.	Run **chkdsk /F /R** from the Recovery Environment.

Identify the Problem	Probable Causes	Possible Solutions
A service failed to start when the computer booted.	The service is not enabled.	Enable the service.
	The service is set to Manual.	Set the service to Automatic.
	The failed service requires another service to be enabled.	Re-enable the required service.
A device did not start when the computer booted.	The external device is not powered on.	Power on the external device.
	The data cable or power cable is not connected to the device.	Secure the data cable and power cable to the device.
	The device has been disabled in BIOS.	Enable the device in BIOS.
	The device has failed.	Replace the device.
	The device has a conflict with a newly installed device.	Remove the newly installed device.
	The driver is corrupted.	Reinstall or roll back the driver.
The computer continually restarts without displaying the desktop.	The computer is set to restart when there is a failure.	Press **F8** to open the Advanced Options menu and choose Disable Automatic Restart on System Failure.
	A startup file has become corrupted.	Run **chkdsk /F /R** from the Recovery Environment.
		Use the Recovery Environment to perform an automatic repair or a system restore.
The computer displays a black or blue screen of death (BSOD).	A driver is not compatible with the hardware.	Research the STOP error and the name of the module that produced the error.
	The RAM is failing.	Perform a memory check.
	The power supply is failing.	Replace any failing devices with known-good devices.

Identify the Problem	Probable Causes	Possible Solutions
The computer locks up without any error messages.	The CPU or FSB settings are incorrect on the motherboard or in the BIOS.	Reset the CPU and FSB settings.
	The computer is overheating.	Check and replace any cooling devices, as necessary.
	An update has corrupted the operating system.	Uninstall the software update or perform a system restore.
	The RAM is failing.	Run **chkdsk /F /R** from the Recovery Environment.
	The power supply is failing.	Replace any failing devices with known-good devices.
An application does not install.	The downloaded application installer contains a virus and has been prevented from installing by virus protection software.	Obtain a new installation disk or delete the file and download the installation file again.
	The installation disk or file is corrupted.	
	The installer is not compatible with the operating system.	Run the installer in Compatibility mode.
	The hardware does not meet the minimum requirements.	Install hardware that meets the minimum installation requirements.
	The software on which the application relies is not installed.	Install any software on which the application relies.
A computer with Windows 7 installed does not run Aero.	The computer does not meet the minimum hardware requirements for running Aero.	Upgrade the processor, RAM, and video card to meet the minimum Microsoft requirements for Aero.
The UAC no longer prompts the user for permission.	The UAC has been turned off.	Turn on the UAC in the User Account applet in the Control Panel.

Identify the Problem	Probable Causes	Possible Solutions
No *gadgets* appear on the desktop.	The gadgets have never been installed or have been uninstalled.	Right-click the desktop > Gadgets > right-click a gadget > Add.
	The XML necessary to render the gadgets is broken, corrupted, or not installed.	Register the file msxml3.dll by entering **regsvr32 msxml3.dll** at the command prompt.
The computer is running slowly and has a delayed response.	A process is using most of the CPU resources.	Restart the process using the Services console (services.msc). If the process is not needed, use Task Manager to end the process. Restart the computer.
The computer displays a "Boot Configuration Data missing" error while booting.	The computer was improperly shut down. A Windows update was unsuccessful.	Boot from Windows 10 installation/recovery media and run the Bootrec tool.

Advanced Troubleshooting for Windows Operating Systems (11.7.3)

OS problems can be attributed to hardware, application, or configuration issues or to some combination of the three. You are likely to need to resolve some types of OS problems more often than others.

Advanced Problems and Solutions for Windows Operating Systems (11.7.3.1)

Table 11-16 lists advanced problems, probable causes, and possible solutions for Windows operating systems.

Table 11-16   Advanced Problems and Solutions for Windows Operating Systems

Identify the Problem	Probable Causes	Possible Solutions
The computer displays an "Invalid Boot Disk" error after the POST.	Media that does not have an operating system is in a drive.	Remove all media from the drives.
	The boot order is not set correctly in the BIOS/UEFI settings.	Change the boot order in the BIOS/UEFI settings to start with the boot drive.
	The hard drive is not detected.	Reconnect the hard drive cables.
	The hard drive does not have an operating system installed.	Install an operating system.
	The MBR/GPT is corrupted.	Use the **bootrec /fixmbr** command from the System Recovery options of Windows 7 or Vista.
	The computer has a boot sector virus.	Recovery options of Windows 7 or Vista.
		Run virus removal software.
	The hard drive is failing.	Replace the hard drive.
		Use the last known good configuration to boot the computer.
The computer displays an "Inaccessible Boot Device" error after the POST.	A recently installed device driver is incompatible with the boot controller.	Boot the computer in Safe mode and load a restore point from before the installation of new hardware.
	BOOTMGR is corrupted.	Restore BOOTMGR using the Windows Recovery Environment.
The computer displays a "BOOTMGR is missing" error after the POST.	BOOTMGR is missing or damaged.	Change the boot order in the BIOS settings to start with the boot drive.
	The boot order is not set correctly in the BIOS/UEFI settings.	Run **chkdsk /F /R** from the recovery console.
	The MBR/GPT is corrupted.	Run **chkdsk /F /R** from the recovery console.
	The hard drive is failing.	

Identify the Problem	Probable Causes	Possible Solutions
A service failed to start when the computer booted.	The service is not enabled.	Enable the service. Set the service to Automatic and re-enable the required service.
	The service is set to Manual, and the failed service requires another service to be enabled.	Set the service to Automatic and re-enable the required service.
	The device has been disabled in the BIOS settings.	Enable the device in the BIOS settings.
A device did not start when the computer booted.	The device has a conflict with a newly installed device.	Remove the newly installed device.
	The driver is corrupted.	Reinstall or roll back the driver.
	The uninstall program did not work correctly.	Reinstall the program and run the uninstall program again.
A program listed in the Registry is not found.	The hard drive has become corrupted.	Run **chkdsk /F /R** to fix the hard drive file entries.
	The computer has a virus.	Scan for and remove the virus.
	The computer is set to restart when there is a failure.	Press **F8** to open the Advanced Options menu and choose Disable Automatic Restart on System Failure.
The computer continually restarts without displaying the desktop.	A startup file has become corrupted.	Run **chkdsk /F /R** from the Recovery Environment. Run Automatic Repair from the Recovery Environment in Windows 8.
	A driver is not compatible with the hardware.	Research the STOP error and the name of the module that produced the error.
The computer displays a black or blue screen of death (BSOD).	There is a hardware failure.	Replace any failing devices with known-good devices.
	The CPU or FSB settings are incorrect on the motherboard or in the BIOS settings.	Check and reset the CPU and FSB settings.

Identify the Problem	Probable Causes	Possible Solutions
The computer locks up without any error messages.	The computer is overheating.	Check and replace any cooling devices, as necessary.
	An update has corrupted the operating system.	Uninstall the software update or perform a system restore.
	There is a hardware failure.	Run **chkdsk /F /R** from the Recovery Environment.
	The computer has a virus.	Replace any failing devices with known-good devices.
		Scan for and remove the virus.
	The installation application is not compatible with the operating system.	Run the installation application in Compatibility mode.
An application does not install.	The index service is not running.	Start the index services by using services.msc.
The search feature takes a long time to find results.	The index service is not indexing in the correct locations.	Change the settings of the index service in the Advanced Options panel.
	A process is using most of the CPU resources.	Restart the process with services.msc.
The computer is running slowly and has a delayed response.	A process is using most of the CPU resources.	If the process is not needed, end the process with Task Manager.
		Restart the computer.
	One or more programs using the DLL file were uninstalled and removed the DLL file that was needed by another program.	Reinstall the program that has a missing or corrupt DLL file.
When you run a program, a missing or corrupt DLL message is displayed.	The DLL file was corrupted during a bad installation.	Reinstall the application that uninstalled the DLL.
		Run **sfc /scannow** in Safe mode.
	Windows does not include the proper drivers to recognize RAID.	Install the proper drivers.

Identify the Problem	Probable Causes	Possible Solutions
RAID is not detected during installation.	RAID settings in BIOS/UEFI are incorrect.	Change the settings in BIOS/UEFI to enable RAID.
	The computer was shut down improperly.	Repair the computer from the Advanced Startup Options menu.
A system file is corrupted.	The computer was shut down improperly.	Boot computer in Safe mode and run **sfc /scannow.**
	The computer has been configured to boot in Safe mode.	Use **msconfig** to adjust the startup settings for the program.
The computer boots to Safe mode.	The computer has a virus.	Scan for and remove any viruses.
A file fails to open.	The file is corrupted.	Restore the file from backup.
	The file type is not associated with any program.	Choose a program to open the file type.

11.7.3.2 Lab: Troubleshoot Operating System Problems

In this lab, you will diagnose the causes of various operating system problems and solve them.

Summary (11.8)

The focus of this chapter was on Windows 7, Windows 8, and Windows 10. Each version comes in several editions, such as Home, Pro, Ultimate, or Enterprise, and comes in 32-bit and 64-bit versions. The Windows editions are tailored for the needs of corporate and personal users. You explored the Windows desktop, Start menu, and taskbar and learned how to work with the Task Manager and File Explorer to monitor system performance and manage files and folders on a computer running Windows in labs.

You learned about the various system tools that are used to configure the Windows operating system and to change settings. You learned that the Control Panel offers many configuration tools that can be used to create and modify user accounts, configure updates and backups, personalize the look and feel of Windows, install and uninstall apps, and configure network settings. You performed several lab exercises using tools in the Control Panel. In these labs, you used the User Accounts control panel to create and modify users, configured Internet settings in Internet Explorer, used the System control panel to configure and manage virtual memory, used Device Manager to display devices and monitor settings, changed region and language options, and conducted many other administrative tasks.

In addition to using the Control Panel GUI, you also learned how to use the Windows CLI and PowerShell command line utility to perform administrative tasks. You also learned system commands that provide the same functions as those found in Task Manager and how to run system utilities from the Windows CLI. To practice what you learned, you performed several labs that involved working with file system commands, disk CLI commands, task and system CLI commands, and other useful commands.

You also learned about the using domains and workgroups for organizing and managing Windows computers on a network. You learned how to share local computer resources, such as files, folders, and printers, on the network and how to configure a wired network connection. You performed labs related to Windows networking in which you created and shared a folder and set permissions, connected your computer to a wireless router and tested the wireless connection, and configured Windows for remote access using Remote Desktop and Remote Assistance.

At the end of the chapter, you learned the importance of following a preventive maintenance plan to decrease downtime, improve performance, improve reliability, and lower repair costs. A good preventive maintenance plan includes detailed information about the maintenance of all computers and network equipment. Preventive maintenance should take place when it causes the least disruption to users. This often means scheduling tasks at night, early in the morning, or over the weekend. You performed a lab in which you scheduled a task using the GUI and at the command line.

Regular scans for viruses and malware are an important part of preventive maintenance. Some programs, such as antivirus scanners and spyware removal tools, do not
automatically start when the computer boots. To ensure that these programs run each
time the computer is booted, you can add them to the Startup folder of the Start
menu. You performed a lab in which you managed startup applications using the Run
key.

Finally, you learned the six steps in the troubleshooting process as they are applied to
Windows operating systems.

Practice

The following activities provide practice with the topics introduced in this chapter.
The labs are available in the companion *IT Essentials v8 Labs & Study Guide* (ISBN
9780138166304). The Packet Tracer activity instructions are also in the *Labs &
Study Guide*. The PKA files are found in the online course.

Labs

11.1.2.5 Lab: Explore the Windows Desktop

11.1.3.4 Lab: Work with Task Manager

11.1.4.11 Lab: Working with File Explorer

11.2.1.5 Lab: Explore Control Panel Categories

11.2.2.3 Lab: User Accounts

11.2.2.4 Lab: Permissions

11.2.3.5 Lab: Configure Browser Settings

11.2.5.8 Lab: Manage Virtual Memory

11.2.6.2 Lab: Use Device Manager

11.2.7.4 Lab: Region and Language Options

Packet Tracer
☐ Activity

Packet Tracer Activity

Check Your Understanding Questions

Complete all the review questions listed here to test your understanding of the topics and concepts in this chapter. Appendix A, "Answers to 'Check Your Understanding' Questions," lists the answers.

1. A user logs into Active Directory on a workstation, and the user's home directory does not redirect to a network share on a file server. A technician suspects that the Group Policy settings are incorrect. Which command can the technician use to verify the Group Policy settings?

   A. tasklist

   B. gpresult

   C. gpupdate

   D. runas

   E. rstrui

2. What are two file attributes in the Windows environment? (Choose two.)

   A. archive

   B. General

   C. Details

   D. read-only

   E. Security

3. Why would an administrator use Windows Remote Desktop and Windows Remote Assistant?

   A. to provide secure remote access to resources on another network

   B. to connect to an enterprise network across an unsecured connection and act as a local client of that network

   C. to enable sharing of files and presentations with a group of users over the Internet

   D. to connect to a remote computer over the network to control its applications and data

4. Which two issues are likely to cause BSOD errors? (Choose two.)

   A. out-of-date browser

   B. power supply failure

   C. lack of antivirus software

   D. device driver errors

   E. RAM failing

5. A technician notices that an application is not responding to commands and that the computer seems to respond slowly when applications are opened. What is the best administrative tool for forcing the release of system resources from the unresponsive application?

   A. System Restore

   B. Add or Remove Programs

   C. Event Viewer

   D. Task Manager

6. In which folder are application files for 32-bit programs typically stored on a computer that is running a 64-bit edition of Windows 7?

   A. C:\Program Files

   B. C:\Program Files (x86)

   C. C:\Users

   D. C:\Application Data

7. Which utility would be used to find the default gateway configured on a host?

   A. **ipconfig**

   B. **ping**

   C. **nslookup**

   D. **tracert**

8. A help desk technician is talking to a user to clarify a technical problem that the user is having. What are two examples of open-ended questions that the technician might use to help determine the issue? (Choose two.)

   A. Has anyone else used the computer recently?

   B. What updates have you performed lately?

   C. Can you boot the operating system?

   D. Can you boot up in Safe mode?

   E. What happens when you try to access your files?

9. Which of the following is true about restore points?

   A. Restore points back up personal data files.

   B. Restore points recover corrupted or deleted data files.

   C. Restore points should always be created before changes are made to a system.

   D. Once System Restore is used to restore a system, the change is irreversible.

10. A user notices that some of the programs that are installed before upgrading to Windows 7 no longer function properly. What can the user do to fix this problem?

    A. Lower the UAC setting in the Change User Account Control settings dialog box of the User Accounts control panel.

    B. Reinstall the programs in Compatibility mode.

    C. Update the driver for the graphics card.

    D. Change the file system to FAT16.

11. A user wants to configure a password on a Windows 10 PC when the PC is woken from hibernation. Where can the user configure this?

    A. Settings, Privacy

    B. Control Panel, User Accounts

    C. Control Panel, Power Options

    D. Settings, Accounts

12. A corporation has expanded to include multiple remote offices around the globe. Which technology should be used to allow the remote offices to communicate and share network resources privately?

    A. Remote Assistance

    B. VPN

    C. Remote Desktop

    D. administrative share

13. Which TCP port number would be used for remotely connecting to a network server and configuring it using an unencrypted connection?

    A. 20

    B. 22

    C. 3389

    D. 443

14. How many libraries are created by default for each user on a new Windows 10 installation?

    A. 5

    B. 6

    C. 4

    D. 2

15. Which Windows utility can be used to schedule a regular backup for preventive maintenance?

    A. Windows Task Manager

    B. Windows Task Scheduler

    C. Disk Cleanup

    D. System Restore

16. After solving a problem on a computer, a technician checks the event log to ensure that there are no new error messages. At which step of the troubleshooting process is this action taking place?

    A. Document the findings.

    B. Verify the solution and full system functionality.

    C. Establish a theory of probable cause.

    D. Determine an exact cause.

17. What are three common causes of operating system problems? (Choose three.)

    A. CMOS battery problem

    B. incorrect IP addressing information

    C. failed service pack installation

    D. a corrupted Registry

    E. loose cable connections

    F. virus infection

18. A technician is designing a hardware preventive maintenance plan for a company. Which strategy should be included in the plan?

    A. Schedule and document routine maintenance tasks.

    B. Avoid performing maintenance operations on Plug and Play devices that are controlled by the operating system.

    C. Avoid performing maintenance operations on components until the equipment malfunctions.

    D. Only clean equipment as requested by the customer.

CHAPTER 12

Mobile, Linux, and macOS Operating Systems

Objectives

Upon completion of this chapter, you will be able to answer the following questions:

- Compare the Android and iOS operating systems.

- Describe the features of the Android touch interface.

- Describe the features of the iOS touch interface.

- Describe operating system features that are common among mobile devices.

- Explain how to configure various types of passcode locks.

- Describe cloud-enabled services for mobile devices.

- Describe software security for mobile devices.

- Describe tools and features of the Linux and Mac operating systems.

- Describe Linux and macOS best practices.

- Define basic CLI commands.

- Explain the six steps of troubleshooting other operating systems.

- Describe common problems and solutions for other operating systems.

Key Terms

This chapter uses the following key terms. You can find the definitions in the glossary at the end of the book.

Android   page 734

Android Application Package (apk)   page 738

Android main home screen   page 740

antivirus   page 772

app   page 737

App Store   page 737

Apple File System (APFS)   page 776

Apple's Software Development Kit (SDK) Xcode   page 737

closed source   page 734

command line interface (CLI)   page 786

cron   page 791

digital assistant   page 760

disk utility   page 790

ext3   page 776

ext4   page 776

Extended Hierarchical File System (HFS Plus)   page 776

firewall app   page 773

firmware   page 793

Introduction (12.0)

The use of mobile devices has grown very rapidly. IT technicians and professionals must be familiar with the operating systems (OSs) on these devices. Like desktops and laptops, mobile devices also use operating systems to interface with the hardware and to run software. The two most commonly used mobile operating systems are Android and iOS. There are also desktop operating systems other than Windows, the two most popular being Linux and macOS.

In this chapter, you will learn about the components, functions, and terminology related to mobile, Linux, and macOS operating systems. First, you will learn about the differences between the open source and customizable Android and the Apple-proprietary and closed source iOS mobile operating systems. You will also learn about common mobile device features, such as screen orientation, screen calibration, Wi-Fi calling, virtual assistants, and GPS. You will work with both the Android and iOS operating systems as part of lab exercises.

The portable nature of mobile devices puts them at risk for theft and loss. You will learn about mobile security features such as screen lock, biometric authentication, remote lock, remote wipe, and patching and upgrading. You will also learn to configure mobile OSs to disable access if too many failed login attempts are made to prevent someone from trying to guess a passcode. Most mobile devices also have a remote lock and remote wipe feature that can be activated if the device is stolen. You will perform a lab exercise securing a mobile device using passcode locks.

Finally, you will learn the six steps in the troubleshooting process as they are applied to mobile, Linux, and macOS operating systems.

Mobile Operating Systems (12.1)

Mobile operating systems are OSs that are designed specifically to run on mobile devices such as smartphones, tablets, and wearables. Just like other operating systems, mobile operating systems manage hardware and software on devices; also as with other OSs, there is not interoperability among device vendor hardware.

Android vs. iOS (12.1.1)

The two most popular mobile operating system are Android and iOS. iOS runs only on Apple products.

Open Source vs. Closed Source (12.1.1.1)

Like desktops and laptops, mobile devices use an OS to run software (see Figure 12-1). This chapter focuses on the two most commonly used mobile operating systems: Android, developed by Google, and iOS, developed by Apple.

Figure 12-1   Mobile Device Operating Systems

In order for users to be able to analyze and modify software, they must be able to see the source code. *Source code* is a sequence of instructions written in human-readable language before it is turned into machine language (zeros and ones). The source code is an important component of free software as it allows users to analyze and eventually modify the code. When a developer chooses to provide the source code, the software is said to be *open source*. If the program's source code is not published, the software is said to be *closed source*.

Android is an open source, Linux-based smartphone/tablet operating system developed by the Open Handset Alliance, primarily driven by Google. Released in 2008 on the HTC Dream, Android OS has been customized for use on a wide range of electronic devices. Because Android is open source and customizable, programmers can use it to operate devices such as laptops, smart TVs, and e-book readers. There have even been Android installations in devices such as cameras, navigation systems, and portable media players. Figure 12-2 shows Android running on a tablet.

Figure 12-2 Android GUI

iOS is a closed source Unix-based operating system for Apple's iPhone smartphone and iPad tablet. iOS was released in 2007 on the first iPhone, though the Apple iOS source code was not released to the public. Copying, modifying, or redistributing iOS requires permission from Apple. Figure 12-3 shows iOS running on an iPhone.

iOS is not the only closed source OS for mobile devices. Microsoft has also created versions of Windows for its mobile devices, including Windows CE, Windows Phone 7, and Windows Phone 8. With the development of *Windows 10 Mobile*, shown in Figure 12-4, Microsoft provides a very similar user interface and use of code on all Microsoft devices, including Windows 10 Mobile phones and Surface tablets. Microsoft ended development and support for Windows 10 Mobile in January of 2020.

Figure 12-3   iOS GUI

Figure 12-4   Windows 10 Mobile

Applications and Content Sources (12.1.1.2)

Apps are programs that are executed on mobile devices. An app is written and compiled for a specific mobile operating system, such as Apple iOS, Android, or Windows. Mobile devices come with a number of different apps preinstalled to provide basic functionality (see Figure 12-5). There are apps to make phone calls, send and receive email, listen to music, take pictures, and play videos or video games.

Apps are used on mobile devices the same way that programs are used on computers. Instead of being installed from an optical disc, apps are downloaded from a content source. Some apps can be downloaded for free, and others must be purchased.

Figure 12-5   Applications

Apps for Apple iOS mobile devices are available for free or purchase from the *App Store*, shown in Figure 12-6. Apple uses a walled garden model for its apps, which means the apps must be submitted to and approved by Apple before they are released to users. This helps prevent the spread of malware and malicious code. Third-party developers can create apps for iOS devices by using *Apple's Software Development Kit (SDK) Xcode* and the *Swift* programming language. Note that Xcode can only be installed on computers running macOS

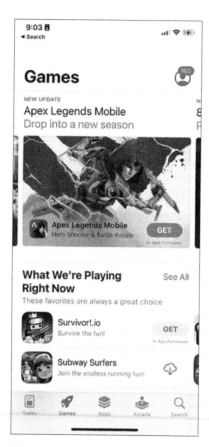

Figure 12-6   iOS Apps

Android apps are available from both *Google Play*, shown in Figure 12-7, and third-party sites, such as Amazon's App Store. Android Studio, a Java-based SDK, is available on Linux, Windows, and macOS. Android apps run in a sandbox and have only the privileges enabled by the user. A prompt appears if an app needs to obtain permissions. Permissions are granted via the app's Settings page.

Third-party or custom programs are installed directly by using an *Android Application Package (apk)* file. This gives users the ability to directly install apps without going through the storefront interface, in a process known as *sideloading*.

Automobile Apps

Many new cars have navigation built into them. Some also have what are known as in-vehicle entertainment systems. A growing trend is to use many of the apps on a mobile device through such an entertainment system, such as Android Auto or Apple CarPlay. A tablet or smartphone is connected to such a system via USB or Bluetooth. Navigation is one of the most common uses for this type of connection. You can also access the music that is on your mobile device and play it over the car stereo. Other features include talk-to-text, hands-free calling, access to digital assistants, and calendar viewing.

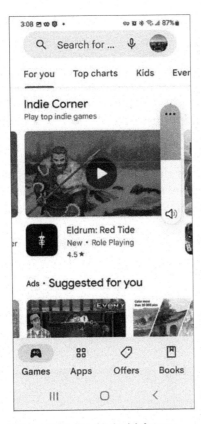

Figure 12-7 Android Apps

12.1.1.3 Check Your Understanding: Compare Android and iOS

Refer to the online course to complete this activity.

Mobile Touch Interface (12.1.2)

Android and iOS support a selection of touchscreens.

Android Home Screen Items (12.1.2.1)

Much like a desktop or laptop computer, a mobile device organizes icons and widgets on multiple screens for easy access (see Figure 12-8).

Figure 12-8 Icon and Widget Organization

One screen is designated as the home screen. Additional screens are accessed by sliding the home screen to the left or right. Each screen contains navigation icons, a main area where icons and widgets are accessed, and notification and system icons, as shown in Figure 12-9. The screen indicator displays which screen is currently active.

Figure 12-9 *Android Main Home Screen*

The Android OS has a system bar for navigating apps and screens, as shown in Figure 12-10. The system bar is always displayed at the bottom of every screen.

Figure 12-10 *Navigation Icons*

The system bar contains the following buttons:

- **Back:** Returns to the previous screen. If the onscreen keyboard is displayed, this button closes it. By continuing to tap the Back button, you can navigate through the previous screens until the home screen is displayed.

- **Home:** Returns to the home screen.

- **Recent Apps:** Opens thumbnail images of recently used apps. To open an app, touch its thumbnail. Swipe a thumbnail to remove it from the list.

- **Menu:** If available, Menu shows additional options for the current screen.

Each Android device has an area that contains system icons, such as the clock, battery status, and radio signal status for Wi-Fi and provider networks. Figure 12-11 shows display status icons indicating communication activity for apps such as email, text messaging, and Facebook.

Figure 12-11 *Notification and System Icons*

To open the notification area on Android devices, swipe down from the top of the screen. You can do the following when notifications are open:

- Respond to a notification by touching it.

- Dismiss a notification by swiping it off the screen to either side.

- Dismiss all notifications with the icon.

- Toggle often-used settings.

- Adjust the brightness of the screen.

- Open the Settings menu with the quick settings icon.

12.1.2.2 Lab: Working with Android

In this lab, you will work with the Android operating system.

iOS Home Screen Items (12.1.2.3)

The *iOS interface* works in much the same way as the Android interface. Screens are used to organize apps (see Figure 12-12), and apps are launched with a touch. There are some very important differences:

- **No navigation icons:** A physical button may have to be pressed instead of touching navigation icons.

- **No widgets:** Only apps and other content can be installed on iOS device screens.

- **No app shortcuts:** Each app on a home screen is the actual app, not a shortcut.

Figure 12-12   iOS Interface

Unlike Android devices, iOS devices do not use navigation icons to perform functions. On iPhone versions prior to the iPhone X, a single physical button called the *Home button*, shown in Figure 12-13, performs many of the same functions as the Android navigation buttons.

Figure 12-13   Home Button

The Home button is at the bottom of the device and can perform many functions. The following are some common functions in iOS:

- **Wake the device:** In versions prior to iPhone X, when the device's screen is off, press the Home button once to turn it on. On iPhone X, you can wake the device using either facial recognition or by raising the phone and tapping the screen. (Raise to Wake is also available on iPhone versions 6s and later.)

- **Return to the home screen:** In versions prior to iPhone X, press the Home button while using an app to return to the last home screen that was used. On iPhone X, return to the home screen by swiping the screen up from the bottom.

- **Start *Siri* or voice control:** In versions prior to iPhone X, press and hold the Home button to start Siri or voice control. Siri is special software that understands advanced voice controls. On iPhone X, launch Siri by pressing and holding the side button.

iOS devices have a notification area called Notification Center that displays all alerts in one location, as shown in Figure 12-14. To open the notification area on iOS devices, touch the top center of the screen and swipe down. Once in Notification Center, you can browse notifications and alerts, dismiss them, clear them, and adjust them as necessary.

Figure 12-14   *iOS Notification Center*

iOS devices allow the user to quickly access common settings and switches, shown in Figure 12-15, even if the device is locked. To access the commonly used settings menu, swipe up from the very bottom of any screen or down from the top (depending on your device) to open the Control Center. From the commonly used settings screen, a user can:

- Toggle commonly used settings such as Airplane mode, Wi-Fi, Bluetooth, Do Not Disturb mode, and screen rotation lock

- Adjust screen brightness

- Control the music player

- Access AirDrop

- Access the Flashlight, Clock, Calendar, and Camera apps

From any screen of an iOS device, touch the screen—any part of the screen except the very top or the very bottom—and drag down to reveal the Spotlight search field, shown in Figure 12-16. When the Spotlight search field is revealed, type what you're looking for. *iOS Spotlight* shows suggestions from many sources, including apps on the device, the Internet, iTunes, the App Store, and nearby locations. Spotlight also automatically updates the results as you type.

Figure 12-15   Commonly Used Settings

12.1.2.4 Lab: Working with iOS

In this lab, you will work with the iOS operating system.

Figure 12-16   iOS Spotlight

Common Mobile Device Features (12.1.3)

A mobile device offers a set of capabilities, services, and applications to the user, and although users have a choice of different vendors and models for the devices, there are common features among them. This section describes capabilities, services, and applications that are common to mobile devices and also describes others that are unique to different vendors' devices.

Screen Orientation (12.1.3.1)

Most mobile devices can be used in either portrait or landscape mode, as shown in Figure 12-17. A sensor inside the device, called an *accelerometer*, detects how the device is being held and changes the *screen orientation* appropriately. Users can choose the viewing mode that is the most comfortable for them for different types of content or applications. Content is automatically rotated to the position of the device. This feature is useful, for example, when taking a photograph. When the device is turned to landscape mode, the Camera app also turns to landscape mode. Also, when a user is writing a text, turning the device to landscape mode automatically turns the app to landscape mode, making the keyboard larger and wider.

Figure 12-17   Screen Orientation

A device may also have a gyroscope to provide more accurate movement readings. A gyroscope allows a device to be used as a control mechanism for driving games where the phone or tablet itself functions as a steering wheel.

Android Screen Auto-Rotation Setting

When using an Android device, to enable auto rotation, open the notifications panel and turn on the auto-rotate function by tapping the screen rotation icon, indicated in Figure 12-18.

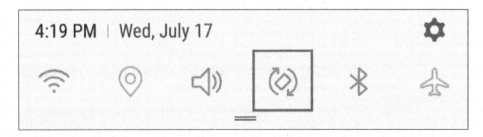

Figure 12-18   Android Screen Auto-Rotation Setting

iOS Screen Auto-Rotation Setting

When using an iOS device, to enable automatic rotation, swipe up from the bottom or down from the top (depending on your device) to open the Control Center. Then tap the screen rotation lock icon, shown in Figure 12-19, until it is turned off.

Figure 12-19 iOS Screen Auto-Rotation Setting

Screen Calibration (12.1.3.2)

When using a mobile device, you may need to adjust the brightness of the screen (see Figure 12-20). When bright sunlight makes the screen difficult to read, increase the brightness level. Inversely, very low brightness is helpful when reading a book on a mobile device at night. Some mobile devices can be configured to automatically adjust the brightness depending on the amount of surrounding light. The device must have a light sensor to use auto-brightness.

The LCD screen component for most mobile devices consumes the most battery power on the device. Lowering the brightness or using auto-brightness helps conserve battery power. Set the brightness to the lowest setting to get the most battery life from the device.

Figure 12-20 *Screen Calibration*

Android Brightness Menu

When using an Android device, to configure screen brightness, swipe down from the very top of the screen and use the path Display > Brightness, then slide the brightness to the desired level, as shown in Figure 12-21.

Alternatively, tap the Adaptive Brightness toggle to allow the device to determine the optimal screen brightness based on the amount of ambient light.

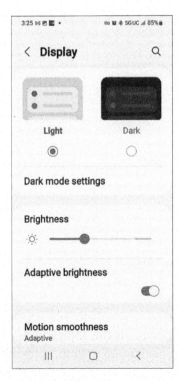

Figure 12-21   Android Brightness Menu

iOS Display & Brightness Menu

When using an iOS device, to configure screen brightness, swipe up from the very bottom of the screen or down from the top (depending on your device) to open the Control Center and slide the brightness bar up or down to vary the brightness. Alternatively, to configure brightness in the Settings menu, tap Settings > Display & Brightness and then slide the brightness to the desired level, as shown in Figure 12-22.

Figure 12-22 iOS Display & Brightness Menu

GPS (12.1.3.3)

Another common feature of mobile devices is the ability to work with the *Global Positioning System (GPS)*. GPS is a navigation system, shown in Figure 12-23, that determines the time and geographical location of the device by using messages from satellites in space and a receiver on Earth. A GPS radio receiver uses at least four satellites to calculate position, based on the messages. GPS is very accurate and can be used under most weather conditions. However, dense foliage, tunnels, and tall buildings can interrupt satellite signals. GPS receivers must have line-of-sight to GPS satellites and do not work indoors. An *indoor positioning system (IPS)* can determine location by triangulating the position of the device based on proximity to other radio signals, such as those from Wi-Fi access points.

Figure 12-23   GPS

GPS services allow app vendors and websites to know the location of a device and offer location-specific services (such as local weather and advertising). This is called *geotracking*.

Android Location Services

To enable GPS on Android devices, tap Settings > Location and then tap on the toggle to turn on location services, as shown in Figure 12-24.

Figure 12-24   Android Location Services

iOS Location Services

To enable GPS on iOS devices, tap Settings > Privacy and then toggle Location Services on, as shown in Figure 12-25.

12.1.3.4 Lab: Mobile Device Features

In this lab, you will learn about mobile device features.

Wi-Fi Calling (12.1.3.5)

Instead of using the cellular carrier's network, a modern smartphone can use the Internet to transport voice calls by taking advantage of a local Wi-Fi hotspot (see Figure 12-26). This is called *Wi-Fi calling*. Locations such as coffee shops, workplaces, libraries, and homes usually have Wi-Fi networks connected to the Internet. A phone can transport voice calls through a local Wi-Fi hotspot. If there is no Wi-Fi hotspot within reach, the phone uses the cellular carrier's network to transport voice calls.

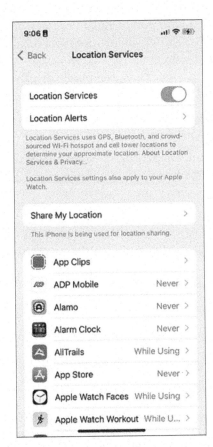

Figure 12-25 iOS Location Services

Figure 12-26 Wi-Fi Calling

Wi-Fi calling is very useful in areas with poor cellular coverage because it uses a local Wi-Fi hotspot to fill the gaps. The Wi-Fi hotspot must be able to guarantee a throughput of at least 1 Mbps to the Internet for a good-quality call. When Wi-Fi calling is enabled and in use during a voice call, the phone displays "Wi-Fi" next to the carrier name.

Enabling Wi-Fi Calling on Android

To enable Wi-Fi calling on Android, tap Settings > More (under the Wireless & Networks section) and tap Wi-Fi Calling, as shown in Figure 12-27, to expose the on/off toggle. Tap the toggle to on to turn it on.

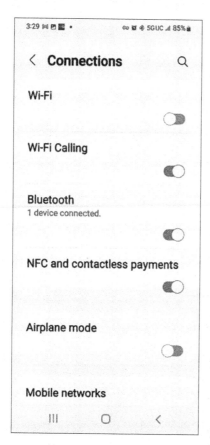

Figure 12-27   Enabling Wi-Fi Calling on Android

Enabling Wi-Fi Calling on iOS

To enable Wi-Fi calling on iOS, tap Settings > Phone > Wi-Fi Calling and then toggle on Wi-Fi Calling on This Phone, as shown in Figure 12-28.

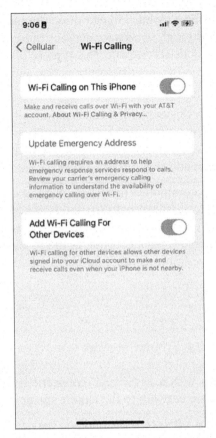

Figure 12-28   Enabling Wi-Fi Calling on iOS

Note

Not all cellular carriers allow Wi-Fi calling. If you cannot enable it on your phone, your carrier or mobile device probably does not support it.

NFC Payment (12.1.3.6)

Mobile payment refers to payment made through a mobile phone. You can make mobile payments in several ways:

- **Premium SMS-based transactional payments:** Consumers send an SMS message to a carrier's special phone number containing a payment request. The seller is informed that the payment has been received and is cleared to release the goods. The charge is then added to the customer's phone bill. Slow speed, poor reliability, and poor security are a few shortcomings of this method.

- **Direct mobile billing:** By using a mobile billing option during checkout, a user identifies themself (usually through two-factor authentication) and allows the charge to be added to the mobile service bill. This type of billing is very popular in Asia and has several benefits: security, convenience, and no need for bank cards or credit cards.

- **Mobile web payments:** With this method, a consumer uses the Web or dedicated apps to complete a payment transaction. This method relies on Wireless Application Protocol (WAP) and usually requires the use of a credit card or a pre-registered online payment solution, such as PayPal.

- **Contactless NFC (fear field communication):** This method is used mostly in physical store transactions. A consumer pays for goods or services by waving the phone near the payment system. Based on a unique ID, the payment is charged directly against a prepaid account, bank account, or credit card. *NFC payments* are also used in mass-transportation services, for public parking, and in many other consumer areas.

Virtual Private Network (12.1.3.7)

A *virtual private network (VPN)* is a private network that uses a public network (usually the Internet) to connect remote sites or users together (see Figure 12-29). Instead of using a dedicated leased line, a VPN uses "virtual" connections routed through the Internet from the company's private network to the remote site or employee.

Many companies create their own VPNs to accommodate the needs of remote employees and distant offices. With the proliferation of mobile devices, it was a natural move to add VPN clients to smartphones and tablets.

Figure 12-29   Virtual Private Network

When a VPN is established from a client to a server, the client accesses the network behind the server as if it were connected directly to that network. Because VPN protocols also allow for data encryption, the communication between client and server is secure.

When VPN information has been added to a device, the VPN connection must be started before traffic can be sent and received through it.

Configuring a VPN Connection on Android

To create a new VPN connection on Android, tap Settings > More (under the Wireless & Networks section) > VPN, tap on the + sign to add a VPN connection, and enter the VPN information (see Figure 12-30).

Figure 12-30   Configuring a VPN Connection on Android

Starting a VPN Connection on Android

To start a VPN connection on Android, tap Settings > General > VPN, select the desired VPN connection, enter the username and password, and tap CONNECT (see Figure 12-31).

Figure 12-31   Starting a VPN Connection on Android

Configuring a VPN Connection on iOS

To create a new VPN connection on iOS, tap Settings > General > VPN & Device Management > VPN > Add VPN Configuration and fill in the screen shown in Figure 12-32.

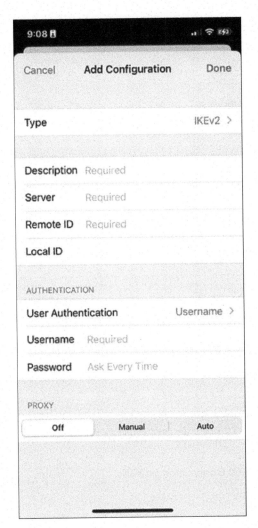

Figure 12-32   Configuring a VPN Connection on iOS

Starting a VPN Connection on iOS

To start a VPN connection on iOS, tap Settings and toggle VPN on, as shown in Figure 12-33.

Figure 12-33   Starting a VPN Connection on iOS

Virtual Assistants (12.1.3.8)

A *digital assistant*, sometimes called a *virtual assistant*, is a program that can understand natural conversational language and perform tasks for the end user. Modern mobile devices are powerful computers, which makes them a perfect platform for digital assistants. Popular digital assistants include Google Now for Android, Siri for iOS, and Cortana for Windows Phone 8.1 and Windows 10 Mobile.

Digital assistants rely on artificial intelligence, machine learning, and voice recognition technology to understand conversational-style voice commands (see Figure 12-34). As the end user interacts with a digital assistant, sophisticated algorithms predict the user's needs and fulfill requests. By pairing simple voice requests with other inputs, such as GPS location, digital assistants can perform tasks such as playing a specific song, performing a web search, taking a note, or sending an email.

Figure 12-34 Virtual Assistants

Google Now

To access Google Now on an Android device, simply say "Okay google," and Google Now begins listening to requests, as shown in Figure 12-35.

Figure 12-35 Google Now

Siri

To access Siri on an iOS device, press and hold the Home button or the side button (depending on the device). Siri begins listening to requests, as shown in Figure 12-36. Alternatively, you can configure Siri to start listening to commands when it hears "Hey Siri." To enable "Hey Siri," tap Settings > Siri & Search and toggle Listen for "Hey Siri" on.

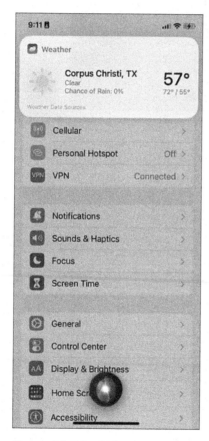

Figure 12-36   Siri

Methods for Securing Mobile Devices (12.2)

Securing mobile devices involves many issues, from physical security to encryption of data. It is easy to forget how vulnerable mobile devices can be, but their ease of use and network access make them targets of threats. There are many ways to secure a mobile device, and knowing them can help ensure that users are practicing good security practices rather than leaving themselves vulnerable due to poor security practices. Mobile device threats are increasing and can result in data loss, security breaches, and regulatory compliance violations.

Passcode Locks (12.2.1)

Setting screen locks and using biometric authentication are methods that can help protect against unauthorized access to a device. Such measures can prevent immediate access to a device for an intruder.

What Do You Already Know? Screen Locks (12.2.1.1)

It is imperative that a mobile device be protected by a screen lock. There are five types of screen locks: face, passcode, pattern, swipe, and fingerprint.

Read the scenarios and select the lock that is used in each case.

Scenarios

Scenario 1: This screen lock requires that a four- or six-digit numeric code be entered to unlock the mobile device.

Scenario 2: This screen lock requires the user to simply swipe the device screen in a predefined direction to unlock the device.

Scenario 3: This screen lock requires the user to join four or more dots in a specific pattern to unlock the device.

Scenario 4: This biometric screen lock can unlock a device by scanning the user's fingerprint.

Scenario 5: This biometric screen lock can unlock a device by scanning the user's face.

Answers

Scenario 1 Answer: Passcode lock. Passcode options can also include setting a custom numeric code or alphanumeric password.

Scenario 2 Answer: Swipe lock (also called Slide to Unlock on many Android devices). Although convenient, this less secure method should be used only if security is unimportant.

Scenario 3 Answer: Pattern lock. This type of lock is available on many Android devices. The screen unlocks when you draw the correct pattern with your finger.

Scenario 4 Answer: Fingerprint lock. This iOS and Android feature converts the user's fingerprint scan into a unique hash. When a user touches the fingerprint sensor, the device recomputes the hash. The device unlocks if the hash values match.

Scenario 5 Answer: Face lock. This iOS and Android feature computes a hash using a picture of the user's face.

12.2.1.2 Lab: Passcode Locks

In this lab, you will use passcode locks.

Restrictions on Failed Login Attempts (12.2.1.3)

When a *passcode* has been properly implemented, unlocking a mobile device requires entering the correct PIN, password, pattern, or another passcode type. In theory, a passcode, such as a PIN, could be guessed given enough time and perseverance. To prevent someone from trying to guess a passcode, mobile devices can be set to perform defined actions after a certain number of incorrect attempts have been made.

For Android devices, shown in Figure 12-37, the number of failed attempts before lockout depends on the device and version of Android OS. It is common for an Android device to lock when a passcode has failed from 4 to 12 times. After a device is locked, you can unlock it by entering the Gmail account information used to set up the device.

Figure 12-37 *Restrictions on Failed Login Attempts*

iOS Erase Data

For iOS devices, you can turn on the Erase Data option, as shown in Figure 12-38. If the passcode fails 10 times, the screen goes black, and all data on the device is deleted. To restore the iOS device and data, if you have backups, use either the Restore and Backup option in iTunes or the Manage Storage option in iCloud.

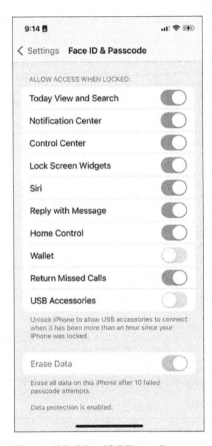

Figure 12-38   *iOS Erase Data*

iOS GUI

On iOS, to increase security, the passcode is used as part of the encryption key for the entire system. Because the passcode is not stored anywhere, no one (including Apple) can gain access to the user data on iOS devices without the passcode. The system depends on the user providing the passcode before the system can be unlocked and decrypted for use. A forgotten passcode renders user data unreachable, as shown in Figure 12-39, and the user must perform a full restore from a backup saved in iTunes or iCloud.

Figure 12-39   *iOS GUI*

12.2.1.4 Check your Understanding: Screen Locks and Biometric Authentication

Refer to the online course to complete this activity.

Cloud-Enabled Services for Mobile Devices (12.2.2)

Cloud-enabled services provide access to data and applications wherever and whenever you want or need them. This on-demand access to storage resources, applications, and services reduces some of the limitations of mobile devices.

Remote Backup (12.2.2.1)

Mobile device data can be lost due to device failure or the loss or theft of the device. Data must be backed up periodically to ensure that it can be recovered, if needed. With mobile devices, storage is often limited and not removable. To overcome these limitations, remote backups can be performed. With a *remote backup*, a device copies its data to cloud storage using a backup app. If data needs to be restored, run the backup app and access the website to retrieve the data.

Most mobile operating systems come with a user account linked to the vendor's cloud service, such as iCloud for iOS (shown in Figure 12-40), Google Sync for Android, or OneDrive for Microsoft. The user can enable automatic backups to the cloud for data, apps, and settings. In addition, third-party backup providers, such as Dropbox, can be used. A mobile device can also be backed up to a PC. iOS supports backups on iTunes running on a PC. Another option is to configure mobile device management (MDM) software to automatically back up user devices.

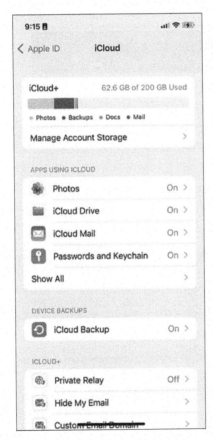

Figure 12-40   iCloud for iOS

Locator Applications (12.2.2.2)

If a mobile device is misplaced or stolen, it is possible to find it by using a *locator application*. A locator app should be installed and configured on each mobile device before it is lost. Both Android and iOS have apps for remotely locating a device.

Apple's Find My iPhone and Android's Device Manager allow a user to locate, ring, or lock a lost device or to erase data from the device. To manage a lost Android device, the user must visit the Android Device Manager Dashboard, hosted at https://www.google.com/android/devicemanager, and log in with the Google account used on the Android device. Android Device Manager is included and enabled by default on Android 5.x and can be found under Settings > Security > Device Administration.

iOS users can use the Find My iPhone app on different iOS devices to help locate lost devices (see Figure 12-41). After installing the app, the user can start it and follow the instructions to configure the software.

Figure 12-41   iOS Find My iPhone

Note

If Find My iPhone is unable to locate the lost device, the device might be turned off or disconnected. The device must be connected to a cellular or wireless network to receive commands from the app or to send location information to the user.

After the device is located, you might be able to perform additional functions, such as sending a message or playing a sound. These options are useful if you have misplaced your device. If the device is close by, playing a sound can help you find it. If the device is at another location, sending a message to display on the screen allows someone to contact you after finding the device.

Remote Lock and Remote Wipe (12.2.2.3)

If attempts to locate a mobile device have failed, other security features can be used to prevent data on the device from being compromised (see Figure 12-42). Usually, the same apps that perform remote location services have security features. Two of the most common remote security features are remote lock and remote wipe.

Figure 12-42   Remote Lock and Remote Wipe

Note

For these remote security measures to function, the device must be powered on and connected to a cellular or Wi-Fi network.

Remote Lock

The *remote lock* feature for iOS devices is called Lost Mode (see Figure 12-43). The Android Device Manager calls this feature Lock. Both of these features allow you to lock the device with a passcode, so others cannot gain access to the data in the device. For example, the user can display custom messages or prevent the phone from ringing to indicate incoming calls or text messages.

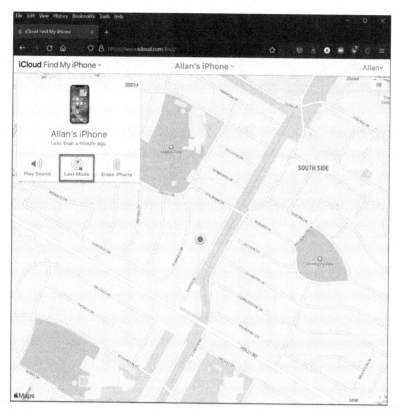

Figure 12-43   Remote Lock

Remote Wipe

The *remote wipe* feature for iOS devices is called Erase iPhone (see Figure 12-44). The Android Device Manager calls this feature Erase. Both Erase iPhone and Erase delete all data from the device and return it to a factory state. To restore data to the device, an Android user must set up the device using a Gmail account, and an iOS user must synchronize the device to iTunes or iCloud.

Most mobile device operating systems provide a full device encryption feature. Full device encryption can prevent anyone in possession of the device from circumventing the device's access controls and reading the raw data stored in memory.

All user data on an iOS device is always encrypted, and the key is stored on the device. When Erase iPhone or Erase is used to wipe the device, the OS deletes the key, and the data becomes inaccessible. Data protection encryption is enabled automatically when a password lock is configured on the device.

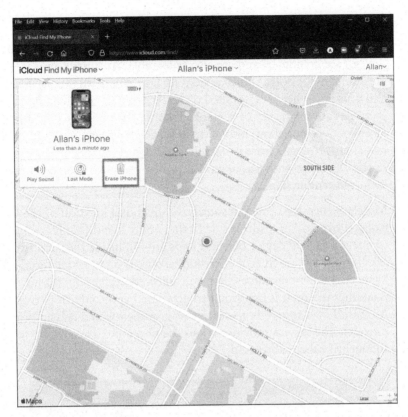

Figure 12-44   Remote Wipe

On Android OS, encryption is enabled through Settings > Security. Android uses full-disk encryption with a passcode-derived key.

Interactive Graphic

12.2.2.4 Check Your Understanding: Cloud-Enabled Services for Mobile Devices

Refer to the online course to complete this activity.

Software Security (12.2.3)

Applications need to be protected from internal design flaws and external threats. Application developers embed security measures inside applications to prevent hackers from compromising a program. Technicians need to take additional measures to keep applications, including operating systems, from being compromised.

Antivirus (12.2.3.1)

All computers are vulnerable to malicious software. Smartphones and other mobile devices are computers and are also vulnerable. *Antivirus* apps (see Figure 12-45) are available for both Android and iOS. Depending on the permissions granted to an antivirus app when it is installed on an Android device, the app might not be able to scan files automatically or run scheduled scans. File scans must be initiated manually. iOS does not allow automatic or scheduled scans. This safety feature prevents malicious programs from using unauthorized resources or contaminating other apps or the OS. Some antivirus apps also provide services such as locator services, remote lock, and remote wipe.

Mobile device apps run in a *sandbox*, which is a location of the OS that keeps code isolated from other resources and other code. It is difficult for malicious programs to infect a mobile device because apps are run inside the sandbox. An Android app asks for permission to access certain resources upon installation. A malicious app has access to any resources that were allowed permission during installation. This is another reason it is important to download apps only from trusted sources. A *trusted app source* is a source that is authenticated and authorized by a service provider. The service provider issues the developer a certificate to use to sign apps and identify them as trusted.

Figure 12-45   Antivirus

Due to the nature of a sandbox, malicious software does not usually damage mobile devices; it is far more likely for a mobile device to transfer a malicious program to another device, such as a laptop or desktop. For example, if a malicious program is downloaded from email, the Internet, or another device, the malicious program could be placed on a laptop the next time it is connected to the mobile device.

To prevent a malicious program from infecting additional devices, a firewall can be used. *Firewall apps* for mobile devices can monitor app activity and prevent connections to specific ports or IP addresses. Because a mobile device firewall must be able to control other apps, it works at a higher (root) permission level. The NoRoot Firewall app works by creating a VPN and then controlling app access to the VPN.

Rooting and Jailbreaking (12.2.3.2)

Mobile operating systems are usually protected by a number of software restrictions. An unmodified copy of iOS, for example, executes only authorized code and allows very limited user access to its file system.

Rooting and jailbreaking are two methods for removing restrictions and protections added to mobile operating systems. They make it possible to circumvent the usual operation of the device operating system to gain superuser or root administrator permissions. *Rooting* is used on Android devices to gain privileged or root-level access for modifying code or installing software that is not intended for the device. *Jailbreaking* is typically used on iOS devices to remove manufacturer restrictions and make it possible to run arbitrary user code and grant users full access to the file system and full access to kernel modules (see Figure 12-46).

Figure 12-46   Rooting and Jailbreaking

Rooting or jailbreaking a mobile device usually voids the manufacturer's warranty. It is not recommended that you modify a customer's mobile device in this way. Nevertheless, a large group of users choose to remove the restrictions on their own devices. Rooting or jailbreaking a mobile device makes it possible to heavily customize the GUI, make modifications to the OS to improve the speed and responsiveness of the device, and install apps from secondary or unsupported sources.

Jailbreaking exploits vulnerabilities in iOS. When a usable vulnerability is found, a program is written. This program is the actual jailbreak software, and it is then distributed on the Internet. Apple discourages jailbreaking and actively works to eliminate vulnerabilities that make jailbreaking possible on iOS. In addition to the OS updates and bug fixes, new iOS releases usually include patches to eliminate known vulnerabilities that allow jailbreaking. When iOS vulnerabilities are fixed by updates, hackers are forced to start over.

Note

The jailbreak process is completely reversible. To remove the jailbreak and bring the device back to its factory state, connect it to iTunes and perform a Restore.

Patching and Updating Operating Systems (12.2.3.3)

As you can update the OS on a desktop or laptop, you can update or patch the OS on a mobile device. *Updates* add functionality or increase performance. *Patches* can fix security problems or issues with hardware and software.

Because there are many different Android mobile devices, updates and patches are not released as one package for all devices. Sometimes a new version of Android cannot be installed on older devices whose hardware does not meet the minimum specifications. These devices might receive patches to fix known issues but may not receive OS upgrades.

Android updates and patches are delivered using an automated process. When a carrier or manufacturer has an update for a device, a notification on the device indicates that an update is ready. Touch the update to begin the download and installation process.

iOS updates also use an automated process for delivery, and devices that do not meet the hardware requirements are excluded. To check for updates to iOS, connect the device to iTunes. A notice to download opens if updates are available, as shown in Figure 12-47. To manually check for updates, click the Check for Update button in the iTunes Summary pane.

Two other types of updates for mobile device radio firmware are important. These baseband updates consist of the *Preferred Roaming List (PRL)* and the *Primary Rate ISDN (PRI)*. The PRL is configuration information that a cellular phone needs to communicate on networks other than its own so that a call can be made outside the carrier's network. The PRI configures the data rates between the device and the cell tower. This ensures that the device is able to communicate with the tower at the correct rate.

Figure 12-47   System Update Notification on iOS

12.2.3.4 Check Your Understanding: Mobile Security Features

Refer to the online course to complete this activity.

Linux and macOS Operating Systems (12.3)

Besides Microsoft Windows, Linux and macOS operating systems are most familiar to users.

Linux and macOS Tools and Features (12.3.1)

Each OS is developed with certain tools and features in mind for the system on which it will run and the people who will use it. This section addresses tools and features such as ease of use, visual aesthetics, security, performance, and compatibility with hardware and software.

Introduction to Linux and macOS Operating Systems (12.3.1.1)

Two file systems (see Figure 12-48) used on most Linux operating systems are *ext3*, which is a 64-bit file system with support for journaling, and *ext4*, which delivers significantly better performance than ext3. Linux can also support FAT and FAT32. In addition, Network File System (NFS) can be used to mount remote storage devices into the local file system.

Figure 12-48   File Systems

Most installations of Linux also support the creation of a swap partition to use as swap space. The OS uses the *swap partition* to supplement system RAM. If applications or data files use up all the available space in RAM, data is written to the swap space on a disk and is treated as if it were stored in RAM.

Apple Mac workstations have their own file system, *Extended Hierarchical File System (HFS Plus)*. This file system supports many of the same features as NTFS in Windows but not native file/folder encryption. macOS High Sierra and later use *Apple File System (APFS)*, which supports native file encryption, instead of HFS Plus. HFS Plus has a maximum volume and file size of 8 EB.

Unix

Unix, shown in Figure 12-49, is a proprietary operating system written in the C programming language. macOS and iOS are based on the Berkeley Standard Distribution (BSD) version of Unix.

Figure 12-49   Unix

Linux

GNU/Linux is an open source, independently developed operating system that is compatible with Unix commands. Android and many OS distributions rely on the Linux kernel.

Linux operating systems are used in embedded systems, wearable devices, smart-watches, cell phones, netbooks, PCs, servers, and supercomputers. There are many different distributions (or *distros*) of Linux, including SUSE, Red Hat, CentOS, Fedora, Debian, Ubuntu (see Figure 12-50), and Mint. Each distro adds specific packages and interfaces to the generic Linux kernel and provides different support options. Most distributions provide a GUI interface.

In most cases, a distro is a complete Linux implementation that includes the kernel, shell, applications, and utilities. Each Linux distribution vendor packages software, distributes installation media, and provides support.

Figure 12-50   Linux

macOS

The operating system for Apple computers, macOS (see Figure 12-51), is developed from the Unix kernel, although macOS is a closed source operating system.

Figure 12-51   macOS

Since its release in 2001, macOS has undergone regular updates and revisions to keep pace with Apple Mac hardware updates. Updates and new OS versions are distributed for free through the App Store. Some older Mac computers may not be able to run the newest macOS versions. You can check support.apple.com/specs for the technical specifications of any macOS release.

macOS supports remote network installation called NetBoot, which is similar to Preboot Execution Environment (PXE).

Overview of Linux GUI (12.3.1.2)

Different Linux distributions ship with different software packages, but users decide what stays in their system by installing or removing packages. The graphical interface in Linux is composed of a number of subsystems that can also be removed or replaced by the user. While the details about these subsystems and their interactions are beyond the scope of this book, it is important to know that the Linux GUI as a whole can be easily replaced by the user. There are many Linux distributions, but this chapter focuses on Ubuntu Linux.

Ubuntu Linux uses Gnome as its default GUI. One feature in the Linux GUI is the ability to have multiple desktops or workspaces. This allows the users to arrange the windows on a particular workspace. The following sections provide a breakdown of the main components of Ubuntu Gnome Desktop: launcher, dash search box, top menu bar, system notification menu, and lenses.

Launcher

The launcher is a dock placed on the left side of the screen that serves as an application launcher and switcher. Right-click any application hosted on the launcher to access a short list of tasks the application can perform (see Figure 12-52).

Figure 12-52   Ubuntu Launcher

Dash Search Box

Dash holds the Search tool and a list of recently used applications (see Figure 12-53). Dash includes lenses at the bottom of the Dash area, which allow the user to fine-tune Dash search results. To access Dash, simply click the Ubuntu button on the top of the Launcher.

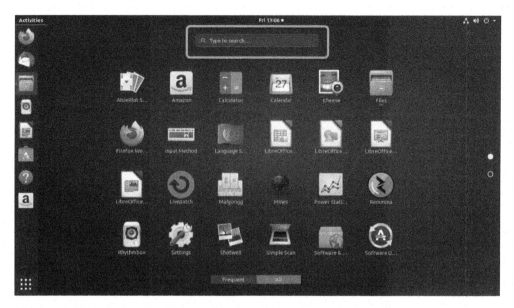

Figure 12-53   Ubuntu Dash Search Box

Top Menu Bar

The top menu bar is a multipurpose menu bar containing the currently running application, buttons to control the active window, and system controls and notifications (see Figure 12-54).

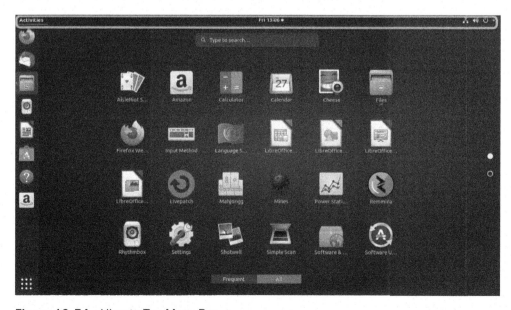

Figure 12-54   Ubuntu Top Menu Bar

System and Notification Menu

Many important functions are located in the indicator menus at the top-right corner of the screen (see Figure 12-55). Use the indicator menu to switch users, shut down the computer, control the volume level, or change network settings.

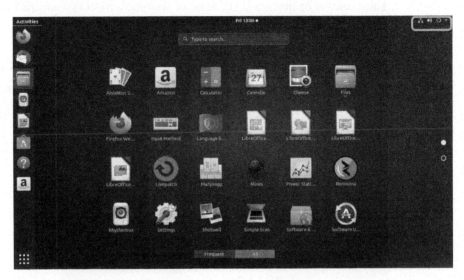

Figure 12-55   Ubuntu System and Notification Menu

Lenses

Lenses allows the user to fine-tune search results (see Figure 12-56).

Figure 12-56   Ubuntu Lenses

Overview of macOS GUI (12.3.1.3)

Among the major differences between older versions of macOS and macOS is the addition of the Aqua GUI. Aqua was designed around the theme of water, with components resembling droplets and deliberate use of reflection and translucency. The latest release of macOS at the time of writing is macOS Ventura 13.2.1. The following sections describe the parts of the macOS Aqua desktop.

Menu Bar

The menu bar contains the Apple menu, currently active application menus, status menus and indicators, Spotlight, and Notification Center (see Figure 12-57).

Figure 12-57 macOS Menu Bar

Apple Menu

The Apple menu allows you to access system preferences, software updates, power controls, and more (see Figure 12-58).

Figure 12-58 macOS Apple Menu

Application Menu

The application menu displays the name of the active application in bold and the menu of the active application (see Figure 12-59).

Figure 12-59   macOS Application Menu

Status Menu

The status menu displays the date, time, and status of your computer and some features, such as Bluetooth and wireless (see Figure 12-60).

Figure 12-60   macOS Status Menu

Spotlight

Spotlight is a file system search feature in macOS. It can be used to find almost anything in macOS. Starting a new search requires clicking the magnifying glass in the menu bar or pressing **Command + Space** to bring up the search box (see Figure 12-61). To change the document type being searched, you need to go to Preferences. To specifically exclude locations from a Spotlight search, click the Privacy button and specify folders or drives to exclude.

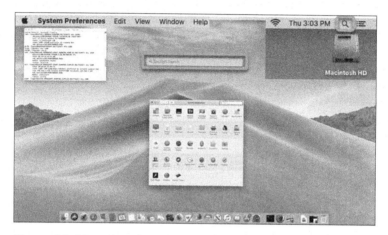

Figure 12-61   macOS Spotlight

Notification Center

Notification Center allows the user to see a variety of notifications (see Figure 12-62).

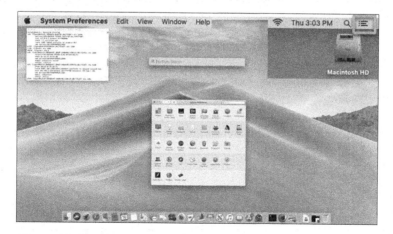

Figure 12-62   macOS Notification Center

Dock

The Dock displays thumbnails of frequently used applications and the running applications that are minimized (see Figure 12-63). One of the important functions included in the Dock is Force Quit. By right-clicking a running application in the Dock, you can choose to close an unresponsive application.

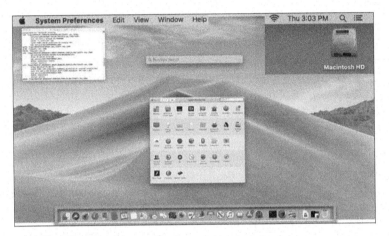

Figure 12-63   macOS Dock

The Apple Magic Mouse and the Magic Trackpad of a MacBook both support gestures to control the user interface. Gestures are finger movements on a trackpad or mouse that enable a user to scroll, zoom, and navigate desktop, document, and application content. Available gestures can be viewed and changed under System Preferences > Trackpad.

With macOS, Mission Control is a quick way to see everything that is currently open on a Mac. Mission Control can be accessed by using a three- or four-finger swipe up gesture, depending on your touch pad or mouse settings. Mission Control allows you to organize your apps on multiple desktops. To navigate the file system, macOS includes Finder. Finder is very similar to Windows File Explorer.

Most Apple laptops do not have an optical drive. To install software from optical media, Remote Disk can be used. Remote Disk is an app that lets the user access a CD/DVD drive on another Mac or Windows computer. To set up Remote Disk, go to System Preferences > Sharing and then check the DVD or CD sharing check box.

macOS also allows screen sharing so that other people using Macs can view your screen and possibly even take control of your computer. This is very useful when you need help or wish to help someone else.

Overview of Linux and macOS CLI (12.3.1.4)

In both Linux and macOS, the user can communicate with the operating system by using the *command line interface (CLI)*. To add flexibility, options and switches that can be used with commands are usually preceded by the dash (-) character. A user enters the options and switches supported by a command along with the command.

Most operating systems include a graphical interface. Although a command line interface is still present, the OS often boots into the GUI by default, hiding the command line interface from the user. One way to access the command line interface in a GUI-based operating system is through a terminal emulator application. These applications provide user access to the command line interface and are often named using some variation of the word *terminal*. The terminal is separated from the kernel by the shell, as shown in Figure 12-64.

A program called a *shell* interprets the commands from the keyboard and passes them to the operating system. When a user logs into the system, the login program checks the username and password; if the credentials are correct, the login program starts the shell. From this point on, an authorized user can begin interacting with the OS through text-based commands.

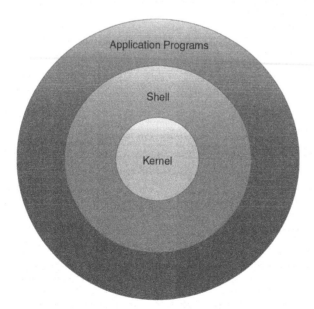

Figure 12-64   Operating System Components

Users interact with the kernel through a shell. Basically, the shell acts as an interface layer between the user and the kernel. The kernel is responsible for allocating CPU time and memory to processes. It also manages the file system and communications in response to system calls.

On Linux, popular terminal emulators are Terminator, eterm, xterm, konsole, and gnome-terminal. Figure 12-65 shows gnome-terminal.

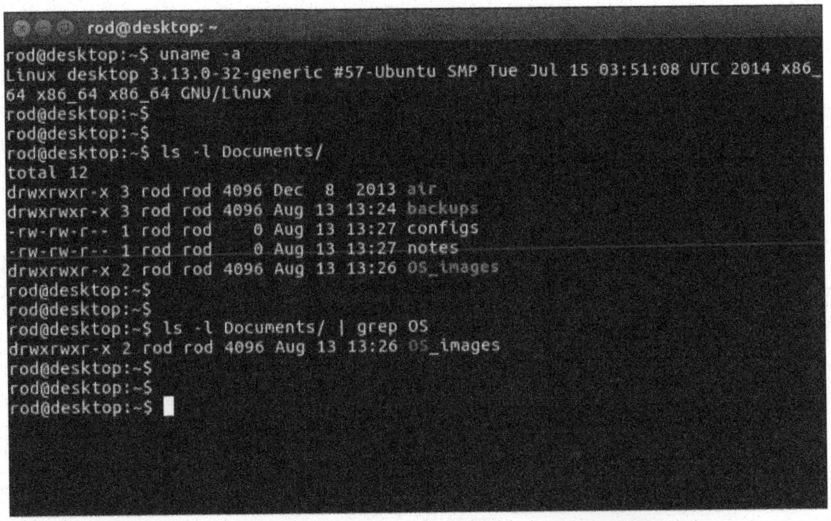

Figure 12-65   The gnome-terminal Linux Terminal Emulator

macOS includes a terminal emulator called Terminal, and a number of third-party emulators are available as well. Figure 12-66 shows Terminal.

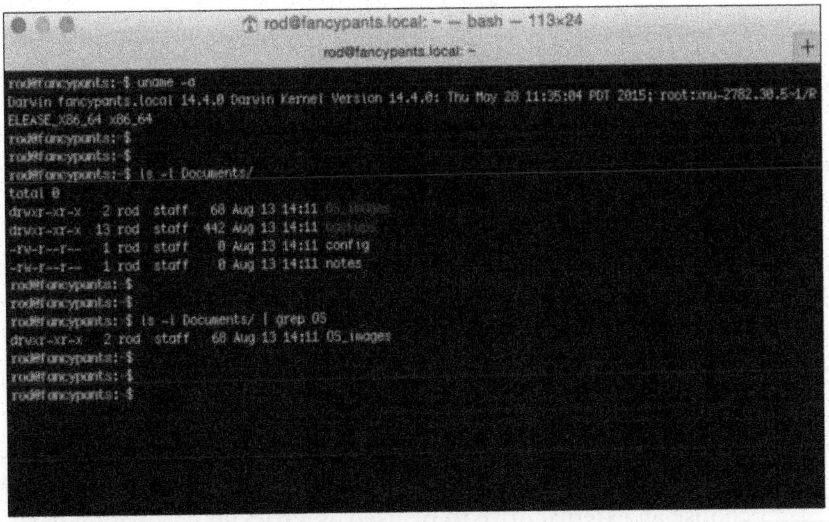

Figure 12-66   The Terminal macOS Terminal Emulator

Linux Backup and Recovery (12.3.1.5)

The process of backing up data involves creating a copy (or multiple copies) of data for safekeeping. When the backup process is complete, the copy is called a *backup*. The primary goal of making backups is to be able to restore or recover data in the event of failure. Gaining access to an earlier version of the data is often seen as a secondary goal of the backup process.

While backups can be achieved with a simple **copy** command, many tools and techniques exist to make the process automatic and transparent to the user.

Linux does not have a built-in backup tool. However, there are many commercial and open source backup solutions for Linux, such as Amanda, Bacula, Fwbackups, and Déjà Dup. Déjà Dup, shown in Figure 12-67, is an easy-to-use and efficient tool for backing up data. Déjà Dup supports a number of features, including local, remote, and cloud backups; data encryption compression; incremental backups; periodic scheduled backups; and GNOME desktop integration. It can also be used to restore from a particular backup.

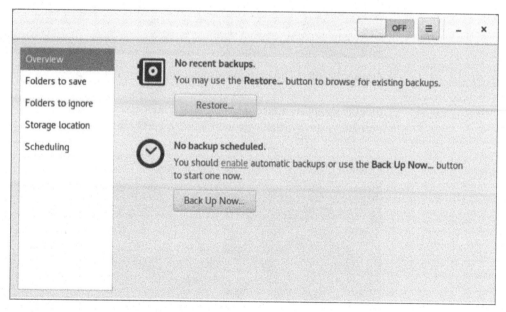

Figure 12-67   Linux Backup and Recovery

macOS Backup and Recovery (12.3.1.6)

macOS includes a backup tool called *Time Machine*. With Time Machine, users choose an external drive to be used as a backup destination device and connect it to the Mac using USB, FireWire, or Thunderbolt. Time Machine prepares the disk to receive backups and, when the disk is ready, it performs incremental backups periodically.

If the user has not specified a Time Machine destination disk, Time Machine asks if the newly connected external disk should be used as the destination backup disk. Time Machine stores some backups on your Mac, and if the Time Machine backup disk is not available, you may be able to restore a backup directly from your Mac. This type of backup is called a *local snapshot*.

To enable Time Machine, go to System Preferences > Time Machine, slide the switch to On, and select the disk where the backups are stored, as shown in Figure 12-68. Clicking the Options button allows the user to select or unselect the files, folders, or drives to back up. By default, Time Machine performs hourly backups for the past 24 hours, daily backups for a month, and weekly backups for all previous months. When the destination backup drive becomes full, Time Machine removes the oldest backup files to free up space.

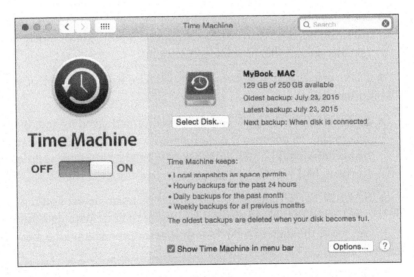

Figure 12-68   macOS Backup and Recovery

To restore data from Time Machine, make sure the destination backup disk is connected to the Mac and click Enter Time Machine in the Time Machine menu. A timeline on the right-hand side of the screen shows the available backups. Time Machine allows the user to restore the data to any previous version currently available in the destination backup disk.

Overview of Disk Utilities (12.3.1.7)

To help diagnose and solve disk-related problems, most modern operating systems include *disk utility* tools. Ubuntu Linux includes a disk utility called Disks. With Disks, users can perform the most common disk-related tasks, including partition management, mounting and unmounting, disk formatting, and query self-monitoring analysis and reporting technology (S.M.A.R.T.). macOS includes Disk Utility. In addition to supporting the main disk maintenance tasks, Disk Utility also supports Verify Disk Permissions and Repair Disk Permissions. Repair Disk Permissions is a common troubleshooting step in macOS. Disk Utility can also be used to back up disks to image files and perform an image recovery to disk from image files. These files contain the entire contents of a disk.

The following are a few common maintenance tasks that can be performed using disk utility software:

- **Partition management:** When working with computer disks, partitions may need to be created, deleted, or resized.

- **Disk partition mounting or unmounting:** On Unix-like systems, mounting a partition refers to the process of binding a partition of a disk or a disk image file (usually an .iso file) to a folder location.

- **Disk formatting:** Before a partition can be used by a user or system, it must be formatted.

- **Bad sector checking:** When a disk sector is flagged as bad, it becomes harmless to the OS because it is no longer used to store data. The existence of many bad sectors could be an indicator of a failing disk. Disk utilities can salvage data stored in bad sectors by moving it to healthy disk sectors.

- **S.M.A.R.T. attribute querying:** S.M.A.R.T. can detect and report attributes about a disk's health. The goal of S.M.A.R.T. is to anticipate disk failure so that the user can move the data to a healthy disk before the failing disk becomes inaccessible.

Interactive Graphic

12.3.1.8 Check Your Understanding: Linux and macOS Operating Systems

Refer to the online course to complete this activity.

Linux and macOS Best Practices (12.3.2)

Computer systems need periodic preventive maintenance to ensure the best performance. Maintenance tasks should be scheduled and performed frequently to prevent or detect problems early. To avoid missing maintenance tasks due to human error, computer systems can be programmed to perform tasks automatically.

Scheduled Tasks (12.3.2.1)

Two tasks that should be scheduled and performed automatically are backups, shown in Figure 12-69, and disk checks.

Figure 12-69   Scheduled Tasks

Backups and disk checks are usually time-consuming tasks. An additional benefit of scheduling maintenance tasks is that it allows the computer to perform these tasks when no users are using the system. The CLI utility known as *cron* can schedule these tasks during off-peak hours.

In Linux and macOS, the cron service is responsible for scheduled tasks. cron runs in the background and executes tasks at specific dates and times. It uses a schedule table called a *cron table* that can be edited with the **crontab** command.

cron Table Format

The cron table is a plaintext file that has six columns, formatted as shown in Figure 12-70. A task is usually represented by a command, a program, or a script. To schedule a task, the user adds a row to the cron table. The new row specifies the minute, hour, day of the month, and the day of the week when the task should be executed by the cron service. When the specified date and time arrives, the task is executed.

Minute	Hours	Days	Months	Weekdays	Commands

Figure 12-70   Cron Table Format

Cron Table Fields

The center column of the cron table shows the data types acceptable for the fields, as shown in Figure 12-71.

minute	0-59	The minute the command executes.
hour	0-23	The hour the command executes.
day	1-31	Day of the month the command executes.
month	1-12	The month the command executes.
weekday	0-6	The day of the week the command executes. 0 = Sunday, 1 = Monday, and so forth.
command	varies	The command or set of commands. This must be compatible with the shell and use.

Figure 12-71   Cron Table Fields

Cron Table Example

The cron table shown in Figure 12-72 has two entries. The first entry tells the cron service to execute the myFirstTask script, located at /myDirectory/, on the first and fifteenth days of each month and also on Mondays, always at midnight (0h0m). The second entry shows that the cron service should execute mySecondTask script, also located at /myDirectory/, every Thursday at 2h37m in the morning.

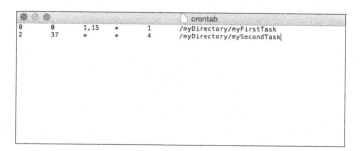

Figure 12-72   Crontab Example

To create or edit the cron table, use the **crontab -e** command from a terminal.

To list the current cron table, use the **crontab -l** command.

To remove the current cron table, use the **crontab -r** command.

Operating System Updates (12.3.2.2)

Despite continued efforts to create a perfectly secure operating system, vulnerabilities still exist. When a vulnerability is found, it can be exploited with a virus or other malicious software.

Measures can be taken to help prevent malicious software from infecting a computer system. The most common of these measures are operating system updates, firmware updates, antivirus, and anti-malware. Also known as *patches*, OS updates are released periodically by OS companies to address any known vulnerabilities in their operating systems. While companies have update schedules, the release of unscheduled OS updates is common when a major vulnerability is found in OS code. Modern operating systems alert the user when updates are available for download and installation, but the user can check for updates at any time. Figure 12-73 shows an update alert window for Apple macOS.

Software Updates Alert on OS

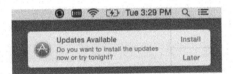

Figure 12-73 Software Updates Alert in macOS

Firmware Updates

Usually held in nonvolatile memory, such as ROM or flash, *firmware* is a type of software designed to provide low-level functionality for a device. Check for firmware updates with the manufacturer and update the system if new versions are available.

Antivirus and Anti-malware

In general, antivirus and anti-malware rely on code signatures to operate. A signature, or *signature file*, is a file that contains a sample of the code used by viruses and malware. Based on signature files, antivirus and anti-malware software can scan the contents of a computer disk and compare the contents of the files stored on the disk with the samples stored in the signature file. If a match is found, the antivirus or anti-malware software alerts the user of the possible presence of malware.

New malware is created and released every day; therefore, the signature files of antivirus and anti-malware programs must be updated just as frequently.

Security (12.3.2.3)

Digital assets are very valuable, and the theft of these assets is a major threat to users and organizations. Proper security practices include methods of protecting credentials that allow access to these assets.

Security Credentials Manager

Usernames, passwords, digital certificates, and encryption keys are just a few of the security credentials associated with a user. Due to the increasing number of necessary security credentials, modern operating systems include a service to manage them. Applications and other services can request and utilize the credentials stored by the *security credentials manager* service.

Security Credentials Service on Ubuntu

GNOME Keyring, shown in Figure 12-74, is a security credentials manager for Ubuntu Linux. To access GNOME Keyring on Ubuntu Linux, select Dash then search for Key > Passwords and Keys.

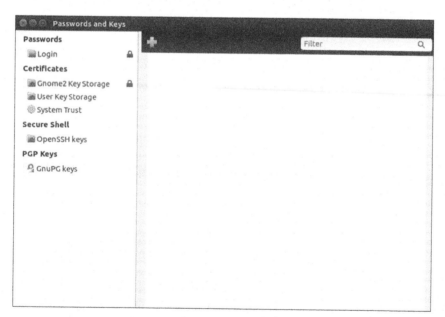

Figure 12-74   Security Credentials Service on Ubuntu

Security Credentials Service on macOS

Keychain, shown in Figure 12-75, is a security credentials manager for macOS. To access Keychain on macOS, select Applications > Utilities > Keychain Access.

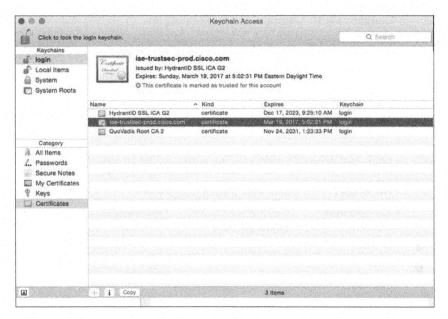

Figure 12-75   Security Credentials Service on macOS

12.3.2.4 Check Your Understanding: Linux and macOS Best Practices

Refer to the online course to complete this activity.

Basic CLI Commands (12.3.3)

The command line interface (CLI) is a user interface that is used to execute commands by typing text at a prompt instead of using a mouse to point and click on icons in a GUI shell. Having a basic understanding of CLI commands allows you to navigate the shell.

12.3.3.1 Syntax Checker: File and Directory Commands

Refer to the online course to complete this activity.

12.3.3.2 Check Your Understanding: File and Directory Commands

Refer to the online course to complete this activity.

The ls -l Command Output (12.3.3.3)

Example 12-1 shows an example of the ls -l command and its output.

Example 12-1   Output of the **ls -l** Command

```
iteuser@iteuser:~$ ls -l
 total 2
 -rwxrw-r-- 1 iteuser staff 11485 Apr 21  2021 My_Awesome_File
 drwx------ 2 iteuser staff  4096 Apr 21  2021 My_Private_Folder
 iteuser@iteuser:~$
```

Table 12-1 describes each of the components of this output.

Table 12-1   ls -l Command Output Components

Component	Component from Example 12-1	Description
Permission	-rwxrw-r-- drwx------	How the user, the group, and others access the files and directories
Link	1 2	The number of links or the number of directories inside this directory (My_Private_Folder in this example)
User	iteuser iteuser	The username of the owner of the file or the directory
Group	staff staff	The name of the group that owns the file or the directory
File Size	11485 4096	The file size, in bytes
Date and Time	Apr 21 2021 Apr 21 2021	The date and time of the last modification
File Name	My_Awesome_File My_Private_Folder	The file or directory name

Basic Unix File and Directory Permissions (12.3.3.4)

To organize the system and reinforce boundaries within the system, Unix uses file permissions. File permissions are built into the file system structure and provide a mechanism to define permissions to every file and directory. Every file and directory on a Unix system carries permissions that define the actions that the owner, the group, and others can do with the file or directory.

The only user who can override file permissions in Unix is the root user. Having the power to override file permissions means the root user can write to any file. Because everything in Unix is treated as a file, the root user has full control over the Unix operating system. Root access is often required to perform maintenance and administrative tasks.

Note

Because Linux and macOS are based on Unix, both operating systems conform with Unix file permissions.

Review the different permission values shown in Figure 12-76. Note how file and directory access is affected by the permissions.

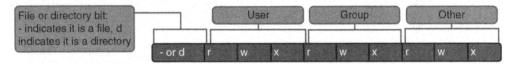

Figure 12-76 Basic Unix File and Directory Permissions

Table 12-2 provides a summary of the Unix file permissions.

Table 12-2 Unix File Permissions Summary

Permission	Description
777 -rwxrwxrwx	There are no restrictions on permissions. Anybody may do anything: read, write, or execute the file. This is generally not a desirable setting.
755 -rwxr-xr-x	With this permission, only the file's owner may read, write, and execute the file. All others may only read and execute the file. This setting is common for programs that are used by all users on the system.
700 -rwx------	The file's owner may read, write, and execute the file. Nobody else has any rights. This setting is useful for programs that only the owner may use and that must be kept private from others.
666 -rw-rw-rw-	All users may read and write the file, but no users can execute the file.
644 -rw-r--r--	Only the file owner may read and write a file, and all others on the system may only read the file. This is a common setting for data files that all the users may read but that only the owner may change.

Permission	Description
600 -rw-------	The owner may read and write a file. All others cannot read, write, or execute the file. This setting is used when the owner wants to keep the data file private.
777 drwxrwxrwx	There are no restrictions on permissions. Anybody may list, add, or delete content in the directory. Generally, this is not a desirable setting.
755 drwxr-xr-x	The directory owner has full access. All others may list the directory but cannot create files or delete them. This setting is common for directories that can be shared with other users.
700 drwx------	The directory owner may list, add, or delete content in the directory. All others have no access, so the directory owner may keep the directory private.

Table 12-3 summarizes the Unix directory and file permissions.

Table 12-3 Directory and File Permissions Summary

Binary	Octal	Permission	Description
000	0	---	No access
001	1	--x	Execute only
010	2	-w-	Write only
011	3	-wx	Write and Execute
100	4	r--	Read only
101	5	r-x	Read and Execute
110	6	rw-	Read and Write
111	7	rwx	Read, Write, and Execute

Interactive Graphic

12.3.3.5 Syntax Checker: File and Directory Permissions

Refer to the online course to complete this activity.

Interactive Graphic

12.3.3.6 Check Your Understanding: File and Directory Permissions

Refer to the online course to complete this activity.

Linux Administrative Commands (12.3.3.7)

Administrators use the terminal, shown in Figure 12-77, to monitor and control users, processes, and IP addresses and to carry out other tasks. Certain commands can be executed by users without any special privileges, while others require elevated privileges.

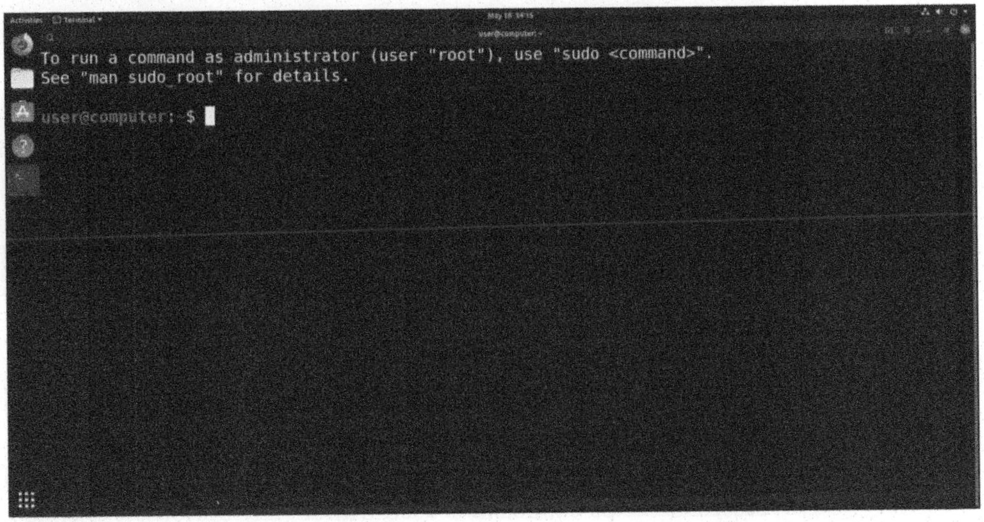

Figure 12-77   Linux Admin Commands

To get to the terminal in an Ubuntu distribution, click Activities in the upper-left corner and type **terminal**. How you open the terminal in other Linux distributions varies depending on the interface.

passwd

The **passwd** command, shown in Figure 12-78, allows users to change their own passwords at the terminal. To change a password, a user must know their current password. For security reasons, neither the password characters nor asterisks are displayed while the user types the password. The **passwd** command is often confused with the **pwd** command, which stands for *print working directory*.

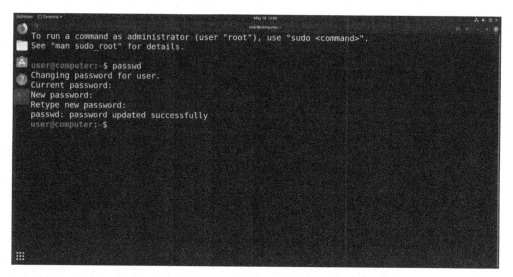

Figure 12-78   passwd Command

ps

The **ps** command, shown in Figure 12-79, allows users to monitor their own processes. If the **ps** command is used without any options, it only shows the programs that are running in the current terminal. The second use of the **ps** command shown in Figure 12-79 includes the **-e** option, indicating *everything*. The output of the command is piped to the **grep** command to search for output lines that match the word gnome (pronounced "GEE-nome").

Figure 12-79   ps Command

kill

The **kill** command, shown in Figure 12-80, allows users to end the processes that they have started. In this example, Firefox was started in the background using the ampersand (&). The **kill** command was used to abruptly end the Firefox process. Use **man kill** to view useful options for the **kill** command.

Figure 12-80   kill Command

ifconfig

The **ifconfig** command, shown in Figure 12-81, is used in much the same way as the Windows **ipconfig** command. Although it is referenced in the CompTIA A+ objectives, this command has been deprecated, and the **ip address** command should be used instead.

Figure 12-81   ifconfig Command

iwconfig

The **iwconfig** command, shown in Figure 12-82, is one of many wireless commands that start with the letters **iw**. The **iwconfig** command allows users to set and view their wireless settings. In the example shown in Figure 12-82, no wireless connections are being used.

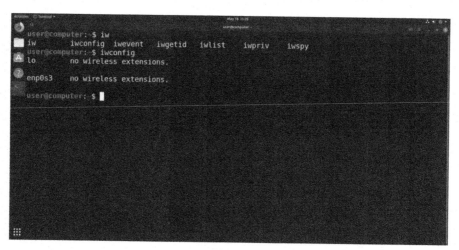

Figure 12-82   iwconfig Commands

chmod

The **chmod** command, shown in Figure 12-83, allows users to change the permissions of files that they own. In the example shown in Figure 12-83, a script is made executable using octal mode, and it is reverted using reference mode.

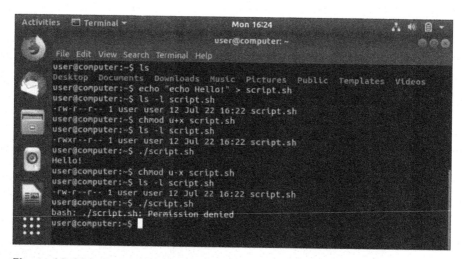

Figure 12-83   chmod Command

Linux Administrative Commands Requiring Root Access (12.3.3.8)

Some commands can be used without special privileges. Other commands require root access some of the time or all of the time, as shown in Figure 12-84. Typically, a user can manipulate the files within their own home directory, but changing files and settings throughout the server requires either **sudo** (superuser DO) or root access.

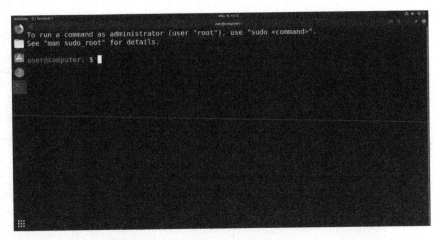

Figure 12-84   Commands Requiring Root Access

sudo

The **sudo** command, shown in Figure 12-85, grants a user root access without actually changing the user's profile. The access is granted for a limited time but only if the user is listed in the /etc/sudoers file. In the example shown in Figure 12-85, **sudo** is needed to kill a process.

Figure 12-85   sudo

chown

The **chown** command, shown in Figure 12-86, allows a user to switch both the owner and the group of a file or files. After using the **su** or **sudo** command, users may see files that don't belong to them in their home directories. Use the **-R** (recursive) option with the **chown** command to revert all files in a user's home directory back to the user.

Figure 12-86   chown

apt-get

The **apt-get** command, shown in Figure 12-87, is used to install and manage software on Debian-based Linux distributions. There are many options available for this command, and you can examine them by simply typing **apt**. The **apt-get** command has been deprecated in favor of simply using **apt**.

Figure 12-87   apt

shutdown

The **shutdown** command, shown in Figure 12-88, is used to halt and reboot the operating system. It can also warn users of an impending shutdown and schedule a shutdown to occur in the future. In a multi-user system, regular users do not have the rights to shut down the system.

Figure 12-88   shutdown

dd

The **dd** (disk duplicate) command, shown in Figure 12-89, is used to copy files and partitions and to create temporary swap files. The **dd** command should be used with extreme caution.

Figure 12-89   dd

12.3.3.9 Check Your Understanding: Administrative Commands

Refer to the online course to complete this activity.

12.3.3.10 Syntax Checker: File Ownership and Permission

Refer to the online course to complete this activity.

Basic Troubleshooting Process for Mobile, Linux, and macOS Operating Systems (12.4)

All OSs are susceptible to errors, freezing up, and other unexpected behaviors. Knowing a basic troubleshooting methodology is critical in helping to correct common OS issues.

Applying the Troubleshooting Process to Mobile, Linux, and macOS Operating Systems (12.4.1)

Follow the steps outlined in this section to accurately identify, repair, and document problems.

The Six Steps of the Troubleshooting Process (12.4.1.1)

The six steps of the troubleshooting process are:

Step 1.   Identify the problem.

Step 2.   Establish a theory of probable cause.

Step 3.   Test the theory to determine the cause.

Step 4.   Establish a plan of action to resolve the problem and implement the solution.

Step 5.   Verify full system functionality and, if applicable, implement preventive measures.

Step 6.   Document findings, actions, and outcomes.

Identify the Problem (12.4.1.2)

When troubleshooting problems with a mobile device, find out if the device is under warranty. If it is, it can often be returned for repair or exchange. If the device is no longer under warranty, determine whether repairing the device would be cost-effective. To determine the best course of action, compare the cost of the repair with the cost of replacing the mobile device.

Mobile device problems can result from a combination of hardware, software, and network issues. Mobile technicians must be able to analyze a problem and determine the cause of the error to repair the mobile device. This process is called *troubleshooting*.

The first step in the troubleshooting process is to identify the problem. Table 12-4 shows a list of open-ended and closed-ended questions to ask the customer for mobile device operating systems and on Linux and macOS.

Table 12-4   Step 1: Identify the Problem

Open-Ended Questions	Closed-Ended Questions
Mobile Device Operating Systems	
■ What is the problem you are experiencing?	■ Has this problem happened before?
■ What is the version of the mobile OS that you are using?	■ Has anyone else used the mobile device?
■ What is your service provider?	■ Is your mobile device under warranty?
■ What apps have you installed recently?	■ Have you modified the operating system on the mobile device?
	■ Have you installed any apps from an unapproved source?
	■ Does the mobile device connect to the Internet?
Linux or macOS	
■ What is the problem you are experiencing?	■ Has this problem happened before?
■ What are the make and model of your computer?	■ Has anyone else used the computer?
■ What version of Linux or macOS is your computer running?	■ Is your computer under warranty?
■ What programs or drivers have you installed recently?	■ Does the computer connect to the Internet?
■ What OS updates have you installed recently?	
■ What system configurations have you changed recently?	

Establish a Theory of Probable Cause (12.4.1.3)

After you have talked to the customer, you can establish a theory of probable cause. Table 12-5 shows a list of some common probable causes for problems with mobile device operating systems, Linux, and macOS.

Table 12-5   Step 2: Establish a Theory of Probable Cause

Common Causes of Linux or macOS Problems	Common Causes of Mobile Device Operating System Problems
■ The computer cannot send or receive email. ■ An application has stopped working. ■ A malicious application has been installed. ■ The computer has stopped responding. ■ The operating system is not up to date. ■ A user has forgotten their login credentials.	■ The mobile device cannot send or receive email. ■ An app has stopped working. ■ A malicious app has been sideloaded. ■ The mobile device has stopped responding. ■ Mobile device software or apps are not up to date. ■ A user has forgotten their passcode.

Test the Theory to Determine the Cause (12.4.1.4)

After you have developed some theories about what is wrong, test your theories to determine the cause of the problem. When the theory is confirmed, you can determine the steps to resolve the problem. Table 12-6 shows a list of quick procedures that can help you determine the exact cause of a problem or even correct the problem. If a quick procedure corrects the problem, you can then verify full system functionality. If a quick procedure does not correct the problem, you might need to research the problem further to establish the exact cause.

Table 12-6   Step 3: Test the Theory to Determine the Cause

Common Steps to Determine the Cause of a Linux or macOS Problem	Common Steps to Determine the Cause of a Mobile Device Operating System Problem
■ Force a running program to close. ■ Reconfigure email account settings. ■ Restart the computer. ■ Restore the computer from a backup. ■ Update the computer's operating system.	■ Force a running app to close. ■ Reconfigure email account settings. ■ Restart the mobile device. ■ Restore the mobile device from a backup. ■ Connect an iOS device to iTunes. ■ Update the operating system. ■ Reset the mobile device to factory defaults.

Establish a Plan of Action to Resolve the Problem and Implement the Solution (12.4.1.5)

When you have determined the exact cause of a problem, establish a plan of action to resolve the problem and implement the solution. Table 12-7 shows some sources you can use to gather additional information to resolve an issue.

Table 12-7   Step 4: Establish a Plan of Action to Resolve the Problem and Implement the Solution

If no solution is achieved in the previous step, further research is needed to implement the solution, using these sources.	■ Help desk repair logs ■ Other technicians ■ Manufacturer FAQs ■ Technical websites ■ Device manual ■ Online forums ■ Internet search

Verify Full System Functionality and, if Applicable, Implement Preventive Measures (12.4.1.6)

After you have corrected the problem, you verify full functionality and, if applicable, implement preventive measures. Table 12-8 shows a list of the steps to verify the solution.

Table 12-8   Step 5: Verify Full System Functionality and, if Applicable, Implement Preventive Measures

Verify Solution and Full System Functionality for Linux and macOS	Verify Solution and Full System Functionality for Mobile Device Operating Systems
■ Reboot the computer. ■ Browse the Internet using Wi-Fi. ■ Browse the Internet using a wired connection. ■ Send a test email. ■ Open different programs.	■ Reboot the mobile device. ■ Browse the Internet using Wi-Fi. ■ Browse the Internet using any carrier network type. ■ Make a phone call. ■ Send a text message. ■ Open different types of apps.

Document Findings, Actions, and Outcomes (12.4.1.7)

In the final step of the troubleshooting process, you must document your findings, actions, and outcomes. Table 12-9 lists the tasks required to document the problem and the solution.

Table 12-9   Step 6: Document Findings, Actions, and Outcomes

Document your findings, actions, and outcomes.	■ Discuss with the customer the solution that was implemented.
	■ Have the customer verify that the problem has been solved.
	■ Provide the customer with all paperwork.
	■ Document the steps taken to solve the problem in the work order and the technician's journal.
	■ Document any components used in the repair.
	■ Document the time spent solving the problem.

Common Problems and Solutions for Other Operating Systems (12.4.2)

To identify and implement solutions to mobile device operating systems, you need to know and understand features of mobile device operating systems. This section will help you identify common issues related to mobile devices and their operation.

Common Problems and Solutions for Mobile Operating Systems (12.4.2.1)

Table 12-10 outlines how you can use the first step of the troubleshooting process (identify the problem) to determine possible solutions to common problems for mobile operating systems.

Table 12-10   Common Problems and Solutions for Mobile Operating Systems

Identify the Problem	Probable Causes	Possible Solutions
The mobile device will not connect to the Internet.	Wi-Fi is turned off.	Turn on Wi-Fi.
	Wi-Fi settings are incorrect.	Reconfigure the Wi-Fi settings.
	Airplane mode is turned on.	Turn off Airplane mode.

Identify the Problem	Probable Causes	Possible Solutions
An app fails to respond.	The app does not work correctly.	Force the app to close.
	The app failed to close.	Restart the mobile device.
	Memory is low.	Reinstall the app.
		Remove and reinsert the battery, if possible.
		Reset the mobile device.
	The mobile device is out of storage space.	Remove unnecessary files.
		Uninstall unnecessary apps.
The mobile device fails to respond.	The operating system has encountered an error.	Restart the mobile device.
	An app has caused the operating system to become unresponsive.	Remove and reinsert the battery, if possible.
	An app has caused the operating system to become unresponsive.	Reset the mobile device.
	The mobile device's memory is low.	Insert a memory card or replace the memory card with a larger one, if possible.
	The mobile device is out of storage space.	Remove unnecessary files.
		Uninstall unnecessary apps.
The mobile device cannot send or receive email.	The mobile device is not connected to the Internet.	Connect the device to a Wi-Fi or cellular data network.
	The email account settings are incorrect.	Reconfigure the email account settings.
The mobile device cannot install additional apps or save photos.	The mobile device is out of storage space.	Insert a memory card or replace the memory card with a larger one, if possible.
		Remove unnecessary files.
		Uninstall unnecessary apps.

Identify the Problem	Probable Causes	Possible Solutions
A mobile device cannot connect or pair with a Bluetooth device.	Bluetooth is not enabled on the mobile device.	Enable Bluetooth on the mobile device.
	The Bluetooth device is out of range of the mobile device.	Move the Bluetooth device within range of the mobile device.
	The Bluetooth device is not turned on.	Turn on the Bluetooth device.
	The PIN code is incorrect.	Enter the correct PIN code.
The mobile device's display looks dim.	Brightness is set too low in the display settings.	Increase the brightness in the display settings.
	Auto-brightness does not work well in well-lit areas.	Turn off auto-brightness.
	Auto-brightness is not calibrated correctly.	Recalibrate the light sensor.
The mobile device cannot broadcast to an external monitor.	No wireless display-capable device is available.	Install a wireless display-capable device or turn it on if there is one available.
	Miracast, Wi-Fi, AirPlay, or other wireless display technology is not enabled.	Enable the wireless display capability.
The mobile device is exhibiting slow performance.	A GPS application is running.	Turn off the GPS or close the GPS application.
	One or more power-intensive apps is running.	Close all unnecessary apps.
	The mobile device's memory is low.	Restart the device.
The mobile device is unable to decrypt email.	The email client is not set up to decrypt email.	Configure the email client to decrypt encrypted email.
	The decryption key is incorrect.	Attain the decryption key from the sender of the encrypted email.

Identify the Problem	Probable Causes	Possible Solutions
The mobile device operating system has frozen.	An app is not compatible with the device.	Uninstall the incompatible app.
	Network connectivity is poor.	Move to an area with better network coverage.
	The device has failing hardware.	Replace any failing hardware.
The mobile device has no sound coming from the speakers.	The volume of the device is set too low in the audio settings or in an app.	Turn up the volume in the audio settings or in the app.
	The volume is muted.	Unmute the volume.
	The speaker has failed.	Replace the speaker.
The mobile device's touchscreen has inaccurate response.	The touchscreen is not calibrated in the display settings or in an app.	Recalibrate the touchscreen in the display settings or in the app.
	The touchscreen is dirty.	Clean the touchscreen.
	The touchscreen is shorting out due to damage or water.	Replace the touchscreen.

Common Problems and Solutions for Mobile OS Security (12.4.2.2)

Table 12-11 outlines how you can use the first step of the troubleshooting process (identify the problem) to determine possible solutions to common problems for mobile operating system security.

Table 12-11   Common Problems and Solutions for Mobile Operating System Security

Identify the Problem	Probable Causes	Possible Solutions
A mobile device has a weak signal, or the signal has been dropped.	There are not enough cell towers in the area.	Move to a more populated area that has more cell towers.
	The area is between coverage areas of the carrier.	Move to an area within the range of the carrier.
	The building that you are in is blocking the signal.	Relocate to a different area in the building or outside.
	Your grip on the mobile device is blocking the signal.	Change your grip on the device.

Identify the Problem	Probable Causes	Possible Solutions
The power of a mobile device is draining more quickly than normal.	The device is roaming between cell towers or areas of coverage.	Move to an area within the range of the carrier.
	The display is set to a high level of brightness.	Set the display to a lower brightness level.
	An app is using too many resources.	Close any unnecessary apps.
	Too many radios are in use.	Turn off any unnecessary radios.
		Reboot the device.
A mobile device has slow data speeds.	The connected cell tower is too far away for high-speed data.	Move closer to a cell tower.
	The mobile device is roaming.	Move to an area within the range of the carrier.
	Data transmission has gone over the usage limit for a device.	Raise the data limit of the device.
	The device is experiencing high resource utilization.	Turn off data usage for the device.
		Close any unnecessary apps.
		Restart the device.
A mobile device connects to a Wi-Fi network unintentionally.	The device is set to automatically connect to unknown Wi-Fi networks.	Set the device so that it will only connect to known Wi-Fi networks.
A mobile device pairs to a Bluetooth device unintentionally.	The device is set to automatically pair with unknown devices.	Set the device to turn off Bluetooth pairing by default.
		Turn off Bluetooth.
A mobile device has leaked personal files and data.	The device has been lost or stolen.	Remote lock or wipe the device.
	The device has been compromised by malware.	Scan for and remove malware from the device.

Identify the Problem	Probable Causes	Possible Solutions
A mobile device's account has been accessed by unauthorized personnel.	Credentials are being stored by default.	Set the device to not store credentials by default.
	No VPN is being used.	Use a VPN connection.
	No passcode is set on the device.	Set a passcode on the device.
	The passcode on the device has been discovered.	Change the passcode to a stronger one.
	The device has been compromised by malware.	Scan for and remove malware from the device.
	The provider database that stores the account credentials has been compromised.	The provider needs to tighten security measures.
An app has achieved unauthorized access to root.	The device has been compromised by malware.	Scan for and remove malware from the device.
A mobile device is being tracked without permission.	GPS is on but is not in use by any apps.	Turn off GPS when not in use.
	An app allows connection to the GPS.	Shut down or remove any unwanted apps that allow connection to the GPS.
	The device has been compromised by malware.	Scan for and remove malware from the device.
A mobile device camera or microphone is being accessed without permission.	An app allows connection to the camera or microphone.	Shut down or remove any unwanted apps that allow connection to the camera or microphone.
	The device has been compromised by malware.	Scan for and remove malware from the device.

Common Problems and Solutions for Linux and macOS Operating Systems (12.4.2.3)

Table 12-12 outlines how you can use the first step of the troubleshooting process (identify the problem) to determine possible solutions to common problems for Linux and macOS operating systems.

Table 12-12   Common Problems and Solutions for Linux and macOS Operating Systems

Identify the Problem	Probable Causes	Possible Solutions
The automatic backup operation does not start.	Time Machine is turned off in macOS.	Turn on Time Machine in macOS.
	Déjà Dup is turned off in Linux.	Turn on Déjà Dup in Linux.
The directory appears to be empty.	The directory is the mount point for another disk or partition.	Remount the disk using the correct directory with Disk Utility for macOS. Remount the disk using the correct directory with Disks for Linux.
	The files were accidentally deleted.	Restore the deleted files from backup by using Time Machine or Déjà Dup.
	The files are hidden.	Use the Show Hidden Files option in the file browser.
An application stops responding in macOS.	The application has stopped working.	Use Force Quit to kill the application.
	The application was using a resource that became unavailable.	Use Force Quit to kill the application.
Wi-Fi is not accessible using Ubuntu.	The wireless NIC driver was not installed correctly.	Install the Linux driver from the manufacturer's website, if available. Install the Linux driver from the Ubuntu repositories, if available. Check the Linux distribution's hardware compatibility list for the wireless card.
macOS cannot read the remote optical disc using Remote Disc.	The Mac already has an optical drive installed.	Place the media in the local optical drive.
	The option to request permission to use the optical drive has been enabled.	Accept the request for permission to use the drive.

Identify the Problem	Probable Causes	Possible Solutions
Linux fails to boot and you receive a "Missing GRUB" or "Missing LILO" message.	GRUB or LILO has been corrupted. GRUB or LILO has been deleted.	Run Linux from the installation media, open a terminal, and install the boot manager with the command **sudo grub-install** or **sudo lilo-install.**
Linux or Mac OS freezes on startup and exhibits kernel panic where there is a stop screen.	A driver has become corrupted.	Update all device drivers from the manufacturer's website.
	Hardware is failing.	Replace any failing hardware.

12.4.2.4 Lab: Troubleshoot Mobile Devices

In this lab, you will learn how to troubleshoot mobile devices.

Summary (12.5)

In this chapter, you learned that, like desktops and laptops, mobile devices use operating systems to interface with the hardware and to run software. The two most commonly used mobile operating systems are Android and iOS. You learned that Android is an open source operating system that is customizable, while iOS is closed source and cannot be modified or redistributed without permission from Apple. Both platforms use apps to provide functionality. You worked with both the Android and iOS operating systems as part of lab exercises.

Mobile devices are easily lost or stolen. Therefore, as an IT professional, you need to be familiar with mobile security features such as screen locks, biometric authentication, remote lock and remote wipe, and patching and upgrading. You learned that mobile devices can be unlocked using facial recognition, fingerprints, passcodes, and swipe patterns. You also learned that mobile OSs can be configured to disable access if too many failed login attempts are made to prevent someone from trying to guess a passcode. Another measure of security is provided by remote lock and remote wipe for devices that have been lost or stolen. These features allow the device to be remotely erased or locked to prevent data on the device from being compromised. You configured passcode locks on a mobile device in a lab.

You learned about the Linux and macOS operating systems and some of the differences between them. Linux supports the ext3, ext4, FAT, and NFS file systems, and macOS supports HFS and APFS. Also, macOS includes a backup tool called Time Machine, and Linux does not have a built-in backup tool. Another major difference between macOS and Linux is that the Linux GUI can be easily replaced by the user.

It is important to not only learn about other operating systems but to build hands-on skills. In this chapter, you worked through a lab to install Linux in a virtual machine and explore the GUI.

Finally, you learned the six steps in the troubleshooting process as they are applied to mobile, Linux, and macOS operating systems.

Practice

The following activities provide practice with the topics introduced in this chapter. The labs are available in the companion *IT Essentials v8 Labs & Study Guide* (ISBN 9780138166304).

Labs

12.1.2.2 Lab: Working with Android

12.1.2.4 Lab: Working with iOS

12.1.3.4 Lab: Mobile Device Features

12.2.1.2 Lab: Passcode Locks

12.4.2.4 Lab: Troubleshoot Mobile Devices

Check Your Understanding Questions

Complete all the review questions listed here to test your understanding of the topics and concepts in this chapter. Appendix A, "Answers to 'Check Your Understanding' Questions," lists the answers.

1. Which feature of an Android or iOS mobile device helps prevent malicious programs from infecting the device?

   A. The phone carrier prevents the mobile device app from accessing some smartphone features and programs.

   B. The passcode restricts the mobile device app from accessing other programs.

   C. Mobile device apps are run in a sandbox that isolates them from other resources.

   D. The remote lock feature prevents malicious programs from infecting the device.

2. Which of the following are features of the Android operating system? (Choose two.)

   A. Android is open source and allows anyone to contribute to its development and evolution.

   B. Android has been implemented on devices such as cameras, smart TVs, and e-book readers.

   C. All available Android applications have been tested and approved by Google to run on the open source operating system.

   D. Each implementation of Android requires a royalty to be paid to Google.

   E. Android applications can only be downloaded from Google Play.

3. Which of the following tasks can be done with an iOS device's Home button? (Choose two.)

   A. wake the device

   B. respond to an alert

   C. display the navigation icons

   D. return to the home screen

   E. open audio controls

   F. place apps into folders

4. Which of the following are types of cloud-enabled services for mobile devices? (Choose two.)

   A. locator apps

   B. remote backup

   C. passcode configuration

   D. screen calibration

   E. screen app locking

5. A company is creating a new website to be hosted on a Linux server. The system administrator creates the group webteam and assigns team members to it. The administrator then creates the directory webpages for storing files. Later that day, one of the team members reports being unable to create files in the webpages directory or subdirectories. The administrator uses the **ls -l** command to view the file permissions. The result displayed is drwxr-xr--. What should the administrator do to allow the team members to add and edit files?

   A. Add the user to the webteam group.

   B. Issue the command **chmod 775 -R webteam**.

   C. Issue the command **chmod 775 -R webpages**.

   D. Make the user the owner of the directory and subdirectories.

6. Which of the following terms describe unlocking Android and iOS mobile devices to allow users full access to the file system and full access to the kernel module? (Choose two.)

   A. patching

   B. rooting

   C. remote wipe

   D. sandboxing

   E. jailbreaking

7. A person with an Android mobile device holds down the power button and the volume down button until the device turns off. The person then turns the device back on. What is this person doing to the device?

   A. a normal power off

   B. a factory reset

   C. a full backup to iCloud

   D. a standard reset of the device

   E. an operating system update

8. True or false: Android and macOS are based on the Unix operating system.

   A. True

   B. False

9. Which of the following methods can be used to unlock a smartphone? (Choose three.)

   A. NFC

   B. passcode

   C. encryption

   D. swipe pattern

   E. QR code scan

   F. biometric information

10. A user taps the Recent Apps icon on an Android-based smartphone to see a list of recently used apps. What should the user do to remove an app from the list?

   A. Swipe the app up.

   B. Double-tap on the app.

   C. Swipe the app down.

   D. Swipe the app to either side.

11. A user has an iOS device. What will happen if the user forgets the passcode to unlock the device?

   A. The user must call Apple to reset the passcode.

   B. The user can visit the Apple website to initiate a passcode reset request.

   C. The user must perform a full restore from a backup saved in iTunes or iCloud.

   D. The user can use the Find My iPhone service on the website www.icloud.com to reset the passcode.

12. Which Linux CLI command removes files?

    A. rm

    B. man

    C. ls

    D. cd

    E. mkdir

    F. moves

13. Which of the following location-specific services can the GPS feature on a mobile device offer? (Choose two.)

    A. playing local songs

    B. delivering local advertising

    C. displaying local weather information

    D. planning a route between two locations

    E. displaying a map of a destination city while driving

14. A system administrator is using the **crontab** command to edit an entry on a Linux server. What is the administrator doing?

    A. editing a shell script to run when the server starts

    B. installing the new BIOS update when it is available

    C. scheduling a task to run at a specific time and date

    D. deleting caches and cookies after the web browser closes

15. Which of the following preventive maintenance tasks should be scheduled to occur automatically? (Choose two.)

    A. executing a backup

    B. scanning the signature files

    C. updating the operating system software

    D. resetting devices by applying the factory reset feature

    E. checking the disks for bad sectors

CHAPTER 13

Security

Objectives

Upon completion of this chapter, you will be able to answer the following questions:

- What are different types of malware?

- What are measures that protect against malicious software?

- What are different types of network attacks?

- What are different social engineering attacks?

- What is a security policy?

- What are physical security measures?

- What are measures that protect data?

- How do you secure a workstation?

- How do you configure security by using the Windows Local Security Policy tool?

- How do you manage users and groups?

- How do you configure security by using Windows Firewall?

- How do you configure a browser for secure access?

- How do you configure security maintenance in Windows?

- How do you configure wireless devices for secure communication?

- What are the six steps of the troubleshooting process for security?

- What are common problems and solutions for security?

Key Terms

This chapter uses the following key terms. You can find the definitions in the glossary at the end of the book.

AAA server page 841

acceptable use policy page 847

Active Directory page 880

ActiveX filtering page 897

Advanced Encryption Standard (AES) page 904

adware page 830

anti-malware program page 832

ASA firewall page 841

asymmetric encryption page 904

authentication method page 907

baiting page 845

biometric lock page 850

BitLocker page 857

blacklist page 883

boot sector virus page 829

Introduction (13.0)

This chapter reviews the types of attacks that threaten the security of computers and the data contained on them. An IT technician is responsible for the security of data and computer equipment in an organization. To successfully protect computers and the network, a technician must understand the threats to physical equipment, such as servers, switches, and wiring, and threats to data, such as authorized access, theft, and loss.

In this chapter, you will learn about the many types of threats to computers and networks, the greatest and most common of which is malware. You will learn about common types of computer malware, such as viruses, Trojan horses, adware, ransomware, rootkits, spyware, and worms, as well as techniques to protect against them. You will also learn about TCP/IP attacks such as denial of service, spoofing, SYN flood, and man-in-the-middle attacks. Cybercriminals often use social engineering techniques to deceive and trick unsuspecting individuals to reveal confidential information or account login credentials. You will learn about the many forms of social engineering attacks, such as phishing, pretexting, baiting, and Dumpster diving, and how to protect against them.

You will also learn about the importance of having a security policy, which is a set of security objectives that ensure the security of a network, the data, and the computers in an organization. A good security policy specifies the persons authorized to access network resources, the minimum requirements for passwords, acceptable uses for network resources, how remote users can access the network, and how security incidents will be handled. You will learn about host-based firewalls such as Windows Defender and how you can configure such a firewall to allow or deny access to specific programs or ports. You will explore the Windows Defender Firewall in a lab and configure advanced firewall settings. You will also learn about wireless security and configure wireless security in a Packet Tracer activity.

Finally, you will learn the six steps in the troubleshooting process as they are applied to security.

13.1 Security Threats (13.1)

This chapter reviews the types of attacks that threaten the security of computers and the data contained on them. A technician is responsible for the security of data and computer equipment in an organization. You will learn how to work with customers to ensure that the best possible protection is in place.

Malware (13.1.1)

This section discusses the various types of malicious software, for which *malware* has become the comprehensive term. Malware can damage and destroy computer systems and data stored on them.

Malware (13.1.1.1)

Many types of threats are created to disrupt computers and networks. The greatest and most common threat for computers and the data contained on them is malware. *Malware* is software developed by cybercriminals to perform malicious acts. In fact, the word *malware* is an abbreviation for *malicious software*.

Malware is typically installed on a computer without the user's knowledge. Once a host is infected, the malware could:

- Change the computer configuration.

- Delete files or corrupt hard drives.

- Collect information stored on the computer without the user's consent.

- Open extra windows on the computer or redirect the browser.

How does malware get on a computer? Cybercriminals use a variety of methods to infect hosts, and a user's system is at risk of being infected for reasons such as these:

- Visiting an infected website

- Having outdated antivirus software

- Having a web browser that is not patched for a new vulnerability

- Downloading a "free" program

- Opening unsolicited email

- Exchanging files on file sharing sites

- Becoming infected by another infected host

- Inserting a USB stick found in a public area

Depending on their goals, cybercriminals use different types of malware. The choice of malware depends on the target and what the criminals are after.

Noncompliant and legacy systems are especially vulnerable to software exploitations. A *noncompliant system* is a system that has not been updated with operating system or application patches or that is missing antivirus and firewall security software. Legacy systems are systems for which the vendor no longer provides support or fixes for vulnerabilities.

What Do You Already Know? - Malware (13.1.1.2)

Malware can come from many different sources. You must know the differences between the seven main types of malware: spyware, adware, rootkit, ransomware, virus, worm, and Trojan horse. Read each scenario and select the malware type in each.

Scenarios

Scenario 1: You just downloaded and installed a free game, and suddenly a new "search" toolbar has appeared in your browser.

Scenario 2: You have booted your computer, and it is displaying a page that states your files are encrypted, and you must send bitcoin to decrypt your hard drive.

Scenario 3: A cybercriminal has installed very hard-to-detect malware on your computer to gain system-level privileges and can now control it remotely.

Scenario 4: Whenever you access a secure site on your computer, a program is secretly capturing the login credentials and sending them to a cybercriminal.

Scenario 5: After visiting a free gaming site, your computer displays a pop-up window saying it discovered several viruses, and to fix it you must download and run the free antivirus software. When you download the software and scan your computer with it, it reports that all viruses have been removed. However, the free antivirus software has installed a backdoor application to give a cybercriminal access to your host.

Scenario 6: You open an email attachment, and suddenly your computer shuts down. You try to reboot it, but it keeps shutting down.

Scenario 7: The corporate network is suddenly very noticeably slow and unresponsive.

Answers

Scenario 1 Answer: Adware. This malware can display unsolicited advertising using pop-up web browser windows or new toolbars, or it can unexpectedly redirect from a web page to a different website.

Scenario 2 Answer: Ransomware. This malware encrypts files on the target and then demands that a ransom be paid for the decryption key needed to decrypt the files.

Scenario 3 Answer: Rootkit. Cybercriminals use this malware to gain Administrator account–level access to a computer and control it remotely.

Scenario 4 Answer: Spyware. This malware monitors user activity and sends information to cybercriminals. Keyloggers do the same thing.

Scenario 5 Answer: Trojan horse. This malware is packaged with legitimate software and is activated when a user installs the legitimate application.

Scenario 6 Answer: Virus. This malware requires human action to spread and infect other hosts. Viruses actively try to make copies of themselves and spread.

Scenario 7 Answer: Worm. This malware exploits network applications to consume bandwidth, crash the device, or install other malware.

Viruses and Trojan Horses (13.1.1.3)

The most common type of computer malware is a *virus*. Viruses require human action to propagate and infect other computers. For example, a virus can infect a computer when a victim opens an email attachment, opens a file on a USB drive, or downloads a file.

The virus hides by attaching itself to computer code, software, or documents on the computer. When opened, the virus executes and infects the computer. These are examples of what can happen when a virus has infected a host:

- Alter, corrupt, or delete files or erase entire computer drives
- Cause computer booting issues and corrupt applications
- Capture and send sensitive information to attackers
- Access and use email accounts to spread themselves
- Lay dormant until summoned by the attacker

Modern viruses are developed for specific nefarious reasons. Table 13-1 lists some of the main types of viruses.

Table 13-1 Types of Viruses

Types of Viruses	Description
Boot sector virus	Attacks the boot sector, file partition table, or file system
Firmware virus	Attacks the device firmware
Macro virus	Uses the Microsoft Office macro feature maliciously
Program virus	Inserts itself in another executable program
Script virus	Attacks the OS interpreter, which is used to execute scripts

Cybercriminals also use Trojan horses to compromise hosts. A *Trojan horse* is a program that looks useful but carries malicious code. Trojan horses are often provided with free online programs such as computer games. Unsuspecting users download and install the game, and they also install the Trojan malware.

There are several types of Trojan horses, as described in Table 13-2.

Table 13-2 Types of Trojan Horses

Type of Trojan Horse	Description
Remote access Trojan	Enables unauthorized remote access
Data-sending Trojan	Provides the attacker with sensitive data, such as passwords
Destructive Trojan	Corrupts or deletes files
Proxy Trojan	Uses the victim's computer as the source device to launch attacks and perform other illegal activities
FTP Trojan	Enables unauthorized file transfer services on end devices
Security software disabling Trojan	Stops antivirus programs or firewalls from functioning
Denial of service (DoS) Trojan	Slows or halts network activity
Keylogger Trojan	Actively attempts to steal confidential information, such as credit card numbers, by recording keystrokes entered into web forms

Viruses and Trojan horses are only two types of malware that cybercriminals use. Many other types of malware have been designed for specific purposes.

To fix some issues caused by viruses, it may be necessary to boot the computer using the Windows product disk and then use the Windows Recovery Console to run commands from a "clean" command environment. The Recovery Console is able to perform functions such as repairing the boot file and writing a new Master Boot Record or Volume Boot Record.

Types of Malware (13.1.1.4)

There are many different types of malware, as described in the list that follows:

- *Adware*

    - Adware is usually distributed by downloading online software.

    - Adware can display unsolicited advertising using pop-up web browser windows and new toolbars, or it can unexpectedly redirect from a web page to a different website.

    - Pop-up windows may be difficult to control as new windows can pop up faster than the user can close them.

- *Ransomware*

  - Ransomware typically denies a user access to their files by encrypting the files and then displaying a message demanding a ransom for the decryption key.

  - Users without up-to-date backups must pay the ransom to decrypt their files.

  - Payment is usually made using wire transfer or cryptocurrencies (such as bitcoin).

- *Rootkit*

  - Cybercriminals use rootkits to gain Administrator account–level access to a computer.

  - A rootkit is very difficult to detect because it can alter firewalls, antivirus protection, system files, and even OS commands to conceal its presence.

  - A rootkit can provide a backdoor to cybercriminals, giving them access to the PC and allowing them to upload files and install new software to be used in a DDoS attack.

  - Special rootkit removal tools must be used to remove a rootkit, or the system may need to be completely reinstalled.

- *Spyware*

  - Spyware is similar to adware but is used to gather information about the user and send it to cybercriminals without the user's consent.

  - Spyware can be a low threat (for example, gathering browsing data), or it can be a high threat (for example, capturing personal and financial information).

- *Worm*

  - A worm is a self-replicating program that propagates automatically without user actions by exploiting vulnerabilities in legitimate software.

  - A worm uses the network to search for other victims with the same vulnerability.

  - The intent of a worm is usually to slow or disrupt network operations.

13.1.1.5 Check Your Understanding: Malware

Refer to the online course to complete this activity.

Preventing Malware (13.1.2)

It is essential for computer systems and networks to be protected against breaches. A technician needs to understand malware, the preventive measures to take, and the technologies available to mitigate attacks.

Anti-Malware Programs (13.1.2.1)

Malware is designed to invade privacy, steal information, damage the operating system, or allow hackers to take control of a computer. It is important to protect computers and mobile devices using reputable antivirus software.

This is the seven-step best practice procedure for malware removal:

Step 1.   Identify and research malware symptoms.

Step 2.   Quarantine the infected systems.

Step 3.   Disable system restore (in Windows).

Step 4.   Remediate infected systems.

Step 5.   Schedule scans and run updates.

Step 6.   Enable system restore and create restore points (in Windows).

Step 7.   Educate the end user.

Antivirus programs are commonly referred to as *anti-malware programs* because many of them can also detect and block Trojans, rootkits, ransomware, spyware, keyloggers, and adware programs, as shown in Figure 13-1.

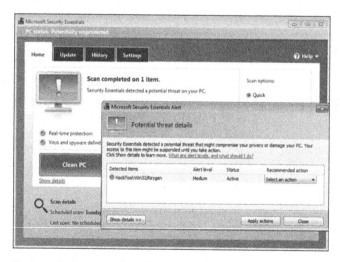

Figure 13-1   Anti-Malware

Anti-malware programs are the best line of defense against malware because they continuously look for known patterns, using a database of known malware signatures. They can also use heuristic malware identification techniques, which can detect specific behavior associated with some types of malware.

An anti-malware program starts when a computer boots, and it checks the system resources, drives, and memory for malware. It then runs continuously in the background, scanning for malware signatures. When a virus is detected, the anti-malware software displays a warning similar to the one shown in Figure 13-1. It may automatically quarantine or delete the malware, depending on software settings.

Anti-malware programs are available for Windows, Linux, and macOS from many reputable security organizations, such as McAfee, Symantec (Norton), Kaspersky, Trend Micro, and Bitdefender.

Note

Using two or more anti-malware solutions simultaneously can negatively impact computer performance.

The most common method of malware delivery is through email. Email filters are a line of defense against email threats, such as spam, viruses, and other malware, because they filter email messages before they reach the user's inbox. Anti-malware software can scan file attachments before they are opened.

Email filtering is available on most email applications, or it can be installed at the organization's email gateway. In addition to detecting and filtering out spam messages, email filters also allow the user to create blacklists of known spammer domains and to whitelist known trusted or safe domains.

Malware can also be delivered through applications that are installed. Installation of software from untrusted sources can lead to the spread of malware such as Trojans. To mitigate this risk, vendors implement various methods to restrict the ability of users to install untrusted software. Windows uses the concept of Administrator and Standard User accounts, along with User Account Control (UAC) and system policies to help prevent installation of untrusted software.

Be cautious of malicious rogue antivirus products that may appear while browsing the Internet. Such a product is likely to display an ad or a pop-up that looks like an actual Windows warning window, as shown in Figure 13-2. Such ads usually state that the computer is infected and must be cleaned. Clicking anywhere inside the window may begin the download and installation of the malware.

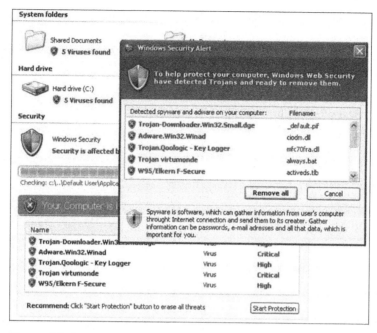

Figure 13-2 Rogue Antivirus

Do not click a warning window that is suspect. Close the tab or the browser to see if the warning window goes away. If the tab or browser does not close, press **Alt+F4** to close the window or use the Task Manager to end the program. If the warning window does not go away, scan the computer using a known good antivirus or adware protection program to ensure that the computer is not infected.

Visit https://zvelo.com/introduction-to-rogue-antivirus/ to read about rogue antivirus malware.

In Linux, users are prompted if they attempt to install untrusted software. The software is signed with a cryptographic private key, and the public key for the repository is needed to install the software.

Mobile OS vendors use the walled garden model to prevent installation of untrusted software. Under this model, apps are distributed from an approved store, such as the Apple App Store or the Microsoft Windows Store.

Signature File Updates (13.1.2.2)

New malware is always being developed; therefore, anti-malware software must be updated regularly. The update process is often enabled by default. However, a technician should know how to manually update anti-malware software signatures.

To update a signature file manually, follow these suggested steps:

Step 1. Create a restore point in case the file you load is corrupt. Setting a restore point allows you to go back to the way things were.

Step 2. Open the anti-malware program. If the program is set to execute or obtain updates automatically, you might need to turn off the automatic feature to perform these steps manually.

Step 3. Click the **Update** button.

Step 4. After the program is updated, use it to scan the computer and then check the report for viruses or other problems.

Step 5. Set the anti-malware program to automatically update its signature file and scan the computer on a regular basis.

Always download signature files from the manufacturer's website to make sure the updates are authentic and not corrupted by malware. This can put a great demand on the manufacturer's website, especially when new malware is released. To avoid creating too much traffic at a single website, some manufacturers distribute their signature files for download to multiple download sites. These download sites are called *mirrors*.

Caution

When downloading signature files from a mirror, ensure that the mirror site is a legitimate site. Always link to the mirror site from the manufacturer's website.

Video

13.1.2.3 Video Explanation: Protecting Against Malware

Refer to the online course to view this video.

Remediating Infected Systems (13.1.2.4)

When a malware protection program detects that a computer is infected, it removes or quarantines the threat. However, the computer is most likely still at risk.

When malware is discovered on your home computer, you should update your anti-malware software and perform full scans of all your media. An anti-malware program can be set to run on system start before loading Windows. This allows the program to access all areas of the disk without being affected by the operating system or any malware.

When malware is discovered on a business computer, you should remove the computer from the network to prevent other computers from becoming infected. Unplug all network cables from the computer and disable all wireless connections. Next, follow the incident response policy that is in place. This may include notifying IT personnel, saving log files to removable media, or turning off the computer.

Removing malware may require that the computer be rebooted into Safe mode to prevent most drivers from loading. Some malware may require that a special tool from the anti-malware vendor be used. Be sure that you download such tools from legitimate sites.

For really stubborn malware, it may be necessary to contact a specialist to ensure that the computer has been completely cleaned. Otherwise, the computer may need to be reformatted and the operating system reinstalled, and you may need to recover your data from the most recent backups.

The OS system restore service may include infected files in a restore point. Therefore, once a computer has been cleaned of any malware, the system restore files should be deleted, as shown in Figure 13-3.

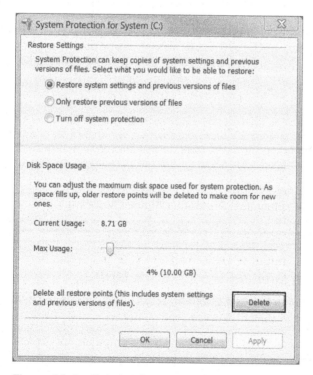

Figure 13-3 Deleting Restore Points

After remediation, you may need to fix some issues caused by viruses; it may be necessary to boot the computer using the Windows product media and then use the Windows Recovery Console to run commands from a "clean" command environment.

The Recovery Console can perform functions such as repairing the boot file and writing a new Master Boot Record or Volume Boot Record.

13.1.2.5 Video Explanation: Remediating an Infected System

Refer to the online course to view this video.

13.1.2.6 Lab: Operating System Security

In this lab, you will configure Microsoft Defender Antivirus and Windows Defender Firewall.

13.1.2.7 Check Your Understanding: Preventing Malware

Refer to the online course to complete this activity.

Network Attacks (13.1.3)

Network attacks take many forms and have many different phases. The common theme among them is that a network attack is an assault on network infrastructures, with the intent to compromise or disrupt the network system and gain unauthorized access to data and systems.

Networks Are Targets (13.1.3.1)

To control communication on the Internet, networks use the TCP/IP protocol suite. Because the TCP/IP protocol suite is the de facto protocol suite, it is widely targeted and has some known vulnerabilities, making networks that use it major targets for attackers.

Attackers look for TCP/IP vulnerabilities. Exploits are used to attack a network and make it or devices unresponsive or to help attackers gain access to internal resources. Many protocols in the TCP/IP suite transmit information in plaintext, which makes them susceptible to various attacks.

Attackers typically do some reconnaissance of target networks. *Reconnaissance*, also referred to as *footprinting*, is the phase of an attack in which the attacker attempts to learn as much about the target network as possible. To accomplish this, an attacker may follow these steps:

Step 1. **Perform an information query of a target:** The attacker looks for network information about a target by using various tools, including Google search, the organization's website, whois, and more.

Step 2.   **Initiate a ping sweep of the target network:** The attacker initiates a ping sweep of the discovered target's public network address to determine which IP addresses are active.

Step 3.   **Initiate a port scan of active IP addresses:** The attacker determines which services are available on the active ports by using tools such as Nmap and SuperScan.

Step 4.   **Run vulnerability scanners:** The attacker runs vulnerability scanners such as Nipper or Secuna PSI to discover the type and version of the application and operating system running on the target host.

Step 5.   **Run exploitation tools:** The attacker attempts to discover vulnerable services that can be exploited, using tools such as Metasploit and Core Impact.

Types of TCP/IP Attacks (13.1.3.2)

There are many different types of TCP/IP attacks, including the following:

- *Denial of service (DoS)*
  - In a DoS attack, the attacker completely overwhelms a target device with false requests to deny service to legitimate users.
  - An attacker could cut or unplug a network cable to a critical network device to cause a network outage.
  - DoS attacks may be caused for malicious reasons or used in conjunction with other attacks.
- *Distributed DoS (DDoS)*
  - A DDoS attack is an amplified DoS attack in which many infected hosts called *zombies* overwhelm a target.
  - Attackers control zombies by using a handler computer.
  - A *botnet* is an army of compromised hosts that remains dormant until instructed by the handler.
  - Botnets can also be used for spam and phishing attacks.
- *DNS poisoning*
  - In a DNS poisoning attack, the attacker has successfully infected a host to accept false DNS records pointing to malicious servers.

- Traffic is diverted to these malicious servers to capture confidential information.

- An attacker can then retrieve the data from that location.

- *Man-in-the-middle (MITM)*

  - In a TCP/IP MITM attack, an attacker intercepts communications between two hosts.

  - If successful, the attacker could capture packets and view their content, manipulate packets, and more.

  - MITM attacks can be created using an ARP poisoning spoofing attack.

- *Replay*

  - A replay attack is a type of spoofing attack in which the attacker has captured an authenticated packet, altered the packet's contents, and sent the packet to its original destination.

  - The goal is to have the target host accept the altered packet as authentic.

- *Spoofing*

  - In a TCP/IP spoofing attack, the attacker forges IP addresses.

  - For example, an attacker might spoof the IP address of a trusted host to gain access to resources.

- *SYN flood*

  - A SYN flood attack is a type of DoS attack that exploits the TCP three-way handshake.

  - The attacker sends continuous false SYN requests to the target.

  - The target is eventually overwhelmed and unable to establish valid SYN requests, creating a DoS attack.

Interactive Graphic

13.1.3.3 Check Your Understanding: Identify the TCP/IP Attack

Refer to the online course to complete this activity.

Zero-Day (13.1.3.4)

The following two terms are commonly used to describe when a threat is detected:

- *Zero-day*: Sometimes also referred to as zero-day attack, zero-day threat, or zero-day exploit, this is the day that an unknown vulnerability is discovered by the vendor. The term is a reference to the amount of time that a vendor has had to address the vulnerability.

- *Zero-hour*: This is the moment when an exploit is discovered.

A network remains vulnerable between the zero-day and the time it takes a vendor to develop a solution.

In the example in Figure 13-4, a software vendor has learned of a new vulnerability. The software can be exploited until a patch that addresses the vulnerability is made available. Notice that in the example, it took several days and a few software patch updates to mitigate the threat.

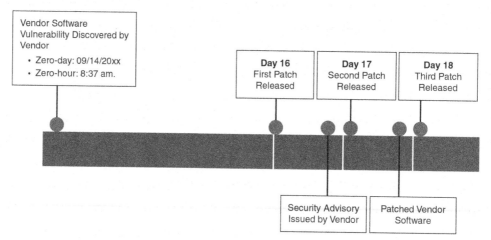

Figure 13-4   Mitigating a Zero-Day Attack

The next section addresses how networks can be protected against threats and zero-day attacks.

Protecting Against Network Attacks (13.1.3.5)

Many network attacks are fast moving; therefore, network security professionals must adopt a sophisticated view of the network architecture. There is no one solution to protect against all TCP/IP or zero-day attacks.

One approach, however, is to use a *defense-in-depth* approach, also known as a layered approach, to security. This requires a combination of networking devices and services working together in tandem.

Consider the network in Figure 13-5.

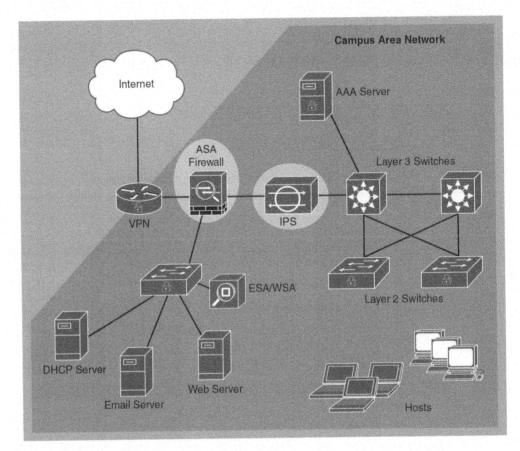

Figure 13-5   Protecting Against Network Attacks

As shown in Figure 13-5, several security devices and services can be implemented to protect users and assets against TCP/IP threats:

- *VPN*: A router can be used to provide secure VPN services with corporate sites and remote access support for remote users, using secure encrypted tunnels.

- *ASA firewall*: This dedicated device provides stateful firewall services. It ensures that internal traffic can go out and come back but external traffic cannot initiate connections to inside hosts.

- An *intrusion prevention system (IPS)*: An IPS monitors incoming and outgoing traffic, looking for malware, network attack signatures, and more. If it recognizes a threat, it can immediately stop it.

- *AAA server*: This server contains a secure database of those who are authorized to access and manage network devices. Network devices authenticate administrative users using this database.

- *Email Security Appliance (ESA)* and *Web Security Appliance (WSA)*: The ESA filters spam and suspicious emails. The WSA filters known and suspicious Internet malware sites.

All network devices, including the router and switches, can also be hardened to prevent attackers from tampering with the devices.

Social Engineering Attacks (13.1.4)

Social engineering is malicious activity achieved through human interactions. It is an art to be able to gain trust and use powers of persuasion to manipulate people to unknowingly give up information that can lead to a security breach. That is exactly how social engineering attacks happen. Exploiting the human consciousness rather than using technical techniques is often a successful method of circumventing security barriers.

Social Engineering (13.1.4.1)

To secure networks and hosts, organizations often deploy network security solutions and anti-malware solutions for their hosts. They also need to address the weakest link: the users.

Social engineering is likely the single most serious threat to a well-configured and well-secured network. Cybercriminals use *social engineering* techniques to deceive and trick unsuspecting targets into revealing confidential information or violating security policies to gain information. Social engineering is an access attack that attempts to manipulate individuals into performing actions or divulging confidential information.

Social engineers prey on people's weaknesses and often rely on human nature and people's willingness to be helpful.

Note

Social engineering is often used in conjunction with other network attacks.

What Do You Already Know? - Social Engineering Techniques (13.1.4.2)

There are many types of social engineering techniques, including impersonation, baiting, pretexting, Dumpster diving, phishing, spam, shoulder surfing, tailgating, spear phishing, and something for something. Read the following scenarios and select the social engineering technique used in each one.

Scenarios

Scenario 1: When you find a USB drive in a parking lot and insert it into your laptop, you unknowingly install malware on your computer.

Scenario 2: An attacker retrieves hard copies of recently outdated device configuration files from a trash bin.

Scenario 3: A person claiming to be from your heating and ventilation contractor asks you if you could let them into a secure area.

Scenario 4: You receive an email from your bank, stating that your account has been compromised and that you should click an enclosed link to rectify the problem. When you click, you install malware on your device.

Scenario 5: Your bank calls to say your account may be compromised and asks you to confirm your identity by providing personal and financial data.

Scenario 6: You notice a colleague purposely looking over your supervisor's shoulder while they are entering their login credentials.

Scenario 7: You received a survey in an email that asks you to provide personal identifiable information in exchange for a cool free t-shirt.

Scenario 8: An attacker sends malicious emails containing harmful links, malware, and deceptive content to a large number of random individuals.

Scenario 9: An attacker has created a targeted phishing attack tailored specifically for the chief executive officer of a large organization.

Scenario 10: A person you have never seen before has quickly followed you into a secure building entrance, saying that they forgot their security badge.

Answers

Scenario 1 Answer: Baiting. With this social engineering technique, an attacker leaves a malware-infected flash drive in a public location (such as a corporate restroom), hoping a victim will find the drive and insert it into a corporate laptop, where it can install the malware.

Scenario 2 Answer: Dumpster diving. With this social engineering technique, an attacker rummages through trash bins to discover confidential documents or old media.

Scenario 3 Answer: Impersonation. With this social engineering technique, an attacker pretends to be someone they are not (such as a new employee, a colleague, or a vendor or partner company employee) to gain the trust of a victim.

Scenario 4 Answer: Phishing. With this social engineering technique, an attacker sends fraudulent email that purports to be from a legitimate, trusted source to trick the recipient into installing malware or sharing personal or financial information.

Scenario 5 Answer: Pretexting. With this social engineering technique, an attacker pretends to need personal or financial information in order to confirm the identity of the person they are talking to.

Scenario 6 Answer: Shoulder surfing. With this social engineering technique, an attacker looks over someone's shoulder to steal their passwords.

Scenario 7 Answer: Something for something. In this social engineering technique, also called *quid pro quo*, an attacker requests personal information from a victim in exchange for something such as a gift.

Scenario 8 Answer: Spam. With this social engineering technique, an attacker sends unsolicited junk mail to thousands or millions of recipients in an attempt to trick them into clicking on an infected link or downloading an infected file.

Scenario 9 Answer: Spear phishing. This social engineering technique is a phishing attack targeting specific individuals (such as executives) or organizations.

Scenario 10 Answer: Tailgating. An attacker uses this social engineering technique, also called piggybacking, to gain access to a secure area.

Social Engineering Techniques (13.1.4.3)

There are many different ways to use social engineering techniques. Some social engineering techniques are used in person, and others involve the telephone or Internet. For example, a hacker could call an authorized employee with an urgent problem that requires immediate network access. The hacker could appeal to the employee's vanity, invoke authority by using name-dropping techniques, or appeal to the employee's greed.

These are the most common social engineering techniques:

- *Pretexting*: An attacker pretends to need personal or financial data in order to confirm the identity of the recipient.

- *Phishing*: An attacker sends fraudulent email, disguised as being from a legitimate, trusted source, to trick the recipient into installing malware on their device or sharing personal or financial information (such as a bank account number and a PIN).

- *Spear phishing*: An attacker creates a targeted phishing attack tailored specifically for an individual or organization.

- *Spam*: Also known as junk mail, this is unsolicited email that often contains harmful links, malware, or deceptive content.

- *Something for something*: With this type of attack, sometimes called *quid pro quo*, an attacker requests personal information from a party in exchange for something such as a free gift.

- *Baiting*: An attacker leaves a malware-infected flash drive in a public location (such as a corporate restroom). A victim finds the drive and inserts it into their laptop, unintentionally installing the malware.

- *Impersonation*: With this type of attack, an attacker pretends to be someone they are not (such as a new employee, a fellow employee, or a vendor or partner company employee) to gain the trust of a victim.

- *Tailgating*: This is an in-person type of attack in which an attacker quickly follows an authorized person into a secure location to gain access to that area.

- *Shoulder surfing*: This is an in-person type of attack in which an attacker inconspicuously looks over someone's shoulder and tries to steal their passwords or other information.

- *Dumpster diving*: This is an in-person type of attack in which an attacker rummages through trash bins, looking for confidential documents.

Protecting Against Social Engineering (13.1.4.4)

Enterprises must train and educate their users about the risks of social engineering and develop strategies to validate identities over the phone, via email, or in person.

These are recommended practices that should be followed by all users:

- Never give your username and password credentials to anyone.

- Never leave your username and password credentials where they can easily be found.

- Never open emails from untrusted sources.

- Never release work-related information on social media sites.

- Never reuse work-related passwords.

- Always lock or sign out of your computer when unattended.

- Always report suspicious individuals.

- Always destroy confidential information according to the organization policy.

Interactive
Graphic

13.1.4.5 Check Your Understanding: Personal and Corporate Social Engineering Techniques

Refer to the online course to complete this activity.

Security Procedures (13.2)

Security procedures, which are built on the security policy of an organization, are the detailed instructions and steps to follow to implement and enforce security rules, as specified in the security policy.

Security Policy (13.2.1)

A security policy is like a blueprint for a company's security plan. It is a plan that outlines the security objectives, goals, and rules established by high-level management. The document is meant to establish the security approach and attitude of an organization.

What Is a Security Policy? (13.2.1.1)

A *security policy* is a set of security objectives that ensure the security of a network, the data, and the computers in an organization. A security policy is a constantly evolving document based on changes in technology, business, and employee requirements.

A security policy is usually created by a committee consisting of management and IT staff. The committee creates and manages a security policy document that identifies the following:

- Which assets require protection
- What the possible threats are
- What to do in the event of a security breach
- What training will be in place to educate the end users

A security policy should consist of the following:

- Identification and authentication policy
- Password policy
- Acceptable use policy
- Remote access policy
- Network maintenance policy
- Incident handling policy

In addition, a security policy should include other items related specifically to the operation of a particular organization. It is up to the IT staff to implement security policy specifications in the network. For example, to implement recommendations on a Windows host, IT staff could use the Local Security Policy feature.

Security Policy Category (13.2.1.2)

The typical items included in a security policy are as follows:

- *Identification and authentication policy*: Specifies authorized persons who can have access to network resources and outlines verification procedures.

- *Password policy*: Specifies minimum requirements for passwords and requires that passwords be changed regularly.

- *Acceptable use policy*: Identifies network resources and usages that are acceptable to the organization. It may also identify ramifications for violation of this policy.

- *Remote access policy*: Identifies how remote users can access a network and what is accessible via remote connectivity.

- *Network maintenance policy*: Specifies network device operating systems and end-user application update procedures.

- *Incident handling policy*: Describes how security incidents are handled.

Securing Devices and Data (13.2.1.3)

The goals of a security policy are to ensure a safe network environment and to protect assets. An organization's assets include data, employees, and physical devices such as computers and network equipment.

A security policy should identify hardware and equipment that can be used to prevent theft, vandalism, and data loss.

Protecting Physical Equipment (13.2.2)

This section examines an often-overlooked aspect of information systems security: physical security. Physical security—including security of personnel, buildings, and equipment—is a vital part of any security plan and foundational to the strength of all security efforts.

Physical Security (13.2.2.1)

Physical security is as important as data security. For example, if a computer is taken from an organization, the data is also stolen or, worse, lost.

Physical security involves securing:

- Access to an organization's premises

- Access to restricted areas

- The computing and network infrastructure

The level of physical security implemented depends on the organization, as some have higher physical security requirements than others.

For example, consider how data centers, airports, and military installations are secured. These organizations use perimeter security including fences, gates, and checkpoints with security guards posted. Entrance to a building's premises and restricted areas is secured using one or more locking mechanism. Building doors typically use self-closing and self-locking mechanisms. The type of locking mechanism required varies based on the level of security required. A visitor accessing a secure building may have to pass through a security checkpoint staffed by security guards. The guards may scan a visitor and their belongings and may have the visitor sign an entry control roster when entering the building and sign out when leaving.

Higher-security organizations have all employees wear identification badges with photographs. A badge could be a smart card containing the user information and security clearance to access restricted areas. For additional security requirements, RFID badges can also be used with proximity badge readers to monitor the location of an individual.

Types of Secure Locks (13.2.2.2)

There are many different types of secure locks, including:

- *Conventional lock*: This type of lock is unlocked by entering the required key into the door handle mechanism (see Figure 13-6).

Figure 13-6   Conventional Lock

■ *Deadbolt lock*: This type of lock is unlocked by entering the required key into a lock separate from the door handle mechanism (see Figure 13-7).

Figure 13-7 Deadbolt Lock

■ *Electronic lock*: This type of lock is unlocked by entering a combination code or PIN into the keypad (see Figure 13-8).

Figure 13-8 Electronic Lock

■ *Token-based lock*: This type of lock is unlocked by swiping a secure card or by using a proximity reader to detect a smart card or wireless key fob (see Figure 13-9).

Figure 13-9   Token-Based Lock

■ *Biometric lock*: This type of lock is unlocked using a biometric scanner such as a fingerprint reader (see Figure 13-10). Other biometric scanners include voice print and retina scanners.

Figure 13-10   Biometric Lock

- *Multifactor lock*: This type of lock uses a combination of mechanisms. For example, a user must enter a PIN and then scan their thumb (see Figure 13-11).

Figure 13-11   Multifactor Lock

Mantraps (13.2.2.3)

In high-security environments, *mantraps* are often used to limit access to restricted areas and to prevent tailgating. A mantrap is a small room with two doors, one of which must be closed before the other can be opened.

Typically, a person enters the mantrap by unlocking one door. Once inside the mantrap, the first door closes, and then the user must unlock the second door to enter the restricted area.

Figure 13-12 illustrates how a mantrap is used to secure access to a restricted area.

In the figure, the person must enter the building using a smart card to open the locked door to the mantrap. Once the person successfully enters the mantrap, the first door locks, and they must now unlock the next door by using the biometric reader. The person must have their thumbprint scanned to unlock the locked door to the secure internal area.

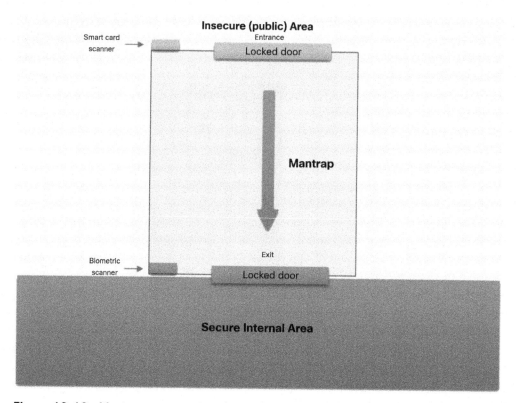

Figure 13-12 Mantrap

Securing Computers and Network Hardware (13.2.2.4)

Organizations must protect their computing and network infrastructure, including cabling, telecommunication equipment, and network devices.

There are several methods of physically protecting computer and networking equipment:

- Use webcams with motion-detection and surveillance software.
- Install physical alarms triggered by motion-detection sensors.
- Label and install RFID sensors on equipment.
- Use locking cabinets or security cages around equipment.
- Fit equipment with security screws.
- Keep telecommunication rooms locked.
- Use cable locks with equipment.

Network equipment should be installed only in secured areas. In addition, all cabling should be enclosed within conduits or routed inside walls to prevent unauthorized access or tampering. Conduit is a casing that protects the infrastructure media from damage and unauthorized access.

To restrict access to physical switch ports and switch hardware to authorized personnel, an organization can use a secure server room and lock hardware cabinets. To prevent the attachment of rogue or unauthorized client devices, switch ports should be disabled through the switch management software.

Factors that determine the most effective security equipment to use to secure equipment and data include:

- How the equipment is used

- Where the computer equipment is located

- What type of user access to data is required

For instance, a computer in a busy public place, such as a library, requires extra protection from theft and vandalism. In a busy call center, a server might need to be secured in a locked equipment room. Server locks can provide physical chassis security by preventing access to power switches, removable drives, and USB ports. Where it is necessary to use a laptop computer in a public place, a security dongle and key fob ensure that the computer locks if the user and laptop are separated. Another tool for physical security is a USB lock, which is locked into place in a USB port and requires a key for removal.

Security policies can be applied to mobile devices in a corporate network through enterprise mobility management (EMM) software. Mobile device management (MDM) software can be used to manage corporate-owned devices and devices used in an environment that has a bring your own device (BYOD) policy. The EMM or MDM software logs use of devices on the network and determines if a particular device should be allowed to connect, through a process known as *onboarding*, based on administrative policies. MDM software sets policies for connectivity, authentication, and the use of features such as the microphone and camera on a device. Mobile application management (MAM) involves setting policies for the applications that are allowed to be used on a device. It keeps corporate data secure and away from applications that are not allowed to process it.

Interactive Graphic

13.2.2.5 Check Your Understanding: Locking Mechanisms

Refer to the online course to complete this activity.

Protecting Data (13.2.3)

One of the most important goals of information security is to protect data. It is critical that the data being stored, processed, and transported be safeguarded. Programs can be reinstalled if damaged, but user data is unique and not easily replaced.

Data—Your Greatest Asset (13.2.3.1)

Data is likely to be an organization's most valuable asset. Organizational data can include research and development data, sales data, financial data, human resources and legal data, employee data, contractor data, and customer data.

Data can be lost or damaged due to theft, equipment failure, or disaster. *Data loss* and *data exfiltration* are terms used to describe data being intentionally or unintentionally lost, stolen, or leaked to the outside world.

Data loss can negatively affect an organization in multiple ways:

- Brand damage and loss of reputation
- Loss of competitive advantage
- Loss of customers
- Loss of revenue
- Legal action resulting in fines and civil penalties
- Significant cost and effort to notify affected parties
- Significant cost and effort to recover from the breach

Losing data, regardless of circumstances, can be detrimental or even catastrophic to an organization.

Data can be protected from data loss using data backups, file and folder encryption, and file and folder permissions.

Data loss prevention (DLP) is the process of preventing data loss or leakage. DLP software uses a dictionary database or an algorithm to identify confidential data and block the transfer of that data to removable media or email if such a transfer does not conform to predefined policy.

Data Backups (13.2.3.2)

Backing up data is one of the most effective ways of protecting against data loss. A data backup stores a copy of the information on a computer to removable backup media that can be kept in a safe place. If the computer hardware fails, the data can be restored from the backup to functional hardware.

Data backups should be performed on a regular basis, as identified in the security policy. Data backups are usually stored offsite to protect the backup media in the event that something happens to the main facility. Windows hosts have a backup and restore utility. This is useful for users to back up their data to another drive or to a cloud-based storage provider. macOS includes the Time Machine utility to perform backup and restore functions.

A number of considerations related to data backup are important:

- **Frequency:** Perform backups on a regular basis, as identified in the security policy. Full backups can be time-consuming, so you might want to perform monthly or weekly full backups with frequent partial backups of changed files.

- **Storage:** Transport backups to an approved offsite storage location on a daily, weekly, or monthly rotation, as required by the security policy.

- **Security:** Protect backups by using strong passwords that are required to restore data.

- **Validation:** Always validate backups to ensure the integrity of the data and validate the file restoration procedures.

File and Folder Permissions (13.2.3.3)

Permissions are rules you configure to limit folder or file access for an individual or for a group of users. The following permissions are available for files and folders in a Windows environment:

- *Full Control*: This permission enables the user to see the content of a file or folder, change and delete existing files and folders, create new files and folders, and run programs in a folder.

- *Modify*: This permission enables the user to change and delete existing files and folders but does not allow the user to create new files or folders.

- *Read and Execute*: This permission enables the user to see the contents of existing files or folders and run programs in a folder.

- *Read*: This permission enables the user to see the contents of a folder and open files and folders.

- *Write*: This permission enables the user to create new files and folders and make changes to existing files and folders.

To configure file- or folder-level permissions in all versions of Windows, right-click the file or folder and select Properties > Security > Edit.

Users should have their permissions limited to only the resources they need in a computer or on a network. For example, they should not be able to access all files on a server if they only need access to a single folder. It may be easier to provide users access to the entire drive, but it is more secure to limit access to only the folder the user needs to perform the job. This is known as the *principle of least privilege*. Limiting access to resources also prevents malicious programs from accessing those resources if the user's computer becomes infected.

Folder redirection allows a user with administrative privileges to redirect the path of a local folder to a folder on a network share. This makes the folder's data available to the user when they log into any computer on the network where the network share is located. With user data redirected from local to network storage, administrators can back up the user data when the network data folders are backed up.

File and network share permissions can be granted to individuals or through membership in a group. These share permissions are different from file- and folder-level NTFS permissions. If an individual or a group is denied permissions to a network share, this denial overrides any other permissions given. For example, if you deny someone permission to a network share, the user cannot access that share, even if the user is the administrator or part of the Administrators group. The local security policy must outline which resources and the type of access allowed for each user and group.

When the permissions of a folder are changed, you are given the option to apply the same permissions to all subfolders. This is known as *permission propagation*. Permission propagation allows you to apply permissions to many files and folders quickly. After parent folder permissions have been set, folders and files that are created inside the parent folder inherit the permissions of the parent folder.

Also, the location of the data and the action performed on the data determine how the permissions are propagated:

- When data is moved to the same volume, it keeps the original permissions.
- When data is copied to the same volume, it inherits new permissions.
- When data is moved to a different volume, it inherits new permissions.
- When data is copied to a different volume, it inherits new permissions.

File and Folder Encryption (13.2.3.4)

Encryption is often used to protect data. With *encryption*, data is transformed using a complicated algorithm that makes the data unreadable. A special key must be used to return the unreadable information back into readable data. Software programs are used to encrypt files, folders, and even entire drives.

Encrypting File System (EFS) is a Windows feature that can encrypt data. EFS is directly linked to a specific user account. Only the user who encrypted the data can access it after it has been encrypted using EFS. To encrypt data using EFS in all Windows versions, follow these steps:

Step 1. Select one or more files or folders.

Step 2. Right-click the selected data and select **Properties.**

Step 3. Click **Advanced.**

Step 4. Select the **Encrypt Contents to Secure Data** check box and click **OK.** Windows displays an informational message stating that it is applying attributes.

Files and folders that have been encrypted with EFS are displayed in green, as shown in Figure 13-13.

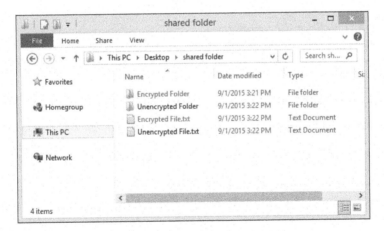

Figure 13-13   Encrypting a File System

Windows BitLocker and BitLocker To Go (13.2.3.5)

You can choose to encrypt an entire hard drive by using *BitLocker.* To use BitLocker, at least two volumes must be present on a hard disk. A system volume is left unencrypted and must be at least 100 MB. This volume holds the files that Windows needs in order to boot.

Note

BitLocker is built into the Windows Enterprise editions, Windows 7 Ultimate, Windows 8 Pro, and Windows 10 Professional.

Before you can use BitLocker, *Trusted Platform Module (TPM)* must be enabled in BIOS. TPM is a specialized chip installed on the motherboard. It stores information specific to the host computer, such as encryption keys, digital certificates, and passwords. Applications such as BitLocker that use encryption can make use of the TPM chip. These are the steps to enable TPM on a Lenovo laptop:

Step 1.   Start the computer and enter the BIOS configuration.

Step 2.   Look for the TPM option in the BIOS configuration screens. Consult the manual for your motherboard to locate the correct screen.

Step 3.   Choose **Enable** or **Activate** for the chip security.

Step 4.   Save the changes to the BIOS configuration.

Step 5.   Reboot the computer.

To turn on BitLocker full disk encryption in all versions of Windows, follow these steps:

Step 1.   Click **Control Panel > BitLocker Drive Encryption.**

Step 2.   On the BitLocker Drive Encryption page, click **Turn On BitLocker** on the operating system volume. (If TPM is not initialized, follow the instructions provided by the wizard to initialize TPM.)

Step 3.   On the Save the Recovery Password page, choose whether to save the password to a USB drive or to a network drive or another location or to print the password. After saving the recovery password, click **Next.**

Step 4.   On the Encrypt the Selected Disk Volume page, select the **Run BitLocker System Check** check box and click **Continue.**

Step 5.   Click **Restart Now.**

When these steps are complete, the Encryption in Progress status bar is displayed. After the computer reboots, you can verify that BitLocker is active, as shown in Figure 13-14.

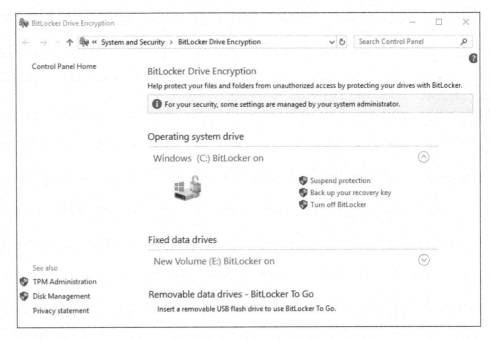

Figure 13-14   Verifying That BitLocker Is Active

You can click TPM Administration to view the TPM details, as shown in Figure 13-15.

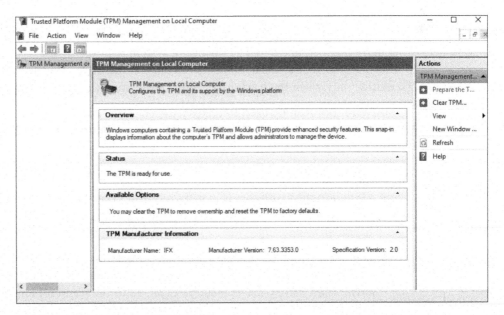

Figure 13-15   Viewing TPM Details

BitLocker To Go makes BitLocker encryption available on removable drives. Bit-Locker To Go does not use a TPM chip but still provides encryption for the data and requires a password.

13.2.3.6 Video Demonstration: BitLocker and BitLocker To Go

Refer to the online course to view this video.

13.2.3.7 Lab: BitLocker and BitLocker To Go

In this lab, you will enable BitLocker encryption on a removable data drive and on the computer system drive.

Data Destruction (13.2.4)

Data destruction or data disposal is a critical part of any security plan. For data that is no longer needed, it is necessary to have a proper disposal strategy to make sure data that you do not want accessed and used for unauthorized purposes is erased and unrecoverable.

Data Wiping Magnetic Media (13.2.4.1)

Protecting data involves removing files from storage devices when they are no longer needed. Simply deleting files or reformatting the drive may not be enough to ensure data privacy. For example, deleting files from a magnetic hard disk drive does not remove them completely. The operating system removes the file reference in the file allocation table, but the actual data remains on the drive. This deleted data is over-written only when the hard drive stores new data in the same location.

Software tools can be used to recover folders, files, and even entire partitions. This can be handy in the case of an accidental erasure, but it can be disastrous in the hands of a malicious user.

Storage media should be fully erased using one or more of the following:

- *Data wiping software*: This software, also known as secure erase, is specifically designed to overwrite existing data multiple times, rendering the data unreadable.

- *Degaussing wand*: A wand with very powerful magnets can be held over exposed hard drive platters to disrupt or eliminate the magnetic field on a hard drive. Hard drive platters must be exposed to the wand for approximately 2 minutes.

- *Electromagnetic degaussing device*: This type of device, which is useful for erasing multiple drives, consists of a magnet with an electrical current applied to it to create a very strong magnetic field that disrupts or eliminates the magnetic field on a hard drive. This method is very expensive but fast, erasing a drive in seconds.

Note

Data wiping and degaussing techniques are irreversible, and the data can never be recovered.

Data Wiping Other Media (13.2.4.2)

SSDs are composed of flash memory instead of magnetic platters. Common techniques used for erasing data, such as degaussing, are not effective with flash memory. Perform a secure erase to fully ensure that data cannot be recovered from an SSD or a hybrid SSD.

Other storage media and documents (such as optical discs, eMMC, and USB sticks) must also be destroyed. Use a shredding machine or an incinerator that is designed to destroy documents and each type of media. When you need to keep sensitive documents, such as those containing classified information or passwords, be sure to keep them locked in a secure location.

When thinking about what devices must be wiped or destroyed, remember that devices besides computers and mobile devices store data. A printer or a multifunction device may also contain a hard drive that caches printed or scanned documents. This caching feature can be turned off in some instances, or the device might need to be wiped on a regular basis to ensure data privacy. It is a good security practice to set up user authentication on the device, if possible, to prevent an unauthorized person from changing any settings that concern privacy.

Hard Drive Recycling and Destruction (13.2.4.3)

Companies with sensitive data should establish and follow clear policies for storage media disposal. There are two choices available when a storage medium is no longer needed:

- **Recycling:** Hard drives that have been wiped can be reused in other computers. A drive can be reformatted, and a new operating system can be installed.

- **Destruction:** Destroying a hard drive fully ensures that data cannot be recovered from it. Specifically designed devices such as hard drive crushers, hard drive shredders, and incinerators can be used for large volumes of drives. Otherwise, physically damaging the drive with a hammer is effective.

Two types of formatting can be performed:

- *Low-level formatting*: The surface of the disk is marked with sector markers identifying tracks where the data will be physically stored on the disk. This type of formatting is most often performed at the factory after the hard drive is assembled.

- *Standard formatting*: This process, also called high-level formatting, involves creating a boot sector and a file system. Standard formatting can be performed only after low-level formatting has been completed.

A company might choose to have an outside contractor destroy its storage media. Such contractors are typically bonded and follow strict government regulations. They might also offer certificates of destruction to provide evidence that the media has been completely destroyed.

Interactive Graphic

13.2.4.4 Check Your Understanding: Data Protection

Refer to the online course to complete this activity.

Securing Windows Workstations (13.3)

Securing workstations should be a significant part of an organization's security strategy. Many organizations store sensitive information that can be used as an access point to the rest of the network system.

Securing a Workstation (13.3.1)

To secure a workstation, you need to consider all facets of its exposure. Physical security, securing user access, and user rights and permissions are a few of the aspects that are discussed in this section.

Securing a Computer (13.3.1.1)

Computers and workstations should be secured against theft. Companies often secure computers in locked rooms.

To prevent unauthorized users from stealing or accessing local computers and network resources, lock your workstation, laptop, or server when you are not present. It is important to use physical security as well as password security. If you must leave a computer in an open public area, use a cable lock to deter theft.

Data displayed on your computer screen should be protected, especially when you're using a laptop in a public location such as an airport, a coffeehouse, or a customer site. Use a privacy screen to protect the information displayed on your laptop from prying eyes. A privacy screen is a clear plastic panel attached to the computer screen that permits only the user directly in front of the screen to see the information displayed.

You also need to protect access to your computer. Three levels of password protection can be used on a computer:

- **BIOS:** Prevents the operating system from booting and changing BIOS settings.

- **Login:** Prevents unauthorized access to the local computer.

- **Network:** Prevents access to network resources by unauthorized personnel.

Securing BIOS (13.3.1.2)

A Windows, Linux, or Mac login password can be bypassed. A malicious user could boot your computer from a CD or flash drive with a different operating system. After it is booted, the malicious user could access or erase your files.

Setting a BIOS or UEFI password can prevent someone from booting the computer. It also prevents someone from altering the configured settings. In Figure 13-16, for example, a user would have to enter the configured BIOS password to access the BIOS configuration.

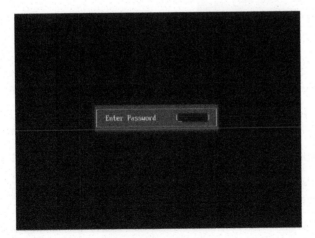

Figure 13-16   BIOS Authentication

All users on a computer share the same BIOS password. UEFI passwords can be set on a per-user basis, but an authentication server is required.

Caution

A BIOS or UEFI password is relatively difficult to reset, so be sure you remember it.

Securing Windows Login (13.3.1.3)

The most common type of password protection is a computer login, where you enter a password and sometimes a username, as shown in Figure 13-17.

Figure 13-17   Windows 10 Login

Depending on your computer system, Windows 10 might also support other sign-in options. Specifically, Windows 10 supports the following sign-in options:

- **Windows Hello:** With this feature, Windows can use facial recognition or your fingerprint to access Windows.

- **PIN:** You may be able to enter a preconfigured PIN to access Windows.

- **Picture password:** You might be able to choose a picture and gestures to use with the picture to create a unique password.

- **Dynamic lock:** This feature causes Windows to lock when a specific paired device such as a cell phone goes out of range of the PC.

Figure 13-18 shows a sample PIN authentication screen instead of the password login option. In this example, a user could change the sign-in option to either password, fingerprint, or facial recognition.

Figure 13-18   Windows 10 PIN Sign-in

If a user chooses to authenticate using their fingerprint, they would scan their finger as shown in Figure 13-19.

Figure 13-19   Laptop Fingerprint Reader

To change sign-in options on a Windows 10 computer, use Start > Settings > Accounts > Sign-in. In the window that appears (see Figure 13-20), you can also change your password, set a PIN, enable picture password, or select to use dynamic lock.

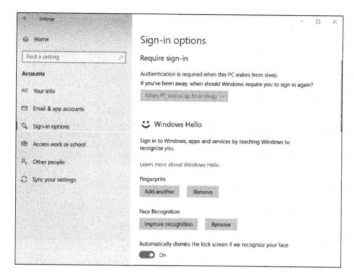

Figure 13-20   Windows 10 Sign-in Options

Local Password Management (13.3.1.4)

Password management for standalone Windows computers can be set locally using the Windows User Accounts tool (see Figure 13-21). To create, remove, or modify a password in Windows, use Control Panel > User Accounts.

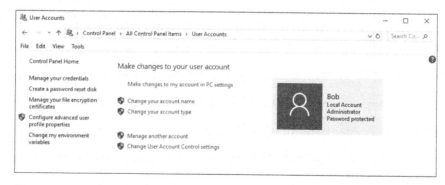

Figure 13-21   User Accounts Tool

It is important to make sure that computers are secure when users are away. A security policy should contain a rule about requiring a computer to lock when the screen saver starts. This ensures that a short time after a user stops using the computer, the screen saver starts, and the computer cannot be used until the user logs in.

In all versions of Windows, use Control Panel > Personalization > Screen Saver to open the dialog shown in Figure 13-22. Choose a screen saver and a wait time and then select the On Resume, Display Logon Screen option.

Figure 13-22   Setting the Screen Saver Lock

Usernames and Passwords (13.3.1.5)

A system administrator usually defines a naming convention for usernames when creating network logins. A common example of a username is the first letter of the person's first name and then the entire last name. Keep the naming convention simple so that people do not have a hard time remembering it. Usernames, like passwords, are important information that should not be revealed.

Password guidelines are an important component of a security policy. Any user who must log onto a computer or connect to a network resource should be required to have a password. Passwords help prevent theft of data and malicious acts. Passwords also help confirm that the logging of events is valid by ensuring that the user is the correct person.

The guidelines for creating strong passwords are as follows:

- **Minimum length:** Use passwords of eight characters or more.

- **Complexity:** Include letters, numbers, and symbols. Avoid passwords based on easily identifiable pieces of information. Deliberately misspell a password.

- **Variety:** Use a different password for each site or computer that you use. Never use the same password twice.

- **Expiration:** Change passwords on a regular basis. The shorter the time period a password is used, the more secure the password will be.

13.3.1.6 Lab: Operating System Login

In this activity, you will explore and configure different types of operating system logins.

Interactive Graphic

13.3.1.7 Check Your Understanding: Secure a Workstation

Refer to the online course to complete this activity.

Windows Local Security Policy (13.3.2)

The Windows Local Security Policy tool enables administration of many system, user, and security settings, such as password policy, audit policy, and user permissions on a local computer. Local Security Policy allows you to control and maintain security policies that are standardized with the organization's policy.

The Windows Local Security Policy (13.3.2.1)

In most networks that use Windows computers, Active Directory is configured with domains on a Windows server. Windows computers are members of a domain. The administrator configures a domain security policy that applies to all computers that join the domain. Account policies are automatically set when a user logs into Windows.

For standalone computers that are not part of an Active Directory domain, the Windows Local Security Policy tool can be used to enforce security settings.

To access the Local Security Policy tool in Windows 7 and Vista, use Start > Control Panel > Administrative Tools > Local Security Policy. In Windows 8, 8.1, and Windows 10, use Search > secpol.msc and then click secpol. The Local Security Policy tool opens, as shown in Figure 13-23.

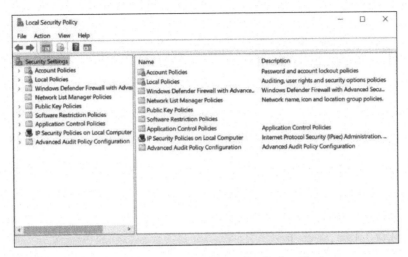

Figure 13-23 The Windows Local Security Policy Tool

Note

In all versions of Windows, you can run the command *secpol.msc* to open the Local Security Policy tool.

Account Policies Security Settings (13.3.2.2)

A security policy should include a password policy. The Windows Local Security Policy tool can be used to set and implement the password policy. When assigning passwords, the level of password control should match the level of protection required.

Note

Use strong passwords whenever possible.

To enforce password requirements, use Account Policies > Password Policy, as shown in Figure 13-24.

Guidelines for the password policy settings in Figure 13-24 are as follows:

- **Enforce Password History:** The user may reuse a password after 24 unique passwords have been saved.

- **Maximum Password Age:** The user must change the password after 90 days.

- **Minimum Password Age:** The user must wait 1 day before changing a password again. This helps reinforce password history by preventing a user from entering a different password 24 times in order to use a previous password again.

- **Minimum Password Length:** The password must be at least eight characters.

- **Password Must Meet Complexity Requirements:** The password must not contain the user's account name or parts of the user's full name that exceed two consecutive characters. The password must contain three of the following four categories: uppercase letters, lowercase letters, numbers, and symbols.

- **Store Passwords Using Reversible Encryption:** Storing passwords using reversible encryption is essentially the same as storing plaintext versions of the passwords. For this reason, this policy should never be enabled unless application requirements outweigh the need to protect password information.

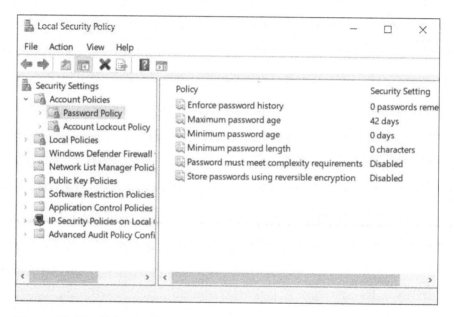

Figure 13-24   Enforcing Password History

To prevent brute-force attacks, use Account Policies > Account Lockout Policy, as shown in Figure 13-25.

The account lockout policy settings in Figure 13-25 can be described as follows:

- **Account Lockout Duration:** If the user exceeds the account lockout threshold (that is, five attempts), the account is locked out for 30 minutes.

- **Account Lockout Threshold:** The user can enter the wrong username and/or password five times.

- **Reset Account Lockout Counter After:** After 30 minutes, the number of attempts is reset to zero, and the user can attempt to log in again.

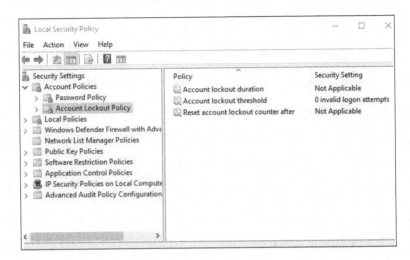

Figure 13-25   Configuring Account Lockout Policies

The account lockout policy shown in Figure 13-25 protects against brute-force attacks, in which the attackers use software that attempts to break a password by trying every possible combination of characters. This account lockout policy also protects against dictionary attacks. A dictionary attack is a type of brute-force attack that tries using every word in a dictionary in hopes of gaining access. An attacker may also use a rainbow table, which is a refinement of a dictionary attack that involves a precomputed lookup table of all probable plaintext passwords and their matching hashes. The hash value of a stored password can be looked up in the table to discover the corresponding plaintext.

Local Policies Security Settings (13.3.2.3)

The Local Policies section in the Local Security Policy tool is used to configure audit policies, user rights policies, and security policies.

It is useful to log successful and unsuccessful login attempts. Use Local Policies > Audit Policy, as shown in Figure 13-26, to enable auditing. In this example, auditing of account logon events is being enabled for all logon events.

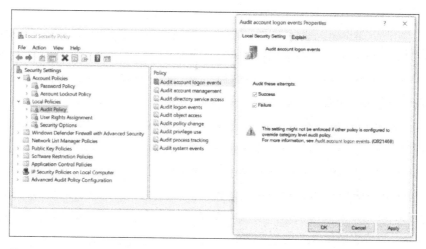

Figure 13-26   Local Policies Security Settings

The User Rights Assignment and Security Options sections of the Local Security Policy tool provide a wide variety of security options that are beyond the scope of this course, but you will explore some settings in a lab (13.3.2.5).

Exporting the Local Security Policy (13.3.2.4)

An administrator might need to implement an extensive local policy for user rights and security options. This policy would most likely need to be replicated on each system. To help simplify this process, the local security policy can be exported and copied to other Windows hosts.

The steps to replicate a local security policy on other computers are as follows:

Step 1.   Use the **Action > Export Policy** feature, as shown in Figure 13-27, to export the policy of a secure host.

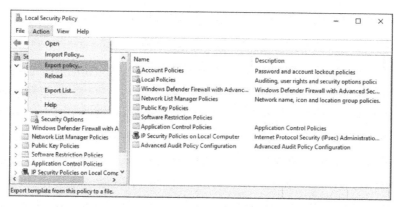

Figure 13-27   Exporting a Local Security Policy

Step 2.   Save the policy to external media with a name such as **workstation.inf.**

Step 3.   Import the local security policy file to other standalone computers.

13.3.2.5 Lab: Configure Windows Local Security Policy

In this lab, you will configure a Windows local security policy. You will modify password requirements, enable auditing, configure some user rights, and set some security options. You will then use Event Manager to view logged information.

13.3.2.6 Check Your Understanding: Local Security Policy

Refer to the online course to complete this activity.

Managing Users and Groups (13.3.3)

Managing who has access to a computer and their access levels is an important part of security. When managing users and groups, you can limit or allow users and groups to perform certain actions by assigning rights and permissions.

Maintaining Accounts (13.3.3.1)

Employees in an organization often require different levels of access to data. For example, a manager and an accountant might be the only employees in an organization with access to the payroll files.

Employees can be grouped by job requirements and given access to files according to group permissions. This process helps manage employee access to the network. Temporary accounts can be set up for employees who need short-term access. Close management of network access can help limit areas of vulnerability that might allow a virus or malicious software to enter the network.

There are several tasks associated with managing users and groups:

- **Terminating employee access:** When an employee leaves an organization, immediately disable the account or change the login credentials on the account.

- **Guest access:**

    - Temporary employees and guests may need limited access to the network, using a guest account.

    - Special guest accounts with additional privileges can be created and disabled as required.

4

- Tracking login times:
  - Employees may only be allowed to log in during specific hours, such as 7 a.m. to 6 p.m.
  - Logins would be blocked during other times of the day. This is known as *logon time restrictions*. The authenticating server periodically checks whether a user has privileges to continue using the network. If the user does not, an automatic logout procedure is activated.
- Logging failed login attempts:
  - Configure a threshold for the number of times a user is allowed to attempt to log in.
  - By default, in Windows the number of failed login attempts is set to zero, which means a user will never be locked out until this setting is changed.
- Configuring the idle timeout and screen lock:
  - Configure an idle timer that will automatically log the user out and lock the screen after a specified period of time.
  - The user must log back in to unlock the screen.
- Changing default admin user credentials:
  - Rename default accounts, such as the default admin user account, so that attackers cannot use the known account names to access the computer.
  - Windows disables the default admin user account by default and replaces it with a named account that is created during the operating system setup process.
  - Some devices ship with a default password such as admin or password. These passwords should be changed during initial device setup.

Managing User Account Tools and User Account Tasks (13.3.3.2)

Regular maintenance tasks for administrators include creating and removing users from the network, changing account passwords, and changing user permissions. You must have administrator privileges to manage users.

To accomplish these tasks, you can use either User Account Control (UAC) or Local Users and Groups Manager. To access UAC, choose User Account Control (UAC) - Control Panel > User Accounts > Manage Another Account. You can use UAC to add, remove, or change attributes of individual users. When logged in as an administrator, use UAC to configure settings to prevent malicious code from gaining administrative privileges.

To access Local Users and Group Manager, choose Local Users and Groups Manager - Control Panel > Administrative Tools > Computer Management > Local Users and Groups. You can use Local Users and Groups Manager to create and manage users and groups that are stored locally on a computer.

User account tasks include creating an account, resetting the account password, disabling or activating an account, deleting an account, renaming an account, assigning a login script to an account, and assigning a home folder to an account.

Local Users and Groups Manager (13.3.3.3)

You can use the Local Users and Groups Manager tool to limit the ability of users and groups to perform certain actions by assigning rights and permissions:

- **Rights:** A right authorizes a user to perform certain actions on a computer. Examples include backing up files and folders and shutting down a computer.

- **Permissions:** A permission is a rule that is associated with an object (usually a file, folder, or printer). It regulates which users can have access to the object and in what manner.

To configure all the users and groups on a computer using the Local Users and Groups Manager tool, type **lusrmgr.msc** in the search box or the Run utility.

The Local Users and Groups > Users window displays the current user accounts on the computer. It includes the built-in administrator and built-in guest accounts, as shown in Figure 13-28.

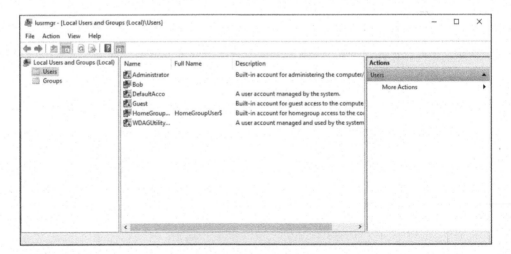

Figure 13-28 Local Users and Groups Manager Window

The Administrator account in Figure 13-28 has the following characteristics:

- Has full control of the computer and is a member of the Administrators group
- Can assign user rights and access control permissions
- Can be renamed or disabled but never deleted or removed from the Administrators group
- Is disabled by default

The Guest account in Figure 13-28 has the following characteristics:

- Is used by users who do not have assigned accounts on the computer
- Is a member of the default Guests group, which allows a user to log on to a computer
- By default, does not require a password
- Is disabled by default

Double-clicking a user or right-clicking and choosing Properties opens the user properties window, as shown in Figure 13-29. This window allows you to change the user options that were defined when the user was created. It also allows you to lock an account and assign a user to a group by using the Member Of tab or control which folders the user has access to by using the Profile tab.

Figure 13-29   User Properties

To add a user, click Action > New User to open the New User window, as shown in Figure 13-30. In this window, you can assign a username, a full name, a description, and account options.

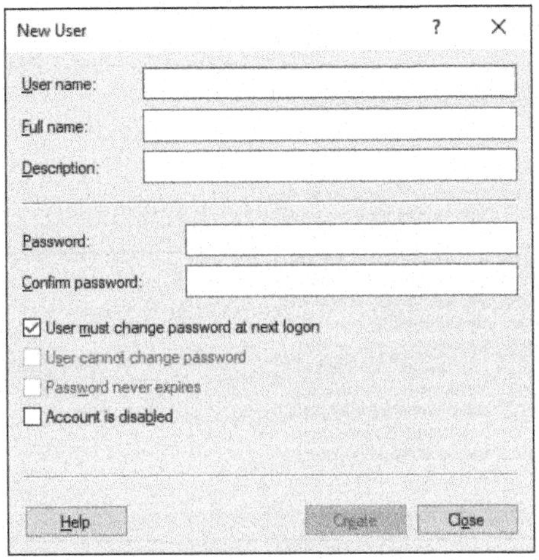

Figure 13-30 Creating a New User

Note

Some versions of Windows also include the built-in Power User account, which possesses most of the power of an administrator but, for security reasons, lacks some of the privileges of an administrator.

Managing Groups (13.3.3.4)

Users can be assigned to groups for easier management. Tasks used to manage local groups include the following:

- Creating a local group
- Adding members to a group
- Identifying members in the local group
- Deleting a group
- Creating a local user account

The Local Users and Groups Manager tool is used to manage local groups on a Windows computer. Use the icon view in Control Panel > Administrative Tools > Computer Management > Local Users and Groups to open the Local Users and Groups Manager tool.

In the Local Users and Groups window, click Groups to list all the local groups on the computer, as shown in Figure 13-31.

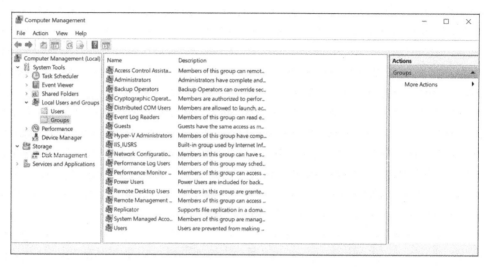

Figure 13-31   Built-in Local Groups

There are many built-in groups available, as shown in Figure 13-31. However, the three most commonly used groups are as follows:

- **Administrators:** Group members who have full control of the computer and can assign user rights and access control permissions. The Administrator account is a default member of this group. Use caution when you add users to this group.

- **Guests:** A member of this group has a temporary profile created at logon, and when the member logs off, the profile is deleted. The Guest account (which is disabled by default) is a default member of this group.

- **Users:** Members of this group can perform common tasks, such as running applications, using local and network printers, and locking the computer. Members cannot share directories or create local printers.

It is important to note that running your computer as a member of the Administrators group makes the system vulnerable to Trojan horses and other security risks. It is recommended that you add your domain user account only to the Users group (and not to the Administrators group) to perform routine tasks, including running programs and visiting Internet sites. When it becomes necessary to perform administrative tasks on the local computer, use Run as Administrator to start a program using administrative credentials.

Double-click a group to view its properties. Figure 13-32, for example, shows the properties of the Guest group.

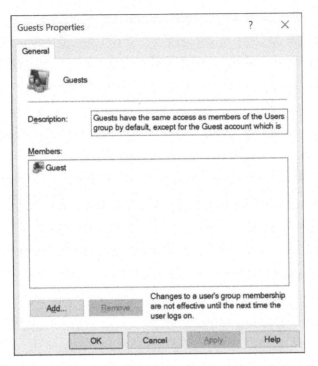

Figure 13-32   Built-in Local Guest Group Properties

To create a new group, click Action > New Group to open the New Group window, as shown in Figure 13-33. In this window you can create new groups and assign users to them.

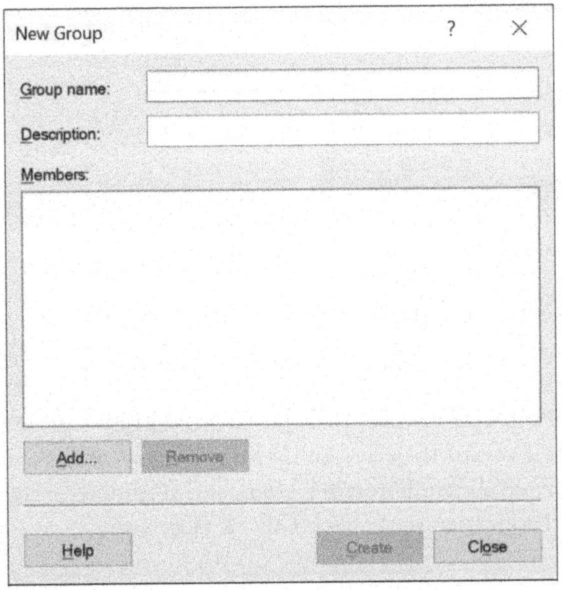

Figure 13-33   Creating a New Group

Active Directory Users and Computers (13.3.3.5)

Whereas local accounts are stored in the Local Security Accounts database of a local machine, domain accounts are stored in Active Directory on a Windows server domain controller (DC) and are accessible from any computer joined to the domain. Only domain administrators can create domain accounts on a domain controller.

Active Directory is a database of all computers, users, and services in an Active Directory domain. The Active Directory Users and Computers console on a Windows server, shown in Figure 13-34, is used to manage Active Directory users, groups, and Organizational Units (OUs). Organizational Units provide a way to subdivide a domain into smaller administrative units. By using Active Directory Users and Computers, an administrator can create more OUs in which to place accounts or add accounts to existing OUs.

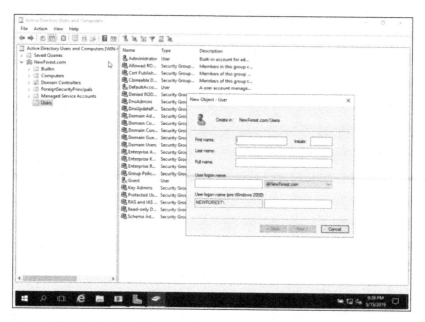

Figure 13-34   Active Directory Users and Computers

To create a new user account, right-click the container or OU that will contain the account and choose New User. Enter the user's information, such as name, last name, and logon name; click Next; and then set an initial password for the user. By default, the option to force the user to reset their password on first sign-in is selected. If a user locks themselves out of their account with too many password attempts, the administrator can open Active Directory Users and Computers, right-click on the user object, select Properties, and check Unlock Account.

To delete a user account, simply right-click the user object and select Delete. Note, however, that once an account is deleted, it may not be retrievable. Another option is to disable an account rather than to delete it. Once an account is disabled, the user is denied access to the network until the administrator reenables the account.

Creating a new group account in Active Directory is similar to creating a new user. Open Active Directory Users and Computers, select the container that will house the group and Action > New > Group. Fill in the group details and click OK.

13.3.3.6 Lab: Configure Users and Groups in Windows

In this lab, you will create users and groups and delete users by using the Local Users and Groups Manager tool. You will also assign group and user permissions to the folders.

Interactive Graphic

13.3.3.7 Check Your Understanding: User Account Tools and User Account Tasks

Refer to the online course to complete this activity.

Windows Firewall (13.3.4)

A firewall selectively denies traffic to a computer or network segment. Firewalls generally work by opening and closing the ports used by various applications. By opening only the required ports on a firewall, you are implementing a restrictive security policy. Any packet not explicitly permitted is denied. In contrast, a permissive security policy permits access through all ports except for those explicitly denied.

Firewalls (13.3.4.1)

A *firewall* protects computers and networks by preventing undesirable traffic from entering internal networks. For instance, the topology at the top of Figure 13-35 illustrates how a firewall enables traffic from an internal network host to exit the network and return to the inside network. The topology illustrated at the bottom of Figure 13-35 shows how traffic initiated by the outside network (that is, the Internet) is denied access to the internal network.

A firewall could allow outside users controlled access to specific services. For instance, servers accessible to outside users are usually located on a special network referred to as the demilitarized zone (DMZ), as shown in Figure 13-36.

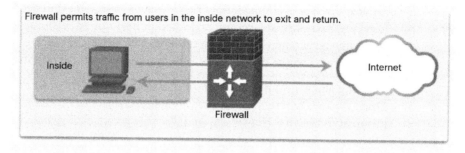

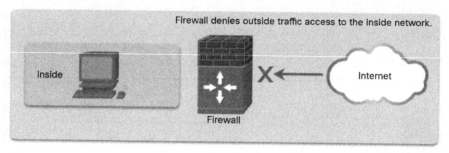

Figure 13-35 Firewall Controls Network Access

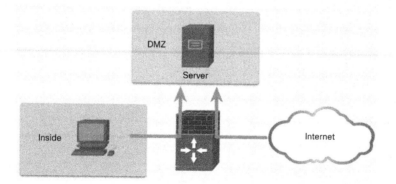

Figure 13-36 Access to the DMZ

The DMZ enables a network administrator to apply specific policies for hosts connected to that network, such as web, FTP, and email services (such as SMTP and IMAP), to external users. The firewall permits access to only those server services and denies all other outside requests, such as traffic to the server from external addresses, inbound ICMP echo request traffic, inbound Microsoft Active Directory queries, or inbound traffic to Microsoft SQL Server inquiries.

Firewall services can be provided as follows:

- *Host-based firewall*: This type of firewall is implemented with software such as Windows Defender Firewall.

- **Small office home office (SOHO):** This network-based solution uses a home or small office wireless router. These devices not only provide routing and WI-FI services but also NAT, DHCP, and firewall services.

- **Small to medium-sized organization:** This network-based solution uses a dedicated device such as a Cisco Adaptive Security Appliance (ASA) or a firewall enabled on a Cisco Integrated Services Router (ISR). These devices use access control lists (ACLs) and advanced features to filter packets based on header information, including source and destination IP addresses, protocol, source and destination TCP/UDP ports, and more.

Routers may also provide many of the following settings:

- *Port Address Translation (PAT)*: PAT is a version of NAT that overloads the router-assigned public IP address. PAT enables internal hosts with private IP addresses to use the public address of the router to traverse the Internet. Return traffic to the router is retranslated to the internal private IP address.

- *Port forwarding*: Port forwarding, also called destination NAT (DNAT), adds an Internet-accessible host on a small router. Internet traffic is forwarded to a specific host/port number.

- **Disabling ports:** You can selectively enable or disable access to specific TCP/UDP ports.

- *MAC address filtering*: You can add known MAC addresses to a whitelist and then permit only whitelisted MAC addresses to connect.

- **Whitelists/blacklists:** A *blacklist* is used to block malicious or disreputable sites based on domain name and IP address. A *whitelist* can be used to identify permitted sites.

- **Parental control:** With parental control, also called content filtering, you can filter traffic based on unacceptable keywords or by website rating.

The focus of this section is on the host-based firewall solution using Windows Firewall.

Software Firewalls (13.3.4.2)

A *software firewall* is a program that provides firewall services on a computer to allow or deny traffic to the computer. The software firewall applies a set of rules to data transmissions through inspection and filtering of data packets.

Windows Firewall is an example of a software firewall that helps prevent cyber-criminals and malware from gaining access to your computer. It is installed by default when the Windows OS is installed.

> **Note**
>
> In Windows 10, Windows Firewall was renamed Windows Defender Firewall. In this section, *Windows Firewall* includes Windows Defender Firewall.

Windows Firewall settings are configured using the Windows Firewall window. To change Windows Firewall settings, you must have administrator privileges to open the Windows Firewall window.

To open the Windows Firewall window, use Control Panel > Windows Firewall. Figure 13-37 shows the Windows 10 Windows Defender Firewall window.

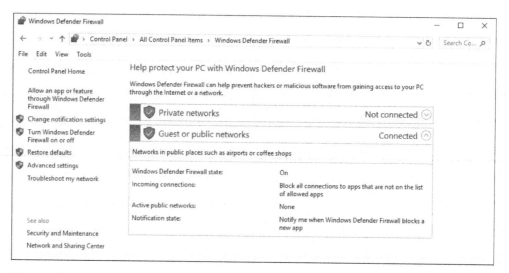

Figure 13-37 Windows Defender Firewall

Windows Firewall (13.3.4.3)

Software firewall features are applied to a network connection. A software firewall has a standard set of inbound and outbound rules that are enabled depending on the location of the connected network.

In the example in Figure 13-38, firewall rules are enabled for a private network, a guest or public network, and a corporate domain network. The window displays the settings for the private network as it is the currently connected network. To display the settings for the domain or guest networks, click on the drop-down arrow beside the Not Connected label.

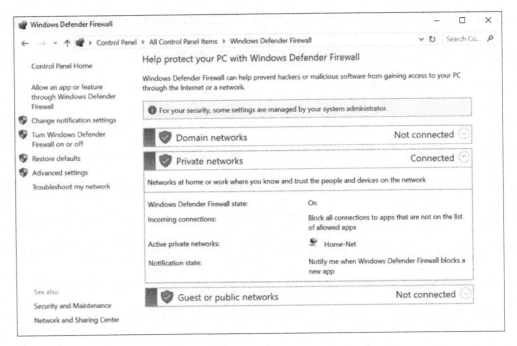

Figure 13-38 Firewall Rules Enabled for a Private Network

From this Windows Firewall window, you can enable or disable Windows Firewall, change notification settings, allow apps through the firewall, configure advanced settings, or restore firewall defaults.

To disable or reenable Windows Firewall or change notifications for a network, click on either Change Notifications Settings or Turn Windows Defender Firewall On or Off to open the Customize Settings window, shown in Figure 13-39.

If you wish to use a different software firewall, you need to disable Windows Firewall.

To disable Windows Defender Firewall in Windows 10, follow these steps:

Step 1. Open **Control Panel > Windows Defender Firewall > Turn Windows Defender Firewall On or Off.**

Step 2. Click on **Turn Off Windows Defender Firewall (not recommended)** for the desired network.

Step 3. Click **OK.**

To disable Windows Firewall in Windows 7 and 8, follow these steps:

Step 1. Open **Control Panel > Windows Firewall > Turn Windows Firewall On or Off.**

Step 2.   Click on **Turn Off Windows Firewall (not recommended)** for the desired network.

Step 3.   Click **OK**.

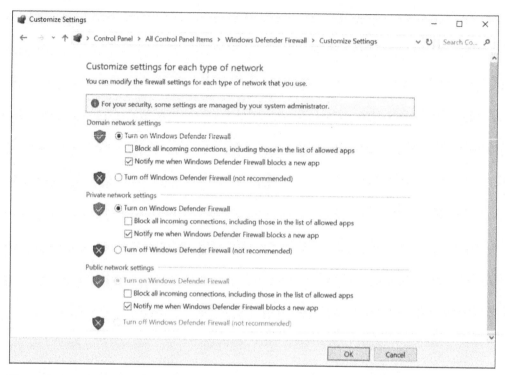

Figure 13-39   Customize Settings Window

Note

Windows Firewall is enabled by default. Do not disable Windows Firewall on a Windows host unless other firewall software is enabled.

Configuring Exceptions in Windows Firewall (13.3.4.4)

You can allow or deny access to specific programs or ports from the Windows Firewall window. To configure exceptions and allow or block applications or ports, click on Allow an App or Feature Through the Windows Firewall to open the Allowed Apps window, shown in Figure 13-40.

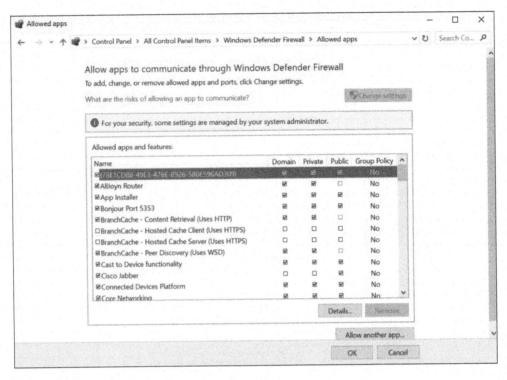

Figure 13-40   Configuring Exceptions

From this window, you can add, change, or remove the allowed programs and ports on the different networks. The steps required to do so are as follows:

To add programs through the Windows Defender Firewall in Windows 10, follow these steps:

Step 1.   Open **Control Panel** > **Windows Defender Firewall** > **Allow an App or Feature Through the Windows Firewall**.

Step 2.   Check the boxes for listed applications or use **Allow Another Program** if a program is not listed.

Step 3.   Click **OK**.

To add programs through the Windows Firewall in Windows 7 and 8, follow these steps:

Step 1.   Open **Control Panel** > **Windows Firewall** > **Allow an App or Feature Through the Windows Firewall**.

Step 2.   Select **Change Settings** > **Allow Another App**.

Step 3.   Click **OK**.

Windows Firewall with Advanced Security (13.3.4.5)

A Windows tool that provides even greater access control with Windows Firewall policies is Windows Firewall with Advanced Security (which is called Windows Defender Firewall with Advanced Security in Windows 10, as shown in Figure 13-41). To open it, in the Windows Firewall window, click on Advanced Settings.

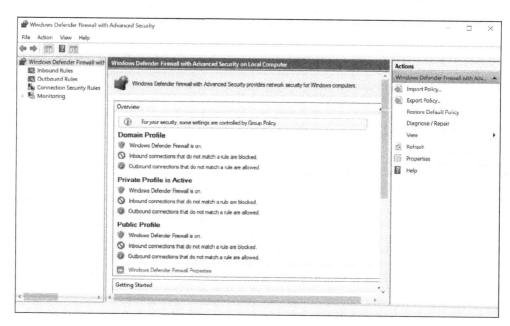

Figure 13-41 Windows Firewall with Advanced Security Window

Note

Alternatively, you can enter **wf.msc** in the search box and press Enter.

Windows Defender Firewall with Advanced Security provides these features:

- **Inbound and outbound rules:** You can configure inbound rules that are applied to incoming Internet traffic and outbound rules that are applied to traffic leaving your computer going to the network. These rules can specify ports, protocols, programs, services, users, or computers.

- **Connection security rules:** Connection security rules secure traffic between two computers. Both computers must have the same rules defined and enabled.

- **Monitoring:** You can display the firewall inbound or outbound active rules or any active connection security rules.

13.3.4.6 Lab: Configure Windows Firewall

In this lab, you will explore Windows Firewall and configure some advanced settings.

Interactive Graphic

13.3.4.7 Check Your Understanding: Windows Firewall

Refer to the online course to complete this activity.

Web Security (13.3.5)

Attackers can use various web tools to install malicious programs on a computer. Web security attempts to mitigate threats that come from the Internet, which is largely an insecure means for data exchange. Web security requires being aware, proactive, and defensive against security vulnerabilities. This section explains some common web vulnerabilities and ways to mitigate the threats they pose.

Web Security (13.3.5.1)

Web browsers are not only used for web browsing; they are also now used to run other applications, including Microsoft 365 and Google Docs, and as interfaces for remote access SSL users. To help support these additional features, browsers use plug-ins to support other content. However, some plug-ins can introduce security problems.

Browsers are targets and should be secured. Some features to secure web browsers include the following:

- InPrivate browsing
- Pop-up blocker
- SmartScreen filter
- ActiveX filtering

When users are browsing, many websites and services require the use of authentication for access. Recently, it has become common to require multifactor authentication instead of using a traditional username and password. *Multifactor authentication* involves using a combination of technologies, such as a password, a smart card, and biometrics, to authenticate a user. For example, two-factor authentication combines something a user has, such as a smart card, with something the user knows, like a password or PIN. Three-factor authentication combines all three: something the user knows, something the user has, and some type of biometric component, such as a thumb or eye retina scan.

Recently, the use of authenticator applications for multifactor authentication has become popular. A service might require both a password and a registered phone number or email address. To access the service, an authenticator application sends a code called a *one-time password (OTP)* to the registered phone or email address. The user must supply their account username and password as well as the OTP code to authenticate.

Once a user is authenticated, the system may grant a software token to the application or device that was used to authenticate. The software token allows the user to perform actions on the system without the need to repeatedly authenticate. If the token system is not secure, a third party may be able to capture it and act as the user. This is known as a *replay attack*. To prevent replay attacks, a token should be time limited or should be usable only once.

Browser Extensions and Plugins (13.3.5.2)

There are many types of browser add-ons that add functionality and features. These are the main types of add-ons:

- **Plug-ins:** These are generally related to multimedia objects on a web page such as video or content created using Flash. They are generally limited in interaction compared to extensions because they are supposed to interact with only media objects. Plug-ins have had many vulnerabilities and are now rarely used, and HTML version 5 is the preferred method to serve this type of role.

- **Extensions:** An extension changes the features of a browser through the use of an application programming interface (API). For example, an extension may block pop-ups, prevent sites from using your computing power for cryptomining, or simply change a menu option within the browser. By default, you must provide the extension permission to perform the intended action. The scripts that the extension executes could be malicious and compromise your browser's security. It is extremely important to only install legitimate extensions from trusted sources.

- **Themes:** The theme affects the look and feel of the browser. It changes the colors and provides custom images for the browser. There is a risk, however, that a theme could inject malicious code into a browser by using an image created by a threat actor.

- **Apps:** Apps allow you to edit documents within the browser. This could be a cloud application that performs the same function as a spreadsheet, word processor, or image editor.

- **Default search provider:** There are many sites that provide search capabilities. You can specify which site you would like to use by default. Specifying a malicious site could redirect you to a site that is spoofed, compromising your browser's security.

Always make sure that you are installing browsers, extensions, and plug-ins from a trusted source. Always keep your software up to date. There have been instances of malicious software being served from trusted stores, so keeping them up to date reduces the risk that they are malicious.

Browser Settings

Browsers maintain settings that you can often change. You can access browser settings through the browser's menu or through an internal URL like about:preferences or chrome://settings. There are also internal URLs like about:config or chrome://flags for adjusting advanced settings.

Another feature of modern browsers is that a user can often sign in and synchronize browser settings (including history, passwords, bookmarks, and other data) across their various devices.

Password Manager

It can be overwhelming trying to remember the myriad passwords used at all the websites that require logins—especially since most sites are requiring more complicated passwords than ever before. Using the same password at multiple sites is a big security risk, and a password manager can be used locally on a device to secure passwords and keep them from being compromised. Once you are signed into the browser, the password manager can populate the password in the credential area. This does not always work, and when it doesn't, you should be able to copy the password from the manager and paste it into the credential area.

Secure Connections and Valid Certificates (13.3.5.3)

Technologies such as Transport Layer Security (TLS) and digital certificates are often used to provide secure connections on the Internet. These technologies ensure that the identity of the host running a website is valid and ensure that the data is encrypted between the server and a user's browser. Certificate authorities (CAs) issue certificates to domains that contain public keys so that the CA that issued a certificate can validate it before signing it. The browser can provide the information associated with the certificate when a site is using HTTPS. Certificate information is shown in Figure 13-42.

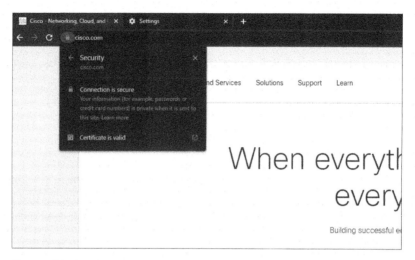

Figure 13-42   Viewing a Certificate in a Browser

There have been cases of certificates being stolen from CAs when weak keys are used in the certificates. It is important to install or update only root certificates that you can verify are safe and legitimate. A root certificate must be trusted, and if a fake certificate is installed, a threat actor could compromise the encryption between your browser and the web server. Microsoft Edge uses the Windows certificate store, but other browsers have separate stores for them. To use internal sites and a third-party browser, ensure that the internal CA root certificate is added directly to the browser. The certificate manager can be found in the browser settings, as shown in Figure 13-43.

Figure 13-43   Browser Certificate Manager

Browser Privacy Settings (13.3.5.4)

Many companies are trying to create profiles of the habits of people online, including their searching and browsing habits. Privacy controls can watch the use of tracking tools like cookies that are used to track online activity. A cookie is a text file that stores data from a browser session. This data could simply be where you were on a web page or who you are. Third-party cookies are often used to provide information to different websites without your knowledge.

Privacy settings can be used to enable cookies, block them, or just not allow cookies from third parties. The following features can be used to block other methods of tracking:

- **Ad blocker:** This is an extension that can be used to block the display of unwanted ads. Such an extension uses rules and algorithms to block items that are not part of the site's main content. It is important to understand that there are some sites that detect ad blockers and prevent the user from viewing the website while an ad blocker is in use.

- **Pop-up blocker:** This is code that prevents a website from creating any windows that are not requested by the user.

A browser also stores data about a user and their activity. This can be configured in two ways:

- **Private browser:** This method disables the caching of information by the browser, such as history, form information, or cookies, so that when the browser is closed, all of the data is erased. This does not make the user anonymous because the websites can still see IP addresses and other information not blocked by the private session.

- **Clearing cache:** This will delete all browsing history. Any files that have been cached in order to speed up the user experience will also be deleted. To stay safe, it is a good practice to delete your cache after every session. This can be done manually or automatically after each session.

InPrivate Browsing (13.3.5.5)

Web browsers retain information about the web pages visited, the searches performed, and identifiable information such as usernames and passwords. Although this information retention is convenient on a personal computer, it is a concern on public computers such as a computer in a library, a hotel business center, or an Internet cafe. The information retained by web browsers can be recovered and exploited to steal your identity or your money or to change your passwords on important accounts.

To improve security when using a public computer, always:

- Clear your browsing history.
- Use the *InPrivate* mode.

Clear Your Browsing History

All web browsers have a way to clear browsing history, cookies, files, and more. The steps to clear the browsing history in Microsoft Edge are listed here and shown in Figure 13-44:

1. Click the **More Actions** icon (…) on the top-right side of Microsoft Edge.

2. Select **Settings** and then click **Privacy, Search, and Services.**

3. Under the Clear Browsing Data subheading, click **Choose What to Clear** to open the Clear Browsing Data menu.

4. Choose a time range, select what to clear, and then click **Clear Now.**

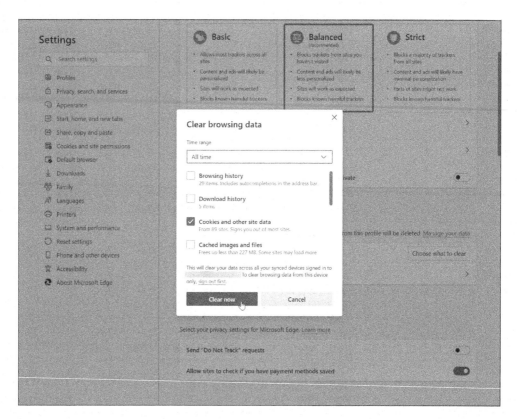

Figure 13-44 Clearing the Browsing History in Microsoft Edge

Use the InPrivate Mode

All web browsers provide the ability to browse the web anonymously without retaining information. Using InPrivate mode causes the browser to temporarily store files and cookies and then delete them when the InPrivate session is ended.

Follow these steps to open an InPrivate window in Microsoft Edge:

1. Click the **More Actions** icon (...) on the top-right side of Microsoft Edge.

2. Select **New InPrivate Windows** to open a new InPrivate browser window.

As you can see in Figure 13-45, the new window is identified with an InPrivate label in the top-right corner of the browser.

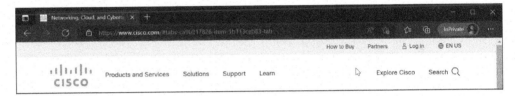

Figure 13-45   Opening an InPrivate Window in Microsoft Edge

Pop-up Blocker (13.3.5.6)

A *pop-up* is a web browser window that opens on top of another web browser window. Some pop-ups are initiated while browsing, as with a link on a page that opens a pop-up to deliver additional information or a close-up of a picture. Other pop-ups are initiated by a website or advertiser and are often unwanted or annoying, especially when multiple pop-ups are opened at the same time on a web page.

Most web browsers offer the ability to block pop-up windows. This enables a user to limit or block most of the pop-ups that occur while browsing the web. Follow these steps to block pop-ups in Microsoft Edge:

1. Click the **More Actions** icon (...) on the top-right side of Microsoft Edge.

2. Select **Settings.**

3. Select **Cookies and Site Permissions** and then click **Pop-ups and Redirects.**

4. Ensure that the **Block** slider is set to **On,** as shown in Figure 13-46.

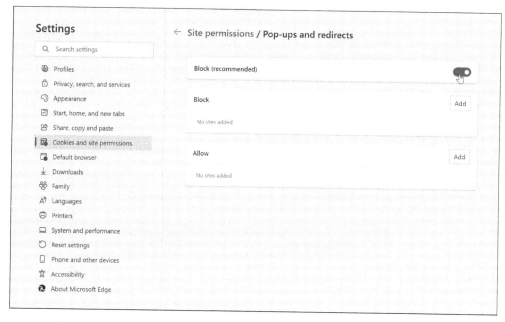

Figure 13-46   Blocking Pop-ups in Microsoft Edge

SmartScreen Filter (13.3.5.7)

Web browsers may offer additional web filtering capabilities. For instance, Microsoft Edge provides the *SmartScreen Filter* feature. This feature detects phishing websites, analyzes websites for suspicious items, and checks downloads against a list of sites and files that are known to be malicious.

Follow these steps to enable SmartScreen Filter in Microsoft Edge:

1. Click the **More Actions** icon (…) on the top-right side of Microsoft Edge.

2. Select **Settings**.

3. Select **Privacy, Search, and Services**.

4. Scroll to the Security section and ensure that **Microsoft Defender SmartScreen** is set to **On**, as shown in Figure 13-47.

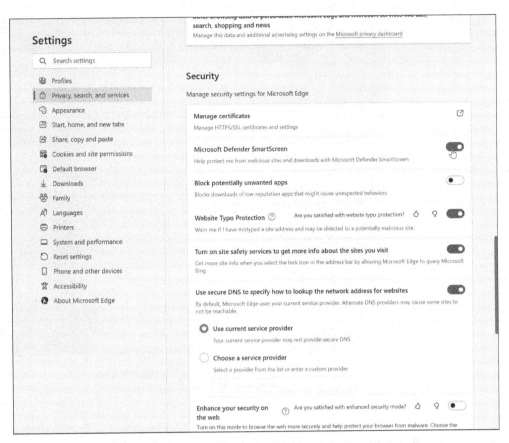

Figure 13-47   Enabling SmartScreen Filter in Microsoft Edge

ActiveX Filtering (13.3.5.8)

Some web browsers require you to install ActiveX controls. The problem is that ActiveX controls can be used for malicious reasons.

After an ActiveX control has been installed for a website, the control runs on other websites as well. This may degrade performance or introduce security risks. *ActiveX filtering* allows for web browsing without running ActiveX controls. When ActiveX filtering is enabled, you can choose which websites are allowed to run ActiveX controls. Sites that are not approved cannot run these controls, and the browser does not show notifications for you to install or enable them.

To enable ActiveX filtering in Internet Explorer 11, use Tools > ActiveX Filtering. The example in Figure 13-48 shows that ActiveX filtering is enabled. Clicking Tools > ActiveX Filtering again disables ActiveX.

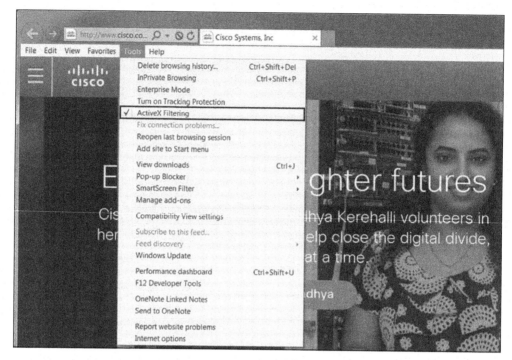

Figure 13-48   Enabling the ActiveX Filtering Feature

To view a website that contains ActiveX content when ActiveX filtering is enabled, click the blue ActiveX Filtering icon in the address bar and click Turn Off ActiveX Filtering.

After viewing the content, you can turn on ActiveX filtering for the website again by following the same steps.

Note

Microsoft Edge does not support ActiveX filtering.

Interactive Graphic

13.3.5.9 Check Your Understanding: Web Security

Refer to the online course to complete this activity.

Security Maintenance (13.3.6)

Maintaining proactive security practices is essential to keeping your devices and network running smoothly and properly. Security maintenance is an ongoing process that requires planning and scheduling.

Restrictive Settings (13.3.6.1)

Devices often come with security features that are not enabled or have security features left set to their defaults. For example, many home users leave their wireless routers with default passwords and open wireless authentication because they think it is easier.

Some devices are shipped with permissive settings, enabling access through all ports except those that are explicitly denied. The problem is that the default permissive settings leave many devices exposed to attackers. Permissive settings are easier to implement, less secure, and easier to hack than more restrictive settings.

Many devices now ship with restrictive settings that must be configured to enable access. Any packet not explicitly permitted is denied. Restrictive settings are harder to implement, more secure, and more difficult to hack than permissive settings.

It is your responsibility to secure devices and configure restrictive settings whenever possible.

Disable Auto-Play (13.3.6.2)

Older Windows hosts used AutoRun to simplify the user experience. When a new medium (for example, a flash drive, a CD, or a DVD) was inserted into the computer, AutoRun would automatically look for a special file called autorun.inf and execute it. Malicious users took advantage of this feature to quickly infect hosts.

Newer Windows hosts now use a feature called AutoPlay that is similar to AutoRun. With AutoPlay, you can determine which media will run automatically. AutoPlay provides additional controls and can prompt the user to choose an action based on the content of the new media.

Use Control Panel > AutoPlay to open the AutoPlay window, shown in Figure 13-49, where you can configure the actions associated with specific media. Even though AutoPlay is less problematic than AutoRun, you are still just one click away from unknowingly running malware through the AutoPlay dialog. Therefore, the most secure solution is to turn off AutoPlay. Follow these steps to disable AutoPlay:

1. Select **Control Panel > AutoPlay**.

2. Uncheck the **Use AutoPlay for All Media and Devices**.

3. Click **Save**.

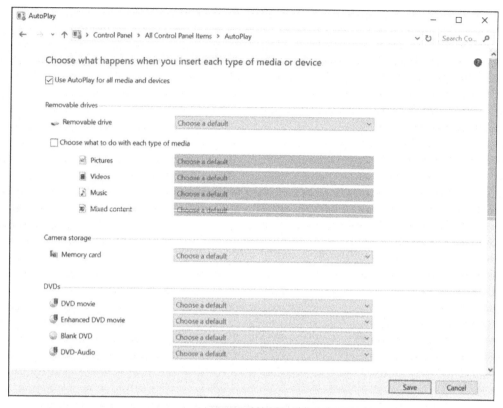

Figure 13-49   Configuring AutoPlay Settings

Operating System Service Packs and Security Patches (13.3.6.3)

Patches are code updates that manufacturers provide to prevent newly discovered viruses or worms from making successful attacks. From time to time, manufacturers combine patches and upgrades into a comprehensive update application called a *service pack*.

It is critical to apply security patches and OS updates whenever possible. Many devastating virus attacks could have been much less severe if more users had downloaded and installed the latest service pack.

Windows routinely checks the Windows Update website for high-priority updates that can help protect a computer from the latest security threats. These updates include security updates, critical updates, and service packs. Depending on the setting you choose, Windows automatically downloads and installs any high-priority updates that your computer needs or notifies you as these updates become available (see Figure 13-50).

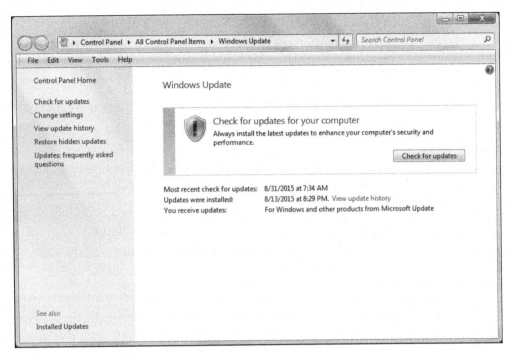

Figure 13-50 Windows Update

13.3.6.4 Check Your Understanding: Security Maintenance

Refer to the online course to complete this activity.

Wireless Security (13.4)

Because wireless networks are easy to implement and more available and less expensive than ever before, wireless network deployment in both home and business environments is growing. Technicians therefore need to understand how to secure wireless networks to prevent unauthorized and malicious access.

Configure Wireless Security (13.4.1)

Wireless network deployment brings new and different security risks to the network infrastructure, and certain security issues particular to wireless communication need special attention.

What Do You Already Know? - Wireless Security (13.4.1.1)

It is vital to protect a network and connected devices. This is true not only for wired networks but also for wireless networks. You need to understand the following terms related to wireless security: SSID, WPA, UPnP, firmware, and firewall.

Read the scenarios and select the term that is most appropriate for each one.

Scenarios

Scenario 1: In a local restaurant, you notice a sign that says "Free Wi-Fi." On your phone, you see a network called ForOurGuests.

Scenario 2: You notice a wireless network named StaffOnly with a lock symbol on it. When you try to connect, a password prompt appears.

Scenario 3: A cybercriminal has requested port forwarding targeting your internal network printer.

Scenario 4: An email from your wireless router manufacturer warns of a vulnerability and recommends that you update the device.

Scenario 5: After learning about remote vulnerabilities, you decide to install a device that carefully monitors and filters network traffic.

Answers

Scenario 1 Answer: SSID. The name of a wireless network can be configured to be broadcast for all devices to see.

Scenario 2 Answer: WPA. Access to wireless networks can be restricted and encrypted with passwords.

Scenario 3 Answer: UPnP. Made for convenience, this protocol opens ports without authentication.

Scenario 4 Answer: Firmware. You can download this file directly from the manufacturer to update your wireless router.

Scenario 5 Answer: Firewall. Threats to your network can come from internal and external sources. It is recommended that all devices filter network traffic.

Common Communication Encryption Types (13.4.1.2)

Communication between two computers may need to be secure communication. There are two major requirements for secure communication: The received information must not have been altered by someone who has intercepted the message and anyone who can intercept the message must be unable to read it. The following technologies can be used to accomplish these requirements:

- Hash encoding

- Symmetric encryption

- Asymmetric encryption

Hash Encoding

Hash encoding, or hashing, ensures the integrity of a message. This means that the message is not corrupt, and it has not been tampered with during transmission. Hashing uses a mathematical function to create a numeric value, called a message digest, that is unique to the data. If even one character is changed, the function output will not be the same. The function can be used only one way. An attacker who knows only the message digest cannot re-create the original message, as a changed message will have a completely different hash output. Figure 13-51 illustrates hash encoding. The most popular hashing algorithm is *Secure Hash Algorithm (SHA)*, which is replacing the older *Message Digest 5 (MD5)* algorithm.

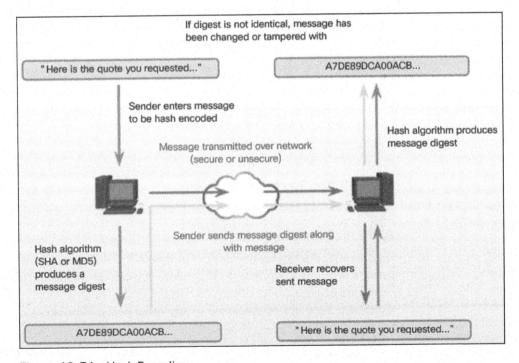

Figure 13-51 Hash Encoding

Symmetric Encryption

Symmetric encryption ensures the confidentiality of a message. If an encrypted message is intercepted, it cannot be understood. It can only be decrypted (that is, read) using the password (that is, key) that it was encrypted with. Symmetric encryption requires both sides of an encrypted conversation to use an encryption key to encode and decode the data. The sender and receiver must use identical keys. Figure 13-52 illustrates symmetric encryption. *Advanced Encryption Standard (AES)* and the older *Triple Data Encryption Algorithm (3DES)* are examples of symmetric encryption.

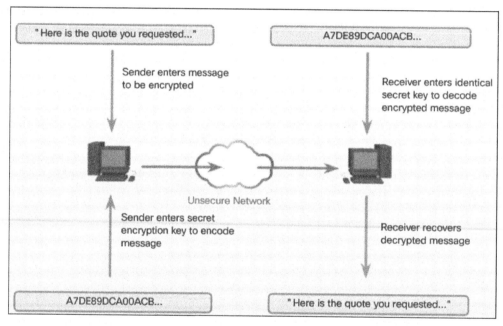

Figure 13-52   Symmetric Encryption

Asymmetric Encryption

Asymmetric encryption ensures confidentiality of a message by using two keys, a *private key* and a *public key*. The public key can be widely distributed, such as by being emailed in plaintext or posted on the Web. The private key is kept by an individual and must not be disclosed to any other party. These keys can be used in two ways:

- Public key encryption is used when a single organization needs to receive encrypted text from a number of sources. The public key can be widely distributed and used to encrypt the messages. The intended recipient is the only party to have the private key, which is used to decrypt the messages. Asymmetric encryption using a public key is shown in Figure 13-53.

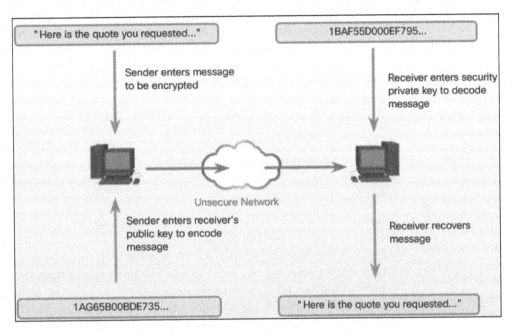

"Here is the quote you requested..."

1BAF55D000EF795...

Sender enters message to be encrypted

Receiver enters security private key to decode message

Unsecure Network

Sender enters receiver's public key to encode message

Receiver recovers message

1AG65B00BDE735...

"Here is the quote you requested..."

Figure 13-53   Asymmetric Encryption

- In the case of digital signatures, a private key is required for encrypting a message, and a public key is needed to decode the message. This approach allows the receiver to be confident about the source of the message because only a message encrypted using the originator's private key can be decrypted using the public key. *RSA* (Rivest-Shamir-Adleman) is the most popular example of asymmetric encryption.

Smart cards also use asymmetric encryption. A digital certificate is stored with a private key on a smart card hardware token. To perform authentication, the card provides the certificate to an authentication server, which checks that it is valid and trusted. The server then uses the public key in the certificate to issue an encrypted challenge to the user. The smart card decrypts the challenge with the private key and sends an appropriate response to the server.

Wi-Fi Configuration Best Practices (13.4.1.3)

Radio waves used to transmit data in wireless networks make it easy for attackers to monitor and collect data without physically connecting to a network. Attackers can gain access to an unprotected wireless network simply by being within range of it.

A technician needs to configure access points and wireless NICs using an appropriate level of security.

A robust wireless network with sufficient coverage for users in all locations requires the proper placement of antenna and access points. If placing an access point in proximity to the provider's cabling does not provide enough coverage, extenders and repeaters can be used to boost the wireless signal to locations where it is weak. A site survey can also be performed to identify signal dead zones.

Reducing the power output on an access point may help prevent war driving, but it may also result in insufficient wireless coverage for legitimate users. Increasing the power output of an access point can increase coverage, but it can also increase the chance of signal bouncing and interference. There may also be legal restrictions on wireless power levels. Because of these potential issues, it is usually best to set power levels to auto-negotiate.

When installing wireless services, apply wireless security techniques immediately to prevent unwanted access to the network. Wireless access points should be configured with basic security settings that are compatible with the existing network security. When you set up an access point on a Wi-Fi network, the management software prompts for a new administrator password. There may also be an option to change the default username of the administrator account, which is slightly more secure than using the default name configured. Also, on smaller networks, you can assign IP addresses statically instead of by using DHCP. This prevents any computer from connecting to the access point unless it is configured with the correct IP address.

Additional security services, such as parental controls or content filtering, may be available in a wireless router. Internet access times can be limited to certain hours or days, specific IP addresses can be blocked, and key words can be blocked. The location and depth of these features varies depending on the router manufacturer and model.

One way to provide basic security on Wi-Fi networks is to change the default service set ID (SSID) and to disable broadcast of the SSID, as shown in Figure 13-54. Access point vendors use a default SSID for each device model. A technician should change the default SSID to something users will recognize that will not get confused with other nearby networks. Most access points broadcast the SSID by default. A level of privacy can be gained by disabling the broadcast of the SSID, which prevents wireless network adapters from finding the network unless they are specifically configured with the name of the network SSID. Disabling the SSID broadcast provides very little security. Someone who knows the SSID of a network can simply enter it manually. A wireless network also broadcasts the SSID during a computer scan, and the SSID can easily be intercepted in transit.

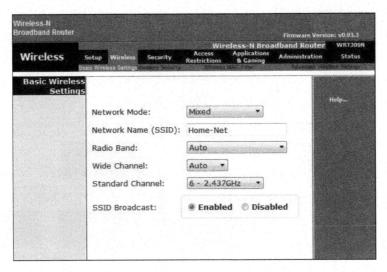

Figure 13-54   Enabling SSID Broadcast

Authentication Methods (13.4.1.4)

There are a variety of *authentication methods*, from unsecured to the most secure, as shown in Figure 13-55. The details of these authentication methods are as follows:

- **Open:** Any wireless device can connect to the wireless network. This method should only be used in situations where security is of no concern.

- **Shared Key:** This method provides mechanisms to authenticate and encrypt data between a wireless client and an AP or wireless router.

- **WEP:** *Wired Equivalent Privacy (WEP)* was the original 802.11 specification for securing WLANs. However, with WEP the encryption key never changes when exchanging packets, making it easy to crack.

- **WPA:** *Wi-Fi Protected Access (WPA)* is a standard that uses WEP but secures the data with the much stronger Temporal Key Integrity Protocol (TKIP) encryption algorithm. TKIP changes the key for each packet, making it much more difficult to crack.

- **WPA2/WPA3:** *WPA2* is now the industry standard for securing WLANs. WPA2 uses Advanced Encryption Standard (AES) for encryption. AES is currently considered the strongest encryption protocol. Since 2006, any device that bears the Wi-Fi Certified logo is WPA2 certified. WPA3 has been ratified since 2018 and is mandatory on Wi-Fi certified devices. WPA3 includes a variety of security over WPA2. However, the currently large install base of WPA2 devices, including Internet of Things (IoT) devices, will probably not be updated. In addition, many users do not understand the new protocol or know how to implement it. Therefore, as of 2023, adoption of WPA3 has been very slow.

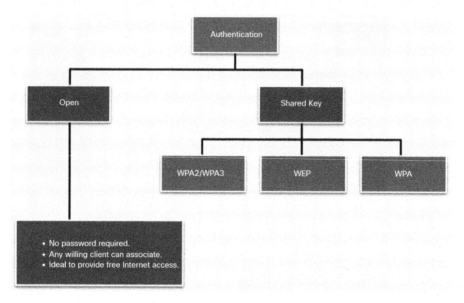

Figure 13-55   Wireless Authentication Methods

Wireless Security Modes (13.4.1.5)

Wi-Fi Protected Setup (WPS) and WPA are different technologies. WPS allows a simplified process for connecting to devices on a wireless home network, and it completes the process of setting up passphrases automatically for the user. WPA can be used with a lot of different protocols, including WPA and WPA2. It is a security and access control technology. Using WPA or WPA2, the user creates and encrypts passwords. WPA2 is the safest option because it has increased security features over WPA. It also offers enterprise options.

WPA2

It is important to use a wireless encryption system to encode the information being sent over a wireless network to prevent unwanted capture and use of data. Most wireless access points support several different security modes. As discussed earlier in this chapter, you should always implement the strongest security mode (WPA2) when possible, as shown in Figure 13-56.

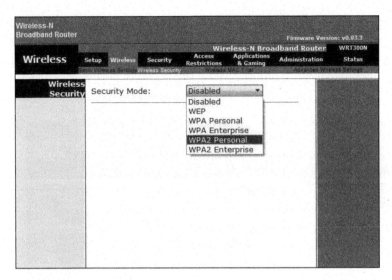

Figure 13-56   WPA2

WPS

Many routers offer WPS, as shown in Figure 13-57. With WPS, both the router and the wireless device have a button that can both be pressed to automatically configure Wi-Fi security between the devices. A software solution using a PIN is also common. It is important to know that WPS is not entirely secure as it is vulnerable to brute-force attack. WPS should be turned off as a security best practice.

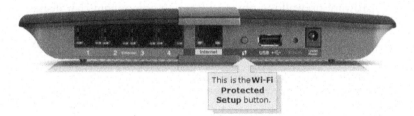

Figure 13-57   WPS

Firmware Updates (13.4.1.6)

Most wireless routers offer upgradable firmware, as shown in Figure 13-58. Firmware releases may contain fixes for common problems reported by customers as well as security vulnerabilities. You should periodically check the manufacturer's website for updated firmware. After it is downloaded, you can use the GUI to upload the firmware to the wireless router, as shown in Figure 13-58. Before installing the upgrade, connect the router to a wired connection because users will be disconnected from the WLAN and the Internet until the upgrade finishes. The wireless router may need to reboot several times before normal network operations are restored.

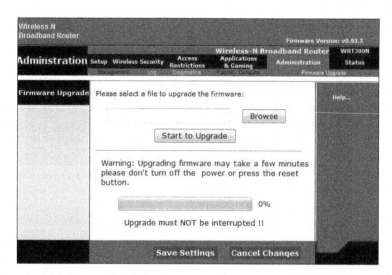

Figure 13-58   Firmware Updates

Firewalls (13.4.1.7)

A hardware firewall is a physical filtering component that inspects data packets from the network before they reach computers and other devices on a network. A hardware firewall is a freestanding unit that does not use the resources of the computers it is protecting, so there is no impact on processing performance. The firewall can be configured to block multiple individual ports, a range of ports, or even traffic specific to an application. Most wireless routers also include an integrated hardware firewall, as shown in Figure 13-59.

A hardware firewall passes two different types of traffic into a network:

- Responses to traffic that originates from inside the network
- Traffic destined for a port that was intentionally left open

Hardware and software firewalls protect data and equipment on a network from unauthorized access. A firewall should be used in addition to security software. Table 13-3 compares hardware and software firewalls.

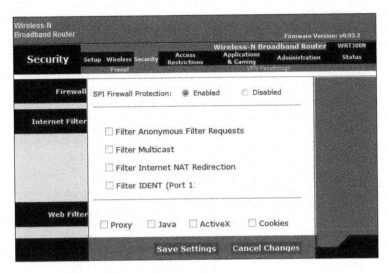

Figure 13-59   SPI Firewall Protection

Table 13-3   Hardware and Software Firewall Comparison

Hardware Firewall	Software Firewall
Dedicated hardware component	Available as third-party software; cost varies
Initial cost for hardware and software updates can be high	Free version included with Windows operating system
Multiple computers can be protected	Typically protects only the computer on which it is installed
No impact on computer performance	Uses computer resources and therefore may potentially have an impact on performance

Table 13-4 describes the different firewall configurations.

Table 13-4   Firewall Configurations

Type	Description
Packet filter	Packets cannot pass through the firewall unless they match the established rule set configured in the firewall. Traffic can be filtered based on different attributes, such as source IP address, source port, or destination IP address or port. Traffic can also be filtered based on destination services or protocols such as WWW or FTP.

Type	Description
Stateful packet inspection (SPI)	This is a firewall that keeps track of the state of network connections traveling through the firewall. Packets that are not part of a known connection are dropped. The SPI firewall is enabled in Figure 13-59.
Application layer	All packets traveling to or from an application are intercepted. All unwanted outside traffic is prevented from reaching protected devices.
Proxy	A firewall can be installed on a proxy server to inspect all traffic and allow or deny packets based on configured rules. A proxy server is a server that is a relay between a client and a destination server on the Internet.

A DMZ, as shown in Figure 13-60, is a subnetwork that provides services to untrusted networks. Email, Web, and FTP servers are often placed into the DMZ so that the traffic using the server does not come inside the local network. This protects the internal network from attacks by this traffic but does not protect the servers in the DMZ in any way. It is common for a firewall or proxy to manage traffic to and from the DMZ.

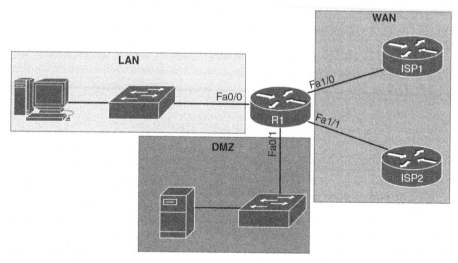

Figure 13-60 Demilitarized Zone

Port Forwarding and Port Triggering (13.4.1.8)

Hardware firewalls can be used to block ports to prevent unauthorized access into and out of a LAN. However, there are situations when specific ports must be opened so that certain programs and applications can communicate with devices on different networks. Port forwarding, shown in Figure 13-61, is a rule-based method of directing traffic between devices on separate networks.

When traffic reaches the router, the router determines whether the traffic should be forwarded to a certain device based on the port number found with the traffic. Port numbers are associated with specific services, such as FTP, HTTP, HTTPS, and POP3. The rules determine which traffic is sent on to the LAN. For example, a router might be configured to forward port 80, which is associated with HTTP. When the router receives a packet with the destination port 80, the router forwards the traffic to the server inside the network that serves web pages. For example, port forwarding could be enabled for port 80, which is associated with the web server at IP address 192.168.1.254.

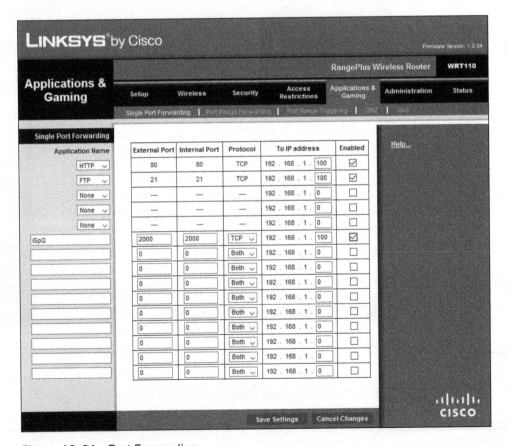

Figure 13-61   Port Forwarding

Port triggering, shown in Figure 13-62, allows the router to temporarily forward data through inbound ports to a specific device. You can use port triggering to forward data to a computer only when a designated port range is used to make an outbound request. For example, a video game might use ports 27000 to 27100 for connecting with other players. These are the trigger ports. A chat client might use port 56 for connecting the same players so that they can interact with each other. In this instance, if there is gaming traffic on an outbound port within the triggered port range, inbound chat traffic on port 56 is forwarded to the computer that is being used to play the video game and chat with friends. When the game is over and the triggered ports are no longer in use, port 56 is no longer allowed to send traffic of any type to this computer.

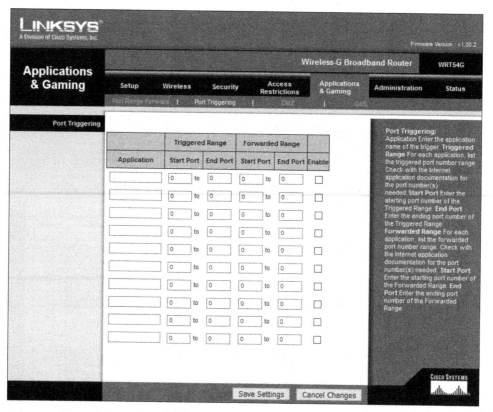

Figure 13-62   Port Triggering

Universal Plug and Play (13.4.1.9)

Universal Plug and Play (UPnP) is a protocol that enables devices to dynamically forward traffic through network ports without the need for user intervention or configuration. Port forwarding, shown in Figure 13-63, is often used for streaming media, hosting games, or providing services from home and small business computers to the Internet.

Although UPnP is convenient, it is not secure. The UPnP protocol has no method for authenticating devices. Therefore, it considers every device trustworthy. In addition, the UPnP protocol has numerous security vulnerabilities. For example, malware can use UPnP to redirect traffic to different IP addresses outside your network, potentially sending sensitive information to a hacker.

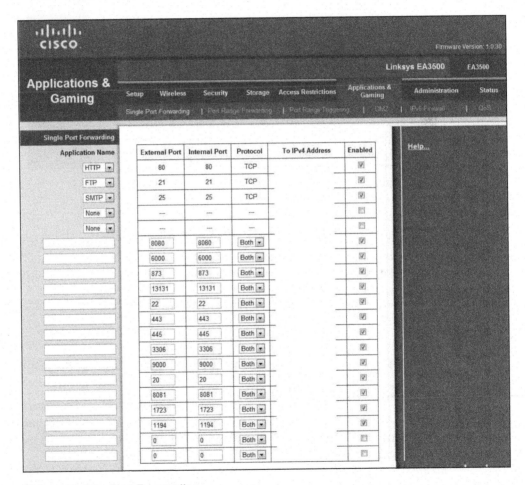

Figure 13-63   Port Forwarding

Many websites host a variety of free browser-based vulnerability profiling tools. Search the Internet for "UPnP router test" and scan your router to determine if yours is subject to UPnP vulnerabilities.

Many home and small office wireless routers have UPnP enabled by default. Therefore, check this configuration, shown in Figure 13-64, and disable UPnP.

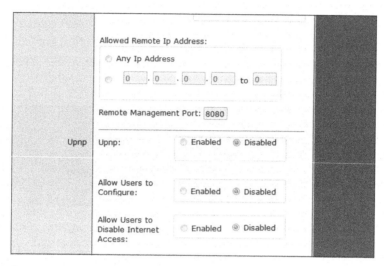

Figure 13-64   Disabling UPnP

13.4.1.10 Packet Tracer: Configure Wireless Security

In this Packet Tracer activity, you will configure a wireless router to use WPA2-Personal as a security method, rely on MAC filtering to increase security, and support single port forwarding.

Basic Troubleshooting Process for Security (13.5)

A technician must be able to effectively troubleshoot security problems. Using the troubleshooting process to identify and correct security problems helps technicians maintain a consistent approach to managing and mitigating threats to data and equipment.

Applying the Troubleshooting Process to Security (13.5.1)

The troubleshooting process is used to help resolve security issues.

The Six Steps of the Troubleshooting Process (13.5.1.1)

The six steps of the troubleshooting process are:

Step 1.   Identify the problem.

Step 2.   Establish a theory of probable cause.

Step 3.   Test the theory to determine the cause.

Step 4.   Establish a plan of action to resolve the problem and implement the solution.

Step 5.   Verify full system functionality and, if applicable, implement preventive measures.

Step 6.   Document findings, actions, and outcomes.

Identify the Problem (13.5.1.2)

Security-related issues can be as simple as preventing shoulder surfing or more complex, such as having to remove infected files from multiple networked computers. Use the troubleshooting steps listed in the preceding section as guidelines to help in diagnosing and repairing security-related problems.

Computer technicians must be able to analyze a security threat and determine the appropriate method to protect assets and repair damage. The first step in the troubleshooting process is to identify the problem. Table 13-5 shows a list of open-ended and closed-ended questions to ask the customer.

Table 13-5   Step 1: Identify the Problem

Open-Ended Questions	Closed-Ended Questions
■ When did the problem start?	■ Is your security software up to date?
■ What problems are you experiencing?	■ Have you scanned your computer for viruses recently?
■ What websites have you visited recently?	■ Have you opened any attachments from suspicious emails?
■ What security software is installed on your computer?	■ Have you changed your password recently?
■ Who else has used your computer recently?	■ Have you shared your password?

Establish a Theory of Probable Cause (13.5.1.3)

After you have talked to the customer, you can begin to establish a theory of probable causes. You may need to conduct additional internal or external research, based on the customer's description of the symptoms. Table 13-6 shows a list of some common probable causes of security problems.

Table 13-6 Step 2: Establish a Theory of Probable Cause

Common causes of security problems	<ul><li>Virus</li><li>Trojan horse</li><li>Worm</li><li>Spyware</li><li>Adware</li><li>Grayware or malware</li><li>Phishing scheme</li><li>Password compromised</li><li>Unprotected equipment rooms</li><li>Unsecured work environment</li></ul>

Test the Theory to Determine Cause (13.5.1.4)

After you have developed some theories about what is wrong, test your theories to determine the cause of the problem. Table 13-7 lists some quick procedures that can help you determine the exact cause of the problem or even correct the problem. If a quick procedure corrects the problem, you can verify full system functionality. If a quick procedure does not correct the problem, you might need to research the problem further to establish the exact cause.

Table 13-7 Step 3: Test the Theory to Determine Cause

Common steps to determine cause	<ul><li>Disconnect from the network.</li><li>Update antivirus and spyware signatures.</li><li>Scan the computer with protection software.</li><li>Check the computer for the latest OS patches and updates.</li><li>Reboot the computer or network device.</li><li>Log in as an administrative user to change a user's password.</li><li>Secure equipment rooms.</li><li>Secure the work environment.</li><li>Enforce the security policy.</li></ul>

Establish a Plan of Action to Resolve the Problem and Implement the Solution (13.5.1.5)

After you have determined the exact cause of the problem, establish a plan of action to resolve the problem and implement the solution. Table 13-8 shows some sources you can use to gather additional information to resolve an issue.

Table 13-8 Step 4: Establish a Plan of Action to Resolve the Problem and Implement the Solution

If no solution is achieved in the previous step, further research is needed to implement the solution, using these sources.	■ Help desk repair logs ■ Other technicians ■ Manufacturer FAQ websites ■ Technical websites ■ News groups ■ Computer manuals ■ Device manuals ■ Online forums ■ Internet search

Verify Full System Functionality and, if Applicable, Implement Preventive Measures (13.5.1.6)

After you have corrected the problem, you need to verify full functionality and, if applicable, implement preventive measures. Table 13-9 shows a list of the steps to verify the solution.

Table 13-9 Step 5: Verify Full System Functionality and, if Applicable, Implement Preventive Measures

Verify solution and full system functionality.	■ Re-scan the computer to ensure that no viruses remain. ■ Re-scan the computer to ensure that no spyware remains. ■ Check the security software logs to ensure that no problems remain. ■ Check the computer for the latest OS patches and updates. ■ Test network and Internet connectivity. ■ Ensure that all applications are working. ■ Verify access to authorized resources such as shared printers and databases. ■ Make sure entries are secured. ■ Ensure that the security policy is enforced.

Document Findings, Actions, and Outcomes (13.5.1.7)

In the final step of the troubleshooting process, you must document your findings, actions, and outcomes. Table 13-10 shows a list of the tasks required to document the problem and the solution.

Table 13-10 Step 6: Document Findings, Actions, and Outcomes

Document your findings, actions, and outcomes	■ Discuss with the customer the solution that was implemented. ■ Have the customer verify that the problem has been solved. ■ Provide the customer with all paperwork. ■ Document the steps taken to solve the problem in the work order and the technician's journal. ■ Document any components used in the repair. ■ Document the time spent solving the problem.

Common Problems and Solutions for Security (13.5.2)

Knowing some of the common problems and solutions related to security can speed the troubleshooting process.

Common Problems and Solutions for Security (13.5.2.1)

Security problems can be attributed to a number of reasons. You will resolve some types of security problems more often than others. Table 13-11 identifies common problems and solutions for security.

Table 13-11 Common Problems and Solutions for Security

Symptoms	Possible Causes	Possible Solutions
A security alert is displayed.	Windows Firewall is disabled.	Enable Windows Firewall.
	Virus definitions are out of date.	Update virus definitions.
	Malware has been detected.	Remove malware.
A user is receiving hundreds or thousands of junk emails each day.	The network is not providing detection or spam protection for the email server.	Install/update antivirus software or email antispam software.

Symptoms	Possible Causes	Possible Solutions
An unauthorized wireless access point is discovered on the network.	A user added a wireless access point to increase the wireless range of the company network.	Disconnect and confiscate the unauthorized device. Enforce the security policy by taking actions against the person responsible for the security breach.
An unknown printer repair person is observed looking under keyboards and on desktops.	Visitors are not being monitored properly or user credentials have been stolen.	Contact security or the police. Educate users to never hide passwords near their work area.
System files have been renamed, applications crash, files are disappearing, or file permissions have changed.	The computer has a virus.	Remove the virus by using antivirus software. Restore the computer from a backup.
Users with flash drives are infecting computers on the network with viruses.	Flash drives are not scanned by the antivirus software when a network computer accesses it.	Set the antivirus software to scan removable media when data is accessed.
Your email contacts report spam coming from you.	Your email has been hijacked.	Change your email password. Contact email service support and reset the account.
Your wireless network is compromised even though 128-bit WEP encryption is used.	WEP can be decrypted using commonly available hacking tools.	Upgrade to WPA encryption. Use MAC address filtering for older wireless clients.
Users are being redirected to malicious websites.	Domain name resolution has been compromised or DNS spoofing is occurring.	Flush the local DNS cache by using **ipconfig /flushdns** to clear malicious entries. Check the HOSTS file for spoofed entries. Check the priority order for name resolution services. Validate the DNS resolvers set as primary and secondary in the client's IP address configuration.

Symptoms	Possible Causes	Possible Solutions
User receives access denied errors when attempting to open files.	Malware has changed the permissions of files.	Quarantine the infected system and investigate closely.
Browser opens a page other than what the user is attempting to access.	Spyware has been installed.	Check the host file for malicious entries. Also verify that the DNS servers the client is using are correct.

13.5.2.2 Lab: Document Customer Information in a Work Order

In this lab, you will document customer information in a work order.

Summary (13.6)

In this chapter, you learned that many types of threats are created to disrupt computers and networks; the greatest and most common threat is malware. Malware is software developed by cybercriminals to perform malicious acts. Malware is typically installed on a computer without user knowledge. You learned about common types of computer malware, such as viruses, Trojan horses, adware, ransomware, rootkits, spyware, and worms, and you also learned about mitigation techniques to protect against malware. You learned about types of TCP/IP attacks, such as denial of service, spoofing, SYN flood, and man-in-the-middle attacks.

Organizations often deploy network security solutions and the latest anti-malware solutions to secure their networks. However, these measures do not address what is likely the single most serious threat to a well-configured and well-secured network: social engineering. You learned that cybercriminals use social engineering techniques to deceive and trick unsuspecting individuals into revealing confidential information or account login credentials. Social engineering attacks take many forms, including phishing, pretexting, baiting, and Dumpster diving.

You learned about the importance of a security policy in defining security objectives that ensure the security of the network, the data, and the computers in an organization. You learned that the policy should specify the persons authorized to access network resources, the minimum requirements for passwords, acceptable uses for network resources, how remote users can access the network, and how security incidents will be handled. Part of the security policy addresses protecting physical equipment. You learned about different types of secure locks and mantraps that can limit access to restricted areas and prevent tailgating.

Data can be easily lost or damaged due to theft, equipment failure, or disasters. The risk of data loss can be mitigated by using data backups, file and folder permissions, and file and folder encryption. You completed a lab using BitLocker encryption to encrypt the data on a removable USB data drive and on the OS drive of a Windows PC.

You learned how to secure a Windows workstation by setting passwords on the BIOS to prevent the operating system from booting and changing BIOS settings, setting login passwords to prevent access to the local computer, and setting network passwords to prevent access to network resources. You also learned how to set local security policies in Windows.

You completed a lab configuring a Windows local security policy to modify password requirements, enable auditing, configure some user rights, and set security options. You also used Event Manager to view logged information in a lab.

You learned about the Windows Defender Firewall host-based firewall included with Windows 10 and how to configure Windows Defender Firewall to allow or deny access to specific programs or ports. You also learned about Windows Defender Firewall with Advanced Security, which provides even greater access control with Windows Firewall policies such as inbound and outbound rules, connection security rules, and monitoring. You explored Windows Firewall and configured advanced settings in a lab.

Wireless networks are particularly vulnerable to attack and must be properly secured. Radio waves used to transmit data in wireless networks make it easy for attackers to monitor and collect data without physically connecting to a network. One way to provide a level of security on Wi-Fi networks is to change the default SSID and to disable broadcast of the SSID. Further levels of security can be gained through authentication and encryption. You practiced configuring wireless security in a Packet Tracer activity.

Finally, you learned the six steps in the troubleshooting process as they are applied to security.

Practice

The following activities provide practice with the topics introduced in this chapter. The labs are available in the companion *IT Essentials v8 Labs & Study Guide* (ISBN 9780138166304). The Packet Tracer activity instructions are also in the *Labs & Study Guide*. The PKA files are found in the online course.

 ## Labs

13.1.2.6 Lab: Operating System Security

13.2.3.7 Lab: BitLocker and BitLocker To Go

13.3.1.6 Lab: Operating System Login

13.3.2.5 Lab: Configure Windows Local Security Policy

13.3.3.6 Lab: Configure Users and Groups in Windows

13.3.4.6 Lab: Configure Windows Firewall

13.5.2.2 Lab: Document Customer Information in a Work Order

Packet Tracer Activity

13.4.1.10 Packet Tracer: Configure Wireless Security

Check Your Understanding Questions

Complete all the review questions listed here to test your understanding of the topics and concepts in this chapter. Appendix A, "Answers to 'Check Your Understanding' Questions," lists the answers.

1. Which type of security threat involves email that appears to be from a legitimate sender and asks the email recipient to visit a website to enter confidential information?

    A. phishing

    B. stealth virus

    C. adware

    D. worm

2. A technician who has recently joined an organization discovers a security breach during the first week on the job. What policy should the technician implement after the security breach has occurred?

    A. acceptable use policy

    B. identification and authentication policy

    C. incident handling policy

    D. remote access policy

3. A technician discovers that an employee has attached an unauthorized wireless router to the company network so that the employee can get Wi-Fi coverage while outside taking a break. The technician immediately reports this to a supervisor. Which of the following actions should the company take in response to this situation? (Choose two.)

    A. Create a guest account for the employee to use when outside the building.

    B. Make sure the wireless router is not broadcasting an SSID.

    C. Immediately remove the device from the network.

    D. Add an authorized wireless access point to the network to extend coverage for the employee.

    E. Consult the company security policy to decide on actions to take against the employee.

4. When a support technician is troubleshooting a security issue on a system, which action should the technician take just before documenting the findings and closing the ticket?

   A. Ask what problem the customer is experiencing.

   B. Boot the system in Safe mode.

   C. Ensure that all applications are working.

   D. Disconnect the system from the network.

5. A corporate executive has asked the IT department to provide a solution to ensure data security of removable drives that are being taken off the premises. Which security solution should be recommended?

   A. TPM

   B. VPN

   C. BitLocker

   D. BitLocker To Go

6. A corporate employee has recently taken the mandated security awareness training and wants to use the correct security term. Which issue can occur when browsing the Internet and is often initiated by the destination website?

   A. autorun

   B. pop-up

   C. phishing

   D. privacy screen

7. When configuring Windows security, which term refers to a rule associated with an object such as a folder or printer?

   A. ActiveX

   B. permission

   C. right

   D. firewall

8. Which characteristics of network traffic are being monitored if a network technician configures the company firewall to operate as a packet filter? (Choose two.)

   A. packet speed

   B. ports

   C. MAC addresses

   D. protocols

   E. packet size

9. A technician in a small business is configuring the local security policy for a computer. Which configuration setting would the technician use to require the user to change the password after 90 days?

   A. Enforce Password History

   B. Password Must Meet Complexity Requirements

   C. Maximum Password Age

   D. Minimum Password Length

10. Which action could be used to determine whether a host is compromised and flooding traffic onto the network?

   A. Examine Device Manager on the host for device conflicts.

   B. Check the host's hard drive for errors and file system issues.

   C. Unseat and then reconnect the hard drive connectors on the host.

   D. Disconnect the host from the network.

11. As data is being stored on a local hard disk, which method would secure the data from unauthorized access?

   A. data encryption

   B. two-factor authentication

   C. deletion of sensitive files

   D. a duplicate hard drive copy

12. Which type of hard drive format is commonly performed at the factory where the drive is assembled?

   A. standard

   B. low-level

   C. EFS

   D. multifactor

13. Which of the following is an example of social engineering?

   A. the infection of a computer by a virus carried by a Trojan

   B. a computer displaying unauthorized pop-ups and adware

   C. an unidentified person claiming to be a technician collecting user information from employees

   D. an anonymous programmer directing a DDoS attack on a data center

14. A technician has recently changed jobs from supporting a small company to supporting a large company, in the security group. Which of the following types of passwords could the larger company use to secure a workstation? (Choose two.)

A. synchronous

B. BIOS

C. multifactor

D. login

E. cryptic

15. When a user turns on their PC on Wednesday, the PC displays a message indicating that all of the user files have been locked. In order to get the files unencrypted, the user is supposed to send an email and include a specific ID in the email title. The message also includes ways to buy and submit bitcoin as payment for the file decryption. After inspecting the message, the technician suspects that a security breach occurred. What type of malware is this?

A. Trojan

B. ransomware

C. spyware

D. adware

CHAPTER 14

The IT Professional

Objectives

Upon completion of this chapter, you will be able to answer the following questions:

- What is the relationship between good communication skills, troubleshooting, and professional behavior?

- What are appropriate communication skills and professional behavior while working with a customer?

- Why is professional behavior at work important?

- What are good customer communications while on a call?

- What are the differences between IT and business documentation?

- How is change managed in an IT environment?

- What are the measures taken by IT organizations to reduce the impact of unplanned outages or data loss?

- What are the ethical and legal issues in the IT industry?

- What are the procedures for dealing with inappropriate content?

- What are the responsibilities of different types of call center technicians?

- What are the basic commands and operation of scripts in different environments?

Key Terms

This chapter uses the following key terms. You can find the definitions in the glossary at the end of the book.

Introduction (14.0)

An IT professional must be familiar with the legal and ethical issues that are inherent in the IT industry. There are privacy and confidentiality concerns that you must take into consideration during every customer encounter as you interact with customers in the field, in the office, or over the phone. If you become a bench technician, although you might not interact with customers directly, you will have access to their private and confidential data. This chapter discusses some common legal and ethical issues.

Call center technicians work exclusively over the phone with customers. This chapter covers general call center procedures and the process of working with customers.

As an IT professional, you will troubleshoot and fix computers, and you will frequently communicate with customers and coworkers. In fact, troubleshooting is as much about communicating with the customer as it is about knowing how to fix a computer. In this chapter, you learn to use good *communication skills* as confidently as you use a screwdriver.

You will also learn about scripting to automate processes and tasks on various operating systems. For example, a script file might be used to automate the process of performing a backup of a customer's data or run a list of standard diagnostics on a broken computer. A script file can save a technician a lot of time, especially when the same tasks need to be performed on many different computers. You will learn about scripting languages and some basic Windows and Linux script commands. You will also learn key scripting terms such as conditional variables, conditional statements, and loops. You will perform a lab writing very basic scripts.

Communication Skills and the IT Professional (14.1)

This section addresses proper communication techniques for working with customers. It is necessary to explore these topics as a technician because they affect customer service. Developing a rapport and establishing a professional relationship with the customer will be beneficial to your information gathering and problem-solving abilities.

Communication Skills, Troubleshooting, and Professional Behavior (14.1.1)

The ability to communicate well with people at all levels of an enterprise, from IT personnel to the CEO, is essential, especially in client-facing roles, such as those at an IT help desk or call center. Whether you're troubleshooting computer issues or managing a team, it's important to know how to interact and communicate well with others at all levels of the organization. You need to be proficient at explaining issues, talking people through solutions, and managing a team efficiently. This section addresses proper communication techniques for working with customers both internal and external to an organization.

Relationship Between Communication Skills and Troubleshooting (14.1.1.1)

Think of a time when you had to call a repair person to get something fixed. Did it feel like an emergency to you? Perhaps you had a bad experience with a repair person. Are you likely to call that same person to fix a problem again? What could that technician have done differently in their communication with you? Did you have a good experience with a repair person? Did that person listen to you as you explained your problem and then ask you questions to get more information? Are you likely to call that person to fix a problem again?

Speaking directly with the customer is usually the first step in resolving a computer problem. To troubleshoot a computer, you need to learn the details of the problem from the customer. Most people who need a computer problem fixed are likely to be feeling some stress. If you establish a good rapport with the customer, the customer might relax a bit. A relaxed customer is more likely to be able to provide the information you need to determine the source of the problem and then fix it.

Follow these guidelines to provide great customer service:

- Set and meet expectations, adhere to the agreed upon timeline, and communicate the status with the customer.

- If necessary, offer different repair or replacement options.

- Provide documentation on the services provided.

- Follow up with customers and users after services are rendered to verify their satisfaction.

Relationship Between Communication Skills and Professional Behavior (14.1.1.2)

Whether you are talking with a customer on the phone or in person, it is important to communicate well and to present yourself professionally.

If you are talking with a customer in person, the customer can see your body language. If you are talking with a customer over the phone, the customer can hear your tone and inflection. Customers can also sense whether you are smiling when you are speaking with them on the phone. Many call center technicians use a mirror at their desk to monitor their facial expressions.

Successful technicians control their own reactions and emotions from one customer call to the next. A good rule for all technicians to follow is that a new customer call means a fresh start. Never carry your frustration from one call to the next.

Working with a Customer (14.1.2)

Customers who seek support from a computer technician are generally doing so because they are experiencing problems. It is the responsibility of the technician to determine the problem while providing a positive customer experience with consideration, respect, and empathy. Listening is an essential part of communication. Ensure that you listen attentively. This section discusses how to identify customer types and relate to customers to provide quality support.

Know, Relate, and Understand (14.1.2.1)

One of your first tasks as a technician is to identify your customer's computer problem. Table 14-1 lists the three general rules for talking with a customer: know, relate, and understand.

Table 14-1   The Know, Relate, and Understand Rules of Customer Service

Rule	Definition	Example
Know	Call the customer by their name. Ask if there is any name in particular that the customer prefers you use.	If the customer tells you their name is Mrs. Johnson, ask if that is what they prefer that you call them. They may say yes, or they may give you their first name. In any case, only use the preferred name with the customer.
Relate	Create a one-to-one connection with the customer.	Find something you may have in common (without giving too much information). If you hear a dog barking in the background of the call and you have a dog, briefly ask about the customer's dog. If you have had to call customer support for your own computer, mention that you understand how frustrating this can be and that you will do everything you can to help the customer. Do not lose control of the call.

Rule	Definition	Example
Understand	Determine the customer's level of knowledge about the computer so you can determine how best to communicate with the customer.	A customer who is very new to computers will not be likely to know all of the jargon that you use every day, so you should use the most common words you can think of to describe aspects of their computer. A more experienced customer probably knows some of the same jargon that you use.

Active Listening (14.1.2.2)

To better enable you to determine the customer's problem, practice *active listening skills*. Allow the customer to tell the whole story. During the time that the customer is explaining the problem, occasionally interject some small words or phrases, such as "I understand," "Yes," "I see," or "Okay." This behavior lets the customer know that you are there and that you are listening.

However, a technician should not interrupt a customer to ask a question or make a statement. Doing so would be rude and disrespectful, and it would create tension. Many times in a conversation, you might find yourself thinking of what to say before the other person finishes talking. When you do this, you are not actively listening. Instead, listen carefully when your customers speak, and let them finish their thoughts.

When you ask a customer to explain a problem to you, you are asking an open-ended question. An open-ended question rarely has a simple answer. In explaining the problem to you, a customer is likely to provide information about what they were doing, what they were trying to do, and why they are frustrated.

After you have listened to the customer explain the whole problem, summarize what the customer has said. This helps the customer know that you have heard and understand the situation. A good practice for clarification is to paraphrase the customer's explanation by beginning with the words "Let me see if I understand what you have told me." This is a very effective tool that demonstrates to the customer that you have listened and that you understand.

After you have assured the customer that you understand the problem, you will probably have to ask some follow-up questions. Make sure that these questions are pertinent. Do not ask questions that the customer has already answered while describing the problem. Doing so would irritate the customer and show that you were not listening.

Follow-up questions should be targeted, closed-ended questions based on the information that you have already gathered. *Closed-ended questions* should focus on obtaining specific information. The customer should be able to answer a closed-ended question with a simple "yes" or "no" or with a factual response, such as "Windows 10."

Use all the information that you have gathered from the customer to complete a work order.

Interactive Graphic

14.1.2.3 Check Your Understanding: Closed-Ended and Open-Ended Questions

Refer to the online course to complete this activity.

Video

14.1.2.4 Video Demonstration: Active Listening and Summarizing

Refer to the online course to view this video.

Professional Behavior (14.1.3)

Courteous and respectful conduct is always expected in the workplace. This is part of what it means to be a professional. Having a well-groomed appearance and exhibiting a positive attitude are other traits of professional behavior. Customers are put at ease by and prefer to deal with people who display professionalism.

Using Professional Behavior with the Customer (14.1.3.1)

Be positive when communicating with a customer. Tell the customer what you can do. Do not focus on what you cannot do. Be prepared to explain alternative ways that you can help, such as by emailing information and step-by-step instructions or using remote control software to solve the problem.

When dealing with customers, it is sometimes easier to explain what you should not do. The following list describes things that you should not do when talking with a customer:

- Do not minimize a customer's problems.

- Do not use jargon, abbreviations, acronyms, and slang.

- Do not use a negative attitude or tone of voice.

- Do not argue with customers or become defensive.

- Do not make culturally insensitive remarks.

- Do not disclose any experiences with customers on social media.

- Do not be judgmental or insulting or call the customer names.

- Avoid distractions and do not interrupt when talking with customers.

- Do not take personal calls when talking with customers.

- Do not talk to coworkers about unrelated subjects when talking with the customer.

- Avoid unnecessary and abrupt phone holds.

- Do not transfer a call without explaining the purpose of the transfer and getting customer consent.

- Do not make negative remarks about other technicians to the customer.

If a technician is not going to be on time, the customer should be informed as soon as possible.

Tips for Hold and Transfer (14.1.3.2)

When dealing with customers, it is necessary to be professional in all aspects of your role. You must handle customers with respect and prompt attention. When on a telephone call, make sure that you know how to place a customer on hold, as well as how to transfer a customer without losing the call, using the tips in Table 14-2 and Table 14-3.

Table 14-2   How to Put a Customer on Hold

Do	Do Not
- Let the customer finish explaining the problem. - Say that you must put the customer on hold and explain why. - Ask the customer for permission to put the call on hold. - When the customer agrees, thank the customer and explain that you expect to be back in just a few minutes. - Explain what you will be doing during that time. - If, after placing the call on hold, it takes longer to return to the customer than expected, quickly get back on the call to explain the situation to the customer. - Always thank the customer for their patience as you work to fix the problem.	- Interrupt the customer. - Put a customer on hold without an explanation. - Put a customer on hold without the customer's consent. - Assume that or act as if your time is more valuable than the customer's time.

Table 14-3 How to Transfer a Call

Do	Do Not
■ Let the customer finish explaining the problem.	■ Interrupt the customer.
■ Say that you must transfer the call and briefly explain why.	■ Transfer the call without an explanation.
■ Tell the customer the name and number of the person they will be speaking with.	■ Transfer the call without the customer's consent.
■ Ask the customer for permission to transfer the call.	■ Assume that or act as if your time is more valuable than the customer's time.
■ When the customer agrees, thank the customer and begin the transfer.	
■ Tell the new technician who will be receiving the transfer your name, the ticket number, and the customer's name.	

14.1.3.3 Video Demonstration: Hold and Transfer

Refer to the online course to view this video.

What Do You Already Know? - Netiquette (14.1.3.4)

As a technician, you should be professional in all communications with customers: respecting people's time and their privacy, being forgiving of others' mistakes, and sharing your expert knowledge. For email and text communications, there is a set of personal and business etiquette rules called *netiquette*. The following list describes some common netiquette dos and don'ts:

- Do be pleasant and polite, even if someone is not being pleasant or polite with you.

- Do begin emails with an appropriate greeting, even within a thread.

- Do check grammar and spelling before you send an email or a text. This is always a good idea. You never know what serious mistake you might have missed.

- Do be ethical. This is true for email and texts, just as it is in all your other interactions with people.

- Do not send or forward chain letters via email.

- Do not send anger-filled, accusatory emails, called "flames."

- Do not reply to flames. Flames never solve a problem but only make it worse.

- Do not use all uppercase in email. Using all uppercase letters is considered SHOUTING.

- Do not email or text anything you would not say to someone's face. Not only is doing so unethical, your emails and texts could possibly be traced back to you.

The Customer Call (14.1.4)

Ensuring a good experience for the customer is essential to you, to them, and to your company because you are the initial link between the customer and the company. Good listening and communication skills are necessary to enhance the customer experience while you answer questions and help to resolve the customer's problems.

Keeping the Customer Call Focused (14.1.4.1)

Part of your job is to focus the customer on the problem during the phone call. When you focus the customer on the problem, you can control the call. The following practices make the best use of your time and the customer's time:

- **Use proper language:** Be clear and avoid technical language that the customer might not understand.

- **Listen and question:** Listen carefully to the customer and let them speak. Use open- and closed-ended questions to learn details about the customer's problem.

- **Give feedback:** Let the customer know that you understand the problem and develop a friendly and positive conversational manner.

Just as there are many different computer problems, there are many different types of customers. By using active listening skills, you may get some hints about what type of customer is on the phone with you. Is this person very new to computers? Is the person very knowledgeable about computers? Is your customer angry? Do not take any comments personally and do not retaliate with any comments or criticism. If you stay calm with the customer, finding a solution to the problem will remain the focal point of the call. Recognizing certain customer traits can help you manage the call accordingly.

Videos 14.1.4.2 through 14.1.4.6 demonstrate strategies for dealing with different types of difficult customers. The list is not comprehensive, and often a customer will display a combination of traits. Each video contains a recording of a technician handling a difficult customer type incorrectly, followed by a recording of the same technician handling the customer professionally. A quiz follows each example.

Video

14.1.4.2 Video Demonstration: The Talkative Customer

Refer to the online course to view this video.

Video

14.1.4.3 Video Demonstration: The Rude Customer

Tips for helping a rude customer:

- Do listen very carefully, as you do not want to ask the customer to repeat any information.

- Do follow a step-by-step approach to determining and solving the problem.

- Do try to contact the customer's favorite technician, if they have one, to see if that technician can take the call. Tell the customer, "I can help you right now, or I can see if your preferred technician is available." If the customer wants the preferred technician and that tech is available, politely transfer the call. If the technician is not available, ask the customer if they will wait. If the customer will wait, note that in the ticket.

- Do apologize for the wait time and the inconvenience, even if there has been no wait time.

- Do reiterate that you want to solve the customer's problem as quickly as possible.

- Do not ask the customer to do any obvious steps if there is any way you can determine the problem without that information.

- Do not be rude to the customer, even if they are rude to you.

Refer to the online course to view this video.

Video

14.1.4.4 Video Demonstration: The Knowledgeable Customer

Tips for helping a knowledgeable customer:

- Do consider setting up a call with a level two technician if you are a level one technician.

- Do describe to the customer the overall approach to what you are trying to verify.

- Do not follow a step-by-step process with the customer.

- Do not ask the customer to check the obvious, such as the power cord or the power switch. Consider suggesting a reboot instead.

Refer to the online course to view this video.

Video

14.1.4.5 Video Demonstration: The Angry Customer

Tips for helping an angry customer:

- Do let the customer tell you their problem without interrupting, even if the person is angry. This allows the customer to release some of their anger before you proceed.

- Do sympathize with the customer's problem.

- Do apologize for the wait time or inconvenience.

- Do not, if at all possible, put the customer on hold or transfer the call.

- Do not spend the call time talking about what caused the problem. It is better to redirect the conversation to solving the problem.

Refer to the online course to view this video.

Video

14.1.4.6 Video Demonstration: The Inexperienced Customer

Tips for helping an inexperienced customer:

- Do allow the customer to talk for about a minute.

- Do gather as much information about the problem as possible.

- Do politely step in to refocus the customer. This is the one exception to the rule of never interrupting a customer.

- Do ask as many closed-ended questions as you need to.

- Do not encourage non-problem-related conversation by asking social questions such as "How are you today?"

Refer to the online course to view this video.

Operational Procedures (14.2)

Operational procedures are guidelines that companies provide employees to give them the specifics of how a task is to be accomplished. They help employees understand the company's expectations of what needs to happen to ensure that work gets done efficiently and with predictability.

Documentation (14.2.1)

Documentation has a multitude of purposes, including but not limited to providing a mechanism for relaying information to coworkers. It can be used in legal matters, it is a way to record problems and solutions for future use, and more. Documentation is another way to provide a good communication channel.

Documentation Overview (14.2.1.1)

Different types of organizations have different operating procedures and processes that govern business functions. Documentation is the main way of communicating these processes and procedures to employees, customers, suppliers, and others.

Purposes for documentation include:

- Providing descriptions for how products, software, and hardware function through the use of diagrams, descriptions, manual pages, and knowledge base articles

- Standardizing procedures and practices so that they can be repeated accurately in the future

- Establishing rules and restrictions on the use of the organization's assets, including acceptable use policies for Internet, network, and computer usage

- Reducing confusion and mistakes, saving time and resources

- Complying with governmental or industry regulations

- Training new employees or customers

Keeping documentation up to date is just as important as creating it. Updates to policies and procedures are inevitable, especially in the constantly changing environment of information technology. Establishing a standard timeframe for reviewing documents, diagrams, and compliance policies ensures that the correct information is available when it is needed.

IT Department Documentation (14.2.1.2)

Keeping documentation current is challenging for even the best-managed IT departments. IT documentation can come in many different forms, including diagrams, manuals, configurations, and source code. In general, IT documentation falls into four broad categories:

- *Policy documents*:

    - Acceptable use policies that describe how technology is to be used within the organization

- Security policies that outline all aspects of information security, including password policies and security incident response methods

- Regulatory compliance policies that describe all federal, state, local, and industry regulations that apply to the organization

- Disaster recovery policies and procedures that provide detailed plans for what must be done to restore services in the event of an outage

- *Operation and planning documents*:

  - IT strategy and planning documents that outline the near- and long-term goals of the department

  - Proposals for future projects and project approvals

  - Meeting presentations and minutes

  - Budgets and purchasing records

  - Inventory management, including hardware and software inventories, licenses, and management methods, such as the use of asset tags and bar codes

- *Project documents*:

  - User requests for changes, updates, or new services

  - Software design and functional requirements, including flow diagrams and source code

  - Logical and physical network topology diagrams, equipment specifications, and device configurations

  - Change management forms

  - User testing and acceptance forms

- *User documentation*:

  - Features, functions, and operation of software, hardware, and services provided by the IT department

  - End-user manuals for hardware and software

  - Help desk ticket database with ticket resolutions

  - Searchable knowledge base articles and FAQs

14.2.1.3 Reports and Procedures

Acceptable Use Policy

An acceptable use policy (AUP) is an agreement between two or more parties that defines the appropriate user access to resources or services. Before the user is granted access, the user must agree to the AUP and follow the policy outlined in the AUP.

For example, splash screens can be used to display the rules and remind the user of data handling procedures before allowing access to a workstation or app.

Incident Report

An incident report, also known as an after-action report (AAR), can be used to document an episode of a critical and major incident, such as a security breach. The report can include investigative information and event analysis from the interested stakeholders. The purpose of the report is to identify potential issues, provide insight for improvements, and allow prompt corrective action to prevent a similar event in the future. Incident reports should be filed promptly in a clear and professional manner. The incident report should be non-biased without personal thoughts, emotions, or solutions.

Standard Operating Procedures

Standard operating procedures (SOP) are step-by-step instructions to guide employees on how to use computers and networked services efficiently, securely, and are informed of expected responsibilities. The main goals of the SOP are to establish uniformity across the company, create high-quality work consistently, and reduce miscommunications. Custom software package installation procedures are an example of SOP.

Procedures for custom installation of a software package:

1. **Verify system requirements:** Verify that the custom software package can be supported and integrated into existing computers and IT infrastructure.

2. **Validate installation files:** After downloading the installation files from the source, verify that the files are not corrupt by comparing hash values generated locally and from the source.

3. **Confirm software license:** Software licensing is a contract between a software company and the end user. It dictates how the software should be used and the number of devices to which the software can be installed. Always verify that the software license can be used for the intended purpose and the number of users.

4. **Update Process:** The new software should be added to any change control and monitoring processes.

5. **Develop up-to-date training and support documentation:** Update support and training documentation after the software installation.

14.2.1.4 User Checklists

SOP can also be in the form of user checklists. Two examples of user checklists are:

- New-user setup checklist
- End-user termination checklist

New-User Setup Checklist

A formal onboarding process helps new hires or employees changing job roles. Some of the typical processes can include:

- Setting up the user accounts with the necessary permissions and security clearance
- Assigning devices and receiving training as necessary
- Learning about security policy and data privacy agreements

End-User Termination Checklist

When an employee retires, changes job roles, or leaves the organization, the end-user termination checklist should be part of the off-boarding process. Some of the typical processes can include:

- Take back the device and wipe all data from the device.
- Transfer or release software licenses.
- Deactivate account access and remove all account permissions.

14.2.1.5 Knowledge Base and Articles

A knowledge base is a centralized repository of articles and documents that allow users to create, share, and manage knowledge across the organization. The articles in the knowledge base can provide these common types of data:

- Answers to frequently asked questions (FAQs)
- Troubleshooting scenarios
- Internal database to support self-service support

- Training documents
- Links to external legitimate and verifiable knowledge base articles

Regulatory Compliance Requirements (14.2.1.6)

Federal, state, local, and industry regulations can have documentation requirements over and above what is normally documented in the company's records. *Regulatory and compliance policies* often specify what data must be collected and how long it must be retained. A few of the regulations may have implications on internal company processes and procedures. Some regulations require keeping extensive records regarding how the data is accessed and used.

Failure to comply with laws and regulations can have severe consequences, including fines, termination of employment, and even incarceration of offenders. It is important to know how laws and regulations apply to your organization and to the work you perform.

14.2.1.7 Asset Databases

Asset management is the tracking and management of assets to ensure that they are used properly, maintained, upgraded, and disposed of responsibly at the end of their lifecycles. The organization needs an inventory of all the deployed hardware assets along with the consumables, spare components in case of hardware failures, and software assets, such as warranty information, licenses, and intellectual property (IP).

Database System

Many software solutions are available for businesses to manage and track their assets. Asset management software can improve the visibility and management of the assets to reduce hardware and software costs.

A simple spreadsheet can track the assets, but it can be difficult to maintain and provide accurate accounting in real time. A centralized asset management database system can be configured to track the assets and store the information, such as device type, serial number, asset ID, deployed location, user history, number of licenses, warranty, and service information. Some asset management software can be configured for network discovery. The software scans the network and retrieves the hardware information, such as make and model and serial numbers, the device configurations, and monitoring data.

Asset Tags and IDs

Asset tags, working in conjunction with an asset management database system, can provide up-to-date and accurate information about an asset. An asset tag identifies the equipment with a unique serial number, barcode, QR code, or radio frequency ID

(RFID) and is typically adhered to the asset. An RFID tag contains encoded digital data that is captured by a scanner using radio waves.

The use of asset tags allows companies to track assets from purchase to disposal and streamline maintenance management. Asset tags with a database system provide visibility and security for your assets.

14.2.1.8 Asset Procurement

Procurement Life Cycle

A procurement life cycle includes the following stages in the use of the asset.

- **Planning:** Analysis of the organization's current and future needs combined with potential asset impact on business, network, daily operations, and implemented devices is needed before requesting a new or upgraded asset.

- **Procurement:** A budget is determined, and a supplier or vendor is identified to deliver the asset.

- **Deployment:** The procured asset can be installed or integrated with the other tools in the business. All of this should occur in a secure manner.

- **Maintenance:** Provisions should be made to keep your assets in operating condition to optimize their use. Some of the maintenance tasks include security updates, data backups, and part replacements.

- **Disposal:** When an asset has reached the end of life, the asset should be sanitized of any data. The sanitized asset can be sold, recycled, donated, or destroyed. The asset management database should be updated to reflect the change in the status of the asset.

Warranty and Licensing

For each hardware asset, the invoice, warranty, support contract, and vendor contact information should be readily available. For each software asset, license information, subscription-based details, and number of allotted users or devices should be readily available.

Assigned Users

Depending on the type of assets, the assets can be assigned to individuals or shared within the entire organization.

Typical assets managed by individual accounts:

- Workstations
- Laptops

- Mobile devices, like smartphones and tablets

- Software license

- Shared assets managed by individuals or security groups within a department:

- Servers

- Routers

- Switches

- Access points

Interactive Graphic

14.2.1.9 Check Your Understanding: Documentation

Refer to the online course to complete this activity.

Change Management (14.2.2)

Change management in the context of this section refers to IT change management. IT change events are a regular function of the IT infrastructure not because of things like unplanned outages, problems, or mandatory design adjustments to increase efficiency and performance but because of all the system dependencies within the infrastructure. Careful planning needs to take place so a change happens with the least possible impact on network service or business operations.

Change Control Process (14.2.2.1)

Controlling changes in an IT environment can be difficult. Changes can be as minor as replacing a printer or as important as upgrading all the enterprise servers to the latest operating system version. Most larger enterprises and organizations have change management procedures in place to ensure that installations and upgrades go smoothly.

A good *change management process* can prevent business functions from being negatively impacted by the updates, upgrades, replacements, and reconfigurations that are a normal part of IT operations. Change management usually starts with a change request from a stakeholder or from within the IT organization itself. Most change management processes include the following:

- *Identification*: What is the change? Why is it needed? Who are the stakeholders?

- *Assessment*: What business processes are impacted by this change? What are the costs related to and resources necessary for implementation? What risks are associated with making (or not making) this change?

- *Planning*: How long will it take to implement this change? Will there be downtime involved? What rollback or recovery process will be used if the change fails?

- *Approval*: Who must authorize this change? Has approval to proceed with the change been obtained?

- *Implementation*: How are stakeholders notified? What are the steps to complete the change, and how will the results be tested?

- *Acceptance*: What are the acceptance criteria, and who is responsible for accepting the results of the change?

- *Documentation*: What updates are required to change logs, implementation steps, or IT documents because of this change?

All the results of the process are recorded on a change request or change control document that becomes part of the IT documentation. Some expensive or complex changes that impact necessary business functions may require the approval of a change board or committee before work can begin.

Figure 14-1 is an example of a change control worksheet.

CHANGE CONTROL WORKSHEET

NAME OF PROJECT	Windows 10 Upgrades	DATE CREATED	06.01.2019
PROJECT MANAGER	IT Manager	DATE APPROVED	06.02.2019
TECHNICIAN	PC Support Technician	DATE STARTED	
STAKEHOLDERS	Payroll Department Manager Payroll Administrative Assistant Payroll Clerks	DATE COMPLETED AND ACCEPTED	

	PROJECT DESCRIPTION
PROPOSED CHANGE	A detailed description of the proposed change. Upgrade six Windows 7 PCs to Windows 10 Professional.
PURPOSE OF CHANGE	A detailed overview of the reasons this change is necessary. Windows 7 is end-of-life and has limited support availability after January 14, 2020.
SCOPE OF CHANGE	Descriptions of all of departments and/or services that will be impacted by this change. Payroll department currently has six Windows 7 PCs running a custom payroll application. These PCs will be upgraded to Windows 10 over a weekend in order to minimize downtime.
INTENDED OUTCOME	Overview of benefits resulting from change. Payroll department PCs will have the latest, most secure version of the operating system. All current programs will function correctly.
ESTIMATED TIME FRAME	Timeframes for preparation, notification, implementation, testing and approval. One week from start to end. Actual downtime will be experienced over a weekend.
RISK ANALYSIS	Detailed analysis of potential risks involved with this change. Critical risks: • Custom payroll app does not run correctly after upgrade and payroll delivery is impacted. • Upgrade fails and PC is unusable. • Software packages do not load or operate. Minor risks: • Systems runs slower than before the upgrade. • Peripheral devices are not recognized or do not operate correctly.

Figure 14-1   Change Control Worksheet Example *(Continues)*

PROJECT DESCRIPTION	
BACK-OUT OR RECOVERY	Detailed steps needed to return system to operational status if the change fails. If post-upgrade testing fails on any PC for any reason: • Restore affected system from pre-upgrade image. • Notify stakeholders and reschedule upgrade. • Continue research and testing to determine the issues.

PROJECT IMPLEMENTATION PLAN	
PLAN FOR CHANGE	Steps necessary to prepare for change. Pre-upgrade preparation: 1) Verify hardware specifications on all six Payroll Department PCs to ensure they meet the Windows 10 specifications. 2) Obtain Win10 images and license keys, if required. 3) Obtain Payroll Department usernames, computer names, and list of installed software. 4) Research software in order to ensure compatibility with Windows 10. Note any software that requires upgrade or new version to run under Windows 10. Order software, if required. 5) Schedule upgrade time with users.
PLANNED IMPLEMENTATION STEPS	Steps to perform change. On-site upgrade steps: 1) Make a backup image of the systems to be upgraded. 2) Perform Win10 In-place upgrade. 3) Verify the operation of the PC, including software and peripheral devices. 4) Review changes with the users. 5) Obtain user approval of the upgrade
ACTUAL STEPS PERFORMED	Detail of the actual implementation of the change. If any unplanned steps are necessary to complete the change, or if there are steps that cannot be completed for any reason, note them here. The following steps were performed: 1) Backup images made for all Payroll Department PCs. 2) Software inventory verified for each PC. 3) Verified hardware compatibility. Note: Signature pad attached to Payroll PC 118 will need to be replaced. Vendor out of business and no driver available. 4) Performed in-place upgrades to Windows 10. 5) Updated printer drivers to latest versions. 6) Tested installed software. Note: Payroll department will continue to test and monitor the custom payroll application. 7) Reviewed changes with Payroll personnel. 8) Obtained acceptance from users in Payroll Department.

PROJECT IMPLEMENTATION PLAN	
DOCUMENTATION AND FOLLOW-UP	Provide a list of current documentation that needs to be updated as a result of this change. 1) Update Help Desk database with new information. 2) Update Inventory with OS change 3) Update User Profile with OS version. 4) Schedule follow-up with department in a week.

AUTHORIZATION AND APPROVALS		
REQUESTOR	Signature of person requesting the change.	Date signed.
PROJECT MANAGER	Signature of the project manager.	Date signed.
PROGRAMMER/TECHNICIAN	Signature of person(s) who performed the change.	Date signed.
FINAL APPROVAL	Signature of person with final approval authority.	Date signed.

Figure 14-1   (Continued)

Disaster Prevention and Recovery (14.2.3)

Businesses increasingly rely on information systems to function. An IT disaster recovery plan (IT DRP) should describe the strategy for protecting the business IT infrastructure from negative events of any type. There should be procedures to follow to allow the IT infrastructure and operations to get back up and running quickly.

Disaster Recovery Overview (14.2.3.1)

We often think of a disaster as being something catastrophic, such as the destruction caused by an earthquake, a tsunami, or a wildfire. In information technology, a disaster can include anything from natural disasters that affect the network structure to malicious attacks on the network itself. The impact of data loss or corruption due to unplanned outages caused by hardware failure, human error, hacking, or malware can be significant.

A *disaster recovery plan* is a comprehensive document that describes how to restore operation quickly and keep critical IT functions running during or after a disaster occurs. The disaster recovery plan can include information such as offsite locations where services can be moved, information on replacing network devices and servers, and backup connectivity options.

Some services may even need to be available during the disaster in order to provide information to IT personnel and updates to others in the organization. Services that might need to be available during or immediately after a disaster include:

- Web services and Internet connectivity
- Data stores and backup files
- Directory and authentication services
- Database and application servers
- Telephone, email, and other communication services

In addition to having a disaster recovery plan, most organizations take steps to ensure that they are ready in case a disaster occurs. These preventive measures can ease the impact of unplanned outages on the operation of the organization.

Preventing Downtime and Data Loss (14.2.3.2)

Some business applications cannot tolerate any downtime. Such businesses use multiple data centers capable of handling all data processing needs, which run in parallel and have data mirrored or synchronized between the centers. Often, these businesses run their applications from cloud servers to minimize the impact of physical damage to their sites.

Data and Operating System Backup

Even the best disaster recovery procedures cannot restore services quickly if there are no current backups of data and operating system environments. It is much easier to restore data from a reliable backup than it would be to re-create it. There are generally two types of backup done for disaster recovery purposes: *image backups* and *file backups*. Image backups record all the information stored on the computer at the time the image is created, and file backups store only the specific files indicated at the time the backup is run. No matter which type of backup is made, it is critical that the restore process be tested frequently to ensure that it will function when it is needed.

Backup files need to be available to the people who will be responsible for restoring and recovering the systems after an unplanned outage. *Backup media* can be stored securely offsite, or backup files can be stored in an online location, such as with a cloud service provider. Locally stored files may be accessible if communication service outages prevent Internet access. Backup files stored online have the benefit of being accessible from anywhere the Internet is available. Table 14-4 outlines the advantages and disadvantages of cloud and local backups.

Table 14-4 Cloud and Local Backups Comparison

Backup Storage Method	Advantages	Disadvantages
Cloud backups	Reliability: Cloud providers use the latest technology and can offer other related services, such as compression and encryption. Scalability: Cloud backups scale easily, so a business doesn't need to worry that it doesn't have the storage capacity or media if the data files increase in size. Accessibility: Cloud backup files are available anywhere the Internet is accessible.	Time: Backing up data and restoring files are dependent on the speed and reliability of the Internet connectivity. In the event of a regional natural disaster, network congestion may cause intermittent loss of connectivity. Discontinuation of service or increase in pricing.

Backup Storage Method	Advantages	Disadvantages
Local backups	Control: An organization has local control of where data files reside and who has access to them. Accessibility: In the event of a disaster that impacts network connectivity, locally stored backup media may be more accessible. Speed of file restores: Locally attached media restore times are usually faster than over the Internet.	Scalability: Keeping local backups often requires manual intervention and handling of the media. The media itself has storage limitations that may cause issues as data file sizes increase. Offsite storage requirements, fire protection, and environmental controls.

Power and Environment Controls

Keeping the power on for a data center or for critical communications infrastructure can prevent data loss caused by interruptions or spikes in electrical power delivery. Sometimes even minor natural disasters can cause power outages that last longer than 24 hours. Small surge protectors and uninterruptible power supplies (UPSs) can prevent damage from minor power problems, but for larger outages, a generator might be required. Data centers require power not only for the computing equipment but also for air conditioning and fire suppression. Large UPS units can keep a data center operational until a fuel-powered generator comes online.

Elements of a Disaster Recovery Plan (14.2.3.3)

The first step in creating a disaster recovery plan is to identify the most critical services and applications that will need to be restored quickly. That information should be used to create a disaster recovery plan. Creating and implementing a disaster recovery plan consists of five major phases, as shown in Figure 14-2 and described in the list that follows:

- *Phase 1: Network design recovery strategy*: Analyze the network design. Some aspects of the network design that should be included in the disaster recovery are:
  - Whether the network is designed to survive a major disaster, whether there are backup connectivity options, and whether there is redundancy in the network design
  - Availability of offsite servers or cloud providers that can support applications such as email and database services

Network Design Recovery
Strategy

Inventory and Documentation

Verification

Approval and Implementation

Review

Figure 14-2   Elements of a Disaster Recovery Plan

- Availability of backup routers, switches, and other network devices
- Location of services and resources that the network needs, whether they are spread over a wide geography, and whether backups are easily accessible in an emergency

- *Phase 2: Inventory and documentation*: Create an inventory of all locations, devices, vendors, services used, and contact names. Verify cost estimates that are created in the risk assessment step.

- *Phase 3: Verification*: Create a verification process to prove that the disaster recovery strategy works. Practice disaster recovery exercises to ensure that the plan is up to date and workable.

- *Phase 4: Approval and implementation*: Obtain senior management approval and develop a budget to implement and maintain the disaster recovery plan.

- *Phase 5: Review*: After the disaster recovery plan has been implemented for a year, review the plan. Information in the plan must be kept up to date, or critical services may not be restored in the event of a disaster.

Interactive Graphic

14.2.3.4 Check Your Understanding: Disaster Recovery

Refer to the online course to complete this activity.

Ethical and Legal Considerations (14.3)

Many legal and ethical issues arise as companies use computers and computer networks in all aspects of business. All types of data are collected and stored about business processes as well as customers and employees. During criminal investigations, audits, and litigation, that data may be required as part of a legal action. This section discusses different ways of handling data for legal purposes.

IT personnel often have access to confidential data and knowledge about individuals' and companies' networks and systems. The work of an IT professional puts them in a position that involves many ethical decisions and challenges, especially involving privacy and confidentiality issues.

Ethical and Legal Considerations in the IT Profession (14.3.1)

For information technology professionals, it is just as important to study ethical and legal concerns as technical skills. It is important to recognize the responsibility and ethical obligations that come from having access to customers' personal and professional information.

Ethical and Legal Considerations in IT (14.3.1.1)

When you are working with customers and their equipment, you should observe some general ethical customs and legal rules. These customs and rules often overlap.

You should always have respect for your customers, as well as for their property. Computers and monitors are property, and property also includes any information or data that might be accessible, including:

- Emails
- Phone lists and contact lists
- Records or data on the computer
- Hard copies of files, information, or data left on a desk

Before accessing computer accounts, including the administrator account, get the permission of the customer. During the troubleshooting process, you might have gathered some private information, such as usernames and passwords. If you document this type of private information, you must keep it confidential. Divulging customer information to anyone else is unethical and might also be illegal. Do not send unsolicited messages to a customer. Do not send unsolicited mass mailings or chain letters to customers. Never send forged or anonymous emails. Legal details of customer information are usually covered under the *service-level agreement (SLA)*. The SLA is a contract between a customer and a service provider that defines the service or goods the customer will receive and the standards with which the provider must comply.

Personally Identifiable Information (PII) (14.3.1.2)

Take particular care to keep *personally identifiable information (PII)* confidential. PII is any data that could potentially identify a specific individual. *NIST Special Publication 800-122* defines PII as "any information about an individual maintained by an agency, including (1) any information that can be used to distinguish or trace an individual's identity, such as name, social security number, date and place of birth, mother's maiden name, or biometric records; and (2) any other information that is linked or linkable to an individual, such as medical, educational, financial, and employment information."

Examples of PII include, but are not limited to:

- Names, such as full name, maiden name, mother's maiden name, or alias
- Personal identification numbers, such as Social Security number (SSN), passport number, driver's license number, taxpayer identification number, or financial account or credit card number, and address information, such as street address or email address
- Personal characteristics, including photographic images (especially of the face or other identifying characteristics), fingerprints, handwriting, or other biometric data (for example, retina scan, voice signature, facial geometry)

PII violations are regulated by several organizations in the United States, depending on the type of data. The *EU General Data Protection Regulation (GDPR)* also regulates how data is handled for personal data, including financial and healthcare information.

Payment Card Industry (PCI) (14.3.1.3)

Payment Card Industry (PCI) information is considered personal information that needs to be protected. We often hear news about breaches of credit card information that impact millions of users. Often it is days or weeks before a merchant realizes a breach has occurred. All businesses and organizations, large or small, need to adhere to strict standards to protect consumer information.

The PCI Security Standards Council was formed in 2005 by the five major credit card companies in an effort to protect account numbers, expiration dates, and magnetic strip and chip data for transactions around the globe. The PCI Security

Standards Council partners with organizations, including NIST, to develop standards and security procedures around these transactions.

In one of the worst breaches in history, malware infected the point-of-sale system of a major retailer, impacting millions of consumers. This breach could potentially have been prevented with adequate software and policies for data breach prevention. As an IT professional, you should be aware of PCI compliance standards.

For more information on the PCI Security Standards Council, visit www.pcisecuritystandards.org.

Protected Health Information (PHI) (14.3.1.4)

Protected health information (PHI) is a particular form of PII that needs to be secured and protected. PHI includes patient names, addresses, dates of visits, telephone and fax numbers, and email addresses. With the move from paper records to electronic records, *electronic protected health information (ePHI)* is also regulated. Penalties for breaches of PHI and ePHI are very severe and are subject to the *Health Insurance Portability and Accountability Act (HIPAA)*.

Examples of ePHI breaches are easily found with an Internet search. Unfortunately, a breach may be undetected for months. Some breaches have occurred from one person giving out information to an unauthorized person. Human error can cause violations. For example, accidentally faxing health information to the wrong party is a violation. Sophisticated attacks also lead to violations. Recent phishing attacks on a California-based health plan went undetected for almost a month before the plan recognized it and then notified 37,000 patients that their data had been breached. As an IT professional, you should be aware of protecting PHI and ePHI.

For more information about PHI and ePHI, visit www.hhs.gov and search for PHI.

Search the Internet for the regulatory agencies in your state, country, or province.

14.3.1.5 Lab: Investigate Breaches of PII, PHI, PCI

In this lab, you will investigate breaches of PII, PHI, and PCI.

Legal Considerations in IT (14.3.1.6)

The laws in different countries and legal jurisdictions vary, but generally, actions such as the following are considered to be illegal:

- It is not permissible to make any changes to system software or hardware configurations without customer permission.

- It is not permissible to access a customer's or coworker's accounts, private files, or email messages without permission.

- It is not permissible to install, copy, or share digital content (including software, music, text, images, and video) in violation of copyright and software agreements or applicable law. Copyright and trademark laws vary between states, countries, and regions.

- It is not permissible to use a customer's company IT resources for commercial purposes.

- It is not permissible to make a customer's IT resources available to unauthorized users.

- It is not permissible to knowingly use a customer's company resources for illegal activities. Criminal or illegal use typically includes obscenity, child pornography, threats, harassment, copyright infringement, Internet piracy, university trademark infringement, defamation, theft, identity theft, and unauthorized access.

- It is not permissible to share sensitive customer information. You are required to maintain the confidentiality of this data.

This list is not exhaustive. All businesses and their employees must know and comply with all applicable laws of the jurisdiction in which they operate.

Licensing (14.3.1.7)

As an IT technician, you might encounter customers who are using software illegally. It is important that you understand the purposes and types of common software licenses in case you determine that a crime has been committed. Your responsibilities are usually covered in your company's corporate end-user policy. In all instances, you must follow security best practices, including documentation and chain of custody procedures.

A *software license* is a contract that outlines the legal use or redistribution of a piece of software. Most software licenses grant end-user permission to use one or more copies of the software. They also specify the end user's rights and restrictions. This ensures that the software owner's copyright is maintained. It is illegal to use licensed software without an appropriate license.

Personal License

Most software is licensed rather than sold. Some personal software licenses regulate how many computers can run a copy of the software. Other licenses specify the number of users who can access the software. Most personal software licenses allow you to run the program on only one machine. Some personal software licenses allow you to copy the software onto multiple computers. These licenses usually specify that the copies cannot be used at the same time.

One example of a personal software license is an *end user license agreement (EULA)*. A EULA is a license between the software owner and an individual end user. The end user must agree to accept the terms of the EULA. Sometimes, accepting a EULA is as simple as opening the physical package that holds a CD of the software or downloading and installing the software. A common example of agreeing to a EULA occurs when updating the software on tablets and smartphones. The end user must agree to accept the EULA when updating the operating system or installing or updating software on the device, as shown in Figure 14-3.

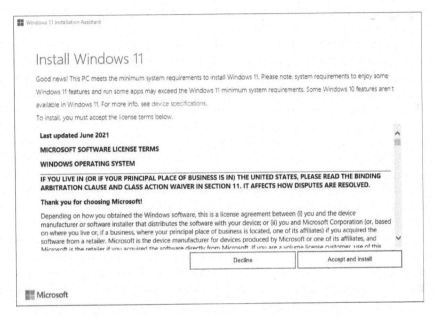

Figure 14-3   Windows 11 License Agreement

Enterprise License

An *enterprise license* is a software site license held by a company. Typically with an enterprise license, the company pays for its employees to use the software. This software does not need to be registered every time it is installed on another employee's computer. In some cases, the employees may need to use a password to activate each copy of the license.

Open Source License

Open source licensing is a copyright license for software that allows developers to modify and share the source code that runs the software. In some cases, an open source license means that the software is free to all users. In other cases, it means that the software can be purchased. In both instances, users have access to the source code. Some examples of open source software are Linux, WordPress, and Firefox.

If the open source licensed software is being used by an individual who is not using it to make money, that person would have a personal license for that software. Personal software licenses are often free or low cost.

Commercial Software License

If a person uses software to make money, that person needs to pay for a *commercial license*. Commercial software licenses are usually more expensive than personal licenses.

Digital Rights Management

In addition to licensing, there is also software that helps control the illegal use of software and content. *Digital rights management (DRM)* software is designed to prevent illegal access to digital content and devices. DRM is used by hardware and software manufacturers, publishers, copyright holders, and individuals. Their purpose for using DRM is to prevent copyrighted content from being copied freely. This helps the copyright holder to maintain control of the content and to be paid for access to that content.

14.3.1.8 Check Your Understanding: Licensing

Refer to the online course to complete this activity.

Legal Procedures Overview (14.3.2)

The laws in different countries and legal jurisdictions vary, but there are many issues considered to be illegal that are held in common. Understanding the laws within the jurisdiction you are working in is paramount to performing your job properly.

Computer Forensics (14.3.2.1)

Data from computer systems, networks, wireless communications, and storage devices may need to be collected and analyzed in the course of a criminal investigation. The collection and analysis of data for this purpose is called *computer forensics*. The process of computer forensics encompasses both IT and specific laws to ensure that any data collected is admissible as evidence in court.

Depending on the country, illegal computer or network usage may include:

- Identity theft
- Using a computer to sell counterfeit goods
- Using pirated software on a computer or network

- Using a computer or network to create unauthorized copies of copyrighted materials, such as movies, television programs, music, and video games

- Using a computer or network to sell unauthorized copies of copyrighted materials

- Pornography

This is not an exhaustive list. Becoming familiar with the signs of illegal computer or network usage can help you identify situations where you suspect illegal activity and report them to the authorities.

Data Collected in Computer Forensics (14.3.2.2)

Two basic types of data are collected when conducting computer forensics procedures:

- *Persistent data*: Persistent data is stored on a local drive, such as an internal or external hard drive, or an optical drive. When the computer is turned off, this data is preserved.

- *Volatile data*: RAM, cache, and the Registry contain volatile data. Data in transit between a storage medium and a CPU is also volatile data. If you are reporting illegal activity or are part of an incident response team, it is important to know how to capture this data because it disappears as soon as the computer is turned off.

In Figure 14-4, the computer forensic expert is examining a hard drive for damage before inspecting it for persistent data.

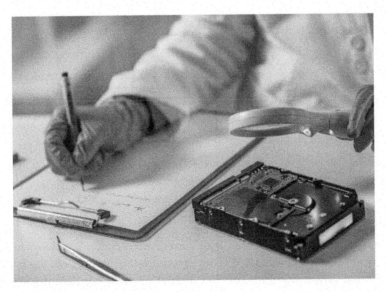

Figure 14-4   Computer Forensics

Cyber Law (14.3.2.3)

There is no single law known as a cyber law. *Cyber law* is a term used to describe the international, regional, country, and state laws that affect computer security professionals. IT professionals must be aware of cyber law so that they understand their responsibility and their liability in relation to cybercrimes.

Cyber law explains the circumstances under which data (evidence) can be collected from computers, data storage devices, networks, and wireless communications. It can also specify the manner in which this data can be collected. In the United States, cyber law has three primary elements:

- Wiretap Act
- Pen/Trap and Trace Statute
- Stored Electronic Communication Act

IT professionals should be aware of the cyber law in their country, region, or state.

First Response (14.3.2.4)

First response is the term used to describe the official procedures employed by people who are qualified to collect evidence. System administrators, like law enforcement officers, are usually the first responders at potential crime scenes. Computer forensics experts are brought in when it is apparent that there has been illegal activity.

Routine administrative tasks can affect the forensic process. If the forensic process is improperly performed, evidence that has been collected might not be admissible in court.

As a field or bench technician, you may be the person who discovers illegal computer or network activity. If this happens, do not turn off the computer. Volatile data about the current state of the computer can include programs that are running, network connections that are open, and users who are logged in to the network or to the computer. This data helps determine a logical timeline of the security incident. It may also help to identify those responsible for the illegal activity. This data could be lost when the computer is powered off.

Be familiar with your company's policy regarding cybercrimes. Know who to call, what to do, and, just as importantly, know what not to do.

Documentation (14.3.2.5)

The documentation required by a system administrator and a computer forensics expert is extremely detailed. They must document not only what evidence was gathered but how it was gathered and with what tools. Incident documentation should use consistent naming conventions for forensic tool output. Stamp logs with the time, date, and identity of the person performing the forensic collection. Document as much information about the security incident as possible. These best practices provide an audit trail for the information collection process.

Even if you are not a system administrator or computer forensics expert, it is a good habit to create detailed documentation of all the work you do. If you discover illegal activity on a computer or network on which you are working, at a minimum, document the following:

- Initial reason for accessing the computer or network

- Time and date

- Peripherals that are connected to the computer

- All network connections

- Physical area where the computer is located

- Illegal material that you have found

- Illegal activity that you have witnessed (or that you suspect has occurred)

- Which procedures you have executed on the computer or network

First responders want to know what you have done and what you have not done. Your documentation may become part of the evidence in the prosecution of a crime. If you make additions or changes to this documentation, it is critical that you inform all interested parties.

Chain of Custody (14.3.2.6)

For evidence to be admitted in legal proceedings, it must be authenticated. A system administrator may testify about the evidence that was collected. They must also be able to prove how this evidence was collected, where it has been physically stored, and who has had access to it between the time of collection and its entry into the court proceedings. This is known as the *chain of custody*. To prove the chain of custody, first responders have documentation procedures in place to track the collected evidence, such as evidence bags, as shown in Figure 14-5. These procedures also prevent evidence tampering so that the integrity of the evidence can be ensured.

Incorporate computer forensics procedures into your approach to computer and network security to ensure the integrity of the data. These procedures help you capture necessary data in the event of a network breach. Ensuring the viability and integrity of the captured data helps you prosecute the intruder.

Figure 14-5   Evidence Bag

Interactive
Graphic

14.3.2.7 Check Your Understanding: Legal Procedures Overview

Refer to the online course to complete this activity.

Call Center Technicians (14.4)

Call center technicians are required to have strong written and verbal communication skills in addition to technical skills. This section describes the call center environment and the responsibilities of a call center technician.

Call Centers, Level One and Level Two Technicians (14.4.1)

Call center technicians answer customer calls and analyze, troubleshoot, and resolve technical issues for customers. Different types of calls are handled by different levels of technicians, providing a basic level to an intermediate level of technical support.

Call Centers (14.4.1.1)

A *call center* environment is usually very organized and professional. Customers call in to receive help for specific computer-related problems. The typical workflow of a call center starts with calls from customers displayed on a callboard. Level one technicians answer these calls in the order in which the calls arrive. If the level one technician cannot solve the problem, it is escalated to a level two technician. In all instances, the technician must supply the level of support that is outlined in the customer's service-level agreement (SLA).

A call center might exist within a company and offer service to the employees of that company as well as to the customers of that company's products. Alternatively, a call center might be an independent business that sells computer support as a service to outside customers. In either case, a call center is a busy, fast-paced work environment, often operating 24 hours a day.

Call centers tend to have a large number of cubicles, as shown in Figure 14-6. Each cubicle has a chair, at least one computer, a phone, and a headset. The technicians working at these cubicles have varied levels of experience with computers, and some specialize in certain types of computers, hardware, software, or operating systems.

Figure 14-6   Call Center Illustration

As calls come in to the call center, they must be prioritized so that the most urgent calls are resolved first. Table 14-5 is an example of a call prioritization system.

Table 14-5   Call Prioritization

Problem Type	Definition	Priority
Down	The company cannot operate any of its computer equipment.	1 (Most urgent)
Hardware	One (or more) of the company's computers is not functioning correctly.	2 (Urgent)

Problem Type	Definition	Priority
Software	One (or more) of the company's computers is experiencing software or operating system errors.	2 (Urgent)
Network	One (or more) of the company's computers cannot access the network.	2 (Urgent)
Enhancement	There has been a request from the company for additional computer functionality.	3 (Important)

All the computers in a call center have support software. The technicians use this software to manage many of their job functions. Technicians use support software to complete the following tasks:

- **Log and track incidents:** The software might manage call queues, set call priorities, assign calls, and escalate calls.

- **Record contact information:** The software might store, edit, and recall customer names, email addresses, phone numbers, location, websites, fax numbers, and other information in a database.

- **Research product information:** The software might provide technicians with information regarding the products supported, including features, limitations, new versions, configuration constraints, known bugs, product availability, links to online help files, and other information.

- **Run diagnostic utilities:** The software might have several diagnostic utilities, including remote diagnostic software, in which the technician can take over a customer's computer while sitting at a desk in the call center.

- **Research a knowledge base:** The software might contain a knowledge database that is programmed with common problems and their solutions. This database might grow as technicians add their own records of problems and solutions.

- **Collect customer feedback:** The software might collect customer feedback regarding satisfaction with the call center's products and services.

Level One Technician Responsibilities (14.4.1.2)

Call centers sometimes have different names for *level one technicians*. These technicians might be known as level one analysts, dispatchers, or incident screeners. Regardless of the title, the responsibilities of a level one technician are fairly similar from one call center to the next.

The primary responsibility of a level one technician is to gather pertinent information from the customer. The technician has to accurately enter all information into the ticket or work order. Examples of the type of information that the level one technician must obtain are as follows:

- Contact information

- What are the manufacturer and model of computer?

- What OS is the computer using?

- Is the computer plugged in to the wall or running on battery power?

- Is the computer on a network? If so, is it a wired or wireless connection?

- Was any specific application being used when the problem occurred?

- Have any new drivers or updates been installed recently? If so, what are they?

- Description of the problem

- Priority of problem

Some problems are very simple to resolve, and a level one technician can usually take care of them without escalating the work order to a level two technician.

When a problem requires the expertise of a level two technician, the level one technician must describe a customer's problem on a work order, using a succinct sentence or two. An accurate description is important because it helps other technicians quickly understand the situation without having to ask the customer the same questions again.

Level Two Technician Responsibilities (14.4.1.3)

As with level one technicians, call centers sometimes have different names for *level two technicians*. These technicians might be known as product specialists or technical-support personnel. The level two technician's responsibilities are generally the same from one call center to the next.

The level two technician is usually more knowledgeable and experienced than the level one technician or has been working for the company for a longer period of time. When a problem cannot be resolved within a predetermined amount of time, the level one technician prepares an escalated work order, as shown in Figure 14-7. The level two technician receives the escalated work order with the description of the problem and then calls the customer back to ask any additional questions and resolve the problem.

Level two technicians can also use remote access software to connect to a customer's computer to update drivers and software, access the operating system, check the BIOS, and gather other diagnostic information to solve the problem.

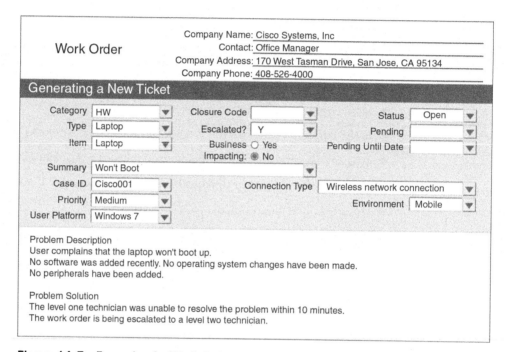

Figure 14-7   Example of a Work Order

14.4.1.4 Lab: Remote Technician - Fix a Hardware Problem

In this lab, you will gather data from the customer and instruct the customer to fix a computer that does not boot.

14.4.1.5 Lab: Remote Technician - Fix an Operating System Problem

In this lab, you will gather data from the customer and instruct the customer to fix a computer that does not connect to the network.

14.4.1.6 Lab: Remote Technician - Fix a Network Problem

In this lab, you will gather data from the customer and instruct the customer to fix a computer that does not connect to the network.

14.4.1.7 Lab: Remote Technician - Fix a Security Problem

In this lab, you will gather data from the customer and instruct the customer to fix a computer that cannot connect to a workplace wireless network.

Basic Scripting and the IT Professional (14.4.2)

This section examines how to write script files that can automate various tasks to save time for a technician or an administrator.

Script Examples (14.4.2.1)

As an IT professional, you will be exposed to many different types of files. One very important type of file is a *script file*, a simple text file written in a scripting language to automate a process or tasks on an operating system. In the field, a script file might be used to automate the process of performing a backup of a customer's data or to run a list of standard diagnostics on a broken computer. The script file can save the technician a lot of time, especially when the same tasks need to be performed on many different computers. You should also be able to identify the many different types of script files because a script file may be causing a problem at startup or during a specific event. Often, preventing the script file from running may eliminate the problem that is occurring.

The commands in a script file might be written on the command line one at a time, but it is more effective to use a script file. The script is designed to be executed line by line, using a command line interpreter in order to perform various commands. A script can be created using a text editor such as Notepad, but an *integrated development environment (IDE)* is often used to write and execute scripts. A Windows batch script is shown in Example 14-1.

Example 14-1 Windows Batch Script

```
@echo off
echo My first batch script!!
echo My hostname is: %computername%
pause
```

The four lines of this Windows batch script do the following:

1. Turn off automatic echoing output at the terminal.

2. Echo the sentence "My first batch script!!" to the terminal.

3. Echo "My hostname is:" followed by the variable **%computername%** to the terminal.

4. Pause the script with the prompt of "Press any key to continue..."

Example 14-2 shows a Linux shell script.

Example 14-2 Linux Shell Script

```
#!/bin/bash
echo My first batch script!!
echo My hostname is: $(hostname)
sleep 2
```

The four lines of this Linux shell script do the following:

1. Identify the shell that the script will be using.

2. Echo the sentence "My first batch script!!" to the terminal.

3. Echo "My hostname is:" followed by the variable **$(hostname)** to the terminal.

4. Pause the script for 2 seconds.

Scripting Languages (14.4.2.2)

A *scripting language* is different from a *compiled language* because each line is interpreted and then executed when the script is run. Examples of scripting languages include Windows batch files, PowerShell, Linux shell script, VBScript, JavaScript, and Python. Compiled languages such as *C*, *C++*, *C#*, and *Java* need to be converted into executable code by a compiler. Executable code is directly readable by the CPU, and scripting languages are interpreted into code that the CPU can read one line at a time by a command interpreter or by the operating system. This makes scripting languages unsuitable for situations in which performance is a significant factor. Table 14-6 lists scripting languages and their extensions.

Table 14-6 Script Types

Scripting Language	Extension	Description
Windows batch file	.bat	Windows command-line interpreted language
PowerShell	.ps1	Windows task-based command-line shell and scripting language
Linux shell script	.sh	Linux shell interpreted language
VBScript	.vbs	Windows Visual Basic script
JavaScript	.js	Client-side scripting language that runs in the browser
Python	.py	An interpreted, object-oriented, high-level language

Table 14-7 shows the comment styles used in various scripting languages.

Table 14-7 Script Styles

Scripting Language	Comment Style
Windows batch file	REM comment
PowerShell	# comment or <# comment #>
Linux shell script	# comment
VBScript	' comment
JavaScript	// comment
Python	# comment

Basic Script Commands (14.4.2.3)

Various commands are available at the terminal of each operating system. Some Windows commands are based on DOS and are accessible through the command prompt. Other Windows commands are accessible through PowerShell. The Windows commands in Table 14-8 were inherited from DOS and work at the Windows command prompt as well as in batch scripts.

Table 14-8 Basic Windows Commands

Command	Output
dir	View the contents of the current directory
cd	Change directories
mkdir	Make a directory
cls	Clear the screen
date	Display/set the date
copy	Copy a file or files

Linux commands are written to be compatible with Unix commands and are often accessed through BASH (Bourne Again shell). The Unix-compatible commands in Table 14-9 are available in most Linux distributions. Note that some of these commands are the same as their DOS counterparts.

Table 14-9   Basic Linux Commands

Command	Output
ls	View the contents of the current directory
cd	Change directories
mkdir	Make a directory
clear	Clear the screen
date	Display/set the date
cp	Copy a file or files

Variables/Environmental Variables (14.4.2.4)

Variables and environmental variables are unique memory locations used by programs.

Variables

Variables are designated places to store information within a computer. A primary function of computers is to manipulate variables. Example 14-3 shows a script in which a user is prompted for their last name (**LNAME**) and where they are from (**PLACE**). The script then shows the execution and output of the script.

Example 14-3 Scripting and Using Variables

```
User@Linux:~$ cat ./script1.sh
#1/bin/bash
echo -n "What is your last name? "
read LNAME
echo -n "Where are you from? "
read PLACE
echo Hello, $LNAME from $PLACE
User@Linux:~$ ./script1.sh
What is your last name? Smith
Where are you from? Michigan
Hello, Smith from Michigan
```

Variable Types

Table 14-10 shows common *data types* used by variables. Some scripting languages require that variables be defined as being integers (numbers), characters, strings, or something else. In code, a string usually contains multiple characters but can also use numbers and spaces. Often, when defining a string, quotes are used to denote the beginning and end of the string (for example, "Dan sold 3 cars yesterday").

Table 14-10 Common Data Type Use by Variables

Data Type	Description	Example
int	Integer numbers	-1,0,1,2,3
float	Numbers with decimals	1234.5678
char	A single character	S
string	Multiple characters	He77o!
bool	True or false	True

Environmental Variables

Some variables are environmental, which means the operating system uses them to keep track of important details such as username, home directory, and language. Example 14-4 shows a shell script with *environmental variables*.

Example 14-4 Calling Environmental Variables

```
User@Linux:~$ cat ./script2.sh
#1/bin/bash
echo The current directory is $PWD
echo The language used is $LANGUAGE
echo The shell being used is $SHELL
User@Linux:~$ ./script1.sh
The current directory is /home/User
The language used is en_US
The shell being used is /bin/bash
```

The Linux variables **PWD**, **LANGUAGE**, and **SHELL** were preset when the user logged into this terminal. To view a list of all environmental variables, use the **env** command. Some useful Windows environmental variables are **%SystemDrive%** (the drive where the system folder is) and **%WinDir%** (exactly where the Windows folder is).

Conditional Statements (14.4.2.5)

Conditional statements are needed for scripts to make decisions. These statements usually come in the form of if-else or case statements. In order for a conditional statement to make a decision, a comparison must be made by using *operators*. The syntax of these commands varies depending on the operator language.

Table 14-11 shows a list of *relational operators* in various scripts. When making a mathematical comparison, use relational operators. Other types of operators include arithmetic (+, -, *, /, %), logical (and, or, not), assignment (+=, -+, *=), and bitwise (&, |, ^) operators.

Table 14-11   Relational Operators

Operator	Batch	PowerShell	BASH	Python
Equal	== or EQU	-eq	-eq	==
Not equal	!= or NEQ	-ne	-ne	!=
Less than	< or LSS	-lt	-lt	<
Greater than	> or GTR	-gt	-gt	>
Less than or equal to	<= or LEQ	-le	-le	<=
Greater than or equal to	>= or GEQ	-ge	-ge	>=

If-Then Statements

Example 14-5 is shell script that determines whether it is currently morning or afternoon.

Example 14-5 If-Then Script

```
User@Linux:~$ date | cut -f 4 -d ' '
09:36:24
User@Linux:~$ cat ./script3.sh
#!/bin/bash
TIME=$(date | cut -f 4 -d ' ' | cut -f 1 -d ':')
declare NOON=12
if [ $TIME -ge $NOON ]
  then echo "Afternoon"
  else echo "Morning"
fi
User@Linux:~$ ./script3.sh
Morning
```

In this script, the **date** command is piped to **cut** until only the hour remains, and the result is placed in a variable. The **if** statement compares the variables **$TIME** and **$NOON** by using the **-ge** operator to determine if the output is going to say "Afternoon" or "Morning."

Case Statements

Example 14-6 is a shell script that determines whether a vowel or a consonant is used.

Example 14-6 case Statement Script

```
User@Linux:~$ cat ./script4.sh
#!/bin/bash
read -p "Give me a letter. " LETTER
case $LETTER in
a|e|i|o|u) echo "$LETTER is a vowel." ;;
*) echo "$LETTER is a consonant." ;;
esac
User@Linux:~$ ./script4.sh
Give me a letter. e
e is a vowel.
User@Linux:~$ ./script4.sh
Give me a letter. b
b is a consonant.
```

The **case** statement is able to lump various comparisons into categories. Note that the letter *b* is not mentioned in the script.

Loops (14.4.2.6)

A loop can be used to repeat commands or tasks. The three main types of *loops* used in scripts are the for loop, the while loop, and the do-while loop.

A *for loop* repeats a section of code a specified number of times. A *while loop* checks a variable to verify whether it is true (or false) before repeating a section of code; this is known as a *pre-test loop*. Finally, a *do-while loop* repeats a section of code and then checks a variable to verify whether it is true (or false); this is known as a *post-test loop*.

For Loops

Example 14-7 is a shell script that outputs five randomly generated binary numbers.

Example 14-7 For Loop Script

```
User@Linux:~$ cat ./script5.sh
#!/bin/bash
for COUNT in 'seq 1 5'; do
  let NUMBER1 = "$RANDOM % 256"
  let NUMBER2 = "$(echo "obase=2; $NUMBER1" | bc)"
```

```
    echo $NUMBER1 = $NUMBER2
done
User@Linux:~$ ./script5.sh
160 = 10100000
71 = 1000111
43 = 101011
187 = 10111011
7 = 111
```

The for loop in this script repeats a sequence exactly five times. The variable **NUM-BER1** is randomly generated to be between 0 and 255. The variable **NUMBER2** is the binary conversion of **NUMBER1**. The spacing between the commands **for** and **done** is optional in some languages, but it helps a programmer understand what code is contained in the loop.

While Loops

Example 14-8 is a shell script that runs until a randomly chosen number is greater than 8.

Example 14-8 While Loop Script

```
User@Linux:~$ cat ./script6.sh
#!/bin/bash
NUMBER=1
while [ $NUMBER -le 8 ]; do
  let NUMBER="$RANDOM % 10+1"
  echo -n "$NUMBER "
done
  echo "> 8 .. loop broken."
User@Linux:~$ ./script6.sh
5 7 9 > .. loop broken.
```

In this script, the loop keeps running until a random number that is chosen is greater than eight. Notice that the variable **NUMBER** was set to **1** before the loop started. This was done to prevent the test **[$NUMBER -le 8]** in the next line from failing.

Do-While Loops

Example 14-9 is a shell script that determines whether a vowel or a consonant is used.

Example 14-9 Do-While Loops

```
User@Linux:~$ cat ./script7.sh
#!/bin/bash
while true ; do
  let NUMBER="$RANDOM % 10+1"
  echo -n "$NUMBER "
  if [ $NUMBER -gt 8 ]; then break; fi
done
  echo "> 8 .. loop broken."
User@Linux:~$ ./script7.sh
3 7 4 1 5 7 6 7 1 7 9 > 8 .. loop broken.
```

Unlike most compiled languages, several scripting languages lack do-while loops. Such languages emulate the post-test function by using an if statement within the loop followed by a **break** statement.

Branch

A branch can be used to have code execute based on the outcome of a formula or logical path. This often happens within a loop when testing multiple outcomes. When a logical statement meets a criterion, the branch is executed. This type of structure adds logical "outs" for the loop and proves a true or false value to a statement or logical test.

14.4.2.7 Lab: Write Basic Scripts in Windows and Linux

In this lab, you will write some basic scripts in different scripting languages to learn how each language handles automating tasks.

Summary (14.5)

In this chapter, you learned about the relationship between communication skills and troubleshooting skills. You need to combine these skills to become a successful IT technician. You learned about the legal aspects and ethics of dealing with computer technology and the property of the customer.

You learned that you should always conduct yourself in a professional manner with your customers and coworkers. Professional behavior increases customer confidence and enhances your credibility. You learned how to recognize the signs of a difficult customer and what to do and what not to do when you are on a call with such a customer.

You must understand and comply with your customer's SLA. If a problem falls outside the parameters of the SLA, find positive ways of telling the customer what you can do to help rather than what you cannot do. In addition to complying with the SLA, you must follow the business policies of the company. These policies include how the company prioritizes calls, how and when to escalate a call to management, and when you can take breaks and lunch. You performed several labs on fixing hardware, operating system, network, and security problems.

You learned about the ethical and legal aspects of working in computer technology. You should be aware of your company's policies and practices. In addition, you might need to familiarize yourself with your local or country's trademark and copyright laws. A software license is a contract that outlines the legal use or redistribution of that software. You learned about the many different types of software licenses, including personal, enterprise, open source, and commercial.

Cyber law explains the circumstances under which data (evidence) can be collected from computers, data storage devices, networks, and wireless communications. *First response* is the term used to describe the official procedures employed by people who are qualified to collect evidence. You learned that even if you are not a system administrator or computer forensics expert, it is a good habit to create detailed documentation of all the work that you do. Being able to prove how evidence was collected and where it has been between the time of collection and its entry into the court proceeding is known as the *chain of custody*.

Finally, you learned about script files, which are files written in scripting languages to automate processes and tasks on various operating systems. A script file can save a technician a lot of time, especially when the same tasks need to be performed on many different computers. You learned about scripting languages and some basic Windows and Linux script commands. You learned about variables, which are designated places to store information within a computer, conditional statements, which are needed for scripts to make decisions, and loops, which repeat commands or tasks.

Learning about scripting is important, and so is experience practicing writing scripts. In this chapter you performed a lab writing some very basic scripts in different scripting languages to learn how each language handles automating tasks.

Practice

The following activities provide practice with the topics introduced in this chapter. The labs are available in the companion *IT Essentials v8 Labs & Study Guide* (ISBN 9780138166304).

Labs

14.3.1.5 Lab: Investigate Breaches of PII, PHI, PCI

14.4.1.4 Lab: Remote Technician - Fix a Hardware Problem

14.4.1.5 Lab: Remote Technician - Fix an Operating System Problem

14.4.1.6 Lab: Remote Technician - Fix a Network Problem

14.4.1.7 Lab: Remote Technician - Fix a Security Problem

14.4.2.7 Lab: Write Basic Scripts in Windows and Linux

Check Your Understanding Questions

Complete all the review questions listed here to test your understanding of the topics and concepts in this chapter. Appendix A, "Answers to 'Check Your Understanding' Questions," lists the answers.

1. A programmer is building a script to calculate the corporate bank account balance to within two decimal places. Which data type would be used in the script to represent the balance?

   A. Bool

   B. int

   C. float

   D. char

2. What category of technician uses remote access software to update a computer belonging to a customer?

   A. level one technicians

   B. level two technicians

   C. field technicians

   D. bench technicians

3. What is the correct way to conduct a telephone call to troubleshoot a computer problem?

   A. Ask personal questions to get better acquainted with the customer.

   B. Maintain professional behavior at all times.

   C. Explain each step to help the customer understand the troubleshooting process.

   D. Always gather information from the customer and escalate the problem.

4. A supervisor receives a complaint that a technician was rude and disrespectful. Which action by the technician most likely caused the customer to complain?

   A. The customer was escalated to a level two technician.

   B. The technician interrupted a number of times to ask questions.

   C. The technician occasionally confirmed an understanding of the problem.

   D. The technician ended the call without saying "Have a nice day."

5. What approach should a technician take when receiving a call from a stressed customer?

   A. Transfer the customer to a level two technician who will ask the customer to explain the problem again.

   B. Try to establish a rapport with the customer.

   C. Ask the customer to telephone back when the customer is feeling less stressed.

   D. Ask the customer to hold and then wait five minutes for the customer to calm down.

6. Which statement best describes a call center?

   A. It is a help desk environment where customers go with their computers to have them fixed.

   B. It is a place to provide computer support to customers.

   C. It is a help desk that customers use to make appointments to report their computer problems.

   D. It is a busy, fast-paced work environment that documents computer problems after they have been repaired by technicians.

7. In which situation would it be appropriate for a technician to back up personal and confidential data from a computer belonging to a customer?

   A. if the technician feels it necessary to back it up

   B. if the customer forgets to sign the work order

   C. if illegal content is discovered on the customer computer

   D. if the customer permits it

8. Which programming language utilizes scripts that are interpreted and executed line by line when the scripts are run?

   A. C++

   B. Java

   C. PowerShell

   D. C#

9. Which of the following are examples of displaying professional communication skills while talking to a customer? (Choose two.)

   A. actively listening, with occasional interjections such as "I see" or "I understand"

   B. interrupting customers with questions to gather more information

   C. asking customers to paraphrase their explanations

   D. focusing on what you cannot do to give customers an idea of the magnitude of the problem

   E. clarifying what customers say after they have finished their explanations

10. Once a technician understands a customer complaint, it is common to ask closed-ended questions. Which question is a close-ended one?

   A. What error messages were displayed when the error occurred?

   B. Is this the first time the error occurred?

   C. What happened after the error occurred?

   D. What happened before the error occurred?

11. A technician working on a computer discovers what is suspected to be illegal activity. Which pieces of information should be immediately documented? (Choose three.)

    A. details of all past users of the computer

    B. location of the computer

    C. technical specifications of the computer

    D. why the computer was accessed by the technician

    E. evidence of the suspected illegal activity

    F. duration of the suspected illegal activity

12. A customer is explaining a problem with a computer to a technician. The technician recognizes the problem before the customer finishes the explanation. What should the technician do?

    A. Ask the customer to repeat the problem so that the technician can document it and verify all the facts.

    B. Interrupt the customer and let the customer know that the technician knows what the problem is.

    C. Wait politely for the customer to finish explaining the problem.

    D. Start working on the PC while listening to the customer at the same time.

13. A customer is upset and wants to speak to a specific technician to resolve a problem immediately. The requested technician is away from the office for the next hour. What is the best way to handle this call?

    A. Ignore the request for the specific technician by walking through a step-by-step process with the customer in an attempt to refocus the customer and solve the problem.

    B. Advise the customer that the requested technician is out of the office and insist on trying to resolve the problem.

    C. Refer the angry customer to a supervisor.

    D. Make an offer to help the customer immediately and advise the customer that otherwise the requested technician will call the customer back within two hours.

14. What is considered ethical behavior by a technician when communicating with a customer?

    A. A technician can send mass emails to customers.

    B. A technician must send only solicited emails.

C. A technician can send forged emails to customers.

D. It is normal to send chain emails to customers.

15. Which situation would require that a support desk call be given the highest priority?

A. A couple of computers have operating system errors.

B. Some computers cannot log in to the network.

C. The company cannot operate because of a system failure.

D. Two users are requesting an application enhancement.

E. A user is requesting a RAM memory upgrade.

16. What action should a technician avoid when dealing with a talkative customer?

A. stepping in and attempting to refocus the customer

B. asking closed-ended questions to regain control of the conversation

C. asking social questions such as "How are you today?"

D. giving the customer a full minute to talk

17. Which of the following roles or tasks are associated with a level two technician? (Choose two.)

A. editing a shell script to run when the server starts

B. installing the new BIOS update when it is available

C. scheduling a task to run at a specific time and date

D. deleting caches and cookies after the web browser closes

18. A programmer uses an operator to compare two variable values within a program. The variable **A** is assigned a value of **5**, and the variable **B** is assigned a value of **7**. Which condition test syntax would provide the result **true**?

A. A == B

B. A > B

C. A != B

D. A >= B

Answers to "Check Your Understanding" Questions

Chapter 1

1. A and B.

   Components such as the BIOS, hard drive, and expansion slots communicate with the CPU via the Southbridge chipset.

2. C.

   High-end desktop and gaming computers use the EPS 12V power supply form factor, which is also used in servers.

3. C.

   Augmented reality (AR) superimposes images and audio over the real world in real time. It does allow ambient light and does not require headsets all the time.

4. D.

   A biometric identification device is an input device that can identify a user based on a unique physical feature, such as a fingerprint or voice. A digitizer is used with a stylus pen to design and create images or blueprints. A scanner is used to digitize an image or a document. A KVM switch can connect multiple computers to one keyboard, monitor, and mouse.

5. D.

   The Mini-ATX motherboard form factor is the smallest form factor (17 cm × 17 cm or 6.7 in. × 6.7 in.) and is used in thin clients and set-top boxes.

6. D.

   A 6/8-pin PCIe power connector is used to supply power to various components of a computer.

7. B.

   The Non-Volatile Memory Express (NVMe) specification provides a standard interface between a compliant SSD, the PCIe bus, and operating systems.

8. C.

   Electrostatic discharge (ESD) can occur when there is a buildup of an electric charge (static electricity) on a surface that comes into contact with another. It can be mitigated by grounding the internal components of the computer to the case.

9. E.

   A keyboard, video, and mouse (KVM) switch is a hardware device that can be used to control more than one computer using a single keyboard, monitor, and mouse. KVM switches provide cost-efficient access to multiple servers using a single keyboard, monitor, and mouse.

10. C.

    An HDMI-to-VGA converter is used to convert digital signals to analog signals.

11. D.

    To help prevent ESD damage, use grounded mats on workbenches and grounded floor mats in work areas. You can also use an antistatic wrist strap to prevent ESD strikes except when working inside power supplies or CRT monitors.

12. C.

The Thunderbolt port enables transmission of high-definition video using the DisplayPort protocol.

13. C and D.

The Northbridge chipset allows the fastest components, such as the RAM and the video card, to interface with the CPU at the front-side bus speed.

14. A, B, and F.

Headphones, monitors, printers, speakers, scanners, fax machines, and projectors are all considered output devices.

15. A.

A solid-state hybrid drive (SSHD) combines a magnetic HDD with onboard flash memory and serves as a nonvolatile cache but costs less than an SSD.

16. C and E.

Fingerprint scanners, keyboards, and mice are all considered input devices, but the two considered the most common are the mouse and keyboard.

Chapter 2

1. B and E.

A network interface card (NIC) upgrade might be done to provide wireless connectivity or to increase bandwidth.

2. D.

550W describes the output power for a power supply.

3. C.

Two form factors used with internal SATA hard drives are 3.5 inch (8.9 cm) and the 2.5 inch (6.4 cm), with the majority of them being 3.5 inch.

4. C.

The job description of a technician commonly lists the need for being able to lift 40 pounds. When lifting heavy objects, it is important to bend at the knees to avoid back injuries.

5. C.

Before working on equipment, remove any watch and other jewelry and secure loose items such as ties and name badges.

6. D.

A RAID card (or RAID controller) controls the data expansion of internal and external drives and also provides fault tolerance for storage devices. The I/O card allows additional I/O ports to be added to a computer. A capture card imports video information into a computer and records it to the storage device. SD storage cards are a form of removable storage used widely in portable devices.

7. A and D.

The data portion of the bus, known as the data bus, carries data between the computer components. The address portion, known as the address bus, carries the memory addresses of the locations where data is read or written by the CPU.

8. A.

Factors to consider when buying a sound card include the slot type, digital signal processor (DSP), port and connection types, and signal-to-noise ratio (SNR).

9. B.

CompactFlash is still used in video cameras because of its high speed and high capacity.

10. A and B.

When building a computer, select a power supply with sufficient wattage to power all the components. Each component inside the computer uses a certain amount of power. Obtain the wattage information for the components from the manufacturer's documentation. When deciding on a power supply, make sure to choose a power supply that has more than enough power for the current components. The shape of the computer case is usually determined by the motherboard, power supply, and other internal components.

11. A.

Before you install a memory module, it is important to verify that there are no compatibility issues. A DDR3 RAM module will not fit in a DDR2 slot. Verification is best done by consulting the motherboard documentation or checking the website of the manufacturer.

12. True.

When installing a hard drive, slightly hand-tighten all the screws to make installation of all screws easier. Do not overtighten the screws when using the screwdriver.

13. C.

Because of the size of cellular phones, a very small storage device such as a MicroSD card is desirable. CompactFlash is an older form of storage device; it is too large for a cellular phone but is widely used in cameras and video recorders because of its large capacity and fast access speed. Similarly, USB flash drives and hard disk drives are too large for a cellular phone.

14. A.

The front-side bus (FSB) is the path between the CPU and the Northbridge. It is used to connect various components, such as the chipset, expansion cards, and RAM. Data can travel in both directions across the FSB.

15. B.

Buffered memory is specialized memory for servers and high-end workstations that use a large amount of RAM. Unbuffered memory is regular memory for computers. With unbuffered memory, the computer reads data directly from the memory banks, which makes it faster than buffered memory. A buffered memory chip has a control chip built into the module. The control chip assists the memory controller in managing large quantities of RAM. Avoid buffered RAM for gaming computers and average workstations because the extra controller chip reduces RAM speed.

Chapter 3

1. D.

An uninterruptible power supply (UPS) helps protect against potential electrical power problems by supplying a consistent level of electrical power to a computer or another device. The battery is constantly recharging while the UPS is in use. The UPS provides a consistent quality of power when brownouts and blackouts occur. Many UPS devices can communicate directly with the computer operating system. This communication allows the UPS to safely shut down the computer and save data prior to the UPS losing all battery power.

2. A.

The resistance of a circuit to the flow of current is measured in Ohms (O). Amps (A) measure the electrons moving through the circuit. Watts (W) measure the work required to move electrons through the circuit. Volts (V) measure the work required to move a charge from one location to another.

3. A.

The BIOS configuration data is saved to a special memory chip called a complementary metal-oxide semiconductor (CMOS).

4. D.

Both RAID 0 and RAID 1 require at least two disks. However, RAID 0 does not provide fault tolerance. The minimum numbers of disks for RAID 5 and RAID 6 are three and four, respectively.

5. D.

Computers designed for audio and video editing need specialized inputs and outputs for recording and playback equipment. This requires an audio and video card that can handle the variety of inputs and outputs needed.

6. B.

Overclocking is a technique that is used to make a processor work at a faster speed than its original specification. Overclocking is not a reliable way to improve computer performance and can result in damage to the CPU.

7. A.

With Hyper-Threading, two pieces of code can be processed simultaneously by a single core, and dual-core is two cores inside a single CPU, where the two cores can process information at the same time.

8. A.

Faster RAM will help the processor keep all the data in sync because the data that it needs to calculate can be retrieved when it is needed. The more RAM the computer has, the less often the computer needs to read from slower storage, such as hard drives or SSDs.

9. A and E.

The BIOS setup program is used to change settings if memory modules, storage devices, and adapter cards are added. Most manufacturers provide the ability to modify boot device options, security and power settings, and adjustments for voltage and clock settings.

10. B.

The safety data sheet (SSD) summarizes information about materials, including hazardous ingredients, fire hazards, and first-aid requirements.

11. D.

The computer time and date are held in CMOS. This requires power from a small battery. If the battery is getting low, the system time and date may become incorrect.

12. D.

Go to the motherboard manufacturer's site to get the correct software to update the BIOS.

13. D.

Native resolution identifies the best monitor resolution for a specific monitor. In Windows

10, the native resolution of a monitor is identified using the keyword (Recommended) beside the monitor resolution.

14. A and D.

One way to increase the power of a computer is to increase the processing speed. You can do this by upgrading the CPU. However, the CPU must meet the following requirements:

❑ The new CPU must operate with the existing motherboard and power supply.

❑ The new CPU must be compatible with the motherboard chipset.

❑ The new CPU must operate with the existing motherboard and power supply.

The new CPU might require a different heat sink and fan assembly. The assembly must physically fit the CPU and must be compatible with the CPU socket. It must also be adequate to remove the heat of the faster CPU.

15. D.

The Lightning connector is a small, proprietary 8-pin connector used by Apple mobile devices such as iPhones, iPads, and iPods for both power charging and data transfer. It is similar in appearance to a USB Type-C connector.

Chapter 4

1. C.

Each light on the front of the case is powered by the motherboard through a cable that attaches somewhere on the board. If this cable comes loose, a particular light on the front of the case will not work.

2. B.

The steps of the troubleshooting process are:

Step 1.   Identify the problem.

Step 2.   Establish a theory of probable cause.

Step 3.   Test the theory to determine the cause.

Step 4.   Establish a plan of action to resolve the problem and implement the solution.

Step 5.   Verify full system functionality and, if applicable, implement preventive measures.

Step 6.   Document findings, actions, and outcomes.

3. A.

Spinning the fan blades with the power off, especially by using compressed air, can damage the fan. The best way to ensure that the fan is working is to visually inspect it with the power on.

4. B.

A failing power supply could also cause a computer to reboot unexpectedly. If the power cord does not attach properly, it is likely that the wrong type of power cord is being used.

5. C.

After the cause of the problem is determined, a technician should research possible solutions, sometimes by visiting various websites and consulting manuals.

6. C.

The CMOS battery maintains the CMOS settings, including the correct date and time. If the CMOS battery is dead or not connected properly, those settings can be lost.

7. D.

   Even though laptops are normally manufactured to operate within a wide range of temperatures, the lower temperature is below freezing and not an optimal environment.

8. C.

   Preventive maintenance includes tasks such as cleaning the device, which can prolong the life of the device.

9. A.

   To remove dust inside a computer, use a can of compressed air.

10. B.

   Before escalating a ticket, document each test that has been performed. Information about the tests is vital if the problem needs to be escalated to another technician.

11. C and D.

   Having a preventive maintenance plan in place can lead to improved reliability, performance, and efficiency in the IT infrastructure. Not having a preventive maintenance plan in place can lead to issues that will cause infrastructure downtime and significant repair costs. A preventive maintenance plan helps ensure that these costly issues are handled before they become problems.

12. B.

   Hold the fan blades in place when you clean the inside of the computer with compressed air to avoid overspinning the rotor or moving the fan in the wrong direction.

13. C.

   Storage device problems are often related to loose or incorrect cable connections.

14. D.

   Always perform a backup before beginning any troubleshooting. Even though the data was backed up to a different partition in this case, the data is still on the same hard drive. If the drive crashes, the data might not be recoverable.

15. D.

   Hardware maintenance tasks include these procedures:

   - Remove dust from fan intakes.

   - Remove dust from the power supply.

   - Remove dust from components inside the computer.

   - Clean the mouse and keyboard.

   - Check for and secure any loose cables.

   Maintenance tasks such as defragmenting a disk and scanning a hard drive for errors are part of a software maintenance routine.

16. A.

   After all repairs have been made, the last step of the troubleshooting process is to verify to the customer the problem and the solutions and demonstrate how the solution corrected the problem.

Chapter 5

1. A and B.

   T568A and T568B are wiring schemes used with Ethernet LAN cabling. IEEE 802.11n and 802.11ac are wireless LAN standards.

Zigbee and Z-Wave are smart home standards.

2. B.

A personal area network (PAN) connects devices, such as mice, keyboards, printers, smartphones, and tablets. These devices are often connected with Bluetooth technology. Bluetooth allows devices to communicate over short distances.

3. D.

A WAN connects multiple LANs that are in geographically separate locations. A MAN connects multiple LANs in a large campus or in a city. A wireless LAN (WLAN) covers a rather small geographical area.

4. A, D, and E.

802.11b and 802.11g operate in the 2.4 GHz range, and 802.11n can operate in either the 2.4 GHz or 5 GHz range. 802.11a and 802.11ac operate only in the 5 GHz range of frequencies.

5. B.

A Zigbee coordinator is a device that manages all the Zigbee client devices to create a Zigbee wireless personal area network (PAN), using the 868 MHz to 2.4 GHz range.

6. A.

Hubs are sometimes called repeaters because they regenerate the signal. All devices connected to the hub share the same bandwidth (unlike with a switch, which gives each device dedicated bandwidth).

7. B.

An IDS is implemented to passively monitor the traffic on a network. Both an IPS and a firewall actively monitor network traffic

and take immediate actions when previously defined security criteria match. A proxy server, when it functions as a firewall, also actively monitors the traffic that travels through it and takes immediate actions.

8. A.

Dynamic Host Configuration Protocol (DHCP) can be used to allow end devices to automatically configure IP information, such as their IP address, subnet mask, DNS server, and default gateway. DNS is used to provide domain name resolution, mapping hostnames to IP addresses. Telnet is a method for remotely accessing a CLI session of a switch or router. Traceroute is a command used to determine the path a packet takes as it traverses the network.

9. B and E.

The TCP/IP model includes four layers: the application layer, the transport layer, the Internet layer, and the network access layer. The functions at each layer include different protocols. The transport layer includes both the TCP and UDP protocols.

10. A.

HTTP uses TCP port 80, and HTTPS uses TCP port 443. HTTP and HTTPS are protocols commonly used to access web pages.

11. B and D.

Common media used in networks include copper, glass or plastic optical fiber, and wireless.

12. C.

A switch maintains a switching table that contains a list of available MAC addresses on the network. The switching table records

MAC addresses by inspecting the source MAC address of every incoming frame.

13. D.

Cable television companies and satellite communication systems both use copper or aluminum coaxial cable for connections between devices.

Chapter 6

1. B and C.

The fact that the web server can be accessed by using its IP address indicates that the web server is working, and there is connectivity between the workstation and the web server. However, the web server domain name is not resolving correctly to its IP address. This could be caused by a misconfiguration of the DNS server IP address on the workstation or the wrong entry of the web server in the DNS server.

2. A.

If a computer is configured with DHCP, but it cannot communicate with the DHCP server in order to obtain an IP address, the Windows OS automatically assigns a link-local IP address in the range 169.254.0.0 to 169.254.255.255. The computer can only communicate with other computers connected to the same 169.254.0.0/16 network and cannot communicate with computers in another network.

3. B.

Forcing a PC to release its DHCP binding allows a new DHCP request operation to occur. The **net**, **tracert**, and **nslookup** commands do not have any effect on DHCP configurations.

4. B.

Port forwarding directs traffic between networks by using forwarding rules. WPA encrypts wireless information, and MAC filtering prevents unauthorized access to the WLAN. Port triggering is a technique used with NAT configurations.

5. B.

Wireless routers usually come with factory default settings. The IP address is often set to 192.168.0.1. The default username and password are often admin. The IP address, username, and password should all be modified to help secure the router.

6. E.

Whitelisting and blacklisting specify which IP addresses are allowed or denied on a network. This is typically done using an access list or access policy.

7. D.

The **ping** command uses Internet Control Message Protocol (ICMP) to test connectivity between network hosts. Address Resolution Protocol (ARP) is used to map IP addresses to MAC addresses. Dynamic Host Configuration Protocol (DHCP) is used to dynamically assign IP addresses to network hosts. Transmission Control Protocol (TCP) is considered a reliable protocol that segments application layer data for transmission.

8. A.

When a computer automatically configures an IP address in the 169.254.x.x range, this is an indication that the DHCP server is inaccessible or down.

9. A.

The manufacturer will maintain up-to-date drivers.

10. D.

Dynamic Host Configuration Protocol (DHCP) can be used to allow end devices to automatically configure IP information, such as their IP address, subnet mask, DNS server, and default gateway. The DNS service is used to provide domain name resolution, mapping hostnames to IP addresses. Telnet is a method for remotely accessing a CLI session of a switch or router. **traceroute** is a command used to determine the path a packet takes as it traverses the network.

11. A.

When workstations are configured to obtain IP addresses automatically but DHCP servers are not available to respond to the requests, a workstation can assign itself an IP address from the 169.254.0.0/16 network.

12. B.

Wireless routers use Network Address Translation to translate internal, or private, addresses into Internet-routable, or public, addresses.

13. C.

The address has a prefix length of /64. The first 64 bits represent the network portion, and the last 64 bits represent the host portion of the IPv6 address. In this example, the network bits are 2001:0db8:cafe:4500.

14. B.

The **nslookup** command was created to allow a user to manually query a DNS server to resolve a given hostname. The **ipconfig /displaydns** command only displays previously resolved DNS entries. The **tracert** command was created to examine the path that packets take as they cross a network

and can resolve a hostname by automatically querying a DNS server. The **net** command is used to manage network computers, servers, printers, and network drives.

15. D.

The fact that the workstation can print at a networked printer indicates that the TCP/IP stack is functional. However, the workstation being unable to communicate with external networks indicates that the most likely problem is the incorrect default gateway address. If the workstation is configured to obtain an IP address automatically, the DHCP server address does not need to be configured.

Chapter 7

1. B.

The default display for any laptop is the laptop display. To output to an external video port such as when a laptop is connected to an external monitor or projector, use the Fn key to change the output to just the external video port or to display both on the laptop display and through the projector.

2. D.

Customer-replaceable units (CRUs) are parts that can be installed by someone who does not have advanced technical skills. Examples of CRUs include a laptop battery and memory.

3. A.

Bluetooth is a low-power, short-range wireless technology that provides connectivity for accessories such as speakers, headphones, and microphones.

4. A.

The first three steps of the troubleshooting process are to identify the problem, establish a theory of probable cause, and test the theory to determine the cause. During the third step, the technician is taking action on what is believed to be the cause of the problem, such as using an AC adapter with a laptop. When a technician is questioning the user, the technician is trying to identify the problem. If the technician suspects that the battery does not have a charge, will not keep a charge, or that there might be loose cable connections, the technician is thinking through common laptop problems.

5. D.

A card reader commonly attaches to a USB port or is integrated into a laptop. It is used to read from or write to flash media of various sizes, including SD.

6. B.

Laptop computers use proprietary form factors, and they are therefore different from one manufacturer to another.

7. D.

Mobile devices typically use either the cellular network or a Wi-Fi network to connect to the Internet. A Wi-Fi connection is preferred because it uses less battery power and is free in many places.

8. C.

With POP, mail is downloaded from the server to the client and then deleted on the server. SMTP is used for sending or forwarding email. Unlike with POP, when a user connects via IMAP, copies of the messages are downloaded to the client application, and the original messages are kept on the server until manually deleted. HTTP is used for web traffic data and is considered insecure.

9. C.

Small outline dual in-line memory modules, or SODIMMs, are designed for the space restrictions of laptops.

10. B.

Liquid-crystal displays (LCDs) use more power than light-emitting diode (LED) or organic LED (OLED) displays. Both LCDs and LEDs use backlights, but LCD screens could use either a cold cathode fluorescent lamp (CCFL) or LED backlight.

11. A.

The Global Positioning System (GPS) is a satellite-based navigation system that transmits signals back to GPS receivers on Earth.

12. C.

To reduce heat and power consumption, CPU throttling can be used. CPU throttling reduces the CPU speed.

13. C and D.

Mobile devices are frequently fitted with GPS radio receivers, enabling them to calculate their position. Some devices do not have GPS receivers. Instead, they use information from Wi-Fi and cellular networks.

14. C.

The Advanced Configuration and Power Interface (ACPI) standard provides support for power states that are very important to mobile devices such as laptops.

15. A.

When removing a SODIMM, make sure to remove the AC adapter and battery first. Then press outward on the clips to release it from the memory slot.

Chapter 8

1. B.

The more complex the structure of the printout, the more time it takes to print. Draft photo–quality pictures, high-quality text, and draft text are less complex than a digital color photograph.

2. C and D.

Using components not recommended by the manufacturer, while they may possibly be less expensive and also more available, might result in poor print quality and void the manufacturer warranty. In addition, the cleaning requirements might vary.

3. B and C.

Some disadvantages of a laser printer include high startup cost, expensive toner cartridges, and a high level of maintenance.

4. C.

Hardware print servers permit several users to connect to a single printer without the need for a computer to share the printer. USB hubs, LAN switches, and docking stations are incapable of sharing printers.

5. B.

Some printers have the capability to perform duplex printing, which is printing on both sides of the paper. IR printing is a form of wireless printing using infrared technology.

Buffering is the process of using printer memory to store print jobs. Spooling puts print jobs into a print queue.

6. D.

If the printer is connected to the wrong computer port, the print jobs will appear on the print queue, but documents will not be printed by the printer.

7. D.

Inkjet print heads cannot usually be effectively cleaned by physical means. Using the vendor-supplied printer software utility is recommended.

8. B.

Virtual printing involves sending the print job to a file (.prn, .pdf, .xps, or image file) or to a remote destination in the cloud. Connecting a printer to the Web using an application such as Google Cloud Print allows virtual printing from any location.

9. A.

Enabling print sharing means allowing a computer to share the printer over the network. Installing a USB hub allows a number of peripheral connections to the same computer. Print drivers do not provide the ability to share printers.

10. D.

Before performing maintenance on a printer, or any computer or peripheral, always disconnect the power source to prevent exposure to dangerous electrical voltages.

11. C and D.

Not requiring the other computers to be cabled directly to the printer is an advantage of printer sharing. To share a printer, computers do not need to be running the same operating system, and more than one computer can send print jobs to the shared printer at the same time. However, the computer directly connected to the printer needs to be powered on, even if not in use. It uses its own resources to manage all the print jobs coming to the printer.

12. A.

Because multiple jobs can be received by a printer while it is busy printing other documents, these jobs must be temporarily stored until the printer is free to print them. This process is called *print buffering*.

13. B.

The greater the number of dots per inch, the better the resolution of the picture and, therefore, the quality of printing.

14. C.

A printer driver is software that allows a computer and a printer to communicate with each other. Configuration software enables users to set and change printer options. Firmware is a set of instructions stored on the printer that controls how the printer operates. Word processing applications are used to create text documents.

15. C and D.

A closed-ended question requires only a yes or no answer that can confirm a fact. An open-ended question requires the user to describe the problem symptoms in detail.

16. A.

Inkjet print heads cannot usually be effectively cleaned by physical means. The vendor-supplied printer software utility is recommended.

Chapter 9

1. D.

Routers, switches, and firewalls are infrastructure devices that can be provided in the cloud.

2. D.

Each virtual machine runs its own operating system. The number of virtual machines that can be made available depends on the hardware resources of the host machine. Like physical computers, virtual machines are susceptible to threats and malicious attacks. To connect to the Internet, a virtual machine uses a virtual network adapter that acts as a physical adapter in a physical computer, connecting through the physical adapter on the host to establish a connection to the Internet.

3. C.

Windows Virtual PC is an example of a Type 2 hypervisor. A Type 2 hypervisor is hosted by an operating system.

4. A.

Cloud computing involves computers, software, servers, network devices, and other services physically held at a remote location. Cloud computing vendors use virtualization to provide multiple servers, networks, applications, operating systems, and so on to clients without the need for equipment for each one. Virtualization of servers, for example, allows multiple servers to be on one physical server. Each server could be for a different client, if necessary.

5. B.

Organizations use cloud-based applications to provide on-demand software delivery.

When a user requests an application, minimal application code is forwarded to the client. The client pulls additional code from the cloud server, as needed.

6. D.

Running Hyper-V on Windows 8 requires a minimum of 4 GB of system RAM.

7. B.

IT as a Service (ITaaS) extends the capability of IT services so that the company does not need to invest in new infrastructure. ITaaS providers also provide training for new personnel and licensing for new software required by the company. These services are available on demand and are delivered economically to any device anywhere in the world without compromising security or function.

8. A and D.

Type 1, or bare-metal, hypervisors are installed directly on host hardware. Therefore, a Type 1 hypervisor has direct access to the host hardware resources and thus has fewer layers of abstraction and is more efficient. However, bare-metal hypervisors do need to have management console software to manage the VM instances.

9. A and D.

OneDrive and Google Drive are cloud-based file storage solutions. Gmail and Exchange Online are cloud-based email services. The virtual desktop solution deploys the entire desktop environment of an organization from a server in a data center to a client.

10. D.

Cloud computing is used to separate an application or a service from the hardware.

Virtualization separates the operating system from the hardware.

11. C and D.

Mission-critical services should use server virtualization technology with a Type 1 hypervisor. VMware vSphere and Oracle VM Server are examples of Type 1 hypervisors. VMware Workstation, Oracle VM VirtualBox, and Windows 10 Hyper-V are examples of Type 2 hypervisors.

12. A and C.

Gmail and Exchange Online are cloud-based email services. OneDrive and Dropbox are cloud-based file storage solutions. A virtual desktop solution deploys the entire desktop environment of an organization from a server in a data center to clients.

13. D.

There is no such thing as BaaS. With Infrastructure as a Service (IaaS), key network devices such as routers and firewalls are leased from a provider. With Wireless as a Service (WaaS), a provider provides wireless connectivity at a fixed monthly cost.

14. A.

Cloud computing allows users to access applications, back up and restore files, and perform tasks without needing additional software or servers. Cloud users access resources through subscription-based or pay-per-use services, in real time, using nothing more than a web browser.

15. A.

Cloud service providers use one or more data centers for services and resources such as data storage. A data center is a data storage facility located inside a company and maintained by the IT staff or leased from a co-location provider, where the maintenance can be done by the provider or the corporate IT staff.

Chapter 10

1. A.

The primary partition that is marked active must carry the boot files for both the operating systems. In this case, the data can be stored in the three logical drives created in the extended partition, leaving one extra primary drive for additional storage.

2. B.

The MBR contains information on how the hard drive partitions are organized. BOOTMGR is a small piece of software loaded from the Volume Boot Record (VBR), the CPU is the electronic circuitry within a computer that carries out the instructions of a computer program, the Registry, which is a database that contains all the information about the computer.

3. A.

On a hard disk, up to four primary partitions can be created. Alternatively, up to three primary partitions plus an extended partition can be created, and the extended partition can be further divided into multiple logical drives, if desired. Only one primary partition can be made the active partition at any time. It is the active partition used by the operating system to boot a PC.

4. A.

During a Windows 8.1 installation, the Administrator account is created automatically. All other accounts have to be created manually.

5. B.

Hard disk drives are organized by several physical and logical structures. Partitions are logical portions of the disk that can be formatted to store data. Partitions consist of tracks, sectors, and clusters. Tracks are concentric rings on the disk surface. Tracks are divided into sectors, and multiple sectors are combined logically to form clusters.

6. E.

The Master Boot Record (MBR) is the boot sector standard that supports a maximum primary partition of 2 TB. The MBR allows four primary partitions per drive. The globally unique identifier (GUID) partition table (GPT) can support enormous partitions with a theoretical maximum of 9.4 ZB (9.4 $\times 10^{21}$ bytes). GPT supports a maximum of 128 primary partitions per drive.

7. A.

NTFS allows the storage of files up to 16 TB in size. The file system exFAT, also known as FAT64, is used to address some of the shortcomings of FAT32 and is mainly used for USB flash drives. CDFS is used for optical drives. FAT32 allows the storage of files up to 4 GB in size.

8. A.

A 32-bit OS cannot be upgraded to a 64-bit OS. Windows XP and Windows Vista cannot be upgraded to Windows 10.

9. A.

Pressing the F8 key during the boot process opens the Windows Advanced Boot Options menu, from which the user can select Last Known Good Configuration.

10. C.

The terms 32-bit and 64-bit refer to the amount of memory space that an OS can address at a time. A 32-bit OS can address 2^{32} bytes of memory, which is 4 GB. A 64-bit OS can address 2^{64} bytes of memory.

11. C.

The Administrator account is used to manage the computer and is very powerful. Best practices recommend that it be used only when it is needed to avoid accidentally performing significant changes to the system.

12. B and D.

The file system has no control over the speed of access or formatting of drives, and the ease of configuration is not file system dependent.

13. C.

NFS (Network File System) is used to access files on other computers across a network. Windows operating systems support several file systems. FAT, NTFS, and CDFS are used to access files stored on drives installed in the computer.

14. C and D.

Two types of computer operating system user interfaces are CLI and GUI. CLI stands for command line interface. In a command line interface, a user enters commands at a prompt using a keyboard. The second type is the GUI, or graphical user interface. With this type of user interface, a user interacts with the operating system by working with icons and menus. A mouse, finger, or stylus can be used to interact with a GUI. PnP is the name of a process by which an OS assigns resources to different

hardware components of a computer. The other answers are examples of application programming interfaces (APIs).

Chapter 11

1. B.

The functions of the listed commands are as follows:

- **tasklist:** Displays currently running applications
- **gpresult:** Displays group policy settings
- **gpupdate:** Refreshes group policy settings
- **runas:** Runs a program or tool with different permissions
- **rstrui:** Starts the System Restore utility

2. A and D.

The file attributes are read-only, archive, hidden, and system. Details, Security, and General are tabs on the file Properties applet.

3. D.

Windows Remote Desktop and Remote Assistant allow an administrator to connect a local computer with a remote computer across the network and to interact with it as though it were the local computer. The administrator sees and can interact with the desktop of the remote computer. With Remote Desktop, the administrator logs onto the remote computer using an existing user account and starts a new user session. No user is required at the remote computer to allow this access. Remote Assistant allows a technician to interact with a remote computer with the assistance of a remote user. The remote user must allow the remote access to the current user session and is able to observe what the technician is doing.

4. D and E.

Device driver errors are the most likely causes of BSOD errors. Failing RAM can also create BSOD errors. Software issues such as browser and antivirus issues do not produce BSOD errors. A power supply failure would prevent the machine from starting.

5. D.

Use the Task Manager Performance tab to see a visual representation of CPU and RAM utilization. This is helpful in determining if more memory is needed. Use the Applications tab to halt an application that is not responding.

6. B.

The C:\Users folder contains all the user profiles. The C:\Application Data folder contains application data related to all users. The 32-bit program files are located in the C:\Program Files (x86) folder, while 64-bit program files are located in the C:\Program Files folder.

7. A.

The functions of the listed commands are as follows:

- **ping:** Determines basic connectivity to the targeted IP address or hostname

- **nslookup:** Finds the successful name resolution of a hostname

- **tracert:** Finds the route taken by a packet

- **ipconfig:** Finds the default gateway configured on a host

8. B and E.

Closed-ended questions generally have a fixed or limited set of possible responses, such as "yes" or "no." Open-ended questions imply no limited or fixed set of replies but rather generally prompt the responder to provide more meaningful feedback.

9. C.

Any change from a system restore is reversible. A restore point only contains information about the system and Registry settings and therefore cannot be used to back up or recover data files.

10. B.

UAC is used to change user account settings while converting the file system to FAT16. Updating the driver for the graphics card will not resolve the issue. Compatibility mode in Windows 7 enables running a program created for previous versions of the Windows environment.

11. D.

In Windows 10, the configuration of a password for a PC woken from hibernation or sleep can be set in Settings > Accounts.

12. B.

A virtual private network (VPN) is used to connect remote sites together securely over a public network.

13. C.

The server listens on TCP port 3389 and UDP port 3389 for remote connections.

14. B.

When Windows 10 is installed, it creates six default libraries for each user.

15. B.

Windows Task Scheduler is a tool that helps in scheduling repetitive tasks, such as backups, antivirus scans, and more.

16. B.

In this situation, the probable cause has been identified, and the exact cause has been acted upon. Documenting the findings is the last action in the process; it happens after checking that the problem has been solved by the solution implemented.

17. C, D, and F.

Typical causes of operating system problems include corrupted or missing system files, incorrect device driver, failed update or service pack installation, corrupted Registry, failing or faulty hard drive, incorrect password, virus infection, and spyware.

18. A.

The types of tasks that need to be scheduled include operating system and antivirus updates as well as hard drive routines.

Chapter 12

1. C.

Because mobile device apps run in a sandbox (an isolated location), it is difficult for malicious programs to infect mobile devices. The passcode and remote lock features secure a device against unauthorized use. The carrier may disable access to some features and programs based on the service contract, but this a commercial function rather than a security function.

2. A and B.

As an open source operating system, Android allows anyone to contribute to the development and evolution of compatible software. Android has been implemented on a wide range of devices and platforms, including cameras, smart TVs, and e-book readers. Royalties are not payable to Google, and Google has not tested and approved all available Android applications. Android applications are available from a range of sources.

3. A and D.

The physical Home button on an iOS device can perform many functions, depending on how it is used. Pressing the button while the device screen is turned off wakes the device. While an app is in use, pressing the Home button returns the user to the Home screen. Double-pressing the Home button while the screen is locked shows the audio controls, which makes it possible to adjust music volume without entering a passcode to enter the system.

4. A and B.

Locator apps and remote backup are two types of cloud-enabled services for mobile devices. Passcode configuration, screen calibration, and screen app locking are performed on a device directly by the user, not as cloud-enabled services.

5. C.

The permissions drwxr-x-r- indicate that the owner of the directory may read, write, and execute the files in the directory, the group members may read and execute the files in the directory but cannot create files, and all users may read files in the directory. By issuing the command **chmod 775 -R**

webpages, the administrator can allow the group members to create and modify files in the directory and subdirectories. The user is already a member in the group because the user can navigate in the directory and subdirectories.

6. B and E.

Rooting and jailbreaking are terms that describe unlocking Android and iOS mobile devices to grant users full access to the file system and full access to kernel modules. Remote wipe, sandboxing, and patching are examples of mobile operating system features and functions related to device security.

7. D.

If a problem with an Android device cannot be solved with a normal power off and on, a user can try a reset of the device. Holding the power button and the volume down keys until the device powers off and then powering it on is one of the ways to reset most Android devices.

8. A.

Both the macOS and Android operating systems use the Unix operating system software as a base.

9. B, D, and F.

A smartphone should use the screen lock feature to protect sensitive information so that to unlock the device, a password or passcode is required. Smartphones also support pattern locks, or swipe locks. Pattern locks eliminate the time it takes to type passwords or PINs. You just need to join the dots (numbers) on the keypad in a specific pattern to unlock the phone. Many modern mobile devices come with biometric authentication capability, such as fingerprint sensors and face recognition, for unlocking the device.

10. D.

By tapping the Recent Apps icon on the system bar, the user can see a list of recently used apps. A user can remove an app by swiping it to either side.

11. C.

On iOS devices, the passcode is used as part of the encryption key for the entire system. The passcode is not stored anywhere, and without it, no one (including Apple) can gain access to the user data on an iOS device. A forgotten passcode renders user data unreachable, forcing the user to perform a full restore from a backup saved in iTunes or iCloud.

12. A.

rm removes files, **man** displays the documentation for a specific command, **ls** displays the files inside a directory, **cd** changes the current directory, **mkdir** creates a directory under the current directory, and **move** moves files to a different directory.

13. B and C.

GPS services allow app vendors and websites to know the location of a device and offer location-specific services such as local weather and advertising.

14. C.

In Linux and OS X, the cron service is responsible for scheduled tasks. cron runs in the background and executes tasks at specific dates and times. cron uses a schedule table called a cron table that can be edited with the **crontab** command.

15. A and E.

To avoid the loss of irreplaceable information, it is critical that regular backups be executed and that the hard drives be checked regularly. The signature files are scanned constantly by anti-malware software. Updating the OS should happen when necessary but should not occur automatically. Because the factory reset of a device deletes all settings and user data, a factory reset should be done only if a major issue requires it.

Chapter 13

1. A.

Phishing attacks use social engineering to obtain personal information from users. Viruses carry malicious executable code that runs on target machines. Worms propagate through a network, consuming bandwidth resources. Adware results in pop-up windows directing users to malicious sites.

2. C.

A company security policy commonly includes incident handling procedures to follow when a security breach occurs.

3. C and E.

Adding an unauthorized wireless router or access point to a company network is a serious potential security threat. The device should be removed from the network immediately in order to mitigate the threat. In addition, the employee should be disciplined. The company security policy, which employees agree to, should describe penalties for behavior that threatens the security of the company.

4. C.

The last step before documenting findings is to verify full system functionality. Ensuring that all of the applications are working would be an example of verifying functionality. Asking what problem the user is experiencing is part of the first step: identifying the problem. Disconnecting from the network and rebooting in Safe mode are both examples of the third step: determining an exact cause.

5. D.

BitLocker To Go supports encrypting removable drives but does not require a TPM chip. However, it does require a password.

6. B.

Most web browsers offer a pop-up blocker. In Internet Explorer, use the Tools icon to enable it.

7. B.

A permission is a rule that is associated with a particular object, such as a file, folder, or printer. A right authorizes a user to perform an action, such as performing backups on a computer.

8. B and D.

Hardware firewalls can be configured as packet filters, application layer firewalls, or proxies. Application layer firewalls read all the traffic data and look for unwanted traffic. Proxies act as relays, scanning traffic and allowing or denying traffic based on established rules. Packet filters only concern themselves with port data, IP address data, and destination services.

9. C.

The Maximum Password Age setting defines the maximum number of days that can pass before the password must be changed.

10. D.

If a network is experiencing an extremely high volume of traffic, disconnecting a host from the network may enable you to confirm that the host is compromised and is flooding traffic onto the network. The other issues are hardware issues and not typically security related.

11. A.

Data encryption is the process of converting data into a form in which only a trusted, authorized person with a secret key or password can decrypt the data and access the original form.

12. B.

The two types of formatting that can be performed on a mechanical hard drive are low level and standard. The low-level format is commonly performed at the factory. The standard format only re-creates the boot sector and file allocation table.

13. C.

A social engineer attempts to gain the confidence of an employee and convince that person to divulge confidential and sensitive information, such as usernames and passwords. DDoS attacks, pop-ups, and viruses are all examples of software-based security threats, not social engineering.

14. B and D.

Three types of password protection that can be used to secure a workstation are the BIOS password configured through the BIOS Setup program; a login password such as a PIN, Windows, or picture password; and a network password that is kept on a server.

15. B.

Ransomware requires payment for access to the computer or files. Bitcoin is a type of digital currency that does not go through a particular bank.

Chapter 14

1. C.

The basic data types used in a script include int to represent integers, char to represent characters, float to represent decimal numbers, strings to represent alphanumeric characters, and Bool to represent true or false.

2. B.

Level one and level two technicians mainly work in call centers, but only level two technicians use remote access software. A bench technician often performs computer warranty service in a central depot or work facility. Field technicians work onsite, in private homes, businesses, and schools.

3. B.

It is important for a technician, when talking by phone with a customer, to be professional. Also, having good communication skills enhances credibility with the customer.

4. B.

When talking with a customer, a technician should allow the customer to tell the whole story. The technician should not interrupt the customer because doing so can be perceived as rude and disrespectful and may create tension between the customer and the technician.

5. B.

Customers who have computer problems probably feel stressed. A technician should establish a good rapport with a customer, which might allow the customer to relax a little bit. A relaxed customer might provide more information to help in troubleshooting the problem.

6. B.

A call center might exist within a company and offer service to the employees of that company as well as to the customers of that company. Alternatively, a call center might be an independent business that sells computer support as a service to outside customers. In either case, a call center is a busy, fast-paced work environment, often operating 24 hours a day.

7. D.

It is important to obtain written consent from the customer prior to backing up any data from the customer's PC.

8. C.

Scripting languages are different from compiled languages because each line is interpreted and then executed when the script is run. Scripting languages include Windows batch files, PowerShell, Linux shell script, VBScript, JavaScript, and Python.

9. A and E.

It is very important to make customers feel that they are being listened to. Interacting with them and using some interjections to let them know that you are listening as well as paraphrasing the problem back to them will show that you are listening. Interrupting them or making them repeat what they have already said and focusing on what you cannot do will make customers angry.

10. B.

During troubleshooting, when a technician listens and understands the computer problems from the customer, some more questions may need to be asked to gather further information. These follow-up questions should be targeted and closed-ended questions based on the information that has already been provided by the customer. The closed-ended questions should be focused on specific aspects, and the customer should be able to answer such a question with a simple "yes" or "no" or with a factual response.

11. B, D, and E.

The initial reason for accessing the computer, the suspected illegal matter or operations, and the location of the computer are immediately apparent to the technician and should be among the first details documented. Details of past computer users and the duration of the illegal activity are matters that the appropriate investigators will determine. The technical specifications of the computer may have little relevance to its illegal use.

12. C.

It is always important to allow the customer to finish explaining the problem at hand. You should always be attentive and actively listen to the customer, without interrupting, and should acknowledge the customer occasionally to affirm that you are actively listening to them.

13. D.

If a customer wants to talk to a specific technician, try to contact that technician and see if they can take the call. If the technician is not available, try to make an effort to help the customer and tell the customer that the favorite technician will contact the customer later if the customer prefers to wait.

14. B.

Sending unsolicited, chain, and forged emails is unethical, and possibly illegal, and a technician must not send them to a customer.

15. C.

Call prioritization is a very important task for a call center. Call prioritization saves time by solving the most important issues first. A failure that stops company operations should be considered a top priority.

16. C.

When dealing with a talkative customer, the technician should not encourage non-problem-related conversation. Instead, the technician should try to get the customer to refocus on the problem.

17. B and C.

A level one technician is primarily tasked with gathering pertinent information from the customer and then accurately entering that information into a trouble ticket or a work order. Sometimes a level one technician must escalate a task or problem to a level two technician if the problem requires a higher level of expertise.

18. C.

== represents equal

!= represents not equal

< represents less than

> represents greater than

<= represents less than or equal to

>= represents greater than or equal to

Because 5 is not equal to 7, the output of **A != is true.**

This glossary defines many of the terms and abbreviations used throughout the course and this book.

Numerics

/?   A basic **cmd** command for getting help on a specific command.

>   In the CLI, a symbol for sending the output of a command to a file.

1G/2G   First-generation (1G) cell phones that handled analog voice calls only and second-generation (2G) networks that handled digital calls.

2.5G   A cell phone generation that supports web browsing, short audio and video clips, games, and application and ring tone downloads.

3D printer   A printer used to create three-dimensional objects.

3G   A cell phone generation that supports faster data speeds as well as full-motion video, streaming music, 3D gaming, and faster web browsing.

3.5G   A cell phone generation that supports high-quality streaming video, high-quality video conferencing, and voice over IP (VoIP).

32-bit bus   A set of wires that transmits 32 bits of data at one time from the processor to RAM or to other motherboard components.

4G   A cell phone generation that supports IP-based voice, gaming services, high-quality streamed multimedia, and IPv6.

5G   A cell phone standard that was ratified in June 2018 and that is currently being implemented in select markets.

64-bit bus   A set of wires that transmits 64 bits of data at one time from the processor to RAM or to other motherboard components.

802.11 collective group   IEEE 802.11 and Wi-Fi group standards that specify the radio frequencies, speeds, and other capabilities for WLANs.

802.11 standard   An IEEE standard that specifies connectivity for wireless networks.

A

AAA server   *See* authentication, authorization, and accounting (AAA) server.

Accelerated Graphics Port (AGP)   A high-speed slot for attaching an AGP video card. AGP has been superseded by PCI.

acceptable use policy   A policy within a security policy that identifies network resources and usages that are acceptable to the organization. It may also identify ramifications of violating this policy.

acceptance   A step in the change management process that involves determining the parties responsible to accept the change.

access point (AP)   A device that connects to a wireless router and that is used to extend the reach of a wireless network.

account credentials   The username that is used to log into a mail or other server and the account password.

Active Directory   A database of all computers, users, and services in a Windows domain.

active listening skills   Skills related to really hearing what is being said and engaging with a person.

active partition   On MBR disks, the partition used to store and boot an operating system.

ActiveX filtering   A type of filtering that allows for web browsing without running ActiveX controls.

adapter   A component that physically connects one technology to another.

adapter card   A device that increases the functionality of a computer by adding controllers for specific devices or by replacing malfunctioning ports.

address bus   A set of wires that carries the memory addresses of the locations where data is read or written by the CPU.

administrative shares   Shares that are hidden from users and accessible only by members of the local administrators' group and identified with a dollar sign ($) at the end of the share name.

administrative tools   Tools that enable users to configure a wide range of system functions, such as general hardware, storage, and encryption settings and operations.

Administrative Tools control panel   A Control Panel item that includes a collection of tools that are used to monitor and configure Windows operation.

Administrator account   An account that has complete control over a computer and that can change settings globally, install programs, and get through User Account Control (UAC) when elevation to perform a task is required.

Administrators   A Windows group that has permissions that give full control of the computer and access to all folders.

Advanced Configuration and Power Interface (ACPI)   An interface that allows the operating system to control power management. Replaces Advanced Power Management (APM). Allows technicians to create power management schemes to get the best performance from a laptop.

Advanced Encryption Standard (AES)   A symmetric encryption method.

Advanced Technology (AT) power supply   The original power supply for legacy computer systems; now considered obsolete.

adware   Software that is usually distributed with downloads of online software. It can display unsolicited advertising using pop-up web browser windows or new toolbars, or it may unexpectedly redirect the user from a web page to a different website. Pop-up windows may be difficult to control as new windows can pop up faster than the user can close them.

AFP Apple Filing Protocol, a proprietary protocol developed by Apple to enable file services for macOS and classic Mac OS.

AirDrop A technology supported by Apple iOS and macOS that uses Bluetooth to establish a direct Wi-Fi connection between devices for file transfer.

Airplane mode A setting that turns off all cellular, Wi-Fi, and Bluetooth radios on a mobile device.

alternating current (AC) A current that changes direction at a uniformly repetitive rate. This type of electricity typically is provided by a utility company and is accessed through wall sockets.

analog telephone A device that can transmit data over standard voice telephone lines for Internet access. This type of service uses an analog modem to place a telephone call to another modem at a remote site. This method of connection is known as dialup.

Android An open source mobile operating system developed by Google.

Android Application Package (.apk) An archive format in which Android applications are packaged that allows third-party or custom programs to be installed directly, without going through the storefront interface.

Android Main Home Screen An Android setting that defines the format of the home screens and the look and feel of icons, buttons, the color scheme, and animations.

answer file A file that contains simple text that instructs Windows Setup how to configure and install the OS.

anti-malware program Software that continuously looks for known patterns against a database of known malware signatures to detect and block Trojans, rootkits, ransomware, spyware, keyloggers, and adware programs.

antivirus Software that relies on code signatures, which are files containing a sample of the code used by viruses and malware. Based on these signature files, the software scans the contents of a computer disk, comparing the contents of the files stored on the disk with the samples stored in the signature file.

App Store The place to download (for free or for purchase) apps for Apple iOS mobile devices.

Appearance and Personalization A Windows configuration category that permits configuration of the taskbar and navigation (via Settings), File Explorer, and available fonts.

Apple File System (APFS) The Apple Mac workstation file system, which supports native file encryption.

Apple ID A username required to set up an iOS device and used to access the Apple App Store, the iTunes Store, and iCloud.

Apple's Software Development Kit (SDK) Xcode A kit that third-party developers can use to create apps for iOS devices.

application programming interface (API) A set of guidelines that programmers follow to ensure that a new application is compatible with an OS.

applications Software programs that enable you to perform specific tasks, such as word processors, databases, spreadsheets, and games.

approval   A step in the change management process that involves verifying approval status.

apps   Applications; programs that are executed on mobile devices. Mobile devices come with a number of different apps preinstalled to provide basic functionality.

ASA firewall   A dedicated Cisco device that provides stateful firewall services. It ensures that internal traffic can go out and come back, but external traffic cannot initiate connections to inside hosts.

aspect ratio   The horizontal to vertical measurement of the viewing area of a monitor.

assessment   A step in the change management process that involves reviewing the impact of a change and the risk assessment.

asymmetric encryption   Encryption that ensures confidentiality of a message by requiring two keys: a private key and a public key. The public key can be widely distributed, including by being emailed in plaintext or posted on the Web. The private key is kept by an individual and must not be disclosed to any other party.

AT Extended (ATX)   A computer desktop power supply form factor. It is an updated version of the AT but still considered to be obsolete.

ATX12V   The most common power supply on the market today. It includes a second motherboard connector to provide dedicated power to the CPU.

audio   The sound system that comes with or can be added to a computer.

audio port   A port used to connect audio devices to a computer.

augmented reality (AR)   Computer technology that creates a simulated environment as it superimposes images and audio over the real world in real time.

authentication, authorization, and accounting (AAA) server   A device that controls who is permitted to access a network (authenticate) and what the user can do while there (authorize) and that tracks what actions the user can perform while accessing the network (accounting).

authentication methods   Ways to accomplish authentication, including using passwords, two-factor authentication, tokens, biometrics, and OTP.

automated   Preconfigured tasks that run according to conditions or timers and that can install software when appropriate without user intervention.

automatic document feeder (ADF)   A slot where an existing document can be placed in a machine in order to make copies of the document. One page of the document is pulled onto the glass surface of the platen, where it is scanned and copies are made. The page on the platen is then automatically removed, and the next page in the original document is pulled onto the platen. This process continues until the entire original document in the feeder has been pulled through.

Automatic Private IP Addressing (APIPA)   A form of addressing in which Windows automatically assigns an address to a computer that cannot communicate with a DHCP server to obtain an IPv4 address.

axis   In a 3D printer, one of several bars on which the hotend nozzle travels to dispense filament. Axes are vertical or horizontal so that the hotend nozzle can be located within a specified location in a 3D environment to "print" the object.

B

Background Intelligent Transfer Service (BITS) A Windows protocol that allows the OS to browse the update site and select updates for download and installation.

backlight A light that supplies the main source of light to the screen of a laptop display. Without it, the image on the screen would not be visible. The backlight shines through the screen and illuminates the display. Two common types of backlights are cold cathode fluorescent lamp (CCFL) and LED.

backup A copy of data that is made to protect the data. A phone backup, for example, includes application settings, text messages, voicemails, and other data types.

backup media A copy of computer data taken and stored locally or stored elsewhere so that it can be used to restore the original after a data loss event.

backup storage location The place where iOS backups are stored; iTunes allows backups to be stored on the local computer hard drive or on the iCloud online service.

Backup Straight from an iOS Device An iOS backup option that allows a user to configure an iOS device to upload a copy of its data directly to iCloud.

baiting An attack in which the attacker leaves a malware-infected flash drive in a public location (such as a corporate restroom), hoping a victim will find the drive and insert it into a laptop, where it installs the malware.

barcode scanner or price scanner A scanner that reads the information contained in the barcodes affixed to most products. These scanners can be handheld, wireless devices, or a stationary device.

basic disk The default disk type in Windows, which contains partitions such as primary and extended as well as logical drives that are formatted for data storage.

basic input/output system (BIOS) An older version of computer firmware that is responsible for hardware initialization, the power-on self-test (POST), and locating the Master Boot Record (MBR).

beep codes An audible reporting system for errors the BIOS finds during the POST.

belt The part that the print head stepper motor uses to move the print head assembly across the page. The belt will then apply the combined layers of ink color uniformly onto the paper.

biometric lock A type of secure lock that is unlocked using a biometric scanner such as a thumbprint reader.

BitLocker A feature that enables a user to encrypt all data on a disk drive or removable drive. Available on Windows 7 Enterprise and Ultimate, Windows 8 Pro and Enterprise, and Windows 10 Pro, Enterprise, and Education Editions.

blacklist A list that specifies which IP addresses are denied on a network and that automatically approves everything else.

blackout A complete loss of AC power.

Bluetooth A wireless industry standard that uses an unlicensed radio frequency for short-range communication, enabling portable devices to communicate over short distances.

Bluetooth Class 1   A type of Bluetooth with maximum permitted power of 100 mW and a power range of 100 meters.

Bluetooth Class 2   A type of Bluetooth with maximum permitted power of 2.5 mW and a power range of 10 meters.

Bluetooth Class 3   A type of Bluetooth with maximum permitted power of 1 mW and a power range of 1 meter.

Bluetooth pairing   The process in which two Bluetooth devices establish a connection to share resources.

Bluetooth Specification 1.0   An older Bluetooth technology with limited capabilities, high power consumption, and a data transfer rate of 1 Mbps.

Bluetooth Specification 2.0   An older Bluetooth technology with limited capabilities, high power consumption, and a data transfer rate of 3 Mbps.

Bluetooth Specification 3.0   An older Bluetooth technology with limited capabilities, high power consumption, and a data transfer rate of 24 Mbps.

Bluetooth Specification 4.0   A newer Bluetooth technology geared toward devices that have limited power and that do not need high data transfer rates; offers a rate of 1 Mbps.

Bluetooth Specification 5.0   A newer Bluetooth technology geared toward devices that have limited power and that do not need high data transfer rates; has four different data rates to accommodate a variety of transmission ranges.

Boot   A tab in System Configuration used to choose the Windows OS version to boot if more than one is present. You can also choose to boot up in Safe boot (formerly Safe mode) with different options regarding the way that Windows starts.

boot loader program   A program that is configured to locate and load an operating system from the boot device.

boot order   The sequence in which a computer should check devices for the operating system's boot files.

boot sector virus   A virus that attacks the boot sector, file partition table, or file system.

booting   The process of turning on a device and beginning the startup sequence, verifying hardware, and loading operating system software.

botnet   An army of compromised hosts.

branch cache   In Windows, a technology that enables remote computers to share access to a single cache of data from shared folders and files or document portals such as SharePoint sites. This can reduce WAN traffic because the individual clients do not each need to download their own copy of cache data.

bridge   A device that divides a LAN into segments. A bridge keeps a record of all the devices on each segment.

brightness   The luminance of a monitor, measured in candelas per square meter (cd/m^2).

broad network access   A type of network access in which capabilities are available over the network and can be accessed using smartphones, tablets, laptops, and workstations.

broadband   A transmission technique that uses different frequencies to send multiple signals over the same medium.

brownout   A temporary drop in AC power.

buffer   A component of fiber-optic cable that helps shield the core and cladding from damage.

buffered memory   A type of memory chip that has a control chip built into the module. The control chip assists the memory controller in managing large quantities of RAM.

bus   A collection of wires through which data travels from one part of a computer to another.

C

C   A compiled language that needs to be converted into executable code using a compiler. It performs almost as efficiently as assembly code.

C#   A compiled language that needs to be converted into executable code using a compiler. It is a high-level, object-oriented programming language that is also built as an extension of C.

C++   A compiled language that needs to be converted into executable code using a compiler. It is a low-level programming language that adds object-oriented features to its base language C.

cable modem   A device that is typically connected to a home or small office router so that multiple users can connect to a cable company's network that provides Internet access.

cable tester   A tool used to check for wiring shorts, faults, or wires connected to the wrong pins.

cache memory   Typically static RAM (SRAM) that is used for storing the data and instructions most recently used by the CPU.

call center   An organization to which customers call in to receive help for specific computer-related problems.

capture card   A device that sends a video signal to a computer so the signal can be recorded to a storage drive with video capture software.

carriage   Where the print head and ink cartridges are located on inkjet printers.

case fan   An active cooling solution to increase the airflow in a computer case to allow more heat to be removed.

cd   A command used to change the current directory to the path specified after the command in Linux, Microsoft CLI, PowerShell, and other CLIs.

cellular   A communications technology that handles the transfer of voice, video, and data. With a cellular WAN adapter installed, a user can access the Internet over the cellular network.

cellular WAN   A wide-area network that has the technology for the use of a cell phone or laptop for voice and data communications.

central processing unit (CPU)   A small microchip that is responsible for interpreting and executing commands.

centronics connector   A connector used for connecting older external SCSI devices such as scanners and printers. This connector came in 36-pin and 50-pin versions.

CGA   Color graphics adapter; an obsolete display standard that IBM introduced in 1981.

chain of custody   Proof of how evidence was collected, where it has been physically stored, and who has had access to it between the time of collection and its entry into the court proceedings.

change management process   A process that can prevent business functions from being negatively impacted by the updates, upgrades, replacements, and reconfigurations that are normally part of IT operations.

charging   A laser printer process in which the image on the drum is removed and the drum is conditioned for the new image. A wire, grid, or roller receives a charge of approximately –600 volts DC uniformly across the surface of the drum.

charms   In Windows 8, a feature that provides quick access to access to Search, Share, Start, Devices, and Settings.

chipset   A collection of integrated circuits on the motherboard that control how system hardware interacts with the CPU and motherboard and determines how much memory can be added to a motherboard and the type of connectors on the motherboard.

chkdsk   A command that checks a file system for errors, including errors with physical media, and repairs some file system errors. It requires Administrator privileges.

cladding   A component of fiber-optic cable that acts like a mirror, reflecting light back into the core of the fiber and keeping light in the core as it travels down the fiber.

clean   An OS installation in which all components of any previous version of the software are removed prior to installation.

clean install   An OS installation in which all components of any previous version of the software are removed prior to installation.

cleaning   In a laser printer, the process in which remaining toner is removed from the drum after an image has been deposited on the paper and the drum has separated from the paper.

client   A host that uses the services provided by servers.

client-side emulator   Both hardware and software that can be used to behave like or imitate a different system. Some uses are running an OS on a hardware platform for which it was not designed, running a Windows program on a Mac, and more.

client-side virtualization   A process in which virtual instances of clients are created on a single system to enable users with specific needs to run VMs on their local computer.

Clock and Region   A Windows category that enables configuration of time and date settings and formats. Location and language can also be configured here in some Windows versions.

clock multiplier   The speed ratio between a computer's front-side bus and the CPU.

clock speed   The speed at which data travels through the bus, measured in MHz or GHz.

closed source   Software for which the source code is not published.

closed-ended question   A question that requires a simple answer, such as yes or no, and that is intended to get the most relevant information in the shortest time.

cloud computing   A technology that separates applications from hardware and provides on-demand delivery of computing services over the network.

cloud computing services The delivery of computing services that are owned and hosted by service providers.

cloud printing The process of sending a print job to a remote printer.

cloud service provider A company that provides various services tailored to meet customer requirements.

cloud storage Online storage that is accessed over the Internet.

cloud-based network controller A device in the cloud that allows network administrators to manage network devices.

cls A command that deletes all command output and moves the command prompt to the top of the command window.

cmd The Windows command line utility, which is a remnant of the very early days of Microsoft, when DOS was the only operating system that Microsoft had to offer.

CMYK Cyan, magenta, yellow, and black; the colors in the inkjet color printing process.

coaxial cable A cable that is constructed of either copper or aluminum and that is used by both cable television companies and satellite communication systems. Coaxial cable is enclosed in a sheath or jacket and can be terminated with a variety of connectors.

color calibration The process of adjusting settings to match the colors on a screen to the colors on a printed sheet.

command line interface (CLI) A prompt at which a user types commands to interact with the OS.

commercial license A software license for a person who receives financial compensation of any sort, in any amount, for use of the software.

communication skills The ability to transfer information from one place to another verbally, in writing, nonverbally, or using a combination of modalities.

community cloud A cloud for exclusive use by specific entities or organizations that is customized for the community.

Compact Disc File System (CDFS) A file system created specifically for optical disc media.

CompactFlash An older type of flash memory that is still in wide use because of its high speed and high capacity.

Compatibility mode A mode that Windows provides to enable older applications to run when they otherwise might not run properly on newer Windows operating systems.

compiled language A language that needs to be converted into executable code using a compiler.

complementary metal-oxide semiconductor (CMOS) RAM that uses a battery to ensure that it maintains its settings while the computer is turned off.

complex instruction set computer (CISC) A CPU architecture that uses a broad set of instructions and requires fewer steps per operation.

Component Services A Windows Administrative Tool used by administrators and developers to deploy, configure, and manage Component Object Model (COM) components.

Computer Management console   A Windows console that enables management of many aspects of a computer and remote computers in one tool.

conditional statement   A statement such as an if-else or a case statement that is needed for scripts to make decisions.

connectivity   When used to describe a computer monitor characteristic, VGA, DVI, HDMI, DisplayPort, and so on.

contrast ratio   A measurement of the difference in intensity of light between the brightest point (white) and the darkest point (black).

Control Panel   A graphical centralized configuration area in Windows that can be used to modify the system in almost every aspect of the hardware and software, including OS functions.

controller card   A hardware component that works as an interface between the motherboard and other computer components.

conventional lock   A type of secure physical lock that is unlocked by entering the required key into the door handle mechanism.

converter   A device that physically connects one technology to another much like an adapter but that also translates the signals from one technology to the other.

copy   A command used to copy files.

core   The light transmission element at the center of optical fiber.

CPU fan   The fan that moves heat away from the metal fins of the heatsink.

CPU throttling   A technique that forces the processor to run at less than the rated speed to conserve power or produce less heat.

CPU virtualization   A hardware feature supported by AMD and Intel CPUs that enables a single processor to act as multiple processors. This hardware virtualization technology allows the operating system to support virtualization more effectively and efficiently than is possible through software emulation.

Credential Manager   A Windows utility that helps manage passwords that are used for websites, Windows applications, and networks.

crimper   A tool used to attach connectors to wires to make a cable.

Critical   An Event Viewer message type that indicates immediate attention is required. Usually related to system or software crashes or lockups.

cron   A CLI utility that can schedule tasks during off-peak hours.

Ctrl+C   A key combination that can be used in the CLI to exit a running command process or script.

Ctrl+Shift+Enter   A key combination that can be used in the CLI to run the command prompt as an administrator.

customer-replaceable units (CRUs)   Parts of a laptop that can be replaced by the customer.

cutoff switch   On the cover of many laptops, a small pin that contacts a switch when the case is closed and turns off the display to conserve power.

cyber law   A term to describe the international, regional, country, and state laws that affect computer security professionals.

D

daisy wheel   An impact printer with print heads that strike an inked ribbon, causing characters to be imprinted on the paper.

data backup   A copy of the data on a computer hard drive that is saved to another storage device or to cloud storage.

data bus   A system of wires that carries data between computer components.

data exfiltration   The process in which data is intentionally or unintentionally lost, stolen, or leaked to the outside world.

data loss prevention (DLP)   A set of tools and processes used to ensure that sensitive data is not lost, misused, or accessed by unauthorized users.

data migration   The process of transferring data and settings.

Data Sources   A tool that administrators use to add, remove, or manage data sources using Open Database Connectivity (ODBC).

data synchronization   The exchange of data between two or more devices while maintaining consistent data on those devices.

data type   A particular data item used by variables. Integers and strings are examples of data types.

data wiping software   Software tools specifically designed to overwrite existing data multiple times, rendering the data unreadable.

data-sending Trojan   Malware that provides the attacker with sensitive data, such as passwords.

Date and Time control panel   In Windows, the Control Panel item that provides the means to change the system time and date.

deadbolt lock   A type of secure physical lock that is unlocked by entering the required key into a lock separate from the door handle mechanism.

default gateway   The router interface that a device uses to access the Internet or another network.

Default Programs control panel   The Windows Control Panel item that provides the means to configure the way that Windows handles files and the applications that are used to work with them.

defense-in-depth   A layered approach to security that requires a combination of networking devices and services working together in tandem.

degaussing wand   A wand with very powerful magnets that is held over exposed hard drive platters to disrupt or eliminate the magnetic field on the hard drive.

del   A command used to delete a file or folder.

demilitarized zone (DMZ)   A network that provides services to an untrusted network so that the traffic using the server does not come inside the local network.

denial of service (DoS) Trojan   Malware that slows or halts network activity.

destination port number   The UDP or TCP port number associated with the destination application on a remote device.

destructive Trojan   Malware that corrupts or deletes files.

detachable touchscreen   A touchscreen that can be removed from a laptop and used like a tablet.

developing   The laser printer process in which toner is applied to the image on the drum.

device driver   Software used by an OS to access and communicate with each hardware component.

Device Manager   A Windows utility that displays a list of all the devices installed in the computer and that allows you to diagnose and resolve device problems.

Devices and Printers control panel   The Windows Control Panel item that provides a high-level view of the devices connected to a computer.

DHCP   *See* Dynamic Host Configuration Protocol (DHCP).

digital assistant   A program that can understand natural conversational language and perform tasks for the end user.

digital camera   An input device that captures images and videos that can be stored, displayed, printed, or altered.

Digital Light Processing (DLP)   A technology that uses a spinning color wheel with an array of mirrors. Each mirror corresponds to a pixel and reflects light toward or away from the projector optics, creating an image of up to 1024 shades of gray. The color wheel then adds the color data to complete the projected image.

digital rights management (DRM)   A type of software that is designed to prevent illegal access to digital content and devices.

digital signal processor (DSP)   A microprocessor chip that measures, filters, and/or compresses analog signals; it should be a factor considered when purchasing a new sound card.

Digital Visual Interface (DVI)   A technology for transmitting uncompressed digital video. A DVI connector consists of as many as 24 pins (3 rows of 8 pins) for digital signals, up to 4 pins for analog signals, and a flat pin called a ground bar.

dir   A command used to display various file attributes and properties.

directory   A location used to store programs and data files, typically displayed in a hierarchical tree structure.

DirectX   A collection of APIs related to multimedia tasks for Microsoft Windows.

DirectX Diagnostic (DxDiag) tool   A tool that displays details for all DirectX components and drivers that are installed in a computer.

Disable a Device   A Device Manager option for disabling a device.

disaster recovery plan   A comprehensive document that describes how to restore operations quickly and keep critical IT functions running during or after a disaster.

discoverable mode   The mode Bluetooth devices must be set to so that they can be detected for pairing. This is also called visible.

disk cloning   A process that involves duplicating all the information on a disk, sector by sector, to another disk.

disk error checking   A process that involves checking the integrity of files and folders by scanning the hard disk surface for physical errors.

Disk Management utility   The part of the Windows Computer Management console that is used for extending and shrinking partitions, viewing drive status, assigning and changing drive letters, adding drives, adding arrays, and designating the active partitions.

disk optimization   Use of tools to perform hard drive defragmentation to gather the noncontiguous data into one place and enable the OS to run faster.

disk utility   A tool used to help diagnose and solve disk-related problems that includes most modern operating systems.

diskpart   A command that starts a separate command interpreter with commands for working with disk partitions.

dism   A command that is used to work with system images before they are deployed.

display colors   The number of colors to display, or the bit depth; the higher the bit depth, the greater the number of colors.

display name   The name that appears to the public when you create an account; can be your real name, nickname, or any other name that you want people to see.

DisplayPort   An interface technology designed to connect high-end graphics-capable PCs and displays, as well as home theater equipment and displays.

distributed DoS   Distributed denial of service; an attack that completely overwhelms a target device by having many infected hosts called zombies send false requests to create a denial of service condition for legitimate users.

DNS   Domain Name System; a system that provides a way to map an IP address to a registered Internet domain for Web, email, and other Internet services.

DNS poisoning   An attack in which an attacker has successfully infected a host to accept false DNS records pointing to malicious servers.

do-while loop   A statement that repeats a section of code and then checks a variable to verify whether it is true (or false). Also known as a post-test loop.

documentation   A step in the change management process that involves determining and monitoring change logs, implementation steps, and collected documents.

domain   A group of computers and electronic devices with a common set of rules and procedures that are administered as a unit.

dot matrix   An impact printer with print heads that strike an inked ribbon, causing characters to be imprinted on the paper.

dot pitch   The distance between pixels on the screen. A lower dot pitch (that is, a smaller distance between dots) produces a better image.

dots per inch (dpi)   A measure of the quality of printing. The larger the dpi number, the better the image resolution.

Double Data Rate 2 SDRAM (DDR2)   A form of memory that runs at higher clock speeds than DDR (553 MHz vs. DDR at 200 MHz) and improves performance by decreasing noise and crosstalk between signal wires.

Double Data Rate 3 SDRAM (DDR3)   A form of memory that expands memory bandwidth by doubling the clock rate of DDR2 and that generates less heat than DDR2.

Double Data Rate 4 SDRAM (DDR4)   A form of memory that quadruples DDR3 maximum storage capacity and consumes less power than DDR3, at 1.2V.

Double Data Rate 5 SDRAM (DDR5)   A form of memory that doubles the speed of the fastest DDR4 and consumes slightly less power, at 1.1V.

Double Data Rate SDRAM (DDR)   A form of memory that can support two writes and two reads per CPU clock cycle and that transfers data twice as fast as SDRAM.

double parity   A RAID type that provides fault tolerance for up to two failed drives.

drive activity LEDs   Lights that indicate when a computer system is reading or writing to hard drives.

drive encryption   A technology that protects information on a hard drive by converting it into unreadable code to prevent data theft.

Drive Status   The part of the Disk Management utility that shows the condition of the drives.

DSL   Digital Subscriber Line; an always-on service that connect to the Internet. With DSL, voice and data signals are carried on different frequencies on the copper telephone wires.

dual channel   A type of memory that has a second channel so it can access a second module at the same time.

dual core CPU   A single CPU with two cores, in which both cores can process information at the same time.

dual inline memory module (DIMM)   A circuit board that holds various memory chips. There are 168-pin SDRAM DIMMs, 184-pin DDR DIMMs, 240-pin DDR2 and DDR3 DIMMs, and 288-pin DDR4 DIMMs.

dual inline package (DIP)   An individual memory chip that has dual rows of pins used to attach it to the motherboard.

dual rail   A power supply that splits the total amperage capability among four circuits. This can allow for safer operation because you're not forcing loads of power through a single rail.

Dumpster diving   An in-person attack in which an attacker rummages through trash bins to discover confidential documents.

duplex multimode LC connector   A fiber-optic connector that accepts both the transmitting and receiving fibers in a single connector.

duplexing assembly   A part of a printer that turns a printed page over and feeds it back through the printer to be printed on the other side.

DVI   *See* Digital Visual Interface (DVI).

dynamic disk   A physical disk that provides features not supported by basic disks and that has the ability to create volumes that span multiple disks.

Dynamic Host Configuration Protocol (DHCP)   A protocol that automatically provides IP addresses to network hosts and provides a way to manage those addresses.

dynamic RAM (DRAM)   An older technology, historically used for main memory, that gradually discharges energy so it must be constantly refreshed in order to maintain the data stored in the chip.

E

Ease of Access   A Windows settings category that provides many options that make Windows easier to use, especially for people who require accommodations for physical or perceptual challenges.

electrically erasable programmable read-only memory (EEPROM)   A form of memory in which information is written to the memory chip after it is manufactured and without being removed from the device. The contents can be "flashed" for deletion. EEPROMs are often used to store a computer system's BIOS.

electromagnetic degaussing device   A tool that is useful for erasing multiple drives. It consists of a magnet with an electrical current applied to it to create a very strong magnetic field that disrupts or eliminates the magnetic field on a hard drive.

electronic lock   A type of secure physical lock that is unlocked by entering a secret combination code or PIN into the keypad.

electronic protected health information (ePHI)   The electronic version of PHI, which includes patient names, addresses, dates of visits, telephone and fax numbers, and email addresses.

electrostatic discharge   The release of a buildup of electric charge on a surface that comes into contact with another, differently charged, surface.

email   Electronic mail; a store-and-forward method of sending, storing, and retrieving electronic messages across a network.

email address   The address people need to send email to you.

email protocol   A protocol used by an incoming email server.

Email Security Appliance (ESA)   A Cisco-proprietary device that filters spam and suspicious emails.

Encrypting File System (EFS)   A file system used on Windows 7 Professional, Enterprise, and Ultimate, Windows 8 Pro and Enterprise, and Windows 10 Pro, Enterprise, and Education Editions that allows the user to configure file- and folder-level encryption. EFS is directly linked to a specific user account. Only the user who encrypted the data can access it after it has been encrypted using EFS.

encryption   A process in which data is transformed using a complicated algorithm to make it unreadable. A special key must be used to turn the unreadable information back into readable data.

end devices   Computers connected to a network that participate directly in network communication.

end user license agreement (EULA)   A license between a software owner and an individual end user.

endpoint management server   A server that is typically responsible for monitoring all the end devices in a network, including desktops, laptops, servers, tablets, and any device connected to the network. An endpoint management server can restrict an end device's connection to the network if the device does not meet certain predetermined requirements.

Enhanced Capabilities Port (ECP)   A parallel port that supports bidirectional communication but offers higher throughput than EPP. *See also* EPP.

Enhanced Parallel Port (EPP)   A parallel port that supports bidirectional communication.

enterprise license   A software site license held by a company. Typically with an enterprise license, the company pays for its employees to use the software.

environmental variable   A variable that an operating system uses to keep track of important details such as username, home directory, and language.

EPS12V   A computer desktop power supply form factor that was originally designed for network servers but that is now commonly used in high-end desktop models.

erasable programmable read-only memory (EPROM)   Nonvolatile memory that can be erased through exposure to strong ultraviolet light. Constant erasing and reprogramming could ultimately render an EPROM chip useless.

e-reader   A special-purpose device with a black-and-white display that has been optimized for reading text.

error   An Event Viewer message type that indicates a problem exists, but no immediate action is required.

error-correcting code (ECC) memory   Data storage that can detect multiple bit errors in memory and correct single bit errors in memory.

eSATA adapter card   An adapter that is installed in a computer to provide eSATA ports.

eSATA cable   A cable that is used to connect external SATA drives. An eSATA port has a key feature to prevent inadvertent insertion of a USB connector.

eSATA card   A card that adds additional internal and external SATA ports to a computer through a single PCI Express slot.

Ethernet   A protocol used to connect devices together in a LAN. An Ethernet cable is a common type of network cable used with wired networks.

Ethernet over Power   A technology called powerline networking that uses existing electrical wiring to connect devices and provides the ability to connect a device to the network wherever there is an electrical outlet.

EU General Data Protection Regulation (GDPR)   A European regulation that governs the handling of personal data, including financial and healthcare information.

Event Viewer   A Windows component that shows the history of application, security, and Windows system events.

execute disable (NX) bit   A technology used in CPUs to protect areas of memory that contain operating system files from malicious attacks by malware.

exFAT   A file system created to address some of the limitations of FAT, FAT32, and NTFS when formatting USB flash drives. One of the primary advantages of exFAT is that it can support files larger than 4GB.

exit   A command used to close the command window.

expansion card   A card that gives a computer additional capabilities.

expansion port   A connection port on a computer that allows various types of peripheral devices to be connected to the system externally.

expansion slot   A computer slot that allows connections to the system bus for the various types of adapter cards, allowing expansion of system performance.

EXPLORER   A shortcut that opens File Explorer or Windows Explorer when typed in the Start Button search box.

exposing   A part of the laser printing process that involves exposing the photosensitive drum with a laser beam. Every portion of the drum that is scanned with the light has the surface charge reduced to about −100 volts DC. This electrical charge has a lower negative charge than the rest of the drum. As the drum turns, an invisible image is created on the drum.

ExpressCard/34   An expansion slot available on some laptops to add functionality. The expansion slot is 34 mm wide and 75 mm long.

ExpressCard/54   An expansion slot available on some laptops to add functionality. The expansion slot is 54 mm wide and 75 mm long.

ext3   A 64-bit Linux file system with support for journaling.

ext4   A Linux file system that delivers significantly better performance than ext3.

Extended Hierarchical File System (HFS Plus)   An Apple Mac file system that supports many of the same features as NTFS in Windows but not native file/folder encryption.

extended partition   A primary partition that has been divided into logical partitions to make more partitions than the four that would otherwise be possible.

external flash drive   A removable storage device that connects to an expansion port such as USB, eSATA, or FireWire.

external Serial ATA (eSATA)   A port that is designed to work with both SATA and USB.

F

F7 key   In the CLI, a shortcut that moves through the previously entered commands.

F8 key   A key that can be pressed during the boot process to open the Windows Advanced Boot Options menu.

facial recognition scanner   A biometric input device used to identify a person based on their unique facial features.

Failure Audit (security only)   A security auditing event enabled in Windows Group Policy (in an Active Directory environment) or Local Security Policy (for a single computer). It is triggered by failed attempts at computer login.

feeder   The part of a 3D printer that takes filament from a feed tube that is placed into the extruder and pulls it down to be heated and then exit through the hotend nozzle.

fiber-optic cable   A cable composed of two kinds of glass (core and cladding), surrounded by insulating material and a protective outer shield (jacket).

fiber to the curb (FTTC)   Fiber-optic cabling that is used in the last mile. At the customer's building or home, the cabling switches to copper coaxial cable.

fiber to the premises (FTTP)   Fiber-optic cabling that is brought into the customer's building or home.

field-replaceable units (FRUs)   Parts of a laptop that should not be replaced by the customer but by a certified service center or the manufacturer.

filament   The material used in 3D printers to create objects.

file   A block of related data that is given a single name and treated as a single unit.

File Allocation Table, 32-bit (FAT32)   A file system that supports partition sizes up to 2 TB or 2048 GB and that is used by Windows XP and earlier OS versions.

file backup   A backup done for disaster recovery purposes that stores only the specific files indicated at the time the backup is run, no matter which type of backup is made.

File Explorer Options   The Windows Control Panel item where many of the most commonly used file and folder options can be found.

File History   A Windows application that backs up the files in the libraries, on the desktop, in the Favorites folders, and in the Contacts folders in Windows 8 and Windows 10.

file system   A process that provides the directory structure that organizes the user's operating system, application, configuration, and data files.

File Transfer Protocol Secure (FTPS)   An encrypted version of FTP.

fingerprint scanner   A biometric input device used to identify a person based on their fingerprint.

firewall   Hardware or software that protects computers and networks by preventing undesirable traffic from entering internal networks.

firewall apps   Apps for mobile devices that can monitor app activity and prevent connections to specific ports or IP addresses.

FireWire   An external connector, similar to a USB port, that provides a high-speed connection between a computer and peripheral devices.

firmware   Permanent software programmed into read-only memory.

firmware virus   A virus that attacks device firmware.

first response   The term used to describe the official procedures employed by those who are qualified to collect evidence.

fitness tracker   A device that is similar to a smartwatch but that is limited to monitoring a person's physical activity, sleep, and exercise.

flash card   A data storage device that uses flash memory to store information.

flash card reader   A peripheral device that reads and writes memory cards, such as Secure Digital (SD) and Secure Digital High Capacity (SDHC) flash cards.

flash memory   A solid-state storage device with no moving parts and nonvolatile memory.

fluorescent backlight   A backlight that shines through an LCD screen and illuminates the display.

folder   A Windows directory.

Folder Options   In Windows 7 and earlier, the Control Panel item where many of the most commonly used file and folder options can be found.

footprinting   The phase of a network attack in which the attacker attempts to learn as much about the target network as possible.

for loop   A statement that repeats a section of code a specified number of times.

form factor   A device's physical design and look.

format   A command used to create a new file system for a disk. It requires Administrator privileges.

formatting   The process of creating a file system on a partition for file storage.

frames per second (FPS)   How many times the computer is creating each frame.

front-side bus (FSB)   The path between the CPU and the Northbridge.

FTP   File Transfer Protocol; a protocol used to transfer files between computers that is considered insecure.

FTP Trojan   Malware that enables unauthorized file transfer services on end devices.

full access   One of the common levels of user access to BIOS, in which all screens and settings are available, except the supervisor password setting.

Full Control   A Windows permission for files and folders that allows users to see the content of a file or folder, change and delete existing files and folders, create new files and folders, and run programs in a folder.

full format   A type of hard drive formatting that removes files from the partition while scanning the disk for bad sectors. It is required for all new hard drives.

function (Fn) key   A keyboard key that can be used to activate a second function on a dual-purpose key.

fuser assembly   A laser printer component that is made up of hot rollers that melt toner into the paper.

fusing   The laser printer process in which toner is permanently fused to the paper.

G

gadgets   In Windows 7, small applications, such as games, sticky notes, a calendar, or a clock on the desktop, that put content, information, and functions in a convenient place.

game port   A device port that connects a joystick or MIDI-interfaced device to a computer.

GDDR Synchronous Dynamic RAM   RAM specifically designed for video graphics that is used in conjunction with a dedicated GPU.

General   The tab in Windows System Configuration that displays three startup selections for troubleshooting: Normal Startup, Diagnostic Startup, and Selective Startup.

Global Positioning System (GPS)   A satellite-based navigation system that transmits signals to Earth.

Global System for Mobile Communications (GSM)   A digital cellular technology used for transmitting mobile voice and data services.

globally unique identifier (GUID) partition table (GPT)   A partition table scheme standard for hard drives that makes use of a number of modern techniques to expand on the older MBR partitioning scheme. GPT is commonly used in computers with UEFI firmware. Most modern operating systems support GPT.

Google Play   The place to get Android apps.

gpresult   A command used to display the Group Policy settings that are in effect for a currently logged in user.

GPS receiver   A device that locks onto GPS signals and constantly calculates its position relative to satellites.

gpupdate   A command that can be used to do a Group Policy update.

graphical user interface (GUI)   An interface that allows a user to interact with the OS by using menus and icons.

graphics card   Computer hardware that produces the images shown on a monitor.

graphics card cooling system   A video adapter card fan that is used to cool the GPU.

guest operating system (guest OS)   The operating system that is running in a VM.

Guests   A Windows group that people can use to access a computer through a temporary profile that is created at logon and deleted on logoff. Guest accounts are disabled by default.

H

hard disk drive (HDD)   A traditional magnetic storage disk device, with speed measured in revolutions per minute (RPM).

hard drive caching   Storing printer files in cache, which poses privacy and security risks because someone with access to the device could recover these files and have access to confidential or personal information.

hardware   The physical components in a computer system.

hardware access   Communication with a hardware component in a computer, which is governed by a device driver.

Hardware and Sound   A Windows settings category that permits configuration of devices such as printers, media devices, power, and mobility.

Hardware control panel   The Windows Control Panel item that contains tools a technician can use to add and remove printers and other types of hardware, configure AutoPlay, manage power, and update drivers.

hash encoding   A type of encoding that ensures the integrity of a message.

HD   High definition; a display standard.

Health Insurance Portability and Accountability Act (HIPAA)   A U.S. regulation that describes penalties for breaches of PHI and ePHI.

health monitoring device   A device that can deliver hospital-quality data to healthcare practitioners by detecting heart attacks, monitoring air quality, or detecting oxygen levels in the blood.

Healthy A Disk Management utility status that indicates a volume that is functioning properly.

heat sink A large surface area with metal fins installed on top of the CPU to dissipate heat into the surrounding air and draw heat away from the CPU core.

help A command that gets information on other commands.

hexa-core CPU A single CPU with six cores inside it.

Hibernate An option that causes documents, applications, and the state of the operating system to be saved to a temporary file on the hard drive. With this option, the computer takes a little longer to power on than from the Sleep state, but it does not use any power to retain the information on the hard drive.

High-Definition Multimedia Interface (HDMI) A digital interface used to transmit audio and video data in a single cable.

hives Multiple database files in the Windows Registry that are associated with each of the top-level registry keys.

HKEY_CLASSES_ROOT A Windows Registry key that contains settings about the file system, file associations, and shortcuts. Information here is used when you ask Windows to run a file or view a directory.

HKEY_CURRENT_CONFIG A Windows Registry key that contains information about the current hardware profile of the machine.

HKEY_CURRENT_USER A Windows Registry key that contains data about the preferences of the currently logged on user, including personalization settings, default devices, and programs.

HKEY_LOCAL_MACHINE A Windows Registry key that contains information about the physical state of the computer, including hardware configuration, network logon and security information, and Plug and Play information.

HKEY_USERS A Windows Registry key that contains all the configuration settings for the hardware and software configured on the computer for all users.

Home button On iPhone versions prior to the iPhone X, a physical button that performs navigation and other functions.

Home Network A network location profile in HomeGroup that allows you to create or join a HomeGroup.

HomeGroup A Windows option that allows computers on the same home network to automatically share files and printers.

host computer A physical computer controlled by a user. VMs use the system resources of the host machine to boot and run an OS.

host operating system (host OS) The operating system of a host computer. Users can use a virtualization emulator on the host OS to create and manage VMs.

host-based authentication A form of authentication in which the client requests authentication with a public key. The server generates a challenge with this key, and the client must decrypt it with the matching private key to complete the authentication.

host-based firewall   A firewall on each individual host computer that controls incoming and outgoing network traffic and determines whether to allow it into a particular device.

hotend nozzle   A part of a 3D printer that extrudes the filament after it is heated to the correct temperature.

HTTP   Hypertext Transfer Protocol; a protocol that provides a set of rules for exchanging text, graphic images, sound, video, and other multimedia files on the World Wide Web.

HTTPS   Hypertext Transfer Protocol Secure; a protocol that provides a set of rules for exchanging text, graphic images, sound, and video on the World Wide Web. HTTPS adds encryption and authentication services using Secure Sockets Layer (SSL) protocol or the newer Transport Layer Security (TLS) protocol.

hub   A device that extends the reach of a network by regenerating the electrical signal. It also receives data on one port and then sends it out to all other active ports. Hubs are legacy devices that do not segment network traffic and should not be used in today's networks.

hybrid cloud   A cloud made up of two or more different cloud types (such as part private and part public), where each part remains a distinctive object, but the parts are connected using a single architecture.

hyper-threading   A process in which multiple pieces of code (threads) are executed simultaneously in the CPU.

HyperTransport   A technology used to enhance CPU performance that provides a high-speed, low-latency connection between the CPU and the Northbridge chip.

hypervisor   Software used on a host computer to create and manage VMs. It is the brain of virtualization.

I

i.LINK   A high-speed communication bus that is platform independent. Also known as FireWire or IEEE 1394.

I/O card   Another term for an expansion card.

IDE   *See* Integrated Drive Electronics (IDE) *and* Integrated Development Environment (IDE).

IDE ribbon cable   A type of cable used for floppy drives, hard drives, and optical drives.

identification   A step in the change management process that defines the change request.

Identification and Authentication Policies   A security policy item that specifies authorized persons who may access network resources and that outlines verification procedures.

IEEE 1284   The standard for parallel printer ports.

IEEE 1394   A high-speed communication bus that is platform independent. Also known as i.LINK.

IEEE 802.11i/WPA2   The industry standard for securing WLANs.

image backup   A backup done for disaster recovery purposes that records all the information stored on the computer at the time the image is created.

image-based internal partition installation   A Windows image stored on an internal (often hidden) partition that can be used to restore Windows to its original state when it was shipped from the factory.

imaging drum The central part of a laser printer, which is a metal cylinder that is coated with light-sensitive insulating material. When a beam of laser light strikes the drum, it becomes a conductor at the point where the light hits it.

impersonation A type of attack in which an attacker pretends to be someone they are not (such as a new employee, a fellow employee, a vendor or partner company employee) to gain the trust of a victim.

implementation The step in the change management process that determines the steps to complete and how to test the results.

incident handling policy A security policy item that describes how security incidents are handled.

incoming and outgoing mail server names The names for mail servers, which are provided by a network administrator or ISP.

indoor positioning system (IPS) A system that can determine device location by triangulating the proximity based on radio signals such as Wi-Fi access points.

Information An Event Viewer message type that indicates a successful event.

infrared (IR) A wireless mobile technology used for device communication over short ranges.

Infrastructure as a Service (IaaS) A service in which a cloud provider manages the network and provides access to network equipment, virtualized network services, storage, software, and supporting network infrastructure.

inkjet printer A type of non-impact printer that creates output by spraying ink onto the material being printed on.

InPrivate mode A browser mode that makes it possible to browse the web anonymously without retaining information. In this mode, the browser temporarily stores files and cookies and deletes them when the InPrivate session is ended.

input device A hardware device, usually outside the computer case, that allow input of raw data for a computer to process.

input/output (I/O) port A port used to connect peripheral devices such as printers, scanners, and portable drives to a computer.

Institute of Electrical and Electronics Engineers (IEEE) standards Standards by a global association and organization of professionals working toward the development, implementation, and maintenance of technology-centered products and services.

Institute of Electrical and Electronics Engineers (IEEE) 802.15.1 standard The Bluetooth standard, which defines physical layer (PHY) and Media Access Control (MAC) specifications for wireless connectivity with fixed, portable, and moving devices within or entering personal operating space.

Integrated Development Environment (IDE) A suite of tools used to write and test scripts.

Integrated Drive Electronics (IDE) A standard type of interface used to connect some hard drives and optical drives to each other and to the motherboard.

integrated graphics processing unit (GPU) A chip that performs the rapid mathematical calculations required to render graphics.

Integrated Services Digital Network (ISDN)   A broadband standard that uses multiple channels to send voice, video, and data over normal telephone wires.

intermediary devices   Devices that exist in between host devices to ensure that data flows from one host device to another host device.

International Mobile Equipment Identity (IMEI)   A unique 15-digit number used to identify a mobile device. This number identifies the device to a carrier's network.

Internet Control Message Protocol (ICMP)   A communications protocol used by devices on a network to send control and error messages.

Internet email   Email service that is hosted on the Internet and controlled by a service provider such as Gmail.

Internet Mail Access Protocol (IMAP)   A communications protocol used to retrieve email messages from a server. It is more advanced than POP3 and offers a number of advantages.

Internet Options   A group of settings used to configure Microsoft Internet Explorer.

Internet Protocol (IP) address   An address assigned as part of connecting to a network. There are two versions: IPv4 and IPv6. *See also* IPv4 address *and* IPv6 address.

intrusion detection system (IDS)   A system that passively monitors traffic on a network.

intrusion prevention system (IPS)   A system that monitors incoming and outgoing traffic, looking for malware and network attack signatures. If it recognizes a threat, it can immediately stop it.

inverter   A device located behind the screen panel on an LCD laptop screen that is used to convert direct current (DC) to alternating current (AC).

iOS   A closed source Unix-based operating system for Apple's iPhone smartphone and iPad tablet.

iOS Erase Data   An iOS data option that causes the device's screen to go black and all the data on the device to be deleted if the wrong passcode is entered a specified number of times (such as 10).

iOS GUI   The user interface on an iOS device.

iOS interface   An iOS screen that is used to organize apps and from which apps are launched with a touch.

iOS Notification Center   A page that displays all iOS alerts in one location. To open the notification area on iOS devices, touch the top center of the screen and swipe down.

iOS Spotlight   An iOS search field that shows suggestions from many sources, including the device itself, the Internet, iTunes, the App Store, and nearby locations.

IoT   Internet of Things; a network of many smart devices that extends Internet connectivity beyond standard devices, like computers and smartphones, to include devices like refrigerators and TVs that are embedded with sensors and other technology to allow them to become part of the network.

IP address   *See* Internet Protocol (IP) address.

ipconfig   A command that displays basic IP configuration information, including the IP address, subnet mask, and default gateway for every network adapter to which TCP/IP is bound.

IPv4 address   An address assigned to a device connected to a computer network that is composed of two parts: a part that identifies the network and a part that identifies the device on the network.

IPv6 address   An address assigned to a device connected to a computer network that is 128 bits and is represented in hexadecimal format.

J

jacket   A component of fiber-optic cable that protects against abrasion, moisture, and other contaminants.

jailbreaking   A process used on iOS devices to remove manufacturer restrictions and make it possible to run arbitrary user code and grant users full access to the file system and full access to kernel modules.

Java   A compiled language that needs to be converted into executable code using a compiler.

Java APIs   A collection of APIs related to the development of Java programming.

JavaScript   A client-side scripting language that runs in a browser.

jump list   A list of tasks that are unique to an application. To open an application's jump list, right-click the application's icon in the taskbar.

K

Kerberos   An authentication protocol that allows for single sign-on (SSO).

keylogger Trojan   Malware that actively attempts to steal confidential information, such as credit card numbers, by recording keystrokes entered into a web form.

keys   A hierarchical arrangement of registry values in the Windows Registry.

KVM switch   A hardware device that can be used to control more than one computer while using a single keyboard, monitor, and mouse.

L

L1 cache   Typically static RAM (SRAM) internal cache that is integrated into the CPU.

L2 cache   External cache originally mounted on the motherboard near the CPU and now integrated into the CPU.

L3 cache   Static RAM (SRAM) memory used on some high-end workstations and server CPUs.

land grid array (LGA)   A chip in which the pins are in the socket instead of on the processor.

laptop   A portable computer.

laptop display   The output device that shows all the onscreen content and is one of the most expensive components of a laptop.

laser printer   A high-quality, fast printer that uses a laser beam to create an image.

Last Known Good Configuration   A setting that loads the configuration settings that were used the last time that Windows started successfully. It requires accessing a copy of the Registry that is created for this purpose.

LDAP   Lightweight Directory Access Protocol; a protocol used to maintain user identity directory information that can be shared across networks and systems.

LED-based backlight   A backlight that shines through an LED screen and illuminates the display.

legacy system   A computer or networking system that is no longer supported but that is still in operation in today's networks.

level one technician   A technician whose primary responsibilities are to gather pertinent information from the customer and accurately enter all the information into a ticket or work order.

level two technician   A technician who is typically more knowledgeable and experienced than a level one technician or who has been working for the company for a longer period of time and receives an escalated work order with the description of the problem and then calls the customer back to ask any additional questions and resolves the problem.

light-emitting diode (LED)   An LCD display that uses LED backlighting. LED consumes less power than standard LCD backlighting.

Lightning   A small proprietary 8-pin connector used by Apple mobile devices such as iPhones, iPads, and iPods for both power charging and data transfer.

Lightning cable   A cable used to connect Apple devices to host computers and other peripherals, such as USB battery chargers, monitors, and cameras.

line-of-sight wireless   An always-on service that uses radio signals for transmitting data and Internet access. A clear path between the transmission tower and customer is required.

link-local address   An address used by a device to communicate with other computers connected to the same network within the same IP address range.

Linux shell script   A Linux shell interpreted language.

liquid crystal display (LCD)   A display that has two polarizing filters with a liquid crystal solution between them. An electronic current aligns the crystals so light can pass through or not pass through, creating the image.

load balancer   A device that can be used to distribute incoming traffic to multiple devices, typically servers.

local area network (LAN)   A network that connects devices using wire cables in a small geographical area. A LAN is typically owned by an individual, such as in a home or small business, or wholly managed by an IT department, such as in a school or corporation.

local backup   A backup that uses local storage such as an external HDD or flash media to store backed up files and that can be accessible if there is no network connectivity.

local email   An email server managed by a local IT department such as a school network, business network, or organizational network.

local installation   An OS installation that occurs from the hard drive, CD, DVD, or USB media.

Local Users and Groups   A Windows administrative tool that provides an efficient way of managing users.

locator application   An Android or iOS app that makes it possible to find a mobile device that is misplaced or stolen.

logical drive   A section of an extended partition that can be used to separate information for administrative purposes.

logical partitions   Areas in a hard drive that provide logical storage units that can be formatted to store information, such as data files or applications.

LoJack   A security feature that is used to find a lost or stolen device.

loop   A device used in coding to repeat commands or tasks.

loopback adapter   A tester that determines the basic functionality of computer ports.

low Earth orbit   A new type of high-speed, low-latency satellite service that has satellites orbiting the Earth in a very low orbit.

low-level formatting   A type of disk formatting in which the surface of the disk is marked with sector markers that identify tracks where the data will be physically stored on the disk.

LTE   A designation for a 4G technology that meets the 4G speed standards.

Lucent connector (LC)   A smaller version of the fiber-optic SC connector, sometimes called a local connector.

M

MAC address filtering   A security method that specifies exactly which device MAC addresses are allowed for or blocked from sending data on a network.

macro virus   A virus that uses the Microsoft Office macro feature maliciously.

magnetic stripe reader   A device that reads information that is magnetically encoded on the back of plastic cards, such as identification badges or credit cards.

malware   Software developed to perform malicious acts.

man-in-the-middle   An attack in which the attacker intercepts communications between two hosts.

mantrap   A small room with two doors, one of which must be closed before the other can be opened; controls physical access to sensitive areas of a building.

mapped drive   A drive that makes it possible to access a single file, specific folders, or an entire drive between different operating systems over a network.

master boot record (MBR)   A kind of boot sector that is stored on a hard disk drive or other storage device that contains the necessary computer code to start the boot process.

maximum speed rating   The maximum speed at which a processor can function without errors.

md   A command used to create a new directory.

mean time between failures (MTBF)   The average length of time a device such as a printer is expected to work without failing.

measured and metered service   Service performance measurements that can be used in a cloud system to automatically control and optimize resources using a metering mechanism.

Media Access Control (MAC) address A physical address that is hard coded onto a network interface card (NIC) by the manufacturer. The address stays with the device regardless of what network the device is connected to. A MAC address is 48 bits and represented in hexadecimal format.

memory module A circuit board that contains integrated circuits and that is installed in a memory slot on a motherboard. A single-sided memory module contains RAM on only one side of the module, and a double-sided memory module contains RAM on both sides.

memory stick A Sony-proprietary Flash memory used in cameras, MP3 players, handheld video game systems, mobile phones, cameras, and other portable electronics.

memory support In a virtual machine, the memory needed for the host OS to meet the requirements of each VM and its guest OS.

Message Digest 5 (MD5) An older hashing algorithm that has been deprecated. Hashing uses a mathematical function to create a numeric value, called a message digest, that is unique to the data.

Messaging Application Programming Interface (MAPI) A proprietary messaging architecture.

metropolitan area network (MAN) A network that spans a large campus or city.

micro-ATX A smaller motherboard form factor designed to be backward compatible with ATX. micro-ATX often uses the same Northbridge

and Southbridge chipsets and power connectors as full-sized ATX boards and therefore can use many of the same components.

microSD A type of removable flash memory card used for storing information mostly in mobile phones and other mobile devices.

Microsoft Backup utility A Windows utility that is used to perform backups.

Microsoft Management Console (MMC) An application that allows the creation of custom management consoles for collections of utilities and tools from Microsoft or other sources.

Microsoft OneDrive A cloud storage service that is available to Microsoft Windows users.

Microsoft Server Exchange Email software that is also contact management and calendaring software.

Microsoft System Preparation (Sysprep) A tool that is used to remove an undesirable Windows setting and that can be used to install and configure the same OS on multiple computers and prepare the OS with different hardware configurations.

Microsoft Windows Update A Windows utility that is used to scan for new software and install service packs and patches.

micro-USB A miniaturized version of the Universal Serial Bus (USB) interface developed for connecting compact and mobile devices.

micro-USB cable A cable used to connect a mobile device with a micro-USB port to an electrical outlet charger or to connect to another device in order to charge and/or transfer data.

mini PCI   A smaller version of PCI used in some laptops.

mini-PCI card   A card that has 124 pins and that is capable of handling 802.11a, 802.11b, and 802.11g wireless LAN connection standards.

mini-PCIe card   A card that has 54 pins and that supports the same standards as mini-PCI as well as 802.11n and 802.11ac wireless LAN standards.

miniSD   A version of SD between the size of an SD card and a microSD card. The format was developed for mobile phones.

mini-USB cable   A cable used to connect a mobile device with a mini-USB port to an electrical outlet charger or to connect to another device in order to charge and/or transfer data.

mirroring   A RAID type that stores duplicate data on one or more other drives.

MMC   *See* Microsoft Management Console (MMC).

mobile device   A device that is handheld and lightweight and that typically has a touchscreen for input.

mobile hotspot   A wireless access point that is created by a mobile device that shares its data connection.

mobile operating system   An operating system designed specifically to run on mobile devices, such as smartphones, tablets, and wearables.

mobility   In information technology, the ability to access information electronically from different locations outside the home or office.

modem   A device that converts signals produced by one type of device to a form compatible with another device, often used to connect a home or small office to the Internet.

Modify   A Windows permission available for files and folders that allows users to change and delete existing files and folders but not create new files or folders.

monitor resolution   The amount of information that can be displayed on a screen. A higher-resolution monitor displays more information on a screen than a lower-resolution monitor does.

more   A command used to display the contents of a file one screen at a time.

motherboard, system board, or main board   The backbone of a computer. It is a printed circuit board (PCB) that contains buses, or electrical pathways, that interconnect electronic components.

mounting   Making a disk image file readable as a drive.

move   A command used to move a file or directory from one directory to another.

mSATA or M.2 module   A family of standards that specify physical aspects of expansion cards such as connectors and dimensions.

MSINFO32   A Windows command that opens the System Information window, which shows a summary of system components, including hardware components and software information.

MSTSC   A Windows command that opens the Remote Desktop utility.

multi rail   A power supply that has a separate printed circuit board (PCB) for each connector of the power supply.

multicore CPU   A single integrated circuit that contains more than one CPU core.

multifactor authentication   Authentication that uses a combination of different technologies, such as a password, a smart card, and biometrics, to authenticate a user.

multifactor lock   A lock that uses a combination of mechanisms.

multimeter   A tool that can take many types of measurements, including AC/DC voltage, electric current, and other electrical characteristics, to test the integrity of circuits and the quality of electricity in computer components.

multimode fiber (MMF)   Fiber-optic cable that consists of a larger core and that uses LED emitters to send light pulses.

multiple displays   Two or more monitors attached to the same computer.

multiprocessing   The running of two or more CPUs.

Multipurpose Internet Mail Extensions (MIME)   An Internet standard that extends the text-based email format to include other formats, such as pictures and word processor documents and that is normally used in conjunction with SMTP.

multitasking   Operating multiple applications at the same time.

multithreading   Dividing a program into smaller parts that can be loaded as needed by the operating system. Multithreading allows individual programs to be multitasked.

multi-user   Programs and peripheral devices that can be used by two or more users with individual accounts at the same time.

N

National Institute of Standards and Technology (NIST)   One of the oldest physical science laboratories in the United States.

native mode   A mode in which the image sent to a monitor by a video adapter card matches the native resolution of the monitor.

native resolution   The best monitor resolution for a specific monitor.

navigation icon   On an Android device, an icon on the system bar that is used for navigating apps and screens.

near field communication (NFC)   A communication protocol that enables two electronic devices to establish communication when they are close to each other.

near letter quality (NLQ)   The highest quality of printing that is produced by a dot matrix printer.

Nearby Sharing   Microsoft's file sharing mechanism, introduced in Windows 10, which provides the ability to share content with a nearby device using both Wi-Fi and Bluetooth.

net use   A command used to display and connect to network resources.

net user   A command used to display and change information about computer users.

NetBIOS (NetBT)   A program through which older computer applications can communicate within a local area network (LAN).

netiquette   Politeness in email, text, forums, and other Internet-based interactions.

network   A group of two or more computers.

Network Address Translation (NAT)   A process used to convert private IPv4 addresses to Internet-routable IPv4 addresses.

Network and Sharing Center   In Windows, a utility that allows an administrator to configure and review nearly all network settings on a computer.

network components   Devices such as wired and wireless network interface cards (NICs) and network devices such as switches, wireless access points (APs), routers, and multipurpose devices.

network design   The way a network is set up and connected to other networks to support the needs of a business.

Network File Sharing   A protocol that enables remote hosts to mount file systems over a network and interact with those file systems as though they are mounted locally.

Network File System (NFS)   A network-based file system that allows file access over the network.

network installation   A type of software installation in which installation files are stored on a server so that a client computer can access the files remotely to begin the installation.

network interface card (NIC)   A device that provides a physical connection to a network using a network cable.

network maintenance policy   A security policy item that specifies network device operating systems and end-user application update procedures.

network media   The channel over which a message travels from source to destination across a network.

network port   Also known as an RJ-45 or 8P8C, a port that has 8 pins and connects hardware devices to a network.

network printer mapping   The process of allowing a user to print over a network without the need for a direct connection to a print device.

network requirements   In a virtual computing environment, the type of virtual machine being used and how it needs to connect to the outside networks.

network service   A service provided using the protocols agreed upon according to the type of service requested.

New Technology File System (NTFS)   A file system that provides improved fault tolerance over traditional file systems and that also provides file-level security.

NFC   *See* near field communication (NFC).

NFC devices and terminals   A system in which tap-to-pay devices, such as credit cards or smartphones, are able to read and write to an NFC chip.

NFC payment   A contactless payment that uses near field communication (NFC) technology to exchange data between readers and payment devices.

NFS (Network File System)   A network-based file system that allows file access over a network.

NIC   *See* network interface card (NIC).

NIST Special Publication 800-122   A publication that addresses PII.

No Authentication (Open)   A wireless network setting in Windows that causes data to be sent unencrypted and with no authentication.

noise   Interference, such as EMI or RFI, that causes unclean power and that may cause errors in a computer system.

noncompliant system   A system that has not been updated with operating system or application patches or that is missing antivirus and firewall security software.

nonparity memory   The most common RAM used for home and business workstations, which does not check for errors in memory.

nonvolatile memory   Memory whose contents are not erased when the computer is powered off.

Non-Volatile Memory Express (NVMe)   A specification that was developed to allow computers to take greater advantage of the features of SSDs by providing a standard interface between SSDs, the PCIe bus, and operating systems.

Northbridge   A chipset that controls high-speed access to the RAM and video card as well as the speed at which the CPU communicates with all the other components in the computer.

NOTEPAD   A command that opens the Notepad basic text editor.

notification and system icons   Icons on an Android device for the clock, battery status, and radio signal status for Wi-Fi and provider networks.

O

octa-core CPU   A single CPU with eight cores inside it.

OLED   *See* organic light-emitting diode (OLED).

on-demand (self-service)   Describes a situation in which individuals can provision or make changes to computing services as needed without human interaction with the service provider.

one-time password (OTP)   An authentication code that is sent to a previously registered email address or phone number for use in multifactor authentication.

Open Database Connectivity (ODBC)   A technology that programs use to access a wide range of databases or data sources.

Open Graphics Library (OpenGL)   A cross-platform standard specification for multimedia graphics.

open source   Software for which users have access to the source code.

open source license   A copyright license for software that allows developers to modify and share the source code that runs the software.

open-ended questions   Questions that allow customers to explain the details of a problem in their own words.

operating system (OS)   A software program that performs general system tasks, such as controlling RAM, prioritizing the processing, controlling input and output devices, and managing files.

operation and planning documents   Proposals for future projects and project approvals, meeting presentations and minutes, and budgets and purchasing records.

operator   In a programming language, a character that is used to make comparisons.

optical fiber   A cable that is composed of two kinds of glass (core and cladding) and a protective outer shield (jacket).

optical fiber connector   A connector that terminates the end of an optical fiber.

optical media   Discs that are written and read by a laser.

optical storage device   A peripheral computer component that can read CD-ROMs or other optical discs using a laser to store and retrieve saved data.

organic light-emitting diode (OLED)   A technology that is commonly used for mobile devices and digital cameras that can also be found in some laptops. Whereas LCD and LED screens use backlights to illuminate their pixels, OLED pixels produce their own light.

orientation   The direction of a display, which can be landscape, portrait, flipped landscape, or flipped portrait.

output device   A hardware device that takes the data processed from input and passes on the information for use.

overclocking   A technique used to make a processor work at a faster speed than its original specification.

P

pages per minute (PPM)   The speed of a printer.

paper orientation   The direction of a printout, which can be landscape or portrait.

parallel   A wider data transfer path in which multiple bits are sent together, as opposed to a serial data transfer path, where one bit follows another.

parallel bus   A channel that sends multiple bits over multiple wires simultaneously.

parallel port   A port that has a 25-pin receptacle and that is used to connect various peripheral devices.

parity   The error-checking bit in the type of RAID that provides basic error checking and fault tolerance.

parity memory   Memory that contains 8 bits for data and 1 bit for error checking.

partition   An area of a hard drive that can be formatted to store information, such as data files or applications.

passcode   The PIN, password, pattern, or another passcode type used to unlock a mobile device.

password policy   A security policy item that ensures passwords meet minimum requirements and are changed regularly.

patch   A code update that a manufacturer provides to prevent a newly discovered virus or worm from making a successful attack.

patch panel   An unpowered or powered device commonly used to collect incoming cable runs from the various networking devices throughout a facility.

Payment Card Industry (PCI)   An organization formed in 2005 by the five major credit card companies in an effort to protect account numbers, expiration dates, and magnetic strip and chip data for transactions around the globe. The PCI Council partners with organizations, including NIST, to develop standards and security procedures around these transactions.

PCI Express (PCIe)   An expansion standard that uses a serial bus that has higher throughput and many other improvements over the older expansion slots. PCIe has x1, x4, x8, and x16 slots, which vary in length from shortest to longest, respectively.

PCI Express micro card   A memory card that has 54 pins and supports the same standards as mini-PCIe.

PCI-Extended (PCI-X)   An updated version of PCI that operates up to four times faster than PCI but that has become mostly obsolete.

PCmover Express   A tool for transferring selected files, folders, profiles, and applications from an old Windows PC to a Windows 10 PC.

peek   To view Windows desktop icons that are behind open windows by placing your cursor over the Show Desktop button at the right edge of the taskbar.

Performance Monitor   A Windows administrative tool that can be used to create customized performance graphs and reports from a wide range of hardware and software components.

Peripheral Component Interconnect (PCI)   A 32-bit or 64-bit expansion slot; PCI is becoming obsolete.

permissions   Rules that limit folder or file access for an individual or for a group of users.

persistent data   Data stored on a local drive, such as an internal or external hard drive or an optical drive, that is preserved when the computer is turned off.

personal area network (PAN)   A network that connects devices, such as mice, keyboards, printers, smartphones, and tablets within the range of an individual person.

Personalize   A setting that enables users to personalize the desktop and other aspects of the Windows GUI.

personally identifiable information (PII)   Any data that could potentially identify a specific individual.

Phase 1: Network design recovery strategy   A phase of a disaster recovery plan that involves analyzing the network design.

Phase 2: Inventory and documentation   A phase of a disaster recovery plan in which you create an inventory of all locations, devices, vendors, used services, and contact names and verify cost estimates that are created in the risk assessment step.

Phase 3: Verification   A phase of a disaster recovery plan in which you create a verification process to prove that the disaster recovery strategy works.

Phase 4: Approval and implementation   A phase of a disaster recovery plan in which you obtain senior management approval and develop a budget to implement and maintain the disaster recovery plan.

Phase 5: Review   A phase of a disaster recovery plan in which you review the plan and ensure that information in the plan is kept up to date to ensure that critical services will be restored in the event of a disaster.

phishing   An attack in which the attacker sends fraudulent email disguised as being from a legitimate, trusted source to trick the recipient into installing malware on a device or to share personal or financial information (such as a bank account number and access code).

physical security   Security related to access to an organization's premise, restricted areas, and computing and network infrastructure.

pickup rollers   Parts in a printer that move a sheet of paper out of the tray or cassette and through the printer during the printing process.

piezoelectric   Crystals that are located in the ink reservoir at the back of an inkjet printer's nozzle. A charge is applied to the crystal, causing it to vibrate. This vibration of the crystal controls the flow of ink onto the paper.

pin grid array (PGA)   An integrated circuit with pins on the underside that are inserted into the motherboard CPU socket using zero insertion force (ZIF).

ping   A command used to test connections between computers that works by sending an ICMP echo request and receiving an ICMP echo reply message to confirm connectivity.

pinned application   An application added to the Windows taskbar for easy access.

pixel   Picture element; a tiny dot capable of displaying the shades red, green, and blue (RGB).

planning   A step in the change management process that involves defining activities and roles, including evaluating the time necessary to implement, the downtimes, and the recovery process during the execute and control stage of a project.

platen   A large roller in a dot matrix printer that applies pressure to keep the paper from slipping.

Platform as a Service (PaaS)   A service in which a cloud provider provides access to operating systems, development tools, programming languages, and libraries used to develop, test, and deliver applications.

plenum-rated cable   A cable made from a special plastic that retards fire and produces less smoke than other cable types.

policy documents   Acceptable use policies, security policies, regulatory compliance policies, and disaster recovery policies.

POP3   *See* Post Office Protocol 3 (POP3).

pop-up   A small window on a website that opens on top of another web browser window and that is often unwanted or annoying.

port   An interface used to track various types of hardware and software communications.

Port Address Translation (PAT)   A version of NAT that overloads the router-assigned public IP address.

port forwarding   A rule-based method of directing traffic between devices on separate networks.

port number   A numeric identifier used to keep track of a specific conversation. Every message that a host sends contains both a source port and a destination port.

port triggering   A process in which a router temporarily forwards data through inbound ports to a specific device when a designated port range is used to make an outbound request.

Post Office Protocol 3 (POP3)   A protocol used by email clients to retrieve messages from an email server.

power button   A physical button that turns a computer on or off.

power management   A system that controls the flow of electricity to the components of a computer.

Power Options control panel   A Windows Control Panel item that allows you to change the power consumption of certain devices or of the entire computer.

power over Ethernet (PoE)   A method for powering devices that do not have a battery or access to a power outlet.

power supply   A critical component used to convert the current provided from an AC outlet into DC current usable by many parts inside a computer case.

power surge   A dramatic increase in voltage above the normal flow of electrical current. A power surge lasts for a few nanoseconds.

power-on self-test (POST)   The hardware check that the BIOS performs on the main components of a computer at boot.

PowerShell   A powerful command line utility in Windows that offers many advanced features, such as scripting and automation.

Preboot Execution Environment (PXE)   An environment that is used to boot a computer, connect to the network, and communicate with the server to begin the installation process when the client computer does not have an operating system installed.

Preferred Roaming List (PRL)   A baseband update for mobile device radio firmware that includes configuration information that a cellular phone needs to communicate on networks other than its own so that a call can be made outside of the carrier's network.

pretexting   An attack in which the attacker pretends to need personal or financial data in order to confirm the identity of the recipient.

preventive maintenance   Regular and systematic inspection, cleaning, and replacement of worn parts, materials, and systems.

preventive maintenance plan   A plan that provides many benefits to users and organizations, such as decreased downtime, improved performance, improved reliability, and lower repair costs. Preventive maintenance plans should include detailed information about the maintenance of all computers and network equipment.

preventive maintenance program   A detailed program that determines maintenance timing, the type of maintenance performed, and the specifics of how the maintenance plan is carried out.

primary partition   A hard drive area that contains the operating system files and is usually the first partition.

Primary Rate ISDN (PRI)   A baseband update for mobile device radio firmware that configures the data rates between a device and a cell tower to ensure that the device is able to communicate with the tower at the correct rate.

print bed   In a 3D printer, the platform onto which the heated filament forms the object.

print head   A core component in a printer that contains the nozzle that sprays ink onto a paper.

print job buffering   A process in which a print job is captured in internal printer memory.

Print Management utility   A Windows utility that provides a detailed view of all the printers that are available to a computer.

print server   A server that enables multiple computer users to access a single printer, regardless of device or operating system.

print spool settings   Settings that enable you to cancel or pause the current print jobs in the printer queue.

Print to File   A Windows setting that enables you to save your data in a file with an extension such as .prn. Print to file can now save in other formats.

Print to Image   A Windows setting that enables you to prevent others from easily copying the content in a document by printing to an image file format, such as JPG or TIFF.

Print to PDF   A Windows setting that enables you to print to Portable Document Format (PDF).

Print to XPS   A Windows setting that enables you to print to the XML Paper Specification (XPS) format, which was meant to be an alternative to PDF.

printed circuit board (PCB)   A circuit board that contains buses, or electrical pathways, that interconnect electronic components.

printer   An output device that creates hard copies of files.

printer sharing   The process of allowing multiple computers and devices connected to the same network to access one or more printers.

Private   A network profile in Windows that allows the user to customize the sharing options. This profile is for use on trusted networks, and the PC is discoverable by other devices.

private key   A key that is used with asymmetric key encryption and that is paired with a public key. Public and private keys are paired for secure communication, such as email. The private key is kept by an individual and must not be disclosed to any other party.

processing   The printer process that involves converting data from the source into a printable form. The printer converts data from common languages, such as Adobe PostScript (PS) or HP Printer Command Language (PCL), to a bitmap image stored in the printer's memory.

processor chip   A collection of transistors interconnected by wires.

processor support   In virtual computing, the ability of CPUs to support virtualization.

program virus   A virus that inserts itself in an executable program.

programmable read-only memory (PROM)   A type of computer memory in which information on the chip is written after the chip is manufactured. Generally, these chips cannot be erased and can be programmed only once.

Programs   A Windows Update category that allows changes to installed programs and Windows updates. Activation or deactivation of a wide range of Windows features can also be accessed here.

Programs and Features control panel   A Windows Control Panel item used to uninstall a program from a computer if you no longer use it or if you want to free up space on your hard disk.

project document A document containing user requests for changes, updates, or new services; software design and functional requirements; logical and physical network topology diagrams; or change management forms.

proprietary or vendor-specific cables Cables used with some mobile devices that are not compatible with other vendor ports but that are often compatible with other products from the same vendor.

protected health information (PHI) A form of PII that includes patient names, addresses, dates of visits, telephone and fax numbers, and email addresses and that needs to be secured and protected.

protocol A standard set of rules that defines how devices on a network communicate with one another.

proxy server A computer system that has the authority to act as another computer to function as a relay between a client and a server.

proxy Trojan Malware that uses the victim's computer as the source device to launch attacks and perform other illegal activities.

PS/2 port A 6-pin connector used for connecting a keyboard and mouse.

Public A network profile in Windows that disables file and printer sharing and network discovery on the link. The PC is hidden from other devices.

public key A key that is used with asymmetric key encryption and paired with a private key.

Public and private keys are paired for secure communication, such as email. The public key can be widely distributed and used to encrypt messages.

public key authentication A type of authentication that provides additional protection over host-based authentication. The user must enter a passphrase to access the private key. This helps prevent the private key from being compromised.

Public Network A network location profile in HomeGroup in which the HomeGroup is not available.

punchdown tool A tool used to terminate wire into termination blocks.

Python An interpreted, object-oriented, high-level language.

Q

quad-core CPU A CPU with four cores inside it.

quality of service (QoS) Refers to prioritization of certain data traffic to reduce packet loss, latency, and jitter on the network.

quick format A disk formatting option that involves removing files from the partition but not scanning the disk for bad sectors.

R

Radio Corporation of America (RCA) A type of connector that has a central plug with a ring around it that is used to carry audio or video. RCA connectors are often found in groups of three, where a yellow connector carries video and red and white connectors carry left and right audio channels.

RADIUS   Remote Authentication Dial-in User Service; an AAA server that performs the authentication on behalf of network devices. The network devices do not store and validate user credentials directly but instead pass the request to the AAA server and forward the response to the user.

rail   The printed circuit board (PCB) inside a power supply to which external cables are connected.

random-access memory (RAM)   Temporary working storage for data and programs being accessed by the CPU. Unlike ROM, RAM is volatile memory, which means the contents are erased every time the computer is powered off.

ransomware   Malware that typically denies a user access to their files by encrypting the files and then displaying a message demanding a ransom for the decryption key.

rapid elasticity   A term that refers to services that can be provisioned when needed and then released very quickly when no longer required.

rd   A command used to delete a directory.

RDP   Remote Desktop Protocol, a desktop protocol developed by Microsoft to provide remote access to the graphical desktop of a remote machine.

Read   A Windows permission available for files and folders that allows users to see the contents of a folder and open files and folders.

Read and Execute   A Windows permission that allows users to see the contents of existing files and folders but not create new files or folders.

read-only memory (ROM)   Nonvolatile memory located on the motherboard and other circuit boards that contains instructions that can be directly accessed by a CPU.

reconnaissance   The phase of an attack in which the attacker attempts to learn as much about the target network as possible.

recovery partition   A section of a disk that is inaccessible to the user and contains an image that can be used to restore the computer to its original configuration.

Reduced Instruction Set Computer (RISC)   A CPU architecture that uses a small set of instructions and executes them very rapidly.

redundant array of independent disks (RAID)   A scheme that provides a way to store data across multiple hard disks for redundancy.

refresh rate   The number of times per second an image on a monitor is rebuilt. A higher refresh rate produces a better image.

regedit   *See* Registry Editor (regedit).

Region control panel   A Windows Control Panel item that allows you to change the format of numbers, currencies, dates, and times.

Registry Editor (regedit)   A Windows tool that allows an administrator to view or make changes to the Registry.

regulatory and compliance policy   A policy that specifies what data must be collected and how long it must be retained.

relational operators   In most programming languages, the operators used to make mathematical comparisons.

Remote   A tab used in Windows to adjust settings for Remote Assistance and Remote Desktop and allow other people to connect to a computer to view or work on it.

remote access policy   A security policy item that identifies how remote users can access a network and what is accessible via remote connectivity.

remote-access Trojan   Malware that includes a backdoor for administrative control over the target computer.

remote authentication   In a wireless network, authentication provided by a scalable authentication architecture using RADIUS or Terminal Controller Access Control System Plus (TACACS+).

remote backup   A copy of a device's data that is stored in the cloud or network location.

Remote Installation Services (RIS)   A Microsoft server that is used to communicate with a client, store the setup files, and provide the necessary instructions for the client to access the setup files, download them, and begin the operating system installation.

remote lock   A tool that allows you to lock a mobile device with a passcode so others cannot gain access to the data in the device.

remote wipe   A tool that deletes all data from a mobile device and returns it to a factory state.

ren   A command used to rename a directory or file.

repair log   A log that helps you determine which equipment is the most or least reliable. It also provides a history of when a computer was last fixed, how it was fixed, and what the problem was.

repeater   A device that regenerates weak signals and extends the distance a signal can travel.

replay   A type of spoofing attack in which the attacker captures an authenticated packet and alters the packet's contents and sends the packet to its original destination with the goal of the target host accepting the altered packet as authentic.

Reset button   A button that restarts a computer without turning it off; not all devices have one.

resistance   Opposition to the flow of current in a circuit.

resolution   The number of horizontal and vertical pixels in a monitor.

resource pooling   A process in which a provider's computing resources are pooled to serve multiple consumers using a multi-tenant model. The tenants (that is, customers) share the different physical and virtual resources that are dynamically assigned and reassigned according to consumer demand.

response time   The amount of time it takes for a pixel to change properties (such as color or brightness).

restore point   A snapshot that contains information about a computer's operating system, installed programs, and Registry settings.

restrictions on failed login attempts   Limitations on the failed login attempts to lock out a user who enters the wrong password more than a specified number of times.

RFID   Radio frequency identification; a form of wireless communication that uses the frequencies in the 125 MHz to 960 MHz range to uniquely identify items.

RG-6   Heavy-gauge cable that has insulation and shielding and is tuned for high-bandwidth, high-frequency applications such as Internet, cable TV, and satellite TV signals.

RG-59   A thinner cable that is recommended for low-bandwidth and lower-frequency applications such as analog video and CCTV applications.

riser card   A card that can be added to a computer to provide additional expansion slots for more expansion cards.

RJ-11 connector   An interface used to connect a computer to a standard telephone line.

RJ-45 connector   A standardized physical network interface for connecting telecommunications or data equipment. The most common twisted-pair connector is an 8-position, 8-contact (8P8C) modular plug and jack.

robocopy   A command used to copy files or entire directory trees; Microsoft recommends using robocopy instead of xcopy.

roll back a driver   To use Device Manager to change the currently installed driver to the previously installed driver.

rollers   In an inkjet print, devices that pull in paper from the feeder.

ROM   *See* read-only memory (ROM).

rooting   A process used on Android devices to gain privileged or root-level access for modifying code or installing software that is not intended for the device.

rootkit   Malware used by cybercriminals to gain administrator account–level access to a computer.

router   A network layer device that forwards data packets between networks. Routers use IP addresses to forward traffic to other networks.

RSA   The most popular example of asymmetric encryption.

S

S0 state   A state in which the computer is on and the CPU is running.

S1 state   A state in which the CPU and RAM are still receiving power, but unused devices are powered down.

S2 state   A state in which the CPU is off, but the RAM is refreshed. The system is in a lower mode than S1.

S3 state   A state in which the CPU is off, and the RAM is set to a slow refresh rate. This mode is often called "save to RAM," and this state is known as suspend mode.

S4 state   A state in which the CPU and RAM are off. The contents of RAM have been saved to a temporary file on the hard disk. It is also called "save to disk" or hibernate mode.

S5 state   A state in which the computer is off.

Safe mode   A diagnostic mode used to troubleshoot Windows and Windows startup issues. Functionality is limited as many device drivers are not loaded.

Safe Mode with Command Prompt   An option that starts Windows and loads the command prompt instead of the GUI.

Safe Mode with Networking An option that starts Windows in Safe mode with networking support.

safety data sheet (SDS) A fact sheet that summarizes information about material identification, including hazardous ingredients that can affect personal health, fire hazards, and first-aid requirements.

sandbox A location in an OS that keeps code isolated from other resources and other code.

SATA Serial AT Attachment; a standard that defines the way data is transferred, the transfer rates, and physical characteristics of the cables and connectors.

SATA data cable A 7-pin data cable that connects a SATA device to a SATA interface. This cable does not supply any power to the SATA device; a separate power cable provides power to the drive.

satellite A connection that uses a satellite dish for two-way communication. The dish transmits and receives signals to and from a satellite that relays these signals back to a service provider.

screen calibration A process that involves adjusting the colors, brightness, and other settings for a screen.

screen orientation The direction of a mobile device screen, which can be either portrait or landscape. A sensor inside the device, known as an accelerometer, detects how the device is being held and changes the screen orientation appropriately.

screen resolution The number of pixels in a screen. A higher number of pixels provides better resolution.

screen size The diagonal measurement of a screen (such as from the top left to the bottom right), typically expressed in inches.

script file A simple text file written in a scripting language to automate processes and tasks on an operating system.

script virus A virus that attacks the OS interpreter, which is used to execute scripts.

scripting language A language that differs from a compiled language in that each line is interpreted and then executed when the script is run.

secpol.msc A Windows administrative tool used to open Local Security Policy. It can be used to enforce security settings on the local computer.

secure boot A UEFI security standard that ensures that the system firmware stops any digitally unsigned drivers from loading and also helps stop malicious software.

Secure Digital (SD) card An ultra-small flash memory card designed for use in portable devices such as cameras, MP3 players, and laptops to provide high-capacity memory in a small form factor.

Secure Hash Algorithm (SHA) A popular hashing algorithm that uses a mathematical function to create a numeric value, called a message digest, that is unique to the data.

Secure Shell (SSH) A TCP protocol that provides strong authentication and encrypted data transport between a client and a remote computer.

Secure Sockets Layer (SSL) A protocol developed to establish authenticated and encrypted links between networked computers, for sending information securely over the Internet.

security credentials manager   An entity that manages usernames, passwords, digital certificates, and encryption keys so that applications and other services can request and utilize those credentials.

security policy   A set of security objectives to ensure the security of a network, the data, and the computers in an organization.

security software disabler Trojan   Malware that stops antivirus programs or firewalls from functioning.

self-monitoring analysis and reporting technology (S.M.A.R.T.)   Technology that enables a PC to predict the future failure of hard disk drives.

Serial AT Attachment (SATA)   *See* SATA.

serial bus   A channel that sends a bit at a time at a much faster rate than would a parallel bus.

serial port   A port that has a 9-pin DB-9 port or a 25-pin port and that is used to connect various peripheral devices.

server   A host that provides services. A server requires server software in order to provide specific application services to the network.

server virtualization   A process that involves creating virtual instances of servers on a single physical server and taking advantage of idle resources to reduce the number of servers required to provide services to users.

service pack   An update distributed by a manufacturer that combines patches and upgrades.

service set identifier (SSID)   The name of a wireless network.

service-level agreement (SLA)   A contract that defines expectations between an organization and a service vendor to provide an agreed-upon level of support.

Services   A tab in Windows System Configuration that is used to display a list of services that are started with the operating system. Allows services running on the computer to be enabled or disabled and can be used to prevent individual services from being loaded on boot for troubleshooting purposes.

Services console (SERVICES.MSC)   A Windows console that allows you to manage all the services on your computer and remote computers.

Settings app   A Windows 10 app that can be used to configure the operating system. From it you can access many system settings.

Setup.exe   The Windows installation program, which can perform an in-place upgrade and automatically preserve all data, settings, applications, and drivers from the existing operating system version or a clean Windows OS installation.

sfc   A command used to verify and repair Windows system files.

shake   A feature in Windows 7, 8, 8.1, and 10 that enables a user to minimize all windows that are not being used by clicking and holding the title bar of one window and shaking it with the mouse. Repeat the action to maximize all of the windows.

shielded twisted-pair (STP)   A two-pair wiring medium used primarily with Token Ring networks. STP cabling has a layer of shielded insulation to reduce electromagnetic interference (EMI).

shoulder surfing   An in-person type of attack in which an attacker looks over someone's shoulder to steal passwords or other information.

shutdown   A command used to power off a local or remote computer.

signature file   A file that contains a sample of the code used by viruses and malware.

signature pad   A device that electronically captures a person's signature.

SIM card   A small card that contains information used to authenticate a device to mobile telephone and data providers. The card can also hold user data, such as personal contacts and text messages.

Simple Mail Transfer Protocol (SMTP)   A protocol used to send email from clients to an email server. It may also be used to relay email messages from the source to destination email servers.

single channel   Memory slots on a motherboard where all the RAM slots are addressed at the same time.

single-core CPU   A single CPU that contains one core that handles all the processing.

Single Inline Memory Module (SIMM)   A small circuit board that holds several memory chips. SIMMs have 30-pin or 72-pin configurations.

single-mode fiber (SMF)   Fiber-optic cable that consists of a very small core and uses laser technology to send a single ray of light in data transmission.

single point of failure   A point in a network where there are no backup servers to handle the failure.

single rail   A power supply that has all the connectors connected to the same printed circuit board (PCB).

single sign-on (SSO)   A type of authentication that enables users to log in once to access all system resources rather than logging in each time they need to access an individual resource.

Siri   A digital assistant program for iOS that can understand natural conversational language and perform tasks for the end user. A special software that understands advanced voice controls.

Sleep   A Windows power option setting that allows a computer to power on quickly but uses power to retain the information in RAM.

SLP   Service Location Protocol; a protocol that allows computers and other devices to locate services on a LAN without previous configuration.

Small Computer Systems Interface (SCSI)   A standard for connecting peripheral and storage devices. It is a bus technology, meaning that all devices connect to a central bus and are daisy-chained together.

small outline DIMM (SODIMM)   A smaller-profile memory module used by most laptops.

smart card   A card that is similar to a credit card but that has an embedded microprocessor that can be loaded with data.

smart card reader   An input device that is typically used on a computer to authenticate a user.

smartphone   A device that is very compact and quite powerful and that runs a special operating system designed for mobile devices. Smartphones use cellular connectivity options for voice, text, and data services.

SmartScreen Filter   A Windows web filtering capability that detects phishing websites, analyzes websites for suspicious items, and checks downloads against a list that contains sites and files that are known to be malicious.

smartwatch   A type of wearable that includes a microprocessor, a special operating system, and apps. Sensors in the smartwatch can gather data about various aspects of the body, such as heart rate, and use Bluetooth to report this information to another device, such as a smartphone.

SMB/CIFS   Protocols that allow for sharing of files, printers, and other resources between nodes on a network. CIFS is a dialect of SMB.

snap   To resize a window by dragging it to one of the edges of the screen.

SNMP   Simple Network Management Protocol; a protocol that enables network administrators to monitor network operations from centralized monitoring stations.

social engineering   An access attack in which the attacker attempts to manipulate individuals into performing actions or divulging confidential information.

socket   A connector on the motherboard that houses a CPU and forms the electrical interface and contact with the CPU.

SODIMM   *See* small outline DIMM (SODIMM).

software   The operating system and programs that run on a computer system.

Software as a Service (SaaS)   A service in which a cloud provider provides access to services, such as email, calendar, communication, and office tools over the Internet on a subscription basis.

software-defined networking (SDN)   An architecture that decouples network control (control plane) from the network devices (forwarding plane). SDN brings automation and programmability into data center, campus, backbone, and wide area networks.

software firewall   A program that provides firewall services on a computer to allow or deny traffic to the computer. It applies a set of rules to data transmissions through inspection and filtering of data packets.

software license   A contract that outlines the legal use or redistribution of software.

solid-state drive (SSD)   A drive that stores data as electrical charges in semiconductor flash memory. It has no moving parts, makes no noise, is energy efficient, and produces less heat than an HDD.

solid-state hybrid drive (SSHD)   A compromise between a magnetic HDD and an SSD that combines a magnetic HDD with onboard flash memory serving as a nonvolatile cache.

something for something   Sometimes called *quid pro quo*, a social engineering attack in which an attacker requests personal information from a party in exchange for something such as a free gift.

sound adapter   An adapter card used to provide audio capability.

sound card   A device that provides audio capability in a computer.

Sound control panel   The Windows Control Panel item for configuring audio devices or changing the sound scheme of a computer.

source code   A sequence of instructions that is written in human-readable language before it is turned into machine language (zeros and ones).

source port number   The number associated with the originating application on the local device.

Southbridge   A chipset that enables the CPU to communicate with slower-speed devices, including hard drives, Universal Serial Bus (USB) ports, and expansion slots.

spam   Also known as junk mail, unsolicited email that often contains harmful links, malware, or deceptive content.

spear phishing   An attack in which the attacker creates a targeted phishing attack tailored specifically for an individual or organization.

spike   A sudden increase in voltage that lasts for a short period and exceeds 100% of the normal voltage on a line. Spikes can be caused by lightning strikes and can also occur when the electrical system comes back on after a blackout.

spoofing   An attack in which the attacker forges IP addresses.

spyware   Malware that is similar to adware but that is used to gather information about the user and send it to cybercriminals without the user's consent.

SSH   *See* Secure Shell (SSH)

SSH File Transfer Protocol (SFTP)   An extension to Secure Shell (SSH) protocol that can be used to establish a secure file transfer session.

standard formatting   A type of disk formatting that involves creating a boot sector and a file system. Standard formatting can only be performed after low-level formatting has been completed.

Standard User account   A Microsoft user account that allows limited control over a computer. Users with this type of account can run applications but cannot install programs.

standby power supply (SPS)   A battery backup that is enabled when voltage levels fall below normal.

standoffs   Non-metallic spacers that provide space between the motherboard and the case to keep it from grounding and short-circuiting.

Start menu   In Windows, the primary place to locate all the applications installed on the computer, a list of recently opened documents, and a list of other elements, such as the search feature, Help and Support, and Control Panel.

Startup   A tab in Windows System Configuration that is used to display a list of all the applications that run automatically when Windows starts.

stateful packet inspection (SPI)   A firewall technology that keeps track of the state of network connections traveling through the firewall.

static IP address   An IP address that is manually configured on a device.

static RAM (SRAM)   Memory that is usually used for cache that uses little power and is much faster than dynamic RAM.

storage   In virtual computing, space for very large files, such as operating systems, applications, and all the VM data.

storage controller   A device that allows for the expansion of internal and external drives for a computer system and that can be integrated or added as an expansion card.

Storage Spaces   A technology that became available in Windows 8 and 10 that can be configured from a Control Panel item. It is the disk array technology that is recommended by Windows that creates pools of physical hard drives from which virtual disks (storage spaces) can be created.

strengthening material   Material that prevents a fiber-optic cable from being stretched when it is being pulled. The material used is often the same material used to produce bulletproof vests.

striping   A RAID method that involves writing data across multiple drives.

stylus   A handheld pen-like tool used to convert analog signals into digital signals to input commands to a computer screen, mobile device, or graphics tablet.

subdirectory   A directory that is located within another directory.

subfolder   A folder that is located within another folder.

subnet mask   A number used to separate an IP address into network and host addresses. It masks the network part of the system's IP address and leaves the host portion to identify the device that is connected to the network.

subscriber connector (SC)   A fiber-optic connector, sometimes referred to as square connector or standard connector, that uses a push/pull mechanism to ensure positive insertion. This connector type is used with multimode and single-mode fiber.

Success Audit (security only)   A message indicating that a Microsoft Event Viewer security event has been successful. For example, a successful logon from a user triggers an event with this level.

supervisor password   A password that, when configured, prevents access to a BIOS setup utility in order to prevent users from changing BIOS settings in the future.

Supervisory Control and Data Acquisition (SCADA)   Part of an industrial control system used to gather data and manage devices remotely.

surge protector   A device that helps protect against damage from electrical surges and spikes.

SVGA (Super Video Graphics Array)   A display standard introduced in 1989 that is still supported on some platforms.

swap partition   An area used by an operating system to supplement system RAM.

Swift   A programming language used with Apple's Software Development Kit (SDK) Xcode to create apps for iOS devices.

switch   A device that microsegments a LAN and that connects multiple devices on a network by receiving data and using filtering and forwarding to send the data to the intended destination device.

symmetric encryption   Encryption that ensures the confidentiality of a message by requiring both sides of an encrypted conversation to use an encryption key to encode and decode the data. The sender and receiver must use identical keys.

SYN flood   A type of DoS attack that exploits the TCP three-way handshake. The attacker sends continuous false SYN requests to the target. The target is eventually overwhelmed and unable to establish valid SYN requests, creating a DoS attack.

Sync   A setting that copies new apps, music, video, or books from iTunes to an iPhone and from an iPhone to iTunes, resulting in full synchronization on both devices.

Sync Center   A Windows utility that allows files to be edited from multiple Windows devices.

Sync over Wi-Fi   A setting that enables iTunes to scan and connect to iOS on the same Wi-Fi network.

synchronous dynamic RAM (SDRAM)   RAM that operates in synchronization with the memory bus.

syslog   A protocol that allows networking devices to send their system messages across the network to syslog servers.

System and Security control panel   A Windows Control Panel item that enables viewing and configuration of security settings such as Windows Defender Firewall and also access to administrative tools that enable configuration of a wide range of system functions, such as general hardware, storage, and encryption settings, and operations.

System Center Configuration Manager (Configuration Manager)   A Windows utility that can be used to automate the process of upgrading Windows 7 or Windows 8.1 to Windows 10. It updates the operating system and migrates apps and settings to the new OS.

System Configuration (MSCONFIG)   A tool used to identify problems that keep Windows from starting correctly.

System control panel   A Windows Control Panel item that allows all users to view basic system information, access tools, and configure advanced system settings.

System Image Manager (SIM)   A utility used to create the setup answer file when customizing a standard Windows 10 installation.

System Information   A tool used to collect and display information about local and remote computers. It is designed to quickly find information about software, drivers, hardware configurations, and computer components.

system panel connectors   The places where the hard disk drive activity lights, case speaker, reset button, power on/off button, computer power on light, and key lock, are connected.

System Protection   The Windows tab to access System Restore, which returns a computer to an earlier configuration and allows you to configure settings to enable system restore points and the amount of disk space that is used for them.

System Restore utility   A Windows tool that allows you to restore a computer to a previous configuration if restore points have been set.

system speaker   A motherboard speaker that indicates the computer's status during the POST.

T

T568A and T568B   Wiring schemes that define the pinout, or order of wire connections, on the end of each cable.

tablet   A mobile device that is similar to a smartphone and uses a special mobile operating system such as Android or iOS.

tailgating   An in-person attack in which an attacker quickly follows an authorized person into a secure location to gain access to the secure area.

tape drive   A drive that uses a magnetic read/write head and removable tape cartridges for archiving data.

Task Manager   A Windows utility that provides a high level of information about how a system is operating, including displaying what programs are running on the computer, the overall resource usage, and detailed statistics about each process.

taskbar   An element of an operating system's GUI typically located at the bottom of the screen. It enables users to locate and launch programs or view any program that is currently open.

taskkill   A command used to kill a running process.

tasklist   A command used to display a list of the processes that are currently running on the local computer or on a remote computer.

TCP   Transmission Control Protocol; a reliable, full-featured transport layer protocol which ensures that all of the data arrives at the destination.

TCP/IP model   A model that consists of layers that perform functions necessary to prepare data for transmission over a network.

Telnet   An insecure remote access protocol that provides a command line on a remote computer.

Terminal Controller Access Control System Plus (TACACS+)   A remote authentication AAA server that performs authentication on behalf of network devices. Rather than the network devices storing and validating user credentials directly, they pass the request to the AAA server and forward the response to the user.

tether   To use a smartphone to share its cellular data connection with other devices.

tethering   Connecting a mobile device to another mobile device or computer to share a network connection.

TFTP   Trivial File Transfer Protocol; a protocol used to transfer files between computers that utilizes less overhead than FTP, is used for transferring small amounts of data, and does not need authentication for communication.

thermal compound   A material that increases the efficiency of heat transfer from the CPU to the heat sink by filling any tiny gaps between the two.

thermal printer   A printer in which a pulse of electrical current is applied to heating chambers around the nozzles to create a bubble of steam in the chamber. The steam forces ink out through the nozzle and onto the paper.

thumbnail preview   A thumbnail image of a running program that is viewed by hovering the mouse over the program icon on the taskbar.

Thunderbolt card   A card that allows for high-speed connection of peripherals such as hard drives, RAID arrays, and network interfaces and that can transmit high-definition video using the DisplayPort protocol.

tiles   Interactive apps on a Windows 8 Start screen that provide dynamic information and quick updates about apps without the need to launch the applications.

Time Machine   A backup tool included with macOS.

token-based lock   A type of secure lock that is unlocked by swiping a secure card or by using a proximity reader to detect a smart card or a wireless key fob.

tone generator and probe   A two-part tool used to trace the remote end of a cable for testing and troubleshooting. The tone generator applies a tone to the wire to be tested.

toner   A negatively charged combination of plastic and metal particles that is used in laser printers.

Tools   A tab in Microsoft System Configuration that is used to display a compact and very comprehensive list of diagnostic tools that can be run to help with troubleshooting.

total cost of ownership (TCO)   A financial estimate intended to help determine the direct and indirect costs of a device such as a printer.

touchscreen   A special glass piece attached to the front of a screen, known as a digitizer, that converts touch actions (press, swipe, and so on) into digital signals that are processed by the laptop or tablet.

tractor feed   Continuous-feed paper that most dot matrix printers use that has perforations between sheets and perforated strips on the sides that are used to feed the paper and to prevent skewing or shifting.

transfer roller   A device in a laser printer that assists in transferring toner from the imaging drum to the paper.

transferring   A laser printer process in which toner, attached to the image, is transferred to paper.

transistor   A semiconductor whose state changes from on to off or off to on, generating a small amount of heat. The amount of heat generated increases as the speed of the processor increases. When the processor becomes too hot, it begins to produce errors.

triple-core CPU   A single CPU with three cores inside it. This is a quad-core processor with one of the cores disabled.

Triple Data Encryption (3DES) algorithm   A legacy symmetric encryption method.

Trojan horse   A program that looks useful but that carries malicious code.

troubleshooting   The systematic process used to locate the cause of a fault in a computer system and correct the relevant hardware and software issues.

Troubleshooting control panel   A Windows Control Panel item that has a number of built-in scripts that are used to identify and solve common problems with many Windows components.

troubleshooting process steps   The steps involved in identifying a problem, establishing a theory of probable cause, testing the theory to determine the cause, establishing a plan of action, verifying full system functionality, and documentation.

trusted app source   An app that is authenticated and authorized by a service provider. The service provider issues the developer a certificate to use to sign its apps and identify them as trusted.

Trusted Platform Module (TPM)   A specialized chip installed on a motherboard and designed to secure hardware by storing encryption keys, digital certificates, passwords, and data.

TV tuner card   A card that provides the ability to watch and record television signals on a PC by connecting a cable television, satellite, or antenna to the installed tuner card.

twisted-pair   A pair of insulated wires wrapped together in a regular spiral pattern to control the effects of electrical noise.

type   A command used to display the contents of a file.

Type 1 (native) hypervisor   A bare-metal hypervisor typically used with server virtualization that runs directly on the hardware of a host and manages the allocation of system resources to virtual operating systems.

Type 2 (hosted) hypervisor   A hypervisor hosted by an OS that is commonly used with client-side virtualization.

U

Ubuntu   A distribution (distro) of Linux.

UDP   User Datagram Protocol; a very simple transport layer protocol that does not provide for any reliability.

unattended   *See* unattended installation.

unattended installation   An installation method in which no prompts or other information is displayed. It is based on an answer file that contains simple text that instructs Windows Setup how to configure and install the OS.

unattended.bat file   A Windows file used on a client machine to prepare the hard drive and install the OS from the server over the network.

unbuffered memory   Conventional memory in a computer. The computer reads data directly from the memory banks, making unbuffered memory faster than buffered memory.

Unified Extensible Firmware Interface (UEFI)   A newer type of BIOS that has many advantages, including a GUI that is user friendly compared to older BIOS versions, the ability to recognize larger hard drives, and a built-in feature called secure boot.

unified threat management (UTM)   A generic name for an all-in-one security appliance. UTMs include all the functionality of an IDS/IPS as well as stateful firewall services.

Uninstall a Driver   In Windows Device Manager, an option to remove a driver.

uninterruptible power supply (UPS)   A device that helps protect against potential electrical power problems by supplying a consistent level of electrical power to a computer or other device. The battery is constantly recharging while the UPS is in use. The UPS provides a consistent quality of power when brownouts and blackouts occur.

Universal Plug and Play (UPnP)   A protocol that enables devices to dynamically add themselves to a network without the need for user intervention or configuration.

Universal Serial Bus (USB)   A standard interface that connects peripheral devices to a computer; these devices are hot swappable, which means users can connect and disconnect the devices while the computer is powered on.

Universal Serial Bus (USB) controller card   A card that provides additional USB ports to connect a computer to peripheral devices.

Unix   A proprietary operating system written in the C programming language.

unshielded twisted-pair (UTP)   A four-pair wire medium used in a variety of networks. UTP is rated in categories, with higher categories providing the best performance and highest bandwidth.

up-arrow keys   A Windows CLI shortcut that moves through the previously entered commands.

update   A new, improved, or fixed version of software that replaces an older version of the same software.

Update a Driver   A Windows Device Manager option to change the currently installed driver.

USB   *See* Universal Serial Bus (USB).

USB 3.0 motherboard connector   A connector that allows the connection of a USB 3.0 module for additional USB 3.0 front or rear panel ports.

USB 3.1 motherboard connector   Also known as a USB header, a group of pins on a motherboard that allows the connection of a USB 3.1 module for additional USB 3.1 front or rear panel ports.

USB mini-B   A connector form factor that is rectangular with small indentations on each side and that is replacing the mini-USB form factor.

USB Type-A   A rectangular connector found on virtually every desktop PC and laptop, as well as TVs, game consoles, and media players.

USB Type-B   A connector form factor that is commonly used to connect printer and external hard drives. It has a square shape with beveled exterior corners and an extra notch at the top.

USB Type-C   A connector form factor that is smaller than the Type-A connector and is rectangular with four rounded corners.

USB-C cable   A cable that can be plugged in in either direction and that is used with mobile devices to connect to an electrical outlet charger or to connect to another device, such as when connecting a smartphone to a laptop in order to charge and/or transfer data.

User Account Control (UAC)   A Windows utility that monitors programs on the computer and warns users when actions might present threats to the computer.

User Accounts   A category that enables administration of Windows user accounts and User Account Control (UAC).

user documentation   Documentation such as searchable knowledge base articles and FAQs, end-user manuals for hardware and software, and help desk ticket databases with ticket resolutions.

user interface   The interface a user uses to interact with software and hardware.

user password   A password that provides access to the BIOS based on a defined level such as full access, limited access, view only access, and no access.

User State Migration Tool (USMT)   A command line utility developed by Microsoft that allows users who are comfortable with scripting languages to transfer files and settings between Windows PCs.

Users A Windows group whose users have permissions that allow them to perform common tasks such as running applications and accessing local or network printers. A user profile is created and persists on the system.

V

variable A designated place to store information within a computer. A primary function of computers is to manipulate variables.

VBScript Windows Visual Basic Scripting Edition; a scripting language developed by Microsoft.

Very High-Speed DSL (VDSL) A form of DSL that attains much higher bit rates than DSL, from 26 Mbps for symmetric links and 52 Mbps download and 6 Mbps upload for asymmetric links. VDSL2 can carry up to 100 Mbps in both directions.

VGA (Video Graphics Array) A connector for analog video that has 3 rows and 15 pins.

video adapter A device that provides video capability.

video port A port for connecting a monitor cable to a computer.

view only access One of the common levels of user access to BIOS, where all screens are available but no settings can be changed.

virtual assistant A program that can understand natural conversational language and perform tasks for the end user.

virtual LAN (VLAN) A broadcast domain that is created on a single switch as if it were multiple switches and that groups a collection of devices from different LANs.

virtual machine (VM) A software program or operating system that acts like a separate computer and that is capable of performing tasks such as running applications and programs as if it were a separate computer. VMs share the resources of the host computer, and virtualization software separates the actual physical hardware.

virtual machine manager (VMM) Another name for a hypervisor, software used on a host computer to create and manage VMs.

virtual memory An area on the hard drive that can be used when a computer does not have enough RAM available to run a program.

virtual printer Software on a computer that has an interface similar to a print driver that is coded to send the output to other applications rather than to a physical device.

virtual private network (VPN) A network used to securely connect to another network over an insecure network, such as the Internet.

virtual reality (VR) Computer technology that creates a simulated, three-dimensional environment that a user feels immersed in and can manipulate.

virtual reality headset A head-mounted device that provides a separate image for each eye and that typically includes head-motion and eye-motion tracking sensors. These devices are also output devices that deliver video and audio to the wearer.

virtualization   A technology that enables a single computer to host multiple independent virtual computers that share the host computer hardware.

virus   Malware that requires human action to propagate and infect other computers.

voice over IP (VoIP)   A technology that applies Internet addressing to voice data.

volatile data   Data that disappears as soon as the computer is turned off.

volatile memory   Memory whose contents are erased every time the computer is powered off.

voltage   A measurement of the work required to move a charge from one location to another. Voltage is measured in volts (V). A computer power supply usually produces several different voltages.

voltage selector switch   A physical switch used to set the input voltage on a power supply to either 110V/115V or 220V/230V.

Volume Boot Record (VBR)   A sector that loads the boot manager, which for Windows is bootmgr.exe.

VPN   *See* virtual private network (VPN).

W

Wake on LAN (WOL)   A setting used to wake up a networked computer from a very low power mode state. Very low power mode means that the computer is turned off but is still connected to a power source. To support WOL, the computer must have an ATX-compatible power supply and a WOL-compatible NIC.

Warning   A Windows Event Viewer message type that indicates a potential problem with a software component not functioning ideally.

water cooling system   A system in which a metal plate is placed over the processor, and water is pumped over the top to collect the heat that the processor generates. The water is pumped to a radiator to disperse the heat into the air, and the water is then recirculated.

watt (W)   A measure of the pressure required to push electrons through a circuit (voltage), multiplied by the number of electrons going through that circuit (current). Computer power supplies are rated in watts.

wearable   A smart device that is meant to be worn on the body or attached to clothing.

Web Security Appliance   A Cisco-proprietary device that filters known and suspicious Internet malware sites.

web server   A server that provides web resources requested by a client using HTTP or HTTPS.

webcam   A video camera that is either embedded into the display on a mobile device or connected externally to a computer, often used for video conferencing or to stream live video onto the Internet.

while loop   A statement that checks a variable to verify whether it is true (or false) before repeating a section of code. This is known as a pre-test loop.

whitelist   A list that specifies which IP addresses are allowed on a network.

whoami   A command that displays the name of the computer on which the prompt is open and the user account.

wide area network (WAN)   A network that connects multiple networks in geographically separated locations, with access contracted from a service provider.

Wi-Fi   A technology that makes use of radio waves in order to provide high-speed connections to users on a local area network (LAN) and that usually has no limit for the amount of data.

Wi-Fi analyzer   A mobile tool for auditing and troubleshooting wireless networks.

Wi-Fi antenna   A device that transmits and receives data carried over radio waves.

Wi-Fi calling   A technology by which modern smartphones use the Internet to transport voice calls by taking advantage of a local Wi-Fi hotspot.

Wi-Fi Protected Access (WPA)   A wireless network setting that uses Pre-Shared Key.

Win+R   In the CLI, a key combination that opens a run box.

Windows 7   A version of Windows that can be installed as an upgrade from Windows XP or Vista.

Windows 8   A version of Windows that introduced the Metro user interface, which unifies the Windows look and feel on desktops, laptops, mobile phones, and tablets.

Windows 8.1   An update for Windows 8 that includes improvements to make Windows more familiar for users with devices that have touch or mouse and keyboard interfaces.

Windows 10   A version of Windows that became available in 2015. Nine editions of Windows 10 are currently offered.

Windows 10 Mobile   A Microsoft user interface used on Windows 10 Mobile phones and tablets.

Windows Advanced Boot Options   A boot screen that lets a user start Windows in advanced troubleshooting modes. The menu can be accessed by turning on the computer and pressing the F8 key before Windows starts.

Windows Advanced Startup Options   A menu that provides a selectable list of Windows startup modes and troubleshooting tools.

Windows API   An API that provides application developers with user interface controls and file management and graphical elements, such as windows, scroll bars, and dialog boxes.

Windows apps   Apps that are distributed through the Microsoft Store.

Windows Automated Installation Kit (AIK)   A collection of tools and technologies designed to help deploy Microsoft Windows operating system images.

Windows Defender   The antivirus functionality included directly in the Windows OS.

Windows Easy Transfer   A tool available to transfer data and settings from an old Windows computer to a new one.

Windows Firewall   A software firewall that helps prevent cybercriminals and malware from gaining access to a computer. It is installed by default when the Windows OS is installed.

Windows Malicious Software Removal Tool   A tool that checks a computer for malicious software.

Windows Media Center   A Microsoft app that allows a computer to be used as a home entertainment appliance for playing DVDs.

Windows Memory Diagnostics   A Windows tool that schedules a memory test that will be executed when the computer starts.

Windows ReadyBoost   A setting that enables Windows to treat an external flash device, such as a USB drive, as hard drive cache. It increases the performance of Windows without installing additional RAM.

Windows Registry   A database that contains settings for Windows and for applications that use the Registry.

Windows Update   A website located at update. microsoft.com that hosts maintenance updates, critical updates, and security patches, as well as optional software and hardware updates for Microsoft Windows versions 7, 8, and 10.

windowsupdate.log   A file stored in the %SystemRoot% directory that contains records of update activity.

wire cutters   A tool used to snip wires, mostly aluminum and copper wires, in a network environment.

wire strippers   A tool used to remove the insulation from wire so that it can be twisted to other wires or crimped to connectors to make a cable. Wire strippers typically have a variety of notches for different wire gauges.

Wired Equivalent Privacy (WEP)   A wireless network setting that provides very weak security and should not be relied upon for confidentiality.

wired network   A network that uses physical media such as copper cables to transfer data between connected devices.

wireless access point (AP)   A device that provides network access to wireless devices, such as laptops and tablets. A wireless AP uses radio waves to communicate with the wireless NIC in the devices and other wireless access points.

wireless adapter   A device that a laptop can use to access the Internet; it can be built into the laptop or attached to the laptop through an expansion port.

wireless LAN (WLAN)   A network that is similar to a LAN but that wirelessly connects users and devices in a small geographical area instead of using a wired connection. A WLAN uses radio waves to transmit data between wireless devices.

wireless mesh network (WMN)   A technology that uses multiple access points to extend a WLAN.

wireless network   A network that uses radio signal frequencies for communication among network devices. Also called a Wi-Fi network or a WLAN.

wireless NIC   A device that connects a computer to a network using radio frequencies.

wireless router   A device that connects multiple wireless devices to a network and that may include a switch to connect wired hosts.

wireless wide area network (WWAN)   A network that requires use of an adapter to link to a cellular provider's network through the nearest base station or transmitter. WWAN adapters can be internal or external (in which case they are connected by USB).

Work Network   A network location profile in HomeGroup for which you are not allowed to create or join a HomeGroup but for which you can view and share resources with other computers.

workgroup   A collection of workstations and servers on a LAN that are designed to communicate and exchange data with one another.

worm   A self-replicating program that propagates automatically without user actions by exploiting vulnerabilities in legitimate software.

WPA2-Enterprise   A wireless network setting with which authentication is passed from the access point to a centralized authentication server running Remote Authentication Dial-in User Service (RADIUS).

WPA2-Personal   A wireless network setting that uses the Advanced Encryption Standard (AES) cipher and Pre-Shared Key (PSK) to encrypt communications.

Write   A Windows permission that allows users to create new files and folders and make changes to existing files and folders.

X

xcopy   A command used to copy files or entire directory trees.

xD   A flash memory card format that is used in digital cameras made by Olympus and Fujifilm.

Z

zero insertion force (ZIF)   Refers to the amount of force needed to install a CPU into the motherboard socket or slot.

zero-day   Also referred to as zero-day attack, zero-day threat, or zero-day exploit, the day that an unknown vulnerability is discovered by the vendor.

zero-hour   The moment an exploit is discovered.

Zigbee   A wireless technology that uses low-power digital radios based on the IEEE 802.15.4 wireless standard for low-rate wireless personal area networks (LR-WPANs). It is meant to be used by low-cost, low-speed devices.

zombies   Many infected hosts that are used to overwhelm a target in a DoS attack and amplify the attack to a DDoS attack.

Z-Wave   A wireless technology that uses low-energy radio waves based on the IEEE 802.15.4 wireless standard for low-rate wireless personal area networks (LR-WPANs). It is meant to be used by low-cost, low-speed devices to let smart devices communicate with one another.

Index

D

S